THE LAW AND PRACTICE OF COMPLEX CONSTRUCTION PROJECTS

Presenting readers with all the need-to-know information on complex construction projects within a single publication, this book expertly focuses on practical issues whilst also providing insights on the law applying to construction projects.

As well as exploring individual subjects such as the negotiation of a contract, the evaluation of a claim or assistance in relation to contractual disputes, the book also creates an overarching understanding of the entire life of a project. It presents an inside view on the various stages of complex projects, from the moment they are conceived to the end of the contractual relation between employer and contractor, including any disputes between the parties. The reader will become familiar with the terminology used in the construction industry, the various phases of complex construction projects, the law applying to each phase and the various deliverables produced by the parties throughout the project. While including sections on the law applying to each phase, the book's primary focus is on the practical aspects faced on a daily basis by practitioners working in the construction industry.

This book is important reading for professionals involved in construction law at every level, including relevant academics, government employees and lawyers. It will also serve as a useful book for students, providing a comprehensive overview of the many factors and phases of a complex construction project.

Fabio Solimene is a qualified solicitor with more than 15 years of experience in the construction sector. He is currently Assistant General Counsel at Honeywell HPS, where he manages the EMEA region. Before that, Fabio was Corporate Head of Legal at the global EPC contractor, Saipem, and lawyer at Watson, Farley & Williams. Since 2018, Fabio has been a Visiting Lecturer on the King's College London M.Sc. in Construction Law and Dispute Resolution.

PRACTICAL LEGAL GUIDES FOR CONSTRUCTION AND TECHNOLOGY PROJECTS
Series Editor: Donald Charrett

The books in this series provide lawyers and construction professionals with the relevant knowledge, resources and practical guidance to understand the contemporary construction industry and the law necessary to achieve successful outcomes for construction projects. The topics covered include front-end issues such as project procurement, the production, negotiation and administration of contracts, and the avoidance of disputes, as well as backend issues such as taking part in, managing or resolving disputes. The series aims to keep abreast of the technologies that have increasing impact in changing traditional ways of working, contracting and resolving disputes.

FIDIC Contracts in Asia Pacific
A Practical Guide to Application
Donald Charrett

Contracts for Construction and Engineering Projects
Second Edition
Donald Charrett

Contracts for Infrastructure Projects
An International Guide to Application
Donald Charrett

FIDIC Contracts in Europe
A Practical Guide to Application
Donald Charrett

FIDIC Contracts in the Americas
A Practical Guide to Application
Donald Charrett

FIDIC Contracts in Africa and the Middle East
A Practical Guide to Application
Donald Charrett

Decision-making in International Construction Arbitration
Haytham Besaiso

Innovative Project Management with FIDIC Contracts
Adriana Spassova

For more information, please visit: www.routledge.com/Practical-Legal-Guides-for-Construction-and-Technology-Projects/book-series/PLGCTP

THE LAW AND PRACTICE OF COMPLEX CONSTRUCTION PROJECTS

FABIO SOLIMENE

informa law
from Routledge

Designed cover image: © Getty Images

First published 2024
by Informa Law from Routledge
4 Park Square, Milton Park, Abingdon, Oxon OX14 4RN

and by Informa Law from Routledge
605 Third Avenue, New York, NY 10158

Informa Law from Routledge is an imprint of the Taylor & Francis Group, an informa business

British Library Cataloguing-in-Publication Data
A catalogue record for this book is available from the British Library

ISBN: 978-1-032-48160-9 (hbk)
ISBN: 978-1-032-48167-8 (pbk)
ISBN: 978-1-00338-771-8 (ebk)

DOI: 10.4324/9781003387718

Typeset in Times New Roman
by ApexCoVantge, LLC

To Chiara, Alessandro and Matteo

CONTENTS

PART FIVE. THE CONTRACT: INTERPRETATION

PART EIGHT. REMEDIES

PART TEN. DISPUTES

PREFACE

When I first embarked on this work, I intended to write an article on delay claims in complex construction projects.

My experience as a construction lawyer, in private practice first and as Head of Legal of a global EPC contractor then, led me to think that delays in high-complexity and high-value construction projects are inevitable and virtually physiological to the very nature of such projects.

Right before I started working on this book, the Covid-19 pandemic severely disrupted construction activities around the globe. This situation has then been further exacerbated by the Russia–Ukraine conflict and its wider geopolitical implications (including sanctions and other restrictions imposed on Russia by the US, the EU and the UK), along with other geopolitical issues and conflicts zones around the world, including terrorist attacks targeting crucial infrastructures and energy production sites, sometimes still under construction.

When framing such events in a time, when the world is experiencing unprecedented natural disasters and extreme weather conditions due to the climate change, one could easily see a "perfect storm" affecting every aspect of our day-to-day life. The construction industry is no exception, with complex construction projects taking the hardest hit.

This "perfect storm" was triggered by a mix of factors, including restrictions on movement of people (which led to shortage of work force) and on the conduct of business with certain companies or countries (which led to a shortage of goods and materials), ports congestion and disruptions to rail freight and air freight transportation (which led to delays in deliveries), projects' suspensions and terminations (due to extreme delays, prolonged suspension or force majeure, or impossibility to carry out operations in certain countries) and financial distress of relevant players (eventually leading to insolvency of less capitalised companies).

From a contractual perspective, the parties to construction contracts found themselves facing unforeseen (and sometimes unforeseeable) and concurring disruptive events with contracts that were often not structured to deal with the relevant consequences. Completion dates became no longer achievable, and the contractual due performance became impractical, uneconomical or even impossible.

However, the more I researched on the subject of delay, the more I realised that I had to take a more holistic and end-to-end approach by looking at complex construction projects from their inception through completion, and beyond. At that point, my article had become a book on complex construction projects.

The book is composed of 10 parts, each covering a different aspect of a complex construction project, from the moment it is conceived up to the resolution of any claims and disputes arising from the contract between employer and contractor.

My hope is that this book could represent a practical tool for stakeholders involved in complex construction projects at various levels to holistically understand such projects and appreciate the plethora of events arising out of them.

However, this book only offers basic guidance and serves as a mere introductory resource for readers exploring the law of construction projects. I invite more specialised readers looking for specific information to seek additional sources for the answer they require.

The views and opinions expressed in this book are mine alone and provided in my personal capacity, and do not represent the official policy or position of any of my past, present or future employers, or organisations I am part of or collaborate with.

INTRODUCTION

1. Complexity in construction projects

Virtually every construction project is intrinsically complex in nature. However, the level of complexity may vary based on a number of factors, including the project's nature (e.g., an offshore wind farm in deep waters, compared to an onshore pipeline in a location with favourable weather conditions), size (e.g., a floating production storage and offloading unit compared to a smaller vessel or a large building complex compared to a small residential home), number of parties' involved (e.g., a large number of contractors and subcontractors working on the same site contemporaneously may create additional complexity), type of parties' involved (e.g., financed projects involving lenders or public entitles with their own needs and rights), and project-specific peculiarities (e.g., a nuclear power plant may involve regulatory, health and security complexities that may not be present in other types of projects).

However, complexity can be managed. Although some events affecting the project may be unpredictable (e.g., a pandemic or a war), the level of expertise and skill of the parties involved and their willingness to cooperate towards the common objective of having the project successfully completed will determine whether or not a highly complex project will ultimately be successful.

2. Main parties of a complex construction project

Complex construction projects involve a multitude of parties. An exhaustive list of all the stakeholders involved in each phase is outside the scope of this book. However, in general terms it can be said that the parties typically involved in a complex construction project could include at least the following:

(i) Engineering companies, giving employers an initial and general overview of the project's feasibility, main features, timing and costs and/or preparing the project's design.

(ii) The contractor, responsible for carrying out the whole or part of the works. When the contract entails the assignment of subcontracts, contractors may be referred to as "main contractors", or "prime contractors", so as to distinguish them from subcontractors. The contractor may either be a single company or a joint venture (where two or more contractors enter into a consortium or joint venture agreement with an aim of performing the contract jointly). The joint venture may either be incorporated or unincorporated. When the joint venture is incorporated,

DOI: 10.4324/9781003387718-1

it will usually be the signatory party to the construction contract. When it is unincorporated, all the parties composing the joint venture will sign the construction contract, and each joint venture member will typically be jointly and severally liable to the employer for all obligations under the contract.

(iii) The subcontractors, appointed to perform a part of the construction works under a subcontract. In the case of EPC projects, subcontractors will be appointed by the main contractor and will only be responsible to it, while not having any obligations to, or rights against, the employer;

(iv) The lenders, who are financing the project and, as a result, have rights reflecting their interest in the project's completion in accordance with their expectations as agreed with the employer.

(v) The various vendors supplying goods and materials necessary for the project, typically, in the case of EPC contracts, to the main contractor.

(vi) The employer (sometimes also referred to as the "owner", the "client" or the "principal"), required to pay for the works, regardless of whether it will be the ultimate user or owner of the works or will be paying for the works with its own resources or through financing.

(vii) The engineer (sometimes also referred to as the employer's representative or another name, depending on the relevant contract, project or qualification), appointed by, and acting on behalf of the employer. Employers may elect to work through a representative having the relevant technical skills to manage and supervise the contract and the project. As the employer's representative, the engineer usually receives all notices, invoices and claims under the contract and decides on the contractor's claims, including determining any amounts due (although an engineer is usually prevented from instructing variations).

3. Main phases of complex construction projects

Every project goes through several phases, which may change in number and content based on the project type and complexity. However, in very broad terms, a typical complex construction project may include at least the following phases:

(i) First, the project is conceived and planned. In this phase a basic and high-level design is prepared to help the employer assess whether the project is feasible in general terms, how it could be developed, how much it could cost and how long it could take to complete the construction. This phase typically ends with the preparation of a basic design which is then used, usually by the main contractor, as a basis for the detailed design ultimately used for the construction phase.

(ii) In the case of turnkey projects (i.e., where a single contractor undertakes to complete all stages of the project, from detail engineering through construction, so that it will be ready for immediate use), the employer will issue an invitation to tenders. The contractors interested in bidding for that project will submit their tender, which will then be collected and reviewed by the employer.

(iii) The employer will then make a shortlist of preferred contractors (or select only one candidate) and start a discussion of the main aspects of the project, including the construction contract that will regulate the parties' relation (the initial contract form is usually provided by the employer).

(iv) The employer will then issue the final letter of award whereby the contract will be awarded to the successful contractor.

(v) The contract will then be entered into between the employer and the successful contractor.

(vi) The next phase is the performance of the contract. In this phase the contractor carries out the scope of work and the employer pays the agreed price, usually in instalments based on progress and achievement of milestones. The construction contract may be amended (e.g., the employer may issue change orders varying the scope of work), discharged and the parties may make claims against each other (e.g., the contractor may claim extensions of time and/or by the employer may claim liquidated damages).

(vii) The next phase commences when the work is completed and the work is complete and the employer accepts and takes it over. In this phase the project will be "substantially complete", although some minor "punch list" items will normally be still outstanding. The contractor normally has a duty to rectify defects within a certain period of time, after which the relation between the contractor and the employer will come to an end (although there may be some outstanding obligations related to latent defects).

(viii) Claims and disputes do not constitute a phase per se as they may occur throughout the project or well after its completion (subject to any applicable statute of limitation). Litigating while the works are still ongoing may spoil the parties' working relationship and ultimately affect the whole success of the project and drain energies that both parties need to dedicate to the project. It is therefore common for the parties to wait until the project's completion before commencing any significant dispute over the works. However, cash flow issues may drive contractors to disregard this aspect and trigger the agreed dispute resolution mechanism during the construction phase, particularly where adjudication is agreed or mandatory.

PART ONE

THE PRE-CONTRACTUAL PHASE

The pre-contractual phase encompasses all activities starting from the moment in which the project is conceived to the execution of the contract.

In this phase, the parties have early discussions on the type of project, the relevant feasibility and costs, and what is needed for the project to be built in a certain way, with a certain output and within a certain timeframe. In the case of a major construction project, the employer may want to obtain a conceptual design before embarking in further expenditure. If the design confirms the employer's general idea of the project, other deliverables for this phase may be the feasibility study and the front-end engineering design ("FEED"),[1] which give the employer more details on the design and costs of the project. It may also be possible for the employer to early-engage contractors and enter into a pre-construction services agreement in order to carry out some initial activities.

As soon as the employer has a clear idea of the project's design and feasibility, it will need to select the contractor. This phase starts with an invitation to tender ("ITT") and concludes with an evaluation of all the tenders received in reply to the ITT. For large projects with numerous tenderers a pre-qualification process is usually ran in order to reduce the number of potential tenders to those that are genuinely appropriate for the project in question. The parties will also negotiate the construction contract so that everything will be ready for the award.

Tendering is a sensible activity for employers as frequently disputes find their source in tender documents. Employers will need to choose one contractor among various tenderers. The choice will be based on a number of factors, including tender price and contractors' experience in projects like the one that is tendered. Tender price is usually the main driver as employers need to make sure that the project budget is respected. However, contractors' technical capacity will also play an important role as a lack of experience may severely affect the project's success.

Once all the tenders are gathered, the employer will evaluate them and award the contract. A construction contract is "awarded" when the employer notifies a tenderer that its tender was successful and that it will be awarded the contract for the project referred to in the ITT. The award is a delicate phase and may give rise to disputes between the parties. At this stage, the employer has chosen the successful contractor and the project is set to start. The parties will probably be under some form of pressure. On the one hand, contractors may need to recover some initial costs and mobilise personnel that they may

1 Although other names may be used such as pre-project planning (PPP), front-end loading (FEL), feasibility analysis, early project planning, etc.

DOI: 10.4324/9781003387718-2

have hired just for the specific project. On the other hand, employers may need to start the works to ensure timely completion for a number of reasons (e.g., because the facility needs to start production or because lenders have lent money on the assumption that the project would start operations within a certain date or because permits are due to expire). This may lead the parties to start some activities based on interim and partial agreements which do not properly allocate the risks between them and lead to uncertainty as to the parties' rights and obligations.

CHAPTER 1

The pre-tender phase

1.1 The conceptual design

The first step employers take when considering the construction of a complex project is having a conceptual design of the project prepared by a specialised engineering company offering such type of services.

The conceptual design is an initial high-level design document which is used as a basis for the feasibility study and the front-end engineering design ("FEED"). The level of detail of a conceptual design is usually low. Nonetheless, the deliverable may carry important liabilities in terms of reliance by employers on the information it contains, albeit it would be very unusual for an employer to take the decision on whether to embark into a large project only on the basis of a conceptual design (i.e., without getting a more detailed feasibility study and/or FEED). Moreover, such documents usually include disclaimers aimed at limiting the liability of the issuing company.

1.2 The feasibility study

1.2.1 Feasibility studies in general

A feasibility study (or feasibility analysis or feasibility report) is a preliminary assessment undertaken at a very early stage of a project (i.e., after a project has been conceived in general, but not yet evaluated in its feasibility, costs, benefits, etc.) whereby employers assess whether a project could be viable and on what conditions. These documents mainly focus on the technical feasibility and commercial profitability of projects analysing the legal, economic, technology, cost and schedule, environmental and other factors up to project completion, as well as the commercial operations which follow the start-up phase. They aim at identifying key project risks at an early stage so to save employers the costs and time of an investment which may eventually be unviable, or viable but at unacceptable cost and/or conditions. The information provided with the feasibility study is usually used by employers as a starting point for detailed FEED studies.

1.2.2 Typical content of a feasibility study

The content of feasibility studies varies sensibly depending on the type of project. By way of example, a feasibility study for an offshore wind farm may include the following:

DOI: 10.4324/9781003387718-3

(i) data for concept design; (ii) selection of potential project site (e.g., based on wind speed, analysis of wave, current and tidal, water depth, distance to coast, seabed analysis); (iii) forecast of expected return on investment based on energy yield and general project net capacity and cost of energy (i.e., the average cost per kilowatt-hour of electrical energy produced by the wind farm); (iv) considerations on electrical aspects such as connection of the wind farm to the onshore substation; (v) considerations on installation and logistics, e.g. availability of ports and vessels in the area; (vi) procurement considerations, including selection of turbines based on wind speed and predicted extreme weather conditions (e.g., likelihood and power of typhoons); (vii) windfarm layout (number and positioning of turbines based on prevailing wind direction); (viii) main project risks (e.g., uncertainty or lack of available data on geotechnical conditions, environmental risks deriving from sensitive marine ecosystems like coral, reefs, marine life, etc.); (ix) need for legal or statutory approvals like planning permissions and environmental impact assessments; (x) aspects of operations and maintenance.

Although feasibility studies contain important information for employers, they do not cover a level of detail which is typically sufficient to allow them to make a final decision on whether the project will be achievable and on what conditions/costs. This is why feasibility studies are usually followed by FEEDs, which set out the basic design of the project.

1.3 The front-end engineering design

1.3.1 Front-end engineering design in general

Once a concept is determined and feasibility is positively assessed, the employer will typically need a FEED. A FEED consists in a set of documents which set forth a project's basic engineering and design parameters. It will typically be based on and develop the results identified in the conceptual design and/or the feasibility study. The aim is to allow employers to have a more accurate cost estimation, which is necessary to come to a final investment decision and allocate the budget for the construction phase.

The project's work scope and cost prediction identified in the FEED may then be used by the employer to tender the work and, after the award, to keep project costs under control. The FEED will also constitute the basis of the detailed design which will be developed in the procurement and construction phase.

1.3.2 Typical content of a front-end engineering design

The content of FEEDs will vary depending on the type of project. A typical FEED may include the following: (i) project overview and background; (ii) development status, including any reference to conceptual design and feasibility studies already performed and any contracts already available; (iii) expected plant performance; (iv) technical and execution planning; (v) provision of a design which meets the employer's and industry standards; (vi) estimate of operation and maintenance costs; (vii) procurement issues (availability and costs of materials, possible inflation, etc.); (viii) confirmation of constructability in line with the employer's expectations; (ix) main risks and hurdles.

1.3.3 Main legal issues with front-end engineering design

FEEDs are often sources of disputes, particularly where: (i) the contract is a lump sum EPC; (ii) the contractor has relied on info/quantities in the FEED to price the project; and (iii) the project results are more costly than expected due to inaccuracies in the FEED.

The outcome of such disputes will typically depend on what party has prepared the FEED. Where the FEED was prepared by the contractor, the contractor will not typically be able to claim such extra costs from the employer for obvious reasons. Where, however, the employer had a specialist engineering company preparing the FEED and the contractor relied on it to quantify its bidding price, the contractor may contend that any inaccuracies in the FEED are the cause of the extra costs it had to bear, and seek recovery of such loss from the employer. On the other hand, the employer may contend that: (i) the FEED was in fact accurate; (ii) the increase of costs is due to flaws in the detailed engineering prepared by the contractor; (iii) the contractor's incapacity to perform the works in a proper manner caused or contributed to the cost increase; (iv) the contractor endorsed the FEED so assuming responsibility for any relevant accuracy. The outcome of such disputes will depend on the language of the contract and the circumstances of the case.

1.4 Contractor's early engagement and pre-construction services agreements

1.4.1 Pre-construction services agreements in general

Design and construction are separate phases. The employer will contract an engineer to design the project, and then award the contract to the contractor, which will carry out the works on the basis of that design (which the contractor might further develop depending on the level of detail). In this scenario, however, the contractor is not given any possibility to participate to the early stages of the project's planning or to contribute to the development of the project design. As the project will be ultimately constructed by the contractor, this structure may lead to disputes on the reliability and correctness of the design prepared by a third party. For this reason, particularly in the case of large and complex projects, employers may seek to involve contractors in since the planning phase, so that they may work in conjunction with the engineer contracted by the employer to prepare the design.

The early engagement of contractors constitutes a clear advantage for both parties as: (i) employers can share part of the risk relevant to the pre-construction phase with contractors and benefit from the contractors' construction experience; while (ii) contractors can become familiar with, and contribute to the project and the relevant design at an early stage. However, employers should be careful not to create any overlap between early contractor's activities and those that the employer has assigned to an engineering company engaged to provide the project's design (if any), as this may create ambiguity as to what the contractor is requested to do, or even a disagreement between the two as to how the project should be designed.

1.4.2 Typical content of a pre-construction services agreement

The services that an early contractor may be asked to perform before the construction work commences are typically regulated by way of so-called pre-construction services agreements ("PCSA"). The content of such contracts varies based on the project and the type of involvement requested by the employer. However, they may include: (i) advising on buildability, sequencing and construction risks; (ii) creating a better integrated project team; (iii) recommending subcontractors and other vendors; (iv) arranging the site layout plan for the construction phase; (v) advising on costs efficiencies.

CHAPTER 2

The tender phase

2.1 The pre-qualification

2.1.1 The pre-qualification in general

It is common in the construction industry for employers to run a pre-qualification process in order to narrow the list of contractors to be invited to tender. In this way, only those meeting the minimum requirements sought by the employer will be allowed to bid for the project. This preliminary scrutiny is beneficial for both employers and contractors as: (i) employers will avoid wasting time in evaluating contractors' bids which are clearly not in line with the project's standards; while (ii) shortlisted contractors, in particular larger ones which bid for more than one project at a time, will be more engaged and focussed on that single project.

2.1.2 The pre-qualification questionnaire

The pre-qualification process is usually implemented through a pre-qualification questionnaire ("PQQ") and pre-tender interviews where the employer evaluates the contractors' suitability for the specific project against different criteria which change based on the type of project. The PQQ is usually a simple box-ticking type of document with clear yes/no questions and a space for notes where the bidding contractors are allowed to give more detail about their answers. By way of example, the questions may include: (i) the bidders' financial soundness (e.g., credit rating, banking arrangements and capacity to obtain bank guarantees from primary banks); (ii) information on whether the bidder is or may be subject to any insolvency proceedings, e.g., because it has passed a resolution or is the subject of an order by a court for the company's winding up or has had a receiver, manager or administrator on behalf of a creditor appointed in respect of the company's business or any part thereof; (iii) information on the bidders' technical capacity (e.g., track record on similar projects and experience/qualifications of key management and personnel that the tenderer proposes to employ on the project); (iv) availability to do the works within a definite deadline and at a definite price level or price range; (v) information on policies and organisation for quality management, including health and safety (e.g., the bidders' incident rate), anticorruption, ESG, etc.; (vi) tenderer's reputation (e.g., previous performances on projects of a different nature, history of the company, prior business relationship or disputes with the same employer); (vii) availability of project management systems appropriate to the successful management of the project; (viii)

DOI: 10.4324/9781003387718-4

availability of equipment (e.g., fabrication yards, intellectual property rights, vessels, machinery, etc.) necessary for the performance of the specific project; (ix) information on equality and diversity (e.g., any policies in compliance with anti-discrimination legislation and any findings of unlawful discrimination); (x) policies and organisation (including training of personnel) for the management of construction-related environmental issues; (xi) information on whether the organisation or directors or key manager have been previously convicted for serious offences like corruption, bribery, money laundering, fraud, failure to pay social security contributions or taxes, etc.

Employers will typically mark a PQQ using a pass/fail scoring methodology with applying specific scores to each section.

2.2 The invitation to tender

2.2.1 Invitation to tender in general

An invitation to tender (or "ITT") is a formal procurement document issued by employers to invite contractors to tender for a project. In such document employers set out the elements that the bidding contractors need to know to evaluate their ability to submit a tender, execute the works and ultimately make a credible offer for the project to which the ITT relates.

2.2.2 Typical content of an invitation to tender

A typical ITT would include the following main items: (i) the instructions to tenderers; (ii) a document containing the summary of the main contractual terms; (iii) the form of agreement; (iv) the heads of agreement; (v) the project's technical documents (scope of work, technical specifications, drawings, etc.).

2.2.2.1 Instructions to tenderer

The instructions to tender is a document giving tenderers information on the project, the tender and the relevant requirements. It may include the following: (i) a general description of the project and the relevant scope of work; (ii) any eligibility requirements for tendering (e.g., whether the tender may be submitted by a joint venture) and any required formalities which the tender should comply with (e.g., date, stamp, signature evidence of the signatory's authority); (iii) information on costs of tendering such as that tendering costs will be borne by the tenderers regardless of the conduct or outcome of the tendering process (albeit less frequently, the document may state that tendering costs will be refunded to the contractor ultimately winning the project); (iv) whether the tenderers are allowed to make site visits before submitting their tenders and/or request information necessary for preparing the tender (e.g., on ground conditions); (v) list of tender documents including any guarantees like performance bonds, advance payment bonds, etc. and the relevant specimen; (vi) requirements applicable to communications (e.g., language, in writing, timing by which the employer will respond, etc.); (vii) employer's right to amend ITT documents prior to the date of opening of tenders and/or prior to the contract award; (viii) formalities to be complied with when submitting the tender (e.g., envelop marked as "confidential"); (ix) any aspects relevant to pricing (e.g. currency); (x) tender timeline; (xi) any required security (e.g., bid bonds) and relevant format (usually a tender security specimen is attached to the ITT), time of validity and regulation; (xii) whether tenderers may qualify or deviate from the ITT and how this may negatively affect the tenderer's evaluated ranking (e.g., specify what specific deviations may disqualify the tenderer); (xiii) any formalities for the submission of tender, including what should be included in the tender envelop and the format to be used (e.g., use a DVD, preference for pdf files, need of and number of hard copies, etc.); (xiv) delivery method (e.g., courier); (xv) deadline for submissions and treatment of late submissions (e.g., returned unopened to tenderer or destroyed); (xvi) whether the tenderers have a right to modify or withdraw their tenders and how to do it (e.g., in writing and prior to submission date); (xvii) information on next steps (e.g., when tenders will be opened, how this will be done and whether the employer may ask for clarifications); (xviii) how the tenders will be evaluated and what selection criteria will be used; (xix) how the successful tenderer will be notified of the contract award (e.g., by courier); (xx) how and when the contract will be entered into with the successful contractor.

2.2.2.2 Form of agreement

The ITT may also include the form of agreement, i.e., the initial document that will be negotiated between the employer and the successful contractor after the project is awarded.

The employer may either use a contract form made available by construction organisations (such as FIDIC, JTC or NEC) or opt for a bespoke document internally drafted and tailored for the specific project.

2.2.2.3 Heads of agreement

As mentioned, in large projects where the tender phase is particularly complex due to the high number of tenderers, the employer will usually shortlist a limited number of bidders and enter into direct discussions with them with the objective of selecting the best contractor for the works. This screening will go on until the employer narrows its choice to a single preferred tenderer. At that point, the employer will engage in one-to-one exclusive negotiations aimed at narrowing any outstanding distances on the offer and to agree on the main terms of the construction contract. The outcome of such negotiations will usually be a binding contract, e.g., an "EPC heads of agreement", to be used as a basis for the detailed EPC contract that the parties will enter into after the award.

EPC heads of agreement are shorter and less detailed than EPC contracts and may include: (i) a description of the parties; (ii) a description of the project; (iii) reference to the tender process; (iv) the contractor's obligation to prepare and submit a technical and commercial proposal for the project by a certain date; (v) exclusivity provisions limiting the employer's right to deal with other contractors in relation to the scope of the heads of agreement until the contractor submits an acceptable proposal; (vi) any good faith obligations; (vii) any conditions precedent to the execution of the contract (e.g., delivery of suitable insurance policies); (viii) an EPC target price or range and the contractor's commitment to use best efforts to meet the target or stay within the range; (ix) contract's boilerplate clauses such as governing law, joint and several liability (in case the contractor is an unincorporated joint venture) etc.

2.2.2.4 Technical documents

The last set of documents which may be included in an ITT is represented by the project's technical documents. These documents are necessary to allow contractors preparing their tenders and will constitute the basis for the technical and commercial offer. They may often become the source of disputes between the parties where contractors suffer losses as a result of such document proving inaccurate (e.g., inaccuracies in design or quantities).

2.2.3 Bid bonds

Organising a tender for a large project will cost the employer a considerable amount of time and money. For this reason, employers will put in place mechanisms aimed at discouraging contractors from withdrawing from ongoing tenders or from an awarded project as this may force the employer to re-open the tender process, so incurring substantial delay and additional expense and losses (e.g., permits may expire, or financing may become unavailable).

This risk is usually covered by requiring tenderers to submit a so-called bid bond ("BB") for a certain sum as stated in the ITT. Where a tenderer breaches the any obligation attached to the BB (e.g., withdraws a tender that has already been submitted or refuses to sign a contract after the relevant award or fails to procure a required performance bond or advance payment bond after the contract has been entered into), the employer may call on the BB and recover part of the loss it may suffer as a result of the breach. In case a tenderer is not successful and has not breached any tender obligations, the BB will be returned immediately. In case of a successful tenderer, the BB will be returned after any obligations for which it was issued are complied with (e.g., providing a performance bond or obtaining the required insurance policies within a certain number of days after the contract is entered into).

2.2.4 Main legal issues with invitations to tender

ITTs are not typically offers to contract in that they do not normally bind the employer to award the contract to the tenderer submitting the tender that best matches the ITT requirements.

An employer issuing an ITT is in fact making an "invitation to treat", i.e., an invitation to contractors to make an offer,[1] so that no binding contract will come into existence until and unless the employer accepts one of the tenders.

Although it is generally thought that it will be unnecessary for employers to include a statement preserving their discretion to reject a tender, it is recommended that the ITT documentation clarifies this point.

In case the ITT expressly states that the employer will be bound to accept the lowest tender, the ITT may amount to an offer or, alternatively, an ITT coupled with an undertaking to accept the best offer, in which case the contract will be concluded as soon as the lowest offer is communicated (subject to the lowest offer being sufficiently detailed to be susceptible of being accepted).[2]

There may also be cases in which it is unclear whether the employer has made an offer or an invitation to treat. A case that gives an idea of such difficulty is *Carlill v Carbolic*

1 *Spencer v Harding* [1870] LR 5 CP at 564.
2 *William Lacey (Hounslow) Ltd v Davis* [1957] 1 WLR 932 at 939.

Smoke Ball Company.[3] Although this is not a construction case, it is still illustrative of the elements necessary for a valid offer and acceptance. The medical firm Carbolic Smoke Ball Company ("Carbolic") advertised that: (i) their smoke ball would prevent those who used it according to the instructions from catching the flu; (ii) in case the smoke ball did not have such effect, buyers would receive £100; (iii) Carbolic had deposited £1,000 in a bank to show their good faith. Mrs Louisa Elizabeth Carlill bought the smoke ball, used it according to the instructions, but still caught a flu. As a result, she brought legal proceedings against Carbolic. Carbolic's defence was that advertisement was not to be taken as a legally binding offer, but was rather an "invitation to treat" and a "mere puff". The court held: (i) that it would appear to a reasonable man that Carbolic had in fact made a serious offer, also considering the reference to the £1,000 deposit; and (ii) that people who bought the smokeball had given good "consideration" for it by going to the "distinct inconvenience" of using a faulty product. The advertisement was to be considered an offer, despite Carbolic used the phrase "invitation to treat".

2.3 The tender

2.3.1 Tenders in general

Contractors invited to tender respond to the ITTs with their tender.[4] A tender is a document where contractors make an offer for construction services based on the information contained in the ITT. Tenders will need to be compliant with the requirements of, and include all the information requested in the ITT.

A typical tender may include the following elements: (i) the tenderer's price for carrying out the works; (ii) details on how the tenderer intends to meet the employer's requirements; (iii) a tender pricing document setting out rates and costs; (iv) demonstration of capability such as track record on similar projects; (v) information on how the tenderer intends to manage health and safety; (vi) any procedures to be adopted; (vii) design proposals (if so requested in the ITT); (viii) a programme of works in which the tenderer highlights how it proposes to sequence the works; (ix) information on key personnel (project directors and project managers, plant and labour resources) that the tenderer proposes to involve in the project and relevant roles and experience.

2.3.2 Main legal issues with tenders

Tenders carry important legal consequences and are often used as evidence in disputes between contractors and employers.

Tenderers shall use particular care in preparing these documents and make sure they are given enough time to prepare them properly as insufficient time may lead to potential mistakes such as errors in the measurement quantities, poor knowledge of work required, underestimation of escalation and even clerical errors in preparing the bid documents.

3 *Carlill v Carbolic Smoke Ball Company* [1893] 1 QB 256.

4 Before issuing the formal tender, employers and contractors may also run mid-tender interviews aimed at providing clarifications on the ITT and avoid the submission of inaccurate tenders.

As employers will award projects based on the tenders they receive, inaccuracies may become the source of complex disputes.

2.3.2.1 Binding effect of tenders

It is vital that the tender clearly states if it is an offer subject of being accepted. In the case of *Crowshaw v Pritchard and Renwick*,[5] the employer sent a drawing and a specification to a contractor and asked for his tender. The contractor sent an "estimate" which included the following language: "*ESTIMATE – Our estimate to carry out the sundry alterations to the above premises, according to the drawings and specifications, amounts to £1,230*". The employer accepted what he defined the contractor's "*offer to execute*" the works. The contractor then contended that his estimate: (i) was not intended to be an offer; and (ii) based on trade custom, a letter in the form sent to the employer could not be treated as an offer. The court held that there was in fact an enforceable contract based on the estimate. In particular, on the contractor's argument that it was customary that estimates would not to be treated as offers, the court held:

> It has been suggested that there is some custom or well-known understanding that a letter in this form is not to be treated as an offer. There is no such custom, and, if there is, it is contrary to law.

2.3.2.2 Recoverability of tendering costs and claims against the employer

In general, tenderers are not supposed to be paid for the tendering costs they sustain to prepare their tender (which may be substantial), unless the employer's requests are beyond the normal work which a tenderer would perform gratuitously and at his own risk.[6]

However, employers issuing ITT shall be very careful how they manage bids as there may be cases in which bidders responding to ITTs may have grounded claims against employers for such costs. Some examples are the following:

2.3.2.2.1 THE EMPLOYER HAD NEVER INTENDED CONTRACTING THE PROJECT

When a tender process is cancelled, and a tenderer can show that the employer had never had any intention of contracting any of or all the tenderers invited to tender, employers may be liable for damages in fraud and the affected tenderers may be able to recover their tendering expenses.[7] Obviously, the situation is completely different in case the tender processes is genuinely cancelled.

2.3.2.2.2 THE EMPLOYER FAILED TO CONSIDER FAIRLY ALL TENDERS MATCHING THE INVITATION TO TENDER CRITERIA

In the context of public procurement, a tenderer may show that the employer has breached an implied contractual duty to consider all compliant tenders, or to consider them fairly on the basis of a collateral contract created by the ITT and compliant tenders.

In the case of *Blackpool and Fylde Aero Club v Blackpool BC*,[8] the defendant, a local authority owning an airport, had granted the claimants a concession allowing them to operate leisure flights out of the airport. When it was time to renew the concession, the

5 *Crowshaw v Pritchard and Renwick* [1899] 16 TLR 45.
6 *William Lacey (Hounslow) Ltd v Davis* [1957] 1 WLR 932 at 934.
7 *Richardson v Silverster* [1873] LR 9 QB.
8 *Blackpool and Fylde Aero Club v Blackpool BC* [1990] 3 All ER 25.

defendant sent ITTs to several companies. The ITT stated that the defendant was not bound to accept any particular tender, and that any tenders delivered beyond a particular date would not be considered. The claimant duly posted its tender. However, the defendant's staff picked it from their inbox only after the deadline had passed. The concession was then awarded to another bidder. The claimant sued the defendant for breach of contract and negligence, contending that: (i) the defendant had a duty to properly consider all tenders which met the ITT criteria; and (ii) as its tender was submitted before the deadline indicated in the ITT, the employer should have considered it with all the other tenders duly submitted. The Court of Appeal held that: (i) ITTs are not offers, but invitations to treat; and (ii) an ITT followed by a compliant tender creates a collateral contract.[9] Lord Justice Bingham said:

> I have no doubt that the parties did intend to create contractual relations to the limited extent contended for . . . I think it plain that the Council's invitation to tender was, to this limited extent, an offer, and the Club's submission of a timely and conforming tender an acceptance.

As a result, it is now accepted that, at least in the public sector, employers are required to consider fairly all tenders properly matching the criteria indicated in the ITT.[10]

Whether this principle can be extended to private procurement contracts is still uncertain. Although not an English case, a first step in this direction was made in *J&A Developments Limited v Edina Manufacturing Limited, Armoura Ltd and Others*.[11] In this case, Edina Manufacturing Limited ("Edina") issued an ITT to some contractors to tender for the erection of workshop offices and other associated works. The ITT incorporated the Code of Procedure for Single Stage Selective Tendering 1996 (the "Code") published by the National Joint Consultative Committee for Building. The ITT also included a clause stating, among other things, that

> any practice which seeks to reduce the tender arbitrarily where the tender has been submitted in free competition and no modification to the specification, quantity or conditions under which the work is to be executed or to be made, or to reduce tenders other than the lowest to a figure below the lowest tender.

J&A Developments Limited ("J&A") submitted the lowest tender. Edina then approached the first three lowest tenderers and asked them to reduce their respective prices. J&A refused to reduce its price and the contract was awarded to another company. J&A challenged the validity of the award on the grounds that Edina had acted unfairly and in breach of the Code. The court found Edina to be in breach of contract as: (i) inviting the tenderers to reduce their prices arbitrarily was a clear breach of the procedure dictated in the Code; and (ii) had the Code been followed correctly, J&A would have been awarded the contract. In reaching its decision, the High Court of Northern Ireland observed that:

> [implied] contracts have only hitherto been found in tendering situations where the party seeking tenders is a public body . . . while there may be a statutory distinction in the

9 *Blackpool and Fylde Aero Club Ltd v Blackpool BC* [1990] 1 WLR 1195.

10 See also *Harmon CFEM Facades (UK) Ltd v The Corporate Officer of the House of Commons* [1999] 67 Con LR 1.

11 *J&A Developments Limited v Edina Manufacturing Limited, Armoura Ltd and Others* [2006] NIQB 86.

position of a public body and a private employer the common law recognises no such distinction.

2.3.2.2.3 FRAUDULENT OR NEGLIGENT MISREPRESENTATION

Employers will usually seek to exclude their responsibility for inaccuracies in statements of fact and information provided in the ITT documents. Despite that, tenderers may have claims for fraudulent or negligent misrepresentation in case tenderers have suffered losses and have relied on those statements. Any clauses purporting to exclude employers' liability will be construed narrowly and may have to satisfy a reasonableness test.

2.3.2.2.4 CORRUPTION

In cases of corruption or bribery, losing tenderers will be entitled to bring actions in deceit or fraud.[12]

2.3.2.2.5 ALTERNATIVE TENDERS

In some cases, tenderers may be allowed to submit two tenders with different contents from which the employer may choose. However, this may generate uncertainties and, ultimately, disputes.

In the case of *Peter Lind & Co v Mersey Docks & Harbour Board*,[13] a contractor submitted two tenders for construction of a new freight terminal, one for a fixed price and the other on a "cost plus" basis. The employer then communicated acceptance of "*your tender*" pending necessary approvals and completion of some formalities. However, in the following months the price of materials rose. The employer then confirmed acceptance of the fixed price tender and prepared the contract on that basis. The contractor refused to sign the agreement but continued working on the project. Cooke J held that there was no contract as the acceptance was imprecise in that it did not specify which tender had been accepted. The contractors were thus entitled to be paid on a quantum meruit basis.

2.3.3 Tender evaluation[14]

2.3.3.1 Tender evaluation in general

Upon expiry of the deadline set in the ITT, the employer will open and examine the received tenders. In order to reduce the risk that the award to a specific tenderer is subsequently challenged: (i) the evaluation process should be carried out in accordance with criteria, or the methodology specified in the ITT; (ii) such criteria and methodology shall be objective; and (iii) possibly, the same team of evaluators should evaluate all bids to guarantee consistency.

12 *Richardson v Silvester* [1873] LR 9 QB 34.

13 *Peter Lind & Co v Mersey Docks & Harbour Board* [1972] 2 Lloyd's Rep 234.

14 The rules of tender evaluations applicable to public entities will vary depending on the nationality of the authority and is outside the scope of this book.

2.3.3.2 Main evaluation criteria

There are various criteria that employers may use to evaluate tenders. In the case of complex construction projects with a high number of tenderers, employers may first exclude extreme tenders (in terms of price and/or technical requirements) and/or tenders that are deviating the most from the ITT requirements. Employers will then proceed with the evaluation, based on a number of criteria.

The main criterion for a tender evaluation is usually price. However, awarding a construction contract to the lowest bidder without considering other factors can lead to cost and time overruns. As a result, employers will usually seek to achieve value for money, i.e., secure the best mix of quality for the least cost by weighting price and non-price factors. This usually means that the lowest upfront price will not automatically win, whilst the price target will be "blended" with quality targets such as technical merit, track record, aesthetic and functional characteristics, accessibility, social characteristics, environmental characteristics, innovative characteristics, delivery conditions, etc.

One of the most widely used methods to evaluate tenders is the MEAT ("Most Economically Advantageous Tender"), based on which each tender is assigned a score calculated by using a formula which takes into account the best price to quality ratio. Each selected criterion is given a relative weighting or order of importance, which is set out in the tender documents, so that each tender is evaluated based on the extent to which it meets that specific criterion.

CHAPTER 3

The award phase

3.1 The letter of award

3.1.1 The letter of award in general

An employer will award a contract through a written letter of award ("LOA"). A LOA will usually be sent together with the letters to all other unsuccessful tenderers.

In the case of private tenders, the LOA will not come as a surprise for the preferred contractor as, at that stage, the employer and the successful contractor may have entered into an "EPC heads of agreement" fixing the main terms of the final EPC contract and may be already negotiating the final EPC contract on the basis of a form of contract and other documents provided by the employer in the ITT. Thus, the LOA will typically have the aim to fix the terms of the forthcoming relation between the parties and make sure that they formally engage in the performance of the project.

3.1.2 Typical content of a letter of award

Letters of award may differ sensibly depending on the project and the number and type of information that the employer intends to convey to the successful contractor. However, a typical LOA may include at least the following key terms: (i) the date of the LOA; (ii) details of the recipient; (iii) information on the project (typically in the subject); (iv) a number of premises usually referring to the whole process, including the ITT, the tender, any negotiation between the parties, any heads of agreement or form of contract (if finalised/entered into); (v) reference to the employer's requirements (or scope of work) and the basis of design which shall guide the contractor in preparing the detailed design (documents may be attached to the LOA); (vi) the contractor's obligation not to amend or depart the offer contained in its tender; (vii) any target that the project shall meet (e.g., production targets) and a representation from the contractor that such target will be achieved; (viii) the contract price for the scope of work; (ix) the commencement date and the indication that works should only commence subject to the employer having issued a formal notice to proceed. The LOA may also state the consequences of the employer not issuing the notice to proceed within a certain date (e.g., it may state that the parties shall engage in good faith negotiations); (x) the agreed completion date (subject to notice to proceed being issued within a certain date) and a representation from the contractor that it is achievable; (xi) any important requirement such as the issuance of guarantees (e.g., advance payment bonds and performance bonds), insurance policies,

DOI: 10.4324/9781003387718-5

access to site, etc.; (xii) the obligation on the parties to enter into good faith negotiations to finalise the construction contract based on the form of agreement already provided to the contractor and the heads of agreement already entered into between the parties (if any) and to have it signed within a certain deadline; (xiii) indication that the heads of agreement (if any) will regulate the parties relation until the formal EPC contract is entered into; (xiv) indication that the LOA is valid only when countersigned by the contractor for acceptance and shall automatically expire when the final construction contract is executed (or when terminated in accordance with any termination clause included in the LOA); (xv) the signature blocks.

3.1.3 Binding nature of letters of award

A LOA in the form of an offer becomes binding upon acceptance. A binding LOA will usually include a request that the LOA is accepted and signed by the successful contractor. Once accepted, the LOA will regulate the relation between the parties until they enter into the final construction contract (which will usually include an "entire agreement clause" to ensure that the parties' relation is regulated only by the construction contract, which supersedes any other agreement between them, including the LOA).

Where, however, a LOA does not contain an offer, but only an indication that the parties will agree on the terms of the award, it may be classified as an unenforceable agreement to agree.

3.1.3.1 Agreements to agree

3.1.3.1.1 AGREEMENTS TO AGREE IN GENERAL

In construction projects a moment comes when the contractor has already been officially selected, but the parties have not yet entered into a binding contract for the work. In this phase, it is not uncommon for the parties to have reached a general understanding on the terms of the final construction contract (e.g., based on a "heads of agreement") and have "agreed to agree" on such terms as soon as the formal contract will be entered into.

The general rule under English law is that an "agreement to agree" is not enforceable as it is too uncertain to be binding on the parties. However, based on the wrong assumption that an agreement to agree is in fact enforceable, contractors may perform some preliminary obligations arising from this general understanding with the employer. In *Courtney and Fairbairn Ltd v Tolaini Brothers (Hotels) Ltd,*[1] Lord Denning posed the question of whether, even if the parties had not entered into a contract to build, a contract to negotiate may be said to have come into existence. He first considered "*not well founded*" the tentative opinion expressed by Lord Wright in *Hillas & Co Ltd v Arcos Ltd*[2] that:

> There is then no bargain except to negotiate, and negotiations may be fruitless and end without any contract ensuing . . . yet even then, in strict theory, there is a contract (if there is good consideration) to negotiate, though in the event of repudiation by one party the damages may be nominal, unless a jury think that the opportunity to negotiate was of some appreciable value to the injured party.

1 *Courtney and Fairbairn Ltd v Tolaini Brothers (Hotels) Ltd* [1975] ADR LR 00/00; WLR 297.
2 *Hillas & Co Ltd v Arcos Ltd* [1932] All ER Rep 494 at 505, 147 LT 503 at [515].

He then held that:[3]

> If the law does not recognise a contract to enter into a contract (when there is a fundamental term yet to be agreed) it seems to me it cannot recognise a contract to negotiate. The reason is because it is too uncertain to have any binding force. No court could estimate the damages because no one can tell whether the negotiations would be successful or would fall through; or if successful, what the result would be. It seems to me that a contract to negotiate, like a contract to enter into a contract, is not a contract known to the law . . . I think we must apply the general principle that when there is a fundamental matter left undecided and to be the subject of negotiation, there is no contract. So I would hold that there was not any enforceable agreement in the letters between the plaintiff and the defendants.

3.1.3.1.2 RECOVERABILITY OF COSTS ON A QUANTUM MERUIT BASIS

The fact that agreements to agree are not enforceable per se does not mean that constrictors have no remedies to recover all or some of their costs. Where a contractor has carried out some woks without a binding contract having been signed, and the courts do not infer one to exist, the contractor will generally be entitled to recover money in quantum meruit in case the employer has requested the works and has gained some benefit from them.

3.1.3.1.3 ENFORCEABLE AGREEMENTS TO AGREE

There are some circumstances in which the courts will enforce an agreement to agree. These include the following:

3.1.3.1.3.1 AGREEMENTS TO AGREE AS PART OF AN ONGOING AGREEMENT Courts are likely to give effect to an obligation to negotiate where it arises as part of an ongoing agreement. It is not uncommon for construction contracts to contain clauses providing for the renegotiation of fees, wages or other payments to account for fluctuations in the costs of raw materials or labour. Such clauses have the effect of shifting the burdens for increasing materials and labour costs from the contractor to the employer. If a construction contract contains such a provision, English courts will seek to uphold renegotiation or price review wherever possible. In the case of *Associated British Ports v Tata Steel UK Ltd*[4] the High Court considered whether a clause to renegotiate price, quantity or other factors over time was an unenforceable "agreement to agree". In that case, the court came to the conclusion that it was not such, but the case gives useful insights as to what makes such clauses enforceable. Associated British Ports ("ABP"), the owner and operator of Tidal Harbour facilities at Port Talbot, Wales, entered into a licence agreement with Tata Steel UK Limited ("Tata"). The licence agreement also set the rights and obligations of the parties as to Tata's use of the Tidal Harbour facilities in relation to the import of steel works through the Tidal Harbour. Clause 22 of the licence agreement contained a renegotiation provision stating:

> It is hereby agreed between the parties that in the event of any major physical or financial change in circumstances affecting the operation of [Tata's] Works at Llanwern or Port Talbot or ABP's operation of the Tidal Harbour on or at any time after the 15th day of September 2007 either party may serve notice on the other requiring the terms of this Licence to be re-negotiated with effect from the date on which such notice shall be served. The parties shall immediately seek to agree amended terms reflecting such change in circumstances and if agreement is not reached within a period of six months from the date of the notice the matter

3 *Courtney and Fairbairn Ltd v Tolaini Brothers (Hotels) Ltd* [1975] ADR LR 00/00; WLR 297.

4 *Associated British Ports v Tata Steel UK Ltd* [2017] EWHC 694 (Ch).

> shall be referred to an Arbitrator (whose decision shall be binding on both parties and who shall so far as possible be an expert in the area of dispute between the parties) to be agreed by the parties or (if the parties shall fail to agree) to be appointed on the joint application of the parties or (if either shall neglect forthwith to join in such application then on the sole application of the other of them) by the President for the time being of the Law Society.

Tata served notice to ABP under Clause 22 based on the fact that a "*major financial change in circumstances*" had occurred in that the competitiveness of UK-manufactured steel had been reduced due to a number of certain factors, including a doubling in the imports of steel to Europe, a quadrupling of imports from China, increased tariffs by the United States and a strong pound. As a result, Tata asked to amend the licence agreement, including providing for a 50% reduction of the fee that Tata had to pay to ABP. ABP contended that such factors did not fall within the definition of "*major financial change in circumstances*" as the steel industry is regularly impacted by circumstances such as the ones indicated by Tata. ABP applied to the High Court requesting a declaration that the clause was an "agreement to agree" and, as such, it was to be held invalid for uncertainty. Tata applied for ABP's claim to be stayed under Section 9 (1) of the Arbitration Act 1996[5] on the grounds that the dispute was to be resolved by arbitration under Clause 22 of the licence agreement. Rose J rejected ABP's arguments holding that Clause 22 of the licence agreement was not so uncertain as to be unenforceable as it contained a clear obligation to refer any dispute regarding renegotiation of licence's terms to arbitration. In reaching this decision, Rose J confirmed that the courts should strive to give some meaning to contractual clauses agreed by the parties. She reported Leggatt J's assertion in *Astor Management AG & ors v Atalaya Mining plc & others*[6] that:

> the role of the court in a commercial dispute is to give legal effect to what the parties have agreed, not to throw its hands in the air and refuse to do so because the parties have not made its task easy. To hold that a clause is too uncertain to be enforceable is a last resort.

3.1.3.1.3.2 AGREEMENTS TO AGREE ON HOW NEGOTIATION SHOULD OPERATE Agreements to agree may also be held enforceable in case the obligation to negotiate is intended to assist in resolving a dispute about how the negotiation should operate. In the case of *Alstom Signalling Ltd v Jarvis Facilities Ltd*,[7] Railtrack contracted Alstom Signalling Ltd ("Alstom") for the works of extension of the Tyne and Wear Metro in England. The contract contained a pain/gain sharing mechanism for cost overruns and underruns based on which: (i) if the final cost of the project resulted to be below the set target cost, then Alstom and Railtrack would share any net gain; whilst (ii) in case of any overrun, the parties would share the net pain. Alstom wished to subcontract the signalling and other works to Jarvis Facilities Ltd ("Jarvis"). The parties engaged into lengthy negotiations where Jarvis accepted in principle that they would enter into a pain/gain sharing arrangement with Alstom, however Alstom's position was that the calculation of the pain/gain with Jarvis should reflect the

5 Section 9 (1) of the Arbitration Act 1996 states:

> A party to an arbitration agreement against whom legal proceedings are brought (whether by way of claim or counterclaim) in respect of a matter which under the agreement is to be referred to arbitration may (upon notice to the other parties to the proceedings) apply to the court in which the proceedings have been brought to stay the proceedings so far as they concern that matter.

6 *Astor Management AG & ors v Atalaya Mining plc & others* [2017] EWHC 425 (Comm).

7 *Alstom Signalling Ltd v Jarvis Facilities Ltd* [2004] EWHC 1232 (TCC).

one under the main contract, while Jarvis wished the pain/gain sharing mechanism to relate only to the subcontract. During the negotiations Alstom sent Jarvis a draft subcontract: (i) containing a clause stating: "*Details of the pain/gain mechanism are to be reviewed and agreed. . . . Once agreed by both parties the details shall be added to the Sub-contract Agreement as an amendment*"; and (ii) providing that any party could refer a dispute or difference to adjudication under the Housing Grants, Construction and Regeneration Act 1996, and that, subject to that, any dispute or difference which arises between the parties should be referred to the Technology and Construction Court. Eventually, the subcontract between Alstom and Jarvis was never signed, but Alstom contended that a valid contract existed between the parties based on which Jarvis had agreed to share any pain or gain in line with the main contract between Alstom and Railtrack. Jarvis' position was that there was nothing more than an agreement to agree in relation to the pain/gain issue, which was therefore not enforceable. When the works under the main contract were completed, and the pain sharing mechanism was applied, Alstom sought to recover some of such costs from Jarvis. The matter was heard by Mr Recorder Reece QC who found in favour of Alstom. He held that, notwithstanding the absence of a signed document, a binding contract between the parties did exist as it contained an unequivocal agreement to participate in pain/gain sharing, even though to an extent and in a manner yet to be agreed. As a result, the parties had an (implied) primary obligation to make reasonable endeavours to agree on the pain/gain provisions. The parties' failure to agree on such term was a "difference" as per the draft subcontract dispute resolution clause. As a result, Alstom was entitled to ask the Technology and Construction Court to determine this difference.

Another case on this subject is *Teekay Tankers Ltd v STX Offshore and Shipbuilding Co Ltd*,[8] where Mr Justice Walker clarified that the law on agreements to agree was considered in *MRI Trading AG v Erdenet Mining Corp LLC*.[9] In that case the Court of Appeal, citing *Mamidoil-Jetoil Greek Petroleum Co SA v Okta Crude Oil Refinery AD*,[10] stated that, subject to the assumption that each case must be decided on its own facts and on the construction of its own agreement, the following principles apply to the subject of agreements to agree:

(i) Where no contract exists the use of an expression such as "to be agreed" in relation to an essential term is likely to prevent any contract coming into existence, and the absence of agreement on essential terms of the agreement may prevent any contract coming into existence, in both cases, on the ground of uncertainty.

(ii) In commercial dealings between parties who are familiar with the trade in question, and where the parties have acted in the belief that they had a binding contract, the courts are willing to imply terms, where that is possible, to enable the contract to be carried out.

(iii) Where a contract has once come into existence, even the expression "to be agreed" in relation to future executory obligations is not necessarily fatal to its continued existence.

8 *Teekay Tankers Ltd v STX Offshore and Shipbuilding Co Ltd* [2017] EWHC 253 (Comm).
9 *MRI Trading AG v Erdenet Mining Corp LLC* [2013] EWCA Civ 156; [2013] 1 Lloyd's Rep 638.
10 *Mamidoil-Jetoil Greek Petroleum Co SA v Okta Crude Oil Refinery AD* [2001] 2 Lloyd's Rep 76.

(iv) In the case of contracts for future performance over a period, where the parties may desire or need to leave matters to be adjusted in the working out of their contract, the courts will assist the parties to do so, so as to preserve rather than destroy bargains, on the basis that what can be made certain is itself certain. This is particularly the case where one party has either already had the advantage of some performance which reflects the parties' agreement on a long-term relationship, or has had to make an investment premised on that agreement.

3.2 Letters of intent

3.2.1 Letters of intent in general

The lapse of time necessary to agree on the formalities of a construction contract may adversely affect the overall project's programme. To avoid this unwanted result, the parties consider entering into a letter of intent ("LOI") whereby the employer expresses its intention to accept the contractor's tender and instructs the contractor to commence some works/activities pending the finalisation of the construction contract. This allows the contractor to start carrying out some early development works or other limited on-site activities (e.g., design, procurement, off-site pre-construction activities, instruction of subcontractors/suppliers) or to start mobilising personnel before a formal contract is entered into.

The following is an example of LOI in a construction case:[11]

> You [the contractor] will proceed with the preparation of a detailed program of details and samples associated with works including liaison and coordination essential to the program. Pending execution of the contract documents, you will accept this as a letter of intent on the understanding that a contract will be placed with your company. If the project is cancelled at any stage by the client prior to the issue of the contract documents, you will be reimbursed your net costs plus overheads and profit on nets costs only which will be agreed by the quantity surveyor. You will not be reimbursed for costs not incurred such as loss of profit et cetera.

LOIs may be a good instrument to set the project in motion in cases where the formal construction contract is concluded shortly after the LOI. However, where the negotiations of the construction contract protract over time, the parties' relation may deteriorate. Moreover, supervening events may occur that will change the circumstances around the specific project. As a result, the chances of successfully concluding the construction contract may decrease.

Even where the parties eventually reach an agreement, disagreements may arise as to the exact terms governing the work carried out under the LOI. In *Cunningham and Others v Collett and Farmer*[12] Coulson J was called to consider whether the use of a LOI had been negligent in the circumstances. The claimants, who were the owners of a large Georgian mansion, alleged that the defendant architects had been negligent in utilising a LOI for the works. In finding that the use of the LOI was not negligent on the part of the defendant architects, Coulson J gave guidance on when a LOI might be properly used,

11 *Structure Consulting v Maroush* [2017] EWHC 962 (TCC).

12 *Cunningham and others v Collett and Farmer* [2006] EWHC 1771 (TCC).

i.e., where: (i) the contract's scope of work and the price are either agreed or there is a clear mechanism for their agreement; (ii) the contract terms are, or are very likely to be, agreed; (iii) the start and finish dates and contract programme are broadly agreed; (iv) there are good reasons to start work in advance of the finalisation of all contract documents.

It is worth highlighting that some contractors may even consider LOIs better than final construction contracts as they give rise to a right to be paid, but do not carry the contractual obligations deriving from a full contract. In the case of *Tesco Stores v Costain Construction*,[13] HHJ Richard Seymour QC has summarised the problem as follows:

> It is part of the folklore of the construction industry that there exists a mythical beast, 'the Letter of Intent', the legal effect of which, if it is acted upon, is that it entitles a contractor to payment for what he does, but does not expose him to any risk because it imposes no contractual obligations upon him . . . in fact the legal effect of a letter of intent depends upon the true construction of the communications between the parties and the effect, if any, of their actions pursuant to those communications.

However, there is not a single rule as to the effect and efficacy of LOI as their content may differ significantly and it is ultimately "*a question upon the facts of each case whether the sending of a letter of intent can give rise to any, and if any, what, liability*".[14] In this regard, in the case of *ERDC Group v Brunel University*,[15] HH Humphrey Lloyd QC held that:

> Letters of intent come in all sorts of forms. Some are merely expressions of hope; others are firmer but make it clear that no legal consequences ensue; others presage a contract and may be tantamount to an agreement 'subject to contract'; others are contracts falling short of the full-blown contract that is contemplated; others are in reality that contract in all but name. There can therefore be no prior assumptions, such as looking to see if words such as 'letter of intent' have or have not been used. The phrase 'letter of intent' is not a term of art. Its meaning and effect depend on the circumstances of each case.

The parties shall be clear as to what effects and efficacy they want to attach to a LOI. They would be ill-advised to allow work to continue in perpetuity under a LOI as such documents do not usually afford the parties a satisfactory degree of protection.

Generally, employers will make clear in the LOI whether it is intended to be binding or not. However, ambiguities often generate disputes and may lead the court to give a LOI an effect the parties had not intended or anticipated. Where possible, contractors should avoid commencing work before a full agreement has been properly executed.

Where, for practical reasons, contractors agree to commence work under a LOI, they should make sure that there are provisions in place to clarify whether the parties intend the LOI to be binding upon the parties.

The LOI shall also clearly allocate risk between the parties and state the terms and conditions which shall regulate their contractual relations until a full contract is entered into (including whether any standard terms referred to in the LOI is intended to be binding). The document should also identify what terms are still open to discussion between the parties and state whether they are considered essential. Moreover, in order to minimise

13 *Tesco Stores v Costain Construction* [2003] EWHC 1487 (TCC).
14 *Tesco Stores v Costain Construction* [2003] EWHC 1487 (TCC).
15 *ERDC Group v Brunel University* [2006] EWHC 687 (TCC).

the risk of giving rise to an estoppel or to an unwanted variation of the contract, once the LOI is agreed the contractors shall not carry out works beyond the agreed scope or continue working after its expiry date.

3.2.2 Binding nature of letters of intent

Depending on the words used in the document and the particular facts surrounding the case, most letters of intent will fall within two categories, i.e., binding interim contracts or non-binding letters of comfort.

A distinction between non-binding and binding LOI can be found in the case of *Cunningham and Others v Collett and Farmer*,[16] in which Coulson J distinguished between two types of LOI:

(i) The first type, which are "*properly so-called, is a document which expresses an intention on the part of party A to enter into a contract in the future with party B, but creates no liability in regard to that future contract. It is expressly designed to have no binding effect whatsoever*".
(ii) The second type, the most common in the modern construction industry, which are "*expressly designed to give rise to some, albeit limited, reciprocal rights and liabilities*".

3.2.2.1 Binding letters of intent

In certain cases, a LOI can give rise to a binding agreement. The binding contract arising from a LOIs can take one of two forms, i.e., an ancillary executory contract or an "if" contract.

In *British Steel Corporation v Cleveland Bridge & Engineering Co Ltd*,[17] Goff J expressed his view on when a binding contract (including a binding LOI) may only come into existence:

> As a matter of analysis the contract (if any) which may come into existence following a letter of intent may take one of two forms: either there may be an ordinary executory contract, under which each party assumes reciprocal obligations to the other; or there may be what is sometimes called an 'if' contract, i.e. a contract under which A requests B to carry out a certain performance and promises B that, if he does so, he will receive a certain performance in return, usually remuneration for his performance. The latter transaction is really no more than a standing offer which, if acted upon before it lapses or is lawfully withdrawn, will result in a binding contract.

Thus, unless the LOI is an executory contract or an "if" contract, it will not be binding on the parties (although the works carried out by the contractor may nonetheless be remunerated in quantum meruit).

More specifically:

(i) An executory contract may be defined as a contract that has not yet been completely performed by either party, in accordance with its terms. In the case of a LOI, this occurs because the parties have agreed to perform their obligations at a future

16 *Cunningham and others v Collett and Farmer* [2006] EWHC 1771 (TCC).
17 *British Steel Corporation v Cleveland Bridge and Engineering* [1984] 1 All ER.

point in time and are bound to this obligation. Thus, under such type of LOI each party assumes reciprocal obligations to the other on what is agreed in the LOI.

(ii) A LOI is an "if" contract when the employer requests the contractor to carry out a certain work and promises that, if he does so, he will receive a certain remuneration. The employer may usually withdraw the offer or put a deadline by which the contractor shall commence the works. If the contractor acts upon the LOI before it lapses or is lawfully withdrawn, the LOI will result in a binding "provisional" contract, which should then be replaced with the formal construction contract. A LOI in this form has the advantage of allowing the work to commence on main general terms (e.g., scope of work, main terms and conditions, dispute resolution method) which the parties have agreed, even though details are yet to be finalised. However, interim contracts also present risks as the parties are not afforded the set of protections that a full contract may give them. In the case of *Hall & Tawse South Ltd v Ivory Gate Ltd*[18] where Judge Thornton QC said:

> A letter of intent is usually a unilateral assurance intended to have contractual effect if acted upon, whereby reasonable expenditure reasonably incurred in reliance upon such a letter will be reimbursed. Such a letter places no obligation upon the recipient to act upon it and there is usually no obligation to continue with the work or to undertake any defined parcel of work, the recipient being free to stop work at any time.
>
> The effect of such a letter is to promise reasonable reimbursement if the recipient does act upon it. However, the letter in question . . . is one which imposes obligations on both parties. It requires the plaintiff to commence the works, being a defined package of work and contract administration. The plaintiff had an option of whether to start or not but, having started, the plaintiff was under an obligation to continue with the works and not to stop, unless the defendant appointed another contractor or gave notice abandoning the work or the contract was superseded by one of the two successor contracts envisaged by the letter. I propose, therefore, to refer to this contract as 'the provisional contract'.

3.2.2.2 Non-binding letters of intent

The general position is that LOIs are documents whereby the parties express a mere intention to enter into a contract at a later date, but they do not result in a contract in themselves as they are too uncertain to have any binding force. Such type of LOI is also sometimes referred to as comfort letters.

In *Turriff Construction Ltd v Regalia Knitting Mills Ltd*, the court had to consider the effects of a LOI stating as follows:

> Dear Sirs, As agreed at our meeting of 2nd June, it is the intention of Regalia to award a contract to Turriff to build a factory including production, stores, offices and canteen facilities to be built in four continuous phases . . . all to be subject to obtaining agreement on the land and leases with the Development Corporation, full building and bye-law consent and the site investigation . . . the whole to be subject to agreement on an acceptable contract.

Judge Fay QC held that a LOI in such terms was:

> no more than an expression in writing of a party's present intention to enter into a contract at a future date. Save in exceptional circumstances it can have no binding effect.[19]

18 *Hall & Tawse South Ltd v Ivory Gate Ltd* [1998] 62 Con LR 117.
19 *Turriff Construction Ltd v Regalia Knitting Mills Ltd* [1971] 9 BLR 20.

In *Courtney and Fairbairn Ltd v Tolaini Bros Hotels Ltd*[20] the court confirmed that absent an agreement on fundamental terms such as price, a contract cannot be said to have come into existence. Lord Denning MR said:

> If the law does not recognise a contract to enter into a contract (when there is a fundamental term yet to be agreed) it seems to me it cannot recognise a contract to negotiate. The reason is because it is too uncertain to have any binding force.

In *Smith and Gordon Ltd v John Lewis Building Ltd*,[21] the contractors, sent a LOI to their subcontractor stating that a form of subcontract (NSC/1) would follow. The subcontractor orally accepted the LOI, but the contractor failed to send the subcontract. The court found that absent the subcontract, the contractor was prevented from relying on the arbitration clause contained in the subcontract form.

3.2.2.3 Letters of intent and "quantum meruit" claims

Even when the LOI is not binding on the parties (i.e., is not an executory or "if" contract), a contractor that has started working upon it will normally be entitled to a reasonable payment for the work done and may claim such payment in restitution (or quantum meruit).

The absence of a contract will entail that both the employer and the contractor may stop the works at any time without notice, and the employer will not be entitled to claim for breach of contract (as there is no contract) in the case of delay or defective work, although courts may consider defects when assessing the quantum meruit claim.

Clearly, this situation creates uncertainties as the contractual risks have not been properly allocated. For example: (i) contractors may be exposed to uncapped liability as no exclusion or limitation of liability clauses or liquidated damages clauses have been agreed on; and (ii) employers may face uncapped quantum meruit claims[22] as a result of contractors carrying on works without a proper contract in place.

Case law has confirmed the preceding.

A famous case on this subject is *British Steel Corporation v Cleveland Bridge & Engineering Co Ltd*.[23] The claimant gave the defendant an estimated price for some steel work that the defendant needed for its construction project. As the estimate was based on incomplete information, the claimant informed the defendant that the parties had yet to agree a final rate. The defendant then sent the claimant a LOI stating that they were willing to award the contract to the claimant based on the estimated price, and that the contract was to be based on the defendant's standard terms (which imposed unlimited liability on the claimants for late delivery). The LOI stated as follows:

> We are pleased to advise you that it is [our] intention to enter into a subcontract with your company, for the supply and delivery of the steel castings which form the roof nodes on this project. . . . We understand that you are already in possession of a complete set of our node detail drawings and we request that you proceed immediately with the works pending the preparation and issuing to you of the official form of sub-contract.

20 *Courtney and Fairbairn Ltd v Tolaini Bros Hotels Ltd* [1975] WLR 295.
21 *Smith and Gordon Ltd v John Lewis Building Ltd* [1993] 44 Con LR 11.
22 *Haden Young Limited v Laing O'Rourke Midlands Limited* [2008] EWHC 1016 (TCC).
23 *British Steel Corporation v Cleveland Bridge and Engineering* [1984] 1 All ER. See also *Monk Construction Ltd v Norwich Union Life Assurance Society* [1992] 62 BLR 107.

The defendant also asked the claimant to commence the works immediately "*pending the preparation and issuing to you of the official form of sub-contract*". The claimant did not respond to the letter but commenced the work. The parties then continued to negotiate over a number of technical aspects on which they were not eventually able to agree. During the negotiations the claimant had also changed the specifications. The claimant then sent the defendant a formal quotation for the price which was significantly higher than the initial estimate. The defendant rejected the quotation and changed the specifications again. The claimant continued the works. The parties then agreed on the price but could not agree on other aspects, including the contractor's liability for late delivery. When the final delivery was delayed, the claimant sued the defendant in quantum meruit, contending that a contract had never been entered into as the they would have never agreed to the defendant's standard terms. The defendant argued that a contract did in fact exist and counterclaimed for breach of contract, including for late delivery. Considering the facts, the court held that no contract had ever formed between the parties as: (i) the negotiations were still ongoing and the parties had not yet agreed on critical terms such as the price and delivery dates; and (ii) it was an expectation of the parties that a formal contract would follow, which was never agreed. As the works were not referable to any contract: (i) the claimant was entitled to recover its costs in quantum meruit; and (ii) the defendant's counterclaim failed as the claimant was under no obligation to continue with or complete the work. Goff J held:

> the true analysis of the situation is simply this. Both parties confidently expected a formal contract to eventuate. In these circumstances, to expedite performance under that anticipated contract, one requested the other to commence the contract work, and the other complied with that request. If thereafter – as anticipated – a contract was entered into, the work done as requested will be treated as having been performed under that contract; if, contrary to their expectation, no contract was entered into, and the performance of the work is not referable to any contract of which the terms can be ascertained, the law simply imposes an obligation on the party who made the request to pay a reasonable sum for such work as has been done pursuant to that request, such an obligation sounding in quasi-contract or, as we now say, in restitution.

In *Hall & Tawse South Ltd v Ivory Gate Ltd*[24] Judge Thornton QC said:

> A letter of intent is usually a unilateral assurance intended to have contractual effect if acted upon, whereby reasonable expenditure reasonably incurred in reliance upon such a letter will be reimbursed. Such a letter places no obligation upon the recipient to act upon it and there is usually no obligation to continue with the work or to undertake any defined parcel of work, the recipient being free to stop work at any time.
>
> The effect of such a letter is to promise reasonable reimbursement if the recipient does act upon it. However, the letter in question . . . is one which imposes obligations on both parties. It requires the plaintiff to commence the works, being a defined package of work and contract administration. The plaintiff had an option of whether to start or not but, having started, the plaintiff was under an obligation to continue with the works and not to stop, unless the defendant appointed another contractor or gave notice abandoning the work or the contract was superseded by one of the two successor contracts envisaged by the letter. I propose, therefore, to refer to this contract as 'the provisional contract'.

24 *Hall & Tawse South Ltd v Ivory Gate Ltd* [1998] 62 Con LR 117.

In *Regalian Properties Plc v London Docklands Development Corporation*[25] it was held Regalian Properties Plc ("Regalian") could not recover the sums claimed as:

> the expenditure for which Regalian claims recompense was for the purpose of satisfying the requirements of the proposed contract . . . or of putting Regalian into a position of readiness to start the development in accordance with the terms of the proposed contract.

3.2.2.4 Letters of intent "subject to contract"

A LOI may also expressly state that its terms are non-binding. This may be achieved by adding express wording suggesting that the parties are still negotiating on matters which they regarded as essential to the existence of a contract, or where the LOI is expressly contingent on an event which is yet to occur. In such cases, the courts may look at the presumed intentions of the parties to establish whether a binding contract was formed, to the extent all the contractual requirements are present. For example, where the parties expressly state in the LOI that it is "subject to contract", the LOI will not typically be regarded as having a binding effect as the parties have expressly indicated that they wish to be bound only if and after a formal contract is entered into between them. The construction of the phrase "subject to contract" is generally straightforward, and the words will be intended to mean what they actually say. In *Fraser Williams (Southern) Ltd. v Prudential Holborn Ltd.*[26] the court held that:

> In order to determine whether a contract had been concluded, it was necessary to examine the course of dealing between the parties bearing in mind that the phrase 'subject to contract' was normally used to prevent a party from being contractually bound. However, when used by experienced businessmen, subject to contract is normally taken as meaning that acceptance must be in writing. On that basis, the proposal was not an offer capable of being accepted.

This was confirmed in *Comyn Ching v Radius Plc*,[27] where the court held that:

> In this instance, I believe that those words ['Subject to Contract'] were intended to mean what they say, and the parties had no reason to think otherwise.

Also, in *IH Rubenstein v Sperry & Hutchinson Company*,[28] in commenting on the expression "*subject to contract*", the judge said:

> It will suffice to say that the instrument speaks for itself . . . the language is plain, clear and unequivocal that the parties did not intend to be bound.

However, in exceptional circumstances the courts, looking to the substance of a relationship to establish whether a contract exists, find that a binding contract has been entered into even though the LOI contained the words "*subject to contract*".

25 *Regalian Properties Plc v London Docklands Development Corporation* [1995] 1 WLR 212.
26 *Fraser Williams (Southern) Ltd. v Prudential Holborn Ltd.* [1993] 64 BLR 1CA (Civ).
27 *Comyn Ching v Radius Plc* [1997] (Unreported).
28 *IH Rubenstein v Sperry & Hutchinson Company* [1969] 222 So 2d 329.

In *The Rugby Group Ltd v Proforce Recruit Ltd*,[29] Proforce Recruit Ltd ("Proforce") and Rugby Group Ltd ("Rugby") had signed a "*subject to contract*" document stating that Proforce was to purchase certain equipment from Rugby and was to provide Rugby with cleaning personnel, while Rugby was to make monthly payments to Proforce. Each party had then performed its respective obligations as specified in the document. When a dispute arose between the parties, Rugby argued that the words "*subject to contract*" showed an intention not to create a binding contract. Field J stated that:

> In general, except in a very strong and exceptional case, the effect of these words in an agreement is to prevent an executory contract from coming into existence because they are taken to mean that until a further contract has been executed neither party is to owe the other any contractual obligation.

However, as in that case the parties had performed their contractual obligations, they were:

> to be taken to have entered into an implied binding contract on the terms of the agreement.

In *RTS Flexible Systems Limited v Molkerei Alos Muller Gmbh & Company KG (UK Production)*[30] the Supreme Court found that the parties had agreed to enter into a binding agreement even though they had used the words "*subject to contract*" during the negotiations. In that case, the employer sent a LOI attaching a draft contract. The LOI contained a "subject to contract" clause stipulating that the terms of the LOI would not be binding unless by both parties signed and executed it. The LOI was not executed, but the parties behaved as if there was an effective binding contract between them. The contractor carried out the works, which the employer paid for. The parties even agreed a variation to the programme. The Supreme Court held that the "subject to contract" clause had been waived by the actions of both parties, thus the LOI was a binding contract. These cases show that even where the parties have expressly stated in the LOI that the relevant terms are "subject to contract" a court may find the LOI being binding on them despite the lack of a formal execution where the parties have acted in a way that shows that they intended to be bound by the LOI's terms.

3.2.3 Main legal issues with letters of intent

3.2.3.1 Absence of important terms

LOIs are normally short documents. As such, they often fail to clearly allocate risks and lack essential clauses which are usually found in construction contracts, e.g., those relevant to variations, extensions of time, defects and liquidated damages. This may lead to unwanted results in case of disputes resulting on works performed under an incomplete LOI. In the case of *Ampleforth v Turner and Townsend*,[31] the contractor carried out the works under the terms of an LOI which did not provide for liquidated damages. When the project fell behind schedule, the employer was prevented from claiming liquidated

29 *The Rugby Group Ltd v Proforce Recruit Ltd* [2005] EWHC 70.

30 *RTS Flexible Systems Limited v Molkerei Alos Muller Gmbh & Company KG (UK Production)* [2010] EWCA Civ 26.

31 *Ampleforth v Turner and Townsend* [2012] EWHC 2137 (TCC).

damages. In this case, however, the employer was able to successfully sue the project manager contending that he had failed to warn on the risks posed by such a LOI.

3.2.3.2 Failure to enter into a final contract

Although this would be uncommon in the case of complex construction projects, the parties may rely on a LOI without ever entering into the final construction contract. This may occur for a number of reasons. For example: (i) the existence of the LOI may somehow relieve the parties from the pressure of having to negotiate and enter into a full agreement; (ii) contractors may do work outside the scope of the LOI or continue work after the LOI has expired confident that a contract will eventually follow; (iii) once the works have started, the parties may lose focus on finalising the contract and consider the LOI sufficient to regulate their relation. Moreover, even when a final construction contract is eventually entered into, disputes may arise on whether the full contract has fully replaced the interim LOI.

In general, when the final construction contract is eventually entered into, the parties' contractual relation will be regulated by it, sometimes even retrospectively. In the case of *Trollope & Colls Ltd. and Holland, Hannen & Cubitt Ltd. v Atomic Power Constructions Ltd.*,[32] a contract entered into some months after work had started was held to have retrospective effects as the parties had, from the outset of their negotiations, contemplated entering into a formal agreement. This concept was also expressed in the case of *Twintec Ltd Volkerfitzpatrick*[33] where Edwards-Stuart J said:

> where two parties enter into an agreement to carry out work in anticipation that they will in future enter into a formal contract in respect of that work, if that formal contract is subsequently entered into it there may well be an implied term that the contract will govern the parties' relationship retrospectively.

In case a subsequent contract is not concluded, the terms of the interim contract will become final, and the contractor will typically be entitled to interim costs. In the case of *Arcadis Consulting v AMEC*[34] Buchan (now AMEC) engaged with Hyder (now Arcadis Consulting), to carry out structural design works for two large projects, Wellcome Building and Castlepoint Car Park. While negotiations were still ongoing, Buchan sent a LOI to Hyder instructing them to commence work on the Castlepoint Car Park project and attaching a Protocol Agreement with relevant schedules and Terms and Conditions. The Terms and Conditions contained a clause stating that:

> The Consultant's liability for defective work under the Agreement shall be limited to whichever is the lesser of the following: (a) The reasonable direct costs of repair, renewal or reinstatement of any part or part of the sub-contract works to the extent that the Client incurs such costs and/or is or becomes liable either directly or by indirect way of financial contribution to such costs (b) The sum stated in Schedule 1 [which was left blank at the time].

Bucher also stressed that "*work done under this instruction is to be on the basis of . . . the conditions and terms detailed in the Protocol Agreement, Design Consultancy Terms*

32 *Trollope & Colls Ltd and Holland & Hannen and Cubitts Ltd. v Atomic Power Constructions Ltd.* (1962) 3 All ER 1035.

33 *Twintec Ltd Volkerfitzpatrick* [2014] EWHC 10 (TCC) at [18].

34 *Arcadis Consulting (UK) Ltd v AMEC (BCS) Ltd* [2018] EWCA 2222.

and Conditions in your possession at present". In a subsequent letter, Buchan sent the complete version of Schedule 1 which limited Hyder's liability to £610,515. Eventually, the anticipated Protocol Agreement was never entered into. When a dispute arose over alleged defects, Buchan claimed damages of £40 million against Hyder. Hyder contended that liability was capped at £610,515. The High Court had to decide whether a contract had been entered into and if so, whether the Terms and Conditions (which defined the liability cap) had been incorporated into it. The High Court held that a contract existed as the letter of instruction had been accepted by Hyder as evidenced by the fact that they had carried out the work in line with the instructions and had received the relevant payment. However, the court found that the liability cap had not been incorporated into the contract as the Terms and Conditions had been superseded by further negotiations. The Terms and Conditions had never been accepted. As Schedule 1 was ancillary to the Terms and Conditions, there was no agreed liability cap. The Court of Appeal disagreed, holding that the liability cap had in fact been incorporated into the contract. Gloster LJ distinguished between the interim contract under which the parties were working and the final contract (i.e., the Protocol Agreement), the terms of which, if agreed, would supersede the interim contract, but which had never been finalised. The High Court was correct in holding that Hyder had not accepted that the Terms and Conditions be incorporated in the final contract, but the interim contract had in fact come into existence. Hyder accepted the LOI by carrying out the works it had been instructed to do, and for which it was paid. In doing so, it accepted the Terms and Conditions and therefore incorporated the liability cap into the interim contract. The fact that the Terms and Conditions were not included into the final contract did not preclude their use under the interim contract. The court observed that the decision of the High Court placed Hyder into an unrealistic scenario in which a "simple" contract ("simple" because it merely provided for performance and payment) had been imposed on Hyder with terms (i.e., an unlimited liability for its contractual performance) that it had never agreed on.

The difference between the two decisions is that the High Court considered that a "simple" agreement existed because, despite the Protocol Agreement was never signed, work was done and paid for, while the Court of Appeal found that the contract between the parties (i.e., the interim contract) existed not because work had been done and paid for, but because the work done evidenced that Hyder had accepted the LOI, which was a standing offer for an independent contract. The terms and conditions of the interim contract were therefore independent the terms and conditions of the final contract which the parties were still negotiating.

3.2.3.3 Incorporation of contract forms

LOIs are generally shorter and less detailed than full construction contracts. As a result, their terms may lack the degree of certainty necessary to make them binding. For this reason, LOIs often refer to standard contract forms such as FIDIC, JCT or NEC, which are incorporated in the LOI by reference. This has the effect of filling the gaps in the LOI and avoiding any risk of vagueness.

However, the parties may not always agree whether such standard terms have in fact been incorporated in their LOI. There may be cases in which one party contends that the agreement was reached only on the simple wording of the LOI, whilst the other claims that the standard terms have been incorporated in the contract and shall regulate the whole contractual relation between the parties. Such situations normally occur when the parties proceed on the assumption that a full contract will be entered into shortly after the LOI. How disputes such as the one just mentioned will be resolved will depend on the circumstances of the case.

In *Killby & Gayford Ltd v Selincourt Ltd*,[35] the architect wrote a letter to the contractor seeking a price for some works. The letter concluded, "*subject to a satisfactory price between us, the general conditions and terms will be subject to the normal RIBA*[36] *contract*". The contractor sent its written estimate, and the architect replied on behalf of the employer accepting it. The letter also included the following phrase: "*please accept this letter as formal instructions to start work*". The parties never signed the contract. Nonetheless, the court held that a binding contract existed and that the exchange of letters incorporated the current RIBA form of contract.

In the case of *Harvey Shopfitters Ltd v ADI Ltd.*,[37] Harvey Shopfitters Ltd ("Harvey") had to carry out refurbishment works on a number of flats owned by ADI Ltd ("ADI"). The architect issued a LOI to a Harvey stating:

> I write to confirm that it is the intention of our client, A.D.I. Limited, to enter into a contract with you on the basis of the tender sum of £339,895.34 exclusive of VAT, for the above project. The main contract documents are currently being prepared for signature. I confirm that the conditions of contract will be those of the JCT Intermediate Form of Building Contract 1994 Edition amended as stated in the tender documents and this contract is to be executed under hand. . . . If you are agreeable to the foregoing please . . . sign the enclosed copy of this letter and return it to me at the above address.

Harvey signed and returned the letter. Harvey then started to perform the refurbishment works, without any formal contract having been entered into. Following completion, a dispute arose between the parties where Harvey claimed extra time and money, and ADI counterclaimed delay damages. The dispute also focused on the LOI. The parties agreed that the LOI was binding, but they disagreed on its terms. Harvey contended that, as the parties had only agreed on the "simple" wording of the LOI, they were not to be bound by the JCT Intermediate Form of Building Contract ("IFC") conditions. As a result, they were entitled to payments for the work done in quantum meruit and would only be obliged to complete the works within a reasonable time. ADI's position was that the LOI incorporated IFC the conditions as the parties had so agreed and because they had acted as though the IFC conditions applied. As a consequence, payment for work done had to be on a lump sum basis and completion of the works had to be as per the contract, with liquidated damages being payable for late completion. The court held that the parties had in fact contracted on the IFC conditions as: (i) Harvey's tendered based on the IFC conditions and did not object to them applying; and (ii) Harvey had conceded that the scope of work under the LOI was the same as that set out in the tender documentation. The court also found that during the performance of the works the parties had acted consistently with the IFC conditions. Harvey was therefore estopped from denying that they applied.

35 *Killby and Gayford v Selincourt* [1973] 3 BLR 104.
36 Royal Institute of British Architects (now JCT).
37 *Harvey Shopfitters Ltd v ADI Ltd.* [2003] All ER (D) 129 (Mar).

This approach was followed in the case of *Bryen and Langley v Martin Rodney Boston.*[38] Bryen & Langley Limited ("B&L"), the claimant, was a building contractor who had entered into a contract for the conversion of two flats into one residential flat. The preliminaries contained in the specification stated that the contract was a JCT Private with Quantities 1998 Edition (the "JTC Form"). On 12 June 2001, a letter was sent stating the contract price and contract duration and confirming that "*the contract will be executed*" in the form of the JCT Form, and that "*contract documents will be drawn up shortly*". The work commenced, but the contract was never signed. A dispute arose when the defendant refused to pay the balance due under final interim certificate. B&L then referred the matter to adjudication. Martin Rodney Boston ("MRB") position was that the contract did not incorporate the JCT Form, and therefore the adjudicator did not have jurisdiction to decide the dispute (and could not decide on his own jurisdiction). The adjudicator found that: (i) the letter dated 12 June 2001 had in fact incorporated the JCT Form and, therefore, the adjudicator did have jurisdiction to decide the dispute; and (ii) the balance of the interim certificate was due to B&L. However, MRB did not pay the sums due, which led B&L to apply for summary judgment. MRB resisted the claim arguing, among other things, that the adjudicator had no jurisdiction to determine the dispute as the contract did not incorporate the JCT Form and that the letter dated 12 June 2001 merely anticipated that the parties would enter into an agreement under a JCT Form of contract. Evidence of this was that: (i) the letter indicated an intention to enter into a contract based on the JCT Form of contract, rather than purporting to be that contract; (ii) the letter used the expressions "*The contract will be executed*" and "*The contract documents will be drawn up shortly*" which suggested that an agreement would be entered into in the future; (iii) the JCT Form included blanks to be filled in and options to be exercised; and (iv) the parties had not agreed on the bonus scheme. B&L submitted that the letter constituted a contract between the parties and that it incorporated the terms of the JCT Form as: (i) the bill of quantities clearly indicated that the parties would enter into a JCT Form of contract; (ii) B&L's tender was made on the basis that a JCT Form of contract would eventually be signed; and (iii) the letter dated 12 June 2001 expressly referred to the JCT Form. As a result, they concluded that: (i) the adjudication provisions had been incorporated in the contract and accepted by the parties; (ii) the adjudicator had jurisdiction on the dispute; and (iii) the adjudicator's decision was validly issued. HH Judge Seymour QC upheld MRB's position stating that: (i) there was no agreement incorporating the adjudication provisions in the JCT Form; (ii) the adjudicator had no jurisdiction to determine the dispute; (iii) B&L's claim to enforce the adjudicator's decision was to fail as the decision was made without jurisdiction. B&L appealed. The Court of Appeal held that the letter did include the JCT Form despite the parties having proposed that their agreement would be contained in a formal contract to be signed in the future. Even though no formal contract had been executed, the parties had acted as if their rights and obligations had been regulated by the JCT Form, and they were therefore bound by it.

A similar decision was reached in *Allen Wilson Shopfitters v Mr Anthony Buckingham.*[39] Also in this case, the LOI provided, *inter alia*, that the works were to be carried out under the terms and conditions of the JCT Private Without Quantities, 1998 Edition,

38 *Bryen & Langley Ltd v Martin Rodney Boston* [2004] EWHC 2450 (TCC).
39 *Allen Wilson Shopfitters v Mr Anthony Buckingham* [2005] EWHC 1165.

which incorporated a detailed set of adjudication provisions. The LOI (which was then followed by a second one which was not signed) was signed and returned to the sender, but no formal contract was ever entered into. The court held that, pursuant to this LOI, there was a contract between the parties. HHJ Coulson QC also added:

> In particular, it seems to me that these disputes arose because there was not in place a clear lump sum contract at the outset covering the proposed works at the property. If work begins on site without a lump sum agreement in place, events can quickly mean that the parties move apart, rather than together and the prospect of ever agreeing a lump sum recedes into the distance.

The preceding cases show that the terms of a standard form referred to in a LOI could be binding on the parties even when the formal contract has not been executed. If the parties do not wish to be bound by the LOI and the standard terms which it purports to incorporate, they should clearly state that there is no contract until the standard form has been formally executed.

PART TWO

INTRODUCTION TO CONSTRUCTION CONTRACTS

A contract is an agreement between two (or more) parties whereby one party makes a legally binding promise to fulfil one or more obligations to the other party (or parties) in return for consideration. The basic elements that a binding contract shall comprise are offer, acceptance, consideration and intent to be legally bound. This definition may apply to any type of contract, including construction contracts.

The type of construction contract the parties will opt for will depend on a number of factors, including the nature of the project and the parties involved, the type of services that the contractor is required to perform, the contractor's specialisation and expertise in relation to that type of project, the risks involved and the parties' respective risk appetite, and the parties' familiarity with projects of the same type. The combination of these and other factors may give rise to several contractual structures in relation to services and pricing, which may vary during the lifespan of the project. Some construction contracts may fall into a specific category, while others will constitute hybrid forms resulting from the parties' negotiation and needs. Moreover, from a drafting perspective, the parties may either opt for a fully negotiated agreement or use a standard form available for the type of project in question.

DOI: 10.4324/9781003387718-6

CHAPTER 4

Elements of an enforceable construction contract

Under English law the elements of an enforceable contract are: (i) offer and acceptance; (ii) consideration; and (iii) intent to be legally bound.[1] Construction contracts make no exception.

4.1 Offer and acceptance

For an agreement to be legally enforceable one party's offer to do or forebear something shall be accepted by the other party.

4.1.1 Offer

An offer is an expression of willingness made by one party (the "offeror") to another party (the "offeree"), that the offeror intends to be bound, on the terms specified in the offer, as soon as the offer is accepted by the offeree.[2] The general principles applying to offers are as follows:

- (i) The test to assess whether the offeror had intention to be bound is an objective one,[3] i.e., the alleged offeror will be bound to stand by his offer if a reasonable person would be induced to believe that the offeror intended to be bound, even if this was not the case.[4]
- (ii) In general, an offer takes effect when it is received by the offeree.
- (iii) In case an offer does not include a term by which it should be accepted, its duration terminates after the lapse of reasonable time.[5] What constitutes a reasonable time depends on the circumstances of the case.
- (iv) The withdrawal of an offer by the offeror must be done before the offer is accepted by the offeree[6] and takes effect from the time when it comes to the notice of the offeree. The notice shall not necessarily come from the offeror, as

1 Other requirements include: (i) the legal capacity to execute the contract; (ii) the required form; (iii) that the contract is not for an illegal purpose; and (iv) that the contract is sufficiently certain.

2 *Storer v Manchester City Council* [1974] 1 WLR 1403.

3 *First Energy (UK) Ltd v Hungarian International Bank Ltd* [1993] 2 Lloyd's Rep 195 at [201].

4 *Maple Leaf Macro Volatility Master Fund v Jacques Rouvroy and Another* [2009] EWHC 701 (Comm), [2009] EWHC 257 (Comm).

5 *Ramsgate Victoria Hotel Co v Montefiore* [1866] LR 1 Ex at [109].

6 *Payne v Cave* [1789] 3 TR 148.

DOI: 10.4324/9781003387718-7

it is sufficient that the offeree learns of the withdrawal from a reliable source[7] (unless the withdrawal is posted, in which case, it takes effect from the time of its receipt by the offeree[8]).

(v) It is possible for the parties to agree that the offer will remain open for a certain period. In such case the offer may be withdrawn at any time before that period has expired unless consideration has been given to the offeror[9] (as consideration will create an option contract[10]).

(vi) For an offer to be such it is not necessary that the word "offer" is used (words such as "estimate" or "quotation"[11] will likewise indicate an intention to make an offer).

(vii) Offers should be distinguished from "invitations to treat", where one party does not make an offer but invites the other to do so. The wording used is not conclusive. A statement may be an invitation to treat even though it is presented as an offer, and vice-versa.

4.1.2 Acceptance

An acceptance is a final and unqualified expression of assent that the accepting party (the offeree) intends to accept the terms of the offer made by the offeror. General principles applying to acceptances are as follows:

(i) The test to assess whether an acceptance is an objective one.

(ii) The acceptance will need to be final, unconditional[12] and unqualified. An acceptance made subject to further negotiations or other events, e.g., "subject to contract" or "subject to management approval", would not create a binding contract (although there may be exceptional cases in which the parties use such words to express their desire as to how a transaction already agreed will have to progress).

(iii) Unless the offeror has expressly waived this requirement,[13] an acceptance will need to be communicated to the offeror.[14] However, a court may find that a contract has been formed if an offer has been accepted by conduct, notwithstanding that the acceptance was not communicated to the offeror. This is not uncommon in construction projects where, having negotiated and agreed the contract terms with the employer, the contractor may start the works before a formal acceptance is communicated to the employer. In such a case the fact that the employer has given access and possession of the site, and that the contractor has commenced the works, may be evidence that both parties have accepted the contract terms and a binding contract has come into existence. In this situation, the employer may be prevented from denying the contract on the grounds that it waived his right to do so or is otherwise estopped from doing it.

7 *Dickinson v Dodds* [1876] 2 ChD 463; *Canwright v Hoogstoel* [1911] 105 LT 618.
8 *Byrne & Co v Leon Van Tien Hoven & Co* [1880] 5 CPD 344.
9 *Byrne & Co v Leon Van Tien Hoven & Co* [1880] 5 CPD 344.
10 *Dickinson v Dodds* [1876] 2 ChD 463.
11 *Crowshaw v Pritchard* [1899] 16 TLR 45.
12 *Nicolene v Simmonds* [1953] 1 QB 543, CA.
13 *Argo Fund Ltd v Essar Steel Ltd* [2005] EWHC 600 (Comm).
14 *M'Iver v Richardson* [1813] 1 M. & S. 557.

(iv) If the party to whom the offer is addressed rejects the offer[15] or makes a counteroffer, that party loses the right to accept the original offer.[16]

(v) The acceptance will not be effective if, before the offeree has communicated his acceptance, the offeror has withdrawn his offer, or the time limit expressly stated in the offer has lapsed.

(vi) Counteroffers shall not be confused with requests for information, which have no legal effect.[17]

4.1.2.1 Determining whether an offer was accepted

The rules of offer and acceptance also apply to invitations to tender ("ITT") and tenders (although an ITT may not necessarily be an offer and a tender may not be an acceptance) and to the negotiation of construction contracts. Employers and contractors may either be offerors or offerees depending on how the negotiation unfolds. Where the contract negotiation is lengthy and chaotic, it may be difficult to understand whose offer was ultimately accepted.

The parties may engage in what is sometimes referred to as a "*battle of the forms*", where each party states to the other that it is going to contract based on its terms and conditions. Where there are several of such exchanges, the courts will have the hard task to determine which party's terms and conditions govern the agreement. To do to, the courts will: (i) use the so-called *last shot* doctrine, based on which, unless it appears otherwise, the contract is formed by the last unchallenged set of terms and conditions which were discussed between the parties; and (ii) look at the so-called prevail or priority clauses, i.e., boilerplate conflict clauses which offer various options for determining priority between conflicting agreements or parts thereof (e.g., a schedule). Ultimately, the courts will apply the fundamental principles of offer and acceptance to the specific case in order to determine whether a binding contract was entered into, and, if so, on what terms. The courts will assess whether the parties had what is referred to as a "*meeting of the minds*". This is done by looking at the various correspondence exchanged between the parties to establish whether they had agreed on the same terms[18] (i.e., whether an apparently unqualified acceptance reached an offer[19] which was capable of being accepted). In more complex cases, the courts may have to amalgamate both parties' proposed terms.[20] There may also be cases where the courts will conclude that a contract was actually entered into, but none of the parties' terms were incorporated into it. An example can be found in the case of *Transformers and Rectifiers Ltd v Needs Ltd.*[21] Transformers and Rectifiers Ltd ("Transformers") contended that its terms and conditions were incorporated in the contract as they were printed on the back of various purchase orders that Transformers had sent to Needs Ltd ("Needs") by fax and subsequently by post. Needs contended that its terms had in fact formed the contract as a result of the

15 *Tinn v Hoffman & Co* [1873] 29 LTR 271 at 278 and *Trollope & Colls Ltd v Atomic Power Construction Ltd* [1963] 1 WLR 333 at [337].

16 *Hyde v Wrench* [1840] 3 Beavan 334; (1840) 49 ER 132.

17 *Stevenson, Jacques Co v McLean* [1880] 5 QBD 346.

18 *Glencore Energy Ltd v Circus Oil Services Ltd* [2014] EWHC 87 (Comm); [2014] 2 Lloyd's Rep 1.

19 *Hussey v Horne-Payne* [1878] 4 App Cas at [311].

20 *Butler Machine Tool v Ex-Cell-O Corporation* [1979] 1 WLR 401 at 404, CA.

21 *Transformers and Rectifiers Ltd v Needs Ltd* [2015] EWHC 269 [2015] EWHC 269.

acknowledgment of order sent to Transformers which stated: "*The quoted prices and deliveries are subject to our normal Terms and Conditions of Sale (copies available on request)*". Mr Justice Edwards-Stuart found that: (i) Transformers' terms had not been incorporated in the contract as the fax sent to Needs did not include the back page and the letters sent by post did not always incorporate the terms that Transformers was seeking to rely upon and, when they did, it was not clear, to a reasonable person in Needs' position, that Transformers sought to rely on such terms; and (ii) Needs' terms did not apply as Needs had failed to bring them to Transformers' attention, which Needs could have done by referring to the terms and conditions on the face of the acknowledgment.

It is worth noting that the fact that the parties continue to negotiate even after an agreement is reached will not typically affect the existence of that agreement,[22] unless the continuing negotiation may be construed as a mutual intention to rescind the agreement.[23]

Moreover, where the parties perform the transaction, it will be then difficult for them to argue that there was no intention to enter into a contract or that the contract shall be considered void for vagueness or uncertainty.[24]

Given the uncertainty that may arise from the usually lengthy and sometimes "chaotic" negotiations which characterise complex construction contracts, the parties may struggle to understand if they have entered into an agreement and on what terms.

Before issuing any type of communication (including ITTs, tenders and comments to the contract) to the other party, the issuer should be sure about what such communication aims to achieve, including if: (i) the issuer would be content to enter into a contract on the terms of that communication; (ii) the communication, alone or combined with any other prior exchange, may suffice to allow a court concluding that a binding agreement was in fact entered into; (iii) the communication clearly brings the terms the issuer seeks to rely on to the attention of the other party; (iv) the issuer intends to be bound by the terms negotiated up to that moment; (v) the issuer had necessary "internal" authority to enter into a binding contract on the terms resulting from the various exchanges between the parties.

Where the parties do not wish (or the party's negotiator does not have the necessary authority) to enter into a binding agreement, they may avoid the unpleasant result of finding themselves subject to unwanted binding terms by always using clear words stating whether they deem a communication exchanged during the negotiation phase being an offer or a counteroffer capable of being accepted. Where the parties do not intend to be bound by the contract version circulating between them, they might use language such as "subject to contract".

4.2 Consideration

Under English law a contract can be binding on the parties only if it is supported by consideration or made in a deed.[25] In *Dunlop v Selfridge*, the House of Lords defined consideration as:

---

22 *Cranleigh Precision Engineering Ltd v Bryant* [1965] 1 WLR 1293.

23 E. Peel, *Treitel: The Law of Contract* (14th edition) Sweet & Maxwell, 2015, at p. 20.

24 *G. Percy Trentham v Archital Luxfer* [1993] 1 Lloyd's Rep 25 at [27].

25 There are special requirements on execution and delivery of deeds. A contract under seal is an example of a deed. No consideration is required for a contract contained in a deed. A person identified in the deed as someone to benefit from a promise in the deed can enforce a promise to pay money or can seek damages if the promise is not

> An act or forbearance of one party, or the promise thereof, is the price for which the promise of the other is bought, and the promise thus given for value is enforceable.[26]

Consideration is a way to show that the parties had the intent to execute a contract. This concept developed to differentiate contracts from gifts. A gratuitous promise does not amount to a contract.[27]

In the case of construction contracts, the employer gives consideration by paying or promising to pay for the works and the contractor by carrying out or promising to carry out the works. The main aspects of consideration, which also apply to construction contracts, are as follows:

(i) Consideration can be either something of benefit to the promisor or some detriment to the promisee.[28]

(ii) Consideration needs to be something of value in the eye of the law,[29] but need not to be adequate.[30] The courts will not interfere with the bargain made by the parties. Thus, an agreement to build something for say £1 would generally be enforceable.

(iii) The general rule is that past consideration is not good consideration. Consideration is considered past consideration when the promisee has already done the act that is said to constitute the consideration. In determining whether consideration is past the courts are not bound to apply a chronological test. However, a past act may entitle the promisee to claim a reasonable sum for his services in quantum meruit in case the past act or service is done upon request of the promisor and payment must be expected and legally recoverable.[31] For example, if the employer and the contractor agree that the latter shall build something, but the contract is silent on the relevant price, which is agreed only after completion, the contractor can recover its reasonable costs. This is because the works were requested by the employer and the promise to pay for the works will be implied from his request. What is reasonable will depend on the circumstances, and the courts will usually consider the price agreed between the parties following completion when deciding on reasonableness. In the case of *Pao On v Lau Yiu Long*[32] the claimant owned shares in a private company which was the owner of a building that the defendants (who were majority shareholders in a public company) intended to buy. The claimant agreed: (i) to sell his shares in the private company in exchange for shares in the public company; (ii) to refrain from selling his shares in the private company for some time. The parties subsequently agreed that this second promise be replaced with one in which the claimant would be indemnified for any fall in share value and would benefit

---

performed. However, it should be noted that equitable remedies (for example, specific performance of obligations other than to pay money) are not available if there is no consideration.

26 *Dunlop v Selfridge* [1915] AC 847.

27 *Williams v Roffey Bros & Nicholls (Contractors) Ltd* [1991] 1 QB 1 at 19. See also *Re Hudson* [1885] 54 LJ Ch 811.

28 *O'Sullivan v Management Agency & Music Ltd* [1985] QB 428 at [459].

29 *Thomas v Thomas* [1842] 2 QB 851 at [859].

30 *High v Brooks* [1840] 10 A & E 309 at 320; *Brady v Brady* [1989] 1 All ER 1686.

31 E. Peel, *Treitel: The Law of Contract* (14th edition) Sweet & Maxwell, 2015, at p. 89.

32 *Pao On v Lau Yiu Long* [1980] AC 614.

from any rise in share value occurring in the interim. When the share value dropped, the claimant sought to rely on the indemnification provision. The defendants refused to comply, claiming that the consideration for the indemnity agreement was past consideration and that they had agreed to that under duress. The case reached the Privy Council which found that good consideration was given as the promise was done at the promisor's request and the parties understood the act was to be paid for at a later date, and the payment or benefit would have been enforceable had it been promised in advance. In reaching this conclusion the Privy Council applied the exception to the doctrine of past consideration in *Lampleigh v Braithwaite*.[33] In this case, Braithwaite, who had killed a man, asked Lampleigh to secure him a pardon from the king. When Lampleigh had already started working to secure pardon, Braithwaite promised to pay Lampleigh £100 in gratitude. However, Braithwaite refused to pay the money when the pardon was eventually obtained. Braithwaite argued that the plaintiff had acted before the promise to pay was given (i.e., he had provided past consideration). The court found in favour of Lampleigh as the original request by the defendant contained an implied promise to pay the plaintiff for his efforts. Lampleigh had acted upon a request made by Braithwaite. Bowen LJ said:

> A mere voluntary courtesie will not have a consideration to uphold an assumpsit. But if that courtiesie were moved by a suit or request of the party that gives the assumpsit, it will bind.

In general, if A does something for B at their request and subsequently B promises to pay A for their trouble, then that promise is good consideration as the later promise is considered being part of the same single transaction and is, therefore, enforceable.

(iv) Performance of an existing duty is not good consideration. The principle was set out in the case of *Stilk v Myrick*[34] where a ship's master promised to divide the wages of two deserters among the remaining crew if they succeeded in sailing home from the Baltic shorthanded. This was held not to be valid consideration as the crew already had a contractual obligation to sail the ship. The principle was then refined in *Williams v Roffey Bros & Nicholls (Contractors) Ltd*, where the Court of Appeal held that a promise to complete the contracted work on time, where this was falling behind, was good consideration for the contractor's promise to pay extra money. In this case, the appellants, the builders Roffey Bros & Nicholls (Contractors) Ltd ("Roffey Bros"), were awarded a contract for the refurbishment of 27 flats belonging to a housing corporation. Roffey Bros subcontracted some work to a carpenter, Williams, who fell behind with the work. This would have had the effect to delay Roffey Bros' works on their main contract with the housing corporation, which included a penalties clause for late completion. To avoid such consequences, Roffey Bros agreed to pay Williams a bonus if he was to finish on time. When Roffey Bros stopped all payments, Williams sued them for breach of contract. Roffey Bros argued that the

33 *Lampleigh v Braithwaite* [1615] Hob 105.
34 *Stilk v Myrick* [1809] 2 Camp 317.

agreement to pay extra was unenforceable as Williams was only agreeing to do what he was already bound to do (i.e., he had provided no consideration). The only benefit for the Roffey Bros was that they would not pay a penalty under their main contract. Roffey Bros' arguments were based on *Stilk v Myrick*. The Court of Appeal held that the doctrine in *Stilk v Myrick* had been refined over time and a promise to pay a bonus to complete work on time was now enforceable if: (a) the promisor obtained a practical benefit (which, in that case, was the benefit of avoiding the penalty clause); and (b) the promise was not given under duress or by fraud (in that case, there was clearly no duress as Roffey Bros had offered the extra payment).

Another important case on this subject is *Foakes v Beer*,[35] where the House of Lords held that a smaller sum of money cannot be good consideration for the release of a larger debt. However, there will be good consideration if the smaller sum is accompanied by some "*new consideration*", i.e., something non-monetary in addition to the smaller sum (e.g., if payment is made early or in some special place or way).

(v) It is also said that consideration must move from the promisee,[36] meaning that consideration must be given by the party who wants to enforce an obligation under the contract. Therefore, if A promises to B to pay a certain amount of money to B if C builds something for A, and C does so, B cannot enforce A's promise. However, it is not necessary that consideration move to the promisor, i.e., it to be provided to, or benefit, the promisor.

(vi) Consideration must be present also in case the parties compromise a dispute or a claim. In this situation, for there to be a valid consideration it is necessary that the claim or the defence being settled is valid or that the claimant believes them being valid, even in case both parties have doubt on the validity.[37] This also applies in the cases of forbearance to sue.[38] This aspect was considered in the recent case of *Simantob v Shavleyan*[39] where the Court of Appeal held that an unmeritorious defence was good consideration for the variation of a settlement agreement, which resulted in payment to the creditor of a lesser sum than the debt due. In this case, the appellant, Dan Simantob, and the respondent, Yacob Shavleyan, were dealers in Islamic antiques. Following a dispute, certain sums became due from Mr Shavleyan to Mr Simantob. The parties then entered into a settlement agreement (the "First Agreement") where they agreed that: (i) Mr Shavleyan would pay Mr Simantob US$1.5 million in full and final settlement of all claims between the parties; and (ii) in the event of non-payment by a certain date, Mr Shavleyan would pay interests in the amount of US$1,000 per day. Mr Shavleyan did not pay the full amount by the agreed date, so that daily interests commenced to accrue. Over the following years Mr Shavleyan made some partial payments and, years later, he agreed to pay US$800,000 to Mr Simantob (the

35 *Foakes v Beer* (1883) LR 9 App Cas 605.

36 *Barber v Fox* [1682] 2 Wms Saund 134. n.(e).

37 I.N. Duncan Wallace QC, *Hudson's Building and Engineering Contracts* (11th edition) Sweet & Maxwell, 1994, at p. 37.

38 *Callisher v Bischoffsheim* [1870] LR 5 QB 449.

39 *Simantob v Shavleyan* [2019] EWCA Civ 1105.

"Second Agreement"). A dispute then arose as Mr Simantob argued that any such payment was made on account of sums due under the First Agreement, while Mr Shavleyan's position was that the Second Agreement had modified the First Agreement, discharging his outstanding liabilities under it. Mr Simantob then issued proceedings against Mr Shavleyan, demanding payment of US$2,378,000 under the First Agreement, all but US$200,000 of which was interest. In response, Mr Shavleyan argued that the clause under which Mr Simantob was claiming interest was a penalty (such defence was however rejected by the Master following Mr Simantob's application for summary judgment) and that the Second Agreement had modified the First Agreement, so he could not be liable for any sums in excess of the Second Agreement. The High Court concluded that Second Agreement had in fact resulted in a variation to the First Agreement and determined that: (i) the payment of a lesser sum than the amount of debt due cannot be a satisfaction of the debt unless there is some added benefit to the creditor; and (ii) the benefit to Mr Simantob was Mr Shavleyan's forbearance the defence that the interest clause was a penalty. It did not matter that, in deciding on Mr Simantob's application for summary judgment, the Master had rejected Mr Shavleyan's penalty defence, as it might have succeeded or at least been found to be arguable. Mr Simantob appealed on the basis that, as a matter of public policy, a promise not to pursue a defence that is later found to have no real prospect of success cannot amount to good consideration. The Court of Appeal dismissed the appeal concluding that by entering into Second Agreement, Mr Shavleyan agreed that he would no longer be able to raise the penalty clause defence and the debt would be consolidated. Simon LJ said that it was immaterial whether the Master was correct in rejecting Mr Shavleyan's penalty defence, as the question of the validity of the consideration for the Second Agreement must be looked at the time that it was made. He held that:

> There cannot be any sensible public policy against encouraging parties to raise . . . defences that they reasonably believe may succeed, even if they eventually turn out to fail.

The court also distinguished between a defence or claim in which the party advancing it had no confidence at all, and a claim or defence which a party was prepared to pursue in court, even though he had doubts on the relevant merits. Simon LJ also added that:

> there is another countervailing public policy that also must be taken into account . . . namely, the public policy in favour of holding people to their commercial bargains.

4.3 Intent to be legally bound

An essential element of a contract is that the parties have the intent to enter into a legal binding relation by way of a contract.

In general, where a contractor and an employer agree that the former will perform certain works on certain terms which are sufficient to create a binding agreement, the courts will have no issue in finding that the parties had an intention to be bound by that agreement. In such a situation, no party may negotiate or change the terms of the agreement unless the parties reach a fresh agreement as to such terms.[40] However, where there is ambiguity as to whether the parties did in fact have intent to be bound, the courts will need to ascertain their intention objectively.

The subjective intentions of the parties will generally be irrelevant.[41] The courts will not look at what the parties actually intended but may consider the surrounding circumstances of the transaction. In the case of *MacInnes v Gross*[42] Mr MacInnes claimed that the parties had agreed over a dinner in a Mayfair restaurant on 23 March 2011 that he would leave his employment with an investment bank (Investec) to personally assist Mr Gross in growing his business, RunningBall, so to maximise any return on its sale. In return, Mr MacInnes would receive remuneration which was to be calculated by looking at the difference between the target price of the business and the actual sale price. Following the dinner, Mr MacInnes sent an email to Mr Gross where he confirmed that there was an agreement "*on headline terms*". When the case ended in dispute, the court held that no binding agreement had been entered into between the parties as there was no intention to create legal relations. In delivering his judgment, Mr Justice Coulson noted:

> The mere fact that the discussion took place over dinner in a smart restaurant does not, of itself, preclude the coming into existence of a binding contract. A contract can be made anywhere, in any circumstances. But I consider that the fact that this alleged agreement was made in a highly informal and relaxed setting means that the court should closely scrutinise the contention that, despite the setting, there was an intention to create legal relations.

In reaching his conclusion, the court considered the following factors: (i) the terms of the purported agreement were too complex and too uncertain to be enforceable as there was no agreement between on important issues of Mr MacInnes' remuneration, the contractual parties and the relevant scope; (ii) moreover, a "*further note of caution*" was required as discussions took place in English, which was not the defendant's first language (Mr Gross was an Austrian national); (iii) the claimant had not produced any written contract or draft and (iv) none of the parties had told anyone else they had reached a binding agreement.

A similar conclusion was reached in the case of *Blue v Ashley*.[43] Mr Blue, investment banker, claimed that he and Mr Ashley, the founder and majority shareholder of Sports Direct, had a conversation in the Horse & Groom public house in central London where Mr Ashley agreed to pay him a certain amount of money if the Sports Direct share price reached a certain value. When Sports Direct shares reached the said price, Mr Blue claimed £15 million from Mr Ashley. The court found that a contract had not been entered into. Leggatt J set out the following reasons which led him to conclude that the parties had no actual intention to make a contract: (i) the informality of the location, although a contract could theoretically be made in an informal setting; (ii) the meeting did not have the purpose to discuss Mr Blue's work or his role at the company; (iii) the nature and tone of the conversation was "jocular" and "mischievous", more akin to "banter"; (iv) the offer to pay such amount of money to Mr Blue made no commercial sense for Mr Ashley. The figure had no basis. Moreover, he did not know him well, and had not made

40 *Tombs v Wilson Connolly Ltd* (2004) 98 Con LR 44 at [54].

41 *Mannai Investment Co Ltd v Eagle Star Life Assurance Co Ltd* [1997] AC 749 at [775]; *Siemens Building Technologies FE Ltd v Supershield Ltd* [2009] EWHC 927 (TCC) at [30].

42 *MacInnes v Gross* [2017] EWHC 46 (QB).

43 *Blue v Ashley* [2017] EWHC 1928 (Comm).

such kind of offers to anyone else; (v) it was not clear what exactly Mr Blue needed to do to double a company's share price; (vi) the alleged offer was too vague for being seriously considered. Three witnesses who were present while the conversation took place confirmed that their perception was that the offer was not a serious one; (vii) Mr Blue did not consider it necessary to make any written record of the alleged agreement but waited nearly a year before mentioning the agreement to Mr Ashley. This confirms that he had probably not perceived the agreement as serious.

A similar case on the subject is *Wright v Rowland*,[44] although this time the conversation took place on a yacht. Also in this case, a financial consultant claimed breach of an oral agreement. Also in this case, the court found that there was no evidence of the parties' intention to create legal relations. Mr Christopher Butcher QC said that he was:

> entirely unpersuaded that there was any commitment" given by the Rowlands to Mr Wright on the yacht and had "Mr Rowland said what Mr Wright alleges or something approximating to it, with a firm commitment on a series of points, I consider that it would have been documented. Had such words been spoken, I consider that it is likely that Mr Wright would have put them in an email, or at least to have made a contemporaneous note.

The three aforementioned cases show that the courts will not lightly infer the existence of a binding contract unless they are confident that the parties had an intention to be bound. To do so, they will look at the surrounding circumstances, including the location and the purpose of the meeting, the tone of the discussions and the level of details of the alleged agreement.

It is not common that construction contracts for large projects be entered into orally. However, it may happen that oral negotiations take place (e.g., on variations) which will lead to disputes on whether what was said orally crystalised and constitutes at least a part of the agreement between the parties. The parties should therefore ensure that any written contractual exchange is marked as "subject to contract" and that clear words are used to state that the agreement will be binding upon the parties only if included in a written document and signed by both parties.[45]

4.4 Certainty of terms

Under English law, for a contract to exist it is necessary that all essential terms have been agreed between the parties. If there is any uncertainty over one or more essential terms, no contract will come into existence.

A term may be essential: (i) because, without it, the agreement would be incomplete; or (ii) because the parties regarded an agreement on such term so important that they could not intend to be bound by the contract without such term being actually agreed.

Some examples applicable to construction contracts for complex projects may be the scope of work, the contract price, payment terms, liquidated damages or completion date.

In *Viridis UK Ltd v Mulalley & Co Ltd*,[46] Mulalley was appointed as the main contractor on a refurbishment project. Viridis tendered for the contract to replace the windows

44 *Wright v Rowlands and another* [2017] EWHC 2478 (Comm).
45 *Intense Investments Ltd v Development Ventures Ltd* [2006] EWHC 1586 (TCC) at [89].
46 *Viridis UK Ltd v Mulalley & Co Ltd* [2014] EWHC 268 (TCC).

and doors. During the negotiations, Mulalley issued six separate orders to Viridis for certain parts of the works. A dispute arose between the parties, and Viridis referred it to adjudication under one of the six contracts (order 24), which Viridis contended contained the agreement between the parties. Mulalley challenged the jurisdiction of the adjudicator, arguing that the dispute arose under six contracts, not just one. The adjudicator concluded that he had jurisdiction and awarded Viridis a certain amount of money, which Mulalley did not pay. Viridis then started legal proceedings to enforce the award. Mulalley argued that Viridis never accepted order 24, thus there were six contracts, not just one. Viridis argued that order 24 was the overarching subcontract order governing all the works and that the other orders were either work orders placed under order 24 or variations to it. The court held that Viridis never accepted order 24 as the parties had never reached agreement on payment terms, liquidated damages and survey costs. Viridis had in fact accepted three of the six orders issued by Mulalley and undertook the works based on such contracts. The adjudicator had no jurisdiction to decide the dispute as the law provides that, absent an express provision to the contrary, a party may refer only one dispute to adjudication.

The case shows that absent an agreement on terms that the parties consider essential to the formation of a binding contract (in that case, payment terms, liquidated damages and survey costs), a court may find that no agreement exists between the parties.

CHAPTER 5

Main categories of construction contracts

5.1 Main categories of construction contracts based on services

5.1.1 "Pure" construction contracts

Pure construction contracts are those in which the project's specifications and design are provided by the employer (or by a third party on behalf of the employer), whilst the contractor agrees to do the work on the basis of the employer's specifications and design. In this case, the risk undertaken by the contractor will be lower (as it assumes responsibility only for the construction of the works) and the pricing mechanism will usually be unit rate or cost plus.

5.1.2 Design-build

With design-build contracts contractors assume responsibility for both the project's design and the construction of the works. With such contracts contractors take more risks compared to pure construction contracts (which do not include the design scope). This is reflected in the price, which will typically be fixed.

5.1.3 Engineering, procurement and construction

With engineering, procurement and construction ("EPC") or "turnkey" contracts, contractors assume full responsibility for the whole project, from design to delivery[1] (i.e., when the project will be ready for use just by "turning the key") for a pre-agreed fixed price. As such, contractors will bear most of the project risk. This is reflected in the contract price, which will normally be higher (due to the inclusion of higher contingencies) and lump sum.

It is worth noting that the name in itself does not seem to have a specific legal meaning and naming a construction contract "EPC" or "turnkey" would not imply any specific rights and obligations as the courts will look at the terms of the contract to assess the nature of the obligations assumed by the parties, which may vary sensibly from contract

1 *High Mark (M) Sdn Bhd v Patco Malaysia Sdn Bhd* [1984] 28 BLR 129 at 134–135. See also *Davy Offshore Ltd v Emerald Field Contracting Ltd* [1991] 55 BLR 1 at 42.

DOI: 10.4324/9781003387718-8

to contract (e.g., the contractor may take on extra activities like advisory services, e.g., on project risks[2]).

Typically, an EPC contractor will be required to perform: (i) engineering functions, which may include basic engineering, detailed engineering, planning and construction engineering; (ii) procurement functions, which may include logistics, transport and purchasing materials and equipment; and (iii) construction functions which may include electrical installation, mechanical erection and civil engineering.

EPC contracts are maybe the most widely used contracts for the construction of complex projects as they afford employers the highest degree of certainty as to time and costs for the project. They are also referred to as "turnkey" contracts in the sense that the EPC contractor agrees to develop the project from commencement to final completion and is obliged to deliver a complete facility to the employer who need only "turn a key" to start operating it.

The contractor promises to perform certain works within a certain completion date for an all-encompassing fixed/lump sum price. The fact that the price is fixed brings about that the scope of work should be clearly defined in the contract documents as any shortfall of costs is a risk that rests with the EPC contractor, unless it is attributable to events that are outside its control.

The EPC contractor will enter into separate agreements with the vendors and subcontractors for which the EPC contractor will take full responsibility, so that the employer will not be required to be a party in any dispute between the EPC contractor and any of its contractual counterparties to such sub-agreements. Any loss or damages resulting from breaches by its subcontractors or vendors (e.g., in case the employer applies liquidated damages to the EPC contractor due to subcontractors' delays) will be recoverable by the EPC contractor under the relevant sub-agreement. This is why subcontracts between EPC contractors and their subcontractors usually mirror EPC contracts between employers and EPC contractors relevant to the same project.

The parties to a turnkey construction contract may opt for different structures depending on their needs and how they intend to allocate risks. For example, the contractor may be only required to carry out engineering, procurement and construction services or additional activities such as installation (in which case the contract would be named "EPCI") or commissioning (in which case the acronym would be "EPCC") or a mix of the two:

(i) EPCI contracts are turnkey contracts whereby contractors agree, typically for a fixed price, to carry out installation works in addition to the usual engineering, procurement and construction services. They shift control over the project to contractors, who assume full responsibility for it. Employers do not have any involvement in the construction process, which is completely handled by the EPC contractor. This means less effort (including economic effort in terms of staffing requirements) and less risk (e.g., in case of increased costs and delays) for employers, but also less control and a higher price.

    EPCI contracts are the most widely used type of construction contracts for offshore works (e.g., for offshore wind projects), where the installation part of the work requires high specialisation and expertise as contractors will leverage

2 See for example *Enertrag (UK) Ltd v Sea & Land Power and Energy Ltd* [2003] 100 Con LR 146 at 190.

on the knowledge of the project acquired during the construction phase for the installation works.

(ii) EPCC[3] contracts are turnkey contracts where contractors agree, typically for a fixed price, to carry out commissioning functions in addition to engineering, procurement and construction services. Commissioning may be defined as the activity encompassing all those services performed after construction and after pre-commissioning[4] (but before the project is taken over by the employer) aimed at establishing the normal operation of the project including the verification of the facility and its components in order to assess that they are designed, installed, tested and operated to meet the project requirements in accordance with the design parameters, and the preparation of the necessary documentation before the start-up in performed. EPCC contracts are common for large-scale and complex infrastructure projects in the private sector.

5.1.4 Engineering, procurement and construction management

EPCM contracts are not construction contracts and shall not be confused with EPC contracts. To avoid any confusion, it should be kept in mind that the letter "C" in the "EPCM" acronym shall be read in conjunction with the "M" to mean "Construction Management".

In other words, EPCM contracts are professional services-only (or primarily) contracts where the EPCM contractor merely provides management services for the whole project on behalf of the employer.

Under an EPCM contract the EPCM contractor may agree (usually on a cost-reimbursable or a unit rate fee basis) to: (i) develop, organise, coordinate and execute the planning, engineering and design, which may either be the complete detailed engineering or (less often) a mere basic engineering; (ii) perform procurement activities by advising the employer on the strategy for the procurement of equipment and materials, and assisting in implementing such strategy (e.g., by preparing invitations to tender for the procurement of services, materials and equipment; organising the tender process; pre-qualifying the vendors; reviewing technical quotations received; advising on the most convenient tenders; recommending the awarding of contracts by the employer; preparing the technical documentation for the award; and negotiating the relevant contracts); (iii) manage, administer, supervise and coordinate the construction process on behalf of the employer in accordance to, and in compliance with the detailed schedule (including, e.g., any planning of the construction elements, costs, logistics and construction team, on-site management of contractors, operatives, equipment, services, office facilities from the beginning of the project through to completion).

The main target for an EPCM contractor will be ensuring that the final project costs and execution time are in line with the employer's expectations. However, although an EPCM contractor creates, manages and administers contracts with various contractors and vendors, it will do so as an "agent" for the employer (i.e., the

3 It is also possible to encounter engineering, procurement, installation and commissioning (EPIC) contracts, where the contractor does not perform construction works but takes care of all the remaining activity.

4 Pre-commissioning may include activities such as inspection of equipment, piping and machinery, checks on units and facilities against designs, pressure testing, functional testing, simulations, etc.

EPCM contractor will not be a party to such contracts, which will be entered into between the employer and the relevant contractor/supplier). As a result, any time and/or money claims and/or disputes under such contracts will be strictly between the relevant contractor/supplier and the employer, which will be ultimately responsible for the relevant outcome.

The EPCM contractor may have a contractual duty to assist the employer in the relevant management and resolution, but it will not normally have any liability arising from such disputes.

Moreover, EPCM contractors will not typically take any responsibility for: (i) the quality of the works performed by the construction contractor or materials supplied by the suppliers; or (ii) compliance with the budgeted price (although EPCM contracts may include incentives to the EPCM contractors for keeping costs within a certain target price and by providing gain sharing mechanisms in case actual costs are eventually lower than the agreed target price); or (iii) completion within a certain date (although, where the construction contractor contends that the delays were due to late, incomplete or erroneous design prepared by the EPCM contractor, the employer may have a claim against the EPCM contractor). As a result, the employer may not usually claim against EPCM contractors in case of breach from contractors or vendors, although the employer may still have a cause of action against the EPCM contractor for any damages arising under the EPCM contract based on an overriding obligation to exercise reasonable skill and care in carrying out its management services. For example, employers may claim damages against EPCM contractors in case of breaches relevant to: (i) the design (where the EPCM contractor had a contractual duty to ensure that the engineering and design of the project is in compliance with the project's technical and functional specifications); (ii) the estimates made by the EPCM contractor on costs and duration of the works; and/or (iii) the management of the procurement and construction activities.

5.2 Main categories of construction contracts based on pricing

Price and payment are central to most commercial transactions, and construction contracts are no exception. Both the employer and the contractor will expect to bear high "project" costs: (i) the employer will expect to pay the contractor the agreed contract price to have the project completed; while (ii) the contractor will expect to bear construction costs to complete the project and gain the agreed margin.

A contract price is usually made up of three elements:

(i) Direct costs, i.e., the actual costs that the contractor has to bear for the specific works. These include costs like the direct labour (including consultants, if needed), materials that are incorporated into the work, equipment purchased or leased specifically for the project.

(ii) Indirect costs or overhead costs, i.e., business-related costs like renting office spaces, job insurances, transport to and from a work site, communication expenses, etc.

(iii) Profit, i.e., the fee or markup or margin the contractor takes for doing the work.

In the case of complex construction projects, the pricing arrangement is arguably the most important decision the parties will have to make as it affects the allocation of risks between the contractor and the employer and has a bearing on the ultimate decision on whether a project is convenient and should be ultimately built.

The main types of pricing arrangements in construction contracts are lump sum, cost plus and unit price, although there may be hybrid forms of these basic arrangements, which are outside the scope of this book.

Understanding these pricing models and the consequences of choosing one over the other is crucial to make the right choice and avoid unpleasant surprises during the execution of the project. The next paragraphs will give more details on these models and outline the pros and cons of each of them for contractors and employers.

5.2.1 Fixed price (or lump sum)

Fixed price (or "lump sum"[5]) construction contracts are the most commonly used type of construction contracts for large-scale and complex construction projects.

As the name suggests, under this type of contract the contractor agrees to complete the construction of the whole project for a pre-agreed "fixed" price which includes any profits and costs (including operating expenses or overheads).

Under this structure, the employer will pay the agreed price and the contractor will perform the agreed works, regardless of the actual cost ultimately incurred (subject to a number of exceptions). As a result: (i) in case the actual cost of the project is underestimated, the contractor's profit will be reduced by that amount, or, in more extreme cases, the contractor may have to complete the project at a loss; while (ii) in case the actual cost is overestimated or the contractor manages to save on costs, the contractor's margin will proportionally increase.

Under a lump sum contract changes in price will only be allowed as a result of a change in the scope of work (or a change order) issued by the employer. In addition, the contractor may claim financial compensation in case the employer interferes with progress or other events for which the employer is responsible occur that result in an increase in the project's costs.

The word lump sum does not mean that the entire sum is paid in a single payment upon completion of the contract. In the case of large projects, where contractors have to undergo substantial expenditure (e.g., mobilisation costs, labour costs, renting or building structures and facilities, etc.), the employer will usually advance a certain amount of money (the repayment of which is usually guaranteed by way of an advance payment bond issued by the contractor) to the contractor, followed by progress payments made over time throughout the work based on the achievement of predefined milestones. In this way, the payment of the lump sum will be tied to the percentage of work completed (so-called progress) by the contractor within specific deadlines. In this model the contractor may be required to prepare a schedule of values which breaks down the work into categories and assign a value to each of them. Throughout the project, the contractor will submit interim payment requests based on the progress achieved. Such requests will be assessed by the employer (and/or the engineer) against the schedule of value to

5 Or, less frequently, a "stipulated sum".

determine whether the activities have been performed and the amount to be paid based on the actual percentage of completion.

In some cases, the employer will have a right to withhold a portion of any amounts due to the contractor to secure fulfilment of the contractor's obligations or may set-off such amounts in whole or in part against any damages (liquidated or unliquidated) suffered by the employer as a result of the contractor having failed to comply with its contractual obligations.

This pricing model provides the employer with the highest degree of certainty as to project cost, while exposing the contractor to the highest risk of extra costs deriving from quantities, labour efficiency, labour and material costs, as well as all neutral and unforeseeable risks which are not expressly dealt with in the construction contract. For this reason, lump sum contracts are usually appealing to employers valuing price certainty above other considerations, including price. Typical examples are: (i) financed projects, where lenders are not willing to sustain costs higher than those envisaged; and (ii) projects in the public sector, where employers are highly sensitive to the political repercussions of substantial cost overruns. By the same token, in case of large and costly projects, contractors, and in particular smaller ones, tend to resist such a pricing method, particularly where the project involves a high level of complexity or there are elements of uncertainty which may lead to an unforeseen increase of costs. This may ultimately result in less contractor bidding for the project and a consequent increase in tendering prices offered by tendering contractors willing to accept this pricing structure. Usually, only the largest contractors will be eager to take on the risks associated with a lump sum contract as these are generally counterbalanced by a higher margin and the inclusion of contingencies in the contract price (usually spread through the various items that compose the tender price).

From a technical point of view, contractors will be more inclined to agree on a lump sum price where they are particularly experienced with the specific type of project or where the project has a clearly defined scope of work (e.g., where the design and drawings are more straightforward) which is unlikely to change during the construction works so that contractors will be able to anticipate the actual costs and project schedule with a high degree of precision. Conversely, where the project carries a higher degree of uncertainty (e.g., because the scope of work is not well defined, the design is not sufficiently developed, the construction is particularly complex or involves the use of recent technologies), contractors will be less likely to accept a lump sum arrangement as all such factors may lead to an unforeseeable increase of costs which may ultimately reduce their margin.

Disputes relevant to lump sum contract often revolve around whether the employer shall pay the contractor any extra money for activities which the contractor contends do not fall within the original scope as they constitute a variation to such scope or became necessary as a consequence of some supervening events for which the employer has assumed responsibility under the contract, so that the contractor shall be compensated for the resulting increase in a project's cost on top of the agreed contract price. Employers may argue that such activities are included in the agreed scope or that the employer shall not bear the relevant responsibility, so that nothing is due to the contractor as the relevant costs are (or should have been) considered in the contract price.

The issue of variations in lump sum construction contracts was considered in the case of *Mascareignes v Chang Cheng*.[6] The parties entered into a fixed price contract for the design and construction of a 13-storey office building in Mauritius. The contract (a JCT Standard Form of Contract 1980) allowed no change for increases in labour or materials costs. The employer radically redesigned the building. In preparing the final account, the quantity surveyor valued the bulk of the contract components by measurement and value, after deducting the original prices, while leaving the preliminaries unchanged. Mascareignes refused to pay the final valuation as calculated by the quantity surveyor arguing that this approach was not consistent with a lump sum contract. A dispute then arose which went through arbitration, the Mauritius courts and, eventually, the Privy Council. The arbitrator's position was that the contract was either a measure and value contract or a lump sum contract which the parties had turned into a measure and value contract by their conduct. As a result, payment had to be quantified accordingly. The Privy Council disagreed. Lord Hodge commented that there was:

> more scope for flexibility in valuing additional or substituted work in a lump sum contract than the parties have submitted. Work which is not expressly or impliedly included in the work for which the contracted lump sum is payable is extra work.

He also noted that under clause 13.5 of the JCT standard form contract used by the parties additional or substituted work carried out within a lump sum contract may be measured and valued by use of the rates and prices set out in the contract bills if the following three conditions are met:

> First, the work must be of a similar character to the work set out in the bills; secondly, the work must be executed in similar conditions to those of the work in the bills; and, thirdly, the work must not significantly change the quantity of the work set out in the bills. If either or both of the second and third conditions are not fulfilled, the valuation can be based on the rates and prices on the bills but a fair allowance must be made for differences in conditions or quantity.

Thus, the use of measurement and value to ascertain the value of additional or substituted work was not inconsistent with a lump sum contract. The contract had not been varied to become a measure and value contract, but remained a lump sum contract (as evidenced by the fact that the quantity surveyor had preserved the preliminaries unchanged). This was not inconsistent with valuing additional work by measurement and value in the final account statement considering the changes that Mascareignes had made to the works since the parties had entered into the contract.

Lump sum contracts have advantages and disadvantages for both parties: (i) employers know in advance how much the project will cost and are not required to cover contractors' overruns. This will save them the time and costs of keeping contractors' costs under control (unless such costs are reimbursable due to some contractual mechanisms which trigger costs claims such as changes in scope of work or unforeseen circumstances). However, as mentioned, as contractors will assume the risk of overruns, employers may have to pay a higher contract price as contractors will usually include contingencies to cover such

6 *Mascareignes Sterling Co Ltd v Chang Cheng Esquares Co Ltd (Mauritius)* [2016] UKPC 21.

risks. Moreover, employers will not be able to make any savings in case the project is completed at a lower budget or prior to the agreed completion date. In extreme cases, contractors may even try maximising their margin by utilising substandard materials or labour force; (ii) on the other hand, contractors will save money on contract administration as they do not need to justify each head of cost and keep track of all their project expenditure, or account for their work or progress against costs. However, if the tender price proves insufficient to cover the actual construction costs, they will bear the relevant consequences and will not typically be able to claim such extra costs from employers.

5.2.2 Cost reimbursable (or cost plus)

Cost reimbursable (or "cost plus" or "time and material") contracts sit at the other end of the risk allocation spectrum. Based on this structure, contractors are reimbursed the actual costs they incur in carrying out the work, plus an additional fee that may be fixed or a percentage of the total construction costs or some combination of the two.

The pricing risk is all on the employer as the project price is not fixed, but is uncertain and variable depending on the actual number of man hours, the applied labour rate, actual quantities, costs of materials, etc. However, as employers bear most of the risk associated with the project, the contract price is usually lower than the one that contractors seek for fixed price contracts, and contractors will not typically include substantial contingencies in their tendered contract price.

Cost plus contracts carry the risk that contractors may feel less incentivised to manage the works to a budget, which may lead to cost overruns. However, such contracts do not necessarily entail that contractors will be reimbursed for any and every expense they bear for the project. Employers will usually seek an increased level of scrutiny of the contractors' costs management. Costs will need to be justified and supported by evidence showing that the specific expense was reasonably incurred in relation to the work. Contractors will be required to diligently record, update, maintain and make available to the employer (or third-party certifier, e.g., a quantity surveyor) all project costs.

There are at least four categories of cost plus contracts:

(i) Cost plus fixed percentage contract, where contractor has all its actual direct costs reimbursed plus the agreed fee calculated as a fixed percentage of its actual costs. The more the costs, the higher the fee. This carries an intrinsic risk that contractors have little incentive to reduce work costs and may even increase them beyond the initial budget so to maximise their revenues. Thus, while very convenient for contractors, such schemes are not advisable to employers unless there are compelling reasons for choosing them, such as urgency or lack of contractors with adequate skills.

(ii) Cost plus fixed fee contracts, where the contractor's compensation is composed by the repayment of the contractor's actual direct costs plus a fixed fee. As the fee is fixed, delays in the project will increase the project costs, but not the fee. As a result, contractors will be incentivised to complete the project more quickly. However, also in this case, employers assume all the risk of direct cost overruns, while the only risk for contractors is the erosion of their profits in case the project is delayed beyond the expected time.

(iii) Cost plus variable percentage contract, which are a pain gain share type of contract where the contractor agrees to pay a penalty if the final actual cost exceeds the estimated cost (and/or the project is dragged beyond the estimated date of completion), or are paid a higher fee in case the final actual cost is below the estimated cost (and/or the works are completed prior to the agreed completion date).

(iv) Guaranteed maximum price ("GMAX") contracts where the employer agrees to reimburse the contractor its direct actual cost plus a fee, but only up to a "guaranteed maximum price" so that costs beyond the GMAX price will not be coverable. Also in this case, the parties may agree that in case the total cost of construction is below the GMAX price, the employer and contractor will share in the savings in pre-agreed percentages.

Cost reimbursable contracts are often employed where the project is such that overheads or delays are likely to occur (e.g., because contractors are asked to use untested or tailored technologies with a high failure rate or where site conditions have not been thoroughly assessed and analysed) or where the employers expect to have a very high degree of involvement in directing the work.

This pricing mechanism has advantages and disadvantages for both parties. Such contracts are usually budget-friendly for contractors, who will not need to worry in case the cost estimate is inaccurate or flawed. However, contractors will need to keep record of all costs and administer the contract in a proper way, which will require additional effort in terms of time and costs. Moreover, contractors will need to ensure that indirect costs are covered in the "plus" component as they will not be reimbursed.

Another issue is that cost plus contracts typically operate via reimbursement. This means that contractors may be required to front their costs (although, in the case of large contracts, the parties will usually agree on advance payments which will be guaranteed by way of advance payment bonds, and whose repayment will be made by way of retentions progress payments up to the advanced amount). On the other hand, employers maintain a higher degree of control over the works and reduce the risk that contractors use low-quality materials for the project. However, these relatively few advantages are counterbalanced by a higher risk deriving from the uncapped nature of cost plus arrangements (unless the parties agree otherwise, e.g., by way of a GMAX arrangement), which may lead to a liability risk for employers as construction costs will be open-ended and indeterminate (which may also affect the employer's capacity to obtain financing).

Disputes over cost plus contracts often revolve around whether: (i) the contractor actually paid the costs which it is claiming from the employer; (ii) such costs were reasonably borne; (iii) such costs were relevant to the project in question; (iv) the contractor put in place mitigating measures aimed at reducing such costs.

From a drafting standpoint these issues may be addressed by including in the contract an audit provision allowing the employer to audit costs and expenses before or after they are incurred and identify the documents, accounting records and financial records whereby the contractor shall prove the existence and reasonableness of the costs and their relevance to the project. Such audit provisions should clearly state when and how the employer may access the documents, including the place and time at which inspections may take place, the frequency and duration of each inspection, and the parties entitled to attend (including any third-party experts which the employer may hire for the specific task). The parties may also consider including provisions stating how and for how long such documents shall be preserved. Of course, contractors will have a convenience in narrowing the categories of documents to prevent a fishing expedition by employers, while employers will seek detailed records to substantiate expenses which will need to be repaid.

5.2.3 Unit price (or unit rate or measurement or remeasurement)

Under a unit price contract: (i) the contractor breaks down each unit (i.e., a block of work, materials or a combination of the two) of work to be completed and assigns a price to each of them (usually, each unit includes a percentage for overheads and profits); whilst (ii) the employer agrees to pay the contractor for any actual unit provided, installed or constructed.

Thus, rather than considering the project as a whole and setting an overall price for the entire work, a unit price contract will determine the price based on single segments of activities that the contractor will be requested to perform in order to complete the project. Once the work or a part thereof is completed the actual amount of work is measured (e.g., by a quantity surveyor). The total contract price will then be the sum of all the remeasured prices of each completed unit.

This pricing method may be used in the case of repetitive projects where tasks are easily quantifiable, but the ultimate quantity of materials or labour are unknown at the outset of the project or when the price is heavily dependent on materials which are expected to fluctuate based on project needs. This is usually not applicable to complex projects which normally involve a huge number of interconnected activities. However, even in such cases the parties may use the unit price method for single portions of the project, provided that such portions can be easily separated from the rest of the project and separately quantified and paid for.

The main advantage of unit price contracts is simplicity. As the project is split into smaller units, both contractors and employers can easily keep control of both costs and works. For this reason, unit price arrangements are often used when the employer is a public entity, e.g., for projects such as road construction or other public utility-like facilities. Moreover, the fact that contractors are paid a fixed unit price for each unit completed will reduce their risk in case the anticipated units are underestimated as the contractor may refuse to complete additional units or ask to renegotiate the relevant unit price.

The main downside of a unit price contract is that throughout the duration of the project the parties will need to "measure" and "remeasure" the original estimate (for this reason unit prices are also referred to as measurement contracts, measure and pay contracts, or remeasurement contracts). However, as costs are so thoroughly broken down, verifying the actual quantities performed, supplied or constructed on the project against the amounts invoiced by the contractor is not usually a complex exercise.

5.2.4 Hybrid models and price conversion

Employers and contractors may also agree on hybrid pricing models which mix one or more contracting models. For example, they may agree that most of the scope will be paid at a fixed price, while the remainder will be cost plus (e.g., because that portion requires materials that are subject to price fluctuation, or the design is not sufficiently developed).

In the case of large-scale projects, it is also common for the parties to start with a certain pricing model and then agree on converting into another pricing model during the construction phase because of some supervening events. For example, the parties may switch: (i) from a lump sum to a cost plus because project costs have increased to such extent that the contractor may not be able to absorb them and may risk becoming insolvent; or (ii) from a cost plus contract to a fixed price contract as in the interim the scope has become clearer (e.g., because the design has become sufficiently developed).

In such cases, contractors may consider approaching their subcontractors to ensure that subcontracts are amended to reflect the new pricing mechanism in the main contract.

5.3 Bespoke contracts and standard contracts

The parties to a construction contract will usually agree on the document they should use as a starting point for the negotiation, although typically the first draft will be provided by the employer and included in the invitation to tender.

In general, the parties may use either a bespoke contract or a standard form contracts. A bespoke contract is a type of agreement that is not based on a standard form (e.g., because it has been developed internally by one of the parties). The advantage of bespoke contracts is that they are usually customised to meet the specific needs or requirements of the parties. However, as they are produced by one of the parties (usually the employer), they may be particularly "one-sided". This will lead to more effort from the parties that will usually engage in heavy negotiations. Standard form contracts, on the other hand, include standardised provisions that commonly apply to specific types of projects. In this case, the "customisation" is not made to advantage one party over the other, but rather to tailor the contract to the specific project and its characteristics.

Standard form contracts are published by organisations such as the International Federation of Consulting Engineers (FIDIC), the Joint Contracts Tribunal ("JCT"), the Royal Institute of British Architects ("RIBA"), the Institution of Civil Engineers[7] ("ICE"), etc.

Such contracts have several advantages for the parties. They will not need to draft the contract "from scratch" but will rather agree on specific changes based on their needs, the specific requirements of the project and their respective bargaining power. Moreover, the parties will usually be more familiar with the content of such contracts and may be more inclined to accept them with less amendments. In addition, their meaning will often be well understood and tested by the courts. On the other hand, standard form contracts may prove less adaptable to the peculiarity of the specific project and their standardisation may make them harder to customise in accordance with the parties' needs.

7 Which publishes the New Engineering Contract (or NEC Engineering and Construction Contract).

PART THREE

CONTRACT NEGOTIATION

Clauses specific to construction contracts

The construction contract negotiation phase is particularly delicate as it determines how a project's risks are allocated between the parties. It usually starts from the tender phase (when employers propose contractual terms in the invitation to tender) and continues up to contract execution and beyond (e.g., when the parties negotiate variations).

Construction contracts for complex projects are typically lengthy and technical documents and should be negotiated by specialised industry experts in possession of the relevant skillset. Before agreeing on each contractual term, each party shall understand in advance the consequences that the inclusion (or absence) of such term may have on the contract, the project and the balance between parties' respective positions. How contractual terms may affect the parties will ultimately depend on the language of such terms and the law applicable to the contract.

Some contractual terms are more general and may be found in all or most contracts, while others are specific to construction contracts.

DOI: 10.4324/9781003387718-9

CHAPTER 6

General contract negotiation issues

6.1 Scope of work

The "scope of work" is the work that the parties agreed the contractor shall perform. It is an essential term of a construction contract as there may be no binding agreement if the scope of work is not agreed in sufficient detail. What is sufficient detail is a matter of interpretation.

For large projects, it would be impracticable for the parties to agree up to the last detail of the works. As a result, the parties are not expected to define the scope of work in a comprehensive way,[1] and the contract will usually not be held incomplete if the parties have left out the details on fixtures, fittings and finishes.

The courts will normally hold that a contractor's scope of works includes any works which the parties obviously intended to form part of the contractor's scope under the contract, even if not mentioned specifically in contract documents. In the case of *Williams v Fitzmaurice*,[2] the claimant was contracted to build a house for the defendant. According to the contract, the house was "*to be completed and dry and fit for . . . occupation*". The specification did not expressly mention floorboards but stated that "*the whole of the materials mentioned or otherwise in the foregoing particulars, necessary for the completion of the work, must be provided by the contractor*". The claimant had brought the floorboards to the site, but had refused to install them without additional payment. The defendant terminated the contract and seized upon the floorboards by taking over the site. The matter ended in court. The court held that the claimant could not recover any amount as the words used in the contract clearly inferred that flooring was necessary to complete the house. In his decision, Pollock CB said:

> It is clearly to be inferred from the language of the specification that the plaintiff was to do the flooring, for he was to provide the whole of the material necessary for the completion of the work; and unless it can be supposed that a house is habitable without any flooring, it must be inferred that the flooring was to be supplied by him. In my opinion, the flooring of a house cannot be considered an extra any more than doors or windows.

Later cases like *Bacal Construction (Midlands) Ltd v Northampton Development Corporation*[3] show that where the employer provides the contractor with the information the

1 *Management Solutions & Professional Consultants Ltd v Bennett (Electrical) Services Ltd* [2006] EWHC 1720 (TCC) at [25].
2 *Williams v Fitzmaurice* [1858] 3 H&N 833 [157 ER 709].
3 *Bacal Construction (Midlands) Ltd v Northampton Development Corporation* [1976] 8 BLR 88.

DOI: 10.4324/9781003387718-10

contractor shall rely on to prepare its tender, the employer will typically be responsible for the relevant content unless the contract or the document itself contains very strong wording to the contrary.

It is therefore crucial that contractors' tenders clearly state what is included and what is excluded in the price they are offering.

Where a tender indicates that the price does not cover a certain part of the scope of work, where the tender is sufficiently clear on the point the courts may infer that such part of the works is within the contractor's scope, but will be charged at an extra cost to the contract price unless the employer decides that it shall be performed by a third party or contract states explicitly or implicitly those works are excluded from the tender price.[4]

The scope of work is a technical matter and is generally included in a schedule which forms part of the contract documents. The contractual clause relevant to the scope of work is sometimes referred to as "contractor's obligations". It will usually state that the contractor undertakes to the employer to carry out and complete the works in conformity with the provisions of the contract in consideration of the payment of the contract price.

6.2 Performance of the works

6.2.1 Performance of the works in general

By entering into a construction contract a contractor undertakes to do a certain work. Depending on the type of project and the agreement between the parties, this may include designing, manufacturing, supplying, constructing, transporting, installing, testing, commissioning the works, remedying any defects, etc. The fulfilment of such obligations is measured against the agreed scope of work and the technical specifications agreed in the contract.

A contractor is normally required to carry out its services with a certain standard of care. In general terms, the standard of care may be defined as the degree of care and caution which the party providing a certain service must exercise when undertaking such service. In other words, the standard of care sets a benchmark for the quality of the services provided by the contractor.

When considering construction projects, the standards of care are "reasonable skill and care" and "fitness for purpose".

6.2.2 Standards of care

6.2.2.1 Reasonable skill and care

Under English law, unless the parties agree otherwise, the standard of care that a contractor must use is "reasonable skill and care" so that a contractor will not be in breach of its obligations if it can demonstrate that it acted with reasonable skill and care when undertaking its services.

What constitutes reasonable skill and care will be assessed applying the common law test for negligence which provides that a professional person is not negligent if he

4 *Boynton v Willers* [2003] EWCA Civ 904.

carries out his work to the same standard that another reasonably competent member of his profession would have met.

The test is the so-called Bolam test which was formulated in *Bolam v Friern Hospital Management Committee*.[5] Based on the Bolam test, where special skill and competence are involved, the professional will neither be required to have the level of skill and competence required to the "*man on the Clapham omnibus*"[6] nor the specific highest skill. The court held that:

> Where you get a situation which involves the use of some special skill or competence, then the test as to whether there has been negligence or not is . . . the standard of the ordinary skilled man exercising and professing to have that special skill. A man need not possess the highest expert skill; . . . it is sufficient if he exercises the ordinary skill of an ordinary competent man exercising that particular art.

It is worth mentioning that in the 2015 medical case of *Montgomery v Lanarkshire Health Board*[7] the Supreme Court formulated a new "*test of materiality*" to determine whether a doctor had acted with reasonable skill and care. This case is of interest as, although not a construction case, it may have an impact on construction disputes. Mrs Montgomery had diabetes. As a result, she was more likely to have a large baby who could also be at risk of shoulder dystocia (the inability of a baby's shoulders to pass through the pelvis) in case of normal birth rather than a Caesarean section. Mrs Montgomery was not advised about the risk as her doctor estimated this as very small. She then had the baby through normal birth. After her baby was born with severe disabilities, she sued the doctor for professional negligence contending that, had she known about the risk, she would have had a Caesarean section. In holding the doctor negligent, the Supreme Court formulated a materiality test based on:

> whether in the circumstances of the particular case, a reasonable person in the patient's position would be likely to attach significance to the risk, or the doctor is or should reasonably be aware that the particular patient would be likely to attach significance to it.

This test, initially confined to the medical sector, has then been applied in other negligence cases, although never in construction disputes. However, as application in construction disputes may not be thoroughly excluded, the parties should at least consider that as a possibility.

Where the construction contract does not include an express provision on the standard of care to be used by the contractor, a duty to act with reasonable skill and care may be implied by virtue of Section 13 of the Supply of Goods and Services Act 1982 which states that "*[i]n a relevant contract for the supply of a service where the supplier is acting in the course of a business, there is an implied term that the supplier will carry out the service with reasonable care and skill*".

However, in the case of complex construction contracts, where the level of skill and care expected from contractors is high, the contract will typically expressly address the issue.

The contract will normally include wording stating that the contractor shall exercise a degree of professional skill and care (but the parties may also include other words such

5 *Bolam v Friern Hospital Management Committee* [1957] 1 WLR 582 (QB).

6 A hypothetical ordinary man which would act as a reasonable person would do in the circumstances.

7 *Montgomery v Lanarkshire Health Board* [2015] UKSC 11.

as competence, diligence, prudence, foresight, etc.) that would reasonably be expected from a professionally qualified, competent and skilled contractor experienced in carrying out works of a similar nature and complexity to those contemplated in the contract.

6.2.2.2 Fitness for purpose

6.2.2.2.1 FITNESS FOR PURPOSE IN GENERAL

A construction contract may state that the works shall be fit for the purpose for which they are intended. Should this be the case, such obligation will usually be construed as a warranty imposing an obligation of result. This means that the contractor will be held to that result even where the works do not meet the intended purpose for reasons beyond its control. This would impose an absolute obligation on the contractor which is well beyond the contractor's general duty to exercise reasonable skill and care in the carrying out of the works. As a result, even where the contractor has conducted itself in accordance with, or even above its professional standards, it may still be liable for damages in breach of a fitness for purpose clause.

In the case of *Viking Grain Storage Ltd v TH White Installations Ltd*,[8] Davies J stated that a fitness for purpose clause:

> prescribes a relatively simple and certain standard of liability based on the reasonable fitness of the finished product, irrespective of considerations of fault and of whether its unfitness derived from the quality of work or materials or design.

The matter of fit for purpose clauses was recently considered in the case of *MT Højgaard A/S v E.On Climate & Renewables UK Robin Rigg East Limited and another*.[9] MT Højgaard ("MTH") was engaged as the design and build contractor for the foundations of the Robin Rigg offshore wind farm, located on the North West coast of Britain, by the operator E.ON Climate and Renewables ("E.ON"). The tender documents sent by E.ON to MTH included E.ON's "Technical Requirements", which laid out minimum requirements that were to be taken into account by MTH. In particular, paragraph 3.2.2.2 of the Technical Requirements stated:

> The detailed design of the foundation structures shall be according to the method of design by direct simulation of the combined load effect of simultaneous load processes (ref: DNV-OS-J101) . . . The design of the foundations shall ensure a lifetime of 20 years in every aspect without planned replacement. The choice of structure, materials, corrosion protection system operation and inspection programme shall be made accordingly.

DNV-OS-J101 is an international standard for the design of offshore wind turbines published by independent classification and certification agency, DNV, which set out certain mathematical formulae to calculate aspects of the foundation structures, but which however does not guarantee performance (including a 20-year foundations' lifetime). Clause 8.1(x) of the construction contract between E.ON and MHT stated that:

> The Contractor shall, in accordance with this Agreement, design, manufacture, test, deliver and install and complete the Works: (i) with due care and diligence expected of appropriately

8 *Viking Grain Storage Ltd v TH White Installations Ltd* [1985] 33 Build LR 108 at [11].
9 *MT Højgaard A/S v E.On Climate & Renewables UK Robin Rigg East Limited and another* [2017] UKSC 59.

> qualified and experienced designers, engineers and constructors (as the case may require) . . . (x) so that each item of Plant and the Works as a whole shall be free from defective workmanship and materials and fit for its purpose as determined in accordance with the Specification using Good Industry Practice.

The fit for purpose obligation was then defined in a way that it included adherence to the Technical Requirements. One of the formulae included in the DNV-OS-J101 was then found to be wrong, which meant that the strength of the foundation structures had been substantially over-estimated. The foundation structures started failing. As a result, the parties agreed to carry out remedial work, leaving the court to decide who would bear the relevant cost. In particular, the courts had to decide whether the clause 8.1(x), when read with clause 3.2.2.2 of the Technical Requirements, meant that MTH had warrantied a 20-year lifetime for the foundations, or that MTH only had to design with reasonable care and diligence following the design methodology in DNV-OS-J101. The High Court found for E.ON as clause 8.1(x) of the contract ultimately referred to the Technical Requirements. As the foundations had proven not to be designed so to have a lifetime of 20 years (as required by paragraphs 3.2.2.2 and para 3b.5.1 of the Technical Requirements), MTH was to be held liable. MTH appealed. The Court of Appeal found that: (i) there was an inconsistency between paragraphs 3.2.2.2 and para 3b.5.1 of the Technical Requirements, on the one hand, and DNV-OS-J101, on the other hand; (ii) there was no fitness for purpose obligation within the contract as the industry expected compliance with the well-known DNV-OS-J101 standard, which did not guarantee that the foundation would have an operational life of 20 years; (iii) while the Technical Requirements included a 20-year warranty, all the other provisions of the contract, including those referring to a "design life" and the requirement to exercise reasonable skill and care in the design of the foundations, pointed the other way. The case landed in the Supreme Court, which found in favour of E.On. Lord Neuberger stated that:

> even if the customer or employer has specified or approved the design, it is the contractor who can be expected to take the risk if he agreed to work to a design which would render the item incapable of meeting the criteria to which he has agreed . . . where different or inconsistent standards were imposed, the correct analysis was that the more rigorous or demanding of the two requirements must prevail.

The decision shows that contractors should be well aware that accepting a fitness for purpose obligation may expose them to liabilities beyond their duty to exercise reasonable skill and care, regardless of whether the employer approved the design which might be incapable of meeting the fitness for purpose agreed between the parties.

Contractors shall expressly accept a duty of result such as a fitness for purpose obligation as the courts will not usually imply one. As stated in *Greaves & Co (Contractors) Ltd v Baynham Meikle & Partners*:[10]

> The law does not usually imply a warranty that [a professional] will achieve the desired result, but only a term that he will use reasonable care and skill. The surgeon does not warrant that he will cure the patient. Nor does the solicitor warrant that he will win the case.

This may affect the contractor's ability to claim under its professional indemnity insurance policy as it is common for insurers to exclude coverage for liabilities arising from

10 *Greaves & Co (Contractors) Ltd v Baynham Meikle & Partners* [1975] 3 ALL ER 99 (CA).

onerous contractual provisions, i.e., obligations which go beyond what would otherwise be implied by common law or statute. The rationale behind this is that insurers are unwilling to indemnify it for liabilities flowing from voluntary assumption of risk.

6.2.2.2.2 FITNESS FOR PURPOSE CLAUSES

Where the parties agree to include such clause in their construction contract, they should ensure that the operative words to achieve such result are clear and unambiguous. It is essential that they exactly define the "purpose" of the works or services. In case no purpose is defined in the contract, they would be ill-advised to including a general fitness for purpose concept as this would create uncertainty and lead to disputes as to what the parties intended with the clause.

6.3 Priority of documents

Priority of documents clauses are common in construction contracts for complex projects as such contracts are typically composed of many documents (the contract, the contractual conditions, the technical schedules, the employer's requirements, etc.).

Considering the high number and the complexity of such documents, inconsistencies are not uncommon and may lead to arguments, and ultimately disputes, between the parties.

Where the contract does not include a priority of documents clause the courts will look at the contract documents and seek to objectively assess what the order of priority the parties intended to give them. This may lead to unexpected and unwanted outcomes. For this reason, construction contracts include priority of documents clauses which list the contract documents and state that, for the purpose of interpretation, the priority shall be in accordance with the sequence in the clause. As a result, in case of inconsistency or ambiguity, the document that is higher on the list takes precedence.

The clause may also provide that in case one party becomes aware of any conflict or discrepancy within each of such documents it shall notify the other.

The parties shall then endeavour to agree on how to resolve such conflict or discrepancy. Normally, where the parties are unable to agree on a possible solution, the decision will ultimately be on the employer, which will exercise it through an instruction. In case the instruction leads to an increase of costs or time for the contractor, the clause may expressly state whether or not it may be treated as a variation (i.e., whether or not the contractor may claim an extension of time and/or additional costs). Where the clause is silent on the point, it will be a matter of interpretation for the courts to decide whether the instruction is in fact a variation.

The courts will rely on common law principles of interpretation, including the most relevant overriding principle that the contract documents will be considered and construed as a whole and effectively despite the presence of a priority of documents clause in the contract.

Where one or more clauses are inconsistent, the courts may simply follow the order of precedence stated in the priority of documents clause if there is a clear and irreconcilable discrepancy between such provisions. Thus, inconsistencies will not be resolved by choosing between one clause over another, but rather by resolving the discrepancies between individual obligations (unless it could be inferred from the contract that the parties intended to abandon the whole of any provision if it was inconsistent in any respect with another).

This was clearly stated by the case of *RWE Npower Renewables Ltd v J N Bentley Ltd.*[11] JN Bentley Ltd ("JN Bentley") agreed to carry out civil engineering works in connection with the construction of a hydro-electricity generating plant in Scotland for RWE Npower Renewables Ltd ("RWE"). The contract was based on standard terms derived from the NEC3 Engineering and Construction Contract, June 2005 edition (with amendments June 2006). Clause 2 of the contract: (i) included a list of documents comprising the contractual documents, the "Contract Data Parts 1 and 2", the "post-tender clarifications" and the "Works Information and Site Information"; and (ii) stated that such documents were to be read and construed in the order of precedence in which they had been listed. When the project fell behind schedule, a dispute arose between the parties on whether JN Bentley's completion of the works was governed by in particular the Works Information or by Part 1 of the Contract Data, which were inconsistent as one identified the works in greater detail, while the other was worded in more general terms. The dispute was referred to adjudication. The adjudicator held that there was an inconsistency between the two documents and that Part 1 of the Contract Data took precedence over the Works Information. RWE issued proceedings in the High Court. Akenhead J held that the contract should be read as a whole and construed so far as possible to avoid inconsistencies between different parts on the assumption that the parties had intended to express their intentions in a consistent and coherent way. In his view there was no significant inconsistency between the documents, which, at least in relation to the completion of that part of the work, were capable of being read together without undue difficulty. JN Bentley appealed to the Court of Appeal, arguing that there was a clear discrepancy between the clauses in question, which meant that the judge should have discarded the whole of the clause in the Works Information. The Court of Appeal unanimously dismissed the appeal and agreed with Akenhead J. In particular Lord-Justice Moor-Pick clarified that: (i) contract documents should as far as possible be read as complementing each other and therefore as expressing the parties' intentions in a consistent and coherent manner; (ii) only in a case of a clear and irreconcilable discrepancy would it be necessary to resort to the contractual order of precedence to resolve it; (iii) in resolving potential discrepancies, one should obtain such assistance as one can from the other parts of the contract and interpret the contract as a whole; (iv) even if there is a clear and irreconcilable difference: (a) deciding the order of precedence of provisions only becomes necessary where different provisions on their true construction impose different obligations in relation to the same subject matter; and (b) the order of precedence should only be looked at in relation to the discrepancy (not by choosing one clause over the other).

It is also crucial that the parties ensure that the various contractual documents include only one priority of documents clause and that it does not conflict with other contractual provisions.

6.4 Care and supply of documents

The production, exchange and storage of the parties' documents before and after commencement of a project is a sensible issue in construction projects.

11 *RWE Npower Renewables Ltd v J N Bentley Ltd* [2014] EWCA Civ 150.

Technical documents are at the core of the project and disputes almost invariably focus on them and how the parties have complied with their content.

Such documents may include permits, estimates, drawings, plans, specifications, technical data, software and any other information or documents of a technical nature, produced or acquired by the parties or on their behalf which the parties are obliged to exchange or render available to each other upon request.

When it comes to contractor's documents, construction contracts usually provide for a number of obligations on contractors, including the obligations to: (i) keep custody and care of the documents at agreed premises unless and until the project is taken over by the employer; (ii) provide the employer with copies (usually electronic, including native files, although hard copies may also be required) in a number to be agreed between the parties; (iii) grant the employer (and in some cases the lenders or their advisers) reasonable access to the contractor's documents as well as other project documentation (e.g., variations).

The contract may state, and have contractors acknowledge, that the employer will rely on the contractor's documents for any works (other than the works performed by the contractor pursuant to the contract), which are performed by third parties engaged by or on behalf of the employer.

This provision carries a particular weight as contractors are in fact taking on a responsibility for any errors in their documents which might have an impact on the works performed by such third parties on the basis of the design, specifications, etc. provided by the contractor to the employer. This means that should such third parties blame the contractor's documents for any defects or other deficiencies on the work they have carried out, the employer may turn to the contractor and seek damages for faulty or erroneous documents upon which the employer (and the third parties) have in fact relied. This, however, will not typically allow such third parties to have a direct claim against the contractor (unless any form of collateral warranty is given).

As to the employer's documents, these may include the project requirements (e.g., those relevant to the purpose, scope, design, etc. for the works), the site data, the design (e.g., where it is performed by a third party that has prepared the FEED), etc.

Also in this case, the clause may provide that: (i) the employer will retain ownership on the documents; (ii) the documents may be used solely for the purpose of performing the works; (iii) the employer will be liable in case of improper use of its documents.

Another key issue is what type of warranty, if any, the employer will give in relation to the accuracy and sufficiency of the information contained in the documents it provides the contractor with. This is an issue of primary importance for contractors who rely on employers' documents to build the work and eventually discover that they contained inaccuracies which ultimately impact the costs and time to complete the project. Where the employer has not warranted the accuracy of such information, and the design procured by the employer, the contractor may find itself in the position of not being able to perform. A court may then find that the contractor shall be deemed to have satisfied itself as to the accuracy and sufficiency of the information included in the documents prepared by the employer. This is even more so in case the clause specifically states that the contractor has examined the contractual documents and is satisfied that they contain no error and expressly takes on the responsibility for any such errors (if any). For this reason, when such clauses are present in a construction contract, the parties usually agree on a set of information (sometimes called "relied upon information" or "RUI") on which the contractor expressly relies and bases the work. The contractor will not be responsible for the consequences of inaccuracies contained in the RUI and may be able to successfully bring an action against the employer if it can prove: (i) that the RUI was inaccurate; and (ii) that it has made the works in compliance with the RUI; and (iii) that it has suffered losses as a consequence thereof.

Care and supply of documents clauses may also deal with intellectual property ("IP") rights.

As to contractors' IP rights, they usually clarify that contractors will retain ownership or licences and IP rights they owned prior to the contract or which the contractor develops during the project based (totally or predominantly) on such pre-existing rights. This might not be easy to assess, in particular where the word "predominantly" is used as it carries a certain degree of uncertainty as to what extent a new IP was developed on the basis of an existing one.

Where necessary, the employer will seek the contractor to grant to the employer (and its affiliates and lenders, where applicable) a (usually non-exclusive) right to use the licence and/or the IP. This right is usually non-exclusive and royalty-free and limited to any purpose in connection with the project. The parties may agree on any time (e.g., up to the actual or intended design life of the project) and space limitations, revocability or terminability of the licence, as well as any right to grant sub-licences to other parties and on what conditions this may be done. This provision is usually intended to allow the smooth operation of the project and the possibility to allow maintenance, adjustments, reparations and demolishing of the project when the contractor will leave the site (unless an operation and maintenance contract is entered into, in which case the contractor will take care of such aspects). Likewise, employer's IP rights which existed prior to the contract (or which the employer has developed during the project) will normally remain the ownership of the employer, which may grant the contractor a (usually non-exclusive) royalty-free licence of such IP rights. The parties may also agree that the contractor may grant sub-licences to subcontractors when necessary.

As to the any IP jointly developed by the employer and the contractor during the project's execution, the parties may for example assign the right to any of them (usually the employer, in case the IP is necessary for the operation of the project) for a fee.

6.5 Instructions

One of the most important rights that employers normally have under construction contracts is the right to instruct (directly or through the employer's representative or persons to whom the authority has been assigned or delegated) the contractor to do activities which may be necessary for the works.

The clause providing for the employer's right to issue instructions will usually state that instructions shall be in writing. The only exception may apply to urgent matters requiring immediate action (e.g., those relating to health, safety or environmental risks).

Instructions may take two forms. They may either be variations (i.e., the instructed activity was not within the original scope of work and/or the result of a non-compliance), in which case they will entitle contractors to extra payments or extensions of time, or be the consequence of a failure by the contractor to comply with the requirements of the contract, in which case they will not normally entitle the contractor to any additional cost or time.

Where the parties agree that an instruction constitutes a variation, the contractor shall follow the specific procedure set out in the contract for variations. Where the parties are not in agreement on the nature of the instruction, the contract may state that the contractor will be obliged to comply (unless the employer withdraws the instruction), and the issue will usually become contentious and be solved through the dispute resolution procedure agreed in the contract.

CHAPTER 7

Price and payment

7.1 Price

7.1.1 Price as fundamental element of the contract

In the case of construction contracts the contract price is the amount the contractor is compensated or remunerated by the employer for the performance of the work as agreed in the contract.

For obvious reasons the contract price is regarded by the parties as an essential term, so that a construction contract would generally not come into existence or be enforceable unless the parties have agreed how much the employer will pay for the works. This position was confirmed in the case of *Courtney & Fairbairn Ltd v Tolaini Brothers (Hotels) Ltd.*[1] Mr Tolaini, a builder who wanted to develop a site in Hertfordshire, contacted Mr Countney, a property developer and a building contractor, who appeared to be well placed to obtain finance for the project. At a meeting that took place at the office of an architect, Mr Sacks, Mr Courtney agreed to find someone who could finance the project, subject to Mr Tolaini employing Mr Courtney (or his company) to do the works. After the meeting, Mr Courtney sent the following letter to Mr Tolaini:

> Re: Thatched Barn Hotel . . . I am now in a position to introduce you to those who: (a) are interested in your proposals, (b) have access to the necessary finance . . . I think I should mention, at this point, that my commercial interest in this matter is that of a Building Contractor. I am interested in it due to the fact that Mr Sacks, whom I have known for some years, is aware that I work for a number of large investing and development concerns, and thought it possible that I might be in a position to be of service to you. You will understand, therefore, that in addition to making myself useful to you, my objective is to build the three projects mentioned, namely, the Motel, the Filling Station, and the future Hotel, or other development, on the 'Green Belt' area of your site. Accordingly I would be very happy to know that, if my discussions and arrangements with interested parties lead to an introductory meeting, which in turn leads to a financial arrangement acceptable to both parties you will be prepared to instruct your Quantity Surveyor to negotiate fair and reasonable contract sums in respect of each of the three projects as they arise. (These would, incidentally be based upon agreed estimates of the net cost of work and general overheads with a margin for profit of 5%) which, I am sure you will agree, is indeed reasonable.

1 *Courtney and Fairbairn Ltd v Tolaini Brothers (Hotels) Ltd* [1975] ADR LR 00/00.

DOI: 10.4324/9781003387718-11

Mr Tolaini sent the following reply letter to Mr Courtney: "*In reply to your letter of the 10th April, I agree to the terms specified therein, and I look forward to meeting the interested party regarding finance*".

Mr Courtney then introduced a source of finance to the Mr Tolani, who instructed his quantity surveyor to negotiate with Mr Courtney. Eventually, the parties did not reach an agreement as differences arose about the price for the works, and Mr Tolani employed other contractors to do the construction work, which he paid for through money lent by the source introduced to him by Mr Courtney. Mr Courtney's company then sued Mr Tolani claiming for the loss of profit which they would have made if they had been employed as builders for the works. At the trial the parties agreed that the court was to decide on whether there was concluded any enforceable agreement in law between the plaintiff and the defendants or one of them, and if yes, who were the parties to the agreement and what were its terms. Shaw J held that there was an enforceable agreement between Mr Courtney and Mr Tolaini and that the relevant terms were the letters exchanged between the parties, which gave rise to:

> a binding and enforceable contract whereby the Defendants undertook to employ the Plaintiffs . . . to carry out the work referred to in [Mr Courtney's first letter referred earlier] at a price to be calculated by the addition of 5 per cent to the fair and reasonable cost of the work and the general overheads relating thereto.

The first instance decision was appealed. Lord Denning found that there could be no contract as there was no agreement of so fundamental a matter as the price. He held:

> I am afraid that I have come to a different view from the judge. The reason is because I can find no agreement on the price or on any method by which the price was to be calculated. The agreement was only an agreement to 'negotiate' fair and reasonable contract sums. The words of the letter are 'your Quantity Surveyor to negotiate fair and reasonable contract sums in respect of each of the three projects as they arise'. Then there are words which show that estimates had not yet been agreed, but were yet to be agreed. The words are: 'These [the contract sums] would, incidentally be based upon agreed estimates of the net cost of work and general overheads with a margin for profit of 5%'. Those words show that there were no estimates agreed and no contract sums agreed. All was left to be agreed in the future. It was to be agreed between the parties themselves. If they had left the price to be agreed by a third person such as an arbitrator, it would have been different. But here it was to be agreed between the parties themselves. Now the price in a building contract is of fundamental importance. It is so essential a term that there is no contract unless the price is agreed or there is an agreed method of ascertaining it, not dependent on the negotiations of the two parties themselves. In a building contract both parties must know at the outset, before the word is started, what the price is to be, or, at all events, what agreed estimates are. No builder and no employer would ever dream of entering into a building contract for over £200,000 without there being an estimate of the cost and an agreed means of ascertaining the price. In the ordinary course of things, the architects and the quantity surveyors get out the specification and the bills of quantities. They are submitted to the contractors. They work out the figures and tender for the work at a named price; and there is a specified means of altering it up or down for extras or omissions and so forth, usually by means of an architect's certificate. In the absence of some such machinery, the only contract which you might find is a contract to do the work for a reasonable sum or for a sum to be fixed by a third party. But here there is no such contract at all. There is no machinery for ascertaining the price except by negotiation. In other words, the price is still to be agreed. Seeing that there is no agreement on so fundamental a matter as the price, there is no contract.

However, the absence of an agreement on price may not be fatal for contractor's right to obtain payment for any work performed under the purported contract as the courts may find that the contractor is entitled to be paid a reasonable price in quantum meruit.

Contractors tendering for large projects calculate the price so to cover their costs and make some variable margin. Sometimes the price is not expressed as a figure, but the parties may agree on a formula or other machinery to precisely calculate it (e.g., in a "cost plus" contract).

If the mechanism agreed between the parties for determining the contract price is an objective one, the courts will not usually find the contract void for uncertainty. Where the agreed mechanism breaks down, for example because one party refuses to comply with it, a court may step in and set or determine a fair and reasonable price for the contract.[2] In the case of *Sudbrook Trading Estate Ltd v Eggleton*[3] the litigants were parties to four separate leases of four industrial properties. One of the leases granted the lessees an option to

> purchase the reversion in fee simple in the premises hereby demised . . . at such price not being less than £12,000 as may be agreed upon by two valuers one to be nominated by the lessor and the other by the lessee and in default of such agreement by an umpire appointed by the . . . valuers.

The other leases contained similar clauses, though the minimum price was different. The lessees then tried to exercise the options, but the landlords refused to appoint a valuer. The lessees then sued for specific performance asking the court to step in and set the price. The landlords contended that the option clauses were void because they were too uncertain as they did not specify an exact price. The House of Lords held that the clauses specified an objective mechanism to calculate the price, which made the option sufficiently certain. As the landlords refused to appoint a valuer, the mechanism for determining the price had broken down. Thus, the court was entitled to substitute its own machinery to determine a fair and reasonable price and grant an order for specific performance. A contract was complete as the parties had agreed on all its essential terms. The mode of ascertaining the value of the land was not necessarily an essential term of the contract. The method chosen by the parties was not the only reasonable way of ascertaining the price.

The mere fact that the parties agree on the price for a certain scope of work does not, per se, determine that a binding agreement is created as the parties may have failed to agree on other necessary terms. As held by Lord Greene in *Clifton v Palumbo*:[4]

> When parties are beginning to negotiate a transaction of this magnitude it is common experience – and, indeed, it is only business – to find that the first thing they begin to think about is the price. . . . The use of the word 'agree' in such a context may or may not involve a contractual result . . . if you say that the price has been agreed when the contract is being negotiated, you do not use the word 'agree' in the sense that any binding contract has been entered into. All you mean is that a particular element in the contract you are negotiating has been decided.

---

2 S. Furst QC, V. Ramsey QC, *Keating on Building Contracts* (7th edition) Sweet & Maxwell, 2001, at [29].
3 *Sudbrook Trading Estate Ltd v Eggleton,* [1983] 1 AC 444 [1982].
4 *Clifton v Palumbo* [1944] 2 All ER 497 at [499].

7.1.2 Contract price clause

A clause setting out the price for the work will usually include the following terms: (i) the agreed pricing method (e.g., fixed lump sum, cost plus, etc.); (ii) in case of a lump sum price,[5] exact amount that the employer agrees to pay to the contractor in consideration of the satisfactory execution and completion of the works as defined in the contract and the fact that it will not be subject to any alteration such as increases due to currency fluctuations, changes in taxation, etc., except where expressly stated in the contract (e.g., in the case of variations, force majeure, etc.).; (iii) the currency (or currencies, where specific part of the scope are paid in a different currency) in which the price shall be paid; (iv) the indication of which party will bear the relevant taxes, customs, duties and fees. In this regard, the contract will usually state whether the sums payable by the employer will be inclusive or exclusive of value added tax (or other equivalent tax) and how value added tax or other equivalent tax is to be treated in case the payment relates to the reimbursement or indemnification of costs incurred by the other party (i.e., where the value added tax (or other equivalent tax) on that amount has already been paid and may be recoverable from the tax authority in the jurisdiction of the party that has made the payment[6]).

7.2 Payment

7.2.1 Payment in general

The work will typically be remunerated by way of a mix of advance payment, interim payments and final payment (or final account) made by the employer to the contractor in accordance to a pre-agreed schedule of payments.

A schedule of payments will usually state: (i) the sums to be paid; (ii) the relevant currency; and (iii) any employer's rights of netting and set-off the amounts due by the employer to the contractor against amount due by it to the employer.

In addition to the three aforementioned categories, a contractor may be entitled to receive payments as a result of successful claims.

7.2.2 Categories of payments

7.2.2.1 Advance payments and proof of funds

Contractors will usually need to bear high initial costs since the project's inception (e.g., to hire and mobilise personnel, purchase materials and equipment needed for the works, make any other initial payments necessary to commence the works such as applying for permits, pay taxes, etc.). This may expose them to cash flow issues or even to the risk not being able to recover such costs (e.g., because the employer becomes insolvent or is unable to fund the project or merely breaches its contractual obligation to repay such initial costs).

5 In case of a cost plus or hybrid model in which all or some part of the works is paid based on quantities or work done, the contract shall clearly indicate how such quantities or work will be measured and evaluated so that the contract price will be determined in accordance with such mechanism.

6 Tax issues applying to construction projects are outside the scope of this book.

To provide for such needs, construction contracts usually include advance payment provisions stating that the employer will pay a certain amount upfront which the contractor shall use to "kick off" the work.

Advance payments would have the effect of shifting the risk entirely on employers, which may find themselves in the condition of having paid an advance, but being unable to recover it in case no work is performed (e.g., in the case of an insolvent contractor). For this reason, advance payments are typically backed by advance payment bonds issued by contractors to guarantee repayment of the advance payment money. The advance payment will be then returned to the employer (usually in instalments) or set-off against the payments due to the contractor. The parties will usually agree that the advance payment bond shall be returned or reduced accordingly. In case the contractor does not perform in compliance with its obligations, the employer will be entitled to immediate restitution of the advance paid on the grounds of total failure of consideration[7] (unless the parties agreed otherwise in the contract), and may recover the sum due by calling on the advance payment bond.

Where a contractor is unable to secure an advance payment an alternative to cover the risk of not being able to recover its initial costs is asking the employer for a proof of funds. As proofs of funds are a mere additional burden on employers, they are less common than advance payments. However, should a contractor succeed obtaining such a term, the typical clause may state that the evidence the employer should give the contractor as to the availability of funds to carry out the project should be "reasonable" and that, lacking such evidence, the contractor would be entitled to terminate the contract. As to what is reasonable, in the case of *NH International (Caribbean) Ltd v National Insurance Property Development Company Ltd (Trinidad and Tobago)*[8] relevant to a FIDIC contract obliging the employer to give reasonable proof of funds, the employer produced a letter from the Project Administration Unit of the Ministry of Health stating that the Cabinet of the Government of Trinidad and Tobago had approved additional funding for the project. The arbitrator found that the evidence did not amount to "*reasonable evidence*" that "*financial arrangements*" had been "*made and maintained*". The contractor was then entitled to terminate the contract.[9]

In the absence of a proof of funds clause in the contract, it will not be easy for a contractor to ask for proof of funds during the course of the project (e.g., because the employer is in a situation of financial distress or the lenders are reluctant to provide further funds in case of extra costs) as the employer may simply contend that nothing has changed in respect of the date in which the contract had been entered into.

7.2.2.2 Interim (or progress) payments

7.2.2.2.1 INTERIM PAYMENTS IN GENERAL

Once the contract price is agreed, and the advance payment and relevant surety are in place, the contractor will commence the works based on the scope of work agreed and be paid for it. In this phase, payments usually will be made on progress (so-called interim

7 *TTI Team Telecom International Ltd v Hutchison 3G UK Ltd* [2005] EWHC 762 (TCC) at [57].

8 *NH International (Caribbean) Ltd v National Insurance Property Development Company Ltd (Trinidad and Tobago)* [2015] UKPC 37.

9 In that case, a FIDIC contract. The decision was upheld by the Privy Council.

or progress payments). The aim of interim or progress payments is to allow the contractor to have sufficient cash flow to the work (e.g., pay workers, buy materials, pay subcontractors, etc.). This was explained by Lord Hoffmann in *Melville Dundas Ltd v George Wimpey UK Ltd*[10] as follows:

> Instalments payments are in their nature provisional liabilities. As has frequently been said, they are to provide the cash flow for the contractor or sub-contractor to enable him to perform his duties under the contract.

For this reason, nearly every construction contract for large projects provides that progress is remunerated in instalments based on milestones achieved by the contractor.

In the absence of such contractual provision, the contractor will usually be prevented from claiming progress payments, in particular when the contract is an "entire contract", unless progress payments are secured by statute.

In England, the Housing Grants, Construction and Regeneration Act states that a party to a construction contract with a duration of more than 45 days is entitled to interim or stage payments and that the parties cannot contract out of this provision.

7.2.2.2.2 INTERIM PAYMENTS CLAUSES

(A) INTERIM PAYMENT REQUEST Where the construction contract provides for the right to be paid upon achievement of certain levels of progress, each interim payment will usually be supported by an interim payment request that the contractor shall submit to the employer (and/or the engineer). The precise form and content of such a request will usually be agreed in the contract.

(B) INTERIM PAYMENT CERTIFICATE Once it receives the payment request, the employer (and/or the engineer) has typically a certain number of days to check the documents and valuate the work performed. The basis of the valuation is usually agreed upfront in the contract usually based on a mix of progress and quality criteria.

(i) The employer disagrees with the contractor's payment request The contract may state that in case the employer disagrees with the payment request or needs clarifications, it may determine the amount it fairly considers due (if any) or ask for further information.

It is worth noting that for a payment to become due it is not usually necessary that the work is performed "precisely" in accordance with the contract. In the case of *BWP (Architectural) Ltd v Beaver Building Systems Ltd*,[11] the employer contended that the work for which a subcontractor had requested payment had been performed tardily. Despite that, the court found that the subcontractor was entitled to the interim payment for the total value of work properly executed.

Depending on the wording of the clause, the interim payment certificate may be considered a condition precedent to an entitlement to the interim payment. Should this be the case, such condition will usually be upheld by English courts and the contractor will

10 *Melville Dundas Ltd v George Wimpey UK Ltd* [2007] 1 WLR 1136 at 1140.

11 *BWP (Architectural) Ltd v Beaver Building Systems Ltd* [1988] 42 BLR 86; see also *Costain Building & Civil Engineering Ltd v Scottish Rugby Union plc* [1993] 69 BLR 80.

be entitled to payment only subject to the certificate being issued, and in line with the relevant content (e.g., as to the sum due to the contractor).[12] This means that the right to payment will be triggered by the interim payment certificate rather than the contractor having carried out the relevant works.[13]

The employer's failure to issue a payment certificate will not necessarily be fatal for the contractor's right to claim the whole amount. Where the parties cannot reach an agreement on the amount due (based on the procedure mandated in the contract), the issue will be ultimately solved through the dispute resolution mechanisms agreed in the contract.

The contract will also usually provide for the consequences of a delayed payment. The most common remedy is the contractor being entitled to receive interest calculated on the basis of a formula agreed in the contract. Should the parties not include anything in the contract as to how interest on late payments will be calculated, the statutory interest based on statutory law. In England, the Late Payment of Commercial Debts (Interest) Act 1998 (the "LPCD Act") will apply. It is worth noting that Section 8 of the LPCD Act states that a contract term which purports to exclude the right to statutory interest in relation to the debt is void unless there is a substantial contractual remedy for late payment of the debt. As to the meaning of "substantial remedy", Section 9 of the LPCD Act states that the agreed remedy for the late payment shall be regarded as a substantial remedy unless: (i) the remedy is insufficient either for the purpose of compensating the supplier for late payment or for deterring late payment; and (ii) it would not be fair or reasonable to allow the remedy to be relied on to oust or (as the case may be) to vary the right to statutory interest that would otherwise apply in relation to the debt. In determining whether a remedy satisfies the "fair and reasonable" test, regard is to be had to: (a) the benefits of commercial certainty; (b) the strength of the bargaining positions of the parties relative to each other; (c) whether the term was imposed by one party to the detriment of the other (whether by the use of standard terms or otherwise); and (d) whether the supplier received an inducement to agree to the term. In determining whether a remedy is not a substantial remedy, regard shall be had to all the relevant circumstances at the time the terms in question are agreed. It is therefore advisable that the contract includes clear wording stating that the remedy is a substantial remedy for late payment of any sum payable under the contract in accordance with Section 8(2) of the LPCD Act. The accrual of interest for late payment (regardless of whether it is statutory interest or interest agreed between the parties) is generally automatic in that the contractor will not need to send any formal notice or obtain any certification from the employer. The parties will also usually agree that the remedy is without prejudice to any other right or remedy the contractor has in the contract or at law.

(ii) The employer agrees with the contractor's payment request If the employer agrees with the payment request made by the contractor, the employer will issue the payment certificate confirming the basis of its calculation and the payment date. The contractor will then issue an invoice in the amount certified for payment in the payment certificate. The payment is then made within the date agreed in the contract.

12 *Milner v Field* [1850] 5 Ex 829 [155 ER 363].
13 *Henry Boot Construction Ltd v Alstom Combined Cycles Ltd* [2005] BLR 437 at 447 [28].

Should the employer fail to make the payment, the contractor will normally be entitled to apply for summary judgment unless there are clear reasons for which payment could be withheld or set-off against another amount due to the employer[14] or because the certificate should not have been issued in the first place (e.g., because it has been obtained due to fraud or improper pressure, etc.).

In some cases, the contract may state that a payment certificate shall not be construed as employer's acceptance that the amount is due or proof of satisfaction as to the works for which payment is made. This language is typically aimed at affording the employer the right to make corrections or modifications to previous payment certificates. In this case, an interim certificate will not be conclusive evidence[15] that an amount paid by the employer was due as errors may still be corrected in later certificates.[16]

(C) THE INTERIM PAYMENT PERIOD The contract will usually include a schedule clearly indicating the payment periods (usually against precise payment milestones).

In the case of entire contracts, absent an agreement of the parties on this point, the contractor will typically be entitled to payment just upon completion of all of its work[17] (subject to statute law stating otherwise).

It is worth noting that, unless the contract provides otherwise, the time when the employer must make the payment is not of the essence in construction contracts[18] so that a delay in making the payment would not normally entitle a contractor to terminate the contract on grounds of a delay in receiving the payment.[19]

7.2.2.3 Final payment (or final account)

A construction contract will usually include a mechanism to calculate any final payment due to the contractor (although payment may be due to the employer, rather than the contractor).

The final account is normally paid once the defect liability period has lapsed, and the deadline that the employer has to notify any defects has expired. In this way, the employer has clarity as to the quality of the works.

The final account is in fact an adjustment to the contract price, in that it is quantified by considering a number of events affecting the contract price such as variations, liquidated damages, claims, retentions yet to be released, etc.

Where the parties have included a final account mechanism in their contract, it will typically provide for the following steps: (i) the contractor prepares a final statement and applies for the final payment certificate within a certain deadline set out in the contract. In case the contract does not provide for an express term, the courts will not usually imply a term that this should be done within a reasonable time.[20] Some construction contracts also state that, in case the contractor fails to submit the final statement and apply for the

14 *Lovell Projects Ltd v Legg* [2003] BLR 452 at 465 [36] – 466 [39].
15 *AG Machin Design & Build Contractors Ltd v Long* [1992] 34 Con LR 121 at [129].
16 *Rupert Morgan Building Services (LLC) Ltd v Jervis* [2004] 1 WLR 1867 at 1870 [8].
17 *Ruttle Plant Hire Ltd v Secretary of State for Environment Food & Rural Affairs* [2009] BLR 301 at [310] – [311].
18 *Alan Auld Associates Ltd v Rick Pollard Associates* [2008] BLR 419 at 423 [12].
19 *Dalkia Utilities Services plc v Celtech International Ltd* [2006] EWHC 63 (Comm) at [130].
20 *Total M & E Services Ltd v ABB Building Technologies Ltd* [2002] Con LR 154 at 163 [39] – [42].

final payment certificate within the deadline set out in the contract, the employer has a duty to request the contractor to do so. In case the contractor remains idle, depending on the contract's terms, this may lead to the contractor being barred from submitting any further payment claim and/or the employer being entitled right to issue the final payment certificate for such amount as he fairly determines to be due. The contract will usually also state that once the final statement has been submitted the employer will carry no liabilities other than those for matters included in the statement unless the contract provides otherwise and except for cases of any case of gross negligence and/or wilful misconduct by the employer; (ii) should the employer have doubts on the final statement prepared by the contractor, the contract will normally entitle the employer to seek further information/clarifications; (iii) the employer (or the engineer/contract administrator) will then make an assessment of the entirety of the works carried out by the contractor and calculate the final account by deducting any amounts due to the employer, e.g., for set-offs, damages (e.g., liquidated damages or unremedied defects), previous overpayments[21] and other deductions from the amount due to the contractor for the works (including those for which payment has already been made). Where the amount to be deducted is higher than the outstanding amount owed for the works, the contractor will have to pay the difference to the employer (although it may challenge the relevant assessment); (iv) the employer/contract administrator will then issue the final payment certificate for the amount owing to the contractor (or owed by the contractor); (v) in case the contractor does not agree with the quantification made by the employer/engineer, the parties may enter into negotiations (which the contract may qualify as "good faith negotiations") to discuss and try clarifying any outstanding issues. If an agreement is not reached, the contract will usually entitle the employer to issue a final payment certificate for any amount that the employer deems due. The dispute will then be solved through the dispute resolution mechanism set out in the contract.

In case the parties have not included a final account mechanism, a court will not necessarily imply one. A similar situation was considered by the Technology and Construction Court in the case of *JSM Construction Ltd v Western Power Distribution (West Midlands) plc*.[22] Western Power Distribution (West Midlands) plc ("WP") and JSM Construction Ltd ("JSM") entered into a contract whereby JSM had agreed to perform some cable and ductwork installation works in Birmingham. The contract provided for interim payments to be made throughout the works, but did not include a final account mechanism. When JSM submitted a "final application" claiming an amount it had calculated by remeasuring the works it had performed, WP refused to make any payment and contended that the contract did not entitle JSM to claim any final account. JSM then sued WP arguing that: (i) according to Section 110 (1) (a) of the Housing Grants, Construction and Regeneration Act 1996 (the "HGCR Act"): "*Every construction contract shall . . . provide an adequate mechanism for determining what payments become due under the contract, and when*"; (ii) according to Section 110 (3) of the HGCR Act: "*If or to the extent that a contract does not contain such provision as is mentioned in subsection (1), the relevant provisions of the Scheme for Construction Contracts apply*"; (iii) as the contract failed to provide for a final account, the payment terms were inadequate. As a consequence, a final payment

21 *Lamprell v Billericay Union* [1849] 3 Exch 283: 18 LJ Ex 282.
22 *JSM Construction Ltd v Western Power Distribution (West Midlands) plc* [2020] EWHC 3583 (TCC).

term should be implied in the contract and be regulated by paragraph 5 of the Scheme for Construction Contracts 1998 (the "Scheme"), which states that:

> The final payment payable under a relevant construction contract, namely the payment of an amount equal to the difference (if any) between (a) the contract price, and (b) the aggregate of any instalment or stage or periodic payments which have become due under the contract, shall become due on the expiry of (a) 30 days following completion of the work, or (b) the making of a claim by the payee, whichever is the later.

WP disagreed and applied to have JSM's claim "struck out" or for a summary judgment to be entered against JSM. The court noted that the sole issue to be decided was whether a final account provision should be implied into the contract. Pepperall J referred to *Grove Developments Ltd v Balfour Beatty Regional Construction Ltd*[23] where, despite the contract provided that the employer could make 23 interim payments, the contractor had applied for a 24th payment, which the employer had refused to make. In that case, the Court of Appeal had rejected the contractor's claim. In particular, Jackson LJ had held that:

> First, the express words used make it clear that the parties were only agreeing a regime of interim payments up to the contractual date for practical completion. . . . Secondly, it is impossible to deduce from the hybrid arrangement what would be the dates for valuations, payment notices, pay less notices and payments after [after the last interim payment]. These were essential matters for the reasons previously stated. Thirdly, this is a classic case of a party making a bad bargain. The court will not, and indeed cannot, use the canons of construction to rescue one party from the consequences of what that party has clearly agreed.

However, Pepperall J noted that *Grove* was not good authority to defend an assertion that a final account provision should be implied in a construction contract as it specifically related to a claim for an additional interim payment. In particular, the judge: (i) concurred with WPD that Section 110 of the HGCR Act does not mandate that the parties include a final account provision in their contract in order for the agreed payment mechanism to be "adequate". Even without a final account, a fixed fee and staged payments mechanism could be "adequate" for the purposes of the Act, also considering that despite the lack of a final account provision "*might put the parties under considerable pressure*", it would also give then the "*considerable advantage of ensuring early payment*" rather than waiting for complex final account negotiations after completion of the works. He also noted, as an overarching principle, that "*the purpose of the [HGCR Act] is not to save a party from an imprudent deal*"; and (ii) disagreed with JSM's position that paragraph 5 of the Scheme was to be considered a model final account clause. JSM's claim was then denied.

23 *Grove Developments Ltd v Balfour Beatty Regional Construction Ltd* [2016] EWCA Civ 990.

CHAPTER 8

Guarantees

8.1 Guarantees in general

Complex construction projects usually carry high risks and liabilities on the parties. For employers, the main risk is the contractor's failure to perform the contract and carry out the works in compliance with the contract. Employers will therefore seek to cover such risk by requesting contractors to provide guarantees in the employer's favour (or in favour of third parties, such as the employer's lenders). Such guarantees may be in the form of corporate guarantees (e.g., when issued by the contractor's parent company) or bank guarantees (e.g., when issued by a bank, insurance company, etc.). Such guarantees may cover different risks such as the correct performance of the work (so-called performance bonds), the return of any advance payments made by the employer (so-called advance payment bonds), the return of any retention made by the employer (so-called retention bonds) and the correction of any defective works (so-called warranty bonds).

Guarantees (with the exception of parent company guarantees) have a cost typically given by an issuing fee and fees payable whenever the guarantee is extended in duration or value. Not all contractors are able to secure bank guarantees as banks will usually look at the contractor's credit rating and capacity to repay any amount in case the bond is enforced by the employer (unless the contractor gives a "collateral", i.e., deposits an equal amount of money on a bank account at the issuing bank or provides other forms of security, e.g., in the form of security over the contractor's fixed and floating assets).

Contractors usually have two possibilities to secure guarantees, i.e.: (i) entering into project-by-project financial arrangement with issuing financial institution; (ii) entering into ad hoc facility agreements with one or more financial institutions regulating the provision of future project guarantees. This second alternative helps contractors reducing screening times and costs. The downside is that such agreements usually contain default clauses stating that a call on an on-demand bond is to be considered an act of default under the agreement, unless the contractor is able to immediately pay to the bank the amount demanded, the bank may be entitled to terminate all loans, lines of credit and security provided under the facility agreement whether related to this construction contract or otherwise and accelerate the relevant reimbursement. This may be a problem in case the contractor has more dealings with the same bank. The situation may be worsened in case the same contractor is a party to other facility agreements with other banks including cross-default provisions stating that a default under one facility agreement constitutes a default under other facility agreements.

DOI: 10.4324/9781003387718-12

8.2 Conditional and on-demand guarantees

Guarantees are divided into the two main categories of conditional (or "see-to-it") guarantees and "on-demand" guarantees, depending on whether they create a secondary or primary obligation on the guarantor.

A conditional guarantee is an undertaking by the secondary obligor or guarantor (e.g., a bank), to be answerable to a beneficiary for the debt or obligation of a primary obligor (e.g., a contractor) in case of the primary obligor's default. The essential feature is that the secondary obligor is only liable to pay out if the primary obligor is found liable to the beneficiary. This is why the liability of the guarantor is said to be "secondary", and the guarantor is said to have the benefit of suretyship defences (i.e., the same defences of the obligor) against the beneficiary.

This means that the guarantor's obligation to pay is dependent on the beneficiary (e.g., the employer) establishing that the primary obligor is in breach of the underlying contract.

An on-demand guarantee (or on-demand bond or performance bond) is payable simply when a demand is made which complies with the requirements of the bond, irrespective of whether or not the liability under the underlying contract is established. In this case, payment can normally only be refused on grounds of clear fraud,[1] and the guarantor does not have the benefit of suretyship defences that usually has a see-to-it guarantor (for example, the guarantor would not be allowed to apply any set-offs which the contractor may be entitled to under the underlying contract in order to reduce the amount payable to the employer under the bond). An on-demand bond is payable merely on demand regardless of whether there was actual default by the contractor[2] or whether such default is disputed.[3] As said by Mance LJ in *Solo Industries UK Ltd v Canara Bank*:[4]

> Banking commitments are to be honoured free from interference, according to their terms and on a documentary basis. Banks are not to be involved in underlying commercial disputes. Beneficiaries are to be paid, regardless of such disputes.

To the extent the communication whereby the employer calls on the bond meets the requirements of the guarantee, the guarantor must pay.[5] For this reason, on-demand bonds have been defined as "*cash in hands*".[6]

In theory, it would be possible for the parties to agree that some conditions be satisfied by the employer in order for it to call on the bond (e.g., to produce specific documents evidencing a breach of the underlying contract and/or the consequent loss). This form of hybrid guarantees should be avoided as it may create uncertainty and difficulties from a practical point of view.

The difference between see-to-it and on-demand guarantees is not always immediate. The matter was considered in the case of *Shanghai Shipyard Co. Ltd. v Reignwood International Investment (Group) Company Ltd.*[7] In 2011, Reignwood (the "Guarantor")

1 A demand guarantee is also not subject to the requirements of the Statute of Frauds on execution.

2 *Trafalgar House Construction (Regions) Ltd v General Surety & Guarantee Co Ltd* [1996] 1 AC 199 at [206] – [207].

3 *Edward Owen Ltd v Barclays Bank* [1978] 1 QB 159 at [169].

4 *Solo Industries UK Ltd v Canara Bank* [2001] 1 WLR 1800 at 1814 [35].

5 *Meritz Fire and Marine Insurance Co Ltd v Jan De Nul NV* [2011] BLR 535 at 542 [27].

6 *Potton Homes Ltd v Coleman Contractors Ltd* [1984] 28 BLR 19 at [31].

7 *Shanghai Shipyard Co. Ltd. v Reignwood International Investment (Group) Company Ltd* [2021] EWCA Civ 1147.

entered into a shipbuilding contract with Shanghai Shipyard ("SS") for the construction of a US$200 million offshore drillship. The price was to be paid in three instalments, with the final instalment of US$170 million to be paid upon delivery. The shipbuilding contract was then novated to Opus Tiger ("OT"), so that the relevant parties became SS and OT, while the Guarantor provided SS with an "*irrevocable and unconditional Letter of Guarantee*" (the "Guarantee") to secure the payment of the final instalment by OT. The Guarantee provided that: (i) in the event of default of OT, the SS could demand payment of the final instalment from the Guarantor, who was obliged to pay immediately on receipt of the demand; (ii) in case there was a dispute between the OT and SS which was referred to arbitration, the Guarantor could withhold payment until the arbitration award was issued. When OT refused to pay the final instalment, SS made a demand under the Guarantee, but the Guarantor refused to pay pending the outcome of arbitration between SS and OT, even though the proceedings had been commenced only after the demand. A preliminary issues' trial then followed in the High Court concerning the proper characterisation of the Guarantee. The Guarantor contended that the Guarantee was a see-to-it guarantee. In doing so, it sought to rely on the so-called Paget's presumption, which can be found in Paget's Law of Banking.[8] The presumption is based on four criteria which, according to the author, if present, will normally lead to the conclusion that the relevant instrument is an on-demand guarantee. In particular, according to the author:

> where an instrument (i) relates to an underlying transaction between the parties in different jurisdictions, (ii) is issued by a bank, (iii) contains an undertaking to pay 'on demand' (with or without the words 'first' and/or 'written') and (iv) does not contain clauses excluding or limiting the defences available to a guarantor, it will almost always be construed as a demand guarantee.[9]

The Guarantor argued that the Guarantee was not issued by a bank or other financial institution. The High Court found in favour of the Guarantor and held that the Guarantee was in fact a see-to-it guarantee. As such, payment could be withheld pending the arbitration award. SS appealed. The Court of Appeal rejected the Guarantor's argument based on the "Paget's Presumption" stating that:

> [There is] futility of seeking to apply a presumption in circumstances in which only some of the conditions for its existence obtain. Which are the important ones if not all are required? Without clear answers to such a question, the court is not by constructing a presumption which is applied in this way assisting the commercial community in promoting certainty as to the nature and legal consequences of their instruments. If resort is to be had to presumptions at all, the utility of which I would respectfully doubt at least outside the classic context of performance bonds, they should, in my view, be confined to circumstances where all the stated conditions are fulfilled.

In Lord Justice Popplewell's view, what was of relevance was the Guarantor's commercial and financial strength and not the fact that it was not a bank. The court also stressed that primary focus must always remain on the words used by the parties in their context. In that particular case, the language used by the parties suggested that the guarantee was in

8 *Paget's Law of Banking* (11th edition) Butterworth & Co., June 1996.

9 The "Paget's presumption" was endorsed by the Court of Appeal in *Wuhan Guoyu Logistics Group Co. Ltd. v Emporiki Bank of Greece S.A.* [2012] EWCA Civ 1629, where the court held that the guarantee in question was a demand guarantee even though not all of the criteria were present.

fact a demand bond. The language pointed out in the specific case was: (i) the use of the capitalised words "*ABSOLUTELY and UNCONDITIONALLY*"; (ii) the words "*[as primary obligor] and not merely as the surety*"; (iii) the words that payment was due immediately "*upon receipt by us of your first written demand*"; (iv) the fact that obligations on the Guarantor were unaffected by any dispute under the construction contract; (v) the fact that interest was payable for a short period (60 days' worth), which seemed to indicate the need for prompt payment on demand (rather than at the end of the arbitration proceedings).

The difference between the two types of guarantees may have important implications on the dispute resolution process followed to enforce a guarantee. As a claim under a see-to-it guarantee can succeed only if the employer proves the contractor's liability under the underlying contract, the guarantor may seek to refuse payment also in case proceedings between the employer and the contractor have concluded with an award or judgment where the contractor has been held liable under the construction contract. This is because the findings in proceedings between the employer and the contractor will not normally bind the guarantor unless the guarantee contains an express provision stating that any such decision will be binding on the guarantor (who might even be entitled to have the issue re-litigated in proceedings the guarantor is a party to[10]). This principle does not apply to on-demand bonds as they are independent of the underlying contract so that any proceedings between the employer and the contractor under such contract should be of no or limited relevance to the guarantor and his obligation to pay under the on-demand guarantee.

8.3 Form and formalities of guarantees

Guarantees are contracts. As such, they must include all the elements necessary for the existence of a contract to be valid and enforceable as such.

Moreover, a guarantee will typically need to be in the form of a deed. The reason is to avoid the guarantee be considered unenforceable for lack of consideration due to the fact that the guarantor will usually not be entitled to any payment or direct benefit under the underlying construction contract. Moreover, according to Section 4 of the Statue of Frauds 1677, a guarantee must be in writing and signed by a person with the requisite authority in order to be enforceable.

8.4 Main categories of guarantees

8.4.1 Parent company guarantees

It is common for contractors to tender through one of their subsidiaries rather than the group's parent company. This choice may be made, for example, for tax planning reasons or to comply with local content requirements. To address employers' concern that the subsidiary may not have the same financial strength of its parent company (i.e., that in case of contractual disputes the employer may be left with the onus to recover damages from an entity which does not have the necessary funds to pay the amount sought by the

10 *Autoridad del Canal de Panamá v Sacyr SA and others* [2017] EWHC 2228 (Comm).

employer), employers may require contractors to provide security of payment in the form of a parent company guarantee ("PCG"), i.e., a contractual promise whereby the contractor's parent company of the contractor's group guarantees that its subsidiary to which the contract has been awarded will performs its obligations to the employer under the contract.

It is worth noting that a PCG does not "improve" the employer's rights under the construction contract. This means that the guarantor takes on obligations which are contingent and dependant on the ones assumed by the obligor under the construction contract. The guarantor's liabilities will usually be no greater in amount and scope than those taken on by the obligor and the guarantee will end if and when the construction contract is terminated, becomes invalid or ends.

A PCG clause will require the contractor to provide a PGC in a certain form (usually based on a template attached to the contract) and within a certain date. The clause will also typically include the contractor's obligation to deliver a legal opinion, issued by a law firm acceptable to the employer, confirming the identity and authority of the PCG's signatory to execute the PCG on behalf of the contractor's parent company, and the validity and enforceability of the PCG. The legal opinion has the scope to reassure the employer that the PCG serves its scope, also considering that, regardless of the law applying to the PCG, the relevant enforcement may need to be done in a jurisdiction which is not familiar to the employer (typically the country where the parent company or its assets are located). The PCG clause will also usually state that the contractor will be obliged to procure that the contractor's parent re-issues the PCG where events occur which affect the guarantor (e.g., in case of reorganisation, insolvency, liquidation, etc.) or the guarantee (e.g., in case of illegality, invalidity, unenforceability, etc.).

8.4.2 Performance bonds

Almost invariably, construction contracts for large and complex projects require the contractors to provide the employer with a performance bond ("PB") guaranteeing performance by the contractor of its contractual obligations under the contract.

Just like PCGs, also PBs cover employers from the risk of contractor's non-compliance. However, PBs offer a better protection as they also cover the risk of parent company's insolvency as the guarantor is a financial institution.

Performance bonds are usually in the form of on-demand guarantees and thus impose a primary obligation on the guarantor, usually a financial institution of solid financial standing such as a bank or an insurance company, to pay the employer on its first demand where the contractor fails to perform the contract. This means that the beneficiary is usually entitled to payment simply on submitting a statement that the primary obligor has failed to perform its obligations under the contract. The guarantee is therefore independent from the underlying contract and the issuer's obligation to pay is not affected by claims or disputes over the underlying contract between the beneficiary and the primary obligor.

The parties will typically set out the PB's terms and conditions in a template attached to the contract. They will also include a clause in the contract stating: (i) that the contractor shall issue a PB; (ii) whether the PB will be a condition precedent to any payments from the employer to the contractor under the contract; (iii) that the PB shall be valid from the date of issue until completion/take over, with the understanding that, in case the terms PB specifies an expiry date and completion/take over is not achieved by a certain number of days before the expiry date, contractor is requested to extend the validity of the PB until take over. Should the contractor fail to do so, this will entitle the employer to call on the PB; (iv) the amount of the PB, which will depend on the parties' agreement (usually between 10% and 20% of the contract price); (v) whether the contractor will be required to provide a replacement PB in case the contract price increases by a certain agreed amount/percentage as a result of variations; (vi) the characteristics that the entity issuing the PB shall have (e.g., a financial institution of standing and of a certain nationality). The parties may also agree on a specific credit rating of the guarantor so that, should the credit rating of the issuing entity fall below the agreed level, the PB will cease to be valid and will need to be replaced within a certain agreed term. The employer may also seek a right to reject a guarantor which is not satisfactory to the employer, in which case it would be advisable to state that the employer shall act reasonably in its decision; (vii) whether the costs of obtaining and maintaining the PB will be borne by the contractor or otherwise.

8.4.3 Advance payment bonds

A contractor will usually have to meet significant start up and procurement costs even before construction begins (e.g., to hire and mobilise personnel, buy equipment or materials, build structures, obtain permits, etc.). A contractor will generally seek an advance payment from the employer to cover such initial costs. Such advance payment is usually repaid by the contractor throughout the project through deductions from interim payments made by the employer to the contractor. An employer paying an advance payment will usually ask the contractors to provide an advance payment bond ("APB"), typically in the form of an on-demand bond issued by a financial institution such as a bank or an insurance company. The APB will serve the scope to protect the employer from the risk that the contractor fails to perform the works for which the advance was made (so preventing the employer from recovering the relevant portion of advance). In this case, the employer will be entitled to call on the APB and force the guarantor to pay an amount equal to the value of unperformed works for which payment was made in advance.

The contract will generally include a clause stating that any advance payment shall be backed by an APB. The language will largely reflect the one relevant to PBs. However, the APB will differ from clauses providing for PBs as they will typically state that: (i) the APB will be valid from the date of issue until the relevant advance payment has been repaid in full; (ii) the APB expiry date shall be extended up to full repayment of the advance; (iii) the amount of the APB will be progressively reduced by the correspondent amount repaid by the contractor.

8.4.4 Retention bonds

As a form of additional security on the correct performance of the works, an employer may reserve a right to retain a certain percentage of the contract price (typically around 5%) pending completion of the work to ensure that the contractor completes the project, including any punch list, and rectifies defects in the warranty period. Part of such retention money (usually around 50%) is then released on completion, while the remainder will be kept by the employer up to the expiry of the warranty period. The parties may however agree that the contractor has a right to have an earlier release of the retention monies if it procures a retention bond ("RB") to the employer for the same amount.

The advantage for the contractor is to have an improved cash flow. Where the RB is in the form of an on-demand guarantee, the employer's security will not be compromised. All aforementioned considerations made in relation to the other forms of guarantees are applicable to RBs.

8.4.5 Warranty bonds

Construction contracts routinely provide that contractors shall warranty that the works are free from defects. Such obligation has a fixed duration (usually around five years, but longer periods, e.g., 10 years, are not uncommon) and starts on completion and takeover of the works (i.e., issue of the relevant taking over certificate). During this period (sometimes also referred to as defects notification period or defects liability period) the employer will be entitled to have the contractor curing any defects which are covered by such warranty at the contractor's costs. The warranty in question usually will be covered by a specific warranty bond ("WB") which will normally replace all other guarantees in place for the relevant project.

The content of a WB will be not dissimilar from the other project guarantees, the only peculiarity being the type of obligations which the bond intends to cover and the timing of coverage of the guarantee.

The contract will generally include a clause which largely reflects the one relevant to other project guarantees. However, peculiarities of a WB clause are that: (i) the contractor is requested to deliver the WB to the employer prior to or on taking-over; (ii) upon delivery of the WB, the employer will release the PB to the contractor; (iii) the WB will be valid from taking-over until the date agreed between the parties as warranty period (e.g., 12 months after the end of the warranty period agreed in the contract); (iv) the amount of the WB, which is generally expressed as a percentage of the contract price (e.g., 5% of the contract price).

CHAPTER 9

Contract participants

9.1 Parties' representatives

Large construction projects involve a plethora of stakeholders from both parties' sides. It is therefore crucial that the parties communicate through the right channels so that there can be no uncertainty as to whether instructions and other communications are made by or to authorised persons. For this reason, construction contracts typically provide for the parties' right (and obligation) to appoint respective representatives to act on their behalf under the contract. The contract will usually include the rights of the representative and any limitations thereof. For example, an employer's representative will not usually be authorised to relieve the contractor of any duties, obligations or responsibilities under the contract and shall not act ultra vires (i.e., beyond the terms of his authority).

The contract will also usually state that when either party makes an appointment (or intends to replace their appointed representative), it shall give notice to the other party stating: (i) that a representative was appointed/replaced; (ii) the representative personal details (e.g., name, contact details and address); (iii) the duties for which the representative has been appointed; (iv) the authority the representative has been delegated and any limits thereof (unless this is covered elsewhere in the contract); (v) whether such duties and authority may be assigned and delegated to third-party assistants (e.g., inspectors).

9.2 Subcontractors

9.2.1 Subcontracts in general

Where allowed to do so, contractors may subcontract the whole or a part of their scope of work to third-party contractors. The reasons behind subcontracting may be as follows: (i) the main contractor does not have the type of specialisation and skill needed for a specific part of the works or sufficient workforce to carry out the entirety of the work; (ii) the costs for the main contractor to carry out a certain part of the work may be higher than the what the main contractor would pay if such works were subcontracted to a third-party contractor; (iii) the main contractor may use a subcontract as a way to pass on performance risks to the subcontractor.

Considering the benefit of subcontracting, almost invariably construction contracts relevant to complex projects allow the main contractor to engage subcontractors to undertake specific parts of the main contractor's works. However, the doctrine of privity

DOI: 10.4324/9781003387718-13

of contract prevents the creation of a direct contractual link between the employer and the subcontractor so that the main contractor will normally remain responsible to the employer for all aspects of the subcontract (e.g., for any delay or defects due to the subcontractor's scope of work). By the same token, an employer may not claim directly against subcontractors (unless the contract or a separate collateral agreement provide otherwise) and vice-versa.

9.2.2 Domestic, nominated and named subcontractors

A distinction is often made between "domestic", "nominated" and "named" subcontractors. In particular: (i) domestic subcontractors are those selected by the main contractor and for whose acts and omissions the main contractor is solely responsible; (ii) nominated subcontractors are those selected by the employer, but employed by the main contractor, and for which the employer may retain some responsibility (depending on the words of the contract and the circumstances of the case). In order to mitigate this risk, employers often seek to specify in the contract that: (a) in case a contractor does not intend to employ a specific nominated subcontractor, the contractor may raise objections. If such objections are reasonable, the contractor will not be obliged to employ the specific nominated subcontractor; (b) the contractor is responsible for the acts or defaults of any nominated subcontractor as if they were the acts or defaults of the contractor; and (iii) named subcontractors, for which the employer expresses a mere preference by naming them, while the final decision on whether to employ them is completely left to the contractor, so that the employer will not retain any liability as to acts or omissions of the named subcontractor in case the contractor has eventually employed one or more of them.

9.2.3 Subcontractors clause

A typical subcontractors clause will: (i) state whether the contractor is allowed to subcontract the works and to what extent (e.g., only a part or a specific part of the work or the totality of them); (ii) state whether consent of the employer is needed before the contractor enters into a subcontract (e.g., consent may not be necessary on nominated subcontractors or where the value of the subcontract is below a certain amount) and whether the employer should not unreasonably withhold or delay its consent; (iii) clarify that, where the whole or part of the works are subcontracted, the contractor will retain full responsibility for the acts or defaults of its subcontractor (the clause may also include a specific indemnity in the employer's favour for claims brought against the employer by any subcontractors); (iv) provide that the contractor shall procure that its subcontractors comply with the quality, health, safety and environmental, and other requirements included in the main contract; (v) provide that subcontracts be executed as deeds (as under English law the statute of limitation for claims under a deed is extended from six to 12 years); (vi) provide that subcontracts shall include specific terms such as those relevant to: (a) the subcontractor's obligation to deliver collateral warranties in the employer's favour; (b) a step-in right of the employer in the contractual rights and obligations of the main contractor in the subcontract for the case in which the main contractor was to become insolvent; (c) provide for the assignment and/or novation of the subcontract and/or the contractor's rights and obligations under it to the employer in case the main contract is terminated; (d) allow further subcontracting or making them subject to the employer's and specify whether such consent should not be unreasonably withheld or delayed; (vii) prescribe that the main contractor shall obtain the employer's consent before the contractor amends or terminates any specific subcontracts and specify whether such consent shall not be unreasonably withheld or delayed.

CHAPTER 10

The site

10.1 The site in general

In general terms, the construction site (sometimes also referred to as building site) is the area of land on which construction works are being carried out. The Construction (Design and Management) Regulations 2015[1] (CDM Regulations) indicate that a construction site is the area that "*includes any place where construction work is being carried out or to which the workers have access, but does not include a workplace within the site which is set aside for purposes other than construction work*". However, what constitutes the site is generally defined in clear terms in the construction contract, which usually specifies the relevant physical boundaries. The site does not usually cover only the place where the project is located and any relevant means of access (the employer usually also guarantees that means of access are suitable for the activities that the contractor has to perform at site, including transportation of equipment to and from the work areas), but, depending on the parties' agreement, it may also include other places which relate to the project such as places where materials are to be delivered or stored, personnel offices and accommodations, etc., including underground land and part of airspace above the site.[2]

For obvious reasons, the site plays an important role in a construction project and the relevant contractual terms are usually heavily negotiated as the site may be the source of major disputes between the parties.

10.2 Access to the site

Construction contracts provide an obligation on employers to give contractors access to and possession of the site (although the employer's obligation does usually extend to acts that are outside the employer's control[3]) within an agreed term. Full access to the site is normally granted from the commencement date (i.e., the date in which the works are to be commenced, which usually coincides with the date in which the employer issues a so-called notice to proceed). The contract may state that access to site shall be subject

1 The CDM Regulations were introduced in 1994 following publication of European Directive 92/57/EEC on minimum safety and health standards for temporary or mobile construction sites. They are intended to ensure that health and safety issues are properly considered during a project's development so that the risk of harm to those who have to build, use and maintain structures is reduced.

2 *Grigsby v Melville* [1974] 1 WLR 80.

3 See for example *LRE Engineering Services Ltd v Otto Simon Carves Ltd* [1981] 24 BLR 127 at 136–137, per Robert, where Goff J stated that "*the building owner does not insure that prompt possession and use of the site shall be given, he undertakes that it shall be so far as his own acts and ability are concerned, but not otherwise*".

DOI: 10.4324/9781003387718-14

to it being necessary to perform the works. Absent of such provision, access will be intended as undisturbed exclusive possession.[4] It is worth noting that the employer's obligation to give the contractor timely access to the site is an implied term of the contract even in the absence of an express provision.[5]

The contractual provision covering access to the site will usually also describe the consequences and remedies in case the employer fails or delays to provide access to site to the contractor in compliance with the contract. Usually, the contractor will be entitled to an extension of time (provided that completion is or will be delayed due to the delayed access to the site) and the compensation of any prolongation borne by the contractor as a consequence thereof, unless the delay was caused by the contractor. However, an employer's failure to grant access to the site does not usually entitle a contractor to terminate the contract: (i) as a result of repudiation of the contract by the employer, unless the employer's conduct clearly indicates that it has no intention at all of providing access to the contractor; or (ii) for breach of contract,[6] unless the breach is sufficiently serious, e.g., where time is stated to be of the essence and the delay in accessing site would have an impact on completion. However, in such case the parties will usually agree on an extension of time, unless a later completion would not make any sense for any of the parties (e.g., because by agreeing on a new completion date the employer would be deprived from the benefit of the project or the contractor would be in breach of a different contract due to an overlap with the project whose completion date was postponed).

10.3 Site responsibility

Upon the contractor taking possession of the site (and until the employer retakes possession), the relevant responsibility, including any responsibility on the equipment, material and any other property present on site, will shift on the contractor so that the contractor will usually be required to indemnify the employer for any damages thereof. For this reason, it is common for contractors to enter into so-called contractors' all risks (C.A.R.) insurance policies against possible risk of physical damages to the site. However, albeit less common in practice, the parties to a construction contract may agree that the employer shall bear the risk of any damages arising during the work, e.g., due to fire or explosion. However, such clauses would be interpreted by the courts as exclusion clauses which may not exempt contractors from the consequence of events covered by the clauses resulting from the contractor's own negligence.[7]

10.4 Site conditions

10.4.1 English law position on responsibility on site conditions

Construction contracts normally specify what party takes this risk in case the site conditions prove unexpectedly more adverse than anticipated. Such a situation would probably

4 *R v Walter Cabbott Construction Ltd* [1975] 21 BLR 42 at [56] – [57].
5 *Lawson v Wallasey Local Board* [1883] 11 QBD 230.
6 *Mercers v New Hampshire Insurance Co Ltd* [1992] 60 BLR 26 at [37].
7 *Dorset County Council v Southern Felt Roofing Co Ltd* [1989] 48 BLR 96.

affect the project and lead to an increase of cost and time required to complete it. For example, in the case of an offshore wind farm, a contractor may be provided by the employer with geotechnical data and information on seabed, sub-surface and hydrological conditions which prove to be inaccurate (e.g., due to the presence of unexpected boulders or unexpected marine conditions). This may result in the need to change the working method (e.g., using a different drilling technique), the working equipment (e.g., using different types of drills), the project's design (e.g., some foundation sites may need to be moved to a different area) or, in extreme cases, the works may need to be abandoned altogether (e.g., where the actual site conditions would render performance impossible or achievable only at a disproportionate cost).

Information on site conditions is normally supplied by the employer to the contractor, who will rely upon it in planning and carrying on the construction works. Unless the parties agree otherwise, employers will not be taken to warrant the accuracy of such information[8] or that the site is fit for the contractor to complete the work. It will usually be an onus of the contractor to investigate the site conditions and make enquiries without relying only on information provided by the employer.[9] Based on such enquiries, the contractor, which is supposed to have the relevant expertise, will decide whether the works are possible and, in case they are, at what price. This was confirmed in the case of *R. v Paradis and Farley Inc*[10] where Taschereau J stated that:

> Expenses incurred for unforeseen difficulties must be considered as being included in the amount of the tender, and the respondent has the legal obligation to execute the contract for the price agreed upon, in the same way as would have been its indisputable right to benefit, if the soil had been more favourable and easier than foreseen.

In *Obrascon Huarte Lain, v H.M. Attorney General for Gibraltar*,[11] it was said that the contractor should have made allowance for a proper investigation so to allow the worst possible scenario in its price despite that the employer had not warranted any data it had provided in the tender phase. In *Van Oord UK Ltd Anor v Allseas UK Ltd*[12] this principle was confirmed in the following terms:

> Every experienced contractor knows that ground investigations can only be 100% accurate in the precise locations in which they are carried out. It is for an experienced contractor to fill in the gaps and take an informed decision as to what the likely conditions would be overall.

Therefore, any inaccuracy in the information provided by employers in relation to the site conditions will typically not shield contractors from their responsibility for not having built what they had warranted to under the contract.[13] The mere fact that an employer provides inaccurate information in an invitation to tender or during the tender phase will not typically excuse contractors from being unable to build the project as providing such information will not typically imply a warranty from the employer as to the relevant accuracy.

8 *Thorn v London County Council* [1896] 1 App Cas 120.
9 *Ranger v Great Western Railway Co* [1854] 5 HLC 72 at 87.
10 *R. v Paradis and Farley Inc* (1942) SCR 10.
11 *Obrascon Huarte Lain, v H.M. Attorney General for Gibraltar* [2015] EWCA CIV 712 at [94].
12 *Van Oord UK Ltd Anor v Allseas UK Ltd* [2015] EWHC 3074 (TCC).
13 *Tharsis Sulphur & Copper Company v McElroy & Sons* [1878] 3 App Cas 1040.

The case law confirming this principle is well established and goes as far back as the nineteenth century.[14] There are however some exceptions to the general principle that the contractor shall be responsible for the consequences of unexpected site conditions: (i) where the works have become impossible due to a supervening event which frustrates the entire contract;[15] or (ii) where the employer has expressly asked the contractor to bid on the specific information provided relevant to ground conditions in the tender. In *Bacal Construction (Midlands) Ltd v Northampton Development Corporation*[16] the contractor was expressly requested to tender on a ground conditions report provided by the employer. In that case, the court found that the risk had to be borne by the employer as there was an implied term or warranty that the ground conditions would accord with the hypothesis upon which the contractors had been contracted; (iii) where the contract includes clear wording expressly addressing the issue. For example, in *Clancy Docwra Ltd v E.ON Energy Solutions Ltd*[17] the parties had expressly excluded supervening site conditions from the scope of the works, so that when the site conditions proved to be different, they were treated as a variation entitling the contractor to extra payment. The rationale of this exception was clearly expressed in the case of *Worksop Tarmacadam v Hannaby*.[18] *The* contractor claimed additional cost due to the unforeseen presence of hard rocks in the subsoil. The contract contained no provisions allowing the contractor to claim for such eventuality. Russell LJ held:

> Had the plaintiffs wished to make such a provision in the event of unforeseen conditions being encountered, it would have been the easiest thing in the world for them so to have provided in specific terms. They did not do so.

It is therefore fundamental that the parties clearly allocate the risk in case the site conditions prove different than those indicated in the contract. In particular, the contract shall clearly state whether the contractor has or has not relied upon the information provided (directly or indirectly) to it by the owner on this aspect. Alternatively, the contract may specifically list the information upon which the contractor is entitled to rely, so excluding the contractor's reliance upon any other information not included in the list of "relied upon information" (or "RUI"). However, such clauses must be considered in the light of the law of misrepresentation, which, subject to certain limitations, may constitute a contractor's only remedy for material misrepresentations contained in the site information provided by the employer. Such clauses are not always apt to exclude or restrict liability for pre-contract misrepresentation in cases where the contractor has had little or no opportunity to analyse the accuracy and sufficiency of the information provided by the employer.[19] Moreover, a "no reliance" provision will be ineffective where the representation about the site was fraudulent, i.e., where the employer knew that the site information was incorrect or was reckless as to whether the information was correct. This is on the

14 *Jackson v Eastbourne Local Bd.* [1886], 2 Hudson's B.C., 4th ed., at 81 (1914); *Bottoms v York Corporation* [1892] HBC (4th ed), Vol 2, at p. 208; *Nuttall and Lynton & Barnstaple Ry. Co., Re* [1899], 82 LT 17.

15 *Wong Lai Ying v Chinachem Investment* Co Ltd [1979] 13 BLR 81.

16 *Bacal Construction (Midlands) Ltd v Northampton Development Corporation* [1975] 8 BLR 88 CA; [1976] 1 EGLR 127.

17 *Clancy Docwra Ltd v E.ON Energy Solutions Ltd* [2018] EWHC 3124 (TCC).

18 *Worksop Tarmacadam v Hannaby* [1995] 66 Con LR 105 (CA) at p. 108.

19 *Watford Electronics Ltd v Sanderson CFL Ltd* [2001] BLR 143 at 155 [41] and [43].

basis that the one party may not limit or avoid its liability for its own fraudulent statement by way of a clause in the contract.

It is worth noting that considering the complexity of construction contracts, site information may be "hidden" outside the main contract document, e.g., in one of the myriads of technical attachments to the contract or even in the tender correspondence. In *Clancy Docwra Ltd v E.ON Energy Solutions Ltd*,[20] E.ON Energy Solutions Ltd ("E.ON") was required to install an underground district heat network, involving excavating trenches into which pipework would be installed. E.ON engaged Clancy Docwra Ltd ("Clancy") as subcontractor for the work. In the tender phase Clancy had communicated to E.ON that its offer was made on the basis that there was no allowance for hand digging, the breaking out of obstructions in the trench and the diversion of mains and services. Such exclusions were also included in some annexes (including some post-tender minutes) to the resulting subcontract entered into between the parties. The subcontract also included a precedence clause giving priority to the subcontract in case of inconsistencies between it and any appendix. When Clancy encountered adverse ground conditions, the parties entered into a dispute on the allocation of risk in respect of ground conditions. E.ON contended that the work that Clancy had undertaken to carry out in the subcontract included "*all civil works*". Clancy's position was that the allocation of this risk was modified by the appended documents and that any works relevant to such unexpected site conditions would entitle Clancy to a variation. The court looked at the contract documents as a whole and found that the scope of work was defined by reference to the documents appended to the subcontract, including the tender clarifications and post-tender minutes. If they were included in the document that meant that they had a role to play in the contractual relation between the parties.

10.4.2 Site conditions clause

Considering the preceding, employers will typically seek to include a specific clause covering the issue of site conditions and clearly allocating the parties' responsibilities on the subject. More specifically, such clauses may state: (i) that the contractor shall be deemed to have inspected the site and obtained all necessary information as to risks which may affect the works; (ii) that the employer has made available to the contractor data on site conditions, but that contractor shall be responsible to scrutinise and interpret such data, and shall notify any errors or inaccuracies to the employer; (iii) that the employer shall not be responsible (i.e., that it makes no promise, representation or warranty) for the accuracy of the site information provided or, in the alternative, that the employer will take responsibility only on an express set of information usually referred to as "relied upon information" ("RUI"); (iv) that in case the contractor suffers delay and/or incurs cost as a result of any errors or inaccuracies in the information provided by the employer, the contractor will not be entitled to any claim. In case the parties have agreed on a set of RUI, that the contractor will be entitled to a claim only provided that the errors or inaccuracies concern the RUI. This may further be qualified by stating that the contractor's entitlement will be subject to the relevant errors or inaccuracies that would not have been discoverable by an experienced contractor with the level of skill and care that would reasonably be expected from a skilled contractor experienced in carrying out works of a similar nature, scope and complexity to those contemplated in the contract.

20 *Clancy Docwra Ltd v E.ON Energy Solutions Ltd* [2018] EWHC 3124 (TCC).

CHAPTER 11

Design

11.1 Design in general

There is no single definition of what constitutes the "design" of a project. In simple words, it can be said that the design relates to the technical characteristics that the project shall have to meet the objectives for which it is built, and the construction methods and materials necessary to achieve that target.

In the absence of any terms and conditions to the contrary, the English law provides that a professional designer has duty to act with reasonable skill and care.[1] However, the parties may agree on a higher standard of care, such as a "fit for purpose" standard, in which case the professional will be required to meet that standard to prove lack of negligence.

Usually, the initial design is prepared by specialised consultants contracted by employers, while contractors are contracted at a later stage to complete the initial design and carry out the construction works. However, the parties may enter into design and build contracts whereby the main contractor is appointed to both design and construct the works. In this case, the design will be carried out by the contractor based on the requirements given by the employer in the tender phase, although the contractor will normally be allowed to make comments and proposals, including observations on the employer's requirements and the forecasted price for the works. The advantage for the employer is that the contractor will be the single point of responsibility for delivering the project.

11.2 Responsibility for the design

What party will be responsible for the consequences on an inaccurate design will depend on a number of factors, including who has prepared the design and how the contract regulates the subject.

Typical scenarios that may occur are as follows:

11.2.1 The design was prepared by the contractor

In case the contractor has prepared the design, the contractor will usually be solely responsible for the consequences of any relevant inadequacy or errors. In such cases, the construction contract may include typical wording stating that: (i) the contractor shall

1 Section 13 of the Supply of Goods and Services Act 1982.

DOI: 10.4324/9781003387718-15

prepare and be responsible for the design of the works; (ii) the design shall be prepared by a qualified professional (the employer may also include specific qualifications and criteria that such professionals should have, e.g., engineers) with the necessary experience and capability; (iii) the design shall be in accordance with all applicable laws and permits, the contract, and any other requirements based on the specific project; (iv) the contractor shall indemnify the employer for any costs and claims incurred by the employer arising out of flaws in the design.

11.2.2 The design was prepared by a third-party consultant engaged by the employer

The position under English law is that, in case the employer provides the contractor with specifications which turn out to be erroneous, the contractor may still face a liability as the courts will not typically imply that the employer has warranted the correctness of the design. This is clearly stated in the following paragraph of *Keating on Construction Contracts*:[2]

> a contractor who has been put to unexpected expense because of inaccurate quantities or drawings or impracticable plans cannot usually recover the expense by bringing an action for breach of an implied warranty that the plans, drawings or bills of quantities are accurate or practicable. Such warranties are not implied merely from the fact that these documents are submitted to the contractor for tender.

In *Thorn v London Corporation*,[3] the specifications for the construction of a bridge contained an error which made the works unbuildable in the way they had been conceived. The contractor obtained the engineer's instruction to a change in the construction method which meant that the bridge would be built in an entirely different way. The court held that that the employer had not impliedly warranted that a project could be built as per the drawings and specifications produced by the engineer and that the contractor:

> ought to have informed himself of all particulars connected with the work and especially as to the practicability of executing every part of the work contained in the specification.

However, the consequences of a faulty design could be different based on whether or not the contractor has expressly assumed responsibility for a third-party design. In particular:

(i) If the parties agree that the contractor takes responsibility for a design prepared by a third party, the courts will typically uphold such provision based on the principle that the parties to a contract are free to bargain and create the terms of their agreement as they desire. This is even more so in the case of complex construction projects where the parties are typically highly specialised companies. However, where the design is subsequently changed upon instruction of the employer, unless the contractor is expressly requested to endorse the change, the employer will typically bear responsibility for the consequences of the change.[4]

2 S. Furst, V. Ramsey, *Keating on Construction Contracts* (10th edition) Sweet & Maxwell, 2017, at para 4–046.
3 *Thorn v London Corporation* [1876] 1 AC 120.
4 *Viking Grain Storage Ltd v TH White Installations Ltd* [1985] 33 BLR 103.

Moreover, where the design is prepared by a subcontractor which was a nominated subcontractor, the contractor will not be considered to have assumed responsibility in case of flawed design where it has expressly refused to accept responsibility for that design. In such cases, where the nominated subcontractor has given the employer a collateral warranty, the employer will be able to sue the nominated subcontractor directly.[5]

(ii) In case the contract is silent on the point of who will be liable for a design prepared by a third-party consultant, the courts will apply the rules of contractual interpretation to allocate the design responsibility. Typically, a court will infer that the contractor has not accepted to assume this risk. This was clearly stated in the case of *John Mowlem & Co Ltd v British Insulated Callenders Pension Trust Ltd*[6] where Judge Stabb QC held:

> I should require the clearest possible contractual condition before I should feel driven to find a contractor liable for a fault in the design, design being a matter which a structural engineer is alone qualified to carry out and for which he is paid to undertake, an over which the contractor has no control.

In interpreting the contract, the court will put a special weight on whether the contractor has undertaken an obligation of result or an obligation of means. If the contractor has promised to achieve a certain result (e.g., that the project will achieve a certain output in a turnkey contract), a court may be more inclined to find the contractor responsible in case the result is not achieved, regardless of whether this was due to an inadequate design provided by third parties. Conversely, where the contractor has relied upon the third-party design without assuming an absolute obligation to achieve a certain result, provided that the contractor has carried out the work in a proper and workmanlike manner,[7] a court may find that the contractor has discharged its obligation even in case the final project does not meet the targets due to inadequacy of the design produced by the third-party consultant. However, also in case the contractor has not expressly assumed liability for a design prepared by a third-party consultant, a court may find the contractor liable for something that relates to such design due to the typical interrelation between design and construction, and the blurred borderline between the two activities. As stated in *Bellefield Computer Services Ltd v E Turner & Sons*:[8]

> The extent of an architect's responsibility for the detailed working out of construction details for which he has provided an underlying design again depends on the express and implied terms of his engagement and its interrelation with the responsibility of others. The scope of any such responsibility depends on the facts of each case. There is a blurred borderline between architectural design and the construction details needed to put it into effect. Borderlines of responsibility cannot be defined in the abstract. A carpenter's choice of a particular nail or screw is in a sense a design choice, yet very often the choice is left to the carpenter and the responsibility

5 *Sinclair v Woods of Winchester Ltd (No 2)* [2006] EWHC 3003 (TCC) at [30] – [33].
6 *John Mowlem & Co Ltd v British Insulated Callenders Pension Trust Ltd* [1977] 3 Con LR 64.
7 *Cable (1956) Ltd v Hutcherson Bros Pty Ltd* [1969] 123 CLR 143.
8 *Bellefield Computer Services Ltd v E Turner & Sons* [2002] EWCA Civ 1823 at [76].

for making it merges with the carpenter's workmanship obligations. In many circumstance [sic], the scope of an architect's responsibility extends to providing drawings or specifications which give full construction details. But responsibility for some such details may rest with other consultants, eg, structural engineers, or with specialist contractors or subcontractors, depending on the terms of their respective contracts and their interrelationship. As with the carpenter choosing an appropriate nail, specialist details may be left to specialist subcontractors who sometimes make detailed 'design' decisions without expecting or needing drawings or specifications telling them what to do. In appropriate circumstances, this would not amount to delegation by the architect of part of his own responsibility. Rather that element of composite design responsibility did not rest with him in the first place.

11.3 Design clause

From a drafting point of view, where the design was prepared by a third party, the construction contract between the contractor and the employer will usually include a duty on the contractor to warn for any inaccuracies in the design provided by the employer. Such clauses will typically state that: (i) if the contractor (but usually the same obligation is assumed by the employer) discovers any error, defect, etc. in the design, it shall immediately inform the employer; (ii) the employer will then have the option to either issue an instruction to the contractor on how to deal with the matter or request the contractor to make a proposal on how to resolve the problem (in which case, the employer will either approve such solution or ask for further proposal until one is approved by the employer). When a solution is found, the employer will instruct the contractor to proceed with such solution, although this will not relieve the contractor from any relevant liabilities. The parties will also agree whether this will lead to any right to extra money and/or extra time.

It is worth noting that, also in cases where such clause is not present in the contract, the courts may imply an obligation on the contractor to promptly inform the employer of any design flaws it has discovered and find it liable in case it fails to do so. In the case of *Plant Construction Ltd v Clive Adams Associates and JMH Construction Services Ltd*,[9] the employer (Ford) successfully sued *Plant Construction Ltd* ("Plant") following a roof collapse which occurred while one of Plant's subcontractors, *JMH Construction Services Ltd* ("JMH"), was carrying out some temporary works. The collapse was due to the position of the roof propping, which had been directed by Clive Adams Associates ("Clive Adams"), Ford's engineers. Plant then sued JMH and Clive Adams. JMH contended that they were not responsible for the design of the temporary works as they were obliged to follow Clive Adams' instructions in this regard. While the court of first instance agreed with JMH's contention, the Court of Appeal held that, although JMH was not responsible for the design works, they had an obligation to perform the contract with the skill and care of an ordinarily competent contractor and this included an obligation to warn of the danger they had seen.

The later decision in *Aurum Investments Ltd v Avonforce Ltd*[10] has clarified that it must be reasonable to impose a duty to warn in the circumstances.

9 *Plant Construction Ltd v Clive Adams Associates and JMH Construction Services Ltd* [2000] BLR 137.
10 *Aurum Investments Ltd v Avonforce Ltd (in liquidation) and Ors.* [2001] Lloyd's Rep PN 285.

CHAPTER 12

Labour, health and safety

12.1 Labour

Construction contracts for large projects will usually include a clause regulating labour aimed at ensuring that the contractor (and its subcontractors) employ personnel with the right skill and experience required for the type and complexity of the works they are required to perform under the contract and that they are not in breach with, and expressly agree to abide by any applicable labour laws.

For example, labour clauses may include the following contractor's obligations: (i) use only personnel who are appropriately qualified and skilled for the function they are assigned to. The contract may also include a list of key personnel who are assigned to specific tasks and/or roles and who the contractor may not replace without the employer's consent (although in this case contractors shall seek to retain the right to replace key personnel in cases where replacement is necessary, such as resignation, dismissal, long-term illness, etc.); (ii) pay wages and observe conditions of labour compliant with the industry standards; (iii) comply with all the applicable labour laws and require also their employees to do it; (iv) prevent any unlawful conduct by their personnel. The parties may also agree that the employer shall have a right to require the contractor to remove from the project any of the contractor's personnel for specific reasons (e.g., in case of misconduct, lack of care, incompetence, etc.) and request the appointment of a suitable replacement.

12.2 Health and safety

12.2.1 Health and safety in general

Health and safety ("H&S") could be defined as the set of statutes, regulations and other procedures intended to prevent accidents or injuries in workplaces or public environments. This is an important part of a project and contractors are particularly sensible on this matter. This is due to both ethical and commercial reasons as a contractor's H&S track record is typically considered an important factor that employer consider when awarding construction contracts.

12.2.2 Health and safety duties

In the UK, H&S duties arise from both common law and statutes.

DOI: 10.4324/9781003387718-16

12.2.2.1 Health and safety duties at common law

At common law, contractors' H&S obligations are aimed at eliminating safety risks or, in case this is not possible, at providing adequate safeguards against the risk that cannot be eliminated. These obligations include, for example: (i) establishing proper precautions and maximising awareness of the need for safety to ensure the construction work is carried out without harm;[1] (ii) ensuring that the place of work is safe for all workers[2] and visitors (e.g., someone employed to collect blocks and bring them to the site[3]); (iii) taking reasonable steps to provide safe plant and equipment;[4] (iv) providing workers with adequate means of carrying out their work.[5]

12.2.2.2 Statutory health and safety duties

The Health and Safety at Work etc Act 1974 is probably the most important UK statute regarding H&S in a workplace. Other various regulations relate to specific pieces of H&S obligations in the UK.[6] In particular, the Construction (Design and Management) Regulations 2015 (the "CDM Regulations") transpose into UK law the European Council Directive 92/57/EEC on the implementation of minimum safety and health requirements at temporary or mobile work sites. The CDM Regulations propose a methodologic approach to the management and implementation of H&S in every phase of a construction project. This approach identifies the H&S risks what may materialise in a construction project and aims at eliminating them (or at least reducing them, in case they cannot be eliminated) to protect the workers' H&S. The CDM Regulations set out the following not all-encompassing list of key elements to securing construction H&S: (i) managing the risks by applying the general principles of prevention; (ii) appointing the right people and organisations at the right time; (iii) ensuring that everyone has the information, instruction, training and supervision they need to carry out their jobs in a way that secures health and safety; (iv) ensuring that dutyholders cooperate and communicate with each other and coordinate their work; and (v) consulting workers and engaging with them to promote and develop effective measures to secure health, safety and welfare. As mentioned, the CDM are based on principles of prevention. Such principles can be summarised in the following three duties: (i) avoiding risks where possible; (ii) evaluating risks that cannot be avoided; and (iii) putting in place proportionate measures that control them at source. Such duties and obligations are imposed on employers, principal designers, designers, main contractors and other contractors. In particular:

(i) Employers must: (a) make suitable arrangements for managing a project, including the allocation of sufficient time and other resources. Arrangements are

1 *Anglian Water Services Ltd v Crawshaw Robbins & Co Ltd* [2001] BLR 173 at 184 [34].
2 *Horton v Taplin Contracts Limited: CA 8 Nov 2002* at 76 [13] – [16].
3 *Moon v Garrett & Ors* [2006] EWCA Civ 1121.
4 *Andar Transport Pty Ltd v Brambles Ltd* [2004] 217 CLR 424 at [34].
5 *O'Connell v Commissioner for Government Transport* [1954] 100 CLR 225 at 229.
6 For example, the Construction (Design and Management) Regulations 2015, the Control of Noise at Work Regulations 2005, the Public Health Acts 1875 to 1961, the Public Health (Scotland) Acts 1867 to 2008, the Control of Substances Hazardous to Health Regulations 2002, the Electricity at Work Regulations 1989, and the Environmental Protection Act 1990, the Work at Height Regulations 2005 and the Control of Asbestos Regulations 2012.

considered suitable if they ensure that the construction work can be carried out, so far as is reasonably practicable, without risks to the health or safety of any person affected by the project and the project facilities are provided in respect of any person carrying out construction work; (b) ensure that these arrangements are maintained and reviewed throughout the project; (c) provide pre-construction information as soon as is practicable to every designer and contractor appointed, or being considered for appointment, to the project; (d) ensure that before the construction phase begins, a construction phase plan is drawn up by the contractor if there is only one contractor, or by the principal contractor, and the principal designer prepares a health and safety file for the project, which complies with the CDM Regulations, is revised from time to time and is kept available for inspection; (e) take reasonable steps to ensure that the principal designer complies with any other principal designer duties in the CDM Regulations.

(ii) Principal designers with control over the pre-construction phase of the project must: (a) plan, manage and monitor the pre-construction phase and coordinate matters relating to health and safety during the pre-construction phase to ensure that, so far as is reasonably practicable, the project is carried out without risks to health or safety; (b) take into account the general principles of prevention and, where relevant, the content of any construction phase plan and health and safety file; and (c) identify and eliminate or control, so far as is reasonably practicable, foreseeable risks to the health or safety of any person carrying out or liable to be affected by construction work, maintaining or cleaning a structure, or using a structure designed as a workplace; (d) ensure all designers comply with their duties in regulation; (e) ensure that all persons working in relation to the pre-construction phase cooperate with the client, the principal designer and each other; (f) assist the client in the provision of the pre-construction information and provide pre-construction information, promptly and in a convenient form, to every designer and contractor appointed, or being considered for appointment, to the project; (g) liaise with the principal contractor for the duration of the principal designer's appointment and share with the principal contractor information relevant to the planning, management and monitoring of the construction phase and the coordination of health and safety matters during the construction phase.

(iii) Designers (these duties may be added to the ones of the main contractor in case they perform both activities under the contract) must: (a) not commence work in relation to a project unless satisfied that the client is aware of the duties owed by the client under the CDM Regulations; (b) when preparing or modifying a design the designer must take into account the general principles of prevention and any pre-construction information to eliminate, so far as is reasonably practicable, foreseeable risks to the health or safety of any person carrying out or liable to be affected by construction work, (c) maintaining or cleaning a structure or using a structure designed as a workplace; (d) if it is not possible to eliminate these risks, the designer must, so far as is reasonably practicable, take steps to reduce or, if that is not possible, control the risks through the subsequent design process, provide information about those risks to the principal designer, and ensure appropriate information is included in the health and safety file; (e) take all reasonable steps to provide, with the design, sufficient information about the design, construction or maintenance of the structure, to adequately assist the client, other designers and contractors to comply with their duties under the CDM Regulations.

(iv) Main (principal) contractors must (a) plan, manage and monitor the construction phase and coordinate matters relating to health and safety during the construction phase to ensure that, so far as is reasonably practicable, construction work is carried out without risks to health or safety; (b) take into account the general principles of prevention; (c) organise cooperation between contractors; (d) coordinate implementation by the contractors of applicable legal requirements for health and safety; (e) ensure that employers and, if necessary for the protection of workers, self-employed persons apply the general principles of prevention in a consistent manner, and in particular when complying with the CDM Regulations, follow the construction phase plan; (f) ensure that a suitable site induction is provided; (g) ensure that the necessary steps are taken to prevent access by unauthorised persons to the construction site; (h) ensure that facilities that comply with the requirements of the CDM Regulations are provided throughout the construction phase; (i) liaise with the principal designer for the duration of the principal designer's appointment and share with the principal designer information relevant to the planning, management and monitoring of the pre-construction phase and the coordination of health and safety matters during the pre-construction phase.

(v) All contractors must: (a) not carry out construction work in relation to a project unless satisfied that the client is aware of the duties owed by the client under CDM Regulations; (b) plan, manage and monitor construction work carried out either by the contractor or by workers under the contractor's control, to ensure that, so far as is reasonably practicable, it is carried out without risks to health and safety; (c) where there is more than one contractor working on a project, comply with any directions given by the principal designer or the principal contractor and with the parts of the construction phase plan that are relevant to that contractor's work on the project; (d) if there is only one contractor working on the project, the contractor must take account of the general principles of prevention when design, technical and organisational aspects are being decided in order to plan the various items or stages of work which are to take place simultaneously or in succession, and estimating the period of time required to complete the work or work stages; (e) if there is only one contractor working on the project, the contractor must draw up a construction phase plan, or make arrangements for a construction phase plan to be drawn up, as soon as is practicable prior to setting up a construction site; (f) the construction phase plan must fulfil the relevant requirements set out in the CDM Regulations; (g) not employ or appoint a person to work on a construction site unless that person has, or is in the process of obtaining, the necessary skills, knowledge, training and experience to carry out the tasks allocated to that person in a manner that secures the health and safety of any person working on the construction site; (h) provide each worker under their control with appropriate supervision, instructions and information so that construction work can be carried out, so far as is reasonably practicable, without risks to health and safety; (i) the information provided must include a suitable site induction (where not already provided by the principal contractor), the procedures to be followed in the event of serious and imminent danger to health and safety, information on risks to health and safety (as identified by the risk assessment under the CDM Regulations or arising out of the conduct of another contractor's undertaking and of which the contractor in control of the worker ought reasonably to be aware) and any other information necessary to enable the worker to comply with the relevant statutory provisions; (j) not begin work on a construction site unless reasonable steps have been taken to prevent access by unauthorised persons to that site; (k) ensure, so far as is reasonably practicable, that the relevant requirements under the CDM Regulations are complied with so far as they affect the contractor or any worker under that contractor's control.

12.2.3 Health and safety clause

H&S clauses are aimed at ensuring that the parties comply with the H&S statutes, regulations and best practices in order to avoid incidents and fatalities at the site. The typical content of an H&S clause for large projects would state that the contractor shall: (i) take all reasonable precautions to maintain the health and safety of all persons in connection with the works (including, e.g., availability of medical staff, first aid facilities, ambulance service, etc.); (ii) appoint a health and safety manager (the clause will usually also set out the relevant experience or membership to specific categories of professions); (iii) report H&S incidents; (iv) represent and warrant that it is competent to perform its duties and functions under the CDM Regulations.

CHAPTER 13

Performance

13.1 Quality

13.1.1 Quality in general

Quality control systems are processes aimed at ensuring that products, materials and services (including work and work units) comply with the relevant requirements. Such processes are typically carried out by measuring the final quality characteristics of the product or service (or any unit of it) by comparing them with the specific quality standards[1] so to find out any differences between the results obtained and the desired results and find solutions to correct any errors. Quality control systems also usually provide for tests and inspections being carried out during the construction process in order to identify and possibly correct errors before a final result is obtained.

Construction contracts also often refer to quality assurance systems, which are processes aimed at ensuring that the quality procedures implemented during the design phase of a construction project effectively meet the employer-established quality standards for service, performance and production of a project (or a unit thereof). This is obtained by creating a set of rules about minimum quality of, for example, materials (e.g., size, shape and composition), equipment (e.g., safety), how quality is measured (e.g., high standards), project management (e.g., bidding procedures), people skills and experience (e.g., certifications, track record), and procedures aimed at ensuring that such rules are complied with in order to meet the required standards.

13.1.2 Quality clauses

A typical quality assurance and quality control clause in a construction contract would set forth the contractor's obligation to institute and maintain quality assurance and quality control systems in line with the requirements of the contract with specific reference to the standards to be met for the specific project and relevant units.

13.2 Commencement

Commencement generally refers to the moment in which a contractor starts the construction works, and will typically be proceeded by pre-construction activities such as design,

1 The most widely used international standards are the so-called ISO 9000, developed and published by the International Organization for Standardization, a worldwide federation of national standards bodies.

DOI: 10.4324/9781003387718-17

procurement and mobilisation, obtaining planning permissions and building regulations approvals, notifying the various competent authorities, etc.

The commencement date may be a fixed date, or the date on which the employer gives the contractor the green light by issuing a so-called notice to proceed (or, usually, as soon as reasonably practicable after that), or a date calculated starting from the occurrence of a certain event (e.g., upon the contractor being given possession of the site or a number of months from the date on which any necessary permissions have been obtained).

The commencement date has important legal implications as from that date the contractor will typically take on a number of obligations such as those relevant to the health and safety of the site.

Where the contract includes a commencement date, and the contractor does not commence the works within that date, this may be construed as a repudiation of the contract entitling the employer to terminate the contract (subject to any conditions under the contract such as the employer's obligation to first send a notice to the contractor urging it to commence the works within reasonable time or within a reasonable certain date). However, where the contractor has a lawful excuse to delay commencement, a court may find that the contractor has not repudiated the contract and hold any resulting termination unlawful. In *Bedfordshire County Council v Fitzpatrick Contractors Ltd*[2] the contractors, Fitzpatrick Contractors Ltd ("FC"), were engaged by the Bedfordshire County Council ("BCC") to carry out maintenance works to highways in Bedfordshire. The agreed commencement date was 1 June 1996. FC sought to defer the start date after becoming worried about the true amount of work under the contract. The parties did not achieve any agreement on the point. FC did not commence the works on 1 June 1996. BCC sent FC a notice stating that unless works commenced by 15 June 1996, BCC would terminate the contract with FC. As FC did not commence the works by 15 June 1996, BCC terminated the contract. In the resulting court proceedings, the court held that it was unreasonable to require FC to commence work on 15 June 1996 as: (i) FC's concerns about the level of work were genuine; (ii) the amount of work to be carried out prior to 15 June 1996 was minimal; and (iii) the BCC was aware that FC was willing to fulfil its contractual obligations, subject to a delayed start.

Where a construction contract does not include a commencement date, the contractor is under no obligation to commence work within a specific date unless such a commencement date may be inferred from the circumstances of the contract. However, the contractor will still be required to complete the work within the completion date stipulated in the contract (or within reasonable time of the employer providing access to the site in case the contract does not include a completion date).[3]

13.3 Programme

A programme is a tool enabling contractors to forward-plan so to ensure a project is delivered on time, within budget and in line with the agreed quality standards. The Society of Construction Law Delay and Disruption Protocol[4] states that:

2 *Bedfordshire County Council v Fitzpatrick Contractors Ltd* [1998] 62 Con LR 64 at 73.

3 *Porter v Tottenham Urban District Council [1914] 1 KB 663 at 669.*

4 *Society of Construction Law Delay and Disruption Protocol* (2nd edition) February 2017, www.scl.org.uk.

to assist in managing progress of the works and to reduce the number of disputes relating to delay and disruption, the Contractor should prepare and the Contract Administrator (CA) should accept a properly prepared programme showing the manner and sequence in which the Contractor plans to carry out the works. The programme should be updated to record actual progress, variations, changes of logic, methods and sequences, mitigation or acceleration measures and any EOTs granted[5].

As such, a programme may include, among other things: (i) the project's scope of work; (ii) the different development phases; (iii) the anticipated timing of each phase; (iv) the order in which the contractor intends to carry out the works (i.e., the activities that can be carried out simultaneously and those that need to be sequenced); (v) reviews and updates made to account for unforeseen changes to schedule, additional requirements, delays, etc., whenever the previous programme is inconsistent with actual progress; (vi) the periods for each review; (vii) any supporting documents (e.g., description of the construction methods, estimate of the number of contractor's personnel dedicated to the various tasks, indication of equipment required on the site for each phase, etc.). In addition, a programme may also include budgets for each activity and expected cash flow for each phase.

The contract may provide that the contractor shall produce the programme. In such case the document produced by the contractor will be considered a statement of the contractor's intention (or best endeavours) that the works will be performed in accordance with that programme.[6] If the contractor fails to produce the programme, this may constitute a breach of contract.

A construction contract may oblige the contractor to "strictly" follow the programme. In such case, the contractor will be in breach of contract in case of failure to adhere to that programme.[7] In this case, when the breach may result in a delay in the completion of the works, the contractor will be typically allowed to take steps to ameliorate the consequences of that breach by taking later accelerative measures.[8] Where, instead, the contract is silent on the binding nature of the programme, the contractor will not be bound to work to that programme.[9] Moreover, in case the programme prepared by the contractor indicates a completion date which is earlier than the one agreed in the contract, the contractor will not be in breach of contract in case completion does not occur within the earlier date indicated in the programme,[10] unless the contract states otherwise.

Employers are not usually obliged to comply with the programme. However, the parties may agree that an employer's failure to comply with the programme will entitle the contractor to submit a revised programme where the employer's failure has had the effect to delay completion. The contract may also state that, in such case, the contractor will also usually be entitled to an extension of time.

Employers are also usually entitled under the contract to ask the contractor to prepare a revised programme in case they consider that the existing one fails to comply with the contract or is inconsistent with actual progress of the works.

5 US contracts, generally use the word "schedule".

6 *Kitsons Sheet Metal Ltd v Matthew Hall Mechanical & Electrical Engineers Ltd* [1989] 47 BLR 90 at 110–111.

7 *Moody v Ellis* [1983] 26 BLR 39 at 48–49.

8 *Sabic UK Petrochemicals Ltd v Punj Lloyd Ltd* [2013] EWHC 2916 (TCC) at [32].

9 *Pigott Foundations Ltd v Shepherd Construction Ltd* [1993] 67 BLR 48.

10 *JF Finnegan Ltd v Sheffield City Council* [1988] 43 BLR 124 at 132–134.

13.4 Progress and obligation to proceed "*regularly and diligently*"

Unless the contract provides otherwise, contractors can programme the works as they deem suitable to achieve completion of the works by the completion date agreed in the contract. However, construction contracts usually include clauses on how contractors should proceed with the works. A typical wording would be that the contractor shall progress the works "*regularly and diligently*". If the contract lacks such (or similar) wording, the relevant obligation will usually not be implied, although the courts may imply an obligation to work efficiently.[11] Where such obligation is expressly included in the contract,[12] it is widely understood to require the contractor to proceed:

> continuously, industriously and efficiently with appropriate physical resources so as to progress the works towards completion substantially in accordance with the contractual requirements as to time, sequence and quality of work.[13]

It is worth noting that, in order to comply with such obligation both elements must be present so that a contractor may be in breach in case it has progressed regularly but not diligently and vice-versa.[14] Both obligations relate to the level of resources allocated by the contractor to achieve the contractual objective.[15] However, where the contractor progresses the works, but not in a "*regular and diligent*" manner, this alone will not suffice to constitute a repudiatory breach of contract by the contractor entitling *per se* the employer to terminate the contract.[16]

In the two cases of *Sabic UK Petrochemicals Ltd v Punj Lloyd Ltd*[17] and *Vivergo Fuels Ltd v Redhall Engineering Solutions Ltd*[18] the Technology and Construction Court has given guidance on how to interpret the obligation to progress "*regularly and diligently*". The main principles which may be inferred from the two cases are the following: (i) delay as well as a contractor's failure to produce a proper programme may suggest and evidence a lack of due diligence, but are not conclusive proof of it; (ii) a failure to achieve the programmed productivity due to inadequate resourcing will typically evidence a breach of the obligation to proceed regularly and diligently; (iii) where an employer requests the contractor to re-deploy resources to higher priority areas in order to try mitigating a delay caused by the contractor, such a request may jeopardise a subsequent employer's claim that the contractor has failed adequately to resource the works even in case the delay was primarily caused by the contractor's general failure to proceed with priority areas; (iv) poor labour management and inadequate supervision are not conclusive of a contractor's failure to proceed regularly and diligently; (v) the obligation of due diligence should be assessed with regard to what was feasible at a relevant time. Therefore, where completion within the date has become impossible, the

11 *Miller v Cannon Hill Estates Ltd* [1931] 2 KB 113 at 122.

12 *Greater London Council v Cleveland Bridge & Engineering Co Ltd* [1986] 34 BLR 50 at 77.

13 *West Faulkner Associates v London Borough of Newham* [1994] 71 BLR 1

14 *West Faulkner Associates v London Borough of Newham* [1994] 71 BLR 1

15 For an example of the obligation to progress regularly, see *M Hill & Sons Ltd v London Borough of Camden* [1980] 18 BLR 31. For an example on the obligation to proceed diligently see *West Faulkner Associates v London Borough of Newham* [1994] 71 BLR 1

16 *Vivergo Fuels Ltd v Redhall Engineering Solutions Ltd* [2013] EWHC 4030 (TCC) at [504] – [513]

17 *Sabic UK Petrochemicals Ltd v Punj Lloyd Ltd* [2013] EWHC 2916 (TCC) at [32]

18 *Vivergo Fuels Ltd v Redhall Engineering Solutions Ltd* [2013] EWHC 4030 (TCC)

separate obligation to proceed diligently survives and applies to the contractor's obligation of mitigating the ongoing breach.

An aspect to be considered on this subject is whether a contractor that has breached its obligation to proceed with diligence has an obligation to adopt accelerative measures at its own cost if the delay threatens the achievement of the completion date. This is primarily a matter of contract. However, if the contract does not expressly provide for an obligation on the contractor to accelerate the works when it is in culpable delay, such obligation will not typically be implied[19] (although contractors still have a right to do it in order to avoid the consequences of a culpable delay).

13.5 Completion

13.5.1 Completion in general

Considering how delays may affect the parties' positions and interests, the parties to construction contracts usually expressly state a time for completion of the works, which may be in the form of a firm date or a number of months or years from the contract execution (or other events).[20] In case the parties do not include a firm completion date, it is essential that they include a clearly identifiable commencement date from which time starts running so that a completion date can be precisely established.

Before entering into the details of how to identify and calculate time for completion, it is necessary to understand what completion is under English law construction contracts. Completion is linked to a number of legal consequences affecting the contract and the parties, including the following: (i) the employer will re-enter in possession of the site, and the relevant risk will pass on the employer, along with the risks for care of the works and the project; (ii) the defects liability period will start running; (iii) if completion has occurred on time and no claims are outstanding between the parties (other than small punch list claims), the employer will lose its entitlement to liquidated damages and will have to return any performance bonds covering performance and delays and release any retention money still in the employer's possession (while any warranty bond will continue to be effective throughout the warranty period); (iv) the contractor's obligations to keep insurances in place will come to an end.

13.5.2 Completion in entire contracts

Construction contracts for complex projects typically state that the contractor shall complete the works in accordance with the contract.[21] When an obligation to carry out and complete the works is not expressly stated, if a priced contract describes the works with sufficient precision, such obligation will be implied.

A contractor is deemed to have "strictly" completed the works when he has fulfilled all his obligations under the underlying contract. In the case of entire contracts, where the entire fulfilment of the contractor's promise to construct the whole project is a condition

19 *Sabic UK Petrochemicals Ltd v Punj Lloyd Ltd* [2013] EWHC 2916 (TCC).
20 E.g., from the employer's notice to proceed.
21 *Nene Housing Society Ltd. v National Westminster Bank Ltd.* [1980] 16 BLR 22.

precedent for the fulfilment of the employer's promise to pay the whole lump sum price, this might still be the case.[22] In *Sumpter v Hedges*,[23] A.L. Smith LJ expressed the concept with the following words:

> The law is that where there is a contract to do work for a lump sum, until the work is completed the price of it cannot be recovered.

Thus, except for the cases of frustration or breach of contract by the employer, and unless the contract provides otherwise, the contractor will not typically have a right to demand payment: (i) if the works are left unfinished; (ii) if the contractor has voluntarily abandoned the works (even if the abandonment occurs when progress is close to completion); or (iii) where defects on the works are discovered after completion. It follows that the contractor will be unable to recover any money due for work done if he has failed to complete the work satisfactorily (unless the contract expressly gives the contractor such right) or if the works are found to be incomplete or defective. Thus, in such cases the employer may get the benefit of the uncompleted works without having an obligation to pay for them (subject to any payment due in quantum meruit).

However, in the case of construction contracts for complex projects, the contractor usually has a right to payment by instalments upon achievement of certain milestones and/or upon reaching a certain progress.[24] In this case, the rules of the entire contract will not apply to the milestones already achieved, but will still apply, for example, to any intermediate instalment or to the last instalment, if the works are abandoned before the relevant completion.

It shall be noted that if the employer accepts the work, it will be held liable to pay for the works performed by the contractor. However, acceptance cannot be implied from the mere fact that the employer has entered into possession and has commenced to use the work which he holds being incomplete or unsatisfactory.[25]

13.5.3 The doctrine of substantial performance and practical completion

The strict application of the entire agreements' rules to construction contracts could lead employers' entitlement to refuse payment on the grounds of minor defects or minimal parts of the project remaining unfinished. This would not be acceptable in the case of large and complex construction projects where the works generally involve a myriad of small activities whose complete fulfilment, or lack thereof, may even be difficult to assess. Moreover, large construction projects stretch through long periods of time. This often leads to changes in the circumstances that existed at the time of the contract, and the necessity to find alternative solutions where certain minor obligations may not be fulfilled

---

22 An example is furnished by the case of *Cutter v Powell* in which the defendant agreed with a sailor that "Ten days after the ship *Governor Pary* . . . arrives at Liverpool I promise to pay to Mr. T. Cutter the sum of thirty guineas, provided he proceeds, continues and does his duty as second mate in the said ship from here to the port of Liverpool". The sailor performed his duty until his death, which occurred before the voyage was completed. The sailor's widow then sought to recover a proportionate of the agreed remuneration, but was unsuccessful.

23 *Sumpter v Hedges* [1898] 1 QB 673, at p. 674.

24 I.N. Duncan Wallace QC, *Hudson's Building and Engineering Contracts* (11th edition) Sweet & Maxwell, 1994, at p. 475. See also *Eshelby v Federated European Bank [1932] 1 KB*.

25 *Appleby v Myers* [1867] LR 2 CP 651.

as a result of such changes. For example, a particular material may no longer be available or unexpected physical conditions make a small part of the project difficult or impossible to construct in line with the initial specifications. As a result, on the assumption that achieving a completion that is absolutely correct is virtually impossible, and provided that the impact of minor discrepancies is not such as to affect the operation of the project, such discrepancies will not necessarily have a bearing on whether the project will be considered as completed.

The complexity of construction projects was well captured in *HHJ Newey OR in Emson Eastern v EME Developments*,[26] where the court said:

> I think the most important background fact which I should keep in mind is that building construction is not like the manufacture of goods in a factory. The size of the project, site conditions, the use of many materials and the employment of various kinds of operatives make it virtually impossible to achieve the same degree of perfection that a manufacturer can. It must be a rare new building in which every screw and every brush of paint is absolutely correct.

The consciousness of such degree of complexity and the paradoxes which this could lead to in case courts were to adopt a strict approach, has led the courts to evolve the doctrine of practical completion or substantial completion/performance.

One of the first cases to elaborate the doctrine was *Broom v Davis*[27] where the parties agreed that the plaintiff would build a booth on Bath race ground for 20 guineas, five of which to be paid in advance, and then take back the materials after the races. The plaintiff fulfilled his obligation, but the booth fell during the races. The court found that the plaintiff might recover the balance due to him for the work performed, but that the respondent was entitled to bring a cross action against the plaintiff for building the booth improperly.

Other cases have followed since *Broom v Davis*. One of these is *Hoenig v Isaacs*,[28] where, commenting on whether the presence of some defects could prevent payment in case of an entire agreement, Denning LJ stated:

> In determining this issue the first question is whether, on the true construction of the contract, entire performance was a condition precedent to payment. It was a lump sum contract, but that does not mean that the entire performance was a condition precedent to payment. When a contract provides for a specific sum to be paid on completion of specified work, the courts leap against a construction of the contract which would deprive the contractor of any payment at all simply because there are some defects or omissions. The promise to complete the work is, therefore, construed as a term of contract, but not as a condition. It is not every breach of that term which absolves the employer from his promise to pay the price, but only a breach which goes to the root of the contract, such as abandonment of the work when it is only half done. Unless the breach does go to the root of the matter, the employer cannot resist payment of the price. He must pay it and bring a cross-claim for the defects and omissions, or alternatively, set them up in diminution of the price. The measure is the amount which the work is worth less by reason of the defects and omissions, and is usually calculated by the cost of making them good.

26 *HHJ Newey OR in Emson Eastern v EME Developments* (1991) 55 BLR 114 at 125.
27 *Broom v Davis* [1794] 7 East 479, at pp. 480n, 484.
28 *Hoenig v Isaacs* [1952] 2 All ER 176.

In *Bolton v Mahadeva*,[29] Cairns LJ made the following comment on the issue of substantial performance:

> In considering whether there was a substantial performance I am of the opinion that it is relevant to take into account both the nature of the defects and the proportion between the cost of rectifying them and the contract price. It would be wrong to say that the contractor is only entitled to payment if the defects are so trifling as to be covered by the de minimis rule.

Another interesting case is *Mears Ltd v Costplan Services (South East) Ltd & Ors*[30] as it shows why the meaning of practical completion often becomes the subject matter of construction disputes. On 20 May 2016, Mears Limited ("Mears") entered into an agreement for lease ("AFL") with Plymouth (Notte Street) Limited ("PNS"), the owner of a development site, and J.R. Pickstock Limited ("Pickstock"). Based on the AFL, PNS engaged Pickstock to build two blocks to be used as student accommodation and Mears agreed to take a 21-year lease of the accommodation blocks within five working days of practical completion. The AFL also included a long stop date (18 September 2018) after which PNSL or Mears could terminate the AFL had Pickstock not achieved practical completion under the construction contract with PNS. Among others, the AFL also included a provision stating that:

> 6.2 The Landlord shall not make any variations to the Landlord's Works or Building Documents which: 6.2.1 materially affect the size (and a reduction of more than 3% of the size of any distinct area shown upon the Building Documents shall be deemed material), layout or appearance of the Property.

In 2018, prior project completion, Mears served several defect notices alleging that around 56 rooms were more than 3% smaller than the contractually agreed size. On 16 August 2018, Costplan Services (South East) Limited ("Costplan") which had been appointed by PNS to act as its construction agent, disagreeing with Mears' allegations and indicated its intention to conduct a pre-completion inspection aimed at issuing the certificate of practical completion notwithstanding the defects notices that Mears had served. To avoid the inspection, Mears sought and obtained an interlocutory injunction preventing certification. Expedited proceedings then took place where Mears sought declarations from the court aimed at assessing: (i) whether Costplan was permitted to certify practical completion; (ii) whether one or more rooms built were, in fact, more than 3% smaller than the size agreed between Mears the parties; and (iii) whether

> on a true construction of the AFL, any failure to construct one or more of the rooms of the Property such that they are not more than 3% smaller than the sizes specified in the . . . drawings contained in the Building Documents . . . or (contrary to Mears' primary case) such alternative room sizes otherwise agreed to by Mears is a material and substantial breach of Clause 6.2 of the AFL [and/or] constitutes a material and substantial defect in the works.

The High Court found that that 56 rooms were, in fact, smaller than the agreed 3% tolerance size range, which had resulted in a breach of the AFL. However, the court held that

29 *Bolton v Mahadeva* [1972] 2 All ER 1322. See also *Williams v Roffey Bros & Nicholls (Contractors) Ltd* [1989] EWCA Civ 5.

30 *Mears Ltd v Costplan Services (South East) Ltd & Ors* [2019] EWCA Civ 502.

such a breach could not be considered so material and substantial as to entitle Mears to terminate the AFL. Waksman J stated as follows:

> 30. The deeming provision in Clause 6.2.1 is not surprising. It avoids, in one important area of the works, a dispute as to what deviation should be regarded as 'material'. And it ties the areas down to those shown in the Building Documents. Materiality, therefore, whether deemed by Clause 6.2.1 or otherwise, goes to the extent of the variation which has occurred. Unless material 'or substantial' any such variation does not amount to a breach. But if it does, the fact that there has been a material variation says nothing about the extent or importance of that breach to the Property or works as a whole.
>
> 31. Accordingly, the fact that there is a material variation for the purposes of Clause 6.2.1 does not mean without more that the resulting breach is itself material or substantial. In contending that it does, it seems to me that Mears is eliding these two quite different concepts: (a) the scale of the variation and (b) the scale of any resultant breach.

The fact that a 3% failure was considered material did not mean that the resulting breach was also material. The court also held that such a discrepancy was not necessarily irremediable and could not prevent practical completion. Mears appealed. The Court of Appeal upheld the decision of the judge at first instance. Coulson LJ clarified that the parties to contracts of that sort are entitled to agree, in advance, that a breach of a particular clause amounts to a material or substantial breach of contract. However, the issue in that case was whether clause 6.2.1 included such term. He concluded that it did not as:

> the parties were not saying that the resulting breach of contract was itself 'material'. The words of clause 6.2.1 do not say that. Materiality is introduced only in relation to room size ('materially affect the size'), and not in relation to the resulting breach. There is nothing in clause 6.2.1 which addresses the character or quality of the breach. The clause simply provides a mechanism by which a breach of contract can be indisputably identified.

The court also held that in case the parties intended to agree that any failure to meet the 3% tolerance, however trivial, was to be considered a material breach of contract, this would have led to a "*draconian result*" for which the parties should have used "*clear words*", which were not used in the AFL. In the absence of such clear language, the decision on whether practical completion had been achieved was on the certifier. Costplan was ready to certify practical completion regardless of the smaller size of some of the rooms on the assumption that such defect was, in fact, a trifling one. Coulson LJ concluded that only a patent defect which is more than trifling can prevent the certification of practical completion, regardless of whether it is capable of remedy. The appeal was therefore dismissed.

In *Mers* Coulson LJ also usefully summarised the law on practical completion as follows:

a) Practical completion is easier to recognise than define . . . there are no hard and fast rules.

b) The existence of latent defects cannot prevent practical completion. . . . In many ways that is self-evident: if the defect is latent, nobody knows about it and it cannot therefore prevent the certifier from concluding that practical completion has been achieved.

c) In relation to patent defects, the cases show that there is no difference between an item of work that has yet to be completed (i.e. an outstanding item) and an item of defective work which requires to be remedied. Snagging lists can and will usually identify both types of item without distinction. . . .

d) Although one interpretation of Viscount Dilhorne in Jarvis[31] and Lord Diplock in Kaye[32] suggests that the very existence of patent defect prevents practical completion, that was emphatically not the view of Salmon LJ in Jarvis,[33] and the practical approach developed by Judge Newey in William Press[34] and Emson[35] has been adopted in all the subsequent cases. As noted in Mariner,[36] that can be summarised as a state of affairs in which the works have been completed free from patent defects, other than ones to be ignored as trifling.

e) Whether or not an item is trifling is a matter of fact and degree, to be measured against "the purpose of allowing the employers to take possession of the works and to use them as intended" (see Salmon LJ in Jarvis[37]). However, this should not be elevated into the proposition that if, say, a house is capable of being inhabited, or a hotel opened for business, the works must be regarded as practically complete, regardless of the nature and extent of the items of work which remain to be completed/remedied. Mariner[38] is a good example of why such an approach is wrong. In consequence, I do not consider that paragraph [187][39] of the judgment in Bovis Lend Lease,[40] with its emphasis on the employer's ability to take possession, should be regarded (without more) as an accurate statement of the law on practical completion.

f) Other than Ruxley,[41] there is no authority which addresses the interplay between the concept of completion and the irremediable nature of any outstanding item of work. And even Ruxley[42] is of limited use because that issue did not go beyond the first instance decision. But on any view, Ruxley[43] does not support the proposition that the mere fact that the defect was irremediable meant that the works were not practically complete.

The preceding summary also shows that the doctrine will not apply in some cases. These are summarised in *Dakin v Lee*:[44]

> Where a builder has supplied work and labour for the erection or the repair of a house under a lump sum contract, but has parted from the terms of the contract, he is entitled to recover for his services unless (1) the work that he has done is of no benefit to the owner; (2) the work he has done is entirely different from the work which he has contracted to do; or (3) he has abandoned the work and left it unfinished.

---

31 *Jarvis & Sons Limited v Westminster Corporation & Another* ([1970] 1 WLR 637.

32 *Kaye v Hosier & Dickinson* [1972] 1 WLR 146.

33 *Jarvis & Sons Limited v Westminster Corporation & Another* [1969] 1 WLR 1448.

34 *H.W. Nevill (Sunblest) Limited v William Press & Son Limited* (1981) 20 BLR 78.

35 *Emson Eastern Limited (in receivership) v E.M.E. Developments Limited* (1991) 55 BLR 114.

36 *Mariner International Hotels Limited & Another v Atlas Limited & Another* [2007] 10 HKCFAR 1.

37 *Jarvis & Sons Limited v Westminster Corporation & Another* [1969] 1 WLR 1448.

38 *Mariner International Hotels Limited & Another v Atlas Limited & Another* [2007] 10 HKCFAR 1.

39 Where Judge Thornton QC said at [187] that "*what is meant by practical completion is that the works as a whole are substantially complete and are in a state that allows the building owner to take possession*".

40 *Bovis Lend Lease Ltd v Saillard Fuller & Partners* (2001) 77 Con LR 134.

41 *Ruxley Electronics & Construction Limited v Forsyth* [1996] 1 AC 344.

42 *Ruxley Electronics & Construction Limited v Forsyth* [1996] 1 AC 344.

43 *Ruxley Electronics & Construction Limited v Forsyth* [1996] 1 AC 344.

44 *Dakin & Co., Ltd. v Lee* [1916] 1 King's Bench, 566.

Therefore, the cases in which the doctrine of substantial performance will not apply include the following:

(i) Where the employer does not get any benefit from the work as executed by the contractor, e.g., in case the works are not suitable for their purposes.

(ii) Where the works promised are substantially different from the works done. In this regard, in *Hoenig v Isaacs*[45] Romer LJ said:

> In certain cases it is right that the rigid rule . . . should be applied, for example if a man tells a contractor to build a 10 foot wall for him in his garden and agrees to pay £X for it, it would not be right that he should be held liable for any part of the contract price if the contractor builds the wall to 2 feet and then renounces further performance of the contract, or builds the wall of a totally different material from that which was ordered, or builds it at the wrong end of the garden.

(iii) Where the contractor has consciously disregarded his obligations under the contract (e.g., by voluntarily repudiating an obligation or abandoning work) or has refused to remedy his breach. As held by Somervell LJ in *Hoenig v Isaacs*:[46] In a contract to erect buildings on the defendant's land for a lump sum, the builder can recover nothing on the contract if he stops work before the work is completed in the ordinary sense – in other words abandons the contract.

13.5.4 Consequences of late completion

The parties' obligations as to completion and the consequences of late completion will vary sensibly based on whether or not the contract provides for a completion date or whether time is considered "of the essence".

13.5.4.1 Time of the essence

Where the contractor fails to complete within the completion date agreed in the contract, the employer may seek damages (liquidated or unliquidated) for breach of contract. However, when time is of the essence, the stated time for completion is considered a condition of the contract, so that the employer may be entitled to terminate the contract (in addition to claiming damages) as the contractor will be considered having repudiated the contract. This is because the delay is considered as a breach that "*goes to root of the contract*", regardless of the relevant magnitude.[47] However, it is worth noting that construction contracts are unlikely to include time of the essence provisions as the usual remedy for delay is liquidated damages.

The general rules on when time is considered of the essence were as set out in *Halsbury's Laws of England*, and then approved by the House of Lords in *United Scientific Holdings Ltd v Burnley Council*.[48] According to such rules, time will not be considered of the essence unless: (i) the parties expressly stipulate those conditions as to time must be strictly complied with; or (ii) the nature of the subject matter of the contract or the

45 *Hoenig v Isaacs* [1952] 2 All ER 176, at 182G.
46 *Hoenig v Isaacs* [1952] 2 All ER 176.
47 *Lombard plc. v Butterworth* [1987] QB 527 at 535, CA.
48 *United Scientific Holding v Burnley Council* [1978] AC 904 at [946].

surrounding circumstances show that time should be considered to be of the essence; or (iii) a party who has been subjected to unreasonable delay gives notice to the party in default making time of the essence.

Where time was not initially of the essence or it was of the essence, but the parties agreed not to consider it as such or it ceased to be of the essence by waiver of the employer, the latter may send a notice to the contractor asking for the contractor to complete within a certain date. In this way, the employer makes time of the essence and implicitly states that failure to complete by the given date will be considered as a repudiation of the contract.[49] As said by Lord Simon in *United Scientific*:[50]

> The notice operates as evidence that the promisee considers that a reasonable time for performance has elapsed by the date of the notice and as evidence of the date by which the promisee now considers it reasonable for the contractual obligation to be performed. The promisor is put on notice of these matters. It is only in this sense that time is made of the essence of a contract in which it was previously non-essential. The promisee is really saying unless you perform by such and such a date I shall treat your failure as repudiation of the contract. To say that time can be made of the essence of a contract by notice except in the limited sense alone would be to permit one party to the contract unilaterally by notice to introduce a new term into it.

An employer shall be very careful in considering the wording of a notice making time of the essence. The matter was considered in *HDK Limited v Sunshine Ventures & Others*,[51] where the contractor, HDK Limited ("HDK"), sought payment of outstanding sums from the employer, Sunshine Ventures ("Sunshine"), which, in turn, claimed damages for delays and defects in the works. Sunshine sent a first letter to HDK asking them to "*complete the work . . . as soon as possible*" and a second one requiring HDK to "*complete the outstanding works as a matter of urgency*". Sunshine eventually terminated the contract. The matter ended in court. The issue before the court was whether the two letters had the effect of making time of the essence and as such to entitle Sunshine terminating the contract. The court held that the two letters had not made time of the essence as they: (i) had not conveyed in clear terms that unless the notice was complied with the employer would treat the contract as at an end; and (ii) did not specify a date by which the contractor had to complete the work. The result was that the termination was effectively to be considered a repudiation of the contract on the part of the employer.

It is worth noting that the English courts are generally reluctant to find time being of the essence in construction contracts in the light of the relevant consequences in case of non-compliance. In *Lucas v Godwin*[52] the court stated that:

> It never could have been the understanding of the parties that if the house were not done by the precise day the plaintiff would have no remuneration; at all events if so unreasonable an engagement had been entered into the parties should have expressed their meaning with a precision which could not be mistaken.

49 *United Scientific Holding v Burnley Council* [1978] AC 904 at [946].
50 *United Scientific Holding v Burnley Council* [1978] AC 904 at [946].
51 *HDK Limited v Sunshine Ventures & Others* [2009] EWHC 2866 (QB).
52 *Lucas v Godwin* [1837] 3 Bing NC 737.

In *Lamprell v Billericay Union*[53] it was said that:

> We are of the opinion that time for completion was not an essential part of the contract; first because there is an expressed provision made for a weekly sum to be paid for every week during which the work should be delayed . . . and secondly, because the deed clearly meant to exempt the plaintiff from the obligation . . . should he be prevented by fire or other circumstances satisfactory to the architect.

Moreover, where the contract includes an extension of time mechanism or a liquidated damages clause, time will not normally be considered of the essence[54] as with such clauses the parties have provided for alternative remedies for the case of delay. However, the parties may expressly state in the contract that, despite the inclusion of alternative remedies for delays, time shall be considered of the essence. In *Peak Construction v McKinney Foundations*[55] the parties entered into a construction contract pursuant to which the claimant was engaged to construct a multi-storey block of flats within 24 months. The contract contained an extension of time clause which empowered the architect to extend time in the event of "*unforeseen circumstances*" and a liquidated damages clause. The contract also contained a clause stating that

> Time shall be considered as of the essence of the contract on the part of the contractor, and in case the contractor shall fail in the due performance . . . shall be liable to pay the corporation, as and for liquidated damages, the sum of.

The defendants were nominated subcontractors who were contracted for the design and construction of piles. During the construction works, it was discovered that one of the piles was constructed from unsuitable materials and was "*useless*". Works were immediately suspended for 58 weeks. Completion of the remedial works eventually took approximately six weeks. The Court of Appeal held that it was impossible to hold the contractor responsible for a delay of 58 weeks when the requisite remedial works took only six weeks to complete. The Court of Appeal held that extension of time and liquidated damages clauses should be construed strictly contra proferentem, and that no liquidated damages would be recoverable where the employer was in any way responsible for a failure to achieve a completion date. In describing the contract, Salomon LJ held:

> The form of this contract has been much criticised during the course of the argument – and not without justification. Indeed if a prize were to be offered for the form of a building contract which contained the most onesided, obscurely and ineptly drafted clauses in the United Kingdom, the claim of this contract could hardly be ignored.

However, the Court of Appeal confirmed that the employer had a right to terminate the contract pursuant to the "time of the essence" clause despite the contract containing extension of time and liquidated damages provisions. In particular, referring to the time of the essence clause, Salomon LJ said that:

> No doubt this gave the corporation the right to determine the contract at the end of the 24 months period as extended by the architect. Had they done so, some other contractors might have been called in to complete the work, or the plaintiffs might have completed it on freshly

53 *Lamprell v Billericay Union* [1849] 3 EX 283.
54 *Lamprell v Billericay Union* [1849] 3 Ex 283 at [308].
55 *Peak Construction v McKinney Foundations* [1971] 1 BLR 111 at 120, CA.

> negotiated terms. But the corporation did not determine the contract. They elected to leave the plaintiffs to complete the work.

This approach was confirmed in the case of *McAlpine Humberoak Ltd v McDermott International Inc (No. 1)*.[56] The claimant was a contractor engaged by the defendant to supply and install steel parts for an offshore drilling rig. The contract contained the following time of the essence clause: "*Time is of the essence of this contract. Contractor shall commence the work after receipt of notice from McDermott and shall complete the work in accordance with the dates set out in Exhibit B SC 5*". The contractor soon fell behind schedule, with both parties blaming each other for the delay. The disputes then arose in relation to some variations which were ordered by the defendant towards the end of the construction process. The contractor contended that "*Since time was of the essence of the contract, and since the [employer] had no power to fix a new completion date, time became at large*". In commenting this position, the Court of Appeal stated that:

> If, in a contract which provides for a lump sum price and a firm delivery date, the employer causes the contractor to miss the delivery date by one day, as he might, for example, by ordering extra work, both the lump sum and the delivery date are displaced. Otherwise the contract remains intact. So the contractor can take as long as he likes, provided only he is not guilty of culpable delay, and can at the end recalculate his price based on the time actually taken.

Another aspect to be considered on this subject is that in circumstances where the contractor has an obligation to complete within reasonable time, before a valid notice making time of the essence may be given it must first be established that the contractor has breached such obligation. This aspect is clarified in *Shawton Engineering Ltd v DGP International Ltd*.[57] The case concerned a contract for the provision of design drawings by the defendant for the engineering and manufacture of box encapsulation plant for the storage of nuclear waste at Sellafield. The court had to decide on the validity of the employer's termination for breach of contract by the contractor. Shawton Engineering Ltd ("Shawton") contended that many of the drawings contained errors which a reasonably competent engineer would not have made. The contract did not contain an extension of time clause, and the employer had ordered a certain number of variations. The Court of Appeal observed that: (i) as the errors were corrected by DGP, they were insufficient to give the claimant the right to terminate the contract; (ii) lacking an extension of time clause, the effect of the variations was to oblige the contractor to complete the works within a reasonable time; (iii) then employer could legitimately terminate a contractor's employment on the grounds of delay on two bases: (a) if a completion date fixed in a reasonable notice making time of the essence was not complied with, in which case the seeking to make time of the essence shall demonstrate that the other party was in breach of its time obligations under the contract at the time of the notice purporting to make time of the essence; and/or (b) if the failure to complete works within a reasonable time was so flagrant that it effectively deprived the innocent party substantially of the whole benefit of the contract.

---

56 *McAlpine Humberoak Ltd v McDermott International Inc (No. 1)* [1992] 58 BLR 1.
57 *Shawton Engineering Ltd v DGP Group International Ltd* [2005] EWCA Civ 1359.

13.5.4.2 The contract includes a valid completion date

Where the contract sets out the time for completion of the works, the contractor is bound to carry out the works and complete them by that time and will be liable for breach of contract if it fails to do so without a good excuse, regardless of whether time was of the essence. Unless otherwise agreed, the contractor shall have until the last hour of the last day to complete the work.[58] There may be cases in which a time is mentioned in the contract, but is intended as an estimate rather than a strict deadline. In such cases the contractor will not be bound to complete within that specific date. An example is where a contractor submits to the employer a programme showing a completion ahead of the contractual completion date. In the absence of clear language, the date shown on the programme is intended to constitute a mere target guide, even in case the employer has approved it. As stated in *Hudson's Building and Engineering Contracts*:[59]

> The purpose of contractual requirements for a programme to be supplied by the contractor is often misunderstood, and is primarily to enable the owner, or his A/E, to plan their own arrangements for giving possession, supplying information and working drawings, and co-ordinating the work of other contractors or nominated sub-contractors, and only secondarily for use in connection with the contractor's extension of time applications or monetary claims, or to impose additional time obligations on him. Against this background, in the absence of clear language such provisions should not be interpreted as altering the substantive rights or obligations of the parties, though no doubt a programme may be some, although not conclusive, evidence as to what is a reasonable time for the discharge of both parties' obligations under the contract.

13.5.4.3 The contract does not include a completion date, or includes an invalid completion date or there is no formal contract

Although it would be unusual for a construction contract for a complex project not to include a completion date, there may be situations in which the date for completion included in the contract is invalid because it may not be calculated in a precise way (e.g., it shall be calculated by using an imprecise formula or based on unclear assumptions) or because the whole contract, including its completion date, is vitiated. In such cases, the parties may be left with no completion date.

In the absence of a completion date, or in case the completion date has lapsed or becomes void by reason of something for which the employer is responsible (i.e., prevention or breach of contract), time is said to be "at large", meaning that the project shall be completed within a reasonable time. In such case, so long as the delay is attributable to causes beyond the contractor's control, and the contractor has not acted negligently and unreasonably, the obligation to complete within reasonable time is fulfilled regardless of the protracted delay.[60] The burden of proving what constitutes "reasonable time" is on the employer.[61] What constitutes reasonable time is a question of fact which was

58 *Startup v McDonald* [1843] 6 Man & G 593.

59 I.N. Duncan Wallace QC, *Hudson's Building and Engineering Contracts* (11th edition) Sweet & Maxwell, 1994, at p. 1129.

60 *Hick v Raymond & Reid* [1893] AC 22 at 32, HL.

61 *Atwood v Emery* [1856] 1 CB (NS) 110 [140 ER 45].

considered in the following terms in *British Steel Corporation v Cleveland Bridge and Engineering*:[62]

> It was common ground between the parties that the principles I had to apply in this connection were those stated by the House of Lords in Hick v Raymond & Reid, viz. that the question what constituted a reasonable time had to be considered in relation to the circumstances which existed at the time when the contractual services were performed, but excluding circumstances which were under the control of the party performing those services. As I understand it, I have first to consider what would, in ordinary circumstances, be a reasonable time for the performance of the relevant services; and I have then to consider to what extent that time for performance . . . was in effect extended by extraordinary circumstances outside their control. . . .
>
> What is reasonable depends upon all the circumstances of the case, including the conditions operating during the period when the work is being done. It would follow that, as to whether a reasonable time has been taken up, in the doing of the works cannot be decided in advance; it can only be decided after the work has been done.

It is worth noting that an obligation to complete within reasonable time would also be implied in case no formal written contract has been entered into between the parties. In the recent case of *Barkby Real Estate Developments Limited v Cornerstone Telecommunications Infrastructure Limited*,[63] Barkby Real Estate Developments Limited ("BREDL") had engaged Cornerstone Telecommunications Infrastructure Limited ("Cornerstone") to do some works. The parties had never entered into a formal written contract. The works were delayed due to inadequate ground conditions. As a result, BREDL claimed delay damages. The court found that: (i) albeit there was no formal written contract between the parties, a binding agreement had formed when BREDL had accepted a quote and Cornerstone acknowledged receipt of a payment from BREDL based on such quote; (ii) despite the absence of any express terms as to time for completion, a term could be implied by operation of Section 14 of the Supply of Goods and Services Act 1982, that the "*supplier will carry out the service within a reasonable time*", an obligation that, looking at the circumstances of the case, Cornerstone had failed to meet as, among other things. Even after the problem with inadequate ground conditions had been identified, Cornerstone had not acted with reasonable promptness to resolve the issue of the inadequate ground conditions; (iii) BREDL was therefore entitled to recover most of its costs.

62 *British Steel Corporation v Cleveland Bridge and Engineering* [1984] 1 All ER 504 at [512].

63 *Barkby Real Estate Developments Limited v Cornerstone Telecommunications Infrastructure Limited* [2022] EWHC 1892 (TCC).

CHAPTER 14

Time

14.1 Extension of time for completion

14.1.1 Extension of time in general

Extension of time clauses have the effect of extending the date by which the works shall be completed, so relieving the contractor of its obligation to pay damages (liquidated or general, according to the contract) for late completion, in cases where the works have (critically) fallen behind schedule for reasons that are not attributable to the contractor (i.e., where the delay is due to acts of the employer or to so-called neutral events, such as a force majeure event). In the absence of an extension of time clause, time will be "at large" and the contractor will be obliged to complete within a reasonable time. EOT clauses are therefore beneficial for both contractors and employers as they: (i) allow contractors more time to complete the works and eliminate or reduce (depending on the length of the extension) their liability for liquidated damages (in case the contract provides for liquidated damages in case of delay); and (ii) set a new completion date, so preserving the employers' entitlement to liquidated damages (if the contract provides for such damages) for delays for which the contractor is culpable (so avoiding time becoming at large).

The benefits of an extension of time are summarised as follows in the SCL Protocol:[1]

> The benefit to the Contractor of an EOT is to relieve the Contractor of liability for damages for delay (usually LDs) for any period prior to the extended contract completion date and allows for reprogramming of the works to completion. The benefit of an EOT for the Employer is that it establishes a new contract completion date, prevents time for completion of the works becoming 'at large' and allows for coordination/planning of its own activities.

Whether a contractor is entitled to an EOT is ultimately a matter of contract. However, in order for an EOT to be afforded it will be necessary that the delay on which basis the EOT is requested be critical, i.e., leading to the contractor's incapacity to complete within the agreed completion date. As a result, in case a contractor has planned to complete the works ahead of the contractual completion date, a delay not attributable to the contractor which prevents it from completing within the planned date of completion is irrelevant and will usually not entitle the contractor to an EOT, unless the delay has also affected the contractor's ability to complete within the contractual completion date.

1 *Society of Construction Law Delay and Disruption Protocol* (2nd edition) February 2017, www.scl.org.uk, at p. 22.

DOI: 10.4324/9781003387718-18

14.1.2 Extension of time clause

As mentioned, whether a contractor is entitled to request an EOT and in what cases will depend on the terms of the contracts. A typical EOT clause may provide as follows: (i) that the contractor shall not be entitled to an EOT where the delay is the result of its own acts, omissions, defaults or negligence (or his subcontractors); (ii) that the contractor will be entitled to EOTs in case of specific events provided in the contract. These will be events for which the employer is responsible such as variations, acts of prevention, employer's failure to give the contractor timely access or possession of the site, suspension of the works instructed by the employer, neutral events such as changes in law, force majeure, exceptionally adverse weather conditions, etc.; (iii) the specific procedure the contractor should comply in case it considers itself to be entitled to an EOT (which will typically be in line with the one provided in the contract for all other contractor's claims); (iv) the contractor requesting an EOT shall mitigate the effects of any delay to the works; (v) the EOT will not affect any delay damages already accrued, even if not yet claimed by the employer; (vi) in case of concurrent delays, any delay for which the employer is responsible which is concurrent with other delays caused by the contractor will not be considered to calculate the EOT.

EOT clauses also include language aimed at covering ownership of the "float". The float is defined in the SCL Protocol[2] as: the amount of time by which an activity or group of activities may be shifted in time without causing Delay to Completion. Therefore, the float is the amount of time that work activities can absorb, in excess of their original intended duration, without impacting on the critical path of the works. Until the float is completely exhausted, a delay to progress will not result in the contract completion date being missed, but merely in an erosion of the float. The float is a resource which is subject to "ownership" by any of the parties (or the project). Both parties will typically seek to own the float and the issue is usually cause of disputes between them. The opposing interests of the parties are clearly summarised as follows in the SCL Protocol:[3]

> The 'ownership' of float causes particular arguments in disputes over entitlement to an EOT. A Contractor may argue that it 'owns' the float, because, in planning how it proposes to carry out the works, it has allowed additional or float time to give itself some flexibility in the event that it is not able to carry out the works as quickly as it planned. If, therefore, there is any delay to the Contractor's progress for which the Contractor is not responsible, it may contend that it is entitled to an EOT, even if the delay to progress will not result in the contract completion date being missed, but merely in erosion of its float. On the other hand, an Employer may typically say that the Contractor has no EOT entitlement unless the delay to progress will result in a contract completion date being missed. So (the Employer may say) the project owns the float.

The approach suggested in the SCL Protocol is that the parties state in the contract which party "owns" the float in the EOT clause as absence or ambiguity about float generates

2 The SCL Protocol distinguishes between: (i) "*Delay to Completion*", which may mean either delay to the date when the contractor planned to complete its works, or a delay to the contract completion date; and (ii) "*Delay to Progress*", which means a delay which will merely cause delay to the Contractor's progress without causing a contract completion date not to be met.

3 *Society of Construction Law Delay and Disruption Protocol* (2nd edition) February 2017, www.scl.org.uk, at p. 28.

uncertainty and disputes are likely to follow. In case the contract does not contain any provisions as to the float, the float will be owned by the project so that, unless the contract states otherwise, in case of non-critical employer delays having the effect of eroding the float, a contractor may not claim an EOT, nor may it recover its acceleration costs in case it sought to accelerate the works to keep the float time. This approach is consistent with the current judicial thinking.[4]

14.2 Acceleration

14.2.1 Acceleration in general

As the word suggests, acceleration in construction projects is the process of working at a faster pace than originally anticipated. However, the precise meaning of the word is somewhat obscure under English law. As stated by Judge Hicks in the case of *Ascon Contracting Ltd v Alfred Mcalpine Construction Isle of Man Ltd*:[5]

> 'acceleration' tends to be bandied about as if it had a precise technical meaning, but I have found nothing to persuade me that this is the case.

Despite that, the issue of acceleration is very often raised in the context of complex construction projects, and claims for additional costs resulting from acceleration measures are quite common.

It is worth noting that acceleration should not be confused with mitigation. The SCL Protocol[6] clarifies that:

> Mitigation simply means to make less severe or lessen delay, disruption and/or the resultant costs and/or loss. Acceleration is a subset of mitigation, and typically refers to the situation where additional costs are incurred to seek to overcome all or part of delay or disruption (for example, to ensure that that the contract completion date is achieved). Where the Employer is responsible for that delay or disruption, the Contractor may claim its acceleration costs from the Employer. This situation is distinct from a Contractor's general duty to mitigate its loss when it suffers delay and disruption or incurs additional cost due to an Employer Risk Event. That general duty to mitigate does not require the Contractor to incur additional costs.

14.2.2 Categories of acceleration

There are three categories of acceleration, i.e., instructed (or directed) acceleration, constructive (or implied) acceleration and voluntary acceleration.

14.2.2.1 Voluntary acceleration

Voluntary acceleration occurs when a contractor unilaterally decides to accelerate its own work, e.g., to recover its own delays. In this case, the contractor will not be entitled to any damages.

---

4 See, e.g., *Ascon Contracting Ltd v Alfred Mcalpine Construction Isle of Man Ltd* [1999] EWHC J1019–10.

5 *Ascon Contracting Ltd v Alfred Mcalpine Construction Isle of Man Ltd* [2000] 66 Con LR 119; 16 Const LJ 216 (TCC).

6 *Society of Construction Law Delay and Disruption Protocol* (2nd edition) February 2017, www.scl.org.uk, at p. 10.

14.2.2.2 Instructed (or directed) acceleration

An instructed acceleration occurs when the employer issues a specific acceleration instruction order to the contractor. In such instruction the employer may direct the contractor: (i) complete the project earlier than the contractually agreed completion date; (ii) re-sequence the work and/or reorganise the works (e.g., by using more or different equipment and/or hiring more labourers and/or having labourers doing overtime or additional shifts) in order to complete the original project scope of the work, plus additional or changed work within the agreed completion date (e.g., in case the contractor has been granted an EOT, but the employer instructs the contractor to complete within the original completion date) or to recover contractor-caused delays that threaten the achievement of the agreed completion date.

The consequences for a contractor that fails to accelerate upon a valid instruction, may be severe. In the case of *Masons v W D King*[7] the court held that in such cases the contractor may be liable for actual loss deriving from the delay over and above the contractually stipulated liquidated damages.

14.2.2.3 Constructive (or implied) acceleration

Constructive acceleration occurs when a contractor encounters excusable delay entitling it to an extension of time, which the employer fails to grant. In such cases, a contractor may decide to accelerate the works to meet the contractually agreed completion date to avoid risk of incurring delay damages (or simply to avoid delaying other projects), but then claim the acceleration costs based on a theory of constructive acceleration. This theory has been developed in the American courts and is now widely recognised. The courts have identified[8] the following elements that a contractor must establish to recover constructive acceleration costs: (i) there must be an excusable delay; (ii) the contractor must have requested an extension of time as a consequence of such delay; (iii) the employer must have refused to grant such extension of time, but it must have expressly or implicitly directed the contractor to complete within the original completion date; (iv) the contractor must have accelerated and incurred the relevant acceleration costs.

English law generally does not recognise the theory of constructive acceleration. Therefore, unless the contract expressly provides otherwise, the courts will be reluctant to be persuaded by construction acceleration claims which rely on American precedents.[9] As stated in the SCL Protocol:

> Where the Contractor is considering implementing acceleration measures to avoid the risk of liquidated damages as a result of not receiving an EOT that it considers is due to it, and then pursuing a constructive acceleration claim, the Contractor should first take steps to have the dispute or difference about entitlement to EOT resolved in accordance with the contract dispute resolution provisions. Otherwise, there is the risk that it will not be entitled to compensation for those acceleration measures.

Under English law construction contracts, contractors that are denied a justified extension of time are therefore left with the dilemma of whether to (i) accelerate, so trying to avoid delay damages, but risk not to recover the acceleration costs; or (ii) continue with the

7 *Masons v W D King* [2003] EWHC 3124 (TCC) at 62–68.

8 See for example *Fraser Construction Co v United States* [2004] 384 F3d 1354, 1361.

9 *Society of Construction Law Delay and Disruption Protocol* (2nd edition) February 2017, www.scl.org.uk, at p. 7.

normal pace and hope for an extension of time, but risk having to pay delay damages. In such cases, contractors may try arguing that, even if no express instruction to accelerate was given, the employer's conduct did amount to an implied instruction to the contractor to accelerate the works. However, English courts are typically reluctant to imply instructions where an employer disputes liability for work allegedly instructed.[10] An alternative may be a breach of contract claim.[11] A possible argument that contractors may use is that the acceleration was aimed at mitigating the consequence of the project's delay arising from the employer's refusal to grant and extension of time.[12] Alternatively, contractors may try recovering acceleration costs by recurring to other contractual mechanisms, such as by submitting variation claims, provided that the circumstances of the facts allow such categorisation. What is certain is that a contractor which has decided to proceed with a constructive acceleration should, before taking any acceleration measures, at least notify the employer of its intention and clearly state the relevant reasons, the measures it is going to take and the costs which will be borne and claimed back from the employer.

14.2.3 Acceleration clause

Construction contracts usually include acceleration clauses to provide for the case of instructed acceleration. Such clauses typically state that (i) the employer may request the contractor to complete the works earlier than the agreed completion date; and (ii) where a contractor considers that it is entitled to an extension of time, it shall submit, together with the extension of time, a proposal regarding the possibility to accelerate. In both cases, the parties shall agree in advance the relevant acceleration costs before the contractor may proceed with the acceleration.

In the absence of an express acceleration clause, the parties may enter into a separate "acceleration agreement". In such case, the agreement should clearly state: (i) the circumstances which led to the acceleration; (ii) the acceleration measures that are to be taken by the contractor; (iii) the new completion date; and (iv) the amount to be paid (if it is a lump sum) or the method to calculate it (e.g., open book/cost reimbursable).

14.3 Delay damages

14.3.1 Delay damages in general

Construction contracts for large and complex projects almost invariably include a clause providing for the consequences of the contractor negligently failing to complete the works by the completion date agreed in the contract. In general, when a contractor fails to achieve practical completion in a timely fashion, absent any circumstances that permit an extension of time, the contractor will be in breach of contract and will have to pay damages to the employer. Damages may be either liquidated or general, depending on

10 *Holland Hannen & Cubitts (Northern) Ltd v Welsh Health Technical Services Organisation* [1981] 18 BLR 80 (QB) 121.

11 *Amec Process & Energy Ltd v Stork Engineers & Contractors BV* [1999] 68 Con LR 17 at 48 [110].

12 *Ascon Contracting Ltd v Alfred McAlpine Construction Isle of Man Ltd* [1999] 66 Con LR 119 (QB) 132.

the parties' agreement. It is worth noting that, for a delay to be relevant, the delay must be critical as only critical delays entitle contractors to extension of time.

14.3.2 Liquidated damages

14.3.2.1 Liquidated damages in general

Liquidated damages are the ordinary remedy for late completion of works in the case of complex construction contracts. Such contracts usually provide for liquidated damages ("LDs") also sometimes also referred to as liquidated and ascertained damages ("LADs"). The SCL Protocol defines LDs as:

> A fixed sum, usually per week or per day, written into the contract as being payable by the Contractor in the event that the works are not completed by the contract completion date (original or extended).[13]

Thus, LDs are a pre-determined sum of money the contractor will have to pay to the employer in case the contractor negligently fails to complete the works (or a key milestone) by the completion date agreed in the contract.

By including an LD clause in the contract, the parties can fix in advance the sum of money that the contractor will have to pay to the employer in case of non-excusable delays.

LD clauses are advantageous for both employers and contractors: (i) employers will be entitled to payment without having to prove causation and the actual loss suffered. Provided that the employer succeeds in establishing an entitlement to LDs, the burden of proof on causation and quantum will shift on the contractor (i.e., the contractor should prove that the critical delay was totally or partly excusable through an extension of time claim); while (ii) contractors will know in advance the maximum exposure in case of culpable delay.

LD clauses were recently analysed in the case of *Triple Point Technology Inc v PTT Public Company Ltd*[14] where the Supreme Court gave a definition of such clauses and clarified the relevant purpose as follows:

> A liquidated damages clause is a clause in a contract which stipulates what amount of money will be payable as damages for loss caused by a breach of the contract irrespective of what loss may actually be suffered if a breach of the relevant kind (typically, delay in performance of the contract) occurs. Liquidated damages clauses are a standard feature of major construction and engineering contracts and commonly provide for damages to be payable at a specified rate for each week or day of delay in the completion of work by the contractor after the contractual completion date has passed. Such a clause serves two useful purposes. First, establishing what financial loss delay has caused the employer would often be an intractable task capable of giving rise to costly disputes. Fixing in advance the damages payable for such delay avoids such difficulty and cost. Second, such a clause limits the contractor's exposure to liability of an otherwise unknown and open-ended kind, while at the same time giving the employer certainty about the amount that it will be entitled to recover as

---

13 *Society of Construction Law Delay and Disruption Protocol* (2nd edition) February 2017, www.scl.org.uk, at p. 66.

14 *Triple Point Technology Inc v PTT Public Company Ltd* [2021] UKSC 29 at [74].

compensation. Each party is therefore better able to manage the risk of delay in the completion of the project.

14.3.2.2 Liquidated damages and penalties

English courts tend to uphold contractual terms which fix the level of damages for breach, in particular in construction contracts for large projects which have been negotiated at arms' length between sophisticated parties of comparable bargaining power. However, LDs clauses will not be upheld where they constitute a penalty. This constitutes a clear exception to the general rule that the courts will enforce the terms of lawfully made contracts and will typically not rewrite contracts or strike out clauses. However, even in case an LD clause is considered a penalty, an employer may still be entitled to pursue a claim for general (or unliquidated) damages.

Traditionally, LD clauses have been considered unenforceable if they did not represent a "*genuine pre-estimate of loss*" but were stipulated as "*in terrorem*" of the contractor, meaning that the provision had the sole scope of ensuring that the contractor complied with the terms of the contract through fear of the consequences of non-compliance. LDs would be calculated by pre-determining, at the time that a contract was entered into, the actual loss that the employer could incur in case of delay. The clause would then be considered penal in case the amount agreed exceeded the innocent party's actual losses arising from the breach. The courts would not look at the circumstances of the case, including at the commercial background and any legitimate interest that the innocent party may have as to the agreed amount.

Penalty clauses were considered in the case of *Dunlop Pneumatic Tyre Company v New Garage and Motor Company Ltd*[15] where the House of Lords stated:

> 4. To assist this task of construction various tests have been suggested, which if applicable to the case under consideration may prove helpful, or even conclusive. Such are:
>
> (a) It will be held to be a penalty if the sum stipulated for is extravagant and unconscionable in amount in comparison to the greatest loss that could conceivably be proved to have followed from the breach . . .
>
> (b) It will be held to be a penalty if the breach consists only in not paying a sum of money, and the sum stipulated is a sum greater than the sum which ought to have been paid . . .
>
> (c) There is a presumption (but no more) that it is a penalty when "a single lump sum is made payable by way of compensation, on the occurrence of one or more or all of several events, some of which may occasion serious and others but trifling damage . . .
>
> On the other hand:
>
> (d) It is no obstacle to the sum stipulated being a genuine pre-estimate of damage, that the consequences of the breach are such as to make precise pre-estimation almost an impossibility. On the contrary, that is just the situation when it is probable that pre-estimated damages was the true bargain between the parties.

However, in the case of *Cavendish Square Holdings BV v Talal El Makdessi*[16] the Supreme Court labelled the doctrine of penalties as an "*ancient, haphazardly constructed edifice which*

15 *Dunlop Pneumatic Tyre Company v New Garage and Motor Company Ltd* [1915] AC 79 at [86] – [88].
16 *Cavendish Square Holding BV v Talal El Makdessi* [2015] UKSC 67.

has not weathered well" and sought to "*reformulate*" the "*genuine pre-estimate of loss*" rule, holding that the true test to determine whether a clause amounts to a penalty is whether:

> it is a secondary obligation[17] which imposes a detriment on the contract-breaker out of all proportion to any legitimate interest of the innocent party in the enforcement of the primary obligation.[18]

The court clarified that although penalties remain illegal, the courts should look at whether the clause is penal, including by looking at the relevant commercial background, and not whether it is a pre-estimate of loss. Applying this test, an LD clause may still be valid in case the level of LD exceeds the innocent party's actual losses arising from the breach, provided that there is a proportion with the innocent party's legitimate interests in having the contract performed. As stated by Lords Sumption and Neuberger:

> in the case of a straightforward damages clause, that interest will rarely extend beyond compensation for the breach . . . but compensation is not necessarily the only legitimate interest.

Thus, based on the new *Makdessi* test a court assessing the validity of an LD clause will: (i) identify the legitimate interest which the LD clause is designed to protect (which should not be merely punishing the contract-breaker) and take into account that compensation alone may not be the only legitimate interest that the employer may have in the performance of the contractor's primary obligation (i.e., a timely completion); (ii) assess whether the secondary obligation imposed on the breaching party (i.e., the payment of the LDs) is out of all proportion to legitimate interest of the non-breaching party in enforcing the primary obligation (i.e., completion within the completion date); and (iii) take into account that in the context of complex construction projects, the parties are usually experienced, sophisticated commercial companies, of equal bargaining power. Such parties are typically properly advised as to the meaning of the LDs provisions they agreed to include in their contract and were therefore able to assess in advance the relevant commercial implications in case of breach. Based on this, there is the strong initial presumption that they had understood and accepted the LD clause and the relevant consequences, including that the LDs may exceed what would be a genuine pre-estimate of the loss.

By applying the Makdessi test, LD clauses should not be deemed penal even in case they exceed the actual financial loss incurred by the employer, to the extent that the detriment imposed by the clause is not out of all proportion to the legitimate interest of having the works completed within the agreed completion date. The fact that a liquidated damages clause may result in the contract-breaker to pay more than a "*genuine pre-estimate of loss*" does not necessarily lead to that clause being construed as a penalty.

The Makdessi test was considered in various subsequent cases:

(i) In the case of *Unaoil Ltd v Leighton Offshore Pte Ltd*[19] the court found that an LD clause was a penalty as following a reduction of the contract price (from US$75 million to US$55 million) LDs of US$40 million had become extravagant and unconscionable.

17 E.g., a liquidated damages clause.
18 I.e., completion within the completion date.
19 *Unaoil Ltd v Leighton Offshore Pte Ltd* [2014] EWHC 2965 (Comm).

(ii) In *GPP Big Field LLP v Solar EPC Solutions SL (formerly Prosolia Siglio XXI)*[20] Solar EPC Solutions SL ("Solar") contended that the LD clauses contained in some contracts between the parties were to be construed as penalties as: (a) the daily rate of LDs accruing under each of the contracts was the same despite the contracts referring to different plants with differing energy outputs; (b) the LD clauses described the sum to be paid as a "penalty"; and (c) the LD clauses had not been negotiated in detail by the parties. The court applied the *Makdessi* test and rejected Solar's arguments. Although the LD clauses did not represent a precise calculation of the financial losses the employer may have suffered in case of breach, they were:

> not in any way extravagant or unconscionable in comparison with the legitimate interest of the [employer] in ensuring timely performance.[21]

Moreover, the court held that the use of the word "penalty" in the LD clauses was immaterial, while the substance of the clause was clear. The court also dismissed the argument that the LD clauses had not been properly negotiated considering that the parties were sophisticated and experienced commercial entities, with equal bargaining power.

(iii) The case of *Eco World Ballymore Embassy Gardens Company Ltd v Dobler UK Limited*[22] relates to the enforceability of a LD clause in construction contract entered into between Eco World Ballymore Embassy Gardens Company Ltd ("EWB") and Dobler UK Limited ("Dobler") relevant to an apartment development commissioned by a local authority to EWB. The contract did not provide for sectional completion, nor did it include a mechanism to reduce LD in case of late completion affecting only one section of the works. Instead, the contract provided only for LD to be paid if Dobler failed to complete the works by "*the relevant Date for Completion of . . . the Works*" (i.e., by practical completion). Therefore, in circumstances where Dobler had completed part of the works (which had been then taken over by EWB) in advance of practical completion but had failed to complete other parts of the work by the agreed completion date, EWB would be entitled to LD at the full rate set out in the contract (i.e., without considering the part of the work already taken over by EWB). For this reason, Dobler argued that the liquidated damages clause was penal and such, void and/or unenforceable. The court disagreed for the following reasons: (i) the LD clause was negotiated by the parties, who were assisted by external lawyers; (ii) late completion of any part of the works was likely to affect the work of the contractors which were to carry out finishing works and lead to delay which may risk exposing EWB to LD to be paid to the local authority which had commissioned the work and losing apartments purchasers; (iii) fixing in advance the rate of LD payable for late completion of the whole works had allowed the parties to avoid the difficulty of quantifying of the damages that would be suffered by EWB were only part of the works completed on time; (iv) the level of

20 *GPP Big Field LLP v Solar EPC Solutions SL (formerly Prosolia Siglio XXI)* [2018] EWHC 2866 (Comm).
21 *GPP Big Field LLP v Solar EPC Solutions SL (formerly Prosolia Siglio XXI)* [2018] EWHC 2866 (Comm) at [63].
22 *Eco World Ballymore Embassy Gardens Company Ltd v Dobler UK Limited* [2021] EWHC 2207 (TCC).

damages agreed in the contract was not unreasonable or disproportionate to the probable losses that EWB would suffer in case of late completion of any part of the works. For this reason, the judge concluded that the LD clause was not extravagant, exorbitant or unconscionable. It was instead a secondary obligation which, in line with the test in *Cavendish Square Holding v Makdessi*, imposed a detriment on Dobler which was proportionate to the legitimate interest of EWB in the enforcement of the primary obligation to complete the Works in accordance with the contract. The case shows that where the parties agree to one rate of LD for late completion of the whole of the works, contractors may become liable for the full amount of LD, even in case the employer has taken possession of parts of the works. Therefore, where the parties intend to allow the employer to take partial possession of the works in advance of practical completion, they should also include any mechanism in the contract for reducing the level of LD to reflect the early possession of the part of work taken over by the employer.

(iv) In the case of *Mansion Place Limited v Fox Industrial Services Limited*[23] Mansion Place Limited ("MPL"), a property developer, had contracted Fox Industrial Services Limited ("Fox") for an extension and refurbishment of student accommodation at Hockley Point in Nottingham, under an amended under a JCT Design and Build Contract 2016. When the works were delayed, MPL manifested its intention to levy LDs. Fox however argued that the LD clause was penal as: (a) there had been no bespoke assessment of loss; (b) there had been no bespoke negotiation in respect of the same; (c) the amount of LD did not reflect the actual loss which would be suffered by MPL, also considering that the contract did not provide for a mechanism to reduce the LD in case of partial possession of the work. The court disagreed with MPL and, having considered *Cavendish Square Holding v Makdessi*,[24] *Eco World-Ballymore Embassy Gardens v Dobler*[25] and *Triple Point Technology v PTT*,[26] determined that the LD clause was not a penalty clause because: (a) Fox was in a negotiating position which was sufficiently strong to obtain a variation in the LD clause, and had even achieved a revision to the drafting of the LD clause during the relevant negotiations; (b) the employer had a legitimate interest in applying LD as student accommodation needs to be ready in time for term. Therefore, the rate of LD was not "*wholly disproportionate*", as evidenced by the fact that it had been "*accepted by the Defendant at the outset as being appropriate*"; (c) the LD clause remained valid and enforceable as there was provision for calculating a proportionate reduction in LD partial possession of the work which, though cumbersome was still possible.

14.3.2.3 Liquidated damages and general (unliquidated) damages

LD clauses are not without drawbacks. As the parties will have to pre-estimate the employer's loss from the outset of the project (which, in case of large and complex projects usually means several years before those damages might become payable), the

23 *Mansion Place Limited v Fox Industrial Services Limited* [2021] EWHC 2972 (TCC).
24 *Cavendish Square Holding BV v Talal El Makdessi* [2015] UKSC 67.
25 *Eco World Ballymore Embassy Gardens Company Ltd v Dobler UK Limited* [2021] EWHC 2207 (TCC).
26 *Triple Point Technology Inc v PTT Public Company Ltd* [2021] UKSC 29.

resulting amount of agreed LDs may be much lower or higher than the actual losses caused by the breach due to changes in the circumstances of the project which may have occurred after its commencement. As LD are usually considered an exclusive remedy for delay, where the amount of LD is significantly less than the actual loss suffered by the employer, the latter will have no other ways to recover such losses. Conversely, in case the agreed LD exceed the actual employer's losses, the contractor will be unable to dispute such amount and will be bound to pay it, unless it can establish that the LD are penal. Therefore, although very uncommon, the parties may not include an LD clause in their construction contract, in which case, in case of contractor's culpable delay the employer will be entitled to recover its general damages, i.e., the damages which flow naturally from the delay and are not too "remote".[27]

It is worth noting that in case the parties are negotiating based on a standard form contract which includes an LD clause, but intend to exclude LDs, they should delete the clause altogether rather than simply insert "nil" as the rate of LD, as this could be construed as implying that also unliquidated damages will be nil and that the contractor will have no liability for delays.[28]

14.3.2.4 Liquidated damages clause

Considering the advantages for both contractors and employers, construction contracts for complex construction projects almost invariably include an LD clause setting out how to calculate LD damages that the contractor will have to pay in case of culpable delay beyond the contractual completion date (or any interim milestone to which liquidated damages are "attached"). A typical LD clause may include the following terms: (i) that the contractor will be liable to pay LD to the employer in case it fails to complete the works (or any part thereof) by the relevant completion date; (ii) the rate at which LD will be calculated; (iii) the parties' acknowledgment that the agreed rate represents a genuine pre-estimate of the employer's losses deriving from the contractor's failure to complete the works (or part thereof) by the agreed completion date(s); (iv) the parties' acknowledgment that LDs are necessary to protect the employer's legitimate business interest deriving from the contract and are proportionate to the loss likely to be suffered by the employer in case the works (or part thereof) are not completed by the agreed completion date(s); (v) the moment when the LD will commence accruing (i.e. the contractual completion date of the work and/or specific parts thereof); (vi) the LDs liability cap (usually around 10% of the contract price); (vii) the fact that LDs are the sole remedy for the case of culpable delay (with the exception, for example, of the employer's right to terminate the contract); (viii) an express declaration that the contractor will not contend that the LDs are in fact a penalty; (ix) whether the employer will be entitled to claim actual/general damages in case the liquidated damages mechanism fails.

The parties may also want to agree in the LD clauses what will happen to LDs already accrued in case the contract is terminated. The issue was recently decided by the Supreme Court in the case of *Triple Point Technology, Inc v PTT Public Company Ltd.*[29] *PTT Public Company Ltd* ("PTT") contracted Triple Point Technology, Inc ("Triple Point") to

27 *Hadley v Baxendale [1854] EWHC Exch J70.*
28 *Temloc v Errill Properties Limited* [1987] 39 BLR 30.
29 *Triple Point Technology, Inc v PTT Public Company Ltd* [2021] UKSC 29.

design, implement, support and maintain a new Commodities Trading and Risk Management business system for its integrated petrochemicals trading, hedging, charterparty and refinery management system for its operations in Bangkok, Dubai and Singapore. The scope of Triple Point was to be implemented in two phases. The contract provided that Triple Point be paid at the completion of defined milestones in respect of each phase and included an LD clause stating as follows:

> If CONTRACTOR fails to deliver work within the time specified and the delay has not been introduced by PTT, CONTRACTOR shall be liable to pay the penalty at the rate of 0.1% (zero point one percent) of undelivered work per day of delay from the due date for delivery up to the date PTT accepts such work, provided, however, that if undelivered work has to be used in combination with or as an essential component for the work already accepted by PTT, the penalty shall be calculated in full on the cost of the combination.

Triple Point soon fell behind schedule and only completed the first milestone of one phase of the works. When PTT refused to make interim payments to Triple Point, the latter suspended the works. As a result, PTT terminated the contract for repudiation, negligent breach and fundamental breach of contract. In the Technology and Construction Court, Triple Point claimed that the LDs clause was a penalty. The court disagreed and found Triple Point liable to pay LDs for works already completed. As Triple Point had only completed one milestone, it was not obliged to pay LDs in respect of the remaining milestones, even though, by the time the contract had been terminated, Triple Point had missed all the contractual milestone completion dates. In particular, the Court of Appeal distinguished three categories of LDs clauses: (i) those where LDs are due only after the works are completed, so that the employer loses entitlement to LDs in case the contract is terminated prior to completion of the contract works; (ii) those where LDs accrue from the contractual completion date to the earlier of actual completion or contract termination; and (iii) those where LDs accrue from the contractual completion date to actual completion of works, even in case the works are completed by a different contractor after and as a consequence of the termination of the original contract. The Court of Appeal conceded that the second category was the "orthodox" one, but added that, based on the Scottish case of *British Glanzstoff Manfacturing Co Ltd v General Accident, Fire and Life Assurance Co Ltd*,[30] the clause in question fell in the first category, where termination extinguishes the entitlement to LDs. The Supreme Court unanimously rejected the judgment of the Court of Appeal. Lady Arden JSC gave the following peremptory guidance on the effect of early termination on LDs:

> Parties must be taken to know the general law, namely that the accrual of liquidated damages comes to an end on termination of the contract (see Photo Production Ltd v Securicor Transport Ltd [1980] AC 827, 844 and 849). After that event, the parties' contract is at an end and the parties must seek damages for breach of contract under the general law. That is well-understood: see per Recorder Michael Harvey QC in Gibbs v Tomlinson (1992) 35 Con LR 86, p. 116. Parties do not have to provide specifically for the effect of the termination of their contract. They can take that consequence as read. . . . The territory is well-trodden, and the liquidated damages clause does not need to provide for it.

The judgment confirms that, unless the parties agree otherwise, LDs cease to accrue once the contract is terminated, and the terminating party may only seek general damages.

30 *British Glanzstoff Manfacturing Co Ltd v General Accident, Fire and Life Assurance Co Ltd* [1913] SC 1 (HL).

However, LDs already accrued before termination will survive termination.[31] Thus, where the parties intend to extend the right to recover LDs for delays occurred after termination or to deprive the employer of the right to levy LDs upon early termination, they should use clear wording to achieve that result.

14.3.2.5 Consequences of an invalid liquidated damages clause

In the case of *Buckingham Group v Peel L & P Investments and Property*[32] Peel L&P Investments and Property Ltd ("Peel") engaged Buckingham Group Contracting Ltd ("Buckingham") to design and build a corrugated cardboard manufacturing plant at Ellesmere Port. The contract between the parties was based on a JCT Design and Build Contract 2016 (with amendments). Due to a significant delay to the completion of the project, Peel notified Buckingham of its intention to deduct liquidated damages for £1,928,253.77, which was equal to the contractual cap on liquidated damages. Buckingham contended that: (i) the liquidated damages mechanism was void for uncertainty and/or unenforceable as there was inconsistency between the Contract Particulars, which identified 1 October 2018 as the "Date for Completion", and Schedule 10, which indicated 30 November 2018 as the "Milestone Date" for "Practical Completion"; and (ii) in case the liquidated damages were not to apply, any general damages would be capped at the same amount of the liquidated damages cap (i.e., £1,928,253.77). In doing so, Buckingham relied on *Eco World Ballymore Embassy Gardens Company Ltd v Dobler UK Limited*[33] where O'Farrell J had taken the position that a liquidated damages provision "*may on true construction be found to operate as a limitation of liability provision*". On the first issue, Mr Alexander Nissen KC, sitting as a Deputy High Court Judge, held that the liquidated damages mechanism was enforceable and that liquidated damages had to be calculated by reference to the date of 30 November 2018. On the second issue (which, considering the decision on the first issue, had become not necessary for the court to consider), the judge distinguished *Eco World* and held that, on true construction, the clause could not be construed as imposing a separate limitation of liability on general damages.

Considering the conflicting judgments on the point, the parties could either expressly exclude general damages for cases of delay or endeavour to expressly state in the contract whether their intention is that a cap on liquidated damages shall also impose a cap to general damages in the event that the liquidated damages mechanism is subsequently found to be unenforceable.

31 As per *Photo Production Ltd v Securicor Transport Ltd* [1980] AC 827.

32 *Buckingham Group v Peel L & P Investments and Property* [2022] EWHC 1842 (TCC).

33 *Eco World Ballymore Embassy Gardens Company Ltd v Dobler UK Limited* [2021] EWHC 2207 (TCC).

CHAPTER 15

Suspension

15.1 Suspension in general

Unless the contract provides otherwise, neither the contractor nor the employer is entitled under a construction contract to suspend the works without a legitimate cause,[1] even in case the parties are in dispute. Nor a right to suspend the works will normally be implied in the contract. For this reason, construction contracts typically include a clause allowing employers (but not also contractors) to suspend the works "at will". This right may serve a number of the employer's needs such as allowing it to reduce costs while reassessing the opportunity of the project before a termination for convenience.

15.2 Suspension clause

A suspension clause entitling the employer to suspend the works will typically state as follows: (i) the employer is entitled to instruct the contractor to suspend part or all of the works by giving notice; (ii) where the contractor suffers delay and/or incurs cost as a consequence the suspension, the contractor will be entitled to an EOT and a payment of such extra costs, unless the suspension arises from a contractor's breach; (iii) unless instructed by the employer, the contractor is required to remain at site and place on stand-by any equipment as such vessels, machinery, etc. (the parties will normally agree on suspension rates to be applied during the suspension period); (iv) as soon as the suspension ceases, the contractor shall resume the works on the basis of the new programme (which will reflect the rescheduling of the work due to the suspension); (v) where the suspension continues for more than a certain number of days (depending on the project and the parties' agreement), the contractor will be entitled to terminate the contract for prolonged suspension.

1 E.g., for safety reasons, such as where the contractor is requested to perform dangerous activities to persons or properties. See *Plant Construction plc v Clive Adams Associates* [2000] BLR 205 at [209].

DOI: 10.4324/9781003387718-19

CHAPTER 16

Variations

16.1 Variations in general

In the case of construction contracts, variations are alterations to the original amount or scope of the works. The subject of a variation may be, for example, a change to quantities or quality of the works/materials, aesthetic changes, changes as to where some works shall be done or some materials shall be positioned, changes in dimensions, changes to the sequence, timing or method by which the works are to be performed, and omissions of a part of the works (so-called negative variations).

Large and complex construction projects will invariably require variations. The need to variate the works may arise for several reasons. For example: (i) the employer's desire to enhance or improve the project (e.g., the employer may want to increase the project's output or improve its quality or aesthetics); (ii) a supervening event which is outside the parties' control (e.g., archaeological findings or unforeseen site conditions which lead to a change in the location of certain works or the method by which the works are to be performed); (iii) a contractor's negligent act in executing the works which prevents the project from being buildable as originally planned and/or delayed completion; (iv) inconsistencies or errors in the design which make the project impossible to be built as it was initially conceived; (v) the employer's desire to reduce costs by reducing the amount of works or the relevant quality standards.

In general, only "extra work" exceeding the contractor's original obligations under the contract (i.e., work which is not already included in the original scope of work) may constitute a variation entitling the contractor to receive extra consideration. However, the parties have complete freedom as to how to regulate the matter. For example, they may agree that the contractor will be paid regardless of which of them is responsible for the variation or that the fixed price will stand even in case the need to variate the works is attributable to the employer's responsibility or desire, although both such provisions would be unusual.

Variations are one of the main sources of disputes in construction projects as very often the parties disagree on whether an instruction given by the employer falls within the original scope of work or imposes additional obligations on the contractor and is thus a variation order. Keeping the variation on hold while waiting for the dispute being resolved through one of the contractual means of dispute resolution may generate delays and ultimately lead to irreparable consequences for the project. For this reason, variation clauses in construction contracts normally give the employer a unilateral right to instruct variations upon which the contractor will be obliged to act (subject to a number

DOI: 10.4324/9781003387718-20

of exceptions listed in the clause) and set out the procedure whereby the variation will be ordered and the monetary consequences.

16.2 Variations clause

A typical variation clause may include the following terms.

16.2.1 Definition of variation

A definition of variation may either be found in the "definitions" clause or in the variation clause. A good definition of what may constitute a variation under the contract is essential to avoid uncertainties as any disputes on whether a change falls within the scope of the clause will be solved by looking at the variation clause in question and determine, depending on what the variation clause covers, whether the extra or altered work falls within it or not.[1]

The scope of the definition is expressly to set out the limits to which the employer's right to vary the contract shall be subjected. For example, the parties may include the following language:

(i) A definition of the scope of variations by listing what can constitute a variation under the contract (e.g., only changes to quantities, quality, sequence, etc.) and the indication of whether the list is exhaustive.

(ii) The exclusion or limitation of the employer's right to "descope" part of the original scope of work assigned to the contractor to have it performed by a third-party contractor (or by the employer).

(iii) A clarification that for an instruction to be considered a variation under the contract it shall be in writing. In this way the parties will avoid the uncertainty of oral variations and prevent disputes that may arise out of misunderstandings on the instructions.

(iv) A limit on the overall amount of the variations both in terms of scope and impact that the variations will have on the agreed completion date. This term may be particularly important for contractors in cases in which, for example, variations may heavily affect the project's completion so affecting other commitments that the contractor may have taken on a different project. Where the parties will not agree on a limit to the scope and number of variations, the contractor will not be typically entitled to consider the contract frustrated due to the large number of variations instructed by the employer.[2]

(v) The exclusion on the contractor's right to make variations of the works unless instructed by the employer. However, a variation clause will normally give the contractor a right to submit written proposals to the employer where the

1 *Supablast (Nationwide) Ltd. v Story Rail Ltd.* [2010] EWHC 56 (TCC) at [3].

2 In *McAlpine Humberoak Ltd v McDermott International Inc (No. 1)* [1992] 58 BLR 1 at 18, Lloyd LJ, rejecting the contractor's frustration claim, stated that the variations in question "*did not 'transform' the contract into a different contract, or 'distort its substance and identity'. It remained a contract for the construction of four pallets*".

contractor believes that such changes may reduce construction costs, accelerate the project's completion or lead to any other benefit for the employer. Where the employer is favourable to the proposal, this may be treated as it was a variation instructed by the employer. The clause may also expressly state how to treat any cost saving, for example whether they should be shared between the parties in equal shares or be for the sole benefit of the employer. Affording the contractor part of the savings will generate a double reward for the contractor (i.e., the additional costs for the variated works plus any resulting percentage of savings). This has the obvious rationale of encouraging the contractor to apply its expertise and skill to the benefit of the project.

(vi) A longstop date limiting the point in time when the employer may instruct further variations. This will typically be the practical completion or takeover of the works. From that moment, the contractor shall not be obliged to act upon the employer's instructions and any additional works will be agreed in a separate contract.

(vii) A provision stating that for the contractor to be obliged to act upon an instruction the employer shall provide some form of security.[3] This would not be a common term in a complex construction contract. However, it may be useful to address any concerns that contractors may have on the employer's financial strength and its capacity to pay for the variation.

(viii) A provision establishing whether a variation may only concern the amount and type of work to be performed or also the method in which the varied works shall be carried out. Obviously, this term may have an impact on the liability of the parties for losses deriving from the performance of the variation. As contractors will normally be better positioned to decide on the best way to achieve a certain result, unless employers have specific construction expertise (on or have engaged a third party capable to opine on construction methods), they should refrain from adding such a qualification.

16.2.2 Employer's right to vary

The employer does not have an implied power to vary the terms of the contract or the relevant works.[4] As stated by Waller LJ in *SWI Ltd v P&I Data Services Ltd*:[5]

> without some term allowing for variations under a fixed price contract to perform works, the paying party is not entitled to vary the contract.

To avoid the impasse of having to agree on each and any variation, construction contracts will typically afford the employer a right to unilaterally vary the works without having to seek the contractor's consent. This will usually be achieved through so-called variation

3 *Curzon Interiors Ltd v Richmond Terrace (Brighton) Ltd* [2004] EWHC 410 (TCC).

4 S. Furst, V. Ramsey, *Keating on Construction Contracts* (10th edition) Sweet & Maxwell, 2017, at para 4–061.

5 *SWI Ltd v P&I Data Services Ltd* [2007] EWCA Civ 663; [2007] BLR 430.

instructions or variation orders. As stated by Lord Blackburn in *Tharsis Sulphur and Copper Company v McElroy & Sons*:[6]

> it is common enough to have provisions . . . saying that no extra work shall be paid for unless it is ordered in writing by the [contract administrator]; and if such conditions are properly made, and there is nothing fraudulent or iniquitous in the way they are carried out, those conditions would be quite sufficient and effectual.

The nature and extent of an employer's right to vary the work will be set out in the variation clause, subject to some general constraints. For example:

(i) Only real "extra works" which are not already included in the contractor's scope of work can constitute a variation. Under English law, it is a well-established principle that where a contractor agrees to complete a certain scope of work for a lump sum price, the courts will infer a promise on its part to provide everything "indispensably necessary" to complete the project.[7] It follows that an employer's instruction to carry out work which is not expressly included in the contract's scope of work but is "indispensably necessary" to complete the project, will not constitute a variation.[8]

(ii) An instruction should align with the type of work contemplated in the contract. In *Thorn v London Corporation*[9] Lord Cairns held that an instruction for a variation which was "*so peculiar, so unexpected, so different from what any person reckoned or calculated upon that it is not in the contract at all*" entitled the contractor to either refuse to do the work or ask for a new price on a quantum meruit basis reflecting the true value of the works. This approach was confirmed in *Blue Circle Industries plc v Holland Dredging Co Ltd*[10] where the court held that the instructed changes must have some connection with the works under the contract. Where this is not the case, the varied work shall be the subject of a new contract and not a variation under the original contract. The problem for the parties will be then to ensure that the scope of the contract and the variation clause are sufficiently clear so that there will be no uncertainty as to whether a variation goes beyond what the parties agreed the contractor may be instructed to do. This might be an easier task in the case of a subcontract as the parties may take the position that the subcontractor may not be obliged to do anything which is beyond the main contract's scope. This position was confirmed in *Costain Civil Engineering Ltd v Zanen Dredging and Contracting Company Ltd*[11] where the court held that:

> The variations clause of a sub-contract cannot oblige the sub-contractor to carry out works which are not part of the . . . obligations under the main contract. The obligations of the sub-contract are fixed to the obligations of the main contract. The

6 *Tharsis Sulphur and Copper Company v McElroy & Sons* [1878] 3 App Cas 1040 at [1050].
7 *Sharpe v San Paulo Railway* [1873] L R 8 Ch App 597. See also *Williams v Fitzmaurice* [1858] 3 H.
8 *Williams v Fitzmaurice* (1858) 3 H&N 833 [157 ER 709].
9 *Thorn v London Corporation* [1876] 1 AC 120.
10 *Blue Circle Industries plc v Holland Dredging Co Ltd* [1987] 37 BLR 40.
11 *Costain Civil Engineering Ltd and another v Zanen Dredging and Contracting Company Ltd* [1996] 85 BLR 77.

sub-contractor has rights and obligations dependent on the main contract and valuations under the main contract and rights to benefit received under the main contract.

(iii) Where an instruction is not formally issued in accordance with the contract but is provided in a draft form, it will not amount to a variation unless the contractor acts upon it. In *Obrascon Huarte Lain, v H.M. Attorney General for Gibraltar*[12] the engineer issued a document titled "*draft fill guidelines*" guiding the contractor on how to carry out certain works, including how to remove contaminated material from site. The contractor did not follow the engineer's guidelines, but rather opted for another accepted method. The Court of Appeal held that:

> the issue of the draft fill guidelines did not constitute a variation instruction.

(iv) Where the contract states that a variation shall be in writing, the contractor will not be obliged to act upon it in case this requirement is not complied with. When clear words are used, the requirement that the instruction shall be in writing will be treated by the court as a condition precedent to the payment.[13] This was confirmed in *Amec Mining Ltd v The Scottish Coal Company Ltd*[14] where it was held that:

> An 'Instruction' is defined . . . as something given in writing. . . . The reason for these terms is clear. It is to define the precise circumstances in which the contractor may or may not be paid for additional work. It gives to the employer a power to instruct additional work and, if that power is exercised in terms of the contract by written 'Instruction', the contractor will come under an obligation to carry out that work but will have a corresponding right to payment for it. . . . Under and in terms of the contract, if there is no formal 'Instruction', there is no obligation on the part of the contractor to carry out any additional work but conversely there is no right to payment if he chooses to do such work.

The meaning of "in writing" will also depend on any formalities agreed in the contract. For example, in the case of *Myers v Sarl*[15] where the contract entitled the architect to issue variations "*in writing under his hand*", unsigned drawings issued by the architect's office were not considered to be sufficient to meet the contractual "*in writing under his hand*" requirement.

(v) In the absence of a clear language to the contrary, where an instruction is issued after the relevant agreed cut-off date has passed, the contractor will not be obliged to act upon it unless the parties enter into a new agreement. This was confirmed in the case of *TFW Printers Ltd v Interserve Project Services Ltd*,[16] where the court, mentioning *Keating on Building Contracts*, stated that:

> I would accept as correct the statement in Keating on Building Contracts (7th edition) para. 18–142. It is there submitted that the architect cannot issue instructions requiring a variation after practical completion, so that if thereafter the employer wishes them to be executed, they should be the subject of a separate agreement.

12 *Obrascon Huarte Lain, v H.M. Attorney General for Gibraltar* [2015] EWCA CIV 712.
13 *Kitsons Sheet Metal Ltd v Matthew Hall Mechanical & Electrical Engineers Ltd* [1989] 47 BLR 82.
14 *Amec Mining Ltd v The Scottish Coal Company Ltd* [2003] ScotCS 223.
15 *Myers v Sarl* [1860] 3 E & E 306.
16 *TFW Printers Ltd v Interserve Project Services Ltd* [2006] EWCA Civ 875.

(vi) For an employer to be entitled to instruct the contractor to omit part of the work under a lump sum contract, the variation clause shall expressly allow negative variations. In *SWI Ltd v P&I Data Services Ltd*[17] it was stated that:

> Normally without some term allowing for variations under a fixed price contract to perform works, the paying party is not entitled to vary the contract by reducing the work to be done; the builder would have a right to say that he had quoted a fixed price to do certain work and he was prepared to carry out all that work in order to receive his payment. If, of course, the paying party simply waives his right to have the complete works performed the builder will be entitled to his full price for what he has done, and . . . would not be in breach of contract for not performing.

The courts will usually construe provisions allowing negative variations carefully as such clauses may result in the contractor being deprived of the opportunity to realise its profit. The subject was considered in the case of *Abbey Developments v PP Brickwork*[18] where the court stated that provisions allowing the employer to omit part of the works had to be construed:

> so as not to deprive the contractor of its contractual right to the opportunity to complete the works and realise such profit as may then be made. . . . The basic bargain struck between the employer and the contractor has to be honoured, and an employer who finds that it has entered into what he might regard as a bad bargain is not allowed to escape from it by the use of the omissions clause so as to enable it then to try and get a better bargain by having the work done by somebody else at a lower cost once the contractor is out of the way . . . the purpose of a variations clause is to enable the employer to alter the scope of the works to meet its requirements. As a project proceeds it may become clear that some change of mind is needed to attain the result now desired. That might be . . . for some other reasons such as lack of money. The test must therefore be whether the variations clause is or is not wide enough to permit the change that was made. If, with the advantage of hindsight, it turns out that the variation was not ordered for a purpose for which the power to vary was intended then there will be a breach of contract.

The judgment confirms that any instruction whereby the employer descopes part of the works with an aim of assigning it to third parties is only valid if the variation clause upon which the employer is acting clearly allows negative variations. Where the contract does not clearly give the employer a right to descope and reassign part of the work, the courts will construe the clause carefully, so as not to deprive the contractor of its right to complete the work and realise the expected profit. This was confirmed in the recent case of *Van Oord UK Ltd v Dragados UK Ltd.*[19] Van Oord UK ("Van Oord") was subcontractor of Dragados UK ("Dragados"), which was the main contractor, in a project for the design, management and construction of the Aberdeen Harbour Expansion. Clause 14.3 of the contract (which incorporated the standard form NEC3 subcontract conditions) stated that "*The Contractor may give an instruction to the*

17 *SWI Ltd v P&I Data Services Ltd* [2007] EWCA Civ 663; [2007] BLR 430 at [18].

18 *Abbey Developments v PP Brickwork* [2003] CILL 2033, TCC. See also *Trustees of the Stratfield Saye Estate v AHL Construction Ltd* [2004] EWHC 3286 and *Multiplex Constructions (UK) Ltd v Cleveland Bridge UK Ltd & Anor* [2008] EWHC 2220.

19 *Van Oord UK Ltd v Dragados UK Ltd* [2020] CSOH 87.

Subcontractor which changes the Subcontract Works Information or a Key Date. The Contractor may, in the event that a corresponding instruction is issued by the Project Manager under clause 14.3 of the Main Contract only, also give an instruction to omit (a) any Provisional Sum and/or (b) any other work, even if it is intended that such work will be executed by Others. The Subcontractor has no claim for loss of revenue, loss of opportunity, loss of any contract, loss of profit or for any indirect loss or damage against the Contractor in relation thereto". A dispute arose on whether Dragados' instructions omitting part of the works had resulted in a breach of contract. Lord Tyre, having considered the decision in *Abbey* held that Clause 14.3 did not afford Dragados a "*clear contractual entitlement*" to omit work from Van Oord and assign them to other third-party contractors. As a result, the instruction was in breach of contract.

The test of the "*basic bargain*" established in *Abbey* was also used in *Stratfield Saye Estate Trustees v AHL Construction Lt*[20] to assess whether an omission of an amount of work is so great as to "*detract from or change this fundamental characteristic of the works*" so amounting to an effective termination of the project.

In the light of the preceding, where the parties wish to give the employer a right to omit work, clarity of drafting is pivotal. Where they intend to allow descoping and reassignment to other contractors, the parties shall also agree and state in the contract a clear mechanism for valuing the value of the omitted work. This will usually mean that the employer will not pay the portion of contract price relevant to the descoped works but will compensate the contractor for any costs already incurred prior to the descoping (including overheads). The recoverability of any loss of profit for the contractor on the omitted work may be controversial and should therefore be addressed in the contractual mechanism for valuing omitted works.

(vii) Where the contract provides for a condition to be satisfied before the contractor will be bound to act upon an instruction, the contractor may withhold any action until such condition is met. For example, where the parties have agreed that no variation may be ordered unless and until the employer has given some form of payment security to the contractor (e.g., in the form of an advance payment, a bank guarantee or a payment into an escrow account), the contractor is entitled to refuse to undertake the variation and is relieved of the obligation to comply with the instruction until the employer will be able to discharge its payment obligation.[21]

(viii) Where an instruction does not vary the type or amount of work but the methodology or procedure that the contractor shall follow in carrying out the works, a court will typically look at the variation clause to assess whether such instruction may constitute a variation under the clause. For example, in case the contract gives the contractor two methods for carrying out the work between which the contractor is free to choose, an instruction limiting the contractor's choice to only one of such methods would typically constitute a compensable variation as it

20 *Stratfield Saye Estate Trustees v AHL Construction Lt* [2004] EWHC 3286 (TCC).
21 *Curzon Interiors Ltd v Richmond Terrace (Brighton) Ltd* [2004] EWHC 410 (TCC).

would result in a reduction of the contract's options. In *English Industrial Estates Corporation v Kier Construction Ltd*[22] the contract regulated how the contractor may procure filling material by giving it the option of either crushing hard materials resulting from the excavation and demolition works or importing suitable filling material. When the engineer instructed the contractor to use the first method, the instruction was held to be a variation as it had limited the contractor's contractual right to freely choose between the two methods. This approach was also confirmed in *Strachan & Henshaw Ltd v Stein Industrie (UK) Ltd and GEC Alstom Ltd.*[23] The contract between the parties defined: (i) the "*Works*" as "*all plant to be provided and work to be done by the Contractor under the Contract*"; (ii) the "*Plant*" as "*machinery, computer hardware and software, apparatus, materials, articles and things of all kinds to be provided under the Contract other than Contractor's Equipment*"; and (iii) "*Variations*" as "*any alteration of the Works whether by way of addition, modification or omission*". The employer instructed to move the location of the facilities a mile away from where they were supposed to be located. This altered how the workforce would reach the workplace. The court held that such instruction was not a variation as:

> the 'work to be done by the Contractor under the Contract' means simply what it says and should not be distorted so as to encompass the arrangements made by the contractor to bring its workforce to the workplace.

(ix) Although variation clauses will typically entitle contractors to change the works unilaterally, they will allow them to suggest variations to the agreed scope of work where the change is needed or desirable (e.g., for costs saving purposes). Employers shall agree with the contractor's suggestion and expressly promise to pay for any additional costs resulting from the changed works as a mere acknowledgment will not normally give rise to a compensable variation. In *Tharsis Sulphur and Copper Company v McElroy & Son*[24] a dispute arose on whether the employer having "*allowed*" the contractor to alter the scope of work by issuing monthly valuation certificates which considered the change (thicker iron girders) could amount to written variation orders under the contract and allow the contractor to the resulting extra compensation. The position of the parties was summarised by Lord Blackburn as follows: (i) while the contractor had made clear that they could not do the work as they had promised to do it unless the employer/engineer permitted them to make the change; (ii) the engineer/employer's position was that they did not object to the change if the work cannot be made as originally envisaged. This however did not imply any promise of additional payment for the change, nor the position of the engineer/employer could be considered an order to change the works. Lord Cairns held that:

> An 'order' would mean an order by the company to the contractors to execute the work in the altered form. But the position of things was perfectly different, it was

22 *English Industrial Estates Corporation v Kier Construction Ltd* [1991] 56 BLR 98.
23 *Strachan & Henshaw Ltd v Stein Industrie* (UK) Ltd and GEC Alstom Ltd [1997] EWCA Civ 2940.
24 *Tharsis Sulphur and Copper Company v McElroy & Son* [1878] 3 App Cas 1040.

> the contractors who were suggesting to the appellants, if they were not requesting them, that the girders should be of a thicker form.

(x) In some cases, the work may be "deemed" varied, even without a formal instruction from the employer, as the parties had agreed in advance that the occurrence of a certain event (e.g., a statutory change affecting the works) would be treated as an instruction of variation. As a result of a deemed variation, the contractor will have a right (and an obligation) to act upon the occurrence of the event and will be entitled to claim any extra costs and any extension of time (if so agreed) resulting from its obligation to carry out the varied works.

16.2.3 Contractor's right to object to a variation

The contractor may not usually refuse to act upon the employer's instruction unless the contractor can show that compliance with the instruction would, for example: (i) be illegal under any applicable laws or violate any permits relevant to the project; (ii) be impossible (e.g., because the timeframe instructed by the employer is impossible to achieve in the circumstances); (iii) force the contractor to breach any of its obligations under the contract (e.g., those relevant to safety of the works).

Typically, the variation clause will state that the contractor may exercise this right within a specific timeframe (typically a certain number of days) by giving notice to the employer. The contract will usually state that, with its notice, the contractor shall: (i) express its inability to perform the variation; (ii) explain the relevant reasons and possibly provide evidence; (iii) make proposals on how the variation may be performed in a viable way. In case the employer agrees with the content of the contractor's notice, it will cancel or modify the instruction so to adapt it to the contractor's recommendations. Where, instead, the employer considers that the contractor explanation and/or evidence are incorrect, and that the variation is achievable as instructed, it may confirm it and expressly request that the contractor acts upon it. Any disagreement will then be solved through the dispute resolution method agreed in the contract.

16.2.4 Variations due to contractor's failure

A variation clause will usually state that the contractor shall not be entitled to receive any additional payment or extension of time in case the variation became required as a result of a contractual breach or other failure by the contractor. This is based on the obvious principle that a party may not benefit from its own wrongdoing.

16.2.5 Variations due to faulty design

The parties may also choose to expressly agree on whether or not a faulty design leading to a change in the works will entitle the contractor to extra money and/or extra time. Typically, employers may want to exclude any right of the contractor to claim extensions of time or costs due to faulty design. Exclusions are normally agreed with regard to any information on which the contractor is entitled to rely in the tender and construction phases. Conversely, contractors may insist on their entitlement to additional money and time in cases where changes become necessary due to flaws in the design (unless the design was prepared by the same contractor).

16.2.6 Variation procedure

A typical procedure to issue variations includes the following steps: (i) the employer instructs a variation (or requests a proposal from the contractor); (ii) the contractor shall then respond to the instruction (or request for proposal) as soon as practicable (and in any case not later than a certain agreed timeframe, e.g., 30 days); (iii) the contractor's response will describe: (a) the extra works necessary to achieve the instructed variation; (b) any information on how the change will affect the programme and the time for completion; and (c) the extra costs necessary to perform the variation and how this will affect the initial contract price. However, in cases where the contractor is entitled to reject the instruction (e.g., because it is impossible to achieve), the contractor will inform the employer accordingly; (iv) the employer shall then, as soon as practicable (and in any case not later than a certain agreed timeframe, e.g., 30 days), approve, reject or provide any comments to arguments set out in the contractor's response.

16.2.7 Valuation of variations

The variation clause will usually state that once a variation is instructed (or approved if it was the result of a suggestion from the contractor), the parties will consult with an aim to agreeing on the amount due to the contractor for the implementation of the varied works. The parties will usually valuate variation using pre-agreed variation rates included in the bill of quantities attached to the contract. Where the contract does not include any no pre-agreed rates for the type of works that are the subject of the specific variation, the parties may either use the contractual rates provided in the contract for works of similar nature and in similar conditions (e.g., rates relevant to works carried out in a cold winter may not be applicable to similar works to be carried out in a mild weather). Where there are no rates applicable to the specific case, the parties shall then try to agree on a fair valuation of the varied work. If the parties are unable to reach an agreement, the contractor will usually be compelled to carry out the works based on the fair valuation unilaterally made by the employer. The issue may then become contentious and be solved through the dispute resolution mechanism agreed in the contract.

CHAPTER 17

Taking over

17.1 Taking over in general

Taking over marks the moment when the employer takes possession of the project, the work and the site, and becomes solely liable for the relevant care. Employers will normally take over the works after having performed the necessary quality tests aimed at certifying that the work is compliant with the contract.

For this reason, construction contracts will typically include a provision stating that once the contractor has completed the works, it shall notify the employer so that the latter may carry out those inspections and tests necessary to assess that the works comply with the contractual specifications.

The type of tests, the relevant procedures and the expected outcomes will depend on the type of project and will usually be agreed in the contract.

Where the expected outcome is in accordance with the contractual provisions, the employer shall issue a taking over certificate ("TOC") evidencing that the works are completed. The TOC may indicate some minor works to be executed (so-called punch lists) which, however, do not affect the overall completion of the works. The TOC will include a takeover date, which is the date on which the employer may start using the works.

Where the employer is not satisfied with the tests' results, the contract will usually set out a procedure to be followed to achieve completion. This may include re-performing the tests or the employer indicating the works which it deems not having been performed or the defects to be remedied before the completion certificate will be issued.

Disagreements and disputes in this phase are common. Employers may be concerned that releasing a completion certificate will reduce their leverage to have the works fully completed. Contractors, on the other hand, are keen to receive final payments and to demobilise workforce to take on different projects. Disputes usually focus on whether the works are substantially complete and the project suitable for taking over. Unless the parties have agreed otherwise, the assessment will be made, in the first instance, by the employer or the certifier, if so agreed. The parameters used for the assessment are not always clear and, unless the parties have agreed otherwise, the decision will be based on the meaning of practical completion (as takeover normally occurs after the project's practical completion). The parties may not be in agreement on whether or not outstanding work or defects are trifling, or they are such that the works cannot be considered as practically completed. As this may be a grey area, the parties may want to attempt to agree on how to evaluate the importance of outstanding works or defects. In the absence of a clear and express qualification, a dispute on whether outstanding works or defects are

DOI: 10.4324/9781003387718-21

to be considered "minor" or "trifling" will be decided by the adjudicator or the tribunal or the courts based on the relevant facts. In case defects will be held trifling, practical completion and takeover will be allowed to take place.[1]

17.2 Taking over clause

As mentioned, once the works are completed, they will typically be tested. The tests will take place in accordance with the contract, so it is crucial that the parties agree the relevant procedures, attendees and parameters. If the tests are successful, the project will be taken over by the employer.

Thus, a typical taking over clause will state that after completion and successful testing of the works (except for any agreed punch lists still outstanding), the contractor may apply for a TOC. The contract will typically provide for a specific format that the contractor shall use for such notice. As soon as the employer receives the contractor's application, it will make its own assessment of the works to determine if they were completed in accordance with the contract. Following such assessment, the employer may: (i) issue the TOC if it finds that the works are completed in compliance with the contract. This will entitle the employer to use the works and the contractor to be paid for them; (ii) consider the works incomplete and reject the contractor's application. In this case, the employer will specify the relevant reasons and set out what works the contractor shall carry out before a TOC may be issued. The contractor then has the option to either challenge the employer's decision or to follow the employer's instructions and re-apply for a TOC; (iii) take over only part of the works, to the extent the contract gives it such right (or the parties so agree); (iv) neither issue the TOC nor reject the contractor's application within the contractual timeframe without a justification, in which case the contractor may be entitled to an extension of time depending on the circumstances and the language of the contract.

1 *Mears Ltd v Costplan Services (South East) Ltd & Ors* [2019] EWCA Civ 502.

CHAPTER 18

Defects

18.1 Defects in general

There is no agreed definition of "defect" under English law. In *Hudson's Building and Engineering Contracts*[1] defective work is described as:

> work which fails to comply with the express descriptions or requirements of the contract, including very importantly any drawings or specifications, together with any implied terms as to its quality, workmanship, performance or design.

The courts have given some guidance on what defects are in the context of employer liability. For example: (i) in *Tate v Latham & Son*[2] a defect was defined as "*lack or absence of something essential to completeness*"; while (ii) in *Yarmouth v France*[3] a defect in a plat was defined as including "*anything which renders the plant, etc unfit for the use for which it is intended, when used in a reasonable way and with reasonable care*".

What ultimately constitutes a defect will depend on: (i) the standards agreed in the contract, e.g., any fitness for purpose obligation or any quality level expected for the materials, goods and workmanship (e.g., that works will be completed in a "*proper and workmanlike manner*") so that works will be considered defective in case they fall short of such standards; (ii) the contractual definition of "completion". In this regard, it is generally accepted that completion in the case of complex projects is to be intended as practical completion, as it could not be reasonably expected that the works would be completely free from defects to the extent such defects would not prevent the employer from taking over and using of the project.

18.2 Defects clause

The parties to a construction contract will typically include an express clause covering the subject of defective works. Absent such clause, under English law a contractor will neither be entitled nor obliged to return to site and rectify the defect but may agree to do so upon payment of a price.

1 I.N. Duncan Wallace QC, *Hudson's Building and Engineering Contracts* (11th edition) Sweet & Maxwell, 1994, at p. 698.

2 *Tate v Latham & Son* [1876] 1 QB 502.

3 *Yarmouth v France* [1887] LR 19 QBD 647.

DOI: 10.4324/9781003387718-22

Defects provisions are beneficial of both parties. In *BHP Petroleum Ltd v British Steel plc*,[4] May LJ stated that defects liability clauses:

> may be seen as benefiting both parties. The employer is entitled to have the defects rectified without having to engage or pay another contractor to carry out the rectification: the contractor or supplier is entitled to carry out the rectification himself which may normally be expected to be less expensive for him than having to reimburse the cost to the employer of having it done by others. Without a clause of this kind, the contractor or supplier would normally have no right to do work after completion, although an employer faced with defects after completion would need to mitigate his loss, if he wished to claim damages, and mitigation would often lead to inviting the contractor or supplier to do the work.

A typical defects clause may include the following.

18.2.1 The definition of "defects"

As the word "defect" does not have a recognised meaning under English law, the parties to a construction contract usually expressly define it in their contract. A defect may be identified as a wear or a failure of the work or any part thereof. However, not all wears or failures will amount to actionable defects under the contract and the parties will normally include a specific threshold beyond which a wear or a failure may entitle the employer to request the defect being remedied. Considering the difficulty in identifying a precise threshold, the parties may use the language "*fair*", so that only wears and tears beyond what is usually considered "*fair*" may trigger a so-called make good obligation on the contractor.

18.2.2 The employer's right to inspect the work

The contract will normally give the employer (or the engineer) a right to inspect the works throughout the project with an aim of allowing it to timely detect any defects and ask the contractor to remedy them. The contractor is usually entitled to attend to such inspections and review the written report resulting from it.

18.2.3 The defects liability period

Upon the employer taking over the works, the so-called defect liability period will start running. This is that period of time between practical completion and final completion during which the employer is no longer entitled to instruct variations but has a right to request the contractor to remedy any defects at the contractor's risk and cost. If defects are detected during this period, the employer will send the contractor a notice to correct in accordance with the contract. The contractor will then be obliged to remedy such defects within a specific timeframe agreed in the contract or, if no timeframe is expressly agreed, within a reasonable time. Any rectification costs will be borne by the contractor.

4 *BHP Petroleum Ltd v British Steel plc* (2001) 74 Con LR 63 (CA).

18.2.4 The contractor's obligation (and right) to remedy the defects

A defects clause will usually state that the contractor has an obligation to remedy, at its own cost and risk and within a reasonable time, the defects which are within its responsibility, provided that such defects were notified by the employer on or before the expiry of the defects liability period.

However, as mentioned, the contractor will not usually be obliged to remedy "any defects", as the clause will usually except "*fair wear and tear excepted*". This language is typically used in the context of landlord/tenant relation and requires the tenant to return the property in the same state it was at the time it was let except for "*fair wear and tear*" resulting from ordinary use of the premises by the tenant and the passage of time.

It is worth noting that the contractor has not only an obligation but also a right to rectify defects attributable to it, so that in case the employer denies the contractor such right and has the defect remedied by a third party, this would amount to a failure to mitigate a loss.[5] In *London and SW Railway v Flower*[6] it was stated:

> it would seem to be contrary to natural justice to hold that the plaintiffs can, without giving the defendants notice of the duty which is sought to be cast upon them, take upon themselves to perform that duty for the defendants and charge them with the expense.

The contractor shall then be notified about the defect and given the possibility to rectify. This approach was confirmed in *AMEC Foster Wheeler Group Ltd v Morgan Sindall Professional Services Ltd & Anor*[7] where the court stated that:

> It is clear from the wording of this part of the clause [providing for a contractor's obligation to remedy] that there can be no liability on [the contractor] in connection with defects unless it was made aware of those defects. In the absence of knowledge of the defects, no liability can arise under this limb of the clause.

As a consequence, where the employer has had a defect remedied by a third party without making the contractor aware that, any recovery claim against the contractor may be limited to the sum that the contractor would have borne to remedy the defects had the employer notified their existence to the contractor in the first place.[8]

18.2.5 The consequences of the contractor's failure to remedy

The clause will state that the contractor that has been requested to remedy a defect shall do so within a specific term indicated by the employer which should be reasonable. In case the employer does not give any indication, the contractor shall make good within a reasonable time. What constitutes a reasonable time to remedy will depend on the circumstances of the specific case.[9]

---

5 *Woodlands Oak Ltd v Conwell* [2011] BLR 365.

6 *London and SW Railway v Flower* [1875] 1 CPD 77.

7 *AMEC Foster Wheeler Group Ltd v Morgan Sindall Professional Services Ltd & Anor* [2016] EWHC 902.

8 *Pearce and High v Baxter and Baxter* [1999] BLR 101 CA and *Mul v Hutton Construction Ltd* [2014] EWHC 1797.

9 In *Go West Ltd. v Spigarolo & Anor* [2003] EWCA Civ 17 (31 January 2003) the Court of Appeal held that what constituted a reasonable time was to be assessed "*having regard to all the circumstances of the particular case*".

Where a contractor fails to remedy within reasonable time, the employer may have different options, including: (i) reducing the contract price by the amount that it would have spent to remedy the defective works or the reduction in the value of the defective work. This option has the clear advantage of giving the employer more freedom on how to deal with the issue of defects (i.e., whether or not to have them remedied); (ii) rectifying the defects, e.g., through a third-party contractor, at the contractor's cost. However, by doing so the employer may expose itself to the contractor's contention that outstanding defect is in fact due to a failure by the third-party contractor, for which the original contractor shall not be held liable. For this reason, employers exercise this option only in limited circumstances, e.g., where they have serious concerns about the contractor's ability to perform the remedial works; (iii) terminating the contract, in case the defect is so serious as to deprive the employer of substantially the whole benefit of the works. However, it is usually difficult for employers to prove that a repudiatory breach has occurred where the works have been in fact performed, although in a defective way. In *Astea (UK) Ltd. v Time Group Ltd*[10] Judge Seymour stated that:

> The application of the test of repudiation formulated by Diplock LJ in Hongkong Fir Shipping Co. Ltd. v Kawasaki Kisen Kaisha Ltd. is most straightforward in a case in which no performance at all of the obligations of one of the contracting parties has taken place and there is a straightforward refusal of performance. In any case in which there has been any degree of performance before the alleged repudiation the application of the test requires a qualitative judgment of whether failure to perform the remainder of the obligations of the relevant party will deprive the other party of substantially the whole benefit of the contract judged against the commercial purpose of the contract. It is likely to be necessary to consider not only what has been done, but also the value of that to the other party if nothing else is done. However, a flat refusal to continue performance will probably amount to a repudiation however much work has been done. On the other hand, if considerable work has been done in performance of a party's contractual obligations and what is alleged to amount to a repudiation is not a flat refusal to perform, but an indication of an intention to continue to perform at a speed considered by the other party to be unreasonably slow, it may be very difficult to conclude that in those circumstances what is being offered will deprive the other party of substantially the whole benefit of the contract. On the contrary, it may appear that the innocent party will eventually gain exactly the benefit contemplated. The question will be whether, by reason of the time which will need to elapse before that happens, in commercial terms the party entitled to performance will be deprived of substantially the whole of the benefit which it was intended he should derive from the contract.

Employers should thus be cautious before considering terminating the contract duc to a contractor's failure to remedy as a court may be reluctant to find such breaches as repudiatory.

18.2.6 The final acceptance certificate

When the defects liability period has elapsed, the employer will issue what is sometimes called the "final acceptance certificate" or "FAC" (although other definitions may be used). It will be on the parties to decide whether or not the certificate will be final and conclusive evidence that the work has been accepted by the employer. Typically, after

10 *Astea (UK) Ltd. v Time Group Ltd* [2003] EWHC 725 (TCC).

the final acceptance is issued any obligation on the contractor to remedy defects will end, although the contractor will usually keep a liability for latent defects.

18.3 Interpretation of defects clauses

The courts have held that defects liability clauses are not to be interpreted as limitation or exclusion clauses so as to limit or exclude the employer's right to claim damages upon expiry of the defects liability period. In *H W Nevill (Sun Blest) Ltd v William Press & Son Ltd*[11] Judge Newey stated that the defects liability clause was not to be read as depriving the injured party of any of his rights, so including any rights to damages up to expiry of any limitation period. As a result, unless the parties expressly provide otherwise, the remedies under defects liability clause are in addition to and not in substitution for the common law rights. This was confirmed in *BHP Petroleum Ltd v British Steel plc*[12] where the court stated that:

> Clauses of this kind do not limit or exclude liability. Typically they confer additional rights and obligations requiring the contractor or supplier to undertake additional work to rectify defects which appear within a defined time after completion usually without additional payment.

11 *H W Nevill (Sun Blest) Ltd v William Press & Son Ltd* [1982] 20 BLR 78.
12 *BHP Petroleum Ltd v British Steel plc* (2001) 74 Con LR 63 (CA).

CHAPTER 19

Insurance

19.1 The contract of insurance in general

The term insurance is not defined by any statute under English law. However, in *Prudential Insurance Co. v IRC*,[1] Channell J gave the following a widely accepted description of what an insurance contract is:

> It must be a contract whereby for some consideration, usually but not necessarily in periodical payments called premiums, you secure to yourself some benefit, usually but not necessarily the payment of a sum of money, upon the happening of some event . . . the event should be one that involves some amount of uncertainty. There must be either uncertainty whether the event will happen or not, or if the event is one which must happen at some time there must be uncertainty as to the time at which it will happen. The remaining essential is . . . that the insurance must be against something.

Therefore, an insurance may be defined[2] as an agreement where one party (the "insurer") agrees to afford a benefit (the "indemnification") to another party (the "insured") which has an interest in the subject of the insurance, in relation to risks and upon occurrence of a certain loss, against the payment of a consideration (the "premium").

The main aspects of an insurance are as follows:

(i) The existence of a contract. The relevant terms will be included in a so-called insurance policy, which is issued by the insurer after the insurance contract is entered into. Insurance contracts follow the general contractual principles and rules.
(ii) The consideration or premium. Although the existence of a premium will not prevent the formation of an insurance,[3] the policy will typically state that the payment of the premium is a condition precedent to the insurer's liability.
(iii) The indemnification, which is the benefit that the insurer affords to the insured. This will typically be money, although, in theory, nothing prevents the parties from agreeing on different types of benefits.
(iv) The loss triggering the payment, which may vary based on whether the insurance is an indemnity-based insurance (e.g., damages in case of fire) or a contingency-based insurance (e.g., payment of a certain amount in case of death).[4]

1 *Prudential Insurance Co. v IRC* [1904] 2 KB 658.
2 The term "reinsurance" instead, refers to the practice of insurers to insure themselves so passing on part of their liability under a policy to a third-party re-insurer.
3 *Hampton v Toxteth Co-operative Provident Society Limited* [1915] 1 Ch 721.
4 *Medical Defence Union v Department of Trade* [1979] 2 AER 421.

DOI: 10.4324/9781003387718-23

(v) The insured risk. This typically translates in the fact that the occurrence of the event causing the insured loss, and ultimately the payment of the benefit, shall be uncertain.

(vi) The interest of the party taking out the insurance, which shall be an insurable interest in the subject matter.

19.2 General insurance principles applicable to complex construction projects

The following general principles apply to insurance policies in the context of complex construction projects.

19.2.1 Insurable interest

To take out insurance the insured shall have an "insurable interest" (i.e., an interest which is recognised and enforceable at law) in the subject matter of the insurance. This is a statutory requirement provided in Section 1 of the Life Assurance Act 1774, which states that:

> From and after the passing of this Act no insurance shall be made by any person or persons, bodies politick or corporate, on the life or lives of any person, or persons, or on any other event or events whatsoever, wherein the person or persons for whose use, benefit, or on whose account such policy or policies shall be made, shall have no interest, or by way of gaming or wagering; and every assurance made contrary to the true intent and meaning hereof shall be null and void to all intents and purposes whatsoever.

In *Chitty on Contracts*[5] it is stated that:

> It is generally true that a person who would foreseeably suffer financial loss from the occurrence of an event has an insurable interest in the subject matter which it is sought to insure against that event.

The consequence is that a party (including any party that has been named or identified as insured in the policy) that has no interest (or no prospect of an interest) in the insurance it is taking out may not enforce that insurance, i.e., it will have no cover under the policy.

19.2.2 Duty of fair presentation

According to Part 2 of the Insurance Act 2015:

(i) Before a contract of insurance is entered into, the insured must make to the insurer a fair presentation of the risk.

(ii) The disclosure shall occur in a manner which would be reasonably clear and accessible to a prudent insurer.

(iii) Every material representation as to a matter of fact shall be substantially correct, and every material representation as to a matter of expectation or belief shall be made in good faith.

5 A.G. Guest, *Chitty on Contracts* (26th edition) Sweet & Maxwell, 1989, at para 4–207.

(iv) Except the insurer already knows or is presumed to know, the disclosure shall comprise every material circumstance which the insured knows or ought to know, or, failing that, disclosure which gives the insurer sufficient information to put a prudent insurer on notice that it needs to make further enquiries for the purpose of revealing those material circumstances.

(v) In the absence of enquiry, the insured is not required to disclose a circumstance if: (a) it diminishes the risk; (b) the insurer knows it; (c) the insurer ought to know it; (d) the insurer is presumed to know it; or (e) it is something as to which the insurer waives information.

19.2.3 Joint names insurance

Construction contracts often require the parties to take out insurance in joint names so that the interests of all such parties will be covered by a single policy. A joint names insurance will be either a true joint insurance or a composite insurance (or co-insurance), depending on whether the interests of the multiple parties in the subject-matter of the insurance are identical or differing (e.g., main contractor and subcontractor). The peculiarity is that under a joint names insurance policy the insurer does not have a subrogation right against any of the multiple insured parties, even where an insured party has caused the damages for which the insurer has made a payment, as this would deprive the insured party of a remedy.[6]

19.2.4 Indemnity

Based on the indemnity principle the insured can only recover what he has lost and no more than that, so that the insured will not be allowed to make a profit out of the insurance. Where the policy does not expressly state the principle, it will be implied. There are however some exceptions, e.g., in case the parties have agreed upfront the value of the subject matter, and this turns up to be higher than the actual loss.

19.2.5 Multiple insurance

Nothing prevents a party from taking out two or more policies in respect of the same risks and covering the same interest. In such case the insured may recover the full amount of his loss from any of the insurers. However, based on the principle of indemnity, the insured will not be allowed to recover more than the total loss. The insurer that has made the payment to the insured will then have a right of contribution allowing him to claim from the other insurers their proportion of the payment.

19.2.6 Subrogation

Based on the subrogation principle, an insurer that made a payment or agreed to make a payment under a policy shall have a right: (i) to avail himself of the rights and remedies

6 See *Simpson v Thompson* [1877] 3 APP Cas 279 HL and *Petrofina (UK) Limited v Magnaload Limited* [1983] 2 Lloyd's Rep 91.

available to the insured against the third parties,[7] including pursuing in the insured's name any claim which the insured is entitled to bring against third-party wrongdoers in order to recover any sums paid to the insured; and (ii) to recover from the insured any benefits that the insured has received from any third-party wrongdoer so reducing the loss covered by the insurance.[8] The principle is aimed at preventing the insured from being overcompensated by claiming from the insurer and the third party which has caused the loss.

As mentioned a subrogation right cannot be exercised against those jointly insured under a joint insurance policy where the loss has been caused by one of the insured parties. Moreover, the employer has no subrogation rights against a person or entity which, although not named as an insured party, has contributed to the premium, to the extent the policy was taken out totally or partially for such person or entity's benefit.[9]

19.2.7 Rights against insurers on insolvency

At common law, a third party cannot claim against another party's insurer even in case the insured has become insolvent. However, under Third Parties (Rights Against Insurers) Act 1930 (as amended by the Third Parties (Rights Against Insurers) Act 2010) a third party is allowed to "step into the shoes" of the insolvent insured party and pursue claims directly against their insurers to the extent the insured's liability to a third party has been confirmed by a judgment, award or admission.[10]

19.3 Categories of construction insurances

The main categories of insurance are the property (or "works" or "construction") insurance and the liability insurance. The first category covers damage to property, the works, equipment, materials, machinery, etc. during construction connected with it. The second category relates to claims by third parties for personal injury and property damage.

19.3.1 Property or construction insurance

The contractors' all-risk insurance or "CAR" (or "contract works insurance") is the most common and comprehensive type of property or construction insurance on the market. It is usually jointly taken out by the contractor and the employer, and covers all risks normally associated with a construction project including unforeseen loss or damage (e.g., due to fire, storm, flood, vandalism, theft, etc.) to building works, goods, materials, machinery and equipment, public liability, business interruption, etc. Under a CAR the contractor is typically allowed to claim for casualties that aren't expressly excluded and fall within the scope of the insurance (as opposed to the so-called named perils insurance, which only allows the insured to claim for certain conditions specified in the policy). More specifically CAR will usually cover: (i) "contract works", i.e., damages to property such as, e.g., scaffolding, cranes, excavators, etc., owned or hired, either used or stored onsite, throughout the

7 *Masons v Sainsbury* [1782] 3 KB 61.

8 *Castellain v Preston* [1883] 11 QBD 380 CA.

9 *Mark Rolands v Bernie Inns Limited* [1985] 3 AER 473.

10 *Post Office v Norwich Union* [1967] 1 AER 577 and *Bradley v Eagle Star Insurance Co Limited* [1989] 1 AER 961.

construction project; (ii) "public liability", i.e., damages to members of the public other than employer and contractor's employees (e.g., suppliers, subcontractors and other members of the public) for injuries, death or property damages suffered while on site; (iii) "employers' liability", i.e., damages to employer and contractor's employees from injury or death suffered while on site. Under the Employer's Liability (Compulsory Insurance) Act 1969 it is mandatory for UK employers to maintain employer's such insurance.

Although the parties may agree otherwise, a CAR insurance will usually exclude: (i) professional indemnity, i.e., mistakes and negligence in advice, design or physical works; (ii) directors and officers ("D&O"), i.e., consequence on directors and officers, including civil, regulatory or criminal proceedings, due to their managerial decisions and actions during the project; (iii) normal wear and tear, i.e., negligible damage or mechanical failure of equipment and materials; (iv) avoidable damages, i.e., damages which may be avoided or prevented by taking normal precautions; (v) loss of profit, i.e., financial losses deriving from project's delay, e.g., due to redesigns or changes; (vi) gross negligence and wilful misconduct.

19.3.2 Other categories of insurance

The parties to a construction contract will usually agree to take out other types of insurance depending on the type and complexity of the project. These may be aimed at recovering damages not covered in the CAR or in excess of the CAR coverage or in favour of a different subject. Examples of other insurance are professional indemnity insurance, latent defects insurance, loss of profit insurance, terrorism insurance, environmental insurance, etc.

19.3.3 Insurance clause

The insurance clause in a construction contract will typically be divided in a general part followed by specific terms for each insurance. In particular: (i) the general part may include the following provisions: (a) the parties' obligation to take out and maintain insurances in accordance with the contract and as per any requirements of the applicable law; (b) the insurance be based on customary terms and conditions; (c) the insurers be reputable and lawfully carrying on their business in the country where the site is located; (d) the parties' obligation to provide evidence to the other party that the insurance has been effected (e.g., a broker's letter or insurance certificate) within a certain term as of the date of commencement of the works, and a copy of the policy, once issued; (e) the parties' obligation to comply with the terms and conditions of the insurance policies applicable to them; (f) the parties' obligation not to make any material changes to their insurances; while (ii) the specific part of the clause may include the following terms: (a) the specific type of insurance policies that the parties agree are necessary for the project; (b) the party responsible for taking out the specific insurance; (c) whether the insurance shall be taken out jointly by the employer and the contractor or on behalf of other parties (e.g., the other party and/or subcontractors and/or projects lenders like banks or individual investors); (d) the term of validity of each policy (e.g., from commencement date to takeover); (e) the subject of each policy; (f) any maximum insured amount for each policy; (g) the agreement on the payment of the insurance premium for each policy.

CHAPTER 20

Indemnities

20.1 Indemnities in general

An indemnity is an agreement whereby the indemnifying party (the "indemnitor") promises to pay money (a fixed sum or a sum to be determined) to the indemnified party (the "beneficiary" or "indemnitee") on the occurrence of a specified indemnified event which may be either due to the indemnitor fault (e.g., a breach of a confidentiality obligation) or be a neutral event (e.g., a change in law). Thus, an indemnity is a primary obligation entitling the indemnified party to recover its losses without having to prove a breach of a contractual obligation by the indemnifying party.

The benefits of having indemnity clauses in the contract are several: (i) the recovery of losses becomes easier for the indemnified party as it will only need to prove that the indemnified event has generated a loss without having to show "fault" on the part of the indemnifying party; (ii) depending on how the indemnity is drafted the clause may simplify an indemnity claim and/or allow a wider recovery for the indemnified party, e.g., by quantifying the prospective losses upfront and/or including legal and other related costs in the indemnity; (iii) the likelihood of disputes is lower as indemnity claims are more straightforward and, as such, more difficult to resist. As a result, indemnifying parties are more likely to make payments spontaneously without the need for the indemnified party to commence legal proceedings.

Indemnities may be "general", where they cover general classes of events (e.g., any damages deriving contractual breaches), or "specific" which are given for specific types of losses which the parties intend to cover by using a more tailored approach due to the peculiarity of the event, the amount at stake or the severe consequences of the breach. These may include, for example, indemnities for breaches relevant to: (i) IP; (ii) anticorruption; (iii) confidentiality; (iv) data protection; (v) environmental law and pollution.

Moreover, indemnities may be divided into the two categories of conventional ("fault-based") indemnities and "knock-for-knock" indemnities.

20.2 Conventional indemnities

20.2.1 Conventional indemnities in general

Conventional indemnities are fault-based indemnities obliging the indemnitor to indemnify the beneficiary in case of losses caused by a fault, negligence or breach of duty.

DOI: 10.4324/9781003387718-24

20.2.2 Conventional indemnity clause

20.2.2.1 The parties

The parties of an indemnity are the indemnifying party and the indemnified party (or beneficiary). The beneficiary may either be the contractual party or, more commonly, a party's "group". The definition of a party's group will typically not be limited to subjects that are part of that party's corporate group (i.e., the company, its affiliates and their employees, directors, officers and agents). In the case of indemnities given by the employer, the "employer group" may also extend to any lenders, the engineer and other contractors which are procured by the employer and are not included in the definition of "contractor's group". Where the indemnity is given by the contractor, the "contractor group" may also extend to the contractor's subcontractors and their respective subcontractors (including the respective affiliates, employees, directors, officers and agents). Sometimes the definition of group may even extend to third parties that are extraneous to the project such as visitors and secondees.

20.2.2.2 The indemnifying party's obligations

An indemnity clause may state that the indemnifying party shall "indemnify, defend and hold harmless" the beneficiary. These terms are sometimes considered interchangeable. However, they may have different meanings. In particular:

(i) "Indemnify" is a wide term which is generally intended as a financial obligation on the indemnifying party to reimburse the losses that the beneficiary has suffered as a result of the specified event without the beneficiary having to show any fault on the indemnifying party.

(ii) "Hold harmless" is intended as an obligation: (a) not to pursue the indemnified party for payment, either by suing it or otherwise; and (b) to prevent third parties from pursuing the indemnified party for payment, to the extent possible.[1]

The words "indemnify" and "hold harmless" are typically used together in indemnity clauses. In *Farstad Supply v Enviroco*[2] the Supreme Court confirmed such a combination provides a defence for the indemnified party in relation to claims made by the indemnifying party as well as an indemnity in respect of the claims of third parties against the indemnified party. The court held that:

> the word 'indemnity' is capable of having a wide meaning but, even assuming that by itself it might (depending upon the context) have a narrow meaning, it does not stand alone in the clause. The owner must 'defend . . . and hold harmless' the charterer, not only against liabilities and causes of action, but also against 'all claims, demands' and proceedings . . . the obligation to hold harmless goes further than the obligation to reimburse because they are words of exception. In some contexts the words 'indemnify' and 'hold harmless' have the same meaning. . . . The word 'indemnify' can sometimes mean indemnify a third party. As ever, all will depend upon the context. Here the context is plain. The expression 'defend, indemnify and hold harmless' is wide enough to include the exclusion of liability for loss incurred

1 *Deepak Fertilisers v (1) Davy McKee and (2) ICI Chemicals* [1999] 1 All ER (Comm) 69, 62 Con LR 86, [1998] EWCA Civ 1753, [1999] 1 Lloyd's Rep 387, (1999) 1 TCLR 200, [1999] BLR 41.

2 *Farstad Supply AS v Enviroco Ltd* [2011] UKSC 16, [2011] WLR 921, [2011] 1 WLR 921, [2011] Bus LR 1108.

> by the owner or charterer . . . [and] is wide enough both to provide a defence for one party to claims made by the other party and to provide an indemnity in respect of the claims of third parties.

As a result, by using these words the indemnifying party would not only promise to pay any losses suffered by the indemnified party, but, in addition to that, would also be prevented from bringing an action against the indemnified party where the indemnifying party considers that the indemnified party has caused or contributed to the loss. Thus, where an indemnifying party intends to keep its right to bring an action against the indemnified party in case such party has caused or contributed to the indemnified loss, it should resist the inclusion of these words in the clause.

The *Farstad* case also seems to suggest that, depending on the language of the clause, the words "indemnify" and "hold harmless" may have in fact the same meaning. If that was the case, this would mean that: (a) the mere use of the word "indemnify" would also automatically lead to an obligation not to sue/prevent others from suing, without the need to add the "hold harmless" language; and (b) the words "hold harmless" would turn the clause into an indemnity without the need to expressly use the words indemnify, indemnity, etc.

(iii) The obligation to "defend" should be intended as an obligation to protect the indemnified party from damages caused by third parties in a dispute (e.g., litigation or arbitration). Therefore, in this case "defending" merely means "protecting from", and the courts will not interpret it as an obligation to hand over the defence to the indemnified party so to allow it to run the case.[3] Where the parties intend the obligation to defend to have such meaning, they should clearly state it in the clause and good practice would be to ensure the clause coupled with a conduct of claims clause.

20.2.2.3 The indemnified losses

The clause will usually state that the indemnifying party shall indemnify, defend and hold harmless the indemnified party for any claims, losses, damages, judgments, awards, costs and expenses (including legal costs and expenses) etc. which are suffered by the indemnified party. In addition, an indemnity clause will usually expressly exclude losses which the parties agree shall not be subject to the indemnity (e.g., indirect losses or consequential damages).

An indemnity would allow the indemnified party to recover in full any losses resulting from the indemnified event without having to prove that such losses are not too remote, foreseeable or reasonable. However, the parties shall consider that the English courts are generally reluctant to award foreseeable and unmitigated losses. As stated by Lord Justice Staughton in *Total Transport Corporation v Arcadia Petroleum Ltd*:[4]

> The word 'indemnity' is . . . used in two senses. It may mean simply damages awarded for tort or breach of contract. . . . Alternatively the word 'indemnity' may refer to all loss suffered which is attributable to a specified cause, whether or not it was in the reasonable

3 *Codemasters Software Co. Ltd v Automobile Club De L'Ouest* [2009] EWHC 2361 (Pat), 17 September 2009.
4 *Total Transport Corporation v Arcadia Petroleum Ltd* [1998] Lloyd's Rep 351.

> contemplation of the parties. There is precious little authority to support such a meaning, but I do not doubt that the word is often used in that sense.

Where the parties intend the indemnity clause to allow the beneficiary's recovery of all losses incurred as a result of an indemnified event, they should use clear and express words evidencing such true intention.[5]

The parties may also state in the clause whether the obligation on the indemnifying party includes or excludes indirect losses. The issue was discussed in *Capita v RFIB Group*[6] where the indemnity stated that "*The Seller undertakes to indemnify . . . the Buyer . . . from any liabilities, costs, claims, demands or expenses which [it] may suffer or incur arising directly or indirectly from . . . any services or products supplied . . . prior to the Transfer Date*". The Court of Appeal held that the causal words "*directly or indirectly*" allowed the court to import the *Hadley* test of remoteness in *Hadley v Baxendale*[7] into the clause and that the words "*or indirectly*" covered liability for losses within the second limb of *Hadley*, but not those which are more remote than the second limb. This means that where an indemnity clause states that the indemnifying party promises to indemnify for direct or indirect losses, the indemnified party may claim losses under the first limb (i.e., those that "*may fairly and reasonably be considered either arising naturally, i.e., according to the usual course of things*") and the second limb (i.e., those that may "*reasonably be supposed to have been in the contemplation of both parties, at the time they made the contract as the probable result of the breach of it*") of *Hadley*, but no more than that. Good practice would be defining what "indirect losses" the parties intend to be covered by or excluded from the indemnity, bearing in mind that courts have held that loss of profits is recoverable as direct loss, unless recovery is expressly excluded. This also applies to "consequential losses", considering that a court may look at the parties' objective intention and hold that they intended to give the words "consequential loss" a broader meaning than "indirect loss".

20.2.2.4 Disputes

An indemnity clause will also usually include a promise to indemnify for legal costs deriving from any disputes between the parties or between the indemnified party and third parties. The courts will be reluctant to allow full recovery of legal costs relevant to disputes between the indemnified party and the indemnifying party where such costs have been unreasonable or where the result of the indemnity would be that the successful party will be required to pay the losing parties' legal costs.[8] Conversely, the courts may be more inclined to allow full recovery of legal costs where the beneficiary is sued by a third party in relation to an indemnified claim. However, also in this case the courts will look at the reasonableness of the legal costs. Any doubts as to whether costs were reasonably incurred or were reasonable in amount will be resolved in favour of the receiving party. In this regard, CPR ("Civil Procedure Rule") 44.3 (1) to (3) states that: (i) where the court is to assess the amount of costs, it will assess those costs on the standard basis or on the indemnity basis, but the court will not in either case allow costs which have

5 *Church Commissioners v Ibrahim* [1997] 1 EGLR 13.
6 *Capita v RFIB Group* [2015] EWCA Civ 131.
7 *Hadley v Baxendale* [1854] EWHC Exch J70.
8 *Woodford v AIG Europe Ltd* [2018] EWHC 358 (QB).

been unreasonably incurred or are unreasonable in amount; (ii) where the amount of costs is to be assessed on the standard basis, the court will only allow costs which are proportionate to the matters in issue (costs which are disproportionate in amount may be disallowed or reduced even if they were reasonably or necessarily incurred) and resolve any doubt in favour of the paying party; while (iii) where the amount of costs is to be assessed on the indemnity basis, the court will resolve any doubt in favour of the receiving party. Moreover, based on Civil Procedure Rule (CPR) 44.4 (a), if it is assessing costs on the standard basis, it will look at whether the costs were proportionately and reasonably incurred or proportionate and reasonable in amount; while (ii) if it is assessing costs on the indemnity basis, the courts will only look at whether the costs were unreasonably incurred or unreasonable in amount. In *Euro-Asian Oil v Credit Suisse*,[9] Euro-Asian, which was awarded a certain amount of legal costs upon successful legal proceedings, sought to recover more than the amount awarded by the court on the basis of an indemnity stating as follows: "*To protect, indemnify and to hold you [Euro-Asian Oil] harmless from and against any and all damages, costs and expenses (including reasonable attorney fees) which you [Euro-Asian Oil] may suffer*". Euro-Asian Oil contended that based on the words "*any and all . . . costs*", the "*attorney fees*" had to be recovered on an indemnity basis (which usually allows a higher recovery as the relevant amount does not have to be proportionate to the amount in dispute or to the complexity of the case, and any doubt is to be resolved in favour of the receiving party). The court, however, favoured Credit Suisse's argument that the costs had to be recovered on a standard basis, with all the relevant consequences in terms of proportionality and assessment in case of doubts.

With specific regard to legal costs for adjudication, the parties shall also consider that, based on Section 108A of the Housing Grants, Construction and Regeneration Act 1996, any contractual provision made between the parties to a construction contract which concerns the allocation as between those parties of costs relating to the adjudication of a dispute arising under the construction contract is ineffective unless: (i) it is made in writing, is contained in the construction contract and confers power on the adjudicator to allocate his fees and expenses as between the parties; or (ii) it is made in writing after the giving of notice of intention to refer the dispute to adjudication.

20.2.2.5 *"As a result of or arising out of or in connection with"*

The parties negotiating an indemnity clause may draft it so to widen or narrow the causal link between the loss and the relevant contract. For example, in the case of *Campbell v Conoco*[10] the indemnity clause stated as follows:

> The Contractor hereby agrees to indemnify and hold harmless the Operator against . . . all claims arising in respect of any injury, death, sickness or ill health caused to or suffered by the Contractor and any Personnel as a result of or arising out of or in connection with the performance or non-performance of the Contract.

The Court of Appeal held that the words "*in connection with*" had widened the causal link in the clause. Based on this, the parties should clearly state whether the indemnity

9 *Euro-Asian Oil v Credit Suisse* [2017] EWHC B7 (Comm).
10 *Campbell v Conoco* [2002] EWCA Civ 704.

covers any incident arising "*out of*" or also "*in connection with*" the performance (or non-performance) of the contract and the works.

20.2.2.6 *"Attributable to"*

An indemnity clause will usually state that the obligation to indemnify shall not apply in case of the beneficiary's own negligence, gross negligence and wilful misconduct. For example, the clause may state that the obligation to indemnify is excluded in case the loss is "*attributable to*" the indemnified party. The meaning of the words "*attributable to*" was considered in *In Central Asbestos Co. Ltd v Dodd*[11] where Lord Pearson suggested that such language:

> refers to causation but it has to cover cases of dual or multiple causation and perhaps another element of responsibility in the case of contributory negligence. . . . In such cases there would have to be an apportionment of the responsibility, and in the case of contributory negligence the apportionment would take into account degrees of blameworthiness as well as causative potency. If this involves another element additional to causation, it is aptly covered by the phrase 'attributable to'.

It is worth noting that the principle that a party cannot, in the absence of clear terms, take advantage of his own wrong is well-established under English law. As stated by Lord Diplock in *Cheall v A.P.E.X.*:[12]

> except in the unlikely case that the contract contains clear express provisions to the contrary, it is to be presumed that it was not the intention of the parties that either party should be entitled to rely upon his own breaches of his primary obligations as bringing the contract to an end, i.e. as terminating any further primary obligations on his part then remaining unperformed.

The principle was further clarified by Patten LJ in *BDW Trading Limited v JM Rowe (Investments) Limited*[13] as follows:

> Although there has been a certain amount of academic discussion as to whether the principle has the status of a rule of law which is imposed upon the parties to a contract almost regardless of what they have agreed, it is now clear as a matter of authority that the application of the principle can be excluded or modified by the terms of the contract and that its scope in any particular case will depend upon the construction of the relevant agreement.

However, there are cases in which this principle will not apply. For example, in *Greenwich Millennium Village Ltd v Essex Services Group plc and others*[14] the Court of Appeal held that a party will not be necessarily prevented from recovering its losses under an indemnity clause even in case they were due to its own negligence. In that case, the court had to decide on recoverability of damages deriving from defective workmanship on the basis of an indemnity clause in a contract between a sub-sub-subcontractor ("A") and sub-subcontractor ("B"). A had been held responsible for defective workmanship and condemned to indemnify B accordingly. A appealed the decision alleging that B had been negligent in failing to detect the defects on inspection. The Court of Appeal held that A's

11 *Central Asbestos Co. Ltd v Dodd* [1972] 3 WLR 333.
12 *Cheall v A.P.E.X.* [1983] 2 AC 180 at [188].
13 *BDW Trading Limited v JM Rowe (Investments) Limited* [2011] EWCA Civ 548.
14 *Greenwich Millennium Village Ltd v Essex Services Group plc and others* [2014] EWCA Civ 960.

contention was not relevant as the parties had neither agreed to limit the indemnity clause only to workmanship breaches which were visible upon reasonable inspection, nor this limit could be presumed.

20.2.2.7 *"On demand"*

Indemnity clauses often state that, once the loss has occurred, the indemnifying party shall make the payment "*on demand*" of the indemnified party. The use of such words, without any further explanation, may create uncertainty as to the moment when the statute of limitation period will start running. In general, the limitation period starts upon occurrence of an event entitling one party to make a claim. In the case of an indemnity claim, unless the clause states otherwise, the indemnified party may advance its indemnity claim as soon as it has suffered the loss that the indemnity was intended to cover. Therefore, the limitation period for the relevant indemnity claim will start running only when the indemnified loss is established. However, when the indemnity clause includes the "*on demand*" words this may cause the limitation period starting in the actual moment in which the demand is made as the indemnified party's right to a cause of action starts with the actual demand. An alternative interpretation is that the words "*on demand*" simply mean that the claim under the indemnity shall be paid by the indemnifying party "*as soon as*" the relevant demand is made (or as soon as the relevant quantum has been established), to the extent the indemnifying party does not dispute that the sum is due under the indemnity. As there is very little case law on the consequences that the inclusion of the language "*on demand*" will have on an indemnity, the parties should try to use precise words as to the effect that they intend to assign to such words.

20.2.2.8 Indemnities and contractual limitation on liability

Another aspect that the parties may want to clarify in the indemnity clause is whether or not the indemnity amount is intended to fall within any cap on liability provided in the contract. In the absence of such express agreement, any amount paid under the indemnity may not necessarily fall outside of the liability cap. As a result, where the indemnified party seeks to impose unlimited liability for an indemnity or have any payment under the indemnity falling into a different basket and liability cap, this should be made clear in the clause.

20.2.2.9 Conduct of claims

As mentioned, under an indemnity clause the indemnifying party may be obliged to indemnify the indemnified party in relation to the legal costs and consequences of claims that third parties bring against the indemnified party in relation to events covered by the indemnity. In such cases, the dispute will typically be conducted in the name of the indemnified party. As the indemnifying party will not be a party to the dispute, but will bear the relevant consequences, it will usually seek to add a "conduct of claims" clause in the contract to ensure that the indemnifying party acts upon the indemnifying party's instructions in relation to the proceedings and any amicable negotiations, and does not take any steps which may jeopardise the indemnifying party's position. To achieve such result, the conduct of claims clause may include the following obligations on the indemnified party: (i) notifying the indemnifying party in writing of any events triggering, or which appears may trigger, the indemnity (typically this will be the receipt of any claim from a third party relevant to matters covered in the indemnity); (ii) allowing the indemnifying party to conduct any negotiations and/or litigation proceedings relevant to the third-party claim at the indemnifying cost. This will typically include any decision on strategies as well as the appointment of lawyers and/or technical experts and/or party's appointed arbitrators, etc., although the appointment is usually subject to the prior consent of the indemnified party, which is in fact the party paying for the relevant fees. The parties may however qualify such consent by stating that it "*shall not be unreasonably withheld or delayed*"; (iii) refrain from doing anything which might prejudice the indemnifying party's position in the litigation proceedings or settlement negotiations prior to the indemnifying party having taken on the negotiation or the proceedings. This will usually include an obligation to refrain from entering into any settlement agreement or making any admission or payment which might prejudice the position of the indemnifying party in the negotiation or the proceedings; and (iv) provide reasonable assistance to the indemnifying party and during the litigation proceedings and settlement negotiations subject to repayment of reasonable costs properly incurred in doing it.

Where the clause states that failure to follow the claims procedure shall prevent the indemnified party from bringing a claim under the indemnity, such language may make compliance with the procedure a condition precedent to the obligation to indemnify. Where the parties intend to attain such a result, they should use clear words (e.g., by stating that the indemnity "*shall not apply unless the procedure in the conduct of claims clause has been fully complied with*"). When in doubt, a court will typically look at the contract as a whole and consider words used in other provisions. In the case of *Heritage Oil v Tullow Uganda*[15] the indemnified party had failed to notify the indemnifying party that a certain indemnified event had occurred. The indemnifying party argued that, as compliance with the correct procedure was a condition precedent to the obligation to indemnify, no payment was due under the indemnity. The court rejected this argument, but on the grounds that, in a different indemnity in the contract, the parties had clearly expressed their intention that the indemnity be a condition precedent by stating that it "*shall not apply unless*".

It is worth noting that making "full" compliance with the claims procedure a condition to the validity of claims under an indemnity may have the effect of preventing the indemnified party from raising claims even in case of trivial misalignments with the claims procedure which have no real or substantial impact on the indemnifying party. Considering this, where the parties intend to ensure that the claims procedure is complied with before any indemnity claims are raised, they should endeavour to draft the clause in a way that does not deprive the indemnified party of the benefit of the indemnity by mandating strict compliance with each and any term of the claims procedure regardless of how trivial it may be.

In addition, the parties should try to align the claims procedure in their contract with those provided in any insurance policies taken out by the parties and covering the damages for which the indemnity claim has been brought.

20.2.2.10 Mitigation

An indemnity clause will usually state that the indemnified party shall be obliged to use reasonable endeavours to mitigate the losses or damages which it is claiming under the indemnity.

15 *Heritage Oil v Tullow Uganda* [2014] EWCA Civ 1048.

20.3 Knock-for-knock indemnities

20.3.1 Knock-for-knock indemnities in general

Typical features of complex construction projects are: (i) the involvement of multiple parties (the employer, the engineer, the contractors, their subcontractors, etc.); (ii) the high amounts at stake; and (iii) the complexity of the works and the site location (e.g., in the case of offshore oil and gas projects), which may increase the chances of significant and costly accidents.

With a "knock-for-knock" indemnity (or "mutual hold harmless" indemnity) each party assumes liability for its own losses regardless of fault, negligence or breach of duty on its part. As a result, any damages and/or losses to property or personnel suffered by one party (or, more commonly, a "group" of parties, e.g., the contractor, its affiliates, subcontractors and vendors) is borne by that party regardless of any fault, even where such party was not to be held liable at common law, or liable for breach of statutory duty.[16] It is also common in the case of more complex multi-party projects for all parties involved in the project to enter into a single "mutual hold harmless agreement" (rather than a number of bilateral agreements) where each party indemnifies all the parties involved in the project on a knock-for-knock basis.

Knock-for-knock indemnities in contracts for complex construction projects offer the primary benefit of giving certainty and clarity to the parties (and their insurers) as to where their liabilities lie and facilitating the settlement of claims. Such results will be attained by: (i) ensuring that all claims are channelled to the indemnifying party (so avoiding a multiplicity of claims between indemnified party contractors, subcontractor, employers, etc., e.g., where it is not clear which party has caused the damages or there have been concurrent causes due to negligence of more parties); and (ii) requiring the claimant to prove only causation and not also fault (i.e., negligence).

The fact that the parties contract out of remedies to which they would otherwise be entitled to against the parties involved in the project, and waive the requirement to show fault, mitigates the complexities of having to allocate liability between contracting parties, and reduces substantially the number of disputes on the damages covered by the knock-for-knock clause, so allowing the parties to save the relevant time and costs. The simplification benefit offered by knock-for-knock clauses with respect to injury or death of employees in the construction sector was summarised by Lord Bingham in *Caledonia North Sea Ltd v British Telecommunications plc*[17] as follows:

> The standard practice during construction is thus described by Sharp, Offshore Oil and Gas Insurance (1994), p. 108:
>
> '(iv) Injury or Death of Employees
>
> The position in respect of employers' liability is invariably dealt with by the exchange of mutual indemnities in respect of injuries to or deaths of employees. There is perhaps a simple reason for this. If an individual is injured he will expect to have a right to sue any party who may have been guilty of negligence leading to the circumstances which caused the injury. This party may be another contractor, the

16 *Caledonia North Sea Ltd v London Bridge Engineering Ltd* [2002] UKHL 4.
17 *Caledonia North Sea Ltd v London Bridge Engineering Ltd* [2002] UKHL 4.

> Principal or his employer, or any combination of all three. The issue can become complicated by reason of contributory negligence. Determining liability and awarding costs can be a lengthy process in these circumstances, and this can only add to the anguish of the injured party, or the dependents of the deceased who may have been the sole breadwinner. The employer therefore accepts a responsibility to provide for his employees and will generally give the party with whom he is contracting a full indemnity in respect of any suit or action brought against that other party'.

Another benefit of knock-for-knock clauses is the costs saving deriving from the fact that the party is not usually requested to take out insurance policies for damages that clearly fall within the liability of the other party under the knock-for-knock clause (e.g., in respect of the other parties' property).

20.3.2 Knock-for-knock indemnity clause

A typical knock will be mutual and consisting of two parts, i.e., "employer's knock-for-knock indemnity" and "contractor's knock-for-knock indemnity". The two parts will substantially mirror each other by stating that the relevant party: (i) accepts liability for losses to its own property or losses suffered by its own employees; and (ii) agrees to indemnify the other party in respect of liability arising from the same.

For example, the employer's part of the clause will state that: (i) the contractor shall not be responsible for any losses or damages to the property of the employer (or the employer's group) or any personal injuries of any member of the employer (or the employer's group) related to the contract; and (ii) the employer shall indemnify and hold harmless the contractor from all claims, costs, expenses, actions, etc. related to such losses, damages or personal injuries, even if such loss, damage or personal injury is due to negligence and/or breach of duty by the contractor (or the contractor's group).

Typically, the events triggering the knock-for-knock indemnity (i.e., claims, losses, damages, etc.) may affect property or people. In relation to "property", the parties should expressly state if this will only regard property that is owned by the party or also property that is leased, hired, chartered or otherwise in the possession of the indemnified party. In relation to "people", the parties should try to define the specific type of harm that the person shall suffer for the indemnity to apply (e.g., death, injury, illness, sickness, disease, etc.) so not to make the indemnity too broad.

Some specific events such as pollution, intellectual property and wilful misconduct are normally excluded from the knock-for-knock mechanism and covered by specific indemnities in the light of their seriousness and the impact they may have on the indemnified party.

CHAPTER 21

Exclusion and limitation of liability

21.1 Exclusion and limitation of liability in general

In the case of EPC contracts for complex projects contractors will usually bear most of the risks of the project. As a result, contractors will usually insist to limit their overall liability under the contract by adding: (i) limitation of liability clauses capping the contractor's liability under the contract to certain amounts, typically tied to the contract price (e.g., 10% of the contract price, although the parties are free to agree on any percentage); and (ii) exclusion of liability provisions, stating that the contractor shall not be liable for certain types of losses (e.g., indirect and consequential damages). On the other hand, employers will typically seek to include carve-outs to such exclusions and limitations for more serious breaches (such as cases of gross negligence and wilful misconduct). Such exclusion or limitation of liability clauses have been scrutinised by the courts and the way the courts have constructed them has changed over the years. Thus, when drafting such clauses, the parties shall bear in mind how the courts may construe them so that the clause is clear enough not to leave doubts as to the real intention of the parties.

21.2 Exclusion of liability clause

As mentioned, the parties to a construction contract will usually seek to exclude each party's liability for indirect or consequential losses which either party may suffer in connection with the contract, to the extent the governing law of the contract allows it. Such provisions are aimed at avoiding liability for losses which are not in the contemplation of the parties at the time of the agreement or which the parties do not agree to assume liability for considering the relevant uncertainty and potential magnitude. However, as the meaning of "indirect" and "consequential" losses is somewhat evolving under English law, unless the parties clearly describe what they mean by "indirect" and "consequential", they should clearly list the types of losses they intend to exclude liability for. These will usually include losses like loss of profit, loss of production, loss of any contract and/or loss of opportunity.

Exclusion of liability clauses will typically include exceptions mainly relevant to cases of fraudulent acts, gross negligence and wilful misconduct, as well as losses deriving from particularly serious breaches such as those related to integrity, IP, data protection, etc.

DOI: 10.4324/9781003387718-25

21.3 Limitation of liability clause

Large construction projects carry high risks for both contractors and employers. However, as in the case of EPC contracts in which contractors typically bear most of the risks, they usually seek to reduce their exposure by limiting their overall liability under the contract to a certain fixed amount or an amount which may be easily calculated (e.g., by referring to a certain percentage of the contract price as amended from time to time). The cap on liability is a vital provision in a construction contract as it allows contractors to estimate their maximum contractual risk with a certain degree of certainty and consider it in the contract price.

A limitation of liability clause will usually state that, to the extent allowed by the governing law of the contract, the parties agree that the total liability of the contractor to the employer under or in connection with the contract shall not exceed a certain amount or a certain percentage of the contract price. The clause may also include a number of exclusions from the limitation of liability such as more serious breaches like those related to integrity, data protection and/or IP, and those deriving from fraudulent acts, gross negligence or wilful misconduct of the contractor. The parties will also typically state whether any liquidated damages for delay paid by the contractor and any amount paid under any indemnities will be included in, or excluded from the limitation of liability cap. Another aspect which the parties may want to agree on is whether the limitation of liability cap will be reduced or increased in case of alterations to the contract price, e.g., due to variations.

21.4 Fraud, gross negligence and wilful misconduct

As mentioned, the parties to contracts for complex construction contracts will typically seek to exclude some conducts such as fraud, wilful misconduct and gross negligence from the limitation of liability, so making the contractor's liability in such circumstances uncapped. Such concepts are different and may generate different consequences:

(i) The term "fraud" is defined in Section 1 of the Fraud Act 2006 (the "Act") which identifies three categories of fraud, i.e.: (a) fraud by false representation, which is committed in case a person dishonestly makes a false (i.e., untrue or misleading where the person making it knows that it is, or might be, untrue or misleading) representation (of fact or law, express or implied) and intends, by making the representation, to make a gain for himself or another, or to cause loss to another or to expose another to a risk of loss; (b) fraud by failing to disclose information, which is committed when a person dishonestly fails to disclose to another person information which he is under a legal duty to disclose, and intends, by failing to disclose the information to make a gain for himself or another, or to cause loss to another or to expose another to a risk of loss; and (c) fraud by abuse of position, which is committed when a person occupies a position in which he is expected to safeguard, or not to act against, the financial interests of another person, dishonestly abuses that position, and intends, by means of the abuse of that position to make a gain for himself or another, or to cause loss to another or to expose another to a risk of loss.

(ii) The words "wilful misconduct" and "gross negligence" are not terms of art under English law. However, while it is generally accepted that wilful misconduct may be identified with a deliberate or reckless wrongful act or omission, with a knowledge that it will cause harm or being reckless as to whether harm will occur, the meaning of "gross negligence" is not crystallised, although it is likely to be interpreted as something more fundamental and involving greater degree of culpability than mere negligence. The meaning of these words will however be interpreted in the context of the clause in which it is included. Several court decisions tried to define the term. In *Red Sea Tankers Ltd and Others v Papachristidis and Others Henderson, Baarma and Bouckley*[1] (the "Hellespont Ardent"), Mance J held:

> If the matter is viewed according to purely English principles of construction . . . 'Gross' negligence is clearly intended to represent something more fundamental than failure to exercise proper skill and/or care constituting negligence . . . as a matter of ordinary language and general impression, the concept of gross negligence seems to me capable of embracing not only conduct undertaken with actual appreciation of the risks involved, but also serious disregard of or indifference to an obvious risk.

In *Great Scottish & Western Railway Co Ltd v British Railways Board*,[2] Beldam LJ said:

> in the context of [this clause], the words 'gross negligence' take their colour from the contrast with 'wilful neglect' and refer to an act or omission not done deliberately, but which in the circumstances would be regarded by those familiar with the circumstances as a serious error. The likely consequences of the error are clearly a significant factor. Thus, whether negligence is gross is a function of the nature of the error and the seriousness of the risk which results from it.

In *Camarata Property v Credit Suisse Securities*[3] Andrew Smith J underlined that the use of both the words "negligence" and "gross negligence" in the contract indicates the parties' intention to draw a distinction between the two terms and held that such distinction is one of degree and not of kind.

In *Marex Financial Limited v Creative Finance Limited*[4] the judge said that:

> 'gross negligence' means something different than 'negligence'. It connotes in my opinion a want of care that is more fundamental than a failure to exercise reasonable care. The difference between the two concepts is one of degree. In reaching this conclusion I adopt the persuasive reasoning of Mance J in Red Sea Tankers Ltd & Ors v Papachristidis & Ors [1997] 2 Lloyd's Rep 547 and Andrew Smith J in Camerata Property Inc v Credit Suisse Securities (Europe) Ltd [2011] EWHC 479 (Comm).

---

1 *Red Sea Tankers Ltd and Others v Papachristidis and Others Henderson, Baarma and Bouckley* [1997] 2 Lloyd's Rep 547.

2 *Great Scottish & Western Railway Co Ltd v British Railways Board*, unreported, 10 February 2000.

3 *Camarata Property v Credit Suisse Securities* [2011] EWHC 479.

4 *Marex Financial Limited v Creative Finance Limited* [2013] EWHC 2155 (Comm).

21.5 Interpretation of exclusion and limitation clauses

Where there is a doubt on whether the parties agreed that a party's common law rights and remedies be excluded or restricted by a contractual provision, the court will generally imply a rebuttable presumption that the parties did not intend to exclude such rights. This presumption may be rebutted only if the contract contains clear unequivocal words to such extent. As said by Lord Diplock in *Gilbert-Ash (Northern) Ltd v Modern Engineering (Bristol) Ltd*:[5]

> So when one is concerned with a building contract one starts with the presumption that each party is to be entitled to all those remedies for its breach as would arise by operation of law, including the remedy of setting up a breach of warranty in diminution or extinction of the price of material supplied or work executed under the contract. To rebut that presumption one must be able to find in the contract clear unequivocal words in which the parties have expressed their agreement that this remedy shall not be available in respect of breaches of that particular contract.

The leading authorities on exclusion and limitation clauses are *Suisse Atlantique Societe d'Armement Maritime SA v N V Rotterdamsche Kolen Centrale*[6] and *Photo Production Ltd v Securicor Transport Ltd*.[7] In these cases, the House of Lords: (i) rejected the so-called doctrine of fundamental breach based on which a party was prevented from relying on an exclusion clause where the contract had been terminated as a result of a fundamental breach of contract (e.g., a repudiation) by that party; and (ii) held that whether the exclusion clause was to apply was a matter of contractual interpretation.

However, for exclusion clauses to apply in case of radical breaches, clear language had to be used. This concept was summarised by Lord Wilberforce in a famous passage in *Suisse Atlantique*[8] where the judge stated that:

> the more radical the breach the clearer must the language be if it is to be covered.

Later cases considered the question of whether the requirement to use clear language to extend the exclusion of liability to radical breaches of contract (including deliberate and intentional breaches) gives rise to an interpretative presumption that the parties did not intend the exclusion clause to cover such breaches.

In *Internet Broadcasting Corporation Ltd & others v MAR LLC*[9] (the "MARHedge") a Deputy Judge held that: (i) there was in fact a strong presumption that the exclusion clause did not cover repudiatory breaches of contract; and (ii) such presumption could only be rebutted by strong and explicit language.

In *AstraZeneca UK Ltd v Albemarle International Corp*[10] Mr Justice Flaux held that: (i) the decision in MARHedge was wrong as it sought to revive the doctrine of fundamental breach which was no longer good law following the following *Swiss Atlantique* and *Photo Production*; and (ii) exclusion clauses were to be construed strictly, *but without any presumption.*

---

5 *Gilbert-Ash (Northern) Ltd v Modern Engineering (Bristol) Ltd* [1974] AC 689 at [718].
6 *Suisse Atlantique Societe d'Armement Maritime SA v N V Rotterdamsche Kolen Centrale* [1967] 1 AC 63.
7 *Photo Production Ltd v Securicor Transport Ltd* [1980] AC 827.
8 *Suisse Atlantique Societe d'Armement Maritime SA v N V Rotterdamsche Kolen Centrale* [1967] 1 AC 63.
9 *Internet Broadcasting Corporation Ltd & others v MAR LLC* [2009] EWHC 844 (Ch).
10 *AstraZeneca UK Ltd v Albemarle International Corporation & another* [2011] EWHC 1574 (Comm).

The issue was recently considered in *Mott MacDonald Ltd v Trant Engineering Ltd.*[11] The case related to a contract for design consultancy services for the upgrade of a power station at the RAF Mount Pleasant military base in the Falkland Islands entered into between Trant Engineering Ltd ("Trant") and Mott MacDonald Ltd ("Mott MacDonald"). Disputes arose between the parties which were settled with a Settlement and Services Agreement (the "Settlement") that also regulated the parties' obligations throughout the continuance of the project. The Settlement contained a standard form exclusion clause, stating:

> Notwithstanding any other term to the contrary in the Agreement or any related document and whether the cause of action for any claim arises under or in connection with the Agreement in contract or in tort, in negligence or for breach of statutory duty or otherwise. in relation to any and all causes of action as aforesaid: a. the total liability of the Consultant in the aggregate for all claims shall be limited to £500,000 (Five hundred thousand Pounds).

The Settlement also included some exclusions on liability and a net contribution clause. When Trant failed to make a payment of approximately £1.6 million, Mott MacDonald revoked Trant's passwords to the Building Information Modelling database and so their access to any of the designs. Trant in turn counterclaimed for £5 million for the cost of having to redo most of the design work and alleged that Mott MacDonald had refused to perform its obligations under the contract, which constituted a "*fundamental, deliberate and wilful*" breach of the Settlement. As a result, the exclusion and limitation clauses in the Settlement would not apply. Mott MacDonald denied breach of the Settlement but applied for summary judgment asking the court to confirm that the exclusion clause shall apply and that, as a result, Mott MacDonald's liability was to be limited to £500,000 regardless of whether there had been deliberate or wilful breach of contract. Trant contended that the exclusion clause did not apply. In doing so, it placed significant reliance on the presumption argument in MARHedge and contended that the presumption had not been rebutted as the clause did not include "strong language" against it. The court granted summary judgment in Mott MacDonald's favour. In its judgment, Judge Eyre QC: (i) held that the MARHedge was wrongly decided on this point; (ii) confirmed that in construing exclusion and limitation clauses the court shall refer to the normal principles of contractual construction; (iii) confirmed that exclusion and limitation clauses do not impose a presumption or require the parties to use any particular wording to achieve the effect of excluding liability even in case the clause aims at excluding or limiting liability for deliberate and repudiatory breaches; and (iv) confirmed that the court shall not read the exclusion or limitation of liability as having the effect to reduce a party's obligations to a mere declaration of intent. Based on this, the court found that the exclusion and limitation clauses in the Settlement were to be upheld as the exclusion clauses were sufficiently clear in establishing Mott McDonald's liability under the contract. The need of clear words was not that an exclusion or limitation regime had to expressly refer to deliberate and repudiatory breaches, but it was sufficient for the clause to be broad enough in its terms and scope, as in that specific case. The court also found that the exclusion and limitation clauses did not reduce Mott MacDonald's obligations to a mere declaration

11 *Mott Macdonald Ltd v Trant Engineering Ltd* [2021] EWHC 754 (TCC).

of intent as in case of a repudiatory breach Mott MacDonald would still remain liable up to the £500,000 liability cap.

In the light of the preceding, when negotiating exclusion and limitation of liability clauses the parties shall seek to use clear words in relation to the scope and application of the clause. However, it will usually not be necessary to use specific language sufficient to rebut a presumption that the clause will not apply in the case of a fundamental, wilful or deliberate breach.

CHAPTER 22

Claims

22.1 Claims in general

A claim in a construction contract may be defined as a request for a benefit (usually money, time or both) which the claimant contends being entitled to, but in relation to which the parties have not yet reached an agreement. Highly complex projects are more probable to generate multidiscipline, multi-party and complicated claims. Moreover, due to the scale of such projects, the risk that these claims will expose the parties to high losses is significant. For this reason, a specific claims clause will usually be included in the contract to define the exact procedure whereby the parties may make claims to enforce their rights under contract. Such provisions are principally aimed at facilitating dispute avoidance by setting the steps that shall be taken and deadlines that shall be met before claims escalate to the level of the dispute resolution procedures agreed in the contract. Thus, agreeing in advance on a precise claims handling procedure will increase the chances of achieving early amicable solutions and help the parties to save costs and reduce delays to the project.

22.2 Contractor claims clause

Contractor's claims mainly relate to time or money (or both) such as extensions of time and/or prolongation claims, breach of contract claims, variations, etc. The provisions of a claims clause relevant to the contractor's claims will usually set out a precise procedure that contractors shall follow.

22.2.1 The initial notice of claim

The claim procedure will usually commence with a written notification that the contractor shall send to the employer in case the contractor considers itself entitled to an extension of time and/or any additional payment under the contract.

The clause should clearly state any required form and content, e.g., be in writing and include any supporting particulars available at the time of the claim aimed at substantiating it. Importantly, the clause shall also set out the term by which the contractor shall send the notice. This will typically be as soon as practicable, and in any case within a certain number of days (typically between one and two months) as of the date on which it has become aware or should have become aware of the event giving rise to its right to make that claim. By adding the language "should have become aware" or similar wording, the

DOI: 10.4324/9781003387718-26

parties agree that the term does not run from the "actual knowledge" of the trigger event but extends to so-called constructive knowledge. This part of the claims clause may also set out the consequences in case the contractor fails to comply with the notice of claim requirements as provided in the contract (e.g., does not send it within the contractual agreed term). In the case of complex construction contracts, the parties will typically want to make the notice requirement a condition precedent to the validity of the claim as this will add certainty to the parties' positions and exposure to contractual claims. In this case, the claims clause usually state that a failure to serve the notice within the agreed period will deprive the contractor of any entitlement to extensions of time and/or payments.

22.2.2 The full claim

As the clause will typically set a very tight time limit for the contractor to give the notice of claim, it will be rare for contractors to be able to provide the employer with full details of the claim in the initial notice.

For this reason, the clause will usually give the contractor additional time to gather supporting documents and information so that a comprehensive claim may be sent to the employer within a certain term (usually between one and two months) to be counted from the date on which the notice was given.

Such final notice setting out the full claim shall include, among other things: (i) the original claim notice; (ii) any details relevant to the event that has generated the claim (the type of event, the date it has occurred, whether its effects are still continuing or are finished, etc.); (iii) the type of claim (extension of time and/or payment of money), the relevant contractual clauses entitling the contractor to make the claim and the relevant consequences in terms of additional time and/or money; (iv) the grounds on which the claim is being made; (v) other information and documents the contractor relies upon. When the claim is for an extension of time, the contractor may also be requested to provide a detailed critical path analysis evidencing the impact of the various delay events on the critical path and the "baseline" programme. However, as root cause analysis of complex claims may be particularly complex and considering that the impact of certain events may be hard to determine in advance (e.g., because the event is too complex to make a proper forecast within the specified deadline), the clause should include a mechanism allowing the contractor to propose a different deadline by which it shall submit the full claim. Moreover, where the event triggering the claim is an evolving event (e.g., a pandemic or a natural event), the detailed claim should be considered provisional, and the contractor should be afforded the right (and the obligation) to update the claim at specified intervals as the event develops so that the contractor may send its final claim within a certain number of days of its effects having finally unfolded.

22.2.3 The employer's response

Having received the fully detailed claim's documents and information the employer will then have a certain number of days (typically between one and two months) to approve or reject the claim, provide detailed comments or ask for further particulars. Also in this case, the clause should set out a mechanism allowing the employer to seek a reasonable extension in case of claims particularly large and/or complex.

The clause will also usually state that until the claim is agreed upon, the contractor shall not be released from performing the contract and that, where the parties fail to agree on any aspects relevant to the claim, the matter shall be resolved through the dispute resolution mechanism envisaged in the contract.

22.3 Employer claims clause

Employer's claims usually relate to delays in completing the works attributable to the contractor and quality issues (defects claims). Just like a contractor claims clause, an employer claims clause will usually state that in case the employer considers itself entitled to any payment and/or reimbursement from the contractor and/or any extension of time in relation to any of its obligations under the contract, it shall notify the contractor within a certain timeframe (the parties may agree on the same timeframe provided for the contractor's claims) after the employer became aware of the event entitling it to make the claim. Also in this case, the clause should set out the content of the notice (contractual clauses on which the claim is based, the grounds for the claim, and the amount of time and/or money it is claiming) and the term by which it shall be sent. The clause should also set out the consequences of a failure to notify within the contractual deadline. For example, the clause may state that the claim shall be considered waived, and the employer will be prevented from claiming on the same grounds. The parties may also expressly state that, where the claim has been validly notified, in the absence of an agreement between the parties on the employer's entitlement, the employer will be entitled to retain the claimed amount from any interim payments or final payment due to the contractor.

PART FOUR

CONTRACT NEGOTIATION

General and "boiler plate" clauses

Some contractual clauses are more general and may be found in almost any type of contracts. In some cases, such general clauses are defined as "boiler plate" to mean that they are routinely included in any contract. Often boiler plate clauses can be found at the very end of the agreement.

There is a tendency to consider such general clauses as "standard" and thus not worth a tough negotiation. Typically, the parties will focus on more construction-specific clauses such as those relevant to price and time. However, boiler plate clauses are at least as important as more specific clauses and deserve the same degree of attention from the parties.

DOI: 10.4324/9781003387718-27

CHAPTER 23

General issues

23.1 Introductory information

The incipit of any construction contract is typically introductory information setting out the following elements: (i) the title of the contract (e.g., EPC or EPCM contract), which indicates the type of agreement that the parties intend to enter into. However, the name the parties give to the agreement is not definitive evidence as to the type of contract. The "label" may not match the content. It is the content that counts, although the title may be one of the circumstances which a court considers in case it is called to interpret an ambiguous contract; (ii) the project name (e.g., Alfa Beta Project). This element is of no particular interest as the project will be usually described in detail in the contract and in particular in the contractual technical documents; (iii) the names of the contractual parties; (iv) the date of execution. In this regard, a contract is binding on the parties when there is an offer and an acceptance. In the case of written construction contracts, the contract becomes biding on the parties on the date of execution, which is typically evidenced by both parties signing the agreement. Thus, the contract is entered into when it is signed to be "executed". However, the "execution date" shall not be confused with the "effective date", and the two may not necessarily coincide. The parties to a contract may agree to sign the contract on a certain date but have the contract to start producing legal effects on a subsequent date which may be a fixed date or the date on which one or more conditions precedent will be satisfied.

23.2 The parties

The contract will then set out the exact commercial name of the relevant parties and add information aimed at precisely identifying them, including their address and registration number. This is clearly an important element of the contract also considering that any definition of "affiliate" will be referred to the specific party signing the contract.

23.3 Recitals

The construction contract will include a number of recitals (sometimes called "whereas") explaining the background of the project, the purpose of the contract and the type of services that the contractor has agreed to carry out. Normally, recitals are not binding on the parties as they are not considered having a promissory nature unless the parties clearly state so (which is almost invariably the case). Recitals may also include reference to

DOI: 10.4324/9781003387718-28

clauses which are of particular importance to one or both parties such as those related to health safety and environment ("HSE") and business ethics. In some cases, recitals may even contain operative provisions,[1] but may not modify or override clear provisions in the operative part of a contract.[2] Despite their relative importance, recitals may nonetheless help the courts when they are called to construe the contract's operative terms.[3] The case of *Blackpool Football Club (Properties) Limited v JSC Baltic International Bank & Anor*[4] shows that, when interpreting a contract, the courts will take into account the contract as a whole, including the recitals. In that case, the Court of Appeal commented on the legal status of the contract's recitals stating that "*although only a recital, provides evidence of the relevant factual matrix*" at the date of execution. Therefore, the stated purpose of the agreement as recorded in the recitals may become relevant when considering the contract's objective commercial coherence.[5]

When drafting and negotiating a construction contract it is vital that the parties treat recitals with special care, even when the contract expressly states that they are not binding operative provisions as they may assume unexpected prominence in a contractual dispute as they are still evidence of the context in which the contract was agreed.

23.4 Description of the contract

In this section, the contract describes the various documents which will be deemed to form and be read and construed as part of the contract between them. This usually includes at least: (i) the construction contract and any relevant conditions (if separate); (ii) the schedules; (iii) the scope of work that the contractor is required to perform; (iv) the contractor's documents as identified in the contract.

23.5 Definitions

Construction contracts usually provide a "definitions" clause where the parties expressly agree the meaning of certain technical terms that are repeated in the contract. This is mainly aimed at: (i) avoiding any uncertainly as to the meaning that the parties intend to give to terms whose significance is not objective. For example: (a) the term "adverse" in the expression "adverse weather conditions" does not have an objective meaning as it may be given different connotations depending on the type of contract, the place where the project is to be developed and the contractor's experience; (b) the expression "business day" refers to days in which it is not a public holiday and on which banks are open for general business. However, unless defined, it does not give any indication about the relevant jurisdiction (e.g., in England or in France); (ii) clarifying the meaning of technical words (e.g., "commissioning", "good industry practice", "milestone", "final acceptance

1 *Aspdin v Austin* [1844] 1 QB 671. Particularly where there was an obvious gap in the main body of the contract. See *J Toomey Motors Ltd and Another v Chevrolet UK Ltd* [2017] EWHC 276 (Comm).

2 *Mackenzie v Duke of Devonshire* [1896]) AC 400.

3 *South East Thames Regional Health Authority v YJ Lovell (London) Ltd* [1985] 32 BLR 127 at 135; See also *AMEC Foster Wheeler Group Ltd v Morgan Sindall Professional Services Ltd* [2015] EWHC 2012 (TCC) at 40.

4 *Blackpool Football Club (Properties) Limited v JSC Baltic International Bank* [2018] EWCA Civ 732. See also *J Toomey Motors Ltd and Another v Chevrolet UK Ltd* [2017] EWHC 276 (Comm).

5 *J Toomey Motors Ltd and Another v Chevrolet UK Ltd* [2017] EWHC 276 (Comm).

certificate", "taking over certificate", etc.); (iii) simplifying the contract by avoiding repetitions of long explanations about the meaning of expressions which are used more than once in the contract (e.g., "contract" to refer to the construction contract, "commencement date" to refer to the date in which the works will start, "contract price" to refer to the price to be paid to the contractor, "HGCR Act" to refer to Housing Grants Construction and Regeneration Act 1996, "works" to refer to the contractor's scope of work, etc.).

Definitions are pivotal as uncertain terms that are not clearly defined (in particular the first two categories) may lead to uncertainly as to the real terms of the contract and ultimately generate claims and disputes.

23.6 Interpretation

An interpretation clause aims at guiding the parties (and the courts, in case of disputes) on how the agreement shall be construed in case of ambiguity or disagreement over specific terms, phrases and concepts expressed in the contract. Examples of interpretation provisions include that: (i) words indicating one gender include all genders; (ii) words indicating the singular also include the plural and vice-versa; (iii) words like "agree", "agreed" or "agreement" require the agreement to be recorded in writing; (iv) "written" or "in writing" means hand-written, type-written, printed or electronically made, and resulting in a permanent record; (v) reference to person shall include natural persons and legal persons of whatever kind; (vi) references to a time of day shall be references to the time in London (UK), New York (USA) etc. Particular attention shall be paid to this last provision as it may have an impact on the functioning of the contract, e.g., when it comes to service of notices. The parties may also expressly exclude the application of construction rules such as "ejusdem generis" rule and the "contra proferentem" principle, in which case it would be advisable to specify that they have had the opportunity to obtain legal advice before agreeing on such exclusions.

23.7 Conditions precedent

23.7.1 Conditions precedent in general

An agreement is said to be conditional when its operation depends on an event whose occurrence is not certain. Conditions are divided into the two categories of "conditions precedent" and "conditions subsequent" (although in practice the expression condition precedent or "CP" is usually used in negotiations and contracts to address both categories). In the case of a condition precedent, the contract is not binding on the parties until and unless the relevant event occurs. For example, the contract is "executed", but will become operative only if and after the employer obtains some necessary permits. A condition is subsequent when a contract which is immediately binding on the parties, subject to their contractual obligations being cancelled in the event the condition does not occur. For example, a contract which is immediately binding will cease to be operative if the contractor does not provide a performance bond within a certain date.

English courts will normally uphold a CP if the "conditional link" between the obligation subject to the CP (e.g., issue of notice to proceed by employer) and the performance of the obligation to which it is linked (e.g., issue of a performance bond by the contractor) is clear,[6] even where this may have harsh consequences. The parties do not need to use specific words such as "condition precedent"[7] (e.g., the expression "subject to" is often used to denote a CP). However, as CP will be subject to the general principles of contractual interpretation (e.g., that words will be given their ordinary meaning and will be construed in the context of the contract as a whole),[8] the parties should use the "condition precedent" wording, in particular where the expression is used elsewhere in the contract.[9]

23.7.2 Conditions precedent clause

A typical CP clause would state that the employer shall not issue the notice to proceed until any CPs are fulfilled (or waived) in accordance with the contract. Typical CPs in construction contracts may be: (i) that the employer has received from the contractor any documents the parties agreed the contractor shall deliver before the works may commence (e.g., a duly executed performance bond, a duly executed parent company guarantee and any legal opinion on the relevant validity, enforceability and powers, etc.); (ii) that the contractor has received from the employer any documents the parties have agreed the contractor shall deliver before the works may commence (e.g., proof of permits necessary for the commencement of the works); (iii) that the parties have procured any insurance policies which are required to be in effect before the works can commence; (iv) in the case of financed projects, that any relevant financing documents (e.g., loan agreements, notes, bonds, etc.) is in force and effect, and the relevant funds are committed and available to be drawn.

The clause may also include: (i) reference as to whether the party benefiting from the CP will be required to confirm that the condition has been fulfilled and on what basis (e.g., at its sole discretion, etc.); and (ii) a longstop date by which the CP should be fulfilled[10] (absent such proviso, the CP may be found non-binding for lack of contractual certainty or be interpreted in favour of the party purportedly barred to fulfil the CP due to the expiry of the longstop date, rather than strictly against it[11]); (iii) the consequences in case the CP is not fulfilled by the longstop date.[12] This may include any termination rights afforded to the innocent party and any consequences thereof (e.g., that the parties are discharged from further obligations and liabilities under the contract, save for those already accrued); (iv) the obligation on the relevant party to use reasonable endeavours to ensure the satisfaction of the CP for which it is responsible; (v) whether any CP may be waived (in writing) and what party has the relevant right (usually the party benefiting from the CP); (vi) an obligation on the parties to update each other on the status of the fulfilment of the CP for which each of them is responsible.

---

6 *Aspen Insurance UK Ltd v Pectel Ltd* [2009] 2 All ER (Comm) 873.

7 *O'Brien v TTT Moneycorp Ltd* [2019] EWHC 1491.

8 *Davy Offshore Ltd v Emerald Field Contracting Ltd* [1991] 55 BLR at [79].

9 See *Heritage Oil and Gas Limited v Tulow Uganda Limited* [2014] EWCA Civ 1048 and *Interserve Construction v Hitachi* [2017] 2633 TCC.

10 *Total Gas Marketing Ltd v Arco British Ltd* [1998] UKHL 22.

11 *Obrascon Huarte Lain SA v Her Majesty's Attorney General for Gibraltar* [2014] EWHC 1028 (TCC).

12 *Foundation Co of Canada Ltd v United Grain Growers Ltd* [1997] BCLR.

23.8 Communications/notices

Complex projects will involve a myriad of communications between the employer (and/or the engineer) and the contractor. Such communication may be oral (e.g., communications on site between the parties' respective project teams) or in writing, and occur at different levels, from project people and up to the companies' top management.

Generally, construction contracts provide that the most significant communications (e.g., those relevant to requests, approvals and consents, certificates, determinations and, most importantly for contractors, notices) shall be in writing, e.g., by hand delivery, courier or email. Email is the most widely used system of electronic transmission for communications. However, it may generate legal issues, for example where the email has not reached the recipient because the sender has typed incorrectly the recipient's email address or has received a notification of failed delivery for any other reason. However, when a communication is particularly important (e.g., notices of suspension, termination, force majeure and disputes), the parties may agree the communication be only delivered by hand or by registered mail or courier, so excluding other means, such as non-registered mail and email. It is also common for the parties to agree on the exact moment when a communication will become effective. For example: (i) a communication delivered by hand may be deemed effective on the date of delivery unless it is received after a certain agreed hour of the day, in which case it will be deemed received on the next business day; (ii) a communication sent by registered mail or courier may be deemed delivered a certain number of business days after the day it was posted (which will be variable based on whether the communication was posted from the same country of the receiver or from abroad); (iii) a communication sent by email will be usually considered received upon sending the email, except if sent after a certain hour of the day as per communications delivered by hand.

An alternative may be agreeing to communicate through systems of electronic transmission like cloud-based operation management programs for the exchange of information and communications between the parties and expressly tailored to the peculiarities of complex construction and engineering projects.

Whatever means the parties agree on, it will be advisable to keep the written receipt (in the case of delivery by hand), the registered receipt of sending (in the case of a communication via registered email or courier) or the delivery confirmation (in the case of delivery via email) so to be able to prove that the communication was sent, the date and time it was sent or received and the correctness of the address to which it was addressed. Moreover, it would be good practice for the parties to indicate at least a second addressee who should be copied in the communication as the primary addressee may overlook a communication, experience technical problems, have health problems or leave the company during the execution of the project.

23.9 Process agent

Process agent clauses state that service shall be made on a process agent located in England and Wales. An agent for the service of process or a "process agent" is the representative of a contractual party authorised to receive service of proceedings (court, arbitration, adjudication, etc.) under a contract. The use of process agents has the main advantage of facilitating the service of proceedings when, for example, the parties agree to litigate or arbitrate in England, but one of the parties is based overseas, thereby removing the costly and time-consuming exercise of having to serve proceedings outside of England and Wales.

Process agent clauses are more frequent in cross-border finance transactions but may also be used in construction contracts. In case of disputes over the validity of service upon a process agent, the English courts have shown a tendency to find the service valid to the extent it was made in compliance with the wording of the clause. For example, in the case of *Banco San Juan Internacional Inc v Petroleos De Venezuela SA*,[13] the court found that Banco San Juan Internacional Inc ("BSJI") had a right to appoint a process agent for Petroleos De Venezuela SA ("PDVSA") as the relevant clause allowed BSJI to do so in case of failure by PDVSA to comply with its obligation to appoint a process agent. In *Aquila WSA Aviation Opportunities II Ltd v Onur Air Tasimacilik As*[14] the court found that failure to renew a process agent's appointment did not affect a claimant's right to serve a claim form at the address of the original process agent because the contract provided that the process agent was appointed "irrevocably".

There are certain rules that a principal appointing a process agent should follow to make sure that any service reaches the principal. For example: (i) the agent shall accept the service immediately and forward the documents on to the principal; (ii) the principal should constantly keep the agent up to date as to the contract details to which address any documents it has been served.

As to the wording of a process agent clause, it is not advisable that the clause gives a right to the other party to appoint the process agent in case the party on which the relevant obligation lies does not do it or does not do it within a certain term. If a clause is silent on the point, the service will normally follow the normal rules. It is also not advisable to accept an irrevocable appointment as this may lead to problems in case there is a need to change the appointed agent.

23.10 Severance

23.10.1 Severance in general

Where the parties are in a hurry to commence the work, they may not pay proper attention to the agreed terms of their contract during the negotiation phase. This may result in certain clauses being void or unenforceable due to illegality, invalidity or unenforceability. In the more extreme cases, this may lead to the entire contract being held void or unenforceable. Alternatively, a clause may become illegal as a consequence of a supervening event. An example is when, after the contract is entered into, a change in regulatory laws makes performance of certain contractual obligations illegal.

In such cases, the general principle is that the courts will be permitted to remove ("sever") the unenforceable provisions, so allowing the contract to survive. In case a whole clause is or has become invalid, the court may simply exclude it from the contract. Where, instead, only part of a clause is invalid, the courts adopt the so-called blue pencil test. The test was first used in the case of *Nordenfelt v Maxim Nordenfelt Guns and Ammunition Co Limited*[15]

13 *Banco San Juan Internacional Inc v Petroleos De Venezuela SA* [2020] EWHC 2937 (Comm).

14 *Aquila WSA Aviation Opportunities II Ltd v Onur Air Tasimacilik As* [2017] EWHC 1259 (Comm).

15 *Nordenfelt v Maxim Nordenfelt Guns e Ammunition Co Limited* [1894] AC 535.

where the House of Lords held that courts have the power to "*strike through with a blue pencil*" portions of a contractual clause that are unenforceable, leaving the remaining part of the clause intact and enforceable. The courts apply a three-fold test based on which a provision will be severed only if: (i) it can be severed without adding or modifying the wording of the remaining terms. The court will not redraft the contract for the parties. Words will not be added, rearranged or substituted with other words; (ii) the remaining terms continue to be supported by adequate consideration; (iii) the severance of the unenforceable provisions does not so change the character of the contract that it becomes not the sort of contract that the parties entered into. Moreover, a court will not sever the offending clause or parts unless it accords with public policy to do so. Where an offending clause or any part thereof is not "severable", the contract may be found entirely void.

23.10.2 Severance clause

Construction contracts usually include severance clauses evidencing the parties' intent to sever illegal provisions from the agreement so that the rest of the contract may survive.

Although the common law already covers the point regardless of the inclusion of such clauses, they remove any doubt as to the parties' intentions to keep the contract alive.

A severance clause will usually provide that if any term or provision of the contract is held to be illegal, void or unenforceable in whole or in part under any laws (as defined in the contract), such term or provisions shall be deemed not to form part of the contract and the enforceability of the remainder of the contract shall not be affected. The clause may also state that the parties shall negotiate in good faith to reach an agreement on how to amend or replace the offending provision with a valid and enforceable one.

It is worth noting that the risk of illegality is normally lower when the parties use a form of contract (e.g., a FIDIC form), although it may increase where the form is heavily negotiated and amended by the parties.

23.11 No waiver

23.11.1 Waiver in general

A waiver occurs where a party to a contract foregoes some of its legal rights under the contract. More specifically, the waiving party waives its remedies for breach of contract by the other party.[16] It is therefore completely different from variation.[17]

As held by Lord Bingham in *Millar v Dickson*:[18]

> In most litigious situations the expression 'waiver' is used to describe a voluntary, informed and unequivocal election by a party not to claim a right or raise an objection which it is open to that party to claim or raise.

16 *Enrico Furst & Co v WE Fischer Ltd* [1960] 2 Lloyd's Rep 340.

17 Other differences are that: (i) while a variation needs to be supported by consideration, a waiver does not; and (ii) while a variation requires an offer and an acceptance, a waiver does not.

18 *Millar v Dickson* [2002] 1 WLR 1615 at 1629.

Waiver is subject to a number of rules and requirements. In particular, where party to a contract (A) waives the obligation of the other party to the contract (B) to perform a stipulation in the contract, for the waiver to be effective it is necessary that: (i) the contract term which is the subject of the waiver was for A's sole benefit;[19] (ii) A had knowledge of the existence of the right or defence he is waiving;[20] (iii) it is not necessary that B has requested A to waive B's obligation. However, in the absence of a request from B, the representation from A to B that A waives the performance of B's obligation must be unequivocal.[21] Such representation "*can be by words or conduct, but does not have to be as blunt as 'I hereby waive' the other party's obligation to perform the stipulation*".[22] Where the representation is made by conduct, such conduct shall be intentional and inconsistent with the existence of the right or defence;[23] (iv) B must have relied upon the conduct that he alleges constitutes the waiver,[24] i.e., he must "*either act on the unequivocal representation of A to his detriment; or he must conduct his affairs on the basis of the waiver*".[25]

23.11.2 No waiver clause

A "no waiver" clause provides that in case a contractual party has breached the contract, inaction on the part of the non-defaulting party does not constitute a waiver of the legal rights that the non-defaulting party has under the contract as a consequence of the defaulting party's breach. Some clauses may also add that: (i) the waiver will be effective only if made in writing and signed; (ii) a failure by the non-defaulting party to exercise, or a delay in exercising, any right, power or remedy under the contract will not operate as a waiver; (iii) where, following the breach/default by the defaulting party, the non-defaulting exercises its contractual rights or remedy only partially, the non-defaulting shall not be prevented from exercising any other right or remedy; (iv) a waiver of any breach or default shall not be deemed to be a waiver of any subsequent breach or default.

The case law on the enforceability of no waiver clauses is limited. In *Tele2 International Card Company SA and others v Post Office Limited*,[26] clause 16 of the agreement ("Agreement") between Post Office ("POL") and Tele2 was a "no waiver" clause providing as follows:

> [I]n no event shall any delay, neglect or forbearance on the part of any party in enforcing (in whole or in part) any provision of this Agreement be or be deemed to be a waiver thereof or a waiver of any other provision or shall in any way prejudice any right of that party under this Agreement.

Tele2 breached the terms of the Agreement (it failed to provide parent company guarantee letters in accordance with the Agreement). POL continued to perform its obligations for nearly a year before terminating the contract for breach. At the trial, Tele2 alleged that

19 *Persimmon Homes (South Coast) Ltd v Hall Aggregates (South Coast) Ltd* [2009] EWCA Civ 1108 at [52].
20 *CMA Maltin Engineering Ltd v J Donne Holdings Ltd* [1980] 15 BLR 61 at [77].
21 *Banning v Wright* [1972] 1 WLR 972 at [979].
22 *Persimmon Homes (South Coast) Ltd v Hall Aggregates (South Coast) Ltd* [2009] EWCA Civ 1108 at [52].
23 *CMA Maltin Engineering Ltd v J Donne Holdings Ltd* [1980] 15 BLR 61 at [77].
24 *Scandinavian Trading Tanker Co AB v Flota Petrolera Escuatoriana* [1983] QB 529 at [534–535].
25 *Persimmon Homes (South Coast) Ltd v Hall Aggregates (South Coast) Ltd* [2009] EWCA Civ 1108 at [52].
26 *Tele2 International Card Company SA and others v Post Office Limited* [2009] EWCA Civ 9.

POL's delay in giving written notice of termination until nearly one year after the parent company guarantees were due, and its performance of the contract in the meantime without any protest as to the lack of the parent company guarantees, meant that POL had affirmed the Agreement by election. POL was therefore not entitled to terminate. The purported termination notice was a wrongful anticipatory renunciation of the Agreement. POL sought to rely on clause 16, arguing that its effect was that any delay by POL to give notice to enforce its rights to terminate could not be used to find an affirmation by election. The judge upheld Tele2's argument that there was no effective affirmation by election. The judge held that, but for clause 16, he would have held that POL had elected to affirm the Agreement. However, the effect of clause 16 was that POL's delay in giving notice could not be held against POL. As a result, POL was entitled to terminate, and Tele2 did not have a claim for repudiatory breach of the Agreement. Tele2 appealed. The Court of Appeal found in Tele2's favour. It held that:

> clause 16 cannot prevent the fact of an election to abandon the right to terminate from existing: either it does or it does not. This conclusion is reinforced, I think, by the terms of clause 16 itself. Although it stipulates that 'in no event shall any delay, neglect or forbearance' on the part of any party in enforcing a provision of the Agreement '. . . be or be deemed to be a waiver' of the provision or '. . . shall in any way prejudice any right of that party under this Agreement', it does not deal at all with the issue of election of whether or not to exercise a contractual right. The general law demands that a party which has a contractual right to terminate a contract must elect whether or not to do so. This clause does not attempt to say that the doctrine of election shall not apply – even assuming that any contractual provision could exclude the operation of the doctrine.

The case shows that a "no waiver" clause may not protect the non-defaulting party in case clear conduct showing an election to waive a right may prevent the non-defaulting party from relying on the waiver clause. Therefore, even if the contract contains a no waiver clause, a non-defaulting party seeking to protect its position should always consider sending a letter reserving its rights as soon as it becomes aware of an event of default. The parties may also wish to consider to expressly exclude the possibility of affirmation of contract by election from their "no waiver"" clause. However, as mentioned in the Tele2 judgment ("*even assuming that any contractual provision could exclude the operation of the* doctrine [of election]"), this approach is by no means guaranteed to succeed.

23.12 Entire agreement

23.12.1 Entire agreements in general

Due to the degree of complexity and length, construction contracts are usually negotiated over a long period.

The negotiations may be particularly harsh and complex, and oral representations are usually made by both during this pre-contractual phase. The risk of one party alleging that part of the agreement shall be found outside the contract and was formed during the negotiation phase is therefore high.

This risk is usually covered by the inclusion of entire agreement clauses stating that the contract, and only it, represents a complete set of rights and obligations between the parties.

The purpose of entire agreement clauses was clarified by Lightman J in the case of *Inntrepreneur Pub Company Ltd v East Crown Ltd*[27] where the judge stated that:

> The purpose of an entire agreement clause is to preclude a party to a written agreement threshing through the undergrowth and finding in the course of negotiations some (chance) remark or statement (often long forgotten or difficult to recall or explain) on which to found a claim such as the present to the existence of a collateral warranty. The entire agreement clause obviates the occasion for any such search and the peril to the contracting parties posed by the need which may arise in its absence to conduct such a search. For such a clause constitutes a binding agreement between the parties that the full contractual terms are to be found in the document containing the clause and not elsewhere, and that accordingly any promises or assurances made in the course of negotiations (which in the absence of such a clause might have effect as a collateral warranty) shall have no contractual force, save in so far as they are reflected and given effect in that document.

While the inclusion of an entire agreement clause will normally prevent the parties from relying on what was said and exchanged in the negotiation phase to prove that the terms of the contract are in fact different from the ones included in the written instrument, such clauses will not normally prevent: (i) the admission into evidence of pre-contract evidence (e.g., oral communications or documents) aimed at proving the meaning of the words used in the contract[28] or agreements made after the contract containing the entire agreement clause;[29] (ii) any request of contract rectification in case the parties agree that the current wording does not reflect their true intention; and (iii) the implication of terms into the contract in case of contract "gaps".[30]

23.12.2 Entire agreement clause

A typical entire agreement clause will state that the contract contains and constitutes the entire agreement between the relevant parties in connection with the works and supersedes all prior correspondence, representations, informal undertakings and other communications (whether oral or written) exchanged between the parties and/or their respective employees, agents, advisers, representatives and others in relation to the subject matter of the contract.

An entire agreement clause may also contain an acknowledgment that, in entering into the contract, the parties have not relied upon any statements or representations made by the other party, other than those set out in the contract.[31] The effect of such additional wording is to prevent one party to raise claims on the basis of pre-contractual misrepresentation so that a party will be estopped (so-called contractual estoppel) from alleging that it was induced to enter into the contract by a representation of the other party (which is not recorded in the written contract, e.g., made orally). Where the clause does not include this language, liability under the Misrepresentation Act 1967 may not be excluded,

27 *Inntrepreneur Pub Company Ltd v East Crown Ltd* [2000] 2 Lloyd's Rep 611 at 613 [7], per Lightman J.

28 *Proforce Recruit Ltd v The Rugby Group Ltd* [2006] EWCA Civ 69 at [40] – [41]. See also *Metronet Rail BCV Ltd v London Underground Ltd* [2007] EWHC 2121 (TCC) at [48] – [52].

29 *Lloyd v Sutcliffe* [2007] EWCA Civ 153 at [26] – [28].

30 *Hart v McDonald* [1910] 10 CLR 417 at 430. See also *Matthews v Kuwait Bechtel Corporation* [1959] 2 QB 57 at [63] and, more recently, *West 3 Mechanical Contractors Ltd v Mizen Design Build Ltd* [2014] EWHC 4004 (TCC) at [87] and *J N Hipwell & Son v Szurek* [2018] EWCA Civ 674.

31 This wording may also be included in a separate "non-reliance" clause.

and misrepresentation claims may be considered admissible.[32] This is confirmed by the following words of Mr Justice Browne-Wilkinson in *Alman and another v Associated Newspapers Group Limited*:[33]

> If it [the entire agreement clause which he was considering] were designed to exclude liability for misrepresentation it would, I think, have to be couched in different terms, for example, a clause acknowledging that the parties had not relied on any representations in entering into the contract.

In *EA Grimstead & Son Ltd v McGarrigan*[34] the contract between the parties stated "*The Purchaser confirms that it has not relied on any warranty representation or undertaking of or on behalf of the Vendors . . . save for any representation or warranty or undertaking expressly set out [in the Agreement]*" and "*no party hereto has entered into this Agreement in reliance on any representation, warranty or undertaking of any other party which is not set out or referred to in this Agreement*". The court held that these acknowledgments of non-reliance were "*capable of operating as an evidential estoppel*" to prevent the party who has given the acknowledgment from subsequently asserting that it had in fact relied upon representations not included in the contract. Chadwick LJJ, in giving effect to a non-reliance clause in a contract, said as follows:

> There are, as it seems to me, at least two good reasons why the courts should not refuse to give effect to an acknowledgement of non-reliance in a commercial contract between experienced parties of equal bargaining power a fortiori, where those parties have the benefit of professional advice. First, it is reasonable to assume that the parties desire commercial certainty. They want to order their affairs on the basis that the bargain between them can be found within the document which they have signed. They want to avoid the uncertainty of litigation based on allegations as to the content of oral discussions at pre-contractual meetings. Second, it is reasonable to assume that the price to be paid reflects the commercial risk which each party – or, more usually, the purchaser – is willing to accept. The risk is determined, in part at least, by the warranties which the vendor is prepared to give. The tighter the warranties, the less the risk and (in principle, at least) the greater the price the vendor will require and which the purchaser will be prepared to pay. It is legitimate, and commercially desirable, that both parties should be able to measure the risk, and agree the price, on the basis of the warranties which have been given and accepted.

This was confirmed in *Watford Electronics Ltd v Sanderson CFL Ltd*[35] where the contract stated:

> The parties agree that these terms and conditions (together with any other terms and conditions expressly incorporated in the Contract) represent the entire agreement between the parties relating to the sale and purchase of the Equipment and that no statement or representations made by either party have been relied upon by the other in agreeing to enter into the Contract.

---

32 *Axa Sun Life Services Plc v Campbell Martin Ltd* [2011] EWCA Civ 133; see also *BSkyB Ltd v HP Enterprise Services UK Ltd* [2010] EWHC 86 (TCC) at [359] – [389].

33 *Alman and another v Associated Newspapers Group Limited* (unreported, 20 June 1980).

34 *EA Grimstead & Son Ltd v McGarrigan* [1999] EWCA Civ 3029.

35 *Watford Electronics Ltd v Sanderson CFL Ltd* [2001] EWCA Civ 317.

When the claimant made a claim based on misrepresentation, the court held that the acknowledgment of non-reliance prevented him from asserting that he had relied upon the defendant's pre-contract representations. The court also added that:

> Where both parties to the contract have acknowledged, in the document itself, that they have not relied upon any pre-contract representation, it would be bizarre (unless compelled to do so by the words which they have used) to attribute to them an intention to exclude a liability which they must have thought could never arise.

23.12.3 Interpretation of entire agreement clauses

The English courts will normally uphold entire agreement clauses. In *Strachan & Henshaw Limited v Stein Industrie (UK) Limited and GEC Alsthom Limited*,[36] the Court of Appeal upheld an entire agreement clause by stating that the express terms of the contract were "*exclusive of the rights, obligations and liabilities of each of [the parties] to the other*" which was sufficient to preclude a claim for common law damages for breach of contract. The court noted that there was commercial common sense in providing expressly for the claims the parties intended to be allowed and excluding all others, even if the effect of that was to reduce important contractual obligations to unenforceable declarations of intent.

However, English courts will construe entire agreement clauses strictly, in the same way as they do with exclusion clauses. In *AXA Sun Life Services Plc v Campbell Martin Ltd and Others*[37] the Court of Appeal confirmed that for liability to be effectively excluded, clear wording to that effect will be required. In case the parties intend to exclude liability for misrepresentation (or restrict the remedies only to the contractual ones) it would be advisable to include clear wording to such extent (possibly specifying that clause does not exclude liability for fraud), although lack of express reference to misrepresentation may not be fatal as the courts will look at the whole contract. In *NF Football Investments Ltd and another v NFCC Group Holdings Ltd and another*[38] the contract between parties stated:

> This agreement (together with the documents referred to in it) constitutes the entire agreement between the parties and supersedes and extinguishes all previous discussions, correspondence, negotiations, drafts, agreements, promises, assurances, warranties, representations and understandings between them, whether written or oral, relating to its subject matter.

The contract expressly included a contractual procedure to deal with misrepresentation claims which provided a complete contractual indemnity for losses incurred by reason of any misstatement. The court held that the clause, when construed in the context of the agreement as a whole, and, in particular, the said contractual procedure, excluded any statutory misrepresentation claim.

It is also worth noting that a court will also assess whether a non-reliance clause included in the contract excludes or restricts liability or it is to be construed as a "basis clause", i.e., a clause setting out the basis on which the parties were dealing. As suggested by Lewison

---

36 *Strachan & Henshaw Limited v Stein Industrie (UK) Limited and GEC Alsthom Limited* [1997] EWCA Civ 2940.

37 *AXA Sun Life Services Plc v Campbell Martin Ltd and Others* [2011] EWCA Civ 133.

38 *NF Football Investments Ltd and another v NFCC Group Holdings Ltd and another* [2018] EWHC 1346 (Ch).

LJ in his judgment in *First Tower Trustees Limited & Intertrust Trustees Limited v CDS (Superstores International) Ltd*,[39] if, but for the non-reliance or basis clause, there would be a claim for misrepresentation, then the clause is an exclusion clause which should be subject to the reasonableness test under Unfair Contract Terms Act 1977 ("UCTA").[40] In that case, the Court of Appeal found that the relevant clause was not reasonable and so was void, notwithstanding that it had been negotiated by commercial parties that appeared to have similar bargaining power and had the benefit of legal advice.[41]

Recent case law seems to confirm that courts tend to uphold entire agreement clauses. In *Goodlife v Hall*[42] and in *Interactive E-solutions JLT v O3b Africa Ltd*,[43] the Court of Appeal upheld a wide exclusion clause as reasonable on the grounds that the parties were of equal bargaining position and that the parties had clearly understood the operation of the exclusion clause. In *Motortrak Ltd v FCA Australia Pty Ltd*[44] the court, in upholding an exclusion clause, gave also weight to the fact that it was reciprocal. However, it is clear that the courts have taken a hard position on the doctrine of contractual estoppel plainly overturning previous case law shielding "basis clauses" from the application of statutory "reasonableness" tests. Thus, the parties to the contract should analyse the extent to which such clauses are "reasonable".

23.13 Independent contractor

23.13.1 Vicarious liability

As a general rule, if a person, acting carelessly, causes another to suffer harm, injury or loss, that person will be held liable in negligence for his conduct. However, in some cases a person can be held vicariously liable for the careless conduct of another. The classic example is the vicarious liability of the employer in respect of careless acts of his employee during the course of his employment and despite the employer possibly not having done anything careless. Where there is not an employment relationship the rule is that the employer will not be vicariously liable. As said by Lord Justice Slesser in *Honeywell and Stein Ltd. v Larkin (London Commercial Photographers) Ltd*:[45]

> [i]t is well established as a general rule of English law that the employer is not liable for the acts of his independent contractor in the same way as he is for the acts of his servants or agents even though these acts are done in carrying out work for his benefit under the contract.

39 *First Tower Trustees Limited & Intertrust Trustees Limited v CDS (Superstores International) Ltd* [2018] EWCA Civ 1396.

40 The UCTA regulates clauses that attempt to exclude or limit a party's liability in commercial contracts where one of the parties is a consumer. The reasonable test is included in Section 11(2) of the UCTA which states a term is reasonable when it was fair and reasonable having regard to the circumstances which were, or ought reasonable to have been, known to or in the contemplation of the parties when the contract was made.

41 In contrast with the court's tendency to support freedom of contract. In *Raiffeisen Zentralbank Osterreich AG v The Royal Bank of Scotland Plc* [2011] 1 Lloyd's Rep, Justice Clarke clarified the point stating that "*[t]he Courts have on several occasions expressed the undesirability, generally speaking, of striking down terms freely agreed between large commercial parties who are usually to be regarded as the best judges of their own interests*".

42 *Goodlife Foods Ltd v Hall Fire Protection Ltd* [2018] EWCA Civ 1371.

43 *Interactive E-solutions JLT v O3b Africa Ltd* [2018] EWCA Civ 62.

44 *Motortrak Ltd v FCA Australia Pty Ltd* [2018] EWHC 990 (Comm).

45 *Honeywell and Stein Ltd. v Larkin (London Commercial Photographers) Ltd* [1933] ALL ER 77.

There are, however, a number of exceptions to this general rule, i.e.: (i) in case the employer authorises the independent contractor to commit a tort;[46] (ii) where the independent contractor is engaged to perform "special hazardous" work,[47] where, depending on the court's approach, hazardous work may be intended as "*a dangerous operation in its intrinsic nature*"[48] or activities which are "*exceptionally dangerous whatever precautions are taken*";[49] and (iii) where the law characterises the employer's duty as non-delegable, e.g. the employer's duty to provide a safe workplace for their employee. Even where a formal employment does not exist, an employer may be held vicariously liable for acts by persons which are not employees, but which have with relationships sufficiently "akin to employment" with the employer. In *Various Claimants v Catholic Child Welfare Society*[50] (aka the Christian Brothers case), Lord Phillips listed "*a number of policy reasons*" usually making it fair, just and reasonable to impose vicarious liability upon an employer for the torts committed by an employee in the course of his employment, i.e.:

> (i) the employer is more likely to have the means to compensate the victim than the employee and can be expected to have insured against that liability; (ii) the tort will have been committed as a result of activity being taken by the employee on behalf of the employer; (iii) the employee's activity is likely to be part of the business activity of the employer; (iv) the employer, by employing the employee to carry on the activity will have created the risk of the tort committed by the employee; (v) the employee will, to a greater or lesser degree, have been under the control of the employer[51].

However, in the case of *Barclays Bank plc v Various Claimants*,[52] the Supreme Court has now held in that vicarious liability will not always be imposed for the acts of an independent contractor. If it is clear that the individual is carrying on business on their own account, then there is no need to consider the five factors listed in the Christian Brothers case, which would only be considered in "doubtful" cases to decide whether an independent contractor was effectively part of the employer's business so as to make it fair, just and reasonable to impose vicarious liability, while they should not be considered "*where it is clear that the tortfeasor is carrying on his own independent business*". However, it may not always be easy to draw a distinction between activities integrated into the employer's business and the activities of a clear independent contractor. What is certain is that the employer's vicarious liability does not only apply to those who can be strictly identified as employees ("*it would be going too far down the road to tidiness for this court to align the common law concept of vicarious liability, developed for one set of reasons, with the statutory concept of 'worker', developed for a quite different set of reasons*"[53]) and that, as clarified by Lady

46 *Ellis v Sheffield Gas Consumers Co.* 1853 2 E&B 767.

47 *Salisbury v Woodland* [1970] 1 QB 324. Examples include working on the highway (*Holliday v National Telephone Co.* [1889] 2 QB 392), grounds works adjacent to a neighbouring property which may undermine its foundations (*Angus v Dalton* [1888] 6 App Cas 740) or work entailing peril like metal welding which may cause fire (*Honeywell and Stein Ltd. v Larkin Brothers (London Commercial Photographers) Ltd* [1933] All ER 77).

48 *Honeywell and Stein Ltd. v Larkin Brothers (London Commercial Photographers) Ltd* [1933] All ER 77.

49 *Biffa Waste Services Ltd v Maschinefabrik Ernst Hese GmbH* [2009] WLR 324.

50 *Various Claimants v Catholic Child Welfare Society* [2012] UKSC 56.

51 This approach was followed in a number of following cases including *Cox v Ministry of Justice* [2016] AC 660 and *Armes v Nottinghamshire County Council* [2018] AC 855. In both cases, Lord Reed clarified that (i) the five factors do not carry the same weight; and (ii) it is open to the court to give different weight to each factor depending on the case.

52 *Barclays Bank plc v Various Claimants* [2020] UKSC 13.

53 *Barclays Bank plc v Various Claimants* [2020] UKSC 13.

Hale in Barclays Bank, "the question therefore is, as it has always been, whether the tortfeasor is carrying on business on his own account or whether he is in a relationship akin to employment with the defendant". This is why, although independent contractor's clauses do not entirely eliminate the risk of the employer being found vicariously liable for the carelessness of acts of a contractor, they are important to reduce such risk.

23.13.2 Independent contractor clause

The purpose of "independent contractor" clauses (also called "no partnership or agency" clauses) is to avoid the consequences of an unwanted legal relationship between the contractor and the employer (e.g., a partnership, a joint venture or an employment relationship), which may lead to undesired consequences such as "duties of loyalty' (e.g., a duty to disclose all conflicts of interest and a duty to subordinate the fiduciary's own interests in favour of those of the other party), financial and tax obligations, or the employer's liability to a third party for negligence or other tortious conduct of the contractor it has engaged for the project.

A typical independent contractor clause would normally state that: (i) the contract does not create any partnership, joint venture or other joint relationship between the employer and the contractor; (ii) the contract does not grant a power or authority of one party to act on behalf of the other party (or to represent that it has such authority); and (iii) neither the contractor nor any of its employees is or shall be deemed to be an employee of the employer. This provision is strictly linked to the issue of vicarious liability.

23.14 Exclusive remedy

23.14.1 Exclusive remedies in general

A typical construction contract will expressly provide specific remedies for some breaches, such as liquidated damages for delay. Normally, unless the contract provides otherwise, such contractual remedies are not exclusive, in the sense that they do not automatically exclude any other remedies available to the parties at common law.

23.14.2 Exclusive remedy clause

The parties to a construction contract may agree to include in their contract an exclusive remedy provision stating that the remedies expressly provided for under the contract (e.g., liquidated damages) exclude any remedies at common law (including any damages at law).

Such a clause may include the following terms: (i) the parties' agreement that their respective rights, obligations and liabilities under the contract are to be considered exhaustive of the rights, obligations and liabilities that each party has against the other under or in connection with the contract and/or the works; (ii) the indication that this applies for any type of rights, obligations and liabilities, including those arising as a result of a breach of contract or of statutory duty or in tort giving rise to a remedy at common law; (iii) the express exclusion of liability in respect of any damages or losses suffered by either party arising out of, under or in connection with the contract or the works.

The result of such a clause would be that: (i) the only remedies available to the innocent party would be those under the contract; and (ii) in case the innocent party cannot identify a specific and express remedy under the contract, it would have no remedy available.

For this reason, the employers often reject contractors' request to include an exclusive remedies clause in the contract or limit the applicability of such clauses by clearly stating what remedy is to be considered exclusive (e.g., liquidated damages).

23.14.3 Interpretation of exclusive remedy clauses

It is now accepted that English courts recognise exclusive remedy clauses as valid and enforceable. The leading case on this subject is *Strachan & Henshaw v Stein Industrie (UK)*.[54] Condition 44.4 of the agreement between the parties contained an exclusive remedy clause that read as follows:

> The Purchaser and the Contractor intend that their respective rights, obligations and liabilities as provided for in the Conditions shall be exhaustive of the rights, obligations and liabilities of each of them to the other arising out of, under or in connection with the Contract or the Works, whether such rights, obligations and liabilities arise in respect or in consequence of a breach of contract or of statutory duty or a tortious or negligent act or omission which gives rise to a remedy at common law. Accordingly, except as expressly provided for in the Conditions, neither party shall be obligated or liable to the other in respect of any damages or losses suffered by the other which arise out of, under or in connection with the Contract or the Works, whether by reason or in consequence of any breach of contract or of statutory duty or tortious or negligent act or omission.

When asked to decide on the validity of such clause, the Court of Appeal observed:

> I do not see why the clear meaning and effect of Condition 44.4 should be cut down. If parties want to limit their potential liability to one another in the manner provided for by Condition 44.4, there is no reason why the law should stand in their way and prevent them from doing so.

Given the established position that courts have taken on the validity of exclusive remedies clauses, direct challenges to such clauses are uncommon. Disputes are less infrequent as to whether a particular type of claim is caught by the exclusive remedy clause or is otherwise permissible on a proper construction of it. In the case of *Modern Engineering (Bristol) Ltd v Gilbert Ash (Northern) Ltd*,[55] the House of Lords considered how to construe an exclusive remedy clause. Lord Diplock said:

> It is, of course, open to parties to a contract . . . to exclude by express agreement a remedy for its breach which would otherwise arise by operation of law. . . . But in construing such a contract one starts with the presumption that neither party intends to abandon any remedies for its breach arising by operation of law, and clear express words must be used in order to rebut this presumption. . . . To rebut that presumption one must be able to find in the contract clear unequivocal words in which the parties have expressed their agreement that this remedy shall not be available in respect of breaches of that particular contract.

However, the courts may take the position that the presumption in question is less strong where the parties do not simply exclude a common law remedy, but rather replace it with

54 *Strachan & Henshaw Limited v Stein Industrie (UK) Limited and GEC Alsthom Limited* [1997] EWCA Civ 2940.

55 *Modern Engineering (Bristol) Ltd v Gilbert Ash (Northern) Ltd* [1974] AC 689, [1973] 3 All ER 195.

a different contractual one. In *Scottish Power UK plc v BP Exploration Operating Company Ltd*,[56] Scottish Power UK plc ("Scottish") Power and BP Exploration Operating Company Ltd ("BP") entered into long-term gas sale and purchase agreements (the "Agreements") in relation to a gas field in the North Sea. The Agreement provided: (i) under Clause 7.1, that BP had to repair, maintain and operate the natural gas facilities to the standards to be expected of a skilled and experienced operator and deliver an agreed daily quantity of gas; (ii) that if BP failed to supply the agreed amount of gas, it was obliged to supply an amount equivalent of unsupplied ("default gas") gas to Scottish Power at a "default gas price" (i.e., a discounted rate equal to 70% of the regular contract price for the gas) once production had restarted; and (iii) at Clause 16.6, that

> The delivery of Natural Gas at the Default Gas Price . . . shall be in full satisfaction and discharge of all rights, remedies and claims howsoever arising whether in contract or in tort or otherwise in law on the part of [Scottish Power] in respect of underdeliveries by [BP] under this Agreement, and save for the rights and remedies set out in Clauses 16.1 to 16.5 . . . [Scottish Power] shall have no right or remedy and shall not be entitled to make any claims in respect of any such underdelivery.

Due to operational reasons, BP closed the gas facilities earlier a few years after the Agreement. As a result, Scottish Power brought proceedings against BP for failure of BP to operate the facilities during the relevant period and claimed approximately £85 million as the difference between the default gas price and the amount it had to pay for the replacement of the natural gas due by BP. The dispute focused on whether Scottish Power's rights and remedies in respect BP's breach of its obligations under Article 7.1 were confined to its entitlement to delivery of natural gas at the default gas price, or it could claim damages for breach of Article 7.1. BP held that the default gas price was intended to provide the sole remedy in respect of underdeliveries and that the damages claimed by the Scottish Power were indeed due to the underdelivery of gas. Scottish Power contended that: (i) its claim was not one "*in respect of underdeliveries*" within the meaning of Clause 16.6 because it was not a necessary part of its cause of action to establish that there had in fact been any underdelivery; (ii) thus, as there were two possible meanings of Clause 16.6, the presumption identified by Lord Diplock would lead to the result that Scottish Power should not be taken to have given up very valuable contractual rights; (iii) the contrary conclusion would render the obligations imposed by Clause 7.1 meaningless or would reduce them to mere statements of intent. The Commercial Court disagreed. Leggatt J ruled that Clause 16.6 was comprehensively drafted and, while the words "*in respect of underdeliveries*" were not precise, the default gas price was an automatic remedy in the case of an underdelivery of gas. As a consequence, allowing Scottish Power an additional remedy for the same breach would be an "*improbable intention*" of Clause 16.6 ("*where a breach of [clause] 7.1 causes loss by way of an underdelivery for which the Buyer* [Scottish Power] *automatically receives compensation pursuant to [clause] 16 in the form of Default Gas, that remedy is in my opinion intended to be the sole remedy available for the loss*"). Leggatt J took the following position on the Gilbert Ash presumption:

> I have not overlooked the presumption that parties do not intend to abandon remedies that arise by operation of law. It seems to me that this presumption must be less strong where the

56 *Scottish Power UK plc v BP Exploration Operating Company Ltd* [2016] EWCA Civ 1043.

> common law remedy is not simply excluded but is replaced by a different (and valuable) contractual one . . . the court should give effect to it even though the interpretation may deprive a party of a right at law which he might otherwise have had. It is open to parties to make an agreement which has that effect.

Scottish Power appealed, but the Court of Appeal confirmed the decision given by the Commercial Court. Clarke LJ stated that:

> The fact that there are two possible meanings is the beginning of the inquiry, not its end. It is then necessary for the court to apply 'all its tools of linguistic, contextual, purposive and common sense analysis to discern what the clause really means' per Briggs LJ in Nobahar-Cookson v The Hut Group Ltd [2016] EWCA Civ 128 [19]. If as a result of so doing the answer becomes clear the court should give effect to it even though the interpretation may deprive a party of a right at law which he might otherwise have had. It is open to parties to make an agreement which has that effect. . . . Further the strength of the presumption is reduced in proportion to the degree of derogation from the common law position. Article 16.6 is not a pure exclusion clause. It is a clause which replaces common law rights with a different contractual remedy, which may, in certain circumstances, be more valuable than the right to damages.

This judgment corroborates the current trend in interpretation of contracts that the courts will treat the natural meaning of language as the best guide to interpretation.[57]

23.15 Further assurance

23.15.1 Duty to cooperate

After a construction contract is entered into the parties will normally need to take further actions to give effect to the relevant provisions (e.g., the contract may oblige the parties to cooperate in securing permits or other rights on the site). Such duty to cooperate has been heavily discussed by courts and scholars. In the 1881 case of *Mackay v Dick*,[58] Lord Blackburn stated that:

> as a general rule . . . where in a written contract it appears that both parties have agreed that something shall be done, which cannot effectually be done unless both concur in doing it, the construction of the contract is that each agrees to do all that is necessary to be done on his part for the carrying out of that thing, though there may be no express words to that effect. What is the part of each must depend on circumstances.

Nowadays, English courts are more reluctant to recognise duty to cooperate (also considering the somewhat unclear distinction between the duty to cooperate and the duty to act in good faith) and tend to confine such duty to long-term relational agreements. As held in *Yam Seng Pte Limited v International Trade Corporation Limited*,[59] such duty may be inferred in contracts requiring:

> a high degree of communication, cooperation and predictable performance based on mutual trust and confidence and involve expectations of loyalty which are not legislated for in the express terms of the contract but are implicit in the parties' understanding and necessary to give business efficacy to the arrangements.

57 See also *Arnold v Britton & ors* [2015] UKSC 36.
58 *Mackay v Dick* [1881] 6 App Cas 251.
59 *Yam Seng Pte Limited v International Trade Corporation Limited* [2013] EWHC 111 (QB) at 142.

For example, in *Swallowfalls Ltd v Monaco Yachting*[60] the Court of Appeal implied a "duty to cooperate" in relation to the confirmation of the achievement of milestones and the counter-signature of stage certificates in a shipbuilding contract and its associated loan agreement. The court held that such:

> proposed implied term is an ordinary implication in any contract for the performance of which co-operation is required" and that "[a] shipbuilding contract is such a contract since . . . the builder only earns a stage payment when the buyer's representative signs a certificate that the relevant stage or milestone has been achieved.

23.15.2 Further assurance clause

Considering the narrow construction of the duty to cooperate, construction contracts often include further assurance clauses compelling each party to exercise all such powers as are available to it, do all such acts (including signing, executing and delivering documents) which may be necessary or required to give full force and effect to the provisions of the contract between them. Absent such a clause, a party might try to escape the contract by withholding or "slowing" assistance to the other party where that assistance is necessary for the contract to be performed. Where possible, the parties should try to clearly identify the obligations that they are required to perform for the contract to properly function (as conceptual legal obligations which are disconnected from a specific legal obligations might be unenforceable) and use the further assurance clause as a "catch all" aimed at covering any obligations not expressly mentioned.

The parties may also want to: (i) clarify if the clause is for the benefit of only one party (e.g., where the further assurances tasks are only on one party); (ii) specify who will be responsible and pay for the costs of carrying out further assurances tasks (i.e., if each party will bear its own costs, parties will share equally or costs will be entirely paid by one party); (iii) consider whether one party has a right to request the other party to undertake the further assurances tasks and how the request should be made; (iv) consider any timing to perform the further assurances tasks (e.g., by adding words such as "promptly" or within a certain number of days of being requested by the other party, etc.) in case such tasks are time sensitive.

23.16 Good faith

23.16.1 Good faith in general

The role of good faith in English law regulated contracts has been highly debated. A definition of good faith can be found in *Interfoto Picture Library Ltd v Stiletto Visual Programmes Ltd*,[61] where Bingham LJ stated that:

> In many civil law systems, and perhaps in most legal systems outside the common law world, the law of obligations recognises and enforces an overriding principle that in making and carrying out contracts parties should act in good faith. This does not simply mean that they

60 *Swallowfalls Ltd v Monaco Yachting* [2014] EWCA Civ 186.
61 *Interfoto Picture Library Ltd v Stiletto Visual Programmes Ltd* [1989] QB 433 at [439].

> should not deceive each other, a principle which any legal system must recognise; its effect is perhaps most aptly conveyed by such metaphorical colloquialisms as 'playing fair', 'coming clean' or 'putting one's cards face upwards on the table'.

Although no overarching principle of good faith exists under English law, the obligation to play fair may, to a certain extent, be inferred into construction contracts on a case-by-case basis in order to overcome situations of unfairness. This however cannot be taken so far as to say that a duty to act in good faith will be implied in English law construction contracts. Rather, English law has developed piecemeal solutions which may guide the courts in cases where contractual fairness is concerned.

As held by Bingham LJ in *Interfoto Picture Library Ltd v Stiletto Visual Programmes Ltd*:[62]

> English law has, characteristically, committed itself to no such overriding principle but has developed piecemeal solutions in response to demonstrated problems of unfairness. Many examples could be given. Thus equity has intervened to strike down unconscionable bargains. Parliament has stepped in to regulate the imposition of exemption clauses and the form of certain hire-purchase agreements. The common law has also made its contribution, by holding that certain classes of contract require the utmost good faith, by treating as irrecoverable what purport to be agreed estimates of damage but are in truth a disguised penalty for breach, and in many other ways.

However, in *Yam Seng Pte Ltd v International Trade Corp Ltd*[63] the High Court suggested a different approach to the issue. Leggatt J suggested that the traditional English hostility towards a doctrine of good faith in the performance of contracts is misplaced as it is hard to envisage any contract which would not reasonably be understood as requiring honesty in its performance. He noted that such a requirement meets the traditional tests for the implication of a term in that: (i) it is so obvious that it goes without saying; and (ii) it is necessary to give business efficacy to commercial transactions. The judge also noted that the obligation extends to other standards of commercial dealing which are so generally accepted that the contracting parties could reasonably be understood to take them as read without explicitly stating them in their contractual document and that another aspect of good faith that can readily be implied into commercial contracts is what may be described as fidelity to the parties' bargain.

This case suggests a shift in the courts' approach in relation to good faith. The court found that English law is in fact capable of recognising an implied duty of good faith in commercial dealings in certain circumstances. The case however refers to "relational contracts" requiring extensive cooperation between the parties such as joint venture agreements, franchise agreements or long-term distribution agreements. This is a proposition, which courts seem to have accepted, as shown by the large amount of case law confirming this interpretation.[64] In

62 *Interfoto Picture Library Ltd v Stiletto Visual Programmes Ltd* [1989] QB 433 at [439].

63 *Yam Seng Pte Ltd v International Trade Corp Ltd* [2013] EWHC 111 (QB).

64 *Globe Motors Inc v TRW LucasVarity Electric Steering Ltd* [2016] EWCA Civ 396 at [67] – [69]. *National Private Air Transport Services Company (National Air Services) Ltd v Creditrade LLP and anor* [2016] EWHC 2144 (Comm), at [132] – [136]. *Property Alliance Group Ltd v The Royal Bank of Scotland plc* [2016] EWHC 3342 (Ch), [275] – [276], in which Asplin J conceded that there are "*recognised categories*" of contracts in which good faith may be implied. *Portsmouth City Council v Ensign Highways Ltd* [2015] EWHC 1969 (TCC), in which Edwards-Stuart J held that a good faith obligation was implied into a 25-year public finance initiative contract for the maintenance of roads, but confirmed that a duty of good faith is not usually implied into commercial contracts under English law.

the recent case of *Alan Bates & ors v Post Office Ltd*,[65] the High Court stated the following characteristics that a contract shall have to be considered a relational contract:

> What then, are the specific characteristics that are expected to be present in order to determine whether a contract between commercial parties ought to be considered a relational contract? I consider the following characteristics are relevant as to whether a contract is a relational one or not:
>
> 1 There must be no specific express terms in the contract that prevents a duty of good faith being implied into the contract.
> 2 The contract will be a long-term one, with the mutual intention of the parties being that there will be a long-term relationship.
> 3 The parties must intend that their respective roles be performed with integrity, and with fidelity to their bargain.
> 4 The parties will be committed to collaborating with one another in the performance of the contract.
> 5 The spirits and objectives of their venture may not be capable of being expressed exhaustively in a written contract.
> 6 They will each repose trust and confidence in one another, but of a different kind to that involved in fiduciary relationships.
> 7 The contract in question will involve a high degree of communication, co-operation and predictable performance based on mutual trust and confidence, and expectations of loyalty.
> 8 There may be a degree of significant investment by one party (or both) in the venture. This significant investment may be, in some cases, more accurately described as substantial financial commitment.
> 9 Exclusivity of the relationship may also be present.

The judge also added that he hesitated "*to describe this as an exhaustive list*" and that:

> No single one of the above list is determinative, with the exception of the first one. This is because if the express terms prevent the implication of a duty of good faith, then that will be the end of the matter. However, many of these characteristics will be found to be present where a contract is a relational one. In other cases on entirely different facts, it may be that there are other features which I have not identified above which are relevant to those cases.

Some judges have been critical of the Yam Seng approach. The Court of Appeal in *MSC Mediterranean Shipping Co SA v Cottonex Anstalt*[66] rejected such a general principle. Moore-Bick LJ said that:

> There is in my view a real danger that if a general principle of good faith were established it would be invoked as often to undermine as to support the terms in which the parties have reached agreement.

Leggatt J then touched again on the issue and confirmed the approach taken in the Yam Seng case in *Sheikh Tahnoon Bin Saeed Bin Shakhboot Al Nehayan v Ioannis Kent*[67] where he said:

> Although the observations that I made in the Yam Seng case about the scope for implying duties of good faith in English contract law have provoked divergent reactions, there appears to be growing recognition that such a duty may readily be implied in a relational contract.

65 *Alan Bates & ors v Post Office Ltd* [2019] EWHC 606 (QB).
66 *MSC Mediterranean Shipping Co SA v Cottonex Anstalt* [2016] EWCA Civ 789.
67 *Sheikh Tahnoon Bin Saeed Bin Shakhboot Al Nehayan v Ioannis Kent* [2018] EWHC 333 (Comm).

Turning to the content of the obligation to act in good faith, he mentioned *inter alia*, the Australian case of *Paciocco v Australia and New Zealand Banking Group Limited*[68] where Allsop CJ had summarised the usual content of the obligation of good faith as: (i) an obligation to act honestly and with fidelity to the bargain; (ii) an obligation not to act dishonestly and not to act to undermine the bargain entered or the substance of the contractual benefit bargained for; and (iii) an obligation to act reasonably and with fair dealing having regard to the interests of the parties and to the provisions, aims and purposes of the contract, objectively ascertained. Leggatt J then added that:

> this summary is also consistent with the English case law as it has so far developed, with the caveat that the obligation of fair dealing is not a demanding one and does no more than require a party to refrain from conduct which in the relevant context would be regarded as commercially unacceptable by reasonable and honest people.

23.16.2 Good faith clause

Considering the uncertainties around good faith in English law, it is common for the parties to construction contracts wanting to achieve that result to include clauses expressly requiring them to act in "good faith".[69]

Should the parties agree on the inclusion of a good faith clause, it is crucial that the clause clearly defines what such obligation means and how it may be complied with. In *Walford v Miles*[70] a clause requiring the parties to generally negotiate in good faith was considered "*unworkable in practice*".

23.16.3 Interpretation of good faith clauses

The principle that the parties have autonomy and freedom of contract means that clear good faith clauses will generally be enforced.[71] As stated by Longmore LJ in *Petromec Inc v Petroleo Brasileiro SA*,[72] where the judge enforced a clause to negotiate certain extra costs in good faith:

> It is not irrelevant that it is an express obligation which is part of a complex agreement drafted by City of London solicitors. . . . It would be a strong thing to declare unenforceable a clause into which the parties have deliberately and expressly entered. . . . To decide that it has 'no legal content' to use Lord Ackner's phrase would be for the law deliberately to defeat the reasonable expectations of honest men.

In *Knatchbull-Hugessen and others v SISU Capital Ltd*[73] the parties agreed to negotiate in good faith during a six-week exclusivity period. Leggatt J rejected one of the parties'

68 *Paciocco v Australia and New Zealand Banking Group Limited* [2015] FCAFC 50 at [288].

69 Other phrases commonly used refer to "mutual trust", "collaboration" or "cooperation".

70 *Walford v Miles* [1992] 2 AC 128.

71 As observed by Leggatt J in *Astor Management AG v Atalaya Mining plc* [2017] EWHC 425 (Comm), [2018] 1 All ER (Comm) 547 at [64]: "*[t]he role of the court in a commercial dispute is to give legal effect to what the parties have agreed, not to throw its hands in the air and refuse to do so because the parties have not made its task easy*".

72 *Petromec Inc v Petroleo Brasileiro SA* [2005] EWCA Civ 891, [2006] 1 Lloyd's Rep 161 at [121].

73 *Knatchbull-Hugessen and others v SISU Capital Ltd* [2014] EWHC 1194 (QB).

argument that a term had to be implied that the duty to negotiate in good faith extended beyond the exclusivity period. However, the decision does not suggest that there is any legal difficulty in implying a term to negotiate in good faith. This was confirmed in *Emirates Trading Agency LLC v Prime Mineral Exports Private Ltd.*[74] A contractual clause required the parties "*to seek to resolve the dispute or claim by friendly discussion*" for four weeks before commencing arbitral proceedings. Teare J first held that such clause imported into the contract an obligation to discuss in good faith, and that such an obligation was in fact enforceable. In doing so the judge distinguished *Walford v Miles*[75] on the grounds that the present case did not relate to a dispute resolution clause and that the distinction was justified by public policy considerations.

However, the courts' approach in construing such clauses has been restrictive. For example, the mere fact that the parties have included a good faith clause in the contract does not mean that the courts will find that the parties have a general duty of good faith. In *Mid Essex Hospital Services NHS Trust v Compass Group UK and Ireland Ltd (t/a Medirest)*[76] clause 3.5 of the contract stated that

> The Trust and the Contractor will co-operate with each other in good faith and will take all reasonable action as is necessary for the efficient transmission of information and instructions and to enable the Trust or, as the case may be, any Beneficiary to derive the full benefit of the Contract.

The Court of Appeal held that the duty to act in good faith was limited to the specific circumstances contemplated by the clause, which therefore did not provide for a general duty to act in good faith. Conversely, the parties are also free to expressly exclude the implied duty of good faith.

23.17 Language

Under English law, there is no general rule that a contract must be written in the English language. The parties may choose the contract to be written in any language of their preference.

In case the parties opt for a language other than English, in case of disputes on the meaning of the contract they would generally be allowed to produce a translation of the contract into English.[77]

In case the contract is drafted in two or more languages (e.g., because this approach is required by the law of one of the countries of the parties or because any of the parties does not feel comfortable in signing a contract in a foreign language without a translated version in its own language in the next column on the same page), the contract should expressly state which of such languages prevails over the others in case of inconsistencies between the two versions (as translations may not always perfectly match and some words are not easy to translate with words having the exact meaning of the original language). The clause shall also state what shall be language of communications and

74 *Emirates Trading Agency LLC v Prime Mineral Exports Private Ltd.* [2014] EWHC 2104 (Comm).

75 *Walford v Miles* [1992] 2 AC 128.

76 *Mid Essex Hospital Services NHS Trust v Compass Group UK and Ireland Ltd (t/a Medirest)* [2013] EWCA Civ 200.

77 *Myers v Sarl* [1860] 3 El & El 306 at [315] – [316].

documents issued and prepared in respect of their contract. Usually, the parties will opt for a language that is common to both of them, or will give preference to an international language which is generally known, usually English. However, it is very common that employers impose a certain language since the tender stage, in which case contractors are left with no choice but to accept if they do not want to be disqualified.

Other aspects the parties shall consider when choosing the contract language are: (i) the applicable law (as some legal terms used in the contract may not have a clear meaning in the specific legal system); and (ii) the jurisdiction of the court or the seat of arbitration chosen to solve any contractual disputes (as some courts may not be familiar with a specific language, which may force the parties to translate all documents that they will submit with the court and having translators assisting witnesses which may not be familiar with that specific language at the trial).

23.18 No oral amendments

23.18.1 Oral amendments in general

Under English law, the parties are free to use any form for their contracts, including not having their agreement in writing. In the same way it is possible for parties to a written contract to vary the terms of their contract by a subsequent oral agreement. This freedom to verbally amend a written contract applies to any provision of the written contract, including those which, by express wording in the contract, are stated to be capable of amendment only in writing only. The rationale of this is in that the parties can verbally amend any provisions of their contract, including those that, according to the contract, may be amended only in writing.

23.18.2 No oral amendment clause

In order to prevent informal and possibly abusive attempts to undermine their written contracts, the parties to a construction contract may include a no oral amendments ("NOA") or no oral modifications ("NOM") clause stating that, save as otherwise expressly provided in their contract, no amendment to the terms and conditions of the contract shall be effective unless it is made in writing and signed by a duly authorised representative on behalf of each of the parties.

23.18.3 Interpretation of oral amendment clauses

English courts' approach to NOA clauses has been somewhat fluctuant. In *United Bank Ltd v Asif,*[78] Sedley LJ refused leave to appeal from a summary judgment on the ground that it was "*incontestably right*" that in the face of a NOA clause "*no oral variation of the written terms could have any legal effect*".

78 *United Bank Ltd v Asif*: CA 11 Feb 2000.

In *World Online Telecom Ltd v I-Way Ltd*[79] the same judge deciding on a very similar issue held that it was a sufficient reason for refusing summary judgment that "*the law on the topic is not settled*".

In *Globe Motors Inc., et al. v TRW Lucas Varity Electric Steering Ltd., et al*[80] the Court of Appeal preferred the reasoning in *World Online* holding that an informal variation could be possible, despite the express contractual wording to the contrary. Beatson LJ argued that it is always open to parties to make and unmake their agreements and to waive compliance with particular provisions, but the court would be likely to require "strong evidence" before finding there has been an oral variation of such a clause.

In the case of *Rock Advertising Limited v MWB Business Exchange Centres Limited*,[81] the effect of NOA clauses was considered and clarified by the Supreme Court. In that case the court found that a contract with a NOA clause had been purportedly varied by a subsequent oral agreement, but the NOA clause had prevented the subsequent oral variation from being effective to amend the written contract.

Lord Sumption's judgment (which was supported by Lady Hale, Lord Wilson and Lord Lloyd-Jones) is also of interest as it noted that:

> The reasons which are almost invariably given for treating No Oral Modification clauses as ineffective are (i) that a variation of an existing contract is itself a contract; (ii) that precisely because the common law imposes no requirements of form on the making of contracts, the parties may agree informally to dispense with an existing clause which imposes requirements of form; and (iii) they must be taken to have intended to do this by the mere act of agreeing a variation informally when the principal agreement required writing.

All of these points were made by Cardozo J in a well-known passage from his judgment in the New York Court of Appeals in Beatty v Guggenheim Exploration Co (1919) 225 NY 380, 387–388:

> Those who make a contract, may unmake it. The clause which forbids a change, may be changed like any other. The prohibition of oral waiver, may itself be waived. 'Every such agreement is ended by the new one which contradicts it' (Westchester F Ins Co v Earle 33 Mich 143, 153). What is excluded by one act, is restored by another. You may put it out by the door; it is back through the window. Whenever two men contract, no limitation self-imposed can destroy their power to contract again.

In line with Lord Sumption, Lord Briggs held that:

> This basic concept, that parties to a contract have complete freedom by further agreement to 'unbind' themselves as to their future conduct, is in principle applicable not merely to their substantive mutual obligations, but also to any procedural restraints upon which they may agree, including restraints as to how they may vary their existing contractual relationship. It is therefore fully applicable to the constraint upon their future conduct imposed by a NOM clause. No-one doubts that parties to a contract containing a NOM clause are at liberty thereafter to remove it from their bargain, temporarily or permanently, by a compliant written variation, following which it will not inhibit them from agreeing further variations purely orally.

However, the Supreme Court also made clear that in case the parties agree an oral variation contrary to the terms of a NOA clause, perform the contract as varied, and one party

79 *World Online Telecom Ltd v I-Way Ltd* [2002] EWCA Civ 413.
80 *Globe Motors Inc., et al. v TRW Lucas Varity Electric Steering Ltd., et al.* [2016] EWCA Civ 396.
81 *Rock Advertising Limited v MWB Business Exchange Centres Limited* UKSC 2016/0152.

has relied on the purported variation to its detriment, the doctrine of estoppel may take effect to prevent the other party enforcing the unvaried (written) contract.

23.19 Stamp duty and other charges

Construction contracts usually deal with the issue of stamp duty, i.e., a land tax paid by the buyer of a UK residential property. The contract generally provides that any stamp duties imposed by law in connection with entry into the contract will be paid by the employer. However, in England construction contracts will not be subject to any stamp duty unless the contract includes a transfer in ownership of real property.

23.20 Counterpart signatures

Construction contracts are sometimes signed in counterpart. This is achieved by creating two originals, one for each party. Such party then signs the original in its possession and sends it to the other party. In this way, each party will have its own original contract.

Signature in counterpart is aimed at ensuring that each party has its own original contract and avoiding the logistic issues carried by the "traditional" way of signing contracts where both parties sign the same original document. Such logistic issues include: (i) forcing parties located in different countries to meet in person in the place of signature; (ii) assessing the validity of e-signature in the specific countries where agreed that signature may occur electronically; (iii) circulating the document via courier, which may delay the entry into force of the document and carry the risk that the document is lost before it is delivered to the other party.

It is worth noting that, where the parties agree to sign in counterpart, they shall ensure that they sign the same version of the document as any discrepancies may give rise to disputes.

It is important each counterpart is a complete document (not simply the signature block). In case more than one person is required to sign the contract (e.g., two directors signing on behalf of the same company), they shall all sign the same counterpart[82] (not necessarily at the same time).

The parties may agree to sign in counterpart also in case the contract lacks a clause, but best practice is to have a specific clause so that there is no risk of arguments on how the contract should be signed.

82 A note on electronic execution published by the joint working party of The Law Society and The City of London Law Society and confirmed in the Law Society's subsequent Q&As on how to use electronic signatures and complete virtual executions seems to endorse the position that each authorised signatory may sign in counterparts. However, as this is not corroborated by English law evidence or authority, it is advisable that the two directors sign the same document.

CHAPTER 24

Other general obligations

24.1 Compliance with laws

Compliance with laws and regulations clauses are standard in construction contracts. They do not pose any particular issues as one could say that such obligation "goes without saying". The main issue with such clauses is how the contract defines "laws". Unless expressly stated otherwise, laws are deemed to include instruments which are somehow binding on the parties. This would include laws issued by parliaments, but also by local authorities such as municipal and regional bodies. It may also include binding regulations issued by governmental authorities such as environmental agencies, as well as court judgments and orders. The parties may also include codes and standards. What is important is that such instruments are binding on the parties, i.e., that the issuing body has jurisdiction over the parties or over the project, including the site and the works. Normally "laws" is intended to also include the relevant interpretation.

A different issue relates to the contractor's obligation to comply with any permits during the performance of the work. Permits are not strictly laws but are usually issued by national or local authorities upon application of either the employer (e.g., planning consents or environmental authorisations) or the contractor (e.g., visas and work permits). Also in this case, the parties, but particularly the contractor, are obliged to act in compliance with such permits. The contract may provide that the contractor shall indemnify and hold the employer harmless against and from the consequences of any failure to comply with his obligations in this regard.

The obligation to comply with the laws is one which is hard to credibly negotiate, unless the clause is clearly "one-sided". However, before agreeing on such obligation, parties shall have a clear understanding of what such laws are and, most importantly, what they are required to do not to breach them.

24.2 Confidentiality

24.2.1 Confidentiality in general

Project documents usually include sensible information about prices, IP, technologies, methods of construction, business opportunities, etc. Disclosure of such information between the parties at different levels may be inevitable considering the size and complexity of such projects and the amount of stakeholder involved.

DOI: 10.4324/9781003387718-29

Confidential information may be disclosed in many circumstances throughout the project, from the tender phase up to the end of the works. The disclosure may take place orally (in face-to-face meetings, in phone calls or video conferences) or in writing (by email or other means to exchange document). Companies should always consider if communications lead to the disclosure of confidential information, whether it would be possible to limit such disclosure in terms of addresses and content, and what type of measures may need to be taken to ensure the information remains confidential. Both the disclosing and the receiving parties may take steps to avoid issues of confidentiality. These may include the following:

(i) The steps that may be taken by the disclosing party include: (a) entering into a written non-disclosure agreement before exchanging any communication (i.e., already in the tender phase) and adding a non-disclosure clause to the contract stating that the non-disclosure agreement covering the previous phase will not cease to have effect; (b) agreeing in writing with the other party on what information is to be regarded as confidential and how to identify it. In this regard, the best practise is to mark as "confidential" all information considered as such. Labelling documents as confidential before providing them to the counterparty will prove that it had actual knowledge that the documents were intended to be confidential. This also applies to emails and other communications, whose headings may include the word "confidential". This would not be conclusive evidence of the confidential nature of the information, but will be part of the circumstances that the courts will consider when assessing if a breach of confidence has occurred; (c) disclosing confidential information (both internally and in respect of the receiving party) to as few persons as possible on a need-to-know basis (i.e., only the information that is essential to them doing their job); (d) keeping records of disclosed confidential information so to be able to quickly identify if any breach has occurred.

(ii) The receiving party may take the following steps: (a) storing confidential information received on company systems only accessible at company premises and using an identification unique to each employee; (b) making employees to whom information is disclosed aware of the confidential nature of the information and instructing them on how to treat and use the information, including making them aware of the prohibition to use the confidential information for any purpose other than in connection with the performance of the project and within the relevant limits. In particular, it should be clear to those who come in the possession of confidential information that the information shall not be used for any competitive or commercial purpose; (c) putting in place processes by which confidential information is recorded and retained (and returned/destroyed at the end of the project, if so agreed) by each employee; (d) limiting the access to the other party's confidential information to as few persons as reasonably necessary within the company; (e) making regular checks of IT password strength to avoid any leak of confidential information received; (f) keeping hard copies (if printing is not forbidden) of confidential documents locked away and labelled as confidential, and electronic copies either encrypted or password protected; (g) putting in place an action plan in case confidential information is lost or unlawfully disclosed.

Another issue relates to press releases which often the parties, and in particular contractors, issue in order to publicise the award of the contract. It is good practice that the parties agree in advance on the possibility to publicise the project and what could be the content of any press release. In case the parties agree that no press release may be issued without the consent of both parties, they should also make sure that their subcontractors take on the same obligation.

24.2.2 The law of confidence

Where the construction contract does not contain a confidentiality clause and the parties have not entered into a separate confidentiality agreement or non-disclosure agreement ("NDA"), they are not left with no protection. The common law duty of confidence, mixed with the protection afforded by intellectual property rights (e.g., patents, copyrights or trademarks) and the statutory protection under the Trade Secrets (Enforcement, etc.) Regulations 2018 (SI 2018/597) provide for a good level of protection regardless of any contractual confidentiality obligations.

24.2.2.1 The common law of confidence

The common law of confidentiality is a principle of law that a person who receives information from another party in confidence cannot take advantage of it. That person must not make use of it to the prejudice of the person who gave the information without obtaining his consent. The leading case in this area is *Coco v AN Clark (Engineers) Ltd,*[1] where the judge indicated that "*three elements are normally required if, apart from contract, a case of breach of confidence is to succeed*", i.e.:

(i) The first requirement is that the information must be of a confidential nature. To explain this element the court referred to *Saltman Engineering Co v Campbell Engineering Co Ltd*[2] where Lord Greene stated that something which is public property and public knowledge cannot per se provide any foundation for proceedings for breach of confidence. However, the judge added that this principle should not be taken too far and that something that has been constructed solely from materials in the public domain may possess the necessary quality of confidentiality. The judge referred to the situation in which someone takes information in the public domain and skilfully creates new information which is in fact of a confidential nature. He also touched the issue where the information is partly public and partly private. In such case, the recipient must somehow segregate the two and, although free to use the former, must take no advantage of the communication of the latter.

Some types of information are easily recognisable as confidential, e.g., business strategies, industrial secrets, data relevant to patents under development, internal rates applied by contractors and in general information that is known only to a select few individuals within the company. When the confidential nature

1 However secret and confidential the*Coco v AN Clark (Engineers) Ltd* [1969] RPC 41.
2 *Saltman Engineering Co v Campbell Engineering Co Ltd* [1948] 65 RPC 203.

is not easy to recognise, the courts will be required to assess it objectively. Labelling or treating information as confidential does not make it such. However, the courts will look at all the surrounding circumstances, and will generally be more likely to be satisfied that the information has the necessary quality of confidence if the party acting for breach of confidence can show that it took steps to maintain its secrecy.

(ii) The second requirement is that the information must have been communicated in circumstances importing an obligation of confidence. According to the court:

> However secret and confidential the information, there can be no binding obligation of confidence if that information is blurted out in public or is communicated in other circumstances which negative any duty of holding it confidential.

As to the test to be applied, the court stated that:

> if the circumstances are such that any reasonable man standing in the shoes of the recipient of the information would have realised that upon reasonable grounds the information was being given to him in confidence, then this should suffice to impose upon him the equitable obligation of confidence. In particular, where information of commercial or industrial value is given on a business-like basis and with some avowed common object in mind, such as a joint venture or the manufacture of articles by one party for the other, I would regard the recipient as carrying a heavy burden if he seeks to repel a contention that he was bound by an obligation of confidence.

Thus, in a breach of confidence case the courts will also assess whether the recipient knew, or ought to have known based on the circumstances in which the information was communicated, that he was under a duty not to disclose the confidential information. Certainly, a confidentiality clause or a non-disclosure agreement would be evidence that the information was in fact communicated in circumstances importing an obligation of confidence. However, where the parties have not contractually agreed on the confidentiality of some of the information they will exchange in relation to a project, an obligation of confidence will arise automatically based on the circumstances of the disclosure (e.g., in case information is communicated in restricted meetings where steps are taken to make sure that people attend on a need-to-know basis) or the relationship between the parties (e.g., information between contractor and employer which is not already in the public domain which relates to how the project will be executed and the rates applied by the contractor or by the other contractors to whom the project has not been awarded).

(iii) The third requirement is that there must be an unauthorised use of the information to the detriment of the person communicating it. The use or the threatened use of the confidential information will be unauthorised where the recipient has used or disclosed the information without the permission of the owner (or the holder) of such information or for an unauthorised purpose (e.g., information was disclosed to allow the employer to evaluate a tender, but the employer discloses it to give an advantage to another contractor). It is also necessary that the confidential information is used in a manner which causes or may cause a detriment to the information owner (or holder). Where the information is not already in the public domain, mere disclosure of the information may be considered sufficient to satisfy the test. Where the information has a limited degree of confidentiality and could be ascertained by reverse engineering, or, by a process of compilation from public sources, the courts will assess whether the engineered or compiled information has in fact provided a "springboard" competitive advantage to the recipient over others. This is based on the so-called spring board doctrine, which Roxburgh J defined as follows in the case of *Terrapin v Builders' Supply Co. (Hayes) Ltd.*[3]:

> As I understand it, the essence of this branch of the law, whatever the origin of it may be, is that a person who has obtained information in confidence is not allowed to use it as a spring-board for activities detrimental to the person who made the confidential communication, and spring-board it remains even when all the features have been published or can be ascertained by actual inspection by any member of the public.

The application of this test was considered in the case of *Kerry Ingredients (UK) Ltd v Bakkavor Group Ltd.* Kerry Ingredients (UK) Ltd ("Kerry") had provided Bakkavor Group Ltd ("Bakkavor") with certain information in order to comply with food safety and labelling requirements. However, Bakkavor had used the information to develop its own competing products. The court found that the confidential information had been provided to Bakkavor for the specific limited purposes (i.e., to comply with regulatory requirements) and should not have been used by Bakkavor as a springboard to develop alternative competing products. The court held that Kerry was entitled to a springboard injunction preventing Bakkavor from using the information. A springboard injunction, however: (i) should have a duration limited to the time it would take someone to reverse engineer or compile the sources; and (ii) could not be used to restrain continued misuse of confidential information once the information has ceased to be confidential.[4]

Moreover, under common law, it is generally accepted that there is no breach of confidentiality where the documents are disclosed in litigation.[5] However, the courts will not allow any documents to be disclosed but would rather balance the interests of the party seeking disclosure and the party whose secrets may be put at risk if documents are disclosed.[6]

24.2.2.2 The Trade Secrets (Enforcement, etc.) Regulations 2018

As mentioned, in the UK there are two overlapping regimes aimed at protecting the confidentiality of business information. The first is the common law regime explained earlier, and the second is under the Trade Secrets (Enforcement, etc.) Regulations 2018 (the "Regulations").

Trade secrets may be protected under both regimes, which are intended to operate in parallel. In addition, protection is afforded by intellectual property rights legislation, which is however outside the scope of this book.

3 However secret and confidential the *Terrapin v Builders' Supply Co. (Hayes) Ltd.* [1960] RPC 1. But see also *Seager v Copydex Ltd.* [1967] RPC 349 and *Coco v AN Clark (Engineers) Ltd* [1969] RPC 41.

4 *Vestergaard Frandsen S/A (now called MVF3 APS) v Bestnet Europe Ltd* [2013] UKSC 31 (22 May 2013).

5 *Chantry Martin & Co v Martin* [1953] 2 QB 286.

6 *Premier Profiles Ltd v Tioxide Europe Ltd* [2000] QB.

The Regulations were introduced to comply with the Directive (EU) 2016/943 of the European Parliament and of the Council of 8 June 2016 on the protection of undisclosed know-how and business information (trade secrets) against their unlawful acquisition, use and disclosure (the "Trade Secrets Directive"), which sought to harmonise the protection of confidential information from misuse across Member States. After Brexit, the Regulations have remained substantially unchanged and continue to apply.

Regulation 2(1) defines as trade secrets any information which: (i) is secret in the sense that it is not, as a body or in the precise configuration and assembly of its components, generally known among, or readily accessible to, persons within the circles that normally deal with the kind of information in question; (ii) has commercial value because it is secret, and (iii) has been subject to reasonable steps under the circumstances, by the person lawfully in control of the information, to keep it secret.

Regulations 11 to 15 entitle the courts to make various interim and final measures including orders providing for: (i) the cessation of, or (as the case may be) the prohibition of, the use or disclosure of the trade secret; or (ii) the destruction of all or part of any document, object, material, substance or electronic file containing or embodying the trade secret, or where appropriate, the delivery up to the applicant of all or part of that document, object, material, substance or electronic file.

24.2.3 Confidentiality clause

As mentioned, one of the ways to ensure confidentiality is adding a confidentiality clause to the contract. Such clauses typically list what "confidential information" means for the purposes of the clause. Obviously, not all project information is considered confidential information, but only information of a commercial and valuable nature. In a construction project, this usually includes all information or data however disclosed in any form between the parties (including orally, visually, in writing and electronically) which relates to the contract or the project and which is of particular importance. Examples include legal and financing information, technical information such as know-how and information relevant to market opportunities, customers and business affairs. The receiving party, i.e., the party to whom the other party (the "disclosing party) discloses the confidential information, is obliged to treat and keep such information as secret and confidential and not disclose it, or allow it to be disclosed, to any other person without the prior written consent of the disclosing party. However, it would be practically impossible to restrict knowledge of confidential information to few people in the case of large construction projects. Such projects will typically involve a high number of internal and external stakeholders such as affiliates of the parties (e.g., subsidiaries and/or shareholders), employees (e.g., project, finance, legal, etc.), external consultants (e.g., outside counsels, auditors, etc.), third parties involved in the project (e.g., insurers and lenders). For this reason, the parties will usually agree that no consent will be needed in case the confidential information is disclosed to the receiving party's affiliates, directors, employees, officers, professional consultants and advisers, insurers and lenders, etc. Although less frequently, a confidentiality clause may also allow disclosure to subcontractors, but usually on a need-to-know basis. Moreover, the clause will normally state that the receiving party disclosing confidential information to such persons shall: (i) ensure that they are made aware of the confidentiality obligations; and (ii) shall procure that such persons observe the terms of the confidentiality clause. This means that the receiving party will be held liable for any breach of confidentiality from such persons. The confidentiality obligation is also usually accompanied by the obligation not to make copies of the confidential information (except where reasonably necessary for the works) and to return or destroy the copies straight after termination of the project or at any time upon the disclosing party's request.

Importantly, confidentiality clauses shall include exceptions to the confidentiality obligation stating that the receiving party will not be in breach in case, for example: (i) the information was already in the public domain; (ii) the information was already lawfully in the possession of the receiving party other than in consequence of breach of the confidentiality obligation; (iii) the information was lawfully obtained from a third party who, to the reasonable knowledge of the receiving party, was under no obligation of confidentiality with respect to such information; (iv) the receiving party was obliged to disclose the information, e.g., by any applicable laws or order issued by a competent court or other judicial authority, regulations of any stock exchange or listing authority, etc. In such cases the clause should state that the party should notify the disclosing party as soon as possible (if allowed to do so) and shall limit the disclosure to the information that is strictly necessary to comply with the relevant order or requirement.

The clause shall also set out a reasonable term by which the confidentiality obligations under than clause will continue to be in force. This will normally depend on the specific project and the type of information. Usually, the term starts from the date the final acceptance certificate is issued or other agreed date.

CHAPTER 25

Liability issues

25.1 Assignment

25.1.1 Assignment in general

An assignment is a transfer of a benefit (or right), but not also an obligation (or burden), that a party, the assignor (or "transferor"), has under a contract, to a third party, the assignee (or "transferee"), which is a stranger to such contract.

Construction contracts, as any other type of contracts, create reciprocal rights and liabilities. More specifically: (i) contractors have the right (or benefit) to receive payment and the liability (or burden) to complete the work (and supply materials, if that is the case) in accordance with the contract; while (ii) employers have the right (or benefit) to have the work done and the liability (or burden) to pay for it. Such rights are assignable subject to limitations. The parties may want to assign their rights under the contract to third parties for a number of reasons. For example: (i) when the project is funded, the lenders may require the employer to agree in the construction contract that the employer is entitled to assign its contractual rights and benefits (including those deriving from performance bonds and parent company guarantees) against the contractor as security to the lenders (so-called assignment by way of security); (ii) when the employer has developed the project, but is not the relevant final user, in which case the employer may assign any rights and benefits deriving from the construction contract against the contractor to the final user; (iii) where the parties seek to reserve an unqualified right to assign the contract to an affiliate without the need to seek the other party's prior consent.

25.1.2 Assignment of burden and assignment of benefit

25.1.2.1 Assignment of burden

Under English law the parties may only assign the benefits of a contract, but not also the burden. The principle was stated in *Tolhurst v Associated Portland Cement Manufacturers*[1] where Collins MR said:

> It is, I think, quite clear that neither at law nor in equity could the burden of a contract be shifted off the shoulders of a contractor onto those of another without the consent of the

1 *Tolhurst v Associated Portland Cement Manufacturers* [1903] 2 KB 660.

DOI: 10.4324/9781003387718-30

> contractee. A debtor cannot relieve himself of his liability to his creditor by assigning the burden of the obligation to somebody else; this can only be brought about by the consent of all three, and involves the release of the original debtor.

The House of Lords confirmed this approach in the case of *Linden Gardens Trust Ltd v Lenesta Sludge Disposals Ltd*[2] where Lord Browne-Wilkinson stated:

> It is trite law that it is, in any event, impossible to assign 'the contract' as a whole, i.e. including both burden and benefit. The burden of a contract can never be assigned without the consent of the other party to the contract in which event such consent will give rise to a novation.

The matter was also clearly treated in *Chitty on Contracts*,[3] as it is stated:

> Everybody has a right to choose with whom he will contract and no-one is obliged without his consent to accept the liability of a person other than him with whom he made his contract. Consequently the burden of a contract cannot in principle be transferred without the consent of the other party, so as to discharge the original contractor.

Thus, there cannot be such thing as an assignment of obligations. A party to a construction contract intending to assign any burden under that contract will need to enter into a new agreement (so-called novation agreement) with the consent of all the other parties.[4]

In case the parties intend to transfer contractual obligations, but not also contractual rights, they may subcontract such obligations (assuming that this is not prohibited under the contract). However, in such cases they will normally remain fully responsible for the work (so-called vicarious performance). Where the agreement is silent on the issue of subcontracting, and it cannot be inferred from the circumstances that the parties did not intend to allow subcontracting, the other party may be obliged to accept the subcontractor's performance unless the contractual obligations are of a special nature that require personal performance by the subcontracting party.

Some construction contracts also provide that the parties may assign "the contract" or "the rights and obligations" thereof. However, the "assignment of a contract" or "assignment of obligations" under a contract will result in the right of one party to assign the burden of a contract without having obtained the other party's consent (i.e., through a novation). This was clearly stated in the case of *Linden Gardens Trust Ltd v Lenesta Sludge Disposals Ltd*[5] where Lord Browne-Wilkinson stated that:

> Although it is true that the phrase 'assign this contract' is not strictly accurate, lawyers frequently use those words inaccurately to describe an assignment of the benefit of a contract since every lawyer knows that the burden of a contract cannot be assigned.

It is generally accepted that, even in case the contract refers to assigning a contract or obligations under a contract, this will not displace the common law rule that consent of the other party is necessary to assign contractual obligations. However, in case the parties

---

2 *Linden Gardens Trust Ltd v Lenesta Sludge Disposals Ltd* [1993] UKHL 4.

3 H.G. Beale, *Chitty on Contracts* (30th edition) Sweet & Maxwell, 2008, at paras 19–077 and 19–078.

4 Alternatively, it will be necessary that the other party has, by some act or conduct, acquiesced in the new arrangement. See *Dr. Jaeger's Sanitary Woollen, &c., Company v Walker* [1897] 77 LT 180.

5 *Linden Gardens Trust Ltd v Lenesta Sludge Disposals Ltd* [1993] UKHL 4.

behave as though they have in fact assigned burden of a commercial contract without entering into a formal novation, a court may find that the parties have successfully transferred the contract by way of a novation, or that the outgoing party has assigned the benefit of the contract to the incoming party and, in parallel, the outgoing party has subcontracted (or delegated), the contract's obligations to the incoming party, in which case the outgoing party will remain liable for the incoming party's actions. The appropriate classification will be of course a matter of construction for the courts.

25.1.2.2 Assignment of benefit

If the construction contract does not expressly prohibit the assignment of a benefit,[6] each party may do it without necessarily seeking the assent from the other party. A result of an assignment: (i) the assignee will not become a party to the contract, but will be entitled to benefits from it and will be able to enforce its rights under it (including the right to bring proceedings, alone or by joining the assignor) against the other contracting party; and (ii) the assignor will keep its contractual obligations (or burdens) to the other contracting party, including any liability to perform any part of the contract that has not yet been performed. The assignee is said to take such right "subject to equities", i.e., subject to all defences available to the debtor against the assignor, including set-off. This means that, if a contractor assigns his right to receive money from the employer to an assignee, the assignee will take subject to any claims that the employer may have under the contract against the contractor (e.g., set-off[7] for defective works or damages for delay).[8] However, after notice of assignment has been given to the debtor, he cannot do anything that would diminish the rights of the assignee as they stood at the time of the notice. For example, if the contractor informs the employer that any payment of money owed to the contractor ought to be paid to a third-party assignee, but the employer pays the contractor, the employer may not use the set-off defence that would otherwise be available to the employer, and might be obliged to pay the assignee (and then try to recover the amount unduly paid to the contractor). In *Brice v Bannister*[9] Gough, the contractor, had agreed to build a ship for Bannister, the employer. Gough then assigned the proceeds of the contract to Brice. Under the assignment agreement, any further advances made by Bannister to Gough had to be paid to Brice. Brice then notified Bannister of the assignment. Bannister ignored the notice and made further advances to Gough. When Bannister refused to pay Brice, the latter sued Bannister under the assignment agreement and was able to recover the relevant amount.

25.1.3 Statutory and equitable assignment

25.1.3.1 Statutory assignment

A statutory (or legal) assignment is an assignment compliant with the law, and specifically with Section 136 of the Law of Property Act 1925 (the "Property Act"). Where an

6 In which case any assignment would be invalid and unenforceable against the employer. See *Linden Gardens Trust Ltd v Lenesta Sludge Disposals Ltd* [1993] UKHL 4, [1994] 1 AC 85.

7 In the case of *Business Computers Ltd v Anglo African Leasing Ltd* [1977] 1 WLR 578, it was held that: "*a debt which accrues due before notice of an assignment is received, whether or not it is payable before that date, or a debt which arises out of the same contract as that which gives rise to the assigned debt, or is closely connected with that contract, may be set off against the assignee*".

8 *Roxburgh v Cox* [1881] LR 17 Ch D 520.

9 *Brice v Bannister* [1878] 3 QBD 569.

assignment fails to comply with the formalities of the Property Act, it may however operate as an equitable assignment. Substantively the two types of assignments are the same. The only difference is one procedure: (i) in the case of a legal assignment, the assignee can sue the debtor in his own name for the money assigned; while (ii) in the case of an equitable assignment, the assignor must take part to the proceedings (either as claimant or as defendant, if he refuses to join the assignee).[10] In *Warner Bros Records Inc v Rollgreen Ltd* Roskill LJ stated:

> the only rights that an equitable assignment can create in the equitable assignee are rights against his assignor who thenceforth becomes the trustee of the benefit of the option for the assignee, and the assignor could, of course, be compelled in equity to exercise those rights for the benefit of the assignee.

This view was shared by Sir John Pennycuick who said:

> Where there is a contract between A and B, and A makes an equitable but not a legal assignment of the benefit of that contract to C, this equitable assignment does not put C into a contractual relation with B, and, consequently, C is not in a position to exercise directly against B any right conferred by the contract on A. The equitable assignment may be converted into a legal assignment by notice to B: see section 136 of the Law of Property Act 1925; but, so long as the assignment remains equitable only, C has no more than a right in equity to require A to protect the interest which A has assigned and to do so by exercising the option himself.

For an assignment to be compliant with the Property Act (i.e., for it to be a statutory assignment), the following formalities shall be complied with:

(i) The assignment shall be absolute. This means that the assignment shall be unconditional, and the assignor shall be left with no interest in the assigned property or right. In *Durham Bros v Robertson*[11] an assignment subject to a condition precedent was found not to be absolute. In *Walter and Sullivan Ltd v J. Murphy & Sons Ltd*, Walter and Sullivan Ltd, who were owed £1808 from J. Murphy & Sons Ltd, asked them to pay £1558 to a third party, H & Co. (to whom they were indebted) "*from the money owing by you to us*". The court held that the arrangement was not absolute as it was an assignment of part of a debt.

(ii) The assignment shall be in writing and signed by the assignor. To create a legal assignment there must be a written document signed by the assignor expressing his clear intention to the assignment. The law does not prescribe any specific wording. The assignment might take the form of a document between the assignor and the assignee where the assignor assigns to the assignee the credit he has vis-à-vis a third-party debtor or a demand from the assignor to the debtor that the latter pays directly the assignee, in which case there should be evidence that the assignee consented to the arrangement.[12]

(iii) The assignment shall refer to a debt or other legal thing in action. A thing (or a "chose") in action is a personal property right to an intangible object. In the case of *Torkington v Magee*[13] this was defined as a personal right of property

10 *Warner Bros Records Inc v Rollgreen Ltd* [1976] 1 QB 430 (CA).
11 *Durham Bros v Robertson* [1898] 1 QB 765.
12 *Curran v Newpark Cinema Ltd.* [1951] 1 All ER 285.
13 *Torkington v Magee* [1902] 2 KB 427.

which can only be claimed or enforced by action, and not taking physical possession. This means that the only way to obtain possession of such thing is to sue for it. The classic example is a debt as it cannot be physically possessed and may only be enforced by suing the debtor.

(iv) Express notice in writing shall be given to the debtor. The law does not require any specific language. Even a document which was not intended to be a notice may constitute a valid notice.[14]

For a legal assignment to take place no consideration will be required.[15]

25.1.3.2 Equitable assignment

Where an assignment fails to comply with the formalities of Section 136 of the Property Act, such defective assignment may still operate as an equitable assignment. An equitable assignment may subsequently become a statutory assignment if the defect is removed, and the assignment becomes compliant with the Property Act as a result. For example, in case notice was not served to the debtor, the assignee may subsequently do it so making it a legal assignment.[16] No specific language is prescribed, provided that the words used are unambiguous. It may be in writing or oral. It need not take any particular form. As stated by Lord Macnaghten in *William Brandt's Sons and Co v Dunlop Rubber Co*:[17]

> It may be addressed to the debtor. It may be couched in the language of command. It may be a courteous request. It may assume the form of mere permission. The language is immaterial if the meaning is plain.

The assignment may concern a legal chose or an equitable chose. Where it relates to an equitable chose, no consideration will be required provided that the assignor has, at the material time, done all that he can to perfect the gift.[18]

An equitable assignment would be binding between assignor and assignee even without notice to the debtor. However, in such case: (i) the debtor may pay the assignor and not to the assignee;[19] (ii) the date of notice will establish the order of priority as between successive assignees;[20] (iii) the date of notice plays a role in relation to set-off as the assignee takes "*subject to equities*" (as explained earlier).

25.1.4 Assignment clause

The parties to construction contracts often add assignment clauses to their agreement in order to exclude or limit the common law right to unilaterally assign the benefit of the

14 *Van Lynn Developments v Pelias Construction Co (formerly Jason Construction Co)* [1969] 1 QB 607. However, in *Herkules Piling Ltd and Another v Tilbury Construction Ltd* [1993] 61 BLR 107 a notice given by way of disclosure of documents in legal proceedings in which the debtor was a party was considered insufficient.

15 *Baytur S.A. v Fingaro Holdings* [1992] QB 610, CA.

16 *William Brandt's Sons and Co v Dunlop Rubber Co* [1905] HL.

17 *William Brandt's Sons and Co v Dunlop Rubber Co* [1905] HL.

18 *Letts v Commissioner of Internal Revenue* 84 F.2d 760 [9th Cir. 1936].

19 To use Lord Macnaghten's words in *William Brandt's Sons and Co v Dunlop Rubber Co* [1905] HL: "*If the debtor ignores such a notice, he does so at his peril. If the assignment be for valuable consideration and communicated to the third person, it cannot be revoked by the creditor or safely disregarded by the debtor*".

20 *Dearie v Hall* [1823] 3 Russ.

contract without the need to obtain the other party's prior consent. In case the right of assignment is excluded, a purported assignment contravening such restriction will constitute a breach of contract and may result in an ineffective assignment. The assignment clause may provide that a party may assign the rights and benefits (including the right to any remedies) of the contract but only with the prior written consent of the other party. In such cases, the parties usually agree that such consent should not be unreasonably withheld or delayed. Whether or not it is reasonable to withhold consent to an assignment is assessed by the courts objectively depending on the circumstances of the case, including the nature and object of the specific contract and the purpose of the non-assignment clause. Generally speaking, consent might be found being unreasonably withheld in case the grounds relied upon by the party withholding its consent are extraneous or disassociated from the subject matter of the contract, materially inconsistent with one or more provisions of the contract or based on collateral or improper considerations. Where the clause does not expressly provide that consent to an assignment shall not be unreasonably withheld, this proviso may be implied by the courts. Accordingly, if the parties intend to agree that a party may withhold its consent to an assignment for any reason whatsoever, including on unreasonable grounds, clear contractual language should be used. Alternatively, the parties may list the specific cases in which it will be reasonable for to withhold its consent, e.g., in case: (i) the other party is not satisfied with the proposed assignee's financial standing or reputation; (ii) the proposed assignee is a competitor of the other party or the other party is in dispute with the proposed assignee; (iii) the proposed assignee does not satisfy anti-bribery and corruption due diligence, or is subject to any applicable sanctions preventing the other party from working with the such proposed assignee.

The parties may also seek to: (i) limit the number of assignments of certain rights (e.g., by providing that a collateral warranty may be assigned only once) or the types of rights that one or both parties may assign (e.g., by excluding the assignment of warranties and indemnities); or (ii) provide a right to assign only to a named assignee or class of assignees.

25.2 Novation

25.2.1 Novation in general

As mentioned earlier, while contractual rights and benefits may be transferred by assignment, contractual obligations and burdens are only transferable by way a novation.[21] A novation occurs when one contract (the original contract) is rescinded, and a fresh contract, supported by consideration, is entered into in substitution of the original contract.[22] A novation agreement usually takes the form of a tripartite agreement whereby an original contracting party is released from his rights and obligations under that contract, which are assumed by a third party.[23] For the novation to be valid all the parties shall consent. No particular formalities are required, and consent may be given in writing, orally, by conduct or by any combination of the three.

21 *Charlotte Thirty Ltd v Croker Ltd* [1990] 24 Con LR 46 at [53–54].

22 *Olsson v Dyson* [1969] 120 CLR 365 at [388].

23 This distinguishes novation from contracts of guarantees or indemnities, where the original parties remain bound.

Importantly, unless the parties agree otherwise, novation does not cancel past rights and obligations under the original contract.

It is worth noting that, unless a novation agreement is executed as a deed, consideration (whether financial or otherwise) by the new party in return for the contract being novated to it must be provided. Alternatively, and to the extent the contract does not exclude or restrict assignment and subcontracting, a party may: (i) assign its rights under the contract to the third party (the assignee); and (ii) subcontract the relevant obligations to the assignee.

25.2.2 Novation clause

Novation clauses are usually coupled with assignment clauses. They have the primary aim to prevent oral consent to a novation, or consent being inferred from a continuing party's conduct. Thus, a novation clause will typically provide that a party cannot novate a contract without the prior written consent of all existing parties. The parties may also agree that the novation be subject to the contractor's consent, not to be unreasonably withheld or delayed, and that the proposed "assignee" satisfies some requirements (e.g., anti-bribery and corruption due diligence, is not subject to any applicable sanctions preventing the contractor from working with the assignee). It is also possible for the parties to prospectively authorise one party to novate the agreement unilaterally to a party chosen by the novating party. For example, contractors pre-authorise a novation to third parties that have an interest in the project, such as lenders or employers' affiliates. In such cases, the courts will look to the substance of what has occurred and give effect to the novation provided it is authorised by the proper construction of the original contract. The case *Habbisons Bank Ltd v Standard Chartered Bank (Hong Kong) Ltd*,[24] albeit not a construction case, shows that, as opposed to assignment, it is possible to provide for future novation in an agreement. The courts will uphold such clauses to the extent the commercial purpose of the novation is clear, and the terms of the clause are not uncertain. These clauses do not remove the requirement for consent, but rather seek to make it clear that transfers may be made as prescribed in the agreement without the need for express consent of the other party, as consent is contained in the agreement itself. However, to avoid the risk of merely ending with a non-binding agreement to agree, a specimen form of the proposed novation agreement should be appended to the original contractual documentation.

25.3 Set-off

25.3.1 Set-off in general

A right to set-off is a right to deduct an amount that a party A owes to the party B from an amount the party B owes to the party A, so as to reduce or extinguish the party B's liability. So, for example, if a contractor has satisfactorily carried out works for £500,000 and is entitled to be paid such amount as a result of that, but has a debt to the employer of £300,000 (e.g., for damages due to defective works carried out on the same project), the employer may offset the two amounts so that it shall only pay the relevant difference (£200,000).

24 *Habbisons Bank Ltd v Standard Chartered Bank (Hong Kong) Ltd* [2010] EWCA Civ 1335.

For set-off to apply it is necessary that the two sums be "*connected*"[25] and "*substantially the same*".[26] Thus, in the earlier example, where employer's credit derived from a different contract concerning a different project, the contractor would be entitled to the full amount, and the employer would need to pursue its claim separately in the appropriate venue unless the parties had expressly agreed on a "*cross-contract set-off*" applying to unrelated transactions.[27]

Set-off must be distinguished from abatement, which is a defence that can be invoked by a defendant where the services (or the goods) supplied by the claimant do not justify the payment agreed between the parties. For example, the employer may reduce the price agreed for the work where it was not carried out in accordance with the contractual standards or it was not completed. The difference with set-off is that the employer does not withhold a payment due to the contractor, but rather adjusts the amount payable to the contractor to the actual value of the work.

25.3.2 Categories of set-off

There are three categories of set-off that are relevant to construction contracts: (i) statutory (or independent) set-off; (ii) equitable (or transaction) set-off; and (iii) contractual set-off.

25.3.2.1 Statutory (or independent) set-off

Where legal proceedings are pending between the employer and the contractor, it may be possible to set-off mutual undisputed[28] debts arising from unrelated transactions (unless the parties have expressly agreed in the contract that legal set-off is precluded). For example,[29] the contractor commences proceedings against the employer to enforce a payment of £300,000 resulting from an unpaid arbitration award in the contractor's favour issued in the context of project X. However, the contractor has not paid the employer £200,000 resulting from a different arbitration award in the employer's favour issued on project Y. As the two cross-claims are in fact mutual debts in liquidated amounts (or amounts that can be ascertained readily and without difficulty[30]), the employer would be entitled to exercise a legal right of set-off, and in effect only pay the employer the relevant difference (£100,000). The employer would not be entitled to do so in case the value of its claim could only be ascertained by arbitration or litigation.[31]

25.3.2.2 Equitable (or transaction) set-off

Equitable (or transaction) set-off applies to claims that are closely connected, so that it would be manifestly unjust for the claim to be enforced without taking account of the cross-claim. However, the parties are allowed to exclude the application of equitable

25 *Green v Farmer* (1768) 4 Burr 2214 at [2221].

26 *In re Paraguassu Steam Tramroad Co* (1872) LR 8 Ch App 254.

27 *Henriksens Rederi A/S v THZ Rolimex* [1974] 1 QB 233 at [246] – [247].

28 Although a legal set-off may apply also in case a claim is liquidated, but disputed, and a dispute cannot be easily or quickly resolved. See *Aectra Refining and Manufacturing Inc v Exmar NV* [1994] 1 WLR 1634 at [1648].

29 *Glencore Grain Ltd v Agros Trading Co* [1999] 2 Lloyd's Rep 410 at [412].

30 *Stooke v Taylor* [1880] 5 QBD 569 at [575].

31 *B Hargreaves Ltd v Action 2000 Ltd* [1992) 62 BLR 72 at [79].

set-off in their contract. So, in the earlier example, in case the two contracts related to the same project, a right of equitable set-off may arise despite both contracts being silent on the issue. In the case of *Geldof Metaalconstructie NV v Simon Carves Ltd*,[32] the contractor, Simon Carves Ltd ("SCL"), entered into a contract with its employer for the construction of a building. SCL then entered into two subcontracts with Geldof Metaalconstructie NV ("GMNV") for the supply of goods (the "Supply Contract") and for installation of other goods (the "Installation Contract"), respectively. The Supply Contract provided that SCL was able to set-off "*any amounts lawfully due*" from GMNV to SCL under the Supply Contract or otherwise. The Installation Contract contained a clause preventing set-off. As SCL alleged that GMNV had breached the Installation Contract, it refused to pay the sums under the Supply Contract. GMNV, in response, stopped the work under the Installation Contract. As a result, SCL terminated the Installation Contract. GMNV then started legal proceedings under the Supply Contract. SCL counterclaimed for damages for repudiation of the Installation Contract. The Technology and Construction Court gave a summary judgment denying equitable set-off because there was not a close enough connection between the contracts. The Court of Appeal disagreed with the court of first instance. The test applied by the Court of Appeal was that equitable set-off should be applied when there is an inseparable connection between claim and counterclaim that it would be manifestly unjust to allow a claimant to enforce payment without taking into account the respondent's cross-claim. The inseparable connection had been confirmed by the fact that GMNV had refused to perform the Installation Contract due to non-payment under the Supply Contract. In that case, however, the Court of Appeal found that the set-off clause under the Supply Contract was sufficient to allow SCL to use contractual set-off as the wording any "*amounts lawfully due*" included amounts which have been adjudicated or agreed to be due, and also amounts claimed to be due and that are recognised at law.

25.3.2.3 Contractual set-off and set-off clause

The parties may agree to exclude, reduce or enhance the common law rights of set-off available to them by including a set-off clause in the construction contract. This provision is usually included for the benefit of employers and serves the scope of allowing them to set-off amounts owing by the contractor to the employer against amounts owing to the contractor by the employer. Depending on the language used in the clause, the parties may agree that a set-off right may be invoked against any claim for money made by the contractor against the employer or restrict the right only to certain types of claims (e.g., by stating that set-off may be invoked only against interim payments, but not against final account payments). The parties may also expressly exclude set-off rights altogether, so that the employer will have to pay any amount due to the contractor and pursue separately the contractor for any counterclaim it has against it. In order to exclude or limit the right of set-off, it is necessary this intention results from clear words.[33]

When drafting a set-off clause, the parties may also agree that the set-off of money due to by the employer to the contractor against money due by the contractor to the employer is conditioned upon the employer (or the engineer/contract administrator) issuing

32 *Geldof Metaalconstructie NV v Simon Carves Ltd* [2010] EWCA Civ 667.

33 *Gilbert-Ash (Northern) Ltd v Modern Engineering (Bristol) Ltd* [1974] AC 689 at [717] – [718].

a set-off notice within a certain term (usually as soon as practicable after the employer has become aware of the event giving rise to the claim). The clause may also define the content of such notice (e.g., that it should describe the basis of the employer's claim and the relevant amount). In such case, where notice is not served within the specific term, the employer may lose its right of set-off, but not its right to bring an independent claim or its right of abatement. The issue of timing and form of notice was considered in the case of *NH International (Caribbean) Ltd v National Insurance Property Development Company Ltd (Trinidad and Tobago)*.[34] Sub-clause 2.5 of the agreement between the parties (a standard FIDIC Red Book form) stated that where the employer considered "*itself to be entitled to any payment under any*" clause of the contract, then it should "*give notice and particulars to the Contractor . . . as practicable after the Employer became aware of the event or circumstances giving rise to the claim*" and that the employer should only be entitled "*to set off against or make any deduction from an amount certified in a Payment Certificate, or to otherwise claim against the Contractor, in accordance with this sub-clause*". In this case the arbitrator, the court of first instance and Court of Appeal took the view that Sub-clause 2.5 could not prevent an employer raising a set-off right to any contractor's claims. In particular, according to the arbitrator, Sub-clause 2.5 was not sufficiently clear "*to exclude common law rights of set-off and/or abatement of legitimate cross-claims*". When the matter arrived before the Privy Council, Lord Neuberger stated that the purpose of Sub-clause 2.5:

> is to ensure that claims which an Employer wishes to raise, whether or not they are intended to be relied on as set-offs or cross-claims, should not be allowed unless they have been the subject of a notice, which must have been given 'as soon as practicable'. If the Employer could rely on claims which were first notified well after that, it is hard to see what the point of the first two parts of clause 2.5 was meant to be. Further, if an Employer's claim is allowed to be made late, there would not appear to be any method by which it could be determined, as the Engineer's function is linked to the particulars, which in turn must be contained in a notice, which in turn has to be served 'as soon as practicable'.

Thus, where the parties agree to include such term in their contract, employers must be aware that, in case they do not submit their set-off claim within the term, and in the form prescribed in the contract, they may lose their entitlement to rely on their right to set-off.

25.4 Joint and several liability

25.4.1 Joint and several liability in general

Where two (or more) parties assume liability under a construction contract for the same obligation, the liability of those parties may be: (i) joint, where such parties jointly promise to do the same thing. In such case each party will be liable in full for the performance of the relevant obligation, and full performance by one party will discharge the other; (ii) several, where such parties separately promise to do the same thing. In such case, each party will be liable for its own obligation so that, should a party be unable to fulfil

34 *NH International (Caribbean) Ltd v National Insurance Property Development Company Ltd (Trinidad and Tobago)* [2015] UKPC 37.

it, the relevant liability will not pass to other; or (iii) joint and several, where parties jointly and severally promise to do the same thing. In such case, the claimant may enforce the relevant contractual obligation, in full, against all the parties or either of them. The party against which the obligation is enforced may then pursue the other jointly liable party to recover its share of any amount paid.

25.4.2 Joint and several liability clause

In some cases, ITTs may allow or request contractors to tender in consortia between two companies, e.g., one performing engineering works and the other construction works. The advantage for employers is to have a single point of contact and responsibility. In such cases, the contract will typically include a joint and several liability clause aimed at clarifying the consortium's liability under the contract. Usually, such clauses provide that the consortium members: (i) are deemed to be jointly and severally liable to the other party for the performance of the contract; (ii) shall indicate a consortium leader with authority to bind the consortium and each of the parties composing the consortium; and (iii) shall not alter the consortium's composition or legal status without the prior consent of the other party (which the parties may agree should not be unreasonably withheld or delayed).

Beyond the case of consortia, where a contract is silent on the issue of liability, the rule at common law is that an employer may sue either its contractor or engineer/consultant for the full amount of a loss which both can be said to have caused. The contractor or engineer/consultant that has paid the loss can then seek contribution from the other party under Section 1(1) of the Civil Liability (Contribution) Act 1978 (the "Act"), which states that:

> any person liable in respect of any damage suffered by another person may recover contribution from any other person liable in respect of the same damage (whether jointly with him or otherwise).

In *Royal Brompton Hospital NHS Trust v Hammond (No 3)*[35] a developer sued a firm of architects for negligently issuing extension certificates to contractors after building work was delayed. The court held that the words "*liable in respect of the same damage*" under Section 1(1) of the Act should receive their ordinary and natural meaning. In the specific case: (i) the contractors were responsible for delayed construction "per se"; while (ii) the architects had caused the developer to lose the opportunity to sue the contractors for liquidated damages in respect of that delay (as they had issued the extension certificates). As a loss of opportunity was not "*the same damage*" as the delay, the architects were held unable to claim a contribution from the contractors under Section 1(1) of the Act.

The amount of contribution awarded under the Act will be "*such as may be found by the court to be just and equitable having regard to the extent of that person's responsibility for the damage in question*". The courts usually take into consideration causative potency and comparative blameworthiness.[36] For example, if an engineer or an architect

35 *Royal Brompton Hospital NHS Trust v Hammond* (No 3) [2002] UKHL 14. See also *Mouchel Ltd v Van Oord (UK) Ltd* [2011] EWHC 72 (TCC).

36 See *Mouchel Ltd v Van Oord (UK) Ltd* [2011] EWHC 72 (TCC) and *Furmedge and others v Chester Le Street District Council* [2011] EWHC 1226 (QB).

has prepared the design and the contractor has constructed the work, and both are liable to the employer for the same defective work, the employer could recover 100% of its damages from the engineer/architect despite the contractor being jointly liable with them, and even where it is clear that the loss was caused in unequal proportions. The engineer/architect will then seek to recover a share of those damages from the contractor under the Act (and/or under the consortium agreement, if entered into). However, the common law presumption in favour of joint liability may be rebutted by clear and specific words of severance.[37]

25.4.3 Net contribution

Net contribution clauses ("NCCs") are provisions whereby the parties agree that in case two or more parties involved in a construction project are jointly liable for the same loss or damage, the liability of each of them will be limited to the amount that would be apportioned to that party on a fair and reasonable basis having regard to their responsibility for the loss or damage.

Employers often resist the inclusion of NCC in contractual documents. The reason is that an employer which has suffered a sensible loss may prefer suing a larger contractor rather than a smaller engineering company as that the contractor may be better placed to pay the claim.

As to the interpretation of NCCs clauses, in *West and another v Ian Finlay & Associates*[38] the court confirmed that they are considered limitation clauses. As such: (i) any ambiguity will be interpreted against the party seeking to rely on the limitation (which is usually the contractor); and (ii) the courts will give effect to such clauses to the extent they have been clearly drafted, and include all the parties sharing liability for the loss. In that case, Mr and Mrs West (the "Wests") appointed Ian Finlay & Associates ("IFA") as architect to design and administer works to their home. The appointment agreement included an NCC stating that "*Our liability for loss or damage will be limited to the amount that it is reasonable for us to pay in relation to the contractual responsibilities of other consultants, contractors and specialists appointed by you*". The Wests also directly appointed a main contractor ("Armour") and certain specialist contractors to design and supply certain elements of the project. The works carried out by Armour proved defective. When Armour became insolvent, the Wests sued IFA for the whole loss, claiming £800,000 on grounds of negligence. The judge decided that both IFA and Armour had breached their respective contractual obligations to the Wests. IFA resisted this argument seeking to rely on the NCC to avoid payment of Armour's share. The judge held that the NCC was ambiguous. The phrase "*other consultants, contractors and specialists appointed by you*" could be interpreted either as consultants, contractors and specialists with whom the claimants had entered into a contract in relation to the project other than IFA (in which Armour would be included), or as limited to the various specialist contractors with whom the Wests were proposing to enter into direct contracts outside the main building contract (in which case Armour would be excluded). Edwards-Stuart J decided that, as there was doubt on the meaning of the NCC, the clause should be interpreted in favour

37 *White v Tyndall* [1888] 13 App Cas 263.
38 *Stephen & Carol West v Ian Finlay & Associates (a firm)* [2013] EWHC 868 (TCC), [2014] BLR 324.

of the Wests, who were the claimants. As the clause did not include Armour, it did not limit the liability of IFA, who were then liable for the whole loss. However, the Court of Appeal overturned Edwards-Stuart J's judgment. The court found that, based on the normal meaning of the words used in the NCC, there was no ambiguity. The references to the "*contractual responsibilities of other consultants, contractors and specialists*" meant any such persons appointed by Wests, including Armour. The case shows that the parties shall take particular care when drafting NCCs as they will be scrutinised by the courts as limitation clauses. As such, clarity of wording will be crucial.

25.5 Rights of third parties and collateral warranties

25.5.1 Privity of contract

The common law principle of privity of contract originates from the 1861 case of *Tweddle v Atkinson*.[39] The doctrine provides that persons who are not parties to a contract are prevented from enforcing the relevant terms, even where the contract was made for the purpose of conferring a benefit on them.

In the case of *Price v Easton*,[40] a builder owed money to Price which he was not able to pay. Easton agreed with the builder that if the builder did some work for him, he would settle the debt that the builder had with Price. The builder accepted and did the work. Easton failed to pay Price. When Price sued Easton to enforce the promise made by him to the builder, the court found that Price was not entitled to enforce the promise as he was not a party to the agreement between Easton and the builder. Under the doctrine of privity of contract, Price had not acquired any legally enforceable rights under the contract between Easton and the builder.

The doctrine is now largely superseded by the Contracts (Rights of Third Parties) Act 1999 (the "CRTP Act")[41] which allows third parties, in their own right, to enforce the terms of a contract subject to some limitations. In particular, Section 1 of the CRTP Act states that a person who is not a party to a contract (a "third party") may in his own right enforce a term of the contract if: (i) the contract expressly provides that he may; or (ii) the term purports to confer a benefit on him, unless on a proper construction of the contract it appears that the parties did not intend the term to be enforceable by the third party. However, it will be necessary that the third party be expressly identified in the contract by name, as a member of a class or as answering a particular description but need not be in existence when the contract is entered into. The last of these requirements has been traditionally interpreted strictly by the courts, as shown in *Avraamides v Colwill*[42] in which Waller LJ held that the claimants, who were seeking to claim under a contract to which they were not a party, were unable to rely on the CRTP Act as: (i) they had not been named in that contract as taking a benefit; (ii) the contract did not identify a class of people said to benefit from the contract in which the claimants may be included; (iii) the word "express" in the CRTP Act did not allow any implication as to such terms. In

39 *Tweddle v Atkinson* [1861] EWHC J57 (QB), (1861) 1 B&S 393.
40 *Price v Easton* [1833] 4 B & Ad 433.
41 Sections (1) and (2) of the Contracts (Rights of Third Parties) Act 1999.
42 *Avraamides v Colwill* [2006] EWCA Civ 1533.

the case of *Chudley v Clydesdale Bank plc*[43] the Court of Appeal clarified the findings in *Avramides*. It confirmed that implication could not be used to assert that a contract confers a benefit on a third party in case such party is not expressly identified in the contract by name, as a member of a class or as answering a particular description. However, the court held that it is possible to determine whether a third party is a member of a class or answers a particular description by a process of construction. That a process of construction was permissible was clear from the decision of the Court of Appeal in *Laemthong International Lines Company Ltd. v Artis and Others* (*The Laemthong Glory (No. 2)*.[44]

Other terms of Section 1 of the CRTP Act are that: (i) the third party can only enforce a term of a contract subject to and in accordance with any other relevant terms of the contract (e.g., it may be bound by a contractual limitation period); and (ii) the third party shall have available any remedy that would have been available to him in an action for breach of contract if he had been a party to the contract (and the rules relating to damages, injunctions, specific performance and other relief shall apply accordingly). So, for example, the contracting party may argue that the loss suffered by the third party was too remote or is excluded by another clause of the contract, or that the third party has failed to mitigate his loss; (iii) where a term of a contract excludes or limits liability in relation to any matter references in the CRTP Act to the third party enforcing the term shall be construed as references to his availing himself of the exclusion or limitation. In other words, the third party right can only be defensive so that in case the third party is sued he can rely upon any exclusion clauses that exist in the contract for his benefit.

Section 2 of the CRTP Act is concerned with variation and rescission of contract. In particular, Section 2 (1) states that, where a third party has a right to enforce a term of the contract, the parties to the contract may not, by agreement, rescind the contract, or vary it in such a way as to extinguish or alter his entitlement under that right, without his consent if: (i) the third party has communicated his assent[45] to the term to the party to the contract against whom the term is enforceable by the third party (the "promisor"); (ii) the promisor is aware that the third party has relied on the term; or (iii) the promisor can reasonably be expected to have foreseen that the third party would rely on the term and the third party has in fact relied on it. It is important to clarify that Section 2 does not intend to limit the right to instruct or agree variations to works in a construction contract. This was clearly stated by the Lord Chancellor's Department in the House of Commons where it was explained that variation in this context only referred to variations in a strict legal sense, i.e., a variation to the terms of the agreement which requires new "consideration".

Section 3 of the CRTP Act deals with defences available to the promisor. It applies where the third party has brought proceedings against the promisor for the enforcement of a term of a contract. In those circumstances the promisor shall have available to him by way of defence or set-off: (i) any matter that arises from or in connection with the contract and is relevant to the term, and would have been available to him by way of defence or set-off if the proceedings had been brought by the promisee (i.e., the party to

43 *Chudley & Ors v Clydesdale Bank PLC* [2019] EWCA Civ 344.

44 *Laemthong International Lines Company Ltd. v Artis and Others* [2005] 1 Lloyd's Rep 688.

45 The assent may be by words or conduct, and, if sent to the promisor by post or other means, shall not be regarded as communicated to the promisor until received by him.

the contract by whom the term is enforceable against the promisor); (ii) any matter if an express term of the contract provides for it to be available to him in proceedings brought by the third party, and it would have been available to him by way of defence or set-off if the proceedings had been brought by the promisee; (iii) any matter, and, by way of counterclaim any matter not arising from the contract, that would have been available to him by way of defence or set-off or, as the case may be, by way of counterclaim against the third party if the third party had been a party to the contract. Also in this case, the parties can agree a waiver of the promisor's rights and expressly exclude rights of set-off, defence or counterclaim. Moreover, where in any proceedings brought against him a third party seeks to enforce a term of a contract (including, in particular, a term purporting to exclude or limit liability), he may not do so if he could not have done so (whether by reason of any particular circumstances relating to him or otherwise) had he been a party to the contract. For example, if the contracting party could not have relied upon an invalid contractual clause, the third party will also be unable to rely upon such clause.

Section 4 of the CRTP Act clarifies that the promisee can enforce any term of the contract, independently of the right of a third party to bring proceedings.

Section 5 of the CRTP Act is designed to protect the promisor from double liability and states that where a term of a contract is enforceable by a third party, and the promisee has recovered from the promisor a sum in respect of the third party's loss in respect of the term, or the expense to the promisee of making good to the third party the default of the promisor, then, in any proceedings brought in reliance on that section by the third party, the court or arbitral tribunal shall reduce any award to the third party to such extent as it thinks appropriate to take account of the sum recovered by the promisee.

Section 6 contains a list of exceptions where the CRTP Act will not apply.

Section 7 contains a number of supplementary provisions. In particular: (i) subsection (1) states that the CRTP Act does not affect any rights or remedies available to a third party apart from the CRTP Act; and (ii) subsection (3) preserves the normal limitation periods of six years for a simple contract and 12 years for a contract executed under seal, and makes these periods applicable to third parties enforcing their rights under a contract, subject to the right of the party to limit these rights and impose a shorter limitation period.

Section 8 of the CRTP Act deals with arbitration provisions in contracts, and states that (i) where a right to enforce a term ("the substantive term") is subject to a term providing for the submission of disputes to arbitration ("the arbitration agreement"), and the arbitration agreement is an agreement in writing for the purposes of Part I of the Arbitration Act 1996, the third party shall be treated for the purposes of that CRTP Act as a party to the arbitration agreement as regards disputes between himself and the promisor relating to the enforcement of the substantive term by the third party; and (ii) where a third party has a right to enforce a term providing for one or more descriptions of dispute between the third party and the promisor to be submitted to arbitration ("the arbitration agreement"), the arbitration agreement is an agreement in writing for the purposes of Part I of the Arbitration Act 1996 (i.e., arbitration pursuant to an arbitration agreement), and (iii) the third party does not fall to be treated as a party to the arbitration agreement (e.g., a tort claim made by the promisor against the third party), the third party shall, if he exercises the right, be treated for the purposes of that CRTP Act as a party to the arbitration agreement in relation to the matter with respect to which the right is exercised, and be treated as having been so immediately before the exercise of the right.

25.5.2 Collateral warranties

A collateral warranty is a contract used to extend a duty of care by one contracting party to a third party, who is extraneous to the original contract, by creating a contractual relationship between parties that would not otherwise exist. In the construction industry, collateral warranties may allow buildings' owners (or occupants, e.g., tenants) to claim damages against contractors (or designers) who worked on the property in case of defective works or create step in rights for funders, extending them the benefit of some rights that the employer has under the contract. Under a collateral warranty, the contractor will warrant to a third party (e.g., a tenant or an employer) that the works comply with the terms of the primary contract between the contractor and the employer so that, should this not be the case, the third party to whom the warranty was made may claim for the works to be corrected, or claim damages flowing from the breach of the warranty. Almost invariably, a collateral warranty contains a clause stating that the obligations taken on by the contractor to the third party, and the possible liability for breach that they carry with them, will not be greater than the ones the contractor would have vis-à-vis the employer under the primary contract. In the case of *Safeway Stores Limited v Interserve Project Services Limited*,[46] Chelverton Properties Ltd ("Chelverton"), a property developer, entered into a contract with Safeway Stores Limited ("Safeway") under which Chelverton was to design and build a supermarket which included a car park. Chelverton entered into a subcontract with Interserve Project Services Limited ("Interserve"), which then entered into a collateral warranty with Safeway and Chelverton. Clause 3.3 of the warranty provided that: "*The Contractor shall owe no duties or have any liability under this deed which are greater or of longer duration in that which it owes to the Developer under the Building Contract*". A dispute arose on the quality of the works. Chelverton and Interserve entered into a compromise agreement whereby Chelverton agreed to pay Interserve around £1.2 million, which Chelverton never paid as they became insolvent. As a result, Safeway had to bear costs in excess of £400,000 for the remedial works, which it sought to recover from Interserve under the warranty. Interserve contended that, based on Clause 3.3 of the warranty, it was entitled to set-off the amount allegedly due by Interserve to Safeway against the higher amount that Interserve was owed by Chelverton. Mr Justice Ramsey took the position that:

> absent clause 3.3, Safeway could have proceeded against Interserve without any consideration of parallel liability to Chelverton. However, in my judgment, the purpose of clause 3.3 is clear: it is to restrict Interserve's liability to Safeway to its equivalent liability to Chelverton under the building contract. It still provides a direct route for Safeway to bring proceedings against Interserve, but it ensures that the extent of that liability is no greater than the liability of Interserve to Chelverton.

The limitation clause in the collateral warranty had extinguished Interserve's liability to Safeway. This was because had Chelverton not gone into liquidation, it would have had to consider the sums it owed to Interserve in settling any claim for defective works with Safeway. Interserve's right to payment constituted an equitable set-off which was to be considered a substantive defence to the claim of Safeway against Interserve.

46 *Safeway Stores v Interserve* [2005] EWHC 3085 (TCC).

25.5.3 Rights of third parties clause

The parties of a construction contract have different possibilities to deal with third party rights. They may:

(i) Remain silent on the point, in which case the CRTP Act will apply in its entirety.

(ii) Apply the CRTP Act selectively to specific third parties, in which case they may state that third parties shall have no right under the Act to enforce any term of the construction contract with the sole exception of any specific provision which is expressed to be in favour of a third party (e.g., the employer may mention lenders in case of financed projects). In such they will want to: (a) identify as clearly as possible (e.g., by name, address, etc.) the third parties or the class of third parties having rights under the contract; (b) clearly indicate that such third parties are entitled to enforce the relevant terms; (c) state if such third parties are allowed or forbidden to assign their rights under the contract and state any restriction thereof in case they are.

(iii) Disapply the whole the CRTP Act by stating that third parties shall have no right under the CRTP Act to enforce any term of the construction contract. This is the approach taken by many of the standard forms. It is worth noting that, even where the CRTP Act is disapplied, the parties may still extend the contract's rights and obligations to third parties by way of assignment or novation, or through collateral[47] warranties.

47 They are called collateral as they are associated with another "primary contract".

CHAPTER 26

Environmental, social and governance issues

26.1 Integrity and anticorruption

26.1.1 Integrity and anticorruption in general

Integrity and anticorruption provisions in construction contracts aim at reassuring the parties to a construction contract about the integrity of their counterparts throughout the project. They are primarily aimed at preventing corruptive practices, such as the payment of bribes.

In the construction industry, corruption may occur, for example, where a project is awarded by a public entity and bribes are paid to influence: (i) a public official's choice on the award of contracts; (ii) the degree of tolerance in cases of breach of contract; or (iii) the awarding entity's decision to accept payment of claims.

Anticorruption laws have been enacted almost everywhere in the world.

Companies involved in construction projects must conduct themselves with the highest degree of integrity and honesty. Having a well-drafted anticorruption clause will not be enough. Other practices which may help companies avoiding risks are: (i) carefully ascertain what anticorruption laws apply to the company and to the contract based on the connection the parties and the project have with a certain jurisdiction; (ii) do nothing that even arguably appears to interfere with the impartial, merit-based awarding and administration of the contracts; (iii) have a culture promoting full compliance with ethical behaviours and have procedures and policies that are comprehensive and up to date. These should include a written code of business ethics and conduct which clearly states that the company will not tolerate unethical conduct, including but not limited to bribery, illegal gifts, kickbacks, false statements or falsification of records, etc.; (iv) train directors and staff on anticorruption and more in general on business ethics and compliance; (v) create a system of internal controls and a matrix of authorisation which ensures that the mistakes and improper practices are timely discovered, reported and disclosed, and that corrective measures are promptly put in place; (vi) have in place a policy that will protect employees who raise issues of concern from possible retaliation; (vii) review insurance policies applying to directors and officers (so-called D&O policies) to ensure that they adequately cover the matter, e.g., by covering the costs of investigating and defending any allegations of bribery or corruption.

DOI: 10.4324/9781003387718-31

26.1.2 The Bribery Act 2010

The Bribery Act 2010 (the "Bribery Act") entered into force on 1 July 2011. The offences covered by the Bribery Act are: (i) paying/offering bribes; (ii) soliciting/accepting bribes; and (iii) failing to prevent bribery.

Under the Bribery Act[1] a person is guilty of a bribing offence where such person (the "offeror"): (i) offers, promises or gives (directly or through a third party) a financial or other advantage to another person (the "offeree") provided that the offeror intends the advantage to induce a person to perform improperly a relevant function or activity, or to reward a person for the improper performance of such a function or activity (regardless of whether the offeree is the same person as the person who is to perform, or has performed, the function or activity concerned); or (ii) offers, promises or gives (directly or through a third party) a financial or other advantage to another person, provided that the offeror knows or believes that the acceptance of the advantage would itself constitute the improper performance of a relevant function or activity.

A function (i.e., any public function or any activity connected with a business, or any activity performed in the course of a person's employment) is performed improperly where performance is contrary to the manner in which a reasonable person based in the United Kingdom would expect a person performing that function in the United Kingdom to behave.

So-called facilitation payments or grease payment, i.e., payments to officials aimed an expediting an official process, which are exempted under the US Foreign Corrupt Practices Act ("FCPA"), are likely to constitute an offence under the Bribery Act unless the paying party demonstrates that the payment was required or permitted by local written law.

The persons which can be liable for committing an offence under the Bribery Act comprise everyone who falls under the jurisdiction of the Courts of the United Kingdom, including: (i) companies and partnerships incorporated in the United Kingdom; (ii) individuals who are citizens of the United Kingdom or the British Overseas territories; (iii) individuals who are ordinarily resident in the United Kingdom; and (iv) companies or individuals, of any nationality, if the act or omission which forms part of any of the offence takes place in the United Kingdom. The Bribery Act also provides for the offence of failing to prevent bribery, based on which a company will be guilty of an offence under the Bribery Act if another person (for example an employee, a subsidiary company or a third-party agent) who performs services on behalf of the company pays a bribe. This applies to companies which are incorporated under the law of the United Kingdom and to companies which carry on a business (or part of a business) in the United Kingdom. Unlike the other offences referred earlier, the person paying the bribe for the benefit of the company does not have to have any connection to the United Kingdom, and the bribe can be paid anywhere in the world. Therefore, the company may be held liable for the offence even where the person paying the bribe is outside the jurisdiction of the Bribery Act. A company may avoid liability if it can show that it has "adequate procedures" in place to prevent bribery. The offence of failing to prevent bribery is particularly relevant to the construction sector where there have been cases in which contractors have sought to limit their potential exposure to anti-corruption laws by employing third-party agents

1 Section 1 of the Bribery Act 2010.

to act on their behalf in parts of the world where the payment of bribes is accepted as necessary for doing business.

26.1.3 Integrity and anticorruption clause

Anticorruption clauses are almost invariably present in competitive tenders, submissions and contracts relevant to large and costly projects. With such clauses the parties commit to comply with anticorruption laws and implement appropriate measures to prevent and fight corruption.

Integrity or anticorruption clauses usually provide for the parties to: (i) comply with all applicable laws, regulations, codes and sanctions relating to anti-bribery and anti-corruption. The parties usually include one or more anticorruption laws by way of example, based on the parties' nationality, location of the project or other link with the parties or the project (the Bribery Act and the FCPA are almost invariably referred to. Other laws and regulations are the 1997 OECD Convention on Combating Bribery of Foreign Public Officials in International Business Transactions and the United Nations Convention against Corruption); (ii) not engage in any conduct which would constitute an offence under the Bribery Act if such activity, practice or conduct had been carried out in the UK. This is aimed at catching corrupt practices that take place in countries other than the UK where the relevant practice, which would be sanctioned in the UK, may not be allowed; (iii) declare that they have in place procedures and policies which do not depart from the principles included in main anticorruption and antibribery legislations; (iv) promptly inform the other party in case they become aware: (a) of any improper request or demand for undue advantages. This is often limited to requests or demands connected with the performance of the contract; (b) that a foreign public official has become an officer or employee of one party (or acquires a direct or indirect interest in that party); (v) ensure that any contract with third-party vendors and/or subcontractors in connection with the contract imposes terms equivalent to those agreed in the construction contract. The clause may also require that the contractual party assumes liability for acts of such third parties; (vi) indemnify, defend and hold harmless each other against and from all claims, damages, losses and expenses in respect of any breach of the clause's provisions.

It is not uncommon for anticorruption clauses to place most of the burden on contractors. However, contractors should insist on employers to take on the same level of liabilities which are expected from the contractor. This is because corruption always involves two parties and may also originate from employers.

26.2 Corporate social responsibility

26.2.1 Corporate social responsibility in general

Corporate social responsibility ("CSR") is now an integral part of many companies' business strategy. Companies are conscious their corporate activities have social and environmental impacts which may ultimately affect how they are perceived by their stakeholders and by the public at large. This led many companies, including those working in the construction industry, to develop and implement CSR-related strategies and policies, in particular when the labour-force is from developed economies or where their activities have an environmental impact (e.g., where a pipeline is constructed through a reserve or a building project brings about the deforestation of large green areas). Companies generally adopt and implement CSR practices and procedures on a voluntary basis. However, an increasing number of governments now require companies to show their compliance with CSR, e.g., by disclosing the company's social and environmental plans and performances (e.g., reduction of emissions). This means that companies are required to balance its pure economic objectives with environmental and social requirements, whilst still addressing the expectations of shareholders and stakeholders.

26.2.2 Corporate social responsibility clause

Construction contracts often include CSR clauses whereby the parties ensure their contractual counterparty has the same level of sensibility and care and puts the same level of effort in relation to environmental and social issues. In CSR clauses the parties usually state: (i) they will not engage in any activity, practice or conduct which could constitute, facilitate or cause an infringement of or offence under the United Nations Declaration of Human Rights, the European Union Charter of Fundamental Rights, the Conventions made under the International Labour Organisation (including those relevant to child labour and forced or obligatory labour) and the Modern Slavery Act 2015; (ii) that they have in place, will maintain and properly enforce throughout the term of the contract, policies and procedures suitable to prevent the infringement of the fundamental principles and rights indicated in the regulations they have declared not to be in breach of, and shall carry out periodic monitoring of their compliance with such policies and procedures; (iii) that, in case any of them engages any third-party vendors and/or subcontractors in relation to the contract, such third parties agree to provisions which are equivalent to those in the construction contract. The parties may also reserve entitlement to enforce the provisions of the CSR clause as against said third party.

26.3 Data protection and privacy

26.3.1 Data protection and privacy in general

The parties to a construction agreement are bound to comply with any laws applicable to them in relation to data privacy. This includes Data Protection Act 2018 (the "DPA 1998"), which implements the General Data Protection Regulation (EU) 2016/679 (the "GDPR").

The GDPR requires that companies ensure their compliance with the GDPR's data protection requirements in respect of personal data,[2] i.e., information that relates to an identified or identifiable natural person. According to the GDPR, personal data which shall be: (i) processed lawfully, fairly and transparently; (ii) collected for specific, explicit and

2 Sensitive data (or "special category data"), the exposure of which could significantly impact the rights and freedoms of data subjects (e.g., relevant to race and ethnic origin, religious or philosophical beliefs, political opinions, trade union memberships, biometric data used to identify an individual, genetic data, health data, data related to sexual preferences, sex life, and/or sexual orientation, but not also financial information like bank account or credit card numbers), will need to be handled with even greater care than personal data, but is probably less likely to be of interest in case of construction projects.

legitimate purposes; (iii) kept for no longer than as is necessary; (iv) accurate (companies must take reasonable steps to rectify data that are inaccurate); (v) kept up to date, where necessary; and (vi) kept secure.

In the construction industry, personal data includes not only information relating to individuals' (e.g., employees) contact details (e.g., telephone numbers, email addresses or home addresses), but also information about salaries, performances, qualifications and biometric data. Privacy issues may also arise in relation to any disclosure of details of suppliers and subcontractors.

The matter of data protection shall not be underestimated as penalties for non-compliance can be particularly high.[3] As a result, companies involved in construction projects are putting more and more efforts on the issue of data protection, and often have internal departments dedicated to the subject. For this reason, construction contracts typically include a data protection clause aimed at defining the parties' rights and obligations on the subject. However, introducing a data protection clause in the contract may not be enough to ensure compliance with data protection obligations. Thus, companies in the construction sector may want to take more steps in this direction such as: (i) training employees and project teams, with a particular emphasis on those who have access to personal data, on their privacy obligations and how to comply with them; (ii) putting in place, maintaining, constantly updating and applying internal privacy procedures and policies; and (iii) carrying out internal audits on personal data they hold and use, and on how they are stored and managed.

26.3.2 Data protection and privacy clause

The parties usually include provisions mandating the parties to comply with privacy laws and regulations in their construction contracts. Such clauses usually limit the number and the nature of personal data that the parties can share between them (usually stating that such data shall be agreed in writing between them from time to time) and provide that such data shall be processed only for the purposes of the contract. The parties also usually give reciprocal assurances that they will put in place appropriate measures to prevent unauthorised or unlawful processing and accidental loss, destruction or damage to such data. These measures may be technical (e.g., protection systems against cyberattacks) and organisational (e.g., training on data protection, appropriate procedures, etc.). The parties may also agree on indemnity obligations in case of losses suffered by one of them as a result of the other party's failure to comply with the terms of the clause or with any data protection laws or regulations applicable to the contract, the project and the parties.

3 Currently, up to €20,000,000 or 4% of a company's global turnover (whichever is greater).

CHAPTER 27

Supervening events affecting the parties' obligations

27.1 Force majeure

27.1.1 Force majeure in general

Force majeure ("FM") is not a term of art[1] in English law; nor does there exist a legal doctrine of FM. An old court case describes FM as a term "*used with reference to all circumstances independent of the will of the man, and which it is not in his power to control*".[2] In *Chitty on Contracts* FM is defined as:

> a contractual term by which one (or both) of the parties is entitled to cancel the contract or is excused from performance of the contract, in whole or in part, or is entitled to suspend performance or to claim an extension of time for performance, upon the happening of a specified event or events beyond his control[3].

The effect of FM is excusing non-performance by the affected party of its contractual obligations. The rationale behind FM is thus that a contractual party may not be held liable for non-performance due to the occurrence of events outside its control. It may be said that FM complements the common law doctrine of frustration in that it can regulate circumstances in which the doctrine of frustration does not apply or may limit the consequences of the doctrine of frustration in situations where there may be an overlap between the two (e.g., by limiting or excluding the rigid consequences that may result from the doctrine of frustration).

27.2 Force majeure clause

As mentioned, under English law FM can only be relied on if the parties have expressly provided for it in their contract. In the absence of a FM provision, the courts will be reluctant to imply one. For this reason, nearly all construction contracts for complex projects include FM clauses. A typical FM clause will include the following elements.

27.2.1 Definition of force majeure

As the term "force majeure" has no recognised meaning in English law, a FM clause with no accompanying definition of FM is unlikely to be effective. In *British Electrical*

1 *Tandrin v Aero* [2010] 2 Lloyd's Rep 668, 43.
2 *Lebeaupin v Richard Crispin & Co* [1920] 2 KB at [714].
3 H.G. Beale, *Chitty on Contracts* (33rd edition) Sweet & Maxwell, 2018, at para 15–152.

 DOI: 10.4324/9781003387718-32

and Associated Industries (Cardiff) Ltd v Patley Pressing Ltd[4] a clause stating that the "*usual 'force majeure' clauses shall apply*" was held void for uncertainty. The parties may choose to have a wide definition of FM or opt for an exhaustive list of events that they intended to trigger the FM clause. Both options present pitfalls. While the former may create uncertainty, the latter may leave the parties unprotected in case of events which are so unexpected that the parties could not have anticipated them at the time the contract was entered into. A third option, which is to be preferred, is combining the two approaches by listing the general requirements that the event shall present to be considered a FM event followed by a non-exhaustive list of events that the parties agree will constitute FM events.

27.2.1.1 General requirements of force majeure events

The typical requirements that an event shall have to be considered a FM event under a construction contract are as follows.

27.2.1.1.1 EXCEPTIONAL

Usually, the FM clause will state that only exceptional events may qualify as FM events. In this context, the word exceptional means extraordinary. A typical example relevant to construction projects is extreme weather conditions. Although FM clauses in construction contracts will typically expressly exclude climatic conditions as FM events, unusually severe weather (such as so-called 100-year storms) will usually be excepted. What constitutes "extreme" or "unusual" in this context will be ascertained by the courts based on the factual circumstances (typically, a court will consider historical weather data such as daily temperature and rainfall at the site and compare them with the weather experienced on the project for which the contractor claiming FM, e.g., based on project log, if available).

27.2.1.1.2 BEYOND REASONABLE CONTROL

A FM clause would not typically require that the relevant event be unforeseeable as FM events are often foreseeable, but uncontrollable. Instead, FM clauses will usually contain sweep up language limiting FM to events which are "*beyond the reasonable control*" of the party seeking to rely on the clause. For example, if the project is to be constructed in an instable country, it may be foreseeable that war or other disorders may occur, but the parties will typically have no control over such events, nor will there be anything they could reasonably do to prevent them from occurring or overcome their effects once they have occurred.

27.2.1.1.3 WITHOUT FAULT OR NEGLIGENCE OF THE AFFECTED PARTY

FM clauses will usually exclude that a party may rely on the clause if the event causing FM was brought about by that party's negligence or wilful default.[5] For example, a fire that was voluntarily or negligently caused by one of the parties should not be relied upon by such party to seek relief from performance of its contractual obligations.

4 *British Electrical and Associated Industries (Cardiff) Ltd v Patley Pressing Ltd* [1953] 1 WLR 280.
5 *Hoecheong Products Co Ltd v Cargill Hong Kong Ltd* [1995] 1 WLR 4040, 409. See also *Seadrill Ghana Operations Ltd v Tullow Ghana Ltd* [2018] EWHC 1640.

27.2.1.1.4 NOT ATTRIBUTABLE TO THE NON-PERFORMED PARTY

Some FM clauses also expressly exclude FM in case an event which could normally be relied upon as a FM event is attributable to the non-performed party. For example, war is normally considered a FM event. However, when a war has been started by a State, which is also the contractual party, that State may not invoke the outbreak of war as a FM event as it has in fact "caused" the event. However, unless one of the parties is a State, this qualification is unlikely to be present in FM clauses.

27.2.1.1.5 AFFECTING PERFORMANCE OF A CONTRACTUAL OBLIGATION

The FM clause will usually state that the FM shall affect the claiming party's ability to perform whole or part of its contractual obligations. The parties will usually agree that the affected party shall be completely prevented from performing its contractual obligation for it to be able to rely on the FM clause. However, some contracts soften such language by using words like "hindered" or "delayed", so setting a lower standard for the party seeking to rely on the FM clause.

27.2.1.1.6 INVOLVING THE TERRITORY WHERE THE SITE IS LOCATED

A FM clause may state that an event may constitute a FM event only where it involves the territory where the site is located. In such case, a contractor may only rely upon events such as a war, a fire, a flood, etc. as FM events where they affect the contractor's ability to perform its obligations "at the site". Based on this language, an event of FM affecting a location other than the site where some activities relevant to the project are carried out (e.g., a contractor's fabrication facility in another country) may not constitute a FM event under the contract unless such location is clearly identified as part of the site in the contract. However, where the parties restrict the "territory" where FM events shall occur to be considered such to a specific country or location, they should bear in mind that many FM events are natural catastrophes that will typically have cross boarder effects on more than one country (e.g., ashes due to a volcanic activity may completely stop transport from and to a certain area covering confining states). Thus, the parties may consider carving out such events so to avoid limiting or preventing the correct functioning of the FM clause.

27.2.1.2 List of force majeure events (and non-force majeure events)

27.2.1.2.1 LIST OF EVENTS CONSTITUTING FORCE MAJEURE

Typically, a FM clause will include a list of events which the parties agree will constitute FM events under the contract. The parties may agree whether such list is exclusive or gives mere examples (e.g., by using language such as "*include, but it is not limited to*") and include some form of "catch-all" language. Typically, the second approach is preferred.

The events which are expressly listed in the clause will normally have the common characteristic of being exceptional. An example is climatic conditions at the site. In case climate conditions turn out to be completely diverse from those that one would normally expect of in the country of the site (e.g., abnormal heavy and continuous rain or extreme heat) in that part of the year, which has the effect of disrupting the works, this could be considered an exceptional event or circumstance which might give a right to claim under a FM clause.

The events the parties agree to include in the list of FM events will vary based on the type of project (e.g., based on complexity), the site location (e.g., onshore offshore vs offshore) and the nature of the contractual parties (e.g., private companies vs state owned companies).

A typical force majeure clause in a contract for a complex construction project may include the following categories of events: (i) natural catastrophes which are non-weather-related such as earthquakes, hurricanes, typhoons volcanic eruptions, landslides, tidal waves, etc.; (ii) governmental and regulatory measures such as embargoes, sanctions, expropriation, confiscation and nationalisation; (iii) acts of war and other violent conflict of various level of seriousness such as general hostilities (declared or undeclared), act of foreign enemies, armed conflicts, invasions, etc.; (iv) situations of internal disorder like rebellions, revolutions, insurrections and civil war, carnage, blockade, military or usurped power, terrorism, etc.; (v) interruption of trade or labour-related disorders such as interruption of transportation, power shortage, shortage of labour, equipment or materials, riots, labour strikes or lockouts, union organised actions, etc. In this case, the FM clause will usually exclude that such events may constitute FM events under the contract in case they are committed by the contractor or subcontractor's employees; (vi) dangerous findings at the site like explosive materials, ammunitions, radioactive contaminating substances, etc.; (vii) events of combustion such as fire, conflagration, explosion and implosion; (viii) sanitary emergencies such as plague, epidemic, pandemic or quarantine; (ix) weather-related issues, e.g., "*unusually severe weather*", "*unusual and unforeseeable weather conditions*", etc. Some construction contracts may also refer to so-called 100-year storm, namely a storm that, based upon site statistics has an estimated probability to occur once in every 100 years in the country where the site is located (i.e., has a 1% chance of occurring in any given year).

One of the terms frequently used in force majeure clauses is "Act of God". In *Transco Plc v Stockport Metropolitan Bolough Council*[6] This language was described as:

> A metaphorical phrase (like 'fate') with a religious origin used to describe those events which involved no human agency and which it was not realistically possible for a human to guard against: an accident which the defendant can show is due to natural causes, directly and exclusively, without human intervention and could not have been prevented by any amount of foresight, pains and care, reasonably to be expected of him.

The parties may also mention economic hardship as a force majeure event if they intend it to trigger the relevant consequences. Where the FM clause does not expressly refer to economic hardship it will be very unlikely that a court will deem it included in any general "catch-all" language in the clause.

The FM clause may also mention that regardless of any provision in the clause, the parties will be relieved from their obligations under the contract in case performance becomes illegal or impossible due to an event which is outside their control.

27.2.1.2.2 LIST OF EVENTS NOT CONSTITUTING FORCE MAJEURE

Force majeure clauses in construction contracts for complex projects will also usually list what events the parties agree not to constitute a force majeure. These may include:

6 *Transco Plc v Stockport Metropolitan Borough Council* [2003] 3 WLR 1467, [59] (HL).

(i) a deterioration of the contractor or subcontractor's economic condition like economic hardship, changes in financial conditions or insolvency; (ii) climatic adverse conditions (which are not exceptionally listed as force majeure events, like 100-year storms); (iii) issues relevant to the procurement and quality of goods used for the project such as unavailability or late delivery of materials or equipment and normal wear or breakdowns of any goods, materials or equipment used for the project; (iv) issues attributable to the contractor or its subcontractors such as shortages of manpower; (v) issues attributable to the contractor's subcontractors, such as delay, default or failure to perform. The parties may also expressly state that a subcontractor's entitlement to claim FM under the subcontract relating to the works shall not entitle the contractor to do the same under the main contract for the same reasons; (vi) Covid-19 pandemic is now often excluded as a FM event on the grounds that the parties are now aware of the relevant risk and may provide for that in the contract rather than covering such risk through the FM clause; (vii) any risks expressly assumed by any of the parties in the contract.

27.2.2 Force majeure not to be invoked to avoid payments

A FM clause will also usually state that FM cannot be invoked by any of the parties to be excused from making a payment which became due under the contract prior to the FM event having occurred. This is to avoid that FM is used to avoid compliance with payment obligations, also considering that the performance relevant of payment obligations is rarely affected by FM events (although, one may concede that a FM event affecting the only bank with which one of the parties has its account may in fact delay the execution of a payment without such party having any reasonable control over the event).

27.2.3 Duty and procedure to notify a force majeure event

FM clauses in construction contracts for complex projects will almost invariably include a duty on the party affected by FM to notify the event, and the relevant procedure. The clause will typically set out: (i) the content of the notice (the FM clause that is being relied upon, a description of the FM event, the obligations and the performance that are affected by the event, etc.); (ii) the term by which the notice should be given and the moment from which the term starts to run (typically, the moment in which the affected party became aware, or should have become aware, of the event).

27.2.4 Consequences of force majeure

FM clauses may also expressly state the consequences that the occurrence of a FM event will have on the contract and the performance of the relevant party's obligations. Such consequences will vary based on the severity of the FM event and the impact that it has on the performance of the contract, i.e., whether the event is affecting the performance of the contract for a limited or longer/indefinite period of time.

The parties should clearly define such periods and the specific consequences keeping in mind that once a FM event occurs its duration and impacts will not be immediately predictable. For this reason, FM clauses typically provide for a gradual approach leading to more severe consequences in case of prolonged delay. A possible structure may be as follows: (i) in case a FM event has prevented (or hindered, depending on the language of the clause) the contractor from performing its obligations under the contract and has caused any delays to the completion of the works, the contractor will usually be excused for the delay and be entitled to an extension of time. The clause may also specify whether the contractor may be entitled to certain costs, although it is common to state that each party will bear its own costs incurred by it as a result of the force majeure event and may not claim any reimbursement or damages; (ii) in case the FM event persists for a certain agreed number of consecutive days starting from the day the FM notice was given, the employer shall instruct the contractor on whether it should demobilise or remain in stand-by on or near the site. In the former case, the parties may agree that the contractor will be entitled to demobilisation costs and could take on any other work which it may have under different contracts, while, in the latter case, the contractor will typically be entitled to lower rates pre-agreed with the employer for such contingent situations plus any costs deriving from the stand-by; (iii) in case the FM event prevents (or hinders) performance for a longer agreed period (e.g., six months or one year from the day the FM notice was given), the FM clause may state that the contract will automatically terminate or that each of the parties will have a right to terminate it (partially or wholly, depending on the circumstances and the language of the contract). The rationale of this provision is to avoid the parties being stuck into a contract indefinitely in a situation where works may never resume or resume when the project will not make any more sense. The main consequences of termination will be that the parties will be discharged from their obligations under the contract. The clause will also usually state that the contractor will be entitled to receive some payments, such as: (a) payment for the work already carried out up to that moment; (b) the costs incurred in the expectation of completing the works (e.g., costs for materials already purchased or ordered, to the extent the order cannot be cancelled), in which case, any material for which the employer has paid will become property of the employer; and (c) payment for any extra works that the employer may ask the contractor to carry out (e.g., removal of temporary works from site). It would however be rare for the parties to agree that the contractor shall be entitled to any indirect or consequential losses (such as loss of profit or loss of contracts) deriving from the termination as FM events are typically considered natural events whose risk is shared between the parties.

27.2.5 Obligations of the parties during and upon cessation of a force majeure event

A FM clause should also set out the parties' obligations during the period in which the FM event affects the project and the parties' obligations to perform under the contract. These obligations will usually have the scope to mitigate delays and damages to the works and the materials.

A FM event may bring the project to a definitive alt or delay completion depending on the degree of severity of the event. Where the event will only delay the performance of contractual obligations (e.g., in the case of temporary events such as severe adverse weather, strikes or acts of terrorism), the contractor will be required to resume the works once the event has ceased to exist. In such cases, the FM clause will usually provide that each party shall use all reasonable endeavours to minimise the delay in the performance of the contract.

The clause will also usually state that the affected party shall provide the other party with regular status updates, such as its reasonable predictions as to how long the FM event will likely last so to allow for forward-planning.

The clause will usually set out the parties' obligations after the FM event has ceased. In particular, the contractor shall usually deliver to the employer a remobilisation plan and a revised programme which considers the delays due to the FM events and the steps the contractor intends to take to minimise the relevant effects, plus any associated costs.

27.3 Interpretation of force majeure clauses

The effect of a FM clause will be wholly dependent on how the clause is worded and how it will be interpreted by the courts. The main principles of interpretation of FM clauses can be summarised as follows: (i) the burden of proof will be on the party seeking to rely on the FM clause; (ii) each FM clause will be construed on its own terms, and in its own context;[7] (iii) words used in the FM clause will typically be given their natural and ordinary meaning; (iv) when determining the meaning of the words of a FM clause the courts will seek to determine objectively what the parties meant with such words at the time they entered into the contract. Evidence around what the parties actually and subjectively intended with those words will not be relevant; (v) in determining the objective meaning of the words the court will look at the language of the clause and the contract as a whole; (vi) elements of the wider context such as the overall purpose of the provision, the facts and circumstances known to the parties at the time of the contract or the market practice may also be considered by a court, provided that the parties give clear evidence.[8] However, the attitude of a court to give more or less weight to such elements in reaching its view as to that objective meaning will depend on the nature, formality and quality of drafting of the contract;[9] (vii) a court may interpret a FM clause in a way that makes the most business common sense, but it will not go as far as to relieve a party from a bad bargain. If the language of the clause is unambiguous language, the courts will apply it as it is; (viii) where the clause includes a list of events followed or preceded by "sweeper" words or catch-all language (such as a reference to *events or circumstances beyond the reasonable control of the parties*), the courts will give such words their wider and natural meaning and consider them in the context of the entire clause,[10] but it will not be bound to limit the application of the clause to the categories of events preceding or following the catch-all language or to events which are similar to those expressly listed in the clause.[11]

27.4 Change in law

27.4.1 Change in law in general

Change in law clauses are aimed at establishing in advance which party should bear the consequences of changes in laws and regulations affecting the project and the contract.

7 *Classic Maritime Inc v Limbungan Makmur Sdn Bhd and another* [2019] EWCA Civ 1102.
8 *Crema v Cenkos Securities Plc* [2010] EWCA Civ 1444.
9 *Wood v Capita Insurance Services Limited* [2017] UKSC 24.
10 *Tandrin Aviation Holdings Ltd v Aero Toy Store LLC and others* [2010] EWHC 40.
11 *Chandris v Isbrandtsen-Moller Co Inc* [1951] 1 KB 240.

Under English law, it is an implied term of a construction contract that the contractor will comply with any laws and regulations. However, where the contract is for a lump sum, in the absence of a specific provision entitling the contractor to a payment for extra costs borne to comply with any change in law or regulation, the contractor will not be entitled to such costs as the lump sum nature of the contract is based on the contractor's promise to provide everything necessary to complete the project, including what is needed to comply with any changed laws or regulations.

However, even in the absence of a change in law clause, a contractor may be entitled to recover its costs, for example where the contractor has carried out the work resulting from the change in law following a specific variation instruction issued by the employer (or on the employer's behalf) or the employer has otherwise promised to pay for the resulting costs.

27.4.2 Change in law clause

Construction contracts will generally expressly include a change in law provision. Such provisions typically put the risk of any change in the law on the employer, entitling the contractor to extra money and/or extensions of time (depending on the parties' agreement) upon occurrence of a change in law event leading to extra costs and/or delays.

A typical change in law clause in a construction contract would include the following terms:

27.4.2.1 Definition of change in law

The parties should consider expressly defining the meaning of change in law in the clause. The definition should extend to both the words "change" and "law".

As to the definition of "change", the parties may agree that:

(i) A change should not only include amendments, but also other events affecting the applicable laws and regulations (such as repeals, re-enactments, etc.). The clause should also extend to the introduction of new laws which somehow affect those applicable to the contract.

(ii) For a party being able to rely on a change in law provision, the change should be unforeseeable at the effective date (see next section). Foreseeability will usually be intended as an excusable lack of knowledge. So, a change in law would be unforeseeable: (a) because the contractor could not have knowledge of it by looking at the contractual documents; or (b) because an experienced contractor exercising the level of standard practice agreed in the contract (e.g., best practice or common practice) could not have reasonably foreseen the change.

(iii) The parties may also agree on a materiality threshold (i.e., a *de minimis*) so that changes resulting in extra costs and/or time below the agreed threshold may not entitle the contractor to rely on the clause.

As to the definition of law, the clause may state that:

(i) Law shall not only include legislation, which, in the case of English law, will typically mean any Act of Parliament or subordinate legislation within the meaning of Section 21(1) of the Interpretation Act 1978, any exercise of the royal prerogative in the United Kingdom, but also other instruments (such as regulations or guidance, e.g., those in the health sector), relevant interpretations (from the government or the judiciary) and judgments of a court resulting in a change to a binding precedent.

(ii) The parties may also consider extending the definition of "law" to instruments not yet formally enacted, such as bills and draft bills (i.e., draft laws which have been proposed and are under consideration by the legislature) so to catch future but inevitable changes.

(iii) When the contractor is expected to comply to certain technical standards and/or practices of professional bodies (e.g., welding standards and/or practices issued by a professional body), "law" may extend to such standards or practices.

(iv) The clause may also state that a change will only be relevant in case it regards the laws of the country where the site is located, or the works are to be performed. In the case of complex construction contracts this may have an impact on the contractor's right to claim extra costs/time following changes affecting other countries' law which however have a bearing on the contractor's performance of its works (e.g., the laws of a place where the contractor procures some materials).

(v) The clause may also expressly indicate the classes of "laws" which the parties agree may not trigger a claim under the provision, e.g., changes to tax laws (e.g., tax increases), labour laws (e.g., any immigration laws affecting foreign personnel working at the site), etc.

27.4.2.2 Effective date

It is crucial that the clause expressly sets out the cut-off date from which changes in law are considered relevant and may be relied upon by the affected party to claim under the relevant clause. The "effective date" may be either a fix date relevant to the tender process (e.g., the date the contractor submitted its binding offer) or the date on which the contract was formally entered into. Contractors will tend to prefer the first option as the second may leave them exposed to changes occurring between tender submission and contract execution.

The parties should also consider agreeing if the cut-off will apply not only to laws already in force but also to draft laws and bills that were existing or under discussion at such date. This is to prevent contractors from raising change in law claims in case such change was already anticipated at the effective date.

27.4.2.3 Causation

A change in law clause will usually state that the contractor may only be entitled to the resulting relief if the change had an impact on the works. Typically, this means that the change should result in an obligation to alter the works and lead to additional time and costs for the contractor.

27.4.2.4 Risk allocation

The change in law clause will also typically allocate the relevant risk between the parties. The parties may agree that the consequence of a change in law will be either borne by the employer or shared between them. If the parties agree that the risk will be solely on the employer (which is the typical scenario in a complex construction project), the clause will usually state that the contract price shall be adjusted to take into account any change in the project price resulting from the change in law. As changes in law may also result in a saving in the cost of performing the contract, the parties may also consider agreeing what party shall benefit from such savings. This will typically be the party bearing the relevant risk of cost increase.

The clause will also typically cover the consequences of change in law events which are of such magnitude that the contractor will no longer be able to perform the contract, even at an increased price. An example is where legislation is passed that makes it illegal to construct certain types of projects (e.g., nuclear plants). In such cases, the typical consequence will be a termination of the contract for illegality of the relevant scope, in which case the contractor will normally be entitled to be compensated for the works carried out up to termination plus any loss of profit (if so agreed).

27.4.2.5 Mitigation

The clause will normally state that the contractor replying on a change in law clause shall be obliged to mitigate the consequences of the change by using its reasonable efforts to anticipate the effects of changes and keeping any resulting cost increases to a minimum.

27.4.2.6 Claim procedure

The change in law clause should provide for a specific procedure that the contractor shall follow to apply for the relevant relief. This will usually include the following steps: (i) when the contractor becomes (or should have become) aware of the change in law event, it should, within a certain agreed timeframe (normally, in the range of days), notify in writing the employer about the change in law and claim any resulting extension of time and/or payment of extra costs deriving from the contractor's obligation to comply with the change; (ii) the parties shall meet to try reaching an agreement on the contractor's claims; (iii) where they fail to reach an agreement, the employer will typically have a right to make a fair determination of any extra time and/or extra money due to the contractor. Should the contractor disagree with the employer's determination, the dispute will be solved in accordance with the contract.

27.5 Sanctions

27.5.1 Sanctions in general

Sanctions are laws, regulations or administrative decisions which directly or indirectly prohibit certain activities or transactions with certain entities or person or in certain territories.

Sanction events may affect construction projects in different ways, for example:[12]

(i) Trade sanctions (e.g., embargoes) may prevent or limit: (a) the import, export, transfer, movement, making available or acquisition of goods and technology; (b) the provision or procurement of services related to goods and technology; (c) the provision or procurement of certain other non-financial services.

12 www.gov.uk.

(ii) Financial sanctions may impose restrictions on designated persons, such as freezing their financial assets, as well as wider restrictions on investment and financial services.
(iii) Transport sanctions may restrict the ownership, registration or movement of ships and aircraft, including restrictions on movements to and from ports, harbours and airports, and the detention of ships and aircraft.
(iv) Immigration sanctions (or travel bans) may prevent the relevant addressees from leaving or entering a country.

Recent case law suggests that English courts will interpret broadly contractual provisions dealing with compliance with foreign laws and regulations.

In the case of *Lamesa Investments Limited v Cynergy Bank Limited*, Cynergy Bank Limited[13] ("CBL") and Lamesa Investments Limited ("LIL") had entered into a framework agreement (the "Contract") dated 19 December 2017 whereby CBL lent £30 million to LIL. The contract between the parties stated that CBL would not be in default if it failed to pay "*in order to comply with any mandatory provision of law, regulation or order of any court of competent jurisdiction*". CBL refused to pay a certain amount to LIL to avoid US secondary sanctions. The Court of Appeal held that US secondary sanctions are an "*effective prohibition*" and constitute a "*mandatory provision of law*" within the meaning of the clause. As a result, the court found that CBL had not breached the contract.

27.5.2 Sanction clause

The English courts will typically uphold a provision stating that a party will be excused from performing its contractual obligations to comply with or avoid being subject to foreign sanctions. However, the parties shall carefully draft such clauses as poor drafting may lead to unwanted consequences. In the case of *Mamancochet Mining Limited v Aegis Managing Agency Limited and others*,[14] the sanctions clause in a marine cargo insurance policy stated that:

> No (re)insurer shall be deemed to provide cover and no (re)insurer shall be liable to pay any claim or provide any benefit hereunder to the extent that the provision of such cover, payment of such claim or provision of such benefit would expose that (re)insurer to any sanction, prohibition or restriction under United Nations resolutions or the trade or economic sanctions, laws, or regulations of the European Union, United Kingdom or the United States of America.

The defendants refused to make a payment on the basis that such paying would have resulted in a violation of US primary sanctions on Iran. However, the High Court held that the mere possibility that US secondary sanctions could be imposed was insufficient to engage sanctions clause. In interpreting the clause, Teare J distinguished between: (i) "*exposure to any sanction*" (which was the language used in the sanctions clause), which required the claimant to prove that the conduct was *actually* prohibited by the applicable laws or regulations; and (ii) "*exposure to the risk of being sanctioned*", which required the

13 *Lamesa Investments Limited v Cynergy Bank Limited* [2019] EWHC 1877 (Comm).
14 *Mamancochet Mining Limited v Aegis Managing Agency Limited and others* [2018] EWHC 2643 (Comm).

claimant to prove a mere risk "*that the agency in question might conclude that there was prohibited conduct (when in law there was not or may not be)*".[15] The court concluded that:

> Before a sanction can lawfully be applied there must be conduct which is prohibited. Further, when there is prohibited conduct the agency charged with the application of sanctions may or may not decide to penalise the prohibited conduct with a sanction. That suggests that it is necessary for the insurer to show that the payment of the claim in question would be conduct which was prohibited by the applicable laws or regulations. If that is shown then the insurer can fairly be said to be laid open to a sanction, to be at risk of a sanction, or to be left unprotected from a sanction. If that is not shown, then it cannot be said that the insurer is laid open to a sanction, or at risk of a sanction, or left unprotected from a sanction. For unless the conduct is prohibited, in law there can be no sanction.[16]

On interpretation of the sanctions clause, the court held that the insurer was not liable to pay a claim only if payment would be in breach of sanctions and not in case of a mere risk that the relevant national authority might conclude that there had been a breach of sanctions. Had the parties had such intention, they should have used clear wording to that effect.

Therefore, when drafting a sanction clause, the parties should use clear words to state what they intend to achieve with the provision. A typical sanction clause may include the following elements:

27.5.2.1 Definition of sanctions

Sanctions may mean laws, regulations and decisions, either administrative or regulatory, which, either directly or indirectly, prohibits certain activities (this may include the import, export, transfer, movement, making available or acquisition of goods and technology, the provision or procurement of services related to goods and technology) adopted, maintained or enforced by any sanctioning authority (as defined in the clause).

27.5.2.2 Definition of sanctioning authorities

These are countries and their relevant governmental authorities (e.g., the Office of Foreign Assets Control – or OFAC – of the US Department of Treasury for the US, the Council of the European Union for the EU or the Department for Business and Trade for the UK), and any supranational organisations such as the United Nations. The relevant countries will depend on the parties' nationality, any connections of the project with certain states and location of the project.

27.5.2.3 Definition of sanctioned goods and technologies

As sanctions may apply to specific goods, software and technology that are used solely or also military applications (so-called dual-use items, i.e., items that may be used for both civilian and military applications) the sanctions clause will define such sanctioned items, normally by reference to specific lists published by certain sanctioning countries or relevant authorities.

15 *Mamancochet Mining Limited v Aegis Managing Agency Limited and others* [2018] EWHC 2643 (Comm) at [49].

16 *Mamancochet Mining Limited v Aegis Managing Agency Limited and others* [2018] EWHC 2643 (Comm) at [47].

27.5.2.4 Representation and warranty that no sanctions are in place and disclosure obligations

The parties should represent and warrant to each other that: (a) no sanctions are in force and applicable that would make performance of the contract unlawful due to contrast with any sanctions; (b) neither the parties nor their respective officers or directors are subject to sanctions or are included in a list of persons targeted by any sanctions, or directly or indirectly owned or controlled by a targeted person.

The parties will also agree that each of them should promptly notify the other if it is included in a list of targeted persons or become directly or indirectly owned or controlled by a targeted person.

The contractor may also be required not to engage subcontractors which are subject to sanctions or are included in a list of targeted persons for the performance of the contract.

27.5.2.5 Duty to comply with sanctions

The sanctions clause will typically state that the parties (including their officers, directors and personnel involved in the contract) shall comply with any sanctions (as defined in the clause).

27.5.2.6 Prohibition to use sanctioned goods and technologies

The sanctions clause will typically include a representation and warranty by the contractor that it will not perform any sanctioned services or use any sanctioned items for the work.

The clause may also state that, in case items that the contractor planned to use for the work become sanctioned, the contractor should: (a) use reasonable efforts to use alternative items having technical characteristics at least equal to the ones that have become sanctioned; or (b) apply to obtain an authorisation to export or use the sanctioned item from the competent authority, as required by the applicable sanctions.

27.5.2.7 Consequences of sanctions

The sanctions clause will typically state that, where a sanction event occurs which makes or might make it illegal for a party to perform some or all the contractual obligations, that party should immediately notify the other party in writing and may suspend the performance of the contractual obligations affected by the sanction event.

Where, thc affected party's performance remains illegal for a certain period of time to be agreed between the parties (e.g., three months) as a result of the sanction event, then either party should have a right to terminate the contract. In such case: (a) the contractor should transfer the work to the employer, which shall pay for it; (b) the contractor should assign any subcontracts and transfer any authorisations to the employer, to the extent this will not be in breach of the sanctions.

27.6 Cost escalation

27.6.1 Cost escalation in general

Events like pandemics, sanctions and wars may lead to materials shortages and volatile pricing for raw materials, fuel, labour, equipment and other inputs to the works. In the case of turnkey contracts where the payment is fixed or where the contract is cost reimbursable but provides for a guaranteed maximum price ("GMP") the contractor will typically bear the risk of any unexpected increase in the cost of materials and labour, so that in the event such increases materialise, they will have the effect of reducing the contractor's margin.

However, the parties may consider agreeing in advance which of them shall bear the risk in cases of price fluctuation by including in their contract a cost escalation clause allowing the contractor to pass through to the employer the increase in the cost of materials and labour. A cost escalation provision will typically stipulate a change in the contract price if the cost for raw materials, fuel, labour equipment, etc. increases beyond a certain agreed level. Employers are often reluctant to accept escalation clauses in their contracts and may even go as far as disqualifying contractors which qualify their tenders by including such clauses. However, at a closer look, escalation clauses may be beneficial for both parties as: (i) contractors will be allowed to partially or wholly shift the risk of increased costs to employers; while (ii) employers will: (a) increase the chances of a successful project as contractors will not be exposed to financial risk for having been forced to work at a loss; (b) reduce the number of change orders from a distressed contractor; (c) be able to avoid the contractor adding contingencies for the risk of price increases into the initial bid; and (d) keep the risk cost increase under control by agreeing on a cost increase methodology which objectively sets the mechanics to calculate the resulting price increase and caps the employer's total liability or entitles it to termination in case prices go beyond certain agreed levels.

27.6.2 Cost escalation clause

Cost escalation clauses may take several forms depending on the type of project, the type and the amount of material and equipment necessary for the relevant completion, and the terms of the contract (e.g., because the risk may be partially covered by using other clauses, such as tailoring a force majeure clause or allowing relief for financial hardship). A typical escalation clause may include the following terms: (i) an express agreement that the contractor will be entitled to an increase to its compensation if the requirements under the clause are met; (ii) a list of items (e.g., raw materials, fuel, labour, etc.) which will be subject to a cost adjustment in case of relevant price increase; (iii) a baseline against which the increase shall be measured (e.g., the prices included in the contractor's bid); (iv) an objective methodology to measure the changes in the relevant prices. This will typically be an agreed price index[17] and a formula which shall be used as the basis for the calculation of the specific increase. Less often, the parties may agree that the changes shall be calculated by deducting the lower costs estimated by the contractor in its bid from the higher actual and documented purchase costs; (v) a threshold for the increase in prices, typically in the form of a percentage (e.g., 5% or 10%) which, if reached, will trigger the contractor's entitlement to the extra compensation; (vi) an undertaking from the contractor that it will use its reasonable efforts to mitigate the employer's exposure, e.g. by turning to alternative suppliers or procuring alternative products where the ones specified in the bid become unavailable or more expensive or, where this is not

17 E.g., the Building Cost Information Service ("BCIS") of the Royal Institution of Chartered Surveyors ("RICS").

achievable, by seeking to obtain lowest possible prices from its suppliers; (vii) a procedure that the contractor shall follows to notify the employer of its intention to trigger the escalation clause, including any timing and content of the relevant notice. The notice will typically give certain information such as: (a) the materials impacted by the price increase; (b) the comparison between the agreed costs and the new costs; (c) the supplier from which the materials shall be procured; (d) evidence of the increase in prices (e.g., invoices or purchase orders); (e) the contractor's claim for an increase in the contract price; (viii) a term entitling the employer to terminate the contract if, following the price increase, the contract price would increase beyond a certain agreed threshold; (ix) a de-escalation mechanism entitling the employer to issue negative change orders having the effect of reducing the contract price in case prices decrease.

CHAPTER 28

Termination

28.1 Termination in general

Termination has the effect of bringing a contractual relationship to an end in situations where the law and/or the contract entitle the terminating party to exit the contract. Depending on the type of termination and the party exercising it, termination will have a different impact on the project and the parties' positions.

A party may be intitled to terminate under the contract (either for breach or for convenience) and at common law (e.g., in cases of contract repudiation).

28.2 Categories of termination

A first distinction shall be drawn between termination for breach (or "default" or "cause") and termination for convenience (or "at will") and between termination under the contract and at law.

28.2.1 Termination for breach

In case of termination for breach, the innocent party's right to terminate the contract results from a breach that, according to the law and/or the contract, is so serious as to entitle the innocent party to free itself from the contract. A right to terminate for breach may arise from the contract or the law.

28.2.1.1 Common law termination rights

Common law termination rights will usually arise in case of particularly serious breaches which go to the roots of the contract, so allowing the other party to consider it repudiated.

Unless the parties use clear words[1] to exclude a party's common law termination rights,[2] these will continue to exist in parallel with the contractual termination rights. This means that the party may choose between contractual termination or termination at common law.

1 *Stocznia Gdynia SA v Gearbulk Holdings Ltd* [2009] EWCA Civ 75 at [23].

2 See, e.g., *Lockland Builders Ltd v Rickwood* [1996] 77 Build LR 38. Although see *Stocznia Gdynia SA v Gearbulk Holdings Ltd* [2009] EWCA Civ 75.

DOI: 10.4324/9781003387718-33

28.2.1.2 Contractual termination rights

Contractual termination rights derive from express termination clauses in the construction contract affording one or both parties to terminate the contract in certain specified circumstances. The main benefit of having a termination clause in a construction contract is that only the parties can identify from the outset of their negotiation the risks which are likely to alter their commercial position in such a fundamental way that the innocent party should be allowed a right to terminate the contract.

28.2.2 Termination for convenience

Unlike a termination for cause clause, a termination for convenience clause allows one party to terminate a contract without having to establish that the other party has committed a breach of contract.

Both employers and contractors may benefit from an entitlement to terminate the contract for convenience. For example: (i) an employer may have reconsidered the profitability of a project or may be unable to secure financing for the project or may have simply ran out of money due to the high number of variations or other overruns; while (ii) a contractor may consider the project unprofitable (e.g., due to an increase of prices for materials and workforce) or too risky (e.g., due to unforeseen ground conditions) or may want to focus its efforts on a different and more profitable project.

However, it would be unusual for a construction contractor relevant to a complex project to allow the contractor a right to terminate for convenience as this would allow contractors an easy way out from unwanted projects and expose the employer to substantial risks (e.g., the risk of having to make payments under duress to dishonest contractors asking for price increases to continue the work).

Despite the limited amount of case law on the subject, some guidelines have been established by the courts on to the limits that should apply in relation to the exercise of a termination at will. For example:

(i) In *Abbey Developments Limited v PP Brickwork Limited*,[3] the contract allowed Abbey Developments Limited ("Abbey"), the employer, to reduce or increase the quantity of work for PP Brickwork Limited ("PPB"), the contractor, and to terminate the contract for convenience. When, relying on these provisions, Abbey removed work from PPB due to insufficient supervision and poor workmanship, the court found that the termination for convenience provision only allowed Abbey to remove work from the contractor when such work was no longer required and not also to descope part of the works and pass it on to another contractor and that a termination for convenience clause should provide for compensation to avoid the risk of being considered unfair and, as such, "*unenforceable as unconscionable*".

(ii) In *Hadley Design Associates v Westminster London Borough Council*[4] the Westminster London Borough Council (the "Council") contracted Hadley Design Associates ("Hadley") on a rolling basis to refurbish some flats. The contract entitled the Council to terminate the contract without giving any reasons. The

3 *Abbey Developments Limited v PP Brickwork Limited* [2003] EWHC 1987 (TCC).

4 *Hadley Design Associates v Westminster London Borough Council* [2003] EWHC 1617 (TCC).

Council terminated the contract based on: (a) the need to go through compulsory competitive tendering; (b) their will to assign the repair services to the same firm that had been appointed to supply maintenance after the competitive tendering process, so to have a single firm supplying both services; (c) the fact that residents were dissatisfied with Hadley's services. On that occasion, the court held that these reasons were "*rational, honest and proper*"; such clauses allowing termination "at will" are enforceable.

(iii) In the case of *TSG Building Services Plc. v South Anglia Housing Limited*[5] the court was called to decide on the relation between good faith terms in the contract and express contractual right, including termination rights. In particular, the court had to decide whether a clause which specifically mandated that the parties work together in "*the spirit of trust, fairness and co-operation . . . within the scope of their agreed roles, expertise and responsibilities . . . and in all matters governed by the Contract they shall act reasonably*" prevented one party from terminating at will in an unreasonable manner. The court disagreed and held that: (a) a right to terminate is unconditional insofar as there are not any conditions mentioned in the contract itself; and (b) to the extent the termination clause has been freely negotiated and agreed, the relevant termination rights are less likely to be restricted or disregarded in favour of a good faith clause. However, the court also stressed that, in determining whether a clause is valid, a court will look at the reasonableness of the financial arrangement of termination for convenience and will be more inclined to uphold a contractual right to terminate for convenience when the compensation for the exercise of the termination right is fair. The concept of fairness in similar situations is not easy to interpret. However, although in the context of NEC3 contracts, it was suggested it is the sum which the employer will be required to pay to the contractor in case of termination at will it may be similar to that which would be payable as damages for breach,[6] so to discourage the employer from exercising termination for convenience lightly.

(iv) In *Optimares SpA v Qatar Airways,*[7] Optimares SpA ("Optimares") and Qatar Airways entered into a purchase agreement whereby Optimares agreed to design, manufacture, sell and deliver seat sets to Qatar Airways. The purchase agreement incorporated Qatar Airways standard conditions which include: (i) at clause 12.2.3, provided that "*Notwithstanding anything to the contrary contained in these Standard Condition or the applicable Purchase Agreement, Qatar Airways shall be entitled to terminate these Standard Conditions, the Purchase Agreement and/or any Purchase Order for its convenience and without incurring any liability by providing three (3) months prior written notice to the Supplier*". The clause also stated that, in such case, Optimares was required to repay "*all sums previously paid by Qatar Airways*"; and (ii) at clause 13.1, provided that, in case of excusable delay in the performance due to causes such as an act of God, natural disaster or epidemic (a) neither party would bear any responsibility, (b) the parties had to try agreeing a

5 *TSG Building Services Plc. v South Anglia Housing Limited* [2013] EWHC 1151.
6 D. Thomas, *Keating on NEC3* (1st edition) Sweet & Maxwell, 2012.
7 *Optimares SpA v Qatar Airways* [2022] EWHC 2461 (Comm).

recovery programme and (c) if Qatar Airways considered unfeasible the recovery programme or the delay could reasonably be expected to last more than 30 days, Qatar Airways had the right to terminate with immediate effect, with no liability other than payment of costs already incurred by Optimares. The standard conditions also included a provision stating that "*both parties shall act in good faith in the performance of their respective responsibilities and obligations*". When the Covid-19 pandemic spread across Italy, Optimares served notices contending that an excusable delay had arisen as manufacture had become impossible due to the Italian Government's response. At that point, Optimares contended that they had incurred significant costs in progressing the works and was "on the cusp" of starting to make some deliveries. Considering the uncertainty as to when the products would be delivered, the next day Qatar Airways gave notice purporting to terminate the purchase agreement for convenience pursuant to clause 12.2.3 and sought to be repaid of all sums that it had previously paid to Optimares. Optimares contended that the termination was wrongful and commenced proceedings against Qatar Airways for lost profits and wasted costs. In particular, Optimares' contentions in the proceedings were that: (i) the right to terminate for convenience: (a) was not available where excusable delay had been invoked pursuant to clause 13.1; and (b) was in any case subject to the contractual duty of good faith, which obliged Qatar Airways to allow Optimares to perform its work or, at the very least, to not frustrate the contract by terminating the it; moreover (iii) even if the termination was valid, Optimares was entitled to its common law damages, i.e., wasted costs. The legal issues that the court had to consider were: (i) whether the existence of an "excusable delay" precluded reliance by Qatar Airways on the termination under clause 12.2.3; (ii) what was the meaning of the words "*without incurring any liability*" in clause 12.2.3 and whether Optimares was entitled to common law damages (i.e. the wasted costs incurred up to termination) as a consequence of Qatar Airways having exercised its contractual right of termination for convenience; and (iii) whether Qatar Airways had an unfettered right to terminate for convenience or such right was to be qualified by a duty of good faith. On the first issue, the court confirmed that clause 12.2.3 clearly and unambiguously entitled Qatar Airways to terminate "*notwithstanding anything to the contrary in the Standard Conditions or the applicable Purchase Agreement*". Based on this, the court concluded that the termination for convenience clause would not cease to operate once an excusable delay had arisen as per clause 13.1, and Qatar Airways could choose which termination clause to rely upon. It was irrelevant that Qatar Airways could also terminate for excusable delay under clause 13.1. The court acknowledged that the two types of termination have different financial consequences as, contrarily to termination for convenience under clause 13.1 (which had immediate effect), termination under clause 12.2.3 was subject to a more onerous notice period of three months during which the contract continued to exist. This difference in notice periods might have had a significant bearing on its decision to terminate under one clause or the other. However, Qatar Airways might have preferred to rely on clause 12.2.3 despite termination for convenience not having an immediate effect as this would have avoided a protracted dispute about whether an excusable delay had, in fact, materialised. On the second issue, the court rejected Optimares' submission that the contractual right of termination for convenience entitled them to wasted costs. Clause 12.2.3, which was the sole source of the consequences of the exercise of the right to terminate for convenience, made no provision for common law damages to be awarded to Optimares in case of termination for convenience. Instead, it provided Qatar Airways could terminate "*without incurring any liability*". Moreover, an obligation on Qatar Airways to pay wasted costs would be inconsistent with the provision relevant to termination for convenience which required Optimares to repay "*all sums previously paid by Qatar Airways*". On the third issue the court held that the exercise of a right to terminate did not constitute a "*performance of its respective responsibilities and obligations*", which was the only case in which the duty of good faith applied. Therefore, the language of clause 12.2.3 clearly granted Qatar Airways an unfettered right to terminate for convenience. The court also referred to previous cases indicating the courts' reluctance to qualify an express right to terminate with a duty to act in good faith. In any event, considering the evidence, the judge did not consider that the Qatar Airways termination was made in bad faith. As a consequence of that, the court dismissed Optimares' claim and upheld Qatar Airways' counterclaim, condemning Optimares to pay nearly US$2.5 million.

In summary, based on the available case law, the parties shall be aware that: (i) termination may not be allowed in case of trivial breaches; (ii) the exercise of a termination for convenience with an aim of transferring work to a third-party contractor may be questioned by the courts; (iii) an employer may not be allowed to partially terminate for convenience (so in fact omitting part of the works) to get out of a bad bargain; (iv) the parties shall make sure that the termination clause provides for a fair compensation to avoid it being considered unfair and, as such, unenforceable; (v) the parties should ensure that the clause is clear and unambiguous as the English courts will not rewrite the parties' negotiated clause even where it is evidently weighted in one party's favour.

28.3 Termination clause

28.3.1 Employer's contractual termination rights

28.3.1.1 Termination for breach

For an employer to be entitled to terminate a contract for cause, the other party's breach shall normally be so serious as to justify the innocent party to bring the contract to an end.

However, the parties are free to contractually determine what events may justify termination and how such termination rights should be exercised by adding termination for cause provisions to their contract.

A clause providing for termination for cause may include the following terms.

28.3.1.1.1 NOTICE TO REMEDY/CORRECT THE BREACH

A termination clause will usually state that, before terminating the contract for cause, the employer shall request the contractor to remedy the breach or breaches giving rise to the termination right within a specified timeframe. Typically, the contract includes such language, and to the extent the breach is remediable, a court will typically not uphold a termination exercised in a case where the employer has failed to send the notice to correct or prior to the time granted to the contractor to correct the breach having lapsed. Where the contractor complies with the notice and remedies the breach, the termination right will not be exercisable. It is worth noting that a mere indication of the contractor's intention to perform will not amount to having remedied the breach.[8] The clause will also usually state that the time specified in the notice to correct shall be reasonable considering all the circumstances prevailing at the time of the notice. The issue was considered in *Obrascon Huarte Lain SA v Her Majesty's Attorney General for Gibraltar*[9] in the context of a FIDIC contract. Akenhead J stated that:

> The specified time for compliance with the Clause 15.1 notice must be reasonable in all the circumstances prevailing at the time of the notice. Thus, if 90% of the workforce had gone down with cholera at that time, the period given for compliance would need reasonably to take that into account, even if that problem was the Contractor's risk. It may well be relevant to take into account whether the Clause 15.1 notice is coming out of the blue or if the subject matter has been raised before and the Contractor has chosen to ignore what it has been told. What is reasonable is fact sensitive.

28.3.1.1.2 OTHER CONDITIONS TO TERMINATION

Although not common in the case of construction contracts, the parties may agree on an escalation process that shall be complied with before the employer may terminate the contract. For example, the clause may require that: (i) the parties shall first discuss the matter (lower management first, and then up to the companies' top management): and/or (ii) that before termination the parties have the issue decided by a third party (e.g., a dispute adjudication board). Depending on the relevant language, such provisions may constitute a condition precedent to the termination. As such terms may have the effect of slowing down the works, the parties should not include them unless time is not an essential element of the project.

28.3.1.1.3 BREACHES ENTITLING THE EMPLOYER TO TERMINATE

Termination for cause clauses will typically include an array of "causes" triggering the employer's termination right. The clause shall be clear on the fact that a certain breach may entitle the employer to terminate the whole contract. The parties may achieve this result by expressly classifying the relevant terms as "conditions" as opposed to "warranties". As only the breach of conditions gives rise to termination rights (while the breach of a warranty will normally only entitle to damages), expressly using such word would remove any uncertainties on whether a breach of such term may justify a valid termination or only give a right to claim damages. The same result will be achieved where the parties do not expressly use the word "condition", but clearly state that breach of a particular provision will justify termination. In *Newland Shipping and Forwarding Ltd v Toba Trading FZC*[10] Leggatt J held that:

> in principle, a contractual right to cancel or terminate a contract (these terms generally being interchangeable) arises when the contract says it arises.

8 *Bains v Arunvill Capital Limited* [2020] EWCA Civ 545.

9 *Obrascon Huarte Lain SA v Her Majesty's Attorney General for Gibraltar* [2014] EWHC 1028 at [318]. See also *Shawton Engineering Ltd v DGP International Ltd* [2005] EWCA Civ 1359 at [69].

10 *Newland Shipping and Forwarding Ltd v Toba Trading FZC* [2014] EWHC 661 (Comm).

This approach was also confirmed in *Firodi Shipping Ltd v Griffon Shipping LLC*,[11] where Tomlinson LJ stated that:

> a contractual right of termination exercisable upon the happening or non-happening of an event usually brooks of less argument [than circumstances of repudiatory breach].

It is worth noting that a court may find that, looking at the whole contract, the breached term was in fact trivial. In such cases, the court may seek to construe the contract in a way that avoids termination in order to avoid a situation of unfairness to the party that has committed the trivial breach.

The employer's contractual termination right will usually be triggered by contractor's breaches that are pivotal for the employer. The parties may use words such as "any breach", "material breach", "substantial breach", "fundamental breach" or "serious breach". These alternative terms do not necessarily equate the concept of "repudiatory breach", and their meaning will depend on the interpretation of those words within the context of the contract and the circumstances of the case. Indeed, when these expressions have been used, the courts have often been called to intervene in order to prevent the consequences which would derive from excessively literal interpretations of the relevant termination rights. For example:

(i) In the case of termination clauses allowing termination in the event of "any breach", the courts have held that "any" breach must mean "any repudiatory" breach. This principle was first coined in *Antaios Compania Naviera SA v Salen Rederierna AB*,[12] where the House of Lords held that any other interpretation would "*flout commercial common sense*" (and it typically does not make much commercial sense for a party to terminate a contract for "any breach", no matter how trivial[13]). Since then, the courts have almost invariably followed this interpretation in later decisions.[14] However, a court intending to interpret the contract literally may, provided that words used are unambiguous, give the language "any breach" its literal meaning, so allowing the relevant party a right to terminate even in case of breach of a warranty or innominate term regardless of the seriousness of the breach. Undoubtedly, where the parties use the "any breach" or similar language, for the breach to justify termination the breach shall not be trivial. This position is supported by prominent commentators. For example, in *Hudson's Building and Engineering Contracts*[15] it is stated that:

> Termination clauses occasionally allow termination on the ground of 'any breach' or 'any default'. Although in principle, parties may agree whatever they wish, the courts will generally be reluctant to read such wording literally. 'Default' will be read as meaning a default relevant to the contract, and the courts will treat matters which are not a breach of contract as excluded from the meaning of default. 'Any

11 *Firodi Shipping Ltd v Griffon Shipping LLC* [2014] 1 Lloyd's Rep 471.

12 *Antaios Compania Naviera SA v Salen Rederierna AB* [1985] AC 191.

13 *University of Wales v London College of Business Ltd* [2015] EWHC 1280.

14 See, for example, *Rice v Great Yarmouth BC* [2003] TCLR 1; *Dominion Corporate Services Ltd v Debenhams Properties Ltd* [2010] EWHC 1193 (Ch). But see also *Leofelis SA v Lonsdale Sports Ltd* [2008] ETMR 63 and *ENE Kos 1 Ltd v Petrolio Brasiliero SA (No 2)* [2012] UKSC 17.

15 N. Dennys, M. Raeside, R. Clay, *Hudson's Building and Engineering Contracts* (12th edition) Sweet & Maxwell, 2010, at para 8.056.

breach' will be held to refer only to important breaches, to exclude minor breaches, and to include only such breaches as are of substantial importance.

(ii) In cases where the parties have used expressions such as "material breach", where the parties have expressly defined the meaning of the word "material", then the clause does not usually give rise to much uncertainty if one party wishes to terminate. In case the clause does not offer any guidance as to what "material" means, the courts have typically held that a "material breach" requires something less than a repudiatory breach,[16] and have even gone as far as to suggest a checklist[17] of considerations when assessing whether a breach is "material". These include, for example: (a) the nature of the contract; (b) the specific obligations involved; (c) the type of breach; (d) the circumstances of the breach (including any explanation given or apparent as to why it has occurred); (e) its consequences of the breach on the innocent party; (f) the consequences of a termination for each party.

(iii) The expression "substantial" breach creates more uncertainty. The issue was considered in *Crane v Wittenborg*[18] where it was held to require a repudiatory breach. However, that conclusion should not be generalised as the concept of "substantiality" does not seem too far from the one of "materiality", which is instead typically interpreted as requiring something less than a repudiatory breach.

(iv) The term "fundamental" breach is generally considered to refer to a repudiatory breach of contract unless the contract expresses a different intention.[19]

(v) A "serious" breach will usually equate to a repudiatory breach, although also in this case, the relevant interpretation will depend on the specific circumstances of the case.

Typical events which the clause may expressly state shall justify the employer's termination right include the contractor:

(i) Having failed to comply with a notice to remedy. However, it is generally accepted that not any type of failure will justify a termination. The failure to remedy should relate to a defect which, if not remedied, deprives the employer of substantially the whole benefit of the works. This interpretation is also backed by case law. In *Obrascon Huarte Lain SA v Her Majesty's Attorney General for Gibraltar*,[20] in the context of a FIDIC contract, the court was called to consider whether a clause (Clause 15.1) giving the employer a right to issue a notice to correct in case the contractor failed to carry out any obligation under the contract (so that, in case of failure to correct, the employer would be entitled to terminate

16 See, for example, *Glolite Ltd v Jasper Conran Ltd and Another*: ChD 28 Jan 1998; *National Power v United Gas*: ChD 3 July 1998; *Phoenix Media v Cobweb Information Limited* [2000] 5 WLUK 424; *Mid Essex Hospital Services NHS Trust v Compass Group UK and Ireland* [2013] EWCA Civ 200.

17 *Phoenix Media v Cobweb Information Limited* [2000] 5 WLUK 424. See also *Dalkia Utilities Services PLC v Celtech International Limited* [2006] EWHC 63 and *Gallagher International v Tias Enterprises* [2008] EWHC 804 (Comm).

18 *Crane Co v Wittenborg A/S* [1999] All ER(D) 1487.

19 *Suisse Atlantique Societe d'Armament SA v NV Rotterdamsche Kolen Centrale* [1967] 1 AC 361.

20 In *Obrascon Huarte Lain SA v Her Majesty's Attorney General for Gibraltar* [2014] EWHC 1028 [318] at [321].

the contract) could be used for any type of breach, irrespective of the relevant seriousness. Akenhead J stated that for such clause a commercially sensible construction is required and that:

> Clause 15.1 relates only to more than insignificant contractual failures by the Contractor. It could be a health and safety failure, bad work, serious delay on aspects of the work or the like. It will need to be established as a failure to comply with the Contract. Something may have not yet become a failure; for instance the delivery to site of the wrong type of cement may not become a failure until the cement is or is about to be used. . . . The parties can not sensibly have thought (objectively) that a trivial contractual failure in itself could lead to contractual termination. Thus, there being one day's culpable delay on a 730 day contract or 1m^2 of defective paintwork out of 10,000m^2 good paintwork would not, if reasonable and sensible commercial persons had anything to do with it, justify termination even if the Contractor does not comply with a Clause 15.1 notice. What is trivial and what is significant or serious will depend on the facts.

(ii) Having abandoned the works or taken a conduct that shows its plain intention not to perform its contractual obligations. These conducts are clear signs of the contractor's intention to repudiate the contract and will therefore justify a termination for breach.

(iii) Having failed to proceed with the works with due expedition and without delay (as in FIDIC standard form contracts) or having failed "*to proceed regularly and diligently*" (as in JCT standard form contracts).

A failure to proceed with the works "with due expedition and without delay" must be critical to the progress of the works for the employer to be entitled to terminate the contract under this provision. In *Obrascon Huarte Lain SA v HM Attorney General for Gibraltar*,[21] the context of a FIDIC contract including such obligation on the contractor, the Court of Appeal held:

> The obligation under clause 8 of the FIDIC Conditions to 'proceed with the works with due expedition and without delay' is not directed to every task on the contractor's to-do list. It is principally directed to activities which are or may become critical.

Anobligation to "proceed regularly and diligently" is broader than one to "proceed expeditiously and without delay". In *West Faulkner v London Borough of Newham*[22] Court of Appeal stated that, where the contract includes such language:

> the obligation upon the contractor is essentially to proceed continuously, industriously and efficiently with appropriate physical resources so as to progress the works steadily towards completion substantially in accordance with the contractual requirements to time, sequence and quality of the works.

In *Vivergo Fuels Limited v Redhill Engineering Solutions Limited*[23] the Technology and Construction Court was called to establish whether a failure to provide the level of resource shown in a programme could lead to failure to proceed

21 *Obrascon Huarte Lain SA v HM Attorney General for Gibraltar* [2015] EWCA Civ 712 (09 July 2015) at [132]. See also *Sabic UK Petrochemicals Ltd (formerly Huntsman Petrochemicals (UK) LTD) v Punj Lloyd Ltd (a company incorporated in India)* [2013] EWHC 2916 (TCC) [2014] BLR 43 at [166].

22 *West Faulkner v London Borough of Newham* [1994] 71 BLR 1.

23 *Vivergo Fuels Limited v Redhill Engineering Solutions Limited* [2013] EWHC 4030 (TCC).

regularly and diligently. Mr Justice Ramsey held that it was, and stated that, in that case, such failure *undoubtedly* resulted in an inability to:

> proceed continuously, industriously and efficiently with appropriate physical resources so as to progress the works towards completion.

(iv) Having subcontracted the whole of the works without the employer's consent (where the contract provides such consent being required). Contractors are selected and paid based on their ability and expertise in relation to the specific type of project. Subcontracting the whole of the works to third parties, which may not have the same level of capabilities of the contractor, without the employer's consent would nullify the rationale behind the employer's choice, and ultimately lead to issues in relation to the subcontractor's capability to duly perform the works and the congruity of the contract price agreed between the parties.

(v) Having breached any applicable laws, including anticorruption laws (e.g., having paid or offered a bribe) in relation to the contract.

(vi) Having failed to provide or maintain or replace any guarantees or insurance policies in accordance with the terms of the contract. These are clearly fundamental breaches as they may affect the employer's ability to recover damages in case of breach of contract by the contractor.

(vii) Having become bankrupt or insolvent, gone into liquidation or other events with a similar effect. The parties typically expressly provide for such a termination right in their construction contract as under common law a party does not have an automatic right to terminate in the event of insolvency. It is worth noting that a contractor's intention to wind up its business in the future without affecting the project may not justify a termination or amount to a repudiation of the contract by the contractor when evidence shows that this is done in the context of a legitimate corporate restructuring which is not intended to affect the completion of an ongoing project.[24] The issue of insolvency is particularly important in construction contracts as it is not uncommon that contractors may find themselves in financial distress and therefore unable to perform their obligations under the contract. For this reason, the parties to construction contracts will need to take into consideration the provisions of the Corporate Insolvency and Governance Act 2020 (the "Act") on the subject. In particular, in the wake of the Covid-19 pandemic, section 14 of the Act introduced a new section 233B to the Insolvency Act 1986, which applies to contracts for the supply of goods and/or services (i.e., also construction contracts[25]) and states that suppliers of goods and/or services (i.e., also contractors and subcontractors) are prevented[26] from terminating a contract (i.e., also a construction contract) in case the company they are

24 *Thomas Barnes & Sons Plc v Blackburn with Darwen Borough Council* [2022] EWHC 2598 (TCC).

25 Exemptions apply to contracts of insurance or guarantee, contracts for the supply of utilities and contracts forming part of a public-private partnership project and to small companies that meet two of the three following criteria: (i) a turnover of under £10.2 million, (ii) net assets on the balance sheet of less than £5.1 million and (iii) less than 50 employees.

26 Unless the appointed administrator, receiver or liquidator agrees to the termination of the contract or the courts grant permission to terminate on grounds of "hardship" which in this case would mean that the contractor/subcontractor would be at risk of insolvency if it was forced to continue.

supplying (i.e., also employers and contractors) is going through insolvency proceedings and, during the insolvency period, cannot make it a condition of future supply that they are paid any outstanding amounts for supplies made to the company prior to it entering insolvency. This, however, does not affect employers or contractors' rights to terminate the contract in case their supplier (i.e., contractors or subcontractors) become insolvent. This may pose some real challenges for contractors and subcontractors as, on the one hand, the employer/main contractor becoming subject to insolvency proceedings would most certainly affect its ability to make payments and, on the other hand, contractors/subcontractors may not stop the works or abandon the site without exposing themselves to important repercussions such as having to pay damages and having the contract terminated for default or repudiatory breach. However, while the provisions of the Act cannot be avoided, the parties may use language allowing the supplier (contractor/subcontractor) to terminate the contract before the insolvency, as defined by Act, occurs, e.g., at the time of the filing of a notice to appoint administrators.

(viii) Having failed to complete the works within a certain number of days/months after completion date (as extended on the basis of any extension of time) has lapsed. In the absence of this term an employer intending to terminate on the grounds of delay needs to consider whether time is of the essence. Even where a contract stipulates a completion date, time will not automatically be considered "of the essence" so that in case contractor fails to complete within the agreed completion date, such default will not amount to a repudiation of the contract and the employer will not have a common law right to terminate. Where the employer intends to make time of the essence, this should result: (i) from an express agreement stating that time is of the essence or stipulating a fixed completion date and stating that such term must be strictly complied with. This will turn the completion date into a condition of the contract so making any delay a repudiatory breach; (ii) from the circumstances of the contract or the nature of the subject matter which may allow an implication that the completion date term be exactly complied with, and that the parties intended even a short delay would trigger a right to terminate; or (iii) from a notice served by the employer (who is ready, willing and able to complete) to the contractor which is late requiring completion in a reasonable time. The effect of the notice (which will not make time of the essence) will be that any further delay will be considered as a breach sufficiently serious (i.e., a breach that goes to the root of the contract so as to deprive the innocent party of a substantial part of the benefit of the contract) to justify a termination at common law.

28.3.1.1.4 TERMINATION NOTICE

The termination clause will usually state that termination shall be communicated to the contractor through a written notice which will also set out the reasons why the employer considers itself entitled to terminate the contract, together with any relevant supporting documents and information aiming at allowing the contractor to evaluate the relevant grounds. The parties shall carefully consider what requirements a termination notice shall comply with (e.g., a specific form, content, timing and method of service). This is because for a termination to be effective, the relevant notice shall normally strictly comply with any contractual requirements agreed between the parties. As ironically observed by Lord Hoffman in *Mannai Investments Co Ltd v Eagle Star Assurance*:[27]

> If the clause had said that the notice had to be on blue paper, it would have been no good serving a notice on pink paper.

This would include, for example, the correct address to which the notice shall be delivered. The issue of a notice of termination sent to the wrong address was recently considered in *Thomas Barnes & Sons Plc v Blackburn with Darwen Borough Council*.[28] In that case, Clause 1.7.4 of the contract (which was based on a JCT standard form) stated:

> Any notice expressly required by this Contract to be given in accordance with this clause 1.7.4 shall be delivered by hand or sent by Recorded Signed for or Special Delivery post. Where sent by post in that manner, it shall, subject to proof to the contrary, be deemed to have been received on the second Business Day after the date of posting.

Clause 8.2.1 extended the requirement to notices relevant to termination and Clause 8.2.2 provided that notice of termination of the contractor's employment "*shall take effect on receipt of the relevant notice*". Clause 1.7.3 stated that:

> subject to . . . clause 1.7.4 any notice . . . may be served by any effective means and shall be duly . . . served if delivered by hand or sent by post to . . . the recipient's address stated in the Contract Particulars, or to such other address as the recipient may from time to time notify to the sender.

It was common ground that the address stated in the "Contract Particulars" was the claimant's registered office. The court held that what clause 1.7.4 required was "*service at the claimant's registered office either by hand or by recorded or special delivery post*" and that nothing less or different would suffice. As the notice was delivered to the site, the court held that the defendant had failed to terminate the contract in accordance with the contractual termination provisions. The court also rejected the defendant's contention that a failure to deliver the notice to the correct address was not fatal to its validity as it was sufficient that the notice was brought to the attention of the claimant, even if not in the manner mandated by the contract. In doing so, the court cited a passage in *Keating on Construction Contracts*[29] stating that:

> The courts will construe a termination clause in accordance with its commercial purpose, but may require strict compliance with any condition precedent to its exercise.

The court agreed with the claimant's position that

> the importance of strict compliance was in that the service of default notices and termination notices are so obviously high up in the list of important communications which may be sent

27 *Mannai Investments Co Ltd v Eagle Star Assurance* [1997] 2 All ER 353 at 377.

28 *Thomas Barnes & Sons Plc v Blackburn with Darwen Borough Council* [2022] EWHC 2598 (TCC) (17 October 2022).

29 S. Furst, V. Ramsey, *Keating on Construction Contracts* (11th edition) Sweet & Maxwell, 2020, at para 11–003.

under the contract, given the drastic consequences which may follow if the defaults specified are not remedied and given the drastic consequences of termination.

The recent case of *Struthers v Davies*,[30] although not relevant to a complex construction project (the works related to a home in Surrey), provides useful guidance on default notices prior to termination of a construction contract, particularly in relation to the person that, under the contract, is entitled to issue the notice. In that case, the contract was a RIBA Building Contract between two homeowners and a building contractor. Based on the RIBA Building Contract, the employer can terminate the contractor's employment in case of abandonment of the works or where the contractor fails to proceed "regularly and diligently". To do so: (i) the "Architect or Contract Administrator" has to issue the contractor with a notice of intention to terminate, specifying the contractor's breach ("Default Notice"); and (ii) where the breach continues for 14 days after the Default Notice has been issued, the employer can then serve a second notice of termination ("Termination Notice"). The contractor failed to meet the contractual completion date and made very little progress thereafter. The contractor also showed a certain disregard for the contract by refusing to purchase materials to complete the works, and using materials destined to the works on other jobs. As a consequence, the homeowners (not the Contract Administrator, as mandated by the contract) sent the Default Notice to the contractor and then purported to terminate the building contract and seek recovery of all the costs they had incurred to rectify the defects and complete the works. The contractor challenged the validity of the termination arguing, among other things, that the Default Notice had to be issued by the Contract Administrator and not by the employer (i.e., the homeowners). The court was then called to decide whether the Default Notice was valid, even though it had been issued by the wrong party. On this issue, the judge agreed with the contractor. However, the court also found that the contractor's conduct, which the court defined as "*a litany of failures to carry out work in time and to give any indication of a final date for already delayed works*", was so wrong that it qualified as a repudiatory breach of the contract entitling the homeowners to terminate the contract. As a result, the homeowners' notice had qualified as an acceptance of that repudiatory breach and had had the effect of terminating the contract. This judgment confirms that the courts will interpret termination clauses strictly when looking at the steps that the innocent party shall take to validly terminating the contract, including any formalities relevant to any notice to correct in case such two-stage procedure applies.

However, whether the notice will be correctly served will depend on the language of the clause and the circumstances of the case. In *Obrascon Huarte Lain SA v Her Majesty's Attorney General for Gibraltar*[31] Akenhead J considered a similar matter with reference to a FIDIC contract, and held that:

> courts in the past have been slow to regard non-compliance with certain termination formalities including service at the 'wrong' address as ineffective, provided that the notice has actually been served on responsible officers of the recipient.

The judge then listed the following general principles applying to the issue and drew the relevant consequences on the specific case.

30 *Struthers v Davies* [2022] EWHC 333.

31 *Obrascon Huarte Lain SA v Her Majesty's Attorney General for Gibraltar* [2014] EWHC 1028 at [368].

(a) Termination of the parties' relationship under the terms of such contracts is a serious step. There needs to be substantive compliance with the contractual provisions to achieve an effective contractual termination.
(b) Generally, where notice has to be given to effect termination, it needs to be in sufficiently clear terms to communicate to the recipient clearly the decision to exercise the contractual right to terminate.
(c) It is a matter of contractual interpretation, first, as to what the requirements for the notice are and, secondly, whether each and every specific requirement is an indispensable condition compliance without which the termination cannot be effective. That interpretation needs to be tempered by reference to commercial common sense.
(d) In the Contract in this case, neither Clause 1.3 nor Clause 15.2 use words such as would give rise to any condition precedent or making the giving of notice served only at OHL's Madrid office a pre-condition to an effective termination. Of course, key elements of the notice procedure involve securing that OHL is actually served with a written notice and receives the notice and it being clear and unambiguous that the notice is one being served under Clause 15.2, namely that 14 days notice of termination is being given by GOG to OHL, such as to enable it to expel the Contractor from the Site.
(e) The primary purpose of Clause 1.3 is to provide an arrangement whereby notices, certificates and other communications are effectively dispatched to and received by OHL. The primary purpose of a Clause 15.2 termination notice is to ensure that OHL is made aware that its continued employment on the project is to be at an end.
(f) In my judgment, the service of a Clause 15.2 notice at the Madrid office of OHL as such is not an indispensable requirement either of Clause 15.2 or Clause 1.3. Provided that service of a written Clause 15.2 notice is actually effected on OHL personnel at a sufficiently senior level, then that would be sufficient service to be effective.

28.3.1.1.5 TERMINATION AS SOLE REMEDY

The parties may expressly agree that termination be a sole remedy which, if exercised, would preclude the employer from claiming damages for loss of bargain or loss of the profit. The rationale of such a provision is that termination already has the double effect of benefiting employers, as they will be freed from the contract, and penalising contractors, as they will be prevented from making the profits expected from the performance of the remaining scope of work. However, such a term is not common in construction contracts. Conversely, the parties often expressly state the employer's election to terminate the contract shall not prejudice its other rights under the contract or otherwise.

28.3.1.1.6 CONTRACTOR'S OBLIGATIONS FOLLOWING TERMINATION

When a contract is terminated, the works will not come to an alt immediately as there will be some tasks that the contractor will be required to perform to enable the employer regaining access to, and control over the site with a view of securing it and completing the work.

A termination clause will usually expressly state any post-termination activities that the contractor shall carry out before leaving the site. These include: (i) demobilising the contractor's personnel from the site; (ii) delivering any goods, documents, design, etc. to the employer; (iii) using reasonable endeavours to cancel the existing commitments which the employer is not interested in taking over (e.g., undelivered materials and/or contracts with subcontractors); (iv) transferring, by assignment, novation or otherwise, any subcontracts or other contracts which the employer is interested in taking over from the contractor; (v) mitigating the losses that may result from the termination (e.g., protecting the works and any goods, equipment or other materials at the site which the employer will need to continue the works).

28.3.1.1.7 EMPLOYER'S RIGHT TO COMPLETE THE WORK OR HAVING IT COMPLETED BY THIRD PARTIES

Depending on why the employer has elected to terminate the contract, the works may either be abandoned or continued. In the latter case, the employer may decide to carry out the works itself (where it has the necessary capabilities) or by one or more third-party contractors.

The termination clause will usually provide for such possibility and state that, as soon as the termination has become effective, the employer shall have a right to complete the works or have it done by third parties. The employer may also reserve a right to request the contractor to complete only part of the works upon the same terms of the terminated contract (which would in fact amount to a partial termination) or on different terms to be agreed between the parties.

28.3.1.1.8 ECONOMIC CONSEQUENCES OF A TERMINATION FOR BREACH

The fact that a contract is terminated does not affect the contractor's right to be paid for any demonstrable and reasonable costs the contractor has borne for the works/goods executed/purchased up to the date of termination. However, as a termination for cause will also typically entitle the employer to claim damages resulting from the contractor's breach entitling the employer's termination, the employer has usually a right to withhold any payments due to the contractor until any employer's damages resulting the contractor's breach is established.

The employer quantifies the damages resulting from the breach and communicates the estimate to the contractor. Where the amount owed to the contractor is higher than the losses suffered by the employer, the employer shall pay the relevant difference. However, as the amount of such damages is not immediately precisely quantifiable (as the employer may incur additional costs for completing the works autonomously or by engaging a third-party contractor), the termination clause may state that any payment to the contractor shall be due only after a certain time. In this way, the employer will be able to set-off any sum spent (or precisely forecasted) against any sum due to the contractor as a result of the termination. Where the amount due to the contractor is less than the amount due to the employer, the contractor will be liable to pay the difference.

28.3.1.2 Termination for convenience

As mentioned, a termination clause allowing the employer to terminate for convenience will usually simply state that the employer is entitled to terminate the contract at any time for its convenience, without adding any specific circumstances or limiting such right.

As in this case the termination right is not justified by a contractor's breach; a notice to correct is not necessary. However, the clause may usually indicate that for the termination to be effective the employer shall give notice of termination and that, upon receipt of such notice, the contractor will not be allowed to continue executing the works and shall take those steps which are necessary to implement the termination (removal of equipment, security of site, etc.).

In terms of economic consequences on the parties, a termination for convenience will normally entitle the contractor to the payment of: (i) a "termination fee", which is agreed in advance as a fix amount or, more often, a formula (e.g., a percentage of the value of the works yet to be executed at the date of the termination). The scope of the termination fee is to provide some equity for the contractor as it may have turned down other projects to perform the one that is being terminated and may not have other projects to which it can redirect its personnel; and/or (ii) the amount of material and services that the contractor has provided up to the date of termination plus any reasonable and documented additional costs incurred by the contractor as a consequence of the termination. In turn, the contractor will typically wave any rights raise claims for lost profits or additional revenue that it might have earned following the date of termination.

28.3.2 Contractor's contractual termination rights

As mentioned, contractors will not usually be afforded any contractual termination for convenience rights, but will normally have contractual termination for breach rights, albeit more limited compared to employers' ones.

28.3.2.1 Termination for breach

A contractor's termination clause may include the following terms.

28.3.2.1.1 BREACHES ENTITLING THE CONTRACTOR TO TERMINATE

Contractors' termination rights are typically more limited in scope than those relevant to the employers. A typical termination clause in a construction contract will allow contractors to terminate the contract only in case of serious breaches committed by the employer. These may include: (i) the employer having failed to comply with its payment obligations. In this case, however, most construction contracts will limit the contractor's termination right by stating that, for the contractor to be allowed to terminate the contract: (a) the amount which the employer has failed to pay shall exceed a certain agreed threshold and be due, owing and undisputed; and (b) the contractor shall first be entitled (and obliged) to suspend the works (by first giving the relevant notice) so that the contractor's termination right will only arise if payment is not received within a certain amount of days as of the date payment became finally due. The clause will also normally state that, in case the contractor suffers any delays or incurs any costs as a result of the suspension, it will be entitled to the relevant extension of time and payment of such costs; (ii) the employer having suspended the works under a contractual clause expressly allowing it to do so, and the suspension having lasted for a time which, according to the said clause, allows the contractor to terminate the contract; (iii) the employer having become bankrupt or insolvent (or subject to similar proceedings or circumstances), (although the parties shall keep in mind the provision of new section 233B to the Insolvency Act 1986); (iv) the employer having committed certain serious offences (e.g., having given or offered bribes or breached any anticorruption laws) in relation to the project; (v) the employer not having taken out or having failed to maintain any insurance it is obliged to have under the contract.

28.3.2.1.2 NOTICE OF TERMINATION

Just as the employer, also the contractor will be mandated to first give a notice of termination to the employer setting out the grounds on which it is terminating the contract.

28.3.2.1.3 RECTIFICATION

The employer will typically be allowed a certain time to rectify (so making such notice not too dissimilar from a notice to correct), where possible (e.g., in case of delayed payment, while it may not be possible in case of prolonged suspension). Once this term has lapsed, the contract will then terminate automatically (unless the parties agreed that a further notice to terminate is necessary).

28.3.2.1.4 CONSEQUENCES OF TERMINATION

The clause will then state the economic consequences of termination. Employers will typically seek to limit such consequence as much as possible. Usually, employers will seek to only pay for: (i) the works carried out and/or the good purchased up to the date of termination; (ii) any personnel demobilisation or equipment removal costs. The parties may also agree that the employer shall pay for the works yet to be completed (e.g., a certain percentage of the relevant value). The clause may also state that such payments will constitute the whole entitlement for the contractor, which shall not have any right to claim any other indirect or consequential losses arising from the termination.

CHAPTER 29

Governing law and dispute resolution

29.1 Governing law

29.1.1 Governing law in general

The choice of the law regulating the construction contract is often wrongly underestimated as proven by the fact that this aspect is often agreed at the end of the negotiations. However, this aspect has important affects on the parties' contractual obligations.

As such, the agreement on the governing law should precede the agreement on any other contractual provisions as it will affect the entire contract and the way it shall be negotiated.

The contract shall certainly state in clear terms which law shall govern it. In the case of construction contracts for complex projects it will be rare for the parties not to include a governing law clause. In the absence of such clause, complex rules of international private law regarding the choice of law will come into play to determine what law should apply to the contract. These rules consider several aspects including the place where the parties are located, and the obligations are to be performed.[1] Where the employer and the contractor are located in different jurisdictions and/or where some contractual obligations are performed in different countries (e.g., where a valve is fabricated in the US for a refinery in Algeria), determining the governing law of the contract may be difficult and lead to disputes between the parties on the right ascertainment criterion. This is the scenario which was presented to Mr Justice Mann in the case of *Apple Corps Ltd v Apple Computer Inc.*[2] where the judge observed that:

> The evidence before me showed that each of the parties was overtly adamant that it did not wish to accept the other's jurisdiction or governing law, and could reach no agreement on any other jurisdiction or governing law. As a result, [the relevant agreement] contains no governing law clause and no jurisdiction clause. In addition, neither party wanted to give the other an advantage in terms of where the agreement was finalised. If their intention in doing so was to create obscurity and difficulty for lawyers to debate in future years, they have succeeded handsomely.

Subject to any limits imposed by any international instruments applicable in the specific circumstances, the parties will usually be free to choose any governing law. They shall

1 The subject of conflict of laws is outside the scope of this book.
2 *Apple Corps Ltd v Apple Computer Inc.* [2004] EWHC 768 (Ch).

 DOI: 10.4324/9781003387718-34

not necessarily opt for the law of the place where the project is located, and the choice shall not be necessarily tied to other elements relevant to the situation at the time of choice. The parties may even choose to apply different laws to different parties of the contract (although this is not advisable unless strictly necessary or imposed by the jurisdiction where the project is located) or change the law regulating the contract during the course of the project (which is not advisable unless strictly necessary, in which case they should check the contract to avoid inconsistencies between the new law and the contractual clauses which were agreed under the previous law).

Typical criteria that the parties may take into account when choosing the law regulating their construction contract include:

(i) The impact of a certain law on key aspects of the contract. This is probably the main aspect to consider as different legal systems may regulate contract terms in completely different ways. For example, while English law does not recognise a general principle of good faith many civil law systems include good faith in civil codes. Other important aspects may be how the specific legal system regulates liquidated damages, legality of interests, statute of limitation, etc.).

(ii) The familiarity of the parties with a specific legal system. Where a party is more familiar with a certain legal system, this will lead to a higher level of control over the contract and a more thorough understanding of the contract.

(iii) The place where the project is located and the contractual obligations are performed. This will reduce the risk that the choice will conflict with any mandatory rules that apply to the work based on the project's location.

(iv) The jurisdiction and dispute forum the parties selected for dispute resolution. This will allow consistency with the law of the place where disputes are going to be heard.

(v) The law applying to subcontracts. For example, a main contractor may have an interest that liquidated damages in the main contract are regulated in the same way as the subcontract to avoid liabilities which may not be passed on to the subcontractors in case of delays or other breaches for which they are responsible.

(vi) The stability of the legal system and low risk of recurrent changes in the law.

However, as it often happens, employers will tend to impose the applicable law already in the tender phase, and frequently disqualify tenderers seeking to qualify such requirement. If this is the case, the tenderer should carefully consider the risks deriving from the law imposed by the employer and include for contingencies in the contract price to provide for such risks.

29.1.2 Governing law clause

A typical governing law clause will state: (i) that the contract and all matters arising from or connected with it, including any contractual or non-contractual obligations, shall be governed by, and construed in accordance with, the laws of a certain country. The parties shall bear in mind that some countries have different laws for different states composing them. So, where, for example, the governing law clause may agree that the contract be regulated by US law (but may opt for the laws of the State of New York) or UK law (but may opt for the laws of England and Wales); and (ii) whether any international private law regarding the choice of law shall apply or not to the contract. Typically, the parties will exclude such laws to avoid unexpected results. However, they should bear in mind that international conventions may limit such choice.[3]

29.2 Dispute resolution

29.2.1 Dispute resolution in general

Complex construction projects may take years to complete, and will typically involve a multitude of parties, such as lenders, employer, designers, contractors, subcontractors, supplies and hundreds or even thousands of workers. For this reason, disputes will be common and various for subject and size. The parties will typically seek for efficient methods of conflict resolution which prioritise the commercial relationship between the various players so that the works may continue smoothly, and the parties may maintain a good relationship for future projects. For this reason, alternative dispute resolution or "ADR" methods are common in the construction industry.

29.2.2 Dispute resolution clause

A dispute resolution clause in a construction contract may include the following elements.

29.2.2.1 The dispute

29.2.2.1.1 DEFINITION OF DISPUTE

A dispute resolution clause in a construction contract will usually define the meaning of "dispute" under the contract. This definition should identify disputes in general terms so to include as many controversies as possible. The definition may therefore include both the words "dispute" and "difference" where the term "dispute" may refer to a more crystalised disagreement, while "difference" would aim at catching less serious conflicts between the parties which nonetheless may require the triggering of the dispute resolution clause.

29.2.2.1.2 SCOPE OF THE DISPUTES

The scope of the "disputes" should also be clearly defined. The clause will typically include language aimed at encompassing any disputes relevant to the contract. Absent special circumstances, the parties are not advised to limit the scope of disputes and should define the scope of the clause broadly. Where, however, the parties intend to exclude some specific disputes from the dispute resolution method they have agreed to apply, they should use clear words. In *Premium Nafta Products Limited (20th Defendant) & others v Fili Shipping Company (14th Claimant) & others*[4] Lord Hoffmann held that:

3 See for example: (i) the Regulation (EC) No 593/2008 of the European Parliament and of the Council of 17 June 2008 on the law applicable to contractual obligations (the "Rome I Regulation") and Regulation (EC) No 864/2007 on the law applicable to non-contractual obligations (the "Rome II Regulation").

4 *Premium Nafta Products Limited (20th Defendant) & others v Fili Shipping Company (14th Claimant) & others* [2007] UKHL 40.

> the construction of an arbitration clause should start from the assumption that the parties, as rational businessmen, are likely to have intended any dispute arising out of the relationship into which they have entered or purported to enter to be decided by the same tribunal. The clause should be construed in accordance with this presumption unless the language makes it clear that certain questions were intended to be excluded from the arbitrator's jurisdiction.

However, the parties will usually seek to broaden the scope of the clause by referring to disputes arising not only "under the" or "out of" contract but also "in relation to" or "in connection with" it. The meaning of the words like "in relation to" and "in connection with" is broader than those "under" and "out of". The consequences of using such words were considered in *L Brown & Sons v Crosby North West Homes*.[5] The parties entered into JCT 98 form (the "JTC Contract") for the construction of 114 residential apartments in Manchester. The dispute resolution clause was composed of two parts: (i) Article 5, which provided that "*if any dispute or difference arises under this Contract*" then either party could refer the dispute to adjudication; and (iii) Article 39A1 (which set out the procedure for referring the dispute to adjudication) which was amended to broaden the scope of the clause so that the right of the parties to refer disputes to adjudication was extended to any dispute "*arising under, out of or in connection with this Contract*". The parties had later varied the JCT contract with two side agreements (the "Side Agreements") which affected liquidated damages and introduced a bonus scheme. When disputes arose between the parties under the side agreements, they were referred to adjudication. The adjudicator issued an award in *L Brown & Sons's* ("LB") favour, which *Crosby North West Homes* ("Crosby") did not fulfil. LB then sought a summary judgment to enforce the adjudicator's award. Crosby argued that the adjudicator had no jurisdiction as: (i) Article 5 conferred the right to adjudicate while Article 39A.1 merely stated the procedure. As a result, it could not broaden the scope of that right; and (ii) the disputes had arisen under the Side Agreements which were separate from the main JTC Contract as they did not constitute a variation to the relevant terms, as shown by the fact that they did not include any express language referring to particular clauses in the JCT Contract. The court was then called to decide whether under the JCT Contract's dispute resolution clause the adjudicator had jurisdiction only in respect of disputes arising "*under the contract*" or also in respect of those "*under, out of or in connection with the contract*". Mr Justice Ramsay held that it was clear that the parties had intended to broaden the scope of the right to cover disputes arising "*out of or in connection with*" the contract. Moreover, he found that the side agreements were variations to the contract. As a result, the disputes under those side agreements were properly categorised as disputes "*under the contract*".

29.2.2.1.3 CAUSE OF ACTION

A dispute under the contract may find its cause of action in the contract (e.g., a breach of a contractual term), in tort (e.g., negligence) or under statutory law (e.g., in case of a breach of a statutory term). For this reason, a dispute resolution clause will usually state that the disputes triggering dispute resolution process will be those "*under the contract, in tort and/or under statutory law*".

---

5 *L Brown & Sons v Crosby North West Homes* [2005] EWHC 3503 (TCC).

29.2.2.1.4 NOTICE OF DISPUTE

A dispute resolution clause shall state that any of the parties seeking to resolve a dispute falling within the meaning of the clause may trigger the dispute resolution process by sending a written notice of dispute. The clause may also state that the notice of dispute shall clearly refer to the contractual dispute resolution clause and briefly describe the nature of the dispute and the remedy sought by the claiming party.

Also in this case, the language of the clause may make issuing the notice of dispute a condition precedent to the commencement of the dispute resolution process.

29.2.2.1.5 "MULTI-TIERED" DISPUTE RESOLUTION PROCESS

Dispute resolution in complex construction projects will typically follow a "multi-tiered" (or "multi-step") approach. This is a phased process that usually starts with one or more rounds of negotiations at different levels (project management, middle/senior management, top management) before the parties are allowed to escalate to the following "tier". The advantage of using a multi-tiered dispute resolution process is that each step functions as a filter for the next one, so that only the most rooted disputes reach the final stage (typically litigation or arbitration), while those where the parties' positions are less entrenched can be resolved through more amicable methods (e.g., negotiation or mediation). This spares the parties from lengthy and expensive legal proceedings which may ultimately affect the success of the project and the parties' commercial relationship. Moreover, a tiered approach will also allow the parties more time to prepare their defence in view of more contentious steps.

Being more structured, multi-tiered dispute resolution clauses require more attention and caution when it comes to their negotiation and drafting. This is even more so as poorly drafted clauses may create problems in terms of certainty and enforceability.

An important aspect that the parties should consider if they intend to follow the multi-tiered approach is whether they intend such "tiers" be: (i) binding, so that a party may not escalate the dispute directly to a certain "tier" without having exhausted all previous mandatory "tiers"; or just (ii) optional, in which case the clause is intended to provide for different alternatives among which the parties are free to choose alternatives regardless of the relevant order in the clause (e.g., by bringing directly litigation or arbitration proceedings without the need of first trying to negotiate or mediate the dispute where negotiation or mediation are tiers preceding litigation or arbitration).

Whether the various steps provided in a multi-tiered dispute resolution clause are binding on the parties will depend on the wording of the clause and the circumstances of the case. However, where the parties have made one or more "tiers" clearly binding, compliance with the relevant process will typically be considered a condition precedent to take the dispute to the next level. In such case, a failure to comply with the mandated steps may have serious consequences on the dispute including a staying of the proceedings wrongly initiated in order to allow the parties to comply with all the preceding mandatory steps.

In *Channel Tunnel Group Ltd. and another v Balfour Beatty Construction Ltd. And others*,[6] the dispute resolution clause provided for any dispute to be first referred to a panel of three independent experts. When the disputes arose between the parties, the employer

6 *Channel Tunnel Group Ltd. and another v Balfour Beatty Construction Ltd. And others* [1993] AC 334.

sought an injunction from the English courts. Lord Mustill held that the process in the clause was enforceable, and the employer could not depart from it:

> Having made this choice I believe that it is in accordance, not only with the presumption exemplified in the English cases . . . that those who make agreements for the resolution of disputes must show good reasons for departing from them, but also with the interests of the orderly regulation of international commerce, that having promised to take their [complaints] to the experts and if necessary to the arbitrators, that is where the [employers] should go. The fact that the [employers] now find their chosen method too slow to suit their purpose, is to my way of thinking, quite beside the point.

This approach was confirmed in *Cable & Wireless v IBM UK*[7] where the clause provided that in the event of disputes the parties had to conduct non-binding ADR. Colman J enforced the ADR mechanism and adjourned the substantive claim pending reference to ADR.

In *Wah (Aka Alan Tang) and Another v Grant Thornton International Limited & Others*[8] the dispute resolution clause stated that disputes had to be first referred to the Chief Executive of Grant Thornton. If the dispute was not so resolved, then it had to be referred to a Reconciliation Panel composed of board members. This step was not optional, as the clause used mandatory words ("shall" as opposed to "may"). The clause also stated that "*no party may commence any arbitration procedures in accordance with this Agreement*" until either the panel had determined that it was not able to resolve the dispute, or a month had lapsed since the dispute had been referred to the panel. The matter was referred to arbitration after attempts to conciliate had proven impossible. The award was issued, but the claimants challenged it arguing that the necessary per-arbitration steps had not been followed, so the reference to arbitration was invalid as the conciliation process was a condition precedent to commencing arbitration. Hildyard J had then to decide whether the parties could skip the conciliation phase and refer the dispute directly to arbitration. After reviewing the leading authorities on the subject, the judge determined that the pre-arbitration procedure was not a condition precedent to arbitration. The matter was appealed, and the Court of Appeal confirmed the judge's decision. The court referred to *Sulamérica CIA National de Seguros v Enesa Engenharia*[9] and held that the general test was whether each part of the ADR clause provided for identifiable legal obligations. This included: (i) a sufficiently certain and unequivocal commitment to commence the ADR process; (ii) discernible steps that each party is required to take to put the process in place; and (iii) a sufficiently clearly defined process to enable a court to determine whether the parties have participated in it and when or how it becomes exhausted or properly concluded without a breach. As to any negative stipulation preventing the parties to commence proceedings until a given event has occurred, the question is whether the event is sufficiently defined and its occurrence "objectively ascertainable" to enable the court to determine whether or not it has actually occurred. In the specific case the court found that the process provided by the clause was too equivocal (as the clause did not give any guidance as to what form the process of conciliation undertaken by the Chief Executive of Grant Thornton and the panel had to take) and the relevant parties' obligations too nebulous (as the clause did not

7 *Cable & Wireless v IBM* [2002] EWHC 2059 (Comm).
8 *Wah (Aka Alan Tang) and Another v Grant Thornton International Limited & Others* [2012] EWHC 3198 (Ch).
9 *Sulamérica CIA National de Seguros v Enesa Engenharia* [2012] EWCA Civ 638.

state what parties had to be involved and what was required from them) to be considered an enforceable condition precedent. Albeit the clause set out the procedure to be followed, the absence of any indication as to the quality or nature of the conciliation attempts that the parties had to make to resolve disputes made it impossible for the court to determine whether the process had been complied with. As to the negative stipulation, the court considered that its purpose was not to prevent the parties from commencing arbitration where the completion of the pre-arbitration process had proved impossible, but only to reinforce the provisions generally and provide a cut-off date.

In the recent case of *Ohpen Operations UK Limited v Invesco Fund Managers Limited*[10] the dispute resolution clause contained an escalation procedure based on which the companies' management had to use reasonable efforts to resolve the dispute failing which it was to be referred to the parties' respective executive committees. Where also the executive committees failed to resolve the dispute, the next step was to mediate the dispute through a CEDR appointed mediator. In case the dispute was not resolved at mediation, then either party would be entitled to commence court proceedings. When Ohpen Operations UK Limited commenced court proceedings without mediation having been attempted, Invesco Fund Managers Limited sought to enforce the mediation provision of the dispute resolution clause. Mrs Justice O'Farrell held that the obligation to mediate could not be disregarded as it was a condition precedent to the commencement of litigation. As a result, the litigation proceedings had to be stayed. Interestingly, the judge considered the earlier cases and provided guidance on the subject to multi-tiered ADR creating a condition precedent:

(i) The agreement must create an enforceable obligation requiring the parties to engage in alternative dispute resolution.
(ii) The obligation must be expressed clearly as a condition precedent to court proceedings or arbitration.
(iii) The dispute resolution process to be followed does not have to be formal but must be sufficiently clear and certain by reference to objective criteria, including machinery to appoint a mediator or determine any other necessary step in the procedure without the requirement for any further agreement by the parties.
(iv) The court has a discretion to stay proceedings commenced in breach of an enforceable dispute resolution agreement. In exercising its discretion, the court will have regard to the public policy interest in upholding the parties' commercial agreement and furthering the overriding objective in assisting the parties to resolve their disputes.

29.2.2.1.5.1 NEGOTIATION CLAUSE Negotiation is typically the first step in a multi-tiered dispute resolution process. Through negotiation the parties endeavour autonomously and directly to achieve an amicable solution of the dispute. Negotiation is the most basic form of dispute resolution as it only involves the parties and/or their advisers. The crucial features are that negotiation is voluntary and non-binding. The parties maintain full control over the process and the relevant outcome. This differentiates negotiation from adjudicative

10 *Ohpen Operations UK Limited v Invesco Fund Managers Limited* [2019] EWHC 2246 (TCC).

forms of dispute resolution like litigation, arbitration and adjudication where a third party is empowered to impose a legally binding decision on the parties.

Normally, a dispute resolution clause will make negotiation mandatory so that the parties shall attempt to solve the dispute amicably before they can escalate the dispute to the next level. Historically, agreements to negotiate were considered unenforceable "agreements to agree" as a matter of English law. However, the view around compulsory negotiation has changed following the decision in *Cable & Wireless v IBM UK*,[11] and the English courts will now consider a contractual duty to negotiate enforceable provided that the clause clearly states the formalities the parties are required to fulfil in order to be compliant with the relevant procedure as set out in the clause. In *Emirates Trading v Prime Mineral Exports*[12] the dispute resolution clause required the parties endeavour resolving a dispute by engaging in "*friendly discussion*" for four continuous weeks, following which the dispute could be referred to arbitration. Teare J found that based on the various authorities in the area the clause would be unenforceable. However, the judge referred to the judgment of Allsop P in the Australian case of *United Group Rail Services v Rail Corporation of New South Wales*,[13] where a dispute resolution clause stating that the parties "*should meet and undertake genuine and good faith negotiation with a view to resolving the dispute*", failing which the dispute could be arbitrated, was held enforceable. Applying such reasoning to the case, he held that the obligation to seek to resolve a dispute by friendly discussions in good faith was in fact enforceable as the agreement was not incomplete as it did not lack any essential terms. Moreover, the obligation to seek to resolve a dispute by "*friendly discussions*" (which imported an obligation to do it in good faith) had an identifiable standard, i.e., the parties engage in "*fair, honest and genuine discussions aimed at resolving a dispute*". As a result, the clause was therefore sufficiently certain to be enforceable.

A dispute resolution clause will typically state that before taking any other steps, the parties shall attempt to settle the dispute amicable through mandatory negotiation.

The relevant provision should state: (i) how many negotiation rounds shall be attempted (typically between two and three) before the dispute may be escalated to the next dispute resolution method; (ii) who should be the negotiator for each round (depending on the number of rounds, these may be project management, mid/senior-management and top management, including CEOs); (iii) how long each round shall last before the dispute may escalate to the next negotiator/negotiation team or to the next dispute resolution method. Typically, the more negotiation rounds the parties agree to the shorter each negotiation round will be. As a guidance, a typical negotiation may last around 30 business days in total, but this number varies depending on the contract and the next methods of dispute resolution agreed in the contract. Where negotiation is followed by other non-adversarial methods (e.g., mediation), the parties may be more inclined to shorten the negotiation phase as the dispute will not go straight to litigation or arbitration but will still be "in their hands".

29.2.2.1.5.2 MEDIATION CLAUSE[14] Mediation is a form of assisted negotiation where a third party, the mediator, helps the parties to reach a mediated agreement.

11 *Cable & Wireless v IBM* [2002] EWHC 2059 (Comm).

12 *Emirates Trading v Prime Mineral Exports* [2015] 1 WLR 1145. See also *DS Rendite Fonds v Titan Maritime SA* [2015] EWHC 2488 (Comm).

13 *United Group Rail Services v Rail Corporation of New South Wales* [2009] 127 Con LR 202.

14 For more details on mediation please refer to Chapter 43.

When drafting a mediation clause, the parties should first attempt to agree on the type of mediation they intend to opt for. In general, the parties may choose between: (i) institutional mediation, in which case the mediation process will be handled by, and in accordance with the rules of an institution providing mediation services such as the Centre for Effective Dispute Resolution ("CEDR"), the International Chamber of Commerce ("ICC"), the London Court of International Arbitration ("LCIA") etc. In this case, the parties may agree on additional requirements and/or specific deviations from the chosen rules. For example, the clause may: (a) state that the mediator shall have a particular background (e.g., experience in the construction industry) or a certain number of years of experience as a mediator; or (b) amend the mediation process set out in the chosen rule (e.g. by setting out specific timing by which the mediation shall be concluded, etc.); or (ii) ad hoc mediation, in which case the parties set out the rules applying to the mediation (including how to appoint the mediator and how to run the mediation process) autonomously and without referring to any pre-existing set of rules or mediation institution.

Regardless of their choice, the mediation provision shall clearly identify the mediator or the mediation provider. In *Sulamerica v Enesa Engenharia*,[15] a mediation clause stating that the parties had to "*seek to have the dispute resolved amicably by mediation*" was held not enforceable as it did not define the mediation process or specify the mediation provider.

The clause shall also clearly identify the correct process that the mediator shall follow or the rules what shall apply to the mediation. In *Holloway v Chancery Mead*,[16] the dispute resolution clause stated that the parties "*shall seek to resolve a dispute through conciliation by the NHBC [the National House Builders Council]*". Ramsey J held that the clause was not sufficiently certain as "*conciliation by the NHBC*" was not an identifiable process. Although not relevant to mediation, the case shows the importance of precisely identifying the process.

The clause may also state whether the mediator should take a mere facilitative approach or could use an evaluative approach (where needed). Mediators in construction disputes are typically trained to facilitate a settlement without going into the technical and legal details of the parties' positions. However, the parties may agree that the mediator could take an evaluative approach if suitable to facilitate the resolution of the dispute (e.g., where a party interprets the facts in dispute unreasonably or has unrealistic expectations as to the relevant outcome). In such cases, where the mediator has the necessary skills and expertise, he may evaluate the facts and provide his opinion about the strengths or weaknesses of the parties' cases and legal arguments and make comments and/or recommendations, so assisting them in managing their expectations about the outcome of their dispute if it was to proceed to adjudication, litigation or arbitration.

29.2.2.1.5.3 ADJUDICATION CLAUSE[17] Adjudication clauses relevant to contract which are not subject to statutory adjudication are usually short and give the adjudicator more freedom to decide on the adjudication procedure.

The parties may also agree to use model clauses which refer to the rules of specific administering entities (e.g., the International Chamber of Commerce's Dispute Board Rules). In this case, such rules will apply entirely unless the parties agree otherwise.

15 *Sulamerica v Enesa Engenharia* [2012] EWCA Civ 638.
16 *Holloway v Chancery Mead* [2007] EWHC 2495 (TCC).
17 For more details on adjudication please refer to Chapter 43.

Moreover, where the parties use a standard form (e.g., a FIDIC contract) they will normally use the clause in the form in its entirety or make amendments to tailor it to their needs.

Where statutory adjudication applies, the parties will face some limitations as to the type and number of amendments they may make to the adjudication clause as, based on Section 108(5) of the HGCR Act, where the contract does not comply with the requirements of subsections (1) to (4), the adjudication provisions of the fallback provisions set out in the Scheme will apply. The parties may either incorporate the default procedure set out by the Scheme in full or opt for a bespoke approach by adopting the procedure set out in the Scheme with some amendments.

Considering the preceding, the next paragraph will consider the possible content of a bespoke adjudication clause using as a starting point the provisions of the Scheme and suggesting some possible amendments.

(a) The right to adjudicate The clause will state that where the dispute is not resolved through negotiation (and mediation, if the parties so agreed), within a certain number of days of when the notice of dispute was served (or of the day the dispute was referred to mediation) the claimant has the right to refer the dispute for adjudication.[18]

The clause shall clearly state whether the adjudication "tier" is mandatory or discretionary (subject to mandatory adjudication based on the HGCR Act). Where adjudication is a binding "tier", it will be a necessary step before the case may be escalated to the next level, regardless of the disputes' size, complexity and number, or the project's stage at which they arise. The issue was recently discussed by the Scottish Courts in the case of *Greater Glasgow Health Board v Multiplex Construction Europe Ltd & Ors.*[19] Greater Glasgow Health Board ("GGHB") and Multiplex Construction Europe Ltd & Ors ("Multiplex") entered into two contracts (a "NEC3 Engineering and Construction Contract, Option C" and a "NEC Professional Services Contract") for the construction of the Queen Elizabeth University Hospital in Glasgow. Both contracts contained the NEC clause W2 on dispute resolution stating as follows:

> (1) A dispute arising under or in connection with this contract is referred to and decided by the Adjudicator. A Party may refer a dispute to the Adjudicator at any time. (11) The Adjudicator's decision is binding on the Parties unless and until revised by the tribunal. . . . (1) A Party does not refer any dispute under or in connection with this contract to the tribunal unless it has first been decided by the Adjudicator in accordance with this contract.

GGHB argued that it had suffered losses for defects in the works and issued court proceedings just before expiry of the limitation period to recover £72,800,000 from Multiplex. However, GGHB did so without first referring the dispute to adjudication. The main point raised by GGHB was that the dispute was not one that the parties had intended be referred for adjudication at the time the parties entered into the contract. In particular, GGHB contended that, in the circumstances, adjudication was an inappropriate method of dispute resolution and the parties should not be taken to have agreed to it as, at the time of contracting, it was foreseeable for the parties: (i) that the project would give rise to

18 In line with Section 108(1) of the HGCR Act.
19 *Greater Glasgow Health Board v Multiplex Construction Europe Ltd & Ors* [2021] CSOH 115.

multiple disputes (as many as 22) of a complex nature (11 categories of defects) against several parties (contractor, lead consultant and project supervisor), which was in contrast with the limit to refer only one dispute at a time to adjudication; and (ii) that such disputes would arise at a late stage of the contract, i.e., when adjudication would be of any help. Multiplex rejected these arguments and sought to have the court proceedings dismissed on the basis that GGHB was bound to first refer the dispute to adjudication. The court disagreed with GGHB. Lord Tyre held that:

> [13] The pursuer's argument is founded rather upon the complexity of the claims made in the present action: 11 categories of defects, for each of which three defenders (contractor, lead consultant and project supervisor) are alleged to be jointly and severally responsible. I am not, however, persuaded that clause W2 ought to be construed as impliedly excluding complex disputes. If the parties to the respective contracts had wished to exclude complex disputes, including disputes in which joint and several liability was asserted, they could have done so. It was foreseeable at the time of contracting that in a project of this scale disputes might arise, but the parties have not seen fit to make any special provision for disputes of any particular complexity. Instead they have entered into contracts in terms of which any dispute may be referred at any time for adjudication.
>
> [14] I am not prepared to accept, on the basis of the detail contained in the summons, that it would be impossible for some or even all of the issues identified to be resolved by an adjudication process. There may have to be multiple adjudications. It is of course generally accepted that only a single dispute can be referred to an adjudicator at any one time, and it is conceivable that difficulties may arise in identifying what is or is not a single dispute. That is not an uncommon difficulty, as the case law demonstrates. It may also be that a particular dispute is so complex that the adjudicator is unable to decide it within the time limit imposed by section 108 of the Housing Grants, Construction and Regeneration Act 1996. But as Judge John Toulmin QC observed in CIB Properties Ltd v Birse Construction Ltd [2005] 1 WLR 2252 at paragraph 24:
>
> The Act confers a general right to refer a dispute or difference to adjudication provided it can be adjudicated in accordance with a procedure complying with section 108(2). This general right exists irrespective of the apparent complexity of the dispute but it does not require an adjudicator to reach a decision if he is unable to do so within the time limits imposed by section 108(2) of the Act.
>
> I consider it would be premature, at a time when no reference for adjudication has yet been made, to conclude that any referral would be bound to fail because no reference could be competently framed, or because no adjudicator could reach a decision within the statutory time limit.
>
> [15] Nor am I prepared to accept at this stage that 22 separate adjudications would necessarily have to take place. I have already noted that the basis of the claim made against each of the first, third and fourth defenders in relation to each of the issues is currently unspecific. The process of reference for adjudication should serve to focus the basis of each claim and may not result in all of the claims being pressed against all of these defenders. Finally, I am not prepared to assume at this stage that none of the issues will be resolved in relation to the first and fourth defenders by adjudication. That would run contrary to the experience described in Bresco (above).

As a result, the court found that, based on clause W2, the parties' disputes could not be referred to litigation without having first been referred to adjudication. Interestingly, in this case the court found that reference to and determination by the adjudicator could not be seen as a "*condition precedent*" of the bringing of a court action. As a result, the court held that the action should not be dismissed, but stayed, pending the outcome of the adjudications. This was because:

> although clause W2.4(1) operates as a contractual bar on referral of a dispute to the court unless it has first been decided by the adjudicator, it is a bar that may be waived by the other party to the contract and which does no more than prevent the court from entertaining the dispute so long as the bar remains unwaived and the matter has yet to be decided by the adjudicator.

It is worth noting that where the clause states that a notice of adjudication may be served "at any time",[20] this may be construed as allowing either party to commence adjudication proceedings immediately, i.e., before and regardless of any procedural step envisaged in the contract and even, subject to certain exceptions,[21] to commence adjudication while the same dispute is being litigated in court or otherwise. In this case, the parties may consider stating in the clause that once a dispute has been referred to adjudication, neither party may commence or continue legal proceedings in respect of the same dispute unless and until the adjudicator has given his decision, which has been fully implemented by the party seeking to commence the legal proceedings.

(b) The nature of the adjudication process The clause may also clarify the nature of the process they intend to agree on, and specifically if they intend something different from arbitration. This is aimed at avoiding any misunderstanding as to the meaning of the word adjudication and leaving no room for argument as to the intended method of dispute resolution. Such result may be achieved by clearly stating that the adjudicator shall not act as an arbitrator.[22]

(c) The notice of adjudication The clause may state that where a party intends to refer a dispute to adjudication, it shall send a notice of adjudication writing to every other party to the contract.[23] Based on how the clause is worded, a compliant notice of adjudication may be a condition precedent to the referral of the dispute to the adjudicator.

The clause may also indicate the content of the notice of adjudication.[24] The notice will usually state: (i) the nature and a brief description of the dispute; (ii) the names and addresses of the parties; (iii) the remedy sought; (iv) the clear request to refer the dispute for adjudication.

(d) The appointment of the adjudicator The parties may either set out in the contract how the adjudicator shall be selected and appointed once a dispute has arisen or appoint the adjudicator (or a dispute board or "DB") since the project's inception.

Where the contract does not expressly name a person or a DB, the adjudication clause will typically state that the parties shall endeavour reaching an agreement on the name of the adjudicator within a certain number of days of the notice of adjudication having been issued, failing which, either party (although this will usually be the referring

20 In line with Paragraph 1(1) of the Scheme.

21 E.g., in the case of *Bresco Electrical Services Ltd (in liquidation) v Michael J Lonsdale (Electrical) Ltd* [2020] UKSC 25 the Supreme Court has clarified that a company in liquidation cannot refer a dispute to adjudication when such dispute relates to the determination of any claim for sums to be paid to that company.

22 E.g., in *Barclays Bank Plc v Nylon Capital LLP* [2011] EWCA Civ 826 the clause stated that the dispute resolver was required to "*act as an expert and not as an arbitrator*".

23 In line with Paragraphs 1(1) and (2) of the Scheme.

24 In line with Paragraphs 1(3) of the Scheme.

party) may ask the nominating body to appoint an adjudicator. A nominating body is the entity in charge of selecting the adjudicator[25] when called upon. Some of the most used nominating bodies are the Royal Institution of Chartered Surveyors ("RICS"), the Royal Institute of British Architects ("RIBA"), the Institution of Civil Engineers ("ICE"), the Institution of Chemical Engineers ("IChemE"), the Centre for Effective Dispute Resolution ("CEDR"), the Chartered Institute of Arbitrators ("CIArb"), the Construction Industry Council ("CIC"), the Chartered Institute of Building (CIOB), the Technology and Construction Solicitors Association ("TECSA"), the Technology and Construction Bar Association ("TECBAR"), the International Federation of Consulting Engineers ("FIDIC"), the London Court of International Arbitration ("LCIA") and the Institution of Mechanical Engineers ("IMechE"). The parties may also set out in advance the specific requirements that the adjudicator shall meet to be appointed (e.g., legal and/or technical background, experience in a specific industry, level of seniority as adjudicator, obligation to disclose and absence of any conflicts of interest, etc.).

When, instead, the parties decide to appoint the adjudicator or DB upon the signature of the contract (or within a certain member of days after the contract is entered into or upon commencement of performance of the works), any disputes between the parties will be immediately referred to such person or the DB. The advantage of having an adjudicator or a DB in place since the contract's inception is that the disputes are decided as they arise so that contractors will be able to secure the necessary cash flow (e.g., in the case of disputes relevant to interim payments) and employers will avoid facing large disputes once the project approaches completion or after it. The downside for the parties is, however, that the parties will start paying adjudicator or DB's fees from day one. Such fees will be due regardless of any meaningful dispute resolution services being performed as they will usually remunerate any time spent by the adjudicator or DB members to become and remain familiar with the progress of the project, make themselves available on short notice for meetings, site visits and hearings, etc., and any costs relevant to the setting up and maintaining of a dedicated office (e.g., secretarial services, photocopying, etc.). In addition to this, the parties will have to reimburse any reasonable expenses sustained by the adjudicator or DB members in the performance of their mandate.

(e) The referral The clause will usually give the referring party a term (the Scheme provides for seven days[26]) to refer the dispute to the adjudicator/DB (and the other parties) through a referral notice in writing. The referral should be accompanied by any relevant documents (e.g., the notice of adjudication, the contract and any other documents the referring party intends to rely on). The clause may also limit the length of the referral (e.g., no more than 50 pages of A4 paper).

The parties may also limit the number of concurrent disputes which may be adjudicated at the same time. For example, the clause may entitle the adjudicator to adjudicate at the same time on more than one dispute under the same contract only with the consent of all the parties to those disputes.[27] If the parties intend to include such a provision, they

25 The procedure relevant to the appointment of the adjudicator is set out in Paragraphs (2) to (11) of the Scheme.

26 In line with Paragraph 7(1) of the Scheme.

27 In line with Paragraph 8(1) of the Scheme.

should bear in mind that in case of multiple concurrent disputes, the refusal of one of the parties to have them resolved together may lead to additional time and costs. As an alternative, the parties may either clarify that the adjudicator may adjudicate more than one dispute at the same time regardless of any agreement of the parties or precisely the number of concurrent disputes that may be referred to adjudication.

This part of the clause will also usually state that a referral will not entitle the contractor to suspend performance of the works, unless instructed otherwise by the employer.

(f) The adjudicator's powers The clause will also usually give the adjudicator extensive powers in relation to the procedure to be followed and the requests that the adjudicator/DB may make to the parties (e.g., to supply documents, to decide the language or languages to be used in the adjudication, to schedule meetings and questioning of the parties to the contract, to make site visits and inspections, to appoint experts, to give directions as to the timetable for the adjudication, any deadlines, or limits as to the length of written documents or oral representations). The parties may, however, consider limiting the adjudicator's powers in this regard, e.g., by: (i) expressly setting out the timetable; (ii) agreeing on specific deadlines (e.g., the parties may consider allowing the responding party a minimum number of days, e.g., 30 days, from the date it receives the referral notice, to submit its response); (iii) agreeing on the length (e.g., maximum number of pages in A4 paper) and number (e.g., limiting the submissions to the referral and response only or allowing only one response) of their submissions; (iv) agreeing on whether oral evidence be admitted and any limitations thereof (e.g., number of experts allowed).

The clause will also typically include some general limits to the adjudicator/DB's powers, such as a duty to: (i) act impartially; (ii) act in accordance with the contract; (iii) reach his decision in accordance with the applicable law in relation to the contract; (iv) avoid incurring unnecessary expense;[28] and (v) keep confidential any information or document he is provided with in connection with the adjudication.

(g) The adjudicator's decision One of the main features of adjudication is that the whole process shall be concluded within a very short timeframe compared to other adversarial methods of dispute resolution. Adjudication clauses typically state in clear words that the adjudicator shall reach a decision not later than a certain term, although it is not unusual for adjudicators to seek extensions to account for the complexity of the typical disputes arising from such contracts. The clause may also set out the consequences in case the adjudicator fails to reach his decision in accordance with the agreed deadline. The parties may allow the adjudicator an extension or commence a new adjudication.[29] It is worth noting that, unless the parties agree otherwise or allow an extension, any decision issued beyond the prescribed time will usually be considered invalid and unenforceable.[30] This will also be the case where the decision is made on time but delivered late absent good

28 In line with Paragraph 12 of the Schedule.

29 In line with Paragraph 19 (2) of the Scheme.

30 *Cubitt Building & Interiors Ltd v Fleetglade Ltd* [2006] EWHC 3413 (TCC); *Paice & Anor v Harding (t/a MJ Harding Contractors)* [2016] EWHC 2945 (TCC). But see also *Simons Construction Ltd v Aardvark Developments Ltd* [2003] EWHC 2474 (TCC), where Judge Seymour held that a late decision was not void unless a fresh notice of referral had been issued.

cause and explanation[31] (although a delay of a day or two will usually be considered within tolerance limits[32]). The parties may avoid any uncertainties by clearly setting out the consequences of late decisions. For example, the clause may state the lapse of the term to issue a decision shall make any late decision null and void or entitle each party to issue a notice of dissatisfaction to the other party and to the adjudicator, so depriving the adjudicator of his entitlement to issue a late decision.

An adjudication clause may clearly set out the matters on which the adjudicator may decide and whether the decision shall include the relevant reasons.

The parties are free to agree on the status they intend to afford to the adjudicator's decision. They may entitle the adjudicator to issue decisions which are immediately binding on the parties and must be complied with immediately or promptly or without delay or recommendations which are not immediately binding but become such if no party objects to it (e.g., through a notice of dissatisfaction) within a certain number of days.

The parties will also typically agree whether the adjudicator's decision will be an "interim" decision, which may be referred to litigation or arbitration (depending on the contract or the parties' agreement) for final determination or a "conclusive" decision, which will definitely decide the dispute without any possible recourse to litigation or arbitration (although this would be rare in the case of construction contracts).

The clause may state the remedies available to the parties in case any of them fails to comply with a decision binding. In such cases, the successful party will usually be entitled to enforce the decision (usually in the Technology and Construction Court) and may apply for summary judgment (also in case of a "provisional" decision still subject to challenge or review).

29.2.2.1.5.4 ARBITRATION CLAUSE[33] Unlike litigation, arbitration is a consensual method of dispute resolution which results from a private agreement between the parties. As a result, the extension of the arbitrator's authority will vary depending on the scope of that agreement.

The arbitration agreement may be contained in a document which is separate from the main contract and is negotiated only after a dispute has arisen or, more commonly, it may be incorporated into the construction contract by including an arbitration clause.

Section 6 (1) of the Arbitration Act 1996 defines an "arbitration agreement" as an agreement to submit to arbitration present or future disputes (whether they are contractual or not). This will also apply to arbitration clauses, which are in fact arbitration agreements in that through them the parties agree to submit their disputes to arbitration.

Section 5 of the Arbitration Act 1996 expressly states that the relevant provisions apply only where the arbitration agreement is in writing, i.e., if it is: (i) made in writing (whether or not it is signed by the parties); (ii) made by exchange of communications in writing; or (iii) evidenced in writing (i.e., an agreement made otherwise than in writing, but recorded by one of the parties, or by a third party, with the authority of the parties to the agreement). Moreover, where the arbitration agreement is not initially in writing, but the parties exchange written submissions in arbitral or legal proceedings where they

31 *Lee v Chartered Properties (Building) Ltd* [2010] EWHC 1540 (TCC). In that case, the decision was delivered with a delay of 72 hours.

32 *Barnes & Elliot Ltd v Taylor Woodrow Holdings Ltd* [2003] EWHC 3100 TCC.

33 For more details on arbitration please refer to Chapter 43.

confirm or do not deny the existence of the agreement, the agreement will be considered as being an agreement in writing between those parties.

It is also worth noting that, based on the principle of separability,[34] unless the parties agree otherwise an arbitration clause which forms or was intended to form part of a construction contract separates from that contract. This means that in case the construction contract terminates for whatever reason, including because it is held invalid, or has never come into existence or has become ineffective, the arbitration clause residing in the contract will survive (i.e., it will not be regarded as invalid, non-existent or ineffective), and the parties will be entitled (and obliged) to refer their claims to arbitration based on that clause.

A typical arbitration agreement/clause in a construction contract will include the following elements.

(a) Right to refer disputes to arbitration Where the dispute resolution clause in which the arbitration provision resides provides for a multi-tiered dispute resolution process, the arbitration provision will usually state that the parties may refer the dispute to arbitration only in case all other remedies listed in the multi-tiered clause have been exhausted. This may mean that exhaustion of all previous "tiers" will be a condition precedent to the right to refer the relevant dispute to arbitration.

(b) Number of arbitrators The issue of the number of arbitrators composing the panel has an impact on the cost and duration of the proceedings, and on the quality of the award. Intuitively, an arbitral tribunal may be composed either of one or three members (in any case, it should be an uneven number of arbitrators). A tribunal composed of three members will be more expensive as the parties will have to pay fees to three arbitrators. However, this disadvantage may be counterbalanced by a number of advantages including the following: (i) the proceedings may be shorter as each arbitrator may focus on specific issues; (ii) where each party appoints its own arbitrator there will be a lower risk of bias and each party will maintain a certain degree of control over the proceedings; (iii) there is a reduced risk of irrational or unfair results as a three-member tribunal will be better equipped to address complex issues. Arguably, having a three-member tribunal may be seen as too expensive for small disputes. For this reason, the parties may include mechanisms in their contract aimed at having one arbitrator deciding smaller or simpler disputes and a three-member panel for disputes above a certain threshold of value or of particular complexity. Such mechanism is now included in almost all the most widely used arbitration rules.

The fallback position in the Arbitration Act 1996 on the number of arbitrators is set out in Section 15. Section 15 (1) states the parties are free to agree on the number of arbitrators to form the tribunal and whether there is to be a chairman or umpire.[35] Under Section 15 (2) of the Arbitration Act 1996, unless otherwise agreed by the parties, an agreement that the number of arbitrators shall be two or any other even number shall be understood as requiring the appointment of an additional arbitrator as chairman of

34 Section 7 of the Arbitration Act 1996.
35 Section 15 (1) of the Arbitration Act 1996.

the tribunal.[36] Section 15 (3) of the Arbitration Act 1996 states that in case there is no agreement as to the number of arbitrators, the tribunal shall consist of a sole arbitrator.[37]

(c) Appointment of the arbitral tribunal The parties to a construction contract are free to agree on how the arbitrator or the tribunal shall be appointed. They may refer to the chosen institution's rules or, in the case of ad hoc arbitration or where the chosen rules are not in line with their needs, agree on a tailored appointment procedure. For example: (i) where the parties opt for a sole arbitrator, the clause will usually provide that they should first try to agree on the arbitrator's name. This may be done in several ways. For example, each of the parties may propose a list of names. Both parties will then try to agree on a name from the list. In case they cannot reach an agreement within a certain number of days (e.g., 30 days) of one party requesting the other to do so, the arbitrator shall be selected and appointed by a nominating entity indicated in the clause; and (ii) where the parties have opted for a three-member arbitral tribunal, they may agree that each party shall appoint one arbitrator, and the two parties' appointed arbitrators then shall appoint the third arbitrator, who shall be the presiding arbitrator (or chairman). In case either party fails to appoint "its" arbitrator within a certain number of days (e.g., 30 days), or where the two parties' appointed arbitrators fail to agree on the third arbitrator within a certain number of days (e.g., 30 days) of their appointment, then the appointment of the party's arbitrator/third arbitrator shall be made by the nominating entity indicated in the clause.

The parties may also add any requirements that the arbitrator/tribunal members shall have (e.g., a certain level of seniority as an arbitrator, experience in a specific industry, nationality, qualification in a certain jurisdiction, etc.).

The fallback position on the appointment of arbitrators can be found in Sections 16 and 17 of the Arbitration Act 1996. Such clauses state that parties are free to agree on the procedure for appointing the arbitrator or arbitrators, including the procedure for appointing any chairman or umpire.[38] Where there is no such agreement: (i) if the tribunal is to consist of a sole arbitrator, the parties shall jointly appoint the arbitrator not later than 28 days after service of a request in writing by either party to do so;[39] (ii) if the tribunal is to consist of two arbitrators, each party shall appoint one arbitrator not later than 14 days after service of a request in writing by either party to do so;[40] (iii) if the tribunal is to consist of three arbitrators: (a) each party shall appoint one arbitrator not later than 14 days after service of a request in writing by either party to do so, and (b) the two so appointed shall forthwith appoint a third arbitrator as the chairman of the tribunal;[41] (iv) if the tribunal is to consist of two arbitrators and an umpire: (a) each party shall appoint one arbitrator not later than 14 days after service of a request in writing by either party to do so, and (b) the two so appointed may appoint an umpire at any time after they themselves are appointed and shall do so before any substantive hearing or forthwith if they cannot agree on a matter relating to the arbitration.[42]

36 Section 15 (2) of the Arbitration Act 1996.
37 Section 15 (3) of the Arbitration Act 1996.
38 Section 16 (1) of the Arbitration Act 1996.
39 Section 16 (3) of the Arbitration Act 1996.
40 Section 16 (4) of the Arbitration Act 1996.
41 Section 16 (5) of the Arbitration Act 1996.
4239 Section 16 (6) of the Arbitration Act 1996.

In case any of the parties fails to appoint an arbitration it is entitled to appoint, the other party, having duly appointed his arbitrator, may give notice in writing to the party in default that he proposes to appoint his arbitrator to act as sole arbitrator. If the failure persists, then the other party may appoint his arbitrator as sole arbitrator.[43]

(d) The seat of arbitration The seat of arbitration (or "*locus arbitri*") is the legal place of the arbitration. It "*indicates a link between the arbitration and a system of law*".[44] Where the seat of the arbitration is in England and Wales or Northern Ireland, the Arbitration Act 1996 will apply.[45] According to Section 3 of the Arbitration Act 1996, where the seat of the arbitration is London (or any other place in England and Wales or Northern Ireland), it is identified as the one designated: (a) by the parties to the arbitration agreement; or (b) by any arbitral or other institution or person vested by the parties with powers in that regard; or (c) by the arbitral tribunal if so authorised by the parties. In the absence of any such designation, the seat will be determined having regard to the parties' agreement and all the relevant circumstances.

The seat has an important bearing on arbitration proceedings as the procedural law of the arbitration will affect many practical aspects of the arbitration including: (i) the national court that is competent to assist and/or supervise the parties and the arbitral tribunal; (ii) the availability of interim remedies; (iii) the national court that has exclusive jurisdiction to hear appeal or other challenge against the arbitral award (including the power to set aside an award); (iv) the "nationality" or "country of origin" for the purposes of recognition and enforcement. However, the seat does not necessarily determine the location where hearings shall take place or tribunal meetings are held. The physical location of an arbitration is not significant from a legal point of view. The parties may agree on the physical location of the hearings based on convenience (e.g., parties' location, legal advisor's location, availability and/or quality of facilities. etc.). However, although in practice hearings often are held at the seat, the location of the arbitration does not need to be the same as the legal seat of the arbitration.

The choice of the seat of arbitration is a crucial issue to consider when drafting and negotiating arbitration clauses. The key factors which they may consider when choosing the seat of arbitration are as follows: (i) the international reputation and recognition of the seat and the whole relevant legal system; (ii) the clarity and "attitude" of the national arbitration law and practice with a particular emphasis on whether the national law and courts: (a) respect the parties' choice to arbitrate their contractual disputes; and (b) are supportive of arbitration (e.g., availability of motions to compel and anti-suit injunctions) and do not tend to subordinate arbitration to court litigation (e.g., the track courts' record shows a tendency not to enforce arbitration agreements or to uphold motions to vacate awards). Ideally, the legal system should avoid or limit at a minimum unnecessary intervention or inappropriate interference by the local court; (iii) the quality of the judiciary with a particular emphasis on independency, neutrality, impartiality

43 Section 17 of the Arbitration Act 1996.

44 *Process & Industrial Developments Ltd v Nigeria* [2019] EWHC 2241 (Comm).

45 Although, based on Section 2 (2) of the Arbitration Act 1996, sections 9 to 11 (stay of legal proceedings, &c.), and Section 66 (enforcement of arbitral awards) will apply even if the seat of the arbitration is outside England and Wales or Northern Ireland or no seat has been designated or determined.

and competence; (iv) whether the seat recognises the immunity of arbitrators from civil liability; (v) any restrictions as to the choice of arbitrators (e.g., as to relevant nationality and qualifications); (vi) whether the country of the seat is a signatory to the New York "Convention on the Recognition and Enforcement of Foreign Arbitral Awards" or other relevant international treaties or agreements regulating the recognition and enforcement of foreign arbitral awards; (vii) where the seat is also the place where hearings will be held, the appropriateness, accessibility and safety of the location (e.g., visas requirements, frequency of flights, adequacy of hotels, transport, protection of documentation and information, hearing rooms, translation services and transcription services); (viii) any fiscal issues concerning the award and/or the proceedings.

The parties should ensure that they use clear words when designating the legal seat of arbitration in the arbitration agreement/clause so to avoid unnecessary procedural disputes on whether the location indicated in the clause is in fact the legal seat or merely the venue where the parties intend hearings and meetings relevant to the proceedings to take place. The case of *Process & Industrial Developments Ltd v Nigeria*[46] shows the importance of using clear words when agreeing on the seat of arbitration. The dispute concerned an agreement between Process & Industrial Developments Ltd ("P&ID") and the Federal Republic of Nigeria ("Nigeria") for the supply and processing of natural gas in Nigeria which was governed by Nigerian law and included a dispute resolution clause providing that: (i) in the event of dispute, either party could serve notice of arbitration under the rules of the Nigerian Arbitration and Conciliation Act 2004 (the "Nigerian Act"); (ii) unless otherwise provided in the agreement, the Act would apply to the dispute; and (iii) "*[t]he venue of the arbitration shall be London, England or otherwise as agreed between the Parties*". When a dispute arose between the parties, P&ID commenced arbitration in London against Nigeria. The arbitral tribunal issued a partial award against Nigeria on liability. The arbitration was then to continue only on quantum. Nigeria then applied to the English courts to set aside the award contending that the arbitration was not seated in England, but in Nigeria. The reference to London as seat was to be intended as the place where hearings would take place. The English courts rejected this argument and the application to set aside the award. Nigeria applied to the Nigerian courts to set aside the award. The arbitral then tribunal issued a procedural order confirming that the seat of arbitration was London, England (i.e., that the Nigerian courts lacked any competence to set aside the award). Despite that, the Nigerian courts upheld Nigeria's application to set aside the award. However, the arbitral tribunal decided to continue the arbitration based on its findings on competence. Nigeria participated to the second phase of the arbitration but maintained its position that the award had been set aside in Nigeria. When the arbitral tribunal issued its final award condemning Nigeria to pay US$6.6 billion, P&ID commenced enforcement proceedings in the English courts. In such proceedings, Nigeria, among other things, insisted that the arbitration was not seated in England and that enforcement in the English court was not possible under Section 66 of the Arbitration Act 1996 (according to which, unless it is shown that the tribunal lacked substantive jurisdiction, an award made by a tribunal pursuant to an arbitration agreement may, by leave of the court, be enforced in the same manner as a judgment or order of the court to the same effect). P&ID maintained that reference to London as the "venue" identified

46 *Process & Industrial Developments Ltd v Nigeria* [2019] EWHC 2241 (Comm).

the legal seat of the arbitration. The court confirmed that the tribunal had reached the correct decision on the seat as: (i) the language venue "of the arbitration" used in the clause implied that the selection of that "venue" would apply to the whole proceedings and not only to the hearings. This was compared with the language used in the Nigerian Act which, with reference to the physical location where the hearing would take place, referred to the place a tribunal may "meet" or "hear witnesses, experts or the parties"; (ii) considering the location of the parties, it was unlikely that they had intended the reference to the "venue" of the arbitration to mean that hearings were to take place in London; (iii) the fact that clause allowed the "venue" to be changed only by the parties, not the tribunal, corroborated that with the word "venue" the parties intended to refer to the legal seat, considering that the place where hearings take place is typically decided by the arbitrators; (iv) the fact that the arbitration clause referred to the rules of the Nigerian Act was not inconsistent with the choice of a seat in England as the consequence would merely be that only the mandatory provisions of the Arbitration Act 1996 would apply to the proceedings.

(e) Procedural law The procedural law of the arbitration regulates the operation of the proceedings. It is normally the law of the "seat" of the arbitration. For example, in the case of an arbitration seated in London, the procedural law of the proceedings will be English law, and in particular the Arbitration Act 1996. Although the parties may agree on a different procedural law from the law of the seat, this is not advisable as it may create uncertainties. Where possible, the parties should also consider aligning the governing law of the contract with the procedural law and the location of the seat so to avoid creating any uncertainties as to the law and the interpretation principles applying to each of those aspects.

(f) Law of the arbitration agreement The law of the arbitration agreement is the law which governs its validity, scope or interpretation of the arbitration agreement/clause. An arbitration clause will not usually expressly specify the governing law of the arbitration agreement. However, such provision may be useful in case the law chosen to govern the arbitration agreement is different from the governing law of the construction contract as in such case the mere indication of the seat will not be determinative. In the case of *Enka Insaat Ve Sanayi AS v OOO Insurance Company Chubb*,[47] the court had to decide how to determine the governing law of the arbitration agreement between the parties in a situation where the law applicable to the contract containing it was different from the law of the "seat" of the arbitration. The head-contractor, engaged by the employer for the construction of a power plant in Russia, had contracted the Turkish engineering company, Enka Insaat ve Sanayi AS ("Enka"), as a subcontractor for the relevant works. The construction contract between the head-contractor and Enka provided for International Chamber of Commerce (ICC) arbitration seated in London. The arbitration clause did not specify any law governing the construction contract, nor did it indicate the law applying to the arbitration agreement. The head-contractor had then transferred its rights and obligations under the construction contract to the owner. When the power plant was severely damaged by a fire which caused around US$400 million of damage, the insurer,

47 *Enka Insaat Ve Sanayi AS v OOO Insurance Company Chubb* [2020] UKSC 38.

the Russian company Chubb Russia Investments Limited ("Chubb Russia"), paid an insurance claim to the employer and assumed subrogated the employer's rights to claim compensation from third parties, including Enka, for the damages caused be the fire. Chubb Russia then brought litigation proceedings against Enka in the Moscow courts. Enka applied to have such proceedings dismissed contending that Chubb Russia's claims should be referred to arbitration. Enka argued that, as London was the seat of arbitration chosen by the parties, the arbitration clause was governed by English law. Chubb Russia contended that: (i) the arbitration agreement was governed by Russian law; (ii) the claim was a claim in tort; (iii) based on Russian law, tort claims would fall outside of the scope of the arbitration agreement. Enka then brought arbitration proceedings in London against Chubb Russia and applied to the High Court in London for an anti-suit injunction. At first instance, the High Court upheld Chubb Russia's contention that the appropriate forum to determine the scope of the arbitration agreement was Russia. On appeal, the Court of Appeal, overturning the judge's decision, held that the general rule to apply in cases the clause does not expressly provide for the law governing the arbitration agreement is that the court will imply that the parties have chosen the arbitration agreement to be governed by the law of the seat. As in that case the seat was in London, it was appropriate to grant an anti-suit injunction to restrain Chubb Russia from pursuing its claim in the Russian courts. Chubb Russia then appealed to the Supreme Court which, by a majority judgment, dismisses the appeal. The Supreme Court (Lord Hamblen and Lord Leggatt, with whom Lord Kerr agreed) set out the following principles governing the determination of the law applicable to the arbitration agreement:

i) Where a contract contains an agreement to resolve disputes arising from it by arbitration, the law applicable to the arbitration agreement may not be the same as the law applicable to the other parts of the contract and is to be determined by applying English common law rules for resolving conflicts of laws rather than the provisions of the Rome I Regulation.
ii) According to these rules, the law applicable to the arbitration agreement will be (a) the law chosen by the parties to govern it or (b) in the absence of such a choice, the system of law with which the arbitration agreement is most closely connected.
iii) Whether the parties have agreed on a choice of law to govern the arbitration agreement is ascertained by construing the arbitration agreement and the contract containing it, as a whole, applying the rules of contractual interpretation of English law as the law of the forum.
iv) Where the law applicable to the arbitration agreement is not specified, a choice of governing law for the contract will generally apply to an arbitration agreement which forms part of the contract.
v) The choice of a different country as the seat of the arbitration is not, without more, sufficient to negate an inference that a choice of law to govern the contract was intended to apply to the arbitration agreement.
vi) Additional factors which may, however, negate such an inference and may in some cases imply that the arbitration agreement was intended to be governed by the law of the seat are: (a) any provision of the law of the seat which indicates that, where an arbitration is subject to that law, the arbitration agreement will

also be treated as governed by that country's law; or (b) the existence of a serious risk that, if governed by the same law as the main contract, the arbitration agreement would be ineffective. Either factor may be reinforced by circumstances indicating that the seat was deliberately chosen as a neutral forum for the arbitration.

vii) Where there is no express choice of law to govern the contract, a clause providing for arbitration in a particular place will not by itself justify an inference that the contract (or the arbitration agreement) is intended to be governed by the law of that place.

viii) In the absence of any choice of law to govern the arbitration agreement, the arbitration agreement is governed by the law with which it is most closely connected. Where the parties have chosen a seat of arbitration, this will generally be the law of the seat, even if this differs from the law applicable to the parties' substantive contractual obligations.

ix) The fact that the contract requires the parties to attempt to resolve a dispute through good faith negotiation, mediation or any other procedure before referring it to arbitration will not generally provide a reason to displace the law of the seat of arbitration as the law applicable to the arbitration agreement by default in the absence of a choice of law to govern it.

(g) Language of the proceedings Under 34 (2) (b) of the Arbitration Act 1996, it is for the tribunal to decide all procedural and evidential matters relevant to the proceedings, including the language (or languages) to be used in the proceedings and whether translations of any relevant documents are to be supplied. In determining the language of the arbitration proceedings, the tribunal will typically consider the language of the contract. However, this is subject to the right of the parties to agree otherwise.

Arbitration clauses in construction contracts almost invariably include a provision on the language of the proceedings as this will determine the language in which parties communicate with the tribunal and make their written and oral submissions.

Model clauses prepared by arbitral institutions almost invariably recommend the parties to specify the language of the proceedings in their arbitration agreement to avoid uncertainty as to the language after an arbitration has crystalised.

When choosing the language of the proceedings the parties should have regard to several aspects, including the language of contract, the project's documents and the language of the parties (in particular, of internal legal department managing the proceedings). This will help the parties saving unnecessary translation costs (including for simultaneous translations for witnesses who are not comfortable with providing testimony in a certain language at the evidentiary hearings) and allow them more control over the proceedings.

(h) Multiple disputes One of the disadvantages of arbitration is that arbitrators, unlike court judges, do not have the authority to: (i) join additional parties to the arbitration proceedings where such parties were not parties to the arbitration agreement; or (ii) consolidate related arbitrations among the same parties.

As a result, the parties may have to engage in separate arbitrations in cases where more disputes arise between: (i) the same parties under different contracts (e.g., a construction contract and an operation and maintenance contract between the same employer and contractor); or (ii) different parties under related contracts (e.g., a subcontract), the general rule is that, absent the consent of all such parties, such disputes may be resolved in the same arbitration proceedings.

The first issue may be dealt with by stating in the arbitration clause that, in case two or more separate disputes arise between them under related contracts or under different contracts, but involving similar facts, such disputes should be consolidated into a single arbitration.

Considering the consensual nature of arbitration, the second issue may not be dealt with by merely adding a specific language to the arbitration clause in the construction contract. However, the parties are free to agree to request any third party which is not involved in the arbitration to join in their arbitration proceedings. However, should the third party refuse to partake, there will usually be no ways to force it to join.

(i) Confidentiality Confidentiality is a great concern for companies operating in the construction industry. Based on the principle of open justice, subject to limited exceptions, court hearings are public, and third parties may typically obtain documents, judgments and court orders relevant to court proceedings. Conversely, confidentiality is considered[48] an essential ingredient of arbitration.[49]

Although the Arbitration Act 1996 is silent on the point of confidentiality, it is a settled principle under English law that confidentiality of arbitration is implied.[50] The status confidentiality (and privacy) in relation to arbitration was summarised as follows in *John Forster Emmott v Michael Wilson & Partners Limited*:[51]

> 103. . . . The conduct of arbitrations is private. That is implicit in the agreement to arbitrate. That does not mean that the arbitration is private for all purposes. . . .
>
> 104. Today there is an increasing trend for the privacy of arbitrations to be protected. That is illustrated by the rules in CPR Part 62 and the Practice Direction allowing arbitration claims to be heard in private and restricting (but not prohibiting) access to the court file by strangers to the arbitration. But it is clear from Moscow City Council v Bankers Trust Co. [2004] EWCA Civ 314, [2005] QB 207 that this policy may have to give way to the public interest. Consequently even under the modern law since the 1996 Act there will still be cases where the details of an arbitral dispute may become public, e.g. where a party seeks an injunction to restrain court proceedings brought in breach of an arbitration agreement (e.g. West Tankers Inc v Ras Riunione Adriatica di Sicurta [2007] UKHL 4, [2007] 1 Lloyd's Rep 391) or where a court deals with a challenge to an award for serious irregularity or an appeal on a point of law (e.g. Lesotho Highlands Development Authority v Impregilo SpA [2005] UKHL 43, [2006] 1 AC 221) or where enforcement of an award is resisted on grounds of public policy (e.g. Westacre Investments Ltd v Jugo-Import-SPDR Holding Co Ltd [2000] QB 288).
>
> 105. But case law over the last 20 years has established that there is an obligation, implied by law and arising out of the nature of arbitration, on both parties not to disclose or use for

48 Along with privacy, there is a certain degree of overlap between the concept of confidentiality and privacy, and the courts have sometimes treated the two separately (e.g., in *Dolling-Baker v Merrett* [1990] 1 WLR 1205) and sometimes as the same (e.g., in *London and Leeds Estates Ltd v Paribas Ltd (No 2)* [1995] 2 EG 134, [1995] 1 EGLR 102).

49 *Hassneh Insurance Co. of Israel and Others v Steuart J. Mew* [1993] 2 Lloyd's Rep 243.

50 See, e.g., *Dolling-Baker v Merrett* [1990] 1 WLR 1205.

51 *John Forster Emmott v Michael Wilson & Partners Limited* [2008] EWCA Civ 184.

> any other purpose any documents prepared for and used in the arbitration, or disclosed or produced in the course of the arbitration, or transcripts or notes of the evidence in the arbitration or the award, and not to disclose in any other way what evidence has been given by any witness in the arbitration. The obligation is not limited to commercially confidential information in the traditional sense.
>
> 106. . . . this is in reality a substantive rule of arbitration law reached through the device of an implied term. . . .
>
> 107. In my judgment the content of the obligation may depend on the context in which it arises and on the nature of the information or documents at issue. The limits of that obligation are still in the process of development on a case-by-case basis. On the authorities as they now stand, the principal cases in which disclosure will be permissible are these: the first is where there is consent, express or implied; second, where there is an order, or leave of the court (but that does not mean that the court has a general discretion to lift the obligation of confidentiality); third, where it is reasonably necessary for the protection of the legitimate interests of an arbitrating party; fourth, where the interests of justice require disclosure, and also (perhaps) where the public interest requires disclosure.

With reference to the "interest of justice", in the case of *Teekay Tankers Ltd v STX Offshore Ltd*,[52] Teekay Tankers Ltd ("TTL") referred to the arbitration awards and the arbitrators' reasons in support of its claim against STX Offshore Ltd ("STX") in proceedings in the English Commercial Court. STX contended that, by doing so, TTL had breached its confidentiality obligations. The court disagreed with STX because the disclosure fell within the "*interests of justice*" exception as TTL's assertion was arguable and in good faith.

With reference to the "public interest", in *Symbion Power LLC v Venco Imtiaz Construction Company*,[53] Symbion Power LLC ("Symbion") applied in the Technology and Construction Court ("TCC") to set aside an arbitration award under Section 68 of the Arbitration Act 1996 (i.e., on grounds of serious irregularity). When the TCC judge provided a copy of the draft judgment to the parties, Symbion argued that the judgment should be anonymised as it revealed the content of a prior award which was not the subject of any challenge and involved a third party which was not a party to the TCC proceedings. The judge, however, declined Symbion's request holding that:

> There is a strong public interest in the publication of judgments, including those concerned with arbitrations, because of the public interest in ensuring appropriate standards in the conduct of arbitrations. That has to be weighed against the parties' legitimate expectation that arbitral proceedings and awards will be confidential to the parties.

However, in that case the judge also based its decision on the fact that; (i) the award was already in the public domain as it had been published on a legal website; (ii) a Symbion representative had referred to the proceedings in a comment; and (iii) Symbion had not proved that a publication in an non-anonymised form would be detrimental.

From a drafting point of view, although under English law an obligation of confidentiality seems to be considered implied in the arbitration agreement, where the parties intend to maintain the proceedings confidential, they are advised to make sure that confidentiality is expressly mentioned.

---

52 *Teekay Tankers Ltd v STX Offshore Ltd* [2017] EWHC 253 (Comm).

53 *Symbion Power LLC v Venco Imtiaz Construction Company* [2017] EWHC 348 (TCC).

(j) Arbitral tribunal's powers Under Section 38 (1) of the Arbitration Act 1996, the parties are free to agree on the powers exercisable by the arbitral tribunal for the purposes of and in relation to the proceedings.

Section 38 (2) of the Arbitration Act 1996 empowers tribunals (unless otherwise agreed between the parties) to: (i) order a claimant to provide security for the costs of the arbitration; (ii) give directions (e.g., inspections, photographing, preservation, custody, detention and taking of samples) in relation to any property which is the subject of the proceedings or as to which any question arises in the proceedings, and which is owned by or is in the possession of a party to the proceedings; (iii) direct that a party or witness shall be examined on oath or affirmation, and administer such oaths or take such affirmations; (iv) give directions to a party for the preservation for the purposes of the proceedings of any evidence in his custody or control.

The powers of arbitral tribunals are sometimes complemented by those of the courts. Under Section 42 (1) of the arbitration Act 1996, unless otherwise agreed by the parties, a court may make an order requiring a party to comply with a peremptory order made by the tribunal. However, such power may be exercised only in case the court is satisfied that: (i) the applicant has exhausted any available arbitral process in respect of failure to comply with the tribunal's order; and (ii) the person to whom the tribunal's order was directed has failed to comply with it within the time prescribed in the order or, if no time was prescribed, within a reasonable time.

Under Section 44 (2) of the Arbitration Act 1996, the courts have wide ranging powers for the purposes of and in relation to arbitral proceedings (e.g., taking witness evidence, preserving evidence, making orders relating to property which is the subject of the proceedings or as to which any question arises in the proceedings, selling any goods which are the subject of the proceedings, granting interim injunction or appointing a receiver), which, however, may be exercised only if or to the extent that the arbitral tribunal, and any arbitral or other institution or person vested by the parties with power in that regard, has no power or is unable for the time being to act effectively.[54] Moreover, pursuant to Section 44 (6) of the Arbitration Act 1996, if the court so orders, an order made by it under this section shall cease to have effect in whole or in part on the order of the tribunal or of any such arbitral or other institution or person having power to act in relation to the subject-matter of the order.

Considering how limited in scope the tribunal's powers under the Arbitration Act 1996 are, the parties to a construction contract will typically seek to expand them by adding specific language in the arbitration agreement, e.g., by granting the tribunal the power to order any interim or conservatory measure that it deems appropriate. Should they fail to do so, the parties will have to apply to the courts, rather than the tribunal, to obtain any interim or conservatory measures.

(k) Disclosure and document production Documents are probably the most reliable source of evidence in construction arbitrations as they usually give an accurate and contemporaneous picture of the facts in dispute. For this reason, a good record-keeping practice may ultimately determine the outcome of a construction dispute. Types of

54 Section 44 (5) of the Arbitration Act 1996.

documents that are typically produced/disclosed in a construction dispute are pre-contractual documents (e.g., specifications, drawings, tender documents and internal reports) and contractual documents (e.g., the construction contract and any annexes, the final specifications, the final drawings and any variation orders), project and commercial correspondence exchanged between the parties (including letters, emails and text messages), cost documentation (e.g., invoices, work rates, payments to subcontractors, financial costs, etc.), other contemporaneous records (e.g., minutes of meetings, progress reports, updates to programmes, site logs, handwritten notes, voice recordings and embedded data).

The number of documents disclosed and/or produced in a complex construction arbitration may be surprisingly high. In the case of English court litigation, standard disclosure of documents is governed by Civil Procedure Rule ("CPR") 31.6 which requires a party to disclose the documents (i) on which the party relies; (ii) which adversely affect his own case, adversely affect another party's case or support another party's case; and (iii) which the party is required to disclose by a relevant practice direction.

However, in arbitration document production is not mandatory and there are no procedural rules clearly setting out the parties' disclosure obligations. Section 34 (d) of the Arbitration Act 1996 gives the tribunal the power to decide all procedural and evidential matters including whether any and if so which documents or classes of documents should be disclosed between and produced by the parties and at what stage. However, this is subject to the right of the parties to agree otherwise.

Considering the unpredictability of the tribunal's decision, the number of documents that are typically disclosed in a complex construction dispute and the time and costs flowing from such activity, the parties may consider agreeing in advance the rules of evidence applying to their arbitrations. For example, the parties may agree to adopt the International Bar Association's Rules on Taking of Evidence in International Arbitration ("IBA Rules") which propose a milder approach to disclosure. Under Article 3 of the IBA Rules: (i) each party shall submit to the tribunal and to the other parties all documents available to it on which it relies; (ii) any party may submit to the tribunal and to the other parties a request to produce, which shall contain: (a) a description of each requested document sufficient to identify it or a description in sufficient detail (including subject matter) of a narrow and specific requested category of documents that are reasonably believed to exist; (b) a statement as to how such documents are relevant to the case and material to its outcome; (c) a statement that such documents are not in the possession, custody or control of the requesting party or a statement of the reasons why it would be unreasonably burdensome for the requesting party to produce such documents; and (d) a statement of the reasons why the requesting party assumes the documents requested are in the possession, custody or control of another party; (iii) the party to whom the request to produce is addressed may object to some or all of the documents requested on the grounds of: (a) lack of sufficient relevance to the case or materiality to its outcome; (b) legal impediment or privilege; (c) unreasonable burden to produce the requested evidence; (d) loss or destruction of the document that has been shown with reasonable likelihood to have occurred; (e) compelling grounds of commercial or technical confidentiality; (f) compelling grounds of special political or institutional sensitivity; (g) compelling considerations of procedural economy, proportionality, fairness or equality of the parties; (h) evidence obtained illegally; (i) a failure to satisfy any of the requirements applying to the request to produce. Adopting the IBA Rules may help the parties avoiding the hurdles of a time-consuming and expensive disclosure. On the other hand, however, a party that has not kept documents in a proper and orderly fashion may struggle to prove its case as it may not be able to rely on the documents in possession of its counterparty except in limited the circumstances seen earlier.

(l) Allocation of costs and fees Complex construction arbitrations can be surprisingly expensive. The costs of the proceedings include the arbitrators' fees and expenses, the fees and expenses of any arbitral institution concerned (unless it is an "ad hoc" arbitration), the legal costs (for solicitors and/or barristers) and other costs of the parties (e.g., any expert fees for delay and quantum analysis and any hearing costs for hearing rooms, transcription services, interpreters, travelling and accommodation, etc.). In addition, there are the internal costs that the parties have to bear in relation to the time that employees involved in the arbitration (e.g., in-house counsels, project personnel, finance departments, risk management departments, etc.) spend on managing various aspects of the dispute from a corporate point of view.

Under Section 61 (2) of the Arbitration Act 1996, unless the parties otherwise agree, the tribunal shall award costs on the general principle that costs should follow the event except where it appears to the tribunal that in the circumstances this is not appropriate in relation to the whole or part of the costs.[55]

Based on the default rule that "costs follow the event", the losing party will have to pay the winning party's costs. However, where a party is successful on some claims but not others, the tribunal may take this into account and allocate the costs accordingly. This approach may also serve as a deterrent against frivolous claims and defences. The tribunal may also take into consideration other aspects when allocating costs such as the conduct of the parties before and during the proceedings (e.g., if any party has acted unreasonably or has used any dilatory tactics) or any so-called *Calderbank* offers (i.e., offers to settle a dispute made on a "*without prejudice save as to costs*" basis, which may not be disclosed to the tribunal until after its decision on merits so that, where a party unreasonably fails to accept the offer, this may be considered by the tribunal when deciding how to allocate costs). An alternative rule to allocate costs, which is rarely applied in English law arbitration, is the "costs lie where they fall" rule (or the "American Rule") based on which each party shall bear its own costs. The rationale of the rule is to discourage the parties from bringing frivolous claims and defences. Where the parties do not intend to adopt the "costs follow the event rule", they should clearly state it in their arbitration agreement. Moreover, they should consider that under Section 60 of the Arbitration Act 1996 any agreement which has the effect that a party is to pay the whole or part of the costs of the arbitration in any event is only valid if made after the dispute in question has arisen.

Under Section 62 of the Arbitration Act 1996, any agreement or award extends only to "recoverable costs", although pursuant to Section 63 (1) of the Arbitration Act 1996 the parties can agree which costs of the arbitration are recoverable. Absent an agreement,

55 However, where the tribunal intends to exercise its discretion to depart from the general "costs follow the event" rule on allocation, it must clearly set out the relevant reasons (see *Lewis v Haverfordwest Rural District Council* [1953] 1 WLR 1486).

the tribunal can determine this issue and shall specify the basis on which it is acting and state the items of recoverable costs and the amount referable to each.[56]

(m) Right to appeal Under Section 69 (1) of the Arbitration Act 1996, unless otherwise agreed by the parties, a party to arbitral proceedings may appeal to the court on a question of law arising out of an award made in the proceedings.

The parties will typically exclude the right to appeal on this basis directly or by referring to specific arbitration rules providing so in their arbitration agreement. However, referring to the "procedural rules" of a certain institution may not suffice. In *National Iranian Oil Co v Crescent Petroleum Co International Ltd,*[57] the arbitration agreement between the parties provided that any dispute, controversy or claim was to be finally settled by arbitration in accordance with the "*Procedures for Arbitration*" as contained in Annex 2 of the contract between the parties. Paragraph 9 of Annex 2 provided that in the case of a gap in the procedural rules of arbitration, then "*the procedural rules of arbitration of the International Chamber of Commerce (ICC) shall apply*". Article 28.6 of the 1998 International ICC Rules 1998 provides that:

> Every Award shall be binding on the parties. By submitting the dispute to arbitration under these Rules, the parties undertake to carry out any Award without delay and shall be deemed to have waived their right to any form of recourse insofar as such waiver can validly be made.

Crescent Petroleum Co International Ltd ("Crescent") contended that National Iranian Oil Co ("NIOC") was not entitled to appeal against a Partial Award under Section 69 of the Arbitration Act 1996 as the agreement contained gap in relation to the right to appeal to the court on points of law as Article 22.2 and Annex 2 of the agreement did not contain any rules on this topic. Thus, under Paragraph 9 of Annex 2, such gap was to be filled by Article 28.6 of the ICC Rules 1998, which excluded the right to appeal on a point of law. The court disagreed and stressed that the default position is that there is a right of appeal and that it was wholly unnecessary and unrealistic to expect that the parties should have explicitly to reserve such right.

Therefore, although the parties are not usually required to expressly refer to Section 69 of the Arbitration Ac 1996, they shall use sufficiently clear words if they intend to exclude such section to apply.

29.2.2.1.5.5 LITIGATION CLAUSE

(a) The "forum" A dispute resolution clause providing for court litigation (or "jurisdiction clause") will express the parties' agreement to have all disputes arising under their construction agreement determined by the courts of a certain country (e.g., the courts of England). When choosing the forum of their contractual disputes, the parties may consider several aspects such as neutrality, affordability, freedom from corruption, freedom from improper government influence (particularly where one of the parties in publicly owned or participated), lack of unreasonable delay, availability of interim and final remedies and effectiveness of enforcement.

56 Section 63 (3) of the Arbitration Act 1996.

57 *National Iranian Oil Co v Crescent Petroleum Co International Ltd* [2016] EWHC 1900 (Comm).

In the absence of a parties' choice (or where the clause is ineffective, e.g., because of any ambiguities) the forum for the determination of a dispute under the contract will be decided by reference to rules of private international law. This will cause uncertainty and lead to additional costs and delay in progressing any dispute.

The parties shall ensure their choice is unambiguous and clearly identifies existing courts. For example, a clause giving jurisdiction to "*the courts of the United Kingdom*" may be ambiguous and even unenforceable as, while England and Wales share the same court system, Scotland has its own court system.

Some clauses even go so far as to refer to courts in specific cities (e.g., the courts of London, UK).[58] This is not generally advisable as, in case one of the contracting parties is from jurisdictions outside the United Kingdom, a foreign court may hold the clause invalid as it refers to a city rather than a country. A typical clause would rather refer to the courts of England or England and Wales.

(b) Exclusive and non-exclusive jurisdiction The parties may either opt for "exclusive" jurisdiction or for "non-exclusive" jurisdiction. An alternative would be opting for a hybrid form of jurisdiction.

(i) By opting for exclusive jurisdiction, the parties agree that the courts indicated in the clause shall exclusively hear their disputes. The advantage of exclusive jurisdiction is certainty as the parties know from the outset where what court will be competent to hear their disputes and reducing the risk that courts other than those having exclusive jurisdiction under the clause (which a party may not trust or be familiar with) may accept jurisdiction despite the clause.
Another advantage of exclusive jurisdiction clauses is that they benefit from the protection of the "*Convention of 30 June 2005 on Choice of Court Agreements*" (the "Hague Convention 2005"). In cases where the Hague Convention 2005 applies, it ensures the effectiveness of choice of court agreements made between parties to international commercial contracts by obliging the relevant signatories to recognise a choice of court agreement between parties in the field of civil law. As a result, any courts other than those chosen in the agreement between the parties will be obliged to stay all proceedings, unless the chosen court refuses to uphold the jurisdiction. This protection will apply to the extent the choice of court agreement is "exclusive". Pursuant to Article 3 (a) of the Hague Convention 2005 an agreement will be exclusive if it appoints only one court with jurisdiction. The Hague Convention 2005 does not require the express use of the word "exclusive" (although the recommendation is to include such express word). Article 3 (b) deems an agreement to be exclusive "*unless the parties have expressly provided otherwise*". Thus, designating a specific court will automatically render their jurisdiction exclusive. Although uncommon in the case of construction contracts, where the parties opt for a clause that gives concurrent exclusive jurisdiction to the courts of two states (e.g., the contractor may sue the employer in England, while the employer may sue the contractor in France),

58 *UBS Securities LLC v HSH Nordbank AG* [2009] EWCA Civ 585; *Sebastian Holdings Inc v Deutsche Bank AG* [2010] EWCA Civ 998.

such agreements will not be considered exclusive for the purposes of the Hague Convention 2005. In cases where the Hague Convention 2005 applies, judgments issued by the court chosen in the agreement must be recognised in all states where the convention is applicable.

(ii) In case the parties opt for non-exclusive jurisdiction of certain courts, they agree to submit their disputes to such particular courts (e.g., English courts), but acknowledge that this will now prejudice either party's right to bring proceedings in the courts of any other jurisdiction, where appropriate or necessary. The advantage of "non-exclusive" jurisdiction clauses is that they are more flexible as they allow disputes to be heard by the most appropriate courts. However, such clauses carry significant risks. The most immediate risk is the uncertainty of not knowing what courts will have jurisdiction over the disputes. Moreover, the parties may engage in a "forum shopping" aimed at choosing courts that may be more inclined to uphold their cases. Ultimately, non-exclusive jurisdiction clauses may lead to parallel proceedings in case the parties do not agree on the nature of the clause. It is worth noting that, as mentioned, the Hague Convention 2005 will not apply to "non-exclusive" agreements on the choice of court (with the sole exception of cases under Article 22).

(iii) "Asymmetric" (or "hybrid" or "one-sided" or "unilateral") jurisdiction clauses create an asymmetry between the parties as they allow one party to submit disputes to the "exclusive" jurisdiction of a particular court and the other (typically the one with more bargaining power) to the "non-exclusive" jurisdiction of another court. The second party will thus retain the right to bring proceedings in any court of competent jurisdiction, e.g., the courts of the place where the counterparty's assets are located. Asymmetric jurisdiction clauses will fall outside the scope of the Hague Convention 2005[59] as confirmed by the Court of Appeal in the case of *Etihad Airways PJSC v Flother*.[60] Asymmetric jurisdiction clauses are uncommon in construction contracts and are typically used in transactions where there is an imbalance of negotiating power between the parties. The parties should try avoiding them if possible as they lead to significant uncertainty and leave one of the parties in a substantially less favourable position.

29.2.3 Related agreements

In case of complex construction projects, it is not unusual for the same parties to have more than one related contractual relationship (e.g., construction and operation and maintenance contracts between the same parties). Where such relationships relate to different aspects of the same project, there may be a risk that some aspects of the disputes arising out of the relevant contracts will overlap and generate conflicting results. For this reason, the parties may consider having all disputes relevant to such parallel contracts to be resolved in the same jurisdiction.

59 However, in *Commerzbank Aktiengesellschaft v Liquimar Tankers Management Inc* [2017] EWHC 161 (Comm) Cranston J suggested a different view, albeit obiter.

60 *Etihad Airways PJSC v Flother* [2020] EWCA Civ 1707.

29.2.4 Obligation to continue the works

Normally, the mere fact that a dispute has arisen under a construction contract does not entitle any of the parties to suspend the performance of the contract (including any obligation to proceed with the works and make any payment of monies due and owing under the contract). The consequence of a wrongful suspension of the contract may be severe and amount to a repudiation leading to a termination of the contract and an obligation to pay substantial damages. Very often construction contracts will expressly state that, regardless of the contractual dispute resolution procedure having been triggered, the parties have a duty to continue to perform their respective obligations under the contract, unless the parties agree otherwise.

PART FIVE

THE CONTRACT

Interpretation

The express language and terms incorporated in a construction contract will form the backbone of the agreement between employer and contractor. However, particularly when contracts are poorly drafted or the parties are not familiar with the concept of "implication of terms", they may find themselves bound to obligations which they did not intend being part of their agreement.

Implied terms and contract interpretation are aspects that the parties need to consider and familiarise themselves with even before they start negotiating their construction contract as clear words will usually be needed to prevent the courts implying and/or misinterpreting contractual terms.

DOI: 10.4324/9781003387718-35

CHAPTER 30

Implied terms

30.1 Implied terms in general

Contractual rights and obligations of the parties are defined by the terms of their contract. Considering the complexity and the magnitude of some construction contracts, the relevant parties often seek to predict and expressly cover all the events and possible scenarios that may arise during the project so to avoid any uncertainties as to their rights and obligations under the contracts. The terms that the parties expressly include in their contracts are called express terms. However, under English law the courts are allowed, in certain circumstances, to imply terms into a contract where the parties failed to expressly deal with a specific subject. Even more so when the implication of a term may save an agreement that would otherwise be invalid. However, a court will not imply a term where doing so would be inconsistent with express wording within the agreement.

In *Teekay Tankers Ltd v STX Offshore and Shipbuilding Co Ltd*[1] the shipping company Teekay Tankers Ltd ("Teekay") and the shipbuilder STX Offshore and Shipbuilding Co Ltd ("STX") entered into an option agreement whereby Teekay was granted the option to purchase ships from STX on certain terms. The agreement provided that the delivery date of the ships was to be "*mutually agreed upon*" and that the shipbuilder would "*make best efforts*" to deliver the ships within a specified time period. When disputes arose between the parties, Teekay terminated the option agreement and claimed for the loss of profits. STX contended that the option agreement was void for uncertainty as the words "*mutually agreed upon*" made it an agreement to agree. Teekay disagreed and argued that it was an implied term of the agreement that the date of delivery would either be the date offered by STX having used its best efforts or an objectively reasonable date to be determined by the court. The court had then to decide whether such term could be implied in the agreement. Mr Justice Walker found in favour of STX and held that:

> For the reasons given above I am satisfied that neither of TT's alleged implied terms is capable of forming part the option agreement. TT has identified no other way in which that agreement, containing as it does express provisions for a future agreement on an essential term, can be saved. It follows that STX's uncertainty defence succeeds.

Therefore, in this case the court refused to imply an essential term such as the delivery date of the works in the agreement. However, the parties may also find themselves in the

1 *Teekay Tankers Ltd v STX Offshore and Shipbuilding Co Ltd* [2017] EWHC 253 (Comm).

DOI: 10.4324/9781003387718-36

opposite situation of being bound by a term that a count implies in the contract and that they did not think they had agreed on.

30.2 Implication of terms under English law

Under English law, contractual terms may be implied into a construction contract: (i) as a matter of common law,[2] in which case the terms will be applied to all contracts of a particular class unless the express terms of the given contract or the surrounding circumstances suggest otherwise. Examples of terms implied by law may be found in the Housing Grants, Construction and Regeneration Act 1996 or in the Late Payment of Commercial Debts (Interest) Act 1998 (UK); or (ii) as a matter of fact (or "*ad hoc*"), i.e. based on the construction of the presumed intention of the parties to a particular contract. The leading case on terms implied in fact is the *Moorcock*[3] case where Bowen LJ stated:

> Now, an implied warranty, or, as it is called, a covenant in law, as distinguished from an express contract or express warranty, really is in all cases founded upon the presumed intention of the parties, and upon reason. The implication which the law draws from what must obviously have been the intention of the parties, the law draws with the object of giving efficacy to the transaction and preventing such a failure of consideration as cannot have been within the contemplation of either side; and I believe if one were to take all the cases, and there are many, of implied warranties or covenants in law, it will be found that in all of them the law is raising an implication from the presumed intention of the parties with the object of giving the transaction such efficacy as both parties must have intended that at all events it should have.

The criteria used by the courts to ascertain whether ad hoc terms may be implied in fact were summarised by Lord Simon in *BP Refinery (Westernpoint) Pty Ltd v Shire of Hastings*[4] as follows:

> (1) it must be reasonable and equitable; (2) it must be necessary to give business efficacy to the contract, so that no term will be implied if the contract is effective without it; (3) it must be so obvious that 'it goes without saying'; (4) it must be capable of clear expression; (5) it must not contradicts any express term of the contract.

More specifically:

(i) As to equity and reasonableness, a court will not imply a term only because it would be reasonable to do so. Both reasonableness and equitability must justify the implication of a term.[5]

(ii) As to the business efficacy test, a term may be implied where the term is necessary to give business efficacy to the contract.[6] It follows that no term may be

2 E.g., the Housing Grants, Construction and Regeneration Act 1996.

3 *The Moorcock* [1889] 14 PD 64.

4 *BP Refinery (Westernpoint) Pty Ltd v Shire of Hastings* [1978] 52 ALJR 20 at [26]. The test was then revised in *Marks and Spencer Plc v BNP Paribas Securities Services Trust Co (Jersey) Ltd and Another* [2015] 3 WLR 1843, 1849–1851.

5 *Throllope & Colls Ltd v NW Metropolitan Hospital Board* [1973] 1 WLR 601 at [609]; *Young & Marten Ltd v McManus Childs Ltd* [1969] 1 AC 454.

6 *Liverpool City Council v Irwin* [1977] AC 239 at [257] – [258].

implied into a contract unless the contract lacks commercial or practical coherence,[7] or the contract will not work in the absence of an implied term.[8]

(iii) As to the officious bystander test, a term will not be implied into a contract, unless it is so obvious to the parties that "it goes without saying".[9] In this case, the law will use the implication of terms to fills obvious gaps and make a contract work.[10] In *Shirlaw v Southern Foundries*[11] an implied term in fact was described as:

> something so obvious that it goes without saying; so that, if while the parties were making their bargain, an officious bystander were to suggest some express provision for it in the agreement, they would testily suppress him with a common 'Oh, of course!'

This test is concerned with notional reasonable people in the position of the parties at the time at which they entered into the relevant contract.[12]

(iv) As to the requirement for clear expression, for a term to be implied in a contract it must be possible to formulate such term with adequate precision.[13]

(v) As to the requirement there should not be any inconsistency with the express terms of the contract, the English courts will not imply a term into a contract if it is inconsistent with the existing express contractual terms.[14] In *Attorney General of Belize v Belize Telecom Ltd*[15] Lord Hoffmann suggested that the process of implication is an exercise of construction:

> It follows that in every case in which it is said that some provision ought to be implied in an instrument, the question for the court is whether such a provision would spell out in express words what the instrument, read against the relevant background, would reasonably be understood to mean. It will be noticed from Lord Pearson's speech that this question can be reformulated in various ways which a court may find helpful in providing an answer – the implied term must 'go without saying', it must be 'necessary to give business efficacy to the contract' and so on – but these are not in the Board's opinion to be treated as different or additional tests. There is only one question: is that what the instrument, read as a whole against the relevant background, would reasonably be understood to mean?

The only question for the courts was whether a reasonable reader of the contract with the relevant background knowledge would understand such term to be implied. That decision led to a great debate as to whether it had changed the law so that reasonableness was now sufficient for implying a term. This was

7 *Marks and Spencer Plc v BNP Paribas Securities Services Trust Co (Jersey) Ltd and Another* [2015] 3 WLR 1843, 1851. See also *Luxor (Eastbourne) Ltd v Cooper* [1941] AC 108 at [137].

8 *Marks and Spencer Plc v BNP Paribas Securities Services Trust Co (Jersey) Ltd and Another* [2015] 3 WLR 1843, 1866.

9 *Shirlaw v Southern Foundries* [1939] 2 KB 206, 227; *Luxor (Eastbourne) Ltd v Cooper* [1941] AC 108 at [137].

10 *Adams Holden & Pearson v Trent Regional Health Authority* [1989] 47 BLR 34 at [49].

11 *Shirlaw v Southern Foundries* (1926) Ltd [1939] 2 KB at [227].

12 *Marks and Spencer Plc v BNP Paribas Securities Services Trust Co (Jersey) Ltd and Another* [2015] 3 WLR 1843, 1850.

13 *Luxor (Eastbourne) Ltd v Cooper* [1941] AC 108 at [137].

14 *Lancore Services Ltd v Barclays Bank plc*, [2009] EWCA Civ 752; *Johnson v Unisys Ltd* [2003] 1 AC 518 at [539].

15 *Attorney General of Belize v Belize Telecom Ltd* [2009] UKPC 10; [2009] 1 WLR 1988.

rejected by Lord Neuberger (with whom Lords Sumption and Hodge agreed) in *Marks and Spencer plc v BNP Paribas*[16] where he said:

> I accept that both (i) construing the words which the parties have used in their contract and (ii) implying terms into the contract, involve determining the scope and meaning of the contract. However, Lord Hoffmann's analysis in Belize Telecom could obscure the fact that construing the words used and implying additional words are different processes governed by different rules.

Lord Neuberger then cited with approval the five principles set out by Lord Simon in *BP Refinery* and highlighted the dangers of reformulating such principles. However, he rejected the idea that fairness or reasonableness alone will suffice to justify the implication of terms into a contract. In doing so, he added six comments on the summary given by Lord Simon in *BP Refinery*:

> First, in Equitable Life Assurance Society v Hyman [2002] 1 AC 408, 459, Lord Steyn rightly observed that the implication of a term was 'not critically dependent on proof of an actual intention of the parties' when negotiating the contract. If one approaches the question by reference to what the parties would have agreed, one is not strictly concerned with the hypothetical answer of the actual parties, but with that of notional reasonable people in the position of the parties at the time at which they were contracting; secondly, a term should not be implied into a detailed commercial contract merely because it appears fair or merely because one considers that the parties would have agreed it if it had been suggested to them. Those are necessary but not sufficient grounds for including a term; thirdly, it is questionable whether Lord Simon's first requirement, reasonableness and equitableness, will usually, if ever, add anything: if a term satisfies the other requirements, it is hard to think that it would not be reasonable and equitable; fourthly, as Lord Hoffmann I think suggested in Attorney General of Belize v Belize Telecom Ltd [2009] 1 WLR 1988, para 27, although Lord Simon's requirements are otherwise cumulative, I would accept that business necessity and obviousness, his second and third requirements, can be alternatives in the sense that only one of them needs to be satisfied, although I suspect that in practice it would be a rare case where only one of those two requirements would be satisfied; fifthly, if one approaches the issue by reference to the officious bystander, it is 'vital to formulate the question to be posed by [him] with the utmost care', to quote from Lewison, The Interpretation of Contracts 5th ed (2011), para 6.09. Sixthly, necessity for business efficacy involves a value judgment. It is rightly common ground on this appeal that the test is not one of 'absolute necessity', not least because the necessity is judged by reference to business efficacy. It may well be that a more helpful way of putting Lord Simon's second requirement is, as suggested by Lord Sumption in argument, that a term can only be implied if, without the term, the contract would lack commercial or practical coherence.

This judgment represents a return to the stringent nature of the legal test for implication of terms into a contract. Fairness or reasonableness alone will not be sufficient.

30.3 Some terms typically implied in construction contracts

Terms that are usually implied in construction contracts include as follows:

16 *Marks and Spencer plc v BNP Paribas* [2015] UKSC 72; [2016] AC 742.

30.3.1 Duty not to prevent completion

There is an implied term that neither party to a contract shall do anything to prevent the other party from performing a contract or delay the other party in performing it.[17]

In *Mackay v Dick*[18] the court stated that, when a written contract provides obligations which are dependant on both parties:

> each agrees to do all that is necessary to be done on his part for the carrying out of that thing, though there may be no express words to that effect.

This includes the obligation not to delay the other party in performing the contract.[19] For example, an employer shall not interfere in the supply of goods necessary for the works.[20] However, the duty cannot be stretched so to include an obligation to assist the other party in performing its obligations. As said by Lord Romer in *Luxor (Eastbourne) Ltd v Cooper*:[21]

> If I employ a man for reward to build a house on my land I subject myself to an implied condition that I will do nothing to prevent him carrying out the work. But I am under no implied obligation to help him earn the reward whether by the supply of building materials or otherwise.

30.3.2 Duty to cooperate

This term was defined in *London Borough of Merton v Leach*[22] as an obligation to:

> do whatever is necessary in order to enable a contract to be carried out.

Also in this case, this duty cannot be taken so far as to oblige one party to cooperate so to enable the other party to perform its contractual obligations.[23] Examples of duties to cooperate that may be implied are the employer's duty to give possession of the site within reasonable time[24] or to cooperate with the contractor when the latter is contractually obliged to obtain statutory approvals for the works and is unable to do it without the assistance of the employer.

30.3.3 Duty to perform the works with all proper skill and care

The contractor has an implied duty to use reasonable skill and care in performing the works.[25]

---

17 *Barque Quilpue Ltd v Brown* [1904] 2 KB 261 at [271]; *London Borough of Merton v Leach* [1986] 32 BLR 51 at [80] – [81].

18 *Mackay v Dick* [1881] 6 App Cas 251.

19 *Barque Quilpué Ltd Brown* [1904] 2 KB 261 at [274].

20 Even though there is no contract between the contractor and the supplier. See *Acrow (Automation) Ltd v Rex Chainbelt Inc.* [1971] 1 WLR 1676 at 1680, CA.

21 *Luxor (Eastbourne) Ltd v Cooper* [1941] AC 108.

22 *London Borough of Merton v Leach* [1986] 32 BLR 51 at [80].

23 *Mona Oil Equipment Co v Rhodesia Railways* [1949] 2 All ER 1014 at [1018]; *London Borough of Merton v Leach* [1986] 32 BLR 51 at [80] – [81].

24 *Freeman v Hensler* [1900] HBC (4th edition), Vol. 2, at p. 292, CA.

25 *Young & Marten v McManus Childs* [1969] 1 AC 454 at [465].

At common law it is an implied term that if the contractor holds himself out as possessing a particular skill, it shall exercise reasonable skill and care when employed to do work that requires the application of that skill.[26] This is confirmed by Section 13 of the Supply of Goods and Services Act 1982 which states:

> In a relevant contract for the supply of a service] where the supplier is acting in the course of a business, there is an implied term that the supplier will carry out the service with reasonable care and skill.

However, this duty cannot be stretched as far as to include a duty to achieve a perfect result. As Dillon LJ held in *Hawkins v Chrysler (UK) Ltd*:[27]

> The general position . . . is that a professional man who is called in to advise is bound, and impliedly undertakes, to use reasonable skill and care in advising, but is not responsible for providing a perfect result or a perfect building.

However, if the contractor has expressly assumed a strict obligation to achieve a particular result, it will be liable for failing to achieve it even if he has acted with reasonable skill and care.[28]

30.3.4 Warranty that supplied materials are reasonably fit for purpose and of good quality

In the case of large construction projects, the relevant contracts usually contain an express term that the materials used are to be new and of satisfactory quality. However, where the contract is silent on this aspect, the common law will imply a warranty from contractors that the materials supplied will be of good and proper quality,[29] unless it can be shown that the parties intended otherwise.[30] This warranty is excluded in case in the selection of the materials the employer did not rely on the contractor's skill and judgment,[31] e.g., because the contract requires the contractor to use materials from a supplier nominated by the employer or where the contractor is obliged under the contract to use those materials and cannot obtain an indemnity from the nominated supplier in case the goods turn out to be unsatisfactory.[32] The warranty as to good quality of materials may have the effect of making the contractor liable for latent defects also in case the employer has chosen the materials or the supplier of the materials or where the contractor was unaware at the time of supply that the materials were inappropriate or defective and could not prevent such defects[33] (for example when the contractor orders materials from a supplier which turn out to be defective, but were not obviously such at the time they were supplied). As a result, contractors will not usually be able to use as a defence the fact that they had no reasonable basis for knowing that the supplied materials were defective. A contractor that is found liable for breach of such warranty would then need to pursue the

26 *Hawkins v Chrysler (UK) Ltd* [1986] 38 BLR 36.
27 *Hawkins v Chrysler (UK) Ltd* [1986] 38 BLR 36 at [53].
28 *Costain Ltd v Charles Haswell & Partners Ltd* [2009] EWHC B25 (TCC) at [52] – [59].
29 *Young & Marten v McManus Childs* [1969] 1 AC 454 at [465].
30 *Miller v Cannon Hill Estates Ltd* [1931] 2 KB 113 at [122].
31 *Young & Marten v McManus Childs* [1969] 1 AC 454 at [465].
32 *Young & Marten Ltd v McManus Childs Ltd* [1969] 1 AC 454 at [466] – [467].
33 *Hancock v BW Brazier (Anerley) Ltd* [1966] 1 WLR 1317 at [1332] – [1333].

supplier of the faulty materials. As to the quality level required to comply with the warranty in question, the courts may look at building standards or legislative requirements,[34] where present. In general, goods or materials will not be considered of satisfactory quality if they fail shortly after use, to the extent they have been used for their normal or intended purpose. Also in this case, there is statutory legislation providing for a similar warranty in contracts for the sale or supply of goods.[35]

30.3.5 Warranty that the works will be reasonably fit for purpose

There is an implied term that the works, once completed, will be reasonably fit for the purpose made known by the employer to the contractor at the time of entering into the contract.[36] This warranty applies to the extent the contractor expressly assumed responsibility for design and construction[37] (in which case the obligation on the contractor will not be the mere exercise of reasonable skill and care, but will amount to a warranty of performance[38]) or where the employer relied on the contractor's skill and judgment in achieving the requisite standard[39] (e.g., in case of residential building work for a dwelling, the contractor impliedly warrants that the dwelling be fit for human habitation[40]). As stated in *Independent Broadcasting Authority v EMI Electronics*:[41]

> In the absence of any terms (express or to be implied) negativing the obligation, one who contracts to design an article for a purpose made known to him undertakes that the design is reasonably fit for the purpose.

Thus, where the contractor agrees to, and assumes responsibility for design, there will usually be an implied warranty that the works will be reasonably fit for the agreed or known purpose, unless the warranty was expressly excluded.[42] It is possible that the contractor was made aware of the general purpose of the design, but not of specific requirements as to the final performance or specification. In such case, the contractor will only be required to exercise reasonable skill and care in performing its obligations and will be obliged to ensure that the design will be suitable for its usual purpose.[43]

One question is whether a contractor, which is bound to comply with a detailed specification but has expressly warranted the fitness of the works, may be held liable in case the works are eventually not fit for the relevant purpose. It has been held that contractors may have a duty to warn employers of obvious defects in the plans provided by the employer in cases where the employer has relied on the experience, judgment and skill of the contractor.[44]

Where the contractor has not assumed responsibility for design but has agreed to supply goods and build a structure based on a given design, the contractor will not impliedly

34 *Trebor Bassett Holdings Ltd v ADT Fire and Security Plc* [2012] EWCA Civ 1158.

35 See for example Section 14(2) of the Sale of Goods Act 1979 and Section 4(2) of the Supply of Goods and Services Act 1982.

36 *Gloucestershire CC v Richardson* [1969] 1 AC 480 at 502.

37 *Hawkins v Chrysler (UK) Ltd* [1986] 38 BLR 36 at 55.

38 *Viking Grain Storage Ltd v TH White Installations Ltd* [1985] 33 BLR 103 at 117–118.

39 *Greaves & Co Ltd v Baynham Meikle* [1975] 1 WLR 1095 at 1098, C.A.

40 *Miller v Cannon Hill Estates Ltd* [1931] 2 KB 113 at [120] – [121].

41 *Independent Broadcasting Authority v EMI Electronics* [1980] 14 BLR 1 at [48] (HL(E)).

42 *Viking Grain v T.H. White* [1985] 33 BLR 103.

43 *Cleightonhills v Bembridge Marine Ltd* [2012] EWHC 3449 (TCC) at [47].

44 *Brunswick Construction Ltd v Nowlan* [1974], 49 DLR (3d) and 21 BLR 27 (Canada SC).

warrant the fitness for purpose of the design, but only the fitness for purpose of the materials supplied and the contractor's workmanship, to the extent that they are within the contractor's control.[45]

It is not uncommon that the parties to construction contracts expressly exclude the fitness for purpose warranty and provide that the contractor only undertakes to exercise reasonable skill and care in performing its obligations. This usually occurs where a contractor's insurance policy does not cover the contractor's liability for breach of a fitness for purpose obligations.

30.3.6 Warranty that works will be completed in a good and workmanlike manner

There is an implied term that the contractor will perform and complete the work[46] and will do it in a good and workmanlike manner.[47] In case a contractor knows, or ought to know based on the level of skill required, that the works it has been asked to perform will be defective or unsatisfactory for their known purpose (e.g., due to physical or environmental limitations), the contractor shall not proceed with the relevant work, shall make the employer aware of this and shall seek instructions on how to proceed before carrying out the work.[48] The benchmark against which this warranty will be measured is the skill and care of an ordinarily competent contractor in the circumstances of the actual contractor. The courts may make the assessment having regard to accepted published industry standards. Regard will be given to the whole of the work performed by the contractor and not just a part of it.[49]

30.3.7 Warranty that design information is accurate

Where, based on the construction contract, the employer is obliged to provide design information to the contractor, it will usually imply a term that such information shall be accurate.[50]

30.4 Avoiding the implication of terms in a contract

The range of implied terms which are capable of being implied in a construction contract is limited, and the courts usually are reluctant to imply a term outside these limits. However, the parties should be mindful of the terms that are capable of being implied into their construction contract as a matter of common law or in fact and endeavour to avoid the implication of those terms that are not in line with their common intention.

The parties may avoid the implication of unwanted terms into their contracts in two ways, i.e., expressly excluding the implication of such terms or by including express

45 *Rotherham MBC v Frank Haslam & Co Ltd* (1996) 78 BLR 1 at [22].

46 *Perry v Sharon Development Co Ltd* [1937] 4 All ER 390 at [396].

47 *City of London v Nash* (1747) 3 Atk 512 at [515]; *Emcor Drake & Scull Ltd v Sir Robert McAlpine Ltd* [2004] EWCA Civ 1733 at [14].

48 *Pearce v Tucker* [1862] 3 F&F 136 [176 ER 61].

49 *Barclays Bank plc v Fairclough Building Ltd* [1994] 68 BLR 1 at [13].

50 *London Borough of Merton v Leach* [1985] 32 BLR 51 at [81] – [83].

terms into the contract that are in contrast with terms that would otherwise be implied (as a court will not imply a term that contradicts an express term). Where they opt for the first method, they should ensure that the language purporting to exclude the implication of a term be clear and unambiguous to minimise the risk of disputes arising on whether the implication was in fact excluded. Where they opt for the second method, they should make sure that the express language clearly covers the subject so that there is no ambiguity as to the intention of the parties. In *Trollope & Colls Ltd and Holland & Hannen and Cubitts Ltd. v Atomic Power Constructions Ltd.*[51] Lord Pearson clarified that the role of the court is to:

> interpret and apply the contract which the parties have made for themselves. If the express terms are perfectly clear and free from ambiguity, there is not choice to be made between different possible meanings; the clear terms must be applied even if the court thinks some other terms would have been more suitable. An unexpressed term can be implied if and only if the court finds that the parties must have intended that term to form part of their contract; it is not enough for the court to find that such a term would have been adopted by the parties as reasonable even if it had been suggested to them; it must have been a term that went without saying, a term necessary to give business efficacy to the contract, a term which, though tacit, formed part of the contract which the parties made for themselves.

51 *Trollope & Colls Ltd and Holland & Hannen and Cubitts Ltd. v Atomic Power Constructions Ltd.* [1962] 3 All ER 1035. See also *Twintec Ltd Volkerfitzpatrick* [2014] EWHC 10 (TCC) at [18].

CHAPTER 31

Interpretation of construction contracts

31.1 Interpretation of contracts in general

When drafting contracts for complex construction projects the parties should strive to regulate as many aspects as possible of their relationship expressly and clearly so that, in case disputes arise, few are left to be interpreted by the courts. This is because the court may take positions which are not in line with the parties' intentions and expectations, for example by implying terms into the contract or interpreting them in case of any ambiguities. Very often large corporations have their internal contract forms or use contract forms (e.g., FIDIC forms). However, such forms are usually heavily negotiated between the parties. As a result of the various negotiations rounds, some contractual terms may become unclear or contradict other express terms. Where a contractual term is not sufficiently clear disputes may arise as to its precise meaning. In such cases, the courts will apply a set of construction rules and principles to resolve such uncertainty. In doing so, they are generally guided by the overarching objective to give effect to the contract, so far as possible, rather than destroying the parties' bargain.[1]

The body of case law that has developed over the years in relation to interpretation and construction of contracts is massive and constantly developing. Such general principles apply to construction contracts which are not subject to special rules of construction.[2]

31.2 Rules of interpretation

31.2.1 Statutory interpretation

How the courts will interpret the statute law relevant to construction contracts may ultimately affect the interpretation such contracts. Specific rules have developed over time for the interpretation of statute law. The main rules are the "literal rule", the "golden rule" and the "mischief rule".

31.2.1.1 The literal (or "plain meaning") rule

According to the so-called literal rule, a court applying a statute to a case shall rely on the exact wording of that statute and may not interpret its meaning. As stated by Lord Diplock in the case of *Duport Steels Ltd and Others v Sirs and Others*:[3]

---

1 *Hillas & Co Ltd v Arcos Ltd* [1932] All ER 494 at [499].

2 *Beaufort Developments v Gilbert-Ash* [1999] AC 266 at [269].

3 *Duport Steels Ltd and Others v Sirs and Others* [1980] UKHL J0201–1.

DOI: 10.4324/9781003387718-37

> Where the meaning of the statutory words is plain and unambiguous it is not then for the judges to invent fancied ambiguities as an excuse for failing to give effect to it's plain meaning because they consider the consequences for doing so would be inexpedient, or even unjust or immoral.

Intuitively, a strict application of the Literal Rule may lead to unjust and absurd results.

31.2.1.2 The golden rule

In the case of *Grey v Pearson*[4] Lord Wensleydale identified the "golden rule" as follows:

> The grammatical and ordinary sense of the words is to be adhered to unless that would lead to some absurdity or some repugnance or inconsistency with the rest of the instrument in which case the grammatical and ordinary sense of the words may be modified so as to avoid the absurdity and inconsistency, but no farther.

In *Rhodes v Rhodes*[5] it is clarified that absurdity arises in case, from reading the document as a whole, it is clear that the parties intended a word to have a special meaning as, giving such a word its ordinary meaning would create an absurdity.

31.2.1.3 The mischief (or "Heydon") rule

The so-called mischief rule was formulated in the *Heydon's Case*[6] where Lord Coke stated:

> For the sure and true interpretation of all statutes in general (be they penal or beneficial, restrictive or enlarging of the common law), four things are to be discerned and considered: (1st). What was the common law before the making of the Act? (2nd). What was the mischief and defect for which the common law did not provide. (3rd). What remedy the Parliament hath resolved and appointed to cure the disease of the commonwealth. And, (4th). The true reason of the remedy; and then the office of all the judges is always to make such construction as shall suppress the mischief, and advance the remedy, and to suppress subtle inventions and evasions for continuance of the mischief, and pro privato commodo, and to add force and life to the cure and remedy, according to the true intent of the makers of the Act, pro bono publico.

31.2.2 Contractual interpretation

31.2.2.1 Contractual interpretation in general

Construction contracts are lengthy and complex documents which are often heavily negotiated. The parties' negotiations will start at the tender phase and go on until the contract is entered into. Even after a contract is executed the parties will typically enter into several amendments to the contract to provide for the various events that usually occur throughout a complex construction project (e.g., variations). Such amendments may be subject to lengthy negotiations and will ultimately form part of the initial construction contract. It is not uncommon that such complicated and lengthy negotiations will result

4 *Grey v Pearson* [1957] 6 HL Cas 61 at [106].
5 *Rhodes v Rhodes* [1882] 7 App Cas 192 at [205].
6 *Heydon's Case* [1584] 76 ER 637 3 CO REP 7a.

in inconsistencies and/or inaccuracies that generate disputes over the exact meaning of some contractual provisions and their consistency with other contractual terms. In interpreting construction contracts the courts will be guided by the contract and aided by a number of rules and principles that developed over time.

The guiding principle of contractual interpretation is that the courts shall give words their grammatical and ordinary meaning unless this would lead to some absurdity or inconsistency. The parties' subjective intentions and their motive, purpose, desire or state of mind shall not influence the courts. Where the parties' subjective intention was different from the one that is in fact stated in the contract (i.e., where they used wrong or unclear words to express a certain concept and obtain a certain result), the courts may not actively intervene and the appropriate remedy for the parties will be rectification, if available in the circumstances. The task of the courts is to objectively ascertain what each party could reasonably conclude from the attitude of the other, without trying to investigate whether that party's intention was in line with the specific attitude. What counts is what a reasonable man in the place of one of the parties would conclude from the other party's attitude.

31.2.2.2 Vague and meaningless terms

An agreement will not be enforceable if it is too vague, and a court will not substitute itself to the parties and make the bargain for them or try to speculate over what their intention was at the time they entered into the contract. In *Scammell v Ouston*[7] Lord Wright held:

> It is a necessary requirement that an agreement, in order to be binding, must be sufficiently definite to enable the court to give it a practical meaning. Its terms must be so definite, or capable of being made definite without further agreement of the parties, that the promises and performances to be rendered by each party are reasonably certain.

However, a distinction should be made between vagueness and meaninglessness as, while a meaningless term would not usually affect the whole contract, vagueness affecting an essential term may mean that such a term was not agreed on in the first place and lead a court to find that there is no contract at all. In *Nicolene Ltd. v Simmonds*[8] Denning LJ said:

> In my opinion a distinction must be drawn between a clause which is meaningless, and a clause which is yet to be agreed. A clause which is meaningless can often be ignored, whilst still leaving the contract good: whereas a clause which has yet to be agreed may mean that there is no contract at all, because the parties have not agreed on all the essential terms.

Therefore, if a contract is sufficiently definite, meaningless expressions can be disregarded, while the contract will still be binding on the parties.

31.2.2.3 Use of extrinsic evidence

Construction disputes often focus on whether and to what extent the parties may rely on material (discussions during negotiations, communications, documents, draft contracts, previous agreements between the same parties, explanatory notes, etc.) which is not included in the written construction contract, but may aid the court in construing ambiguous clauses.

7 *Scammell v Ouston* [1941] AC 251 at [268].
8 *Nicolene Ltd. v Simmonds* [1953] 1 QB 543 at [551].

The English courts are reluctant to accord contractual force to such extrinsic evidence when a party seeks to use such evidence to contradict or vary the terms of a written agreement. Such reluctancy (sometimes referred to as the "parol evidence" rule) is a direct consequence of the principle that in construing a contract the courts should only look at the words used in the instrument and not be concerned with the parties' actual and subjective intentions.

The basic rule is that where the parties have entered into a final written contract external evidence cannot be referred to for the purpose of explaining the parties' intentions.[9] An application of this rule can be found in the case of *Davis Contractors Ltd v Fareham Urban District Council*.[10] The appellants were awarded a contract for the construction of 28 houses for eight months. The tender was accompanied by a letter stating that the tender was subject to certain requirements (adequate supplies of materials and labour). The appellants then entered into a contract with the respondents to build the houses at a fixed price. The letter was not incorporated into the contract. The work was delayed due, inter alia, to the lack of skilled labour. The appellants then claimed that they were entitled to claim in quantum meruit as the price in the contract was not binding because it was subject to an overriding condition contained in the letter. The court dismissed the appeal on the grounds that the letter in the tender, and the condition which it stipulated, were not incorporated in the contract.

There are, however, some exceptions to the "parol evidence" rule which developed over time:

(i) When courts are called at solving contractual ambiguity or at deciding whether contractual terms are to be implied, they might have to depart from pure internal linguistic considerations as to the meaning of the words used by the parties, put the agreement into its context and look at the surrounding circumstances at the time the agreement was made. The courts place themselves in the same factual situation in which the parties were at the time they entered into the contract and consider such factual matrix to construe any ambiguous terms. In the case of *Prenn v Simmonds*[11] Lord Wilberforce held that:

> The time has long passed when agreements, even those under seal, were isolated from the matrix of facts in which they were set and interpreted purely on internal linguistic considerations. We must inquire beyond the language and see what the circumstances were with reference to which the words were used, and the object appearing from those circumstances, which the person using them had in view.

The courts may look at surrounding circumstances such as the commercial object of the transaction to explain parties' aim, which may aid them choosing one interpretation over the other. In *Prenn*[12] Lord Wilberforce clarified this point as follows:

> It may be said that previous documents may be looked at to explain the aims of the parties. In a limited sense this is true:, the commercial, or business object, of the transaction, objectively ascertained, may be a surrounding fact. Cardozo J. thought

9 S. Furst QC, V. Ramsey QC, *Keating on Building Contracts* (7th edition) Sweet & Maxwell, 2001, at para 44.
10 *Davis Contractors Ltd v Fareham Urban District Council* [1956] AC 696 [1956] 2 All ER 145.
11 *Prenn v Simmonds* [1971] 1 WLR 1381.
12 *Prenn v Simmonds* [1971] 1 WLR 1381.

> so in the Utica Bank case. And if it can be shown that one interpretation completely frustrates that object, to the extent of rendering the contract futile, that may be a strong argument for an alternative interpretation, if that can reasonably be found. But beyond that it may be difficult to go: it may be a matter of degree, or of judgment, how far one interpretation, or another, gives effect to a common intention: the parties, indeed, may be pursuing that intention with differing emphasis, and hoping to achieve it to an extent which may differ, and in different ways. The words used may, and often do, represent a formula which means different things to each side, yet may be accepted because that is the only way to get 'agreement' and in the hope that disputes will not arise. The only course then can be to try to ascertain the 'natural' meaning. Far more, and indeed totally, dangerous is it to admit evidence of one party's objective – even if this is known to the other party. However strongly pursued this may be, the other party may only be willing to give it partial recognition, and in a world of give and take, men often have to be satisfied with less than they want.

Thus, documents not included in the contract may be helpful for the court in that they may give the court information on the commercial or business objective of the parties. If, looking at such documents, a court finds that a certain literal interpretation of ambiguous contractual terms would completely frustrate the objective of the parties at the time when they entered into the contract, the court may be inclined to prefer a different interpretation which is more in line with such surrounding circumstances, to the extent it is supported by the contract as a whole. However, the courts shall be very careful in inferring common intention from extrinsic evidence as such evidence may only partially reflect the true intention of each party (e.g., because such documents may have meant something different to each of the parties or because one party may have made concessions only to get the deal done).

The test that courts shall apply in construing extrinsic facts is an objective one. The intention and aim of the parties shall be ascertained objectively. The parties may not give direct evidence of what their intention and aim was at the time of the contract. Rather, a court shall ascertain what would be the intention and aim which reasonable people would have had if placed in the situation of the parties.[13]

In *Investors Compensation Scheme Ltd v West Bromwich Building Society*[14] Lord Hoffman held that the "*background*" which was referred to by Lord Wilberforce as the "*matrix of fact*":

> includes absolutely anything which would have affected the way in which the language of the document would have been understood by a reasonable man.

The Supreme Court's case of *Arnold v Britton*[15] has signed a return to the orthodox position on this subject. Lord Neuberger (with whom Lord Sumption and Lord Hughes agreed) held that:

> surrounding circumstances . . . should not be invoked to undervalue the importance of the language of the provision which is to be construed. . . . When interpreting a contractual provision, one can only take into account facts or circumstances which existed at the time that the contract was made, and which were known or reasonably

13 *Reardon-Smith Line Ltd. v Hansen-Tangen* [1976] 1 WLR 989, 889, 995/6.
14 *Investors Compensation Scheme Ltd v West Bromwich Building Society* [1998] 1 WLR 896.
15 *Arnold v Britton* [2015] UKSC 36; [2015] AC 1619.

> available to both parties. Given that a contract is a bilateral, or synallagmatic, arrangement involving both parties, it cannot be right, when interpreting a contractual provision, to take into account a fact or circumstance known only to one of the parties.

A distinct issue is when pre-contractual statements made by any of the parties were expressly incorporated in the contract. In such cases, the parties can rely on those statements in case of breaches. It is worth noting that construction contracts for large and complex projects will usually include entire agreement clauses aimed at ensuring that the entirety of the contractual relationship is governed by the written agreement the parties have formally entered into. This will help minimising the admissibility of extrinsic evidence having contractual effect.

Where, instead, the parties agree that a specific term of the contract was agreed on but has not been entirely or correctly reflected in the written contract, they may apply for rectification so to include the term in the form and extent they had agreed at the time of the contract.

(ii) To prove that the words in a contract were used according to a special custom or usage known to the trade or locality applicable to the contract.

(iii) To prove a pre-contractual misrepresentation or make a claim for rectification of a written agreement.[16]

(iv) To prove that the parties acted on a shared assumption that may operate as an "estoppel by convention" preventing any of them from asserting contractual rights that are contrary to that shared assumption.

(v) Where a party alleges that the written contract does not contain the whole agreement between the parties as there is a collateral warranty (i.e., an agreement, which is associated with another "primary" contract), in which case the asserting party may give evidence of such agreement.[17]

(vi) To prove what the real contractual consideration is in case: (a) the contract includes no consideration or a nominal consideration; (b) the consideration is expressed in general or ambiguous terms; or (c) the contract states a substantial consideration, but a party intends to show that an additional consideration exists which is inconsistent with the contract.[18]

(vii) To prove that a condition precedent was not fulfilled.

(viii) To prove that a contract is void or voidable or has been varied or rescinded.[19]

(ix) To prove that the parties habitually used words in an unconventional sense (a so-called private dictionary) and, therefore, the words in the contract should be interpreted in light of that dictionary. However, the private dictionary exclusion should not extend to cases where a word or phrase is expressly defined in the contract itself.[20]

(x) To prove the meaning of foreign or technical words.

(xi) To prove that the liquidated damages clause is a penalty.[21]

---

16 *Proforce Recruit Ltd v The Rugby Group Ltd* [2006] EWCA Civ 69 at [53].

17 *Tekdata Interconnections Ltd v Amphenol Ltd* [2009] EWCA Civ 1209 at [19].

18 *Pao On v Lau you Long* [1980] AC 614 at 631, PC. See also S. Furst QC, V. Ramsey QC, *Keating on Building Contracts* (7th edition) Sweet & Maxwell, 2001, at para 50.

19 S. Furst QC, V. Ramsey QC, *Keating on Building Contracts* (7th edition) Sweet & Maxwell, 2001, at para 49.

20 *Chartbrook Ltd v Persimmon Homes Ltd* [2007] EWHC 409 (Ch).

21 *Murray v Leisureplay Plc*, CA 28 Jul 2005.

31.2.2.4 Subsequent conduct

Traditionally, the position on subsequent conduct was that where a written contract contained an ambiguity evidence of the parties' subsequent conduct was admissible as an aid of construction to the extent that it unequivocally supported the interpretation suggested.

In the case of *Watcham v Attorney-General of the East Africa Protectorate*[22] the Watchams were the owners of held land along the bank of the Nairobi River which had been conveyed to them by the Crown. The conveyance certificate indicated a transfer of '66 3/4 acres, or thereabouts', but included a physical description which would have resulted in an area of 160 acres. There was evidence that the Watchams had never occupied the more extensive area, part of which had been occupied without objection from them by someone else. The Privy Council held that evidence of such subsequent conduct was admissible as an aid to construction, to show that the description in the certificate must be "*falsa demonstration*".

However, in *James Miller & Partners Ltd v Whitworth Street Estates (Manchester) Ltd*[23] the House of Lords ruled against the admissibility of evidence of subsequent conduct unless it were being used to prove an estoppel or a new contract. The case concerned a dispute on a building contract entered into between the English company Whitworth Street Estates ("Whitworth") and the Scottish company James Miller and Partners Ltd. ("JMP") The contract did not contain an express choice of law clause. Among other things, the House of Lords was called to decide on what was the law applying to the contract (English law or Scottish law). The question was whether an intention could reasonably be inferred. Both the Court of Appeal and the House of Lords (by a majority) held that the contract was regulated by English law. The Court of Appeal relied, inter alia, on the subsequent conduct of the parties, who had on two occasions acted on the basis that English law applied. The court, however, failed to explain that the subsequent conduct of the parties is merely indicative of the parties' intention at the time of the contract, which is where the focus of the court's enquiry should be. The House of Lords held that seeking to establish the parties' actual intention at the time of the contract was of no use as the parties had given no thought to the matter of the law applicable to the contract at that time, thus they had no actual intention on this point. The court was rather called to establish what intention could be reasonably attributed to the parties based on the terms of the contract and the surrounding circumstances at the time the contract was entered into. The question of the parties' subsequent conduct became then irrelevant. Subsequent conduct could provide an indication of what meaning the parties had intended to give to a contractual provision. However, in the case at hand there was no term to be ascertained and no actual intention on the specific subject at the time of the contract. Lord Raid clarified the point as follows:

> It has been assumed in the course of this case that it is proper, in determining what was the proper law, to have regard to actings of the parties after their contract had been made. Of course the actings of the parties (including any words which they used) may be sufficient to show that they made a new contract. If they made no agreement originally as to

22 *Watcham v Attorney-General of the East Africa Protectorate* [1919] AC 533. See also *Neilson v Poole* ChD 1969.

23 *James Miller & Partners Ltd v Whitworth Street Estates (Manchester) Ltd* [1970] UKHL J0303-1.

> the proper law, such actings may show that they made an agreement about that at a later stage. Or if they did make such an agreement originally such actings may show that they later agreed to alter it. But with regard to actings of the parties between the date of the original contract and the date of Mr. Underwood's appointment I did not understand it to be argued that they were sufficient to establish any new contract, and I think they clearly were not. As I understood him, counsel sought to use those actings to show that there was an agreement when the original contract was made that the proper law of that contract was to be the law of England. I must say that I had thought that it is now well settled that it is not legitimate to use as an aid in the construction of the contract anything which the parties said or did after it was made. Otherwise one might have the result that a contract meant one thing the day it was signed, but by reason of subsequent events meant something different a month or a year later.

In the later case of *Schuler A.G. v Wickman Machine Tool Sales*[24] Schuler A.G. ("Schulers") had appointed Wickman Machine Tool Sales ("Wickmans") as their United Kingdom distributor for panel presses made by them. Based on Clause 7(b) of the contract it was "a condition" of the agreement that Wickmans had to send their representatives to visit certain motor manufacturers at least once a week to solicit orders for the panel presses. Several communications exchanged between the parties following the execution of the contract seemed to evidence an understanding that in case of material breach of the visiting obligation Schulers would have a right to terminate if Wickmans failed to remedy such breach within 60 days of notice being given. Schulers then terminated the contract on the ground that clause 7(b) was a condition which entitled them to terminate the contract for any breach, however minor. Both the Court of Appeal and the House of Lords (the case was first arbitrated) rejected this argument. Lord Denning MR said:

> The arbitrator . . . found that Schulers intended the use of the word 'condition' in clause 7(b) to have the effect that a failure by Wickmans to make a single visit by the scheduled representative would entitle Schulers to treat the agreement as at an end. But the arbitrator also found that Wickmans did not share Schulers' intention and would not have signed the agreement had they supposed that the use of the word 'condition' had that effect. So the evidence was not helpful, save to show that we must go by the reasonable interpretation of the words, and not by any supposed common intent.

Thus, the current position under English law is that what is done and said after a construction contract is entered into cannot be legitimately used as an aid in the construction of that contract, even in case the contract or a part thereof is ambiguous. Any subsequent conduct may not have any relevance to the interpretation of the contract, unless it gives rise to an estoppel or new binding contract.

31.2.2.5 Commercial common sense

When the terms of a contract are ambiguous and one construction would lead to an unreasonable result, the court will be unwilling to adopt such a construction[25] and may

24 *Schuler A.G. v Wickman Machine Tool Sales* [1974] AC 235 at 252, 255, HL.
25 *Dodd v Churton* [1897] 1 QB 562 at [566].

construe the contract in a way which is consistent with the business common sense. In *Antaios Compania Naviera SA v Salen Rederierna AB*[26] Lord Diplock held:

> If detailed and syntactical analysis of words in a commercial contract is going to lead to a conclusion that flouts business common sense it must yield to business common sense.

In *Mannai Investment Co v Eagle Star Life Assurance*[27] Lord Steyn said:

> Words are . . . interpreted in the way in which a reasonable commercial person would construe them. And the standard of the reasonable commercial person is hostile to technical interpretations and undue emphasis on niceties of language.

In *Investors Compensation Scheme Ltd v West Bromwich Building Society*[28] Lord Hoffman clarified that:

> The meaning which a document (or any other utterance) would convey to a reasonable man is not the same thing as the meaning of its words. The meaning of words is a matter of dictionaries and grammars; the meaning of the document is what the parties using those words against the relevant background would reasonably have been understood to mean. The background may not merely enable the reasonable man to choose between the possible meanings of words which are ambiguous but even (as occasionally happens in ordinary life) to conclude that the parties must, for whatever reason, have used the wrong words or syntax. . . . The 'rule' that words should be given their 'natural and ordinary meaning' reflects the common sense proposition that we do not easily accept that people have made linguistic mistakes, particularly in formal documents. On the other hand, if one would nevertheless conclude from the background that something must have gone wrong with the language, the law does not require judges to attribute to the parties an intention which they plainly could not have had. Lord Diplock made this point more vigorously when he said in The Antaios Compania Neviera S.A. v Salen Rederierna AB 19851 AC 191, 201: '. . . if detailed semantic and syntactical analysis of words in a commercial contract is going to lead to a conclusion that flouts business commonsense, it must be made to yield to business commonsense'.

The issue was also discussed in the case of *Chartbrook Ltd v Persimmon Homes Ltd*[29] which related to the development of a building site in Wandsworth. The dispute arose over the amount of a payment due by the developer to the landowner under a schedule to the contract. In construing the clause defining such payment the House of Lords departed from the literal interpretation of that clause, so reversing the majority decision of the Court of Appeal. In doing so, Lord Hoffmann stated that:

> There is no dispute that the principles on which a contract (or any other instrument or utterance) should be interpreted are those summarised by the House of Lords in Investors Compensation Scheme Ltd v West Bromwich Building Society [1998] 1 WLR 896, 912–913. They are well known and need not be repeated. It is agreed that the question is what a reasonable person having all the background knowledge which would have been available to the parties would have understood them to be using the language in the contract to mean. The House emphasised that 'we do not easily accept that people have made linguistic mistakes, particularly in formal documents' . . . but said that in some cases the context and background drove a court to the conclusion that 'something must have gone wrong with the language'. In such a case, the law did not require a court to attribute to the parties an intention which a reasonable

26 *Antaios Compania Naviera SA v Salen Rederierna AB* [1985] AC 191.
27 *Mannai Investment Co Ltd v Eagle Star Life Assurance Co Ltd* [1997] AC 749, HL.
28 *Investors Compensation Scheme Ltd v West Bromwich Building Society* [1998] 1 WLR 896.
29 *Chartbrook Ltd* v *Persimmon Homes Ltd* [2009] UKHL 38, [2009] 1 AC 1101.

> person would not have understood them to have had. . . . All that is required is that it should be clear that something has gone wrong with the language and that it should be clear what a reasonable person would have understood the parties to have meant.

In *Rainy Sky SA v Kookmin Bank*,[30] which concerned the construction of a bank guarantee, the Court of Appeal limited the role of business common sense in the construction of contracts. Lord Clarke clarified that where the parties have used unambiguous language, the court must apply such language. He said:

> The language used by the parties will often have more than one potential meaning. I would accept the submission made on behalf of the appellants that the exercise of construction is essentially one unitary exercise in which the court must consider the language used and ascertain what a reasonable person, that is a person who has all the background knowledge which would reasonably have been available to the parties in the situation in which they were at the time of the contract, would have understood the parties to have meant. In doing so, the court must have regard to all the relevant surrounding circumstances. If there are two possible constructions, the court is entitled to prefer the construction which is consistent with business common sense and to reject the other.

Rainy Sky confirms that having regard to the commercial purpose of the agreement is not conditional upon the court concluding that a particular construction will produce an absurd or irrational result. Where the language of the contract is capable of more than one construction and the court is called to resolve the question of what a reasonable person would have understood the parties to mean and may adopt the interpretation which is most consistent with business common sense.

In *Arnold v Britton*[31] Lord Neuberger stated the following principles of contractual interpretation:

> 17. First, the reliance placed in some cases on commercial common sense and surrounding circumstances (eg in Chartbrook, paras 16–26) should not be invoked to undervalue the importance of the language of the provision which is to be construed. The exercise of interpreting a provision involves identifying what the parties meant through the eyes of a reasonable reader, and, save perhaps in a very unusual case, that meaning is most obviously to be gleaned from the language of the provision. Unlike commercial common sense and the surrounding circumstances, the parties have control over the language they use in a contract. And, again save perhaps in a very unusual case, the parties must have been specifically focussing on the issue covered by the provision when agreeing the wording of that provision.
>
> 18. Secondly, when it comes to considering the centrally relevant words to be interpreted, I accept that the less clear they are, or, to put it another way, the worse their drafting, the more ready the court can properly be to depart from their natural meaning. That is simply the obverse of the sensible proposition that the clearer the natural meaning the more difficult it is to justify departing from it. However, that does not justify the court embarking on an exercise of searching for, let alone constructing, drafting infelicities in order to facilitate a departure from the natural meaning. If there is a specific error in the drafting, it may often have no relevance to the issue of interpretation which the court has to resolve.
>
> 19. The third point I should mention is that commercial common sense is not to be invoked retrospectively. The mere fact that a contractual arrangement, if interpreted according to its natural language, has worked out badly, or even disastrously, for one of the parties is not a reason for departing from the natural language. Commercial common sense is only relevant

30 *Rainy Sky SA v Kookmin Bank* [2011] UKSC 50; [2011] 1 WLR 2900 at [21].
31 *Arnold v Britton* [2015] UKSC 36; [2015] AC 1619 at [17] – [20].

> to the extent of how matters would or could have been perceived by the parties, or by reasonable people in the position of the parties, as at the date that the contract was made. Judicial observations such as those of Lord Reid in Wickman Machine Tools Sales Ltd v L Schuler AG [1974] AC 235, 251 and Lord Diplock in Antaios Cia Naviera SA v Salen Rederierna AB (The Antaios) [1985] AC 191, 201, quoted by Lord Carnwath at para 110, have to be read and applied bearing that important point in mind.
>
> 20. Fourthly, while commercial common sense is a very important factor to take into account when interpreting a contract, a court should be very slow to reject the natural meaning of a provision as correct simply because it appears to be a very imprudent term for one of the parties to have agreed, even ignoring the benefit of wisdom of hindsight. The purpose of interpretation is to identify what the parties have agreed, not what the court thinks that they should have agreed. Experience shows that it is by no means unknown for people to enter into arrangements which are ill-advised, even ignoring the benefit of wisdom of hindsight, and it is not the function of a court when interpreting an agreement to relieve a party from the consequences of his imprudence or poor advice. Accordingly, when interpreting a contract a judge should avoid re-writing it in an attempt to assist an unwise party or to penalise an astute party.

The *Arnold* decision seems to depart from previous decisions, and to represent a return to the orthodox principle that the commercial common sense and surrounding circumstances should not undervalue the language of the contract. The language of the contract is therefore the main aspect courts should rely on when ascertaining the meaning of the contract as it would appear to a reasonable man. If the contract is not clearly written and contains "*drafting infelicities*" the court is not allowed to resort to common sense to correct such drafting errors. Commercial common sense can be used to ascertain how reasonable people in the position of the parties could have perceived the matter at the time the contract was made, but not to correct a term of the contract because it looks a very imprudent term in the light of commercial common sense. If a party were imprudent or poorly advised in relation to a term, a court would not be under a duty to relieve that party from the relevant consequences.

It is worth noting that in *Wood v Capita*[32] the Supreme Court dismissed the idea that the approaches taken in *Rainy Sky* and *Arnold* were incompatible. Lord Hodge observed that *Arnold* in fact confirmed *Rainy Sky* in that both approaches could coexist. He said that:

> where there are rival meanings, the court can give weight to the implications of rival constructions by reaching a view as to which construction is more consistent with business common sense. But, in striking a balance between the indications given by the language and the implications of the competing constructions the court must consider the quality of drafting of the clause (Rainy Sky para 26, citing Mance LJ in Gan Insurance Co Ltd v Tai Ping Insurance Co Ltd (No 2) [2001] 2 All ER (Comm) 299 paras 13 and 16); and it must also be alive to the possibility that one side may have agreed to something which with hindsight did not serve his interest: Arnold (paras 20 and 77). Similarly, the court must not lose sight of the possibility that a provision may be a negotiated compromise or that the negotiators were not able to agree more precise terms.

Lord Hodge agreed and held that:

> Textualism [adopted in Arnold] and contextualism [adopted in Rainy Sky] are not conflicting paradigms in a battle for exclusive occupation of the field of contractual interpretation. Rather,

32 *Wood v Capita Insurance Services Ltd* [2017] UKSC 24 at [11].

the lawyer and the judge, when interpreting any contract, can use them as tools to ascertain the objective meaning of the language which the parties have chosen to express their agreement. The extent to which each tool will assist the court in its task will vary according to the circumstances of the particular agreement or agreements.

Turning to the most recent case law, in *Palliser v Fate*[33] Andrew Burrows QC suggested that the modern approach to contract interpretation is that:

> The court must ascertain the meaning of the words used by applying an objective and contextual approach. The court must ask what the term, viewed in the light of the whole contract, would mean to a reasonable person having all the relevant background knowledge reasonably available to the parties at the time the contract was made (excluding the previous negotiations of the parties and their declarations of subjective intent). Business common sense and the purpose of the term (which appear to be very similar ideas) may also be relevant. Important cases recognising the modern approach include Investors Compensation Scheme Ltd v West Bromwich Building Society, HL, especially at 912–913 (per Lord Hoffmann giving the leading speech), and Rainy Sky SA v Kookmin Bank. The Supreme Court in Arnold v Britton clarified that the words used by the parties are of primary importance so that one must be careful to avoid placing too much weight on business common sense or purpose at the expense of the words used; and one must be astute not to rewrite the contract so as to protect one of the parties from having entered into a bad bargain. In Wood v Capita Insurance Services Ltd, at [14], Lord Hodge, with whom the other Supreme Court Justices agreed, said that there was no inconsistency between the approach in Rainy Sky and that in Arnold v Britton: 'On the approach to contractual interpretation, Rainy Sky and Arnold were saying the same thing'.

31.2.2.6 Considering the document as a whole

In interpreting a construction contract, the courts shall examine the whole instrument before construing any individual part thereof. The agreement should be constructed in line with its language and in a way that will best effectuate the intention of the parties, which is to be collected from the whole agreement.[34] This means that a court must look at the contract's main purpose and may reject words if they are inconsistent with what it assumes to be the main purpose of the contract.[35]

31.2.2.7 Blanks

Where a material part of a contract is left completely blank evidence will not be admissible to fill those blanks. In *Kemp v Rose*[36] the parties omitted to include in the contract the date from which liquidated damages were supposed to run. The oral evidence before the court as to the agreed completion date was contradictory. The court then refused to fix such a date and held that liquidated damages were not payable. The court suggested that if oral evidence was clear (or agreed), and the omission was explained as an "oversight", then the court may grant rectification so to give effect to the parties' intentions and allow liquidated damages to be recoverable.

33 *Palliser Ltd v Fate Ltd & Ors* [2019] EWHC 43 (QB).
34 *Ford v Beech* [1848] 11 QB 852 at [866].
35 *Glynn v Margetson & Co.* [1893] AC 351 at [357].
36 *Kemp v Rose* [1858] 32 LT, (OS) 51.

In *Temloc Ltd v Errill Properties*[37] the parties had entered into a contract for the development of a shopping centre in Plymouth pursuant to the JCT Standard Form of Building Contract (1980 edition). The parties had inserted "£nil" in clause 24.2 of the appendix of the contract relevant to liquidated damages. The Court of Appeal held that no damages would be recoverable for delayed completion (be they liquidated or unliquidated). This also considering that the employer conceded that the sum "£nil" was entered as a "bonus" to incentivise timely completion. The court held that:

> I think it clear, both as a matter of construction and as one of common sense, that if (1) clause 24 is incorporated in the contract and (2) the parties complete the relevant part of the appendix, either by stating a rate at which the sum is to be calculated or, as here, by stating that the sum is to be nil, then that constitutes an exhaustive agreement as to the damages which are, or are not, to be payable by the contractor in the event of his failure to complete the works on time.

31.2.2.8 Deleted words

Construction contracts for large and complex projects are usually heavily negotiated. During the various exchanges of comments between the parties, terms are amended, deleted and/or replaced. Where the parties use printed forms which show deletions, the courts which are called to interpret the contract shall decide what bearing, if any, such deleted words shall have on the contract and the parties' positions. There are two schools of thought as to how courts should deal with deleted words:[38]

(i) One school of thought is that courts shall not consider deletions at all. As the parties have clearly expressed the intention to exclude a specific term from their agreement, that term shall be treated as if it has never formed part of the concluded contract, so that it may not be used to construe other terms. This view was accepted in several cases,[39] including the case of *A&J Inglis v John Buttery & Co.*[40] relevant to a shipbuilding contract. During the contract negotiations the term "*but if any new plaiting is required, the same is to be paid for extra*" was deleted from the contract. When a dispute arose between the shipowner and the contractor the former rejected any liability for the new plaiting. The House of Lords observed that once removed deleted words cease to exist for all intent and purposes. Lord Gordon noted that:

> It is quite fixed, and no more wholesome or salutary rule relative to written contracts can be devised, that where parties agree to embody, and do actually embody, their contract in a formal written deed, then in determining what the contract really was and really meant a Court must look at the formal deed and to that deed alone.

37 *Temloc Ltd v Errill Properties* [1987] 39 BLR 30.

38 S. Furst QC, V. Ramsey QC, *Keating on Building Contracts* (7th edition) Sweet & Maxwell, 2001, at para 45.

39 *Ambatielos v Jurgens* [1923] AC 175 at 185, HL; *M.A. Sassoon & Sons v International Banking Corp* [1927] AC 711 at 712, PC; *City & Westminster Properties* [1934]; *Ltd v Mudd* [1959] Ch. 129; *Prenn v Simmonds* [1971] 1 WLR 1381; *HL. Compania Naviera Termar v Tradax Export* [1965] 1 Lloyd's Rep 198 at [204]; *Ben Shipping v An-Boad Bainne* [1986] 2 Lloyd's Rep 285 at [291]; *Wates Construction v Franthom Property* [1991] 53 BLR 23, CA.

40 *A&J Inglis v John Buttery & Co.* [1878] 3 App Cas 552, HL.

Similarly, Lord Blackburn noted that deleted sentences, being part of prior negotiations, cannot be resorted for interpretation of a particular term of a contract as the formal contract supersedes all previous communications between the parties.

(ii) The other school of thought is that deleted terms are part of the surrounding circumstances which courts are allowed to look at to solve any ambiguity in words retained in the contract. A court could then use such words as a construction aid (e.g., to infer that the parties directed their minds to the specific question) or to negate the implication of terms inconsistent with the deletion. In *Mottram Consultants Ltd v Bernard Sunley and Sons Ltd*[41] Lord Cross of Chelsea said:

> When the parties use a printed form and delete parts of it one can, in my opinion pay regard to what has been deleted as part of the surrounding circumstances in the light of which one must construe what they have chosen to leave in. The fact that they deleted (iii) shows that these parties directed their minds (inter alia) to the question of deductions under the principle of *Mondel v Steel* [(1841) 8 M. and W. 858] and decided that no such deductions should be allowed.

Such conflicting authorities and the question of whether it is permissible to have regard to deleted words in construing a contract were considered in *Mopani Copper Mines Plc v Millennium Underwriting Ltd.*[42] Having listed the various conflicting authorities on the subject[43] the court expressed the view that:

> The tenor of the authorities appears to be that in general such recourse is illegitimate, save that (a) deleted words in a printed form may resolve the ambiguity of a neighbouring paragraph that remains; and (b) the deletion of words in a contractual document may be taken into account, for what (if anything) it is worth, if the fact of deletion shows what it is the parties agreed that they did not agree and there is ambiguity in the words that remain. This is classically the case in relation to printed forms (Mottram Consultants, Timber Shipping, Jefco Mechanical Services), or clauses derived from printed forms (Team Service), but can also apply where no printed form is involved (Punjab National Bank Ltd).

The judge also mentioned that support for that view may be found in the then current edition of *Keating* on *Building Contracts* which contained the following passage:

> In this confusion the second school is generally to be preferred. Where parties have made a contract in a document that contains deletions, to look at the deletions does not offend the principle discussed above which prevents reference to preliminary

41 *Mottram Consultants Ltd v Bernard Sunley and Sons Ltd* [1975] 2 Lloyd's Rep 197.

42 *Mopani Copper Mines Plc v Millennium Underwriting Ltd* [2008] EWHC 1331 (Comm).

43 See [100] to [120] where the judge cites the following cases: *Louis Dreyfus & Cie v Parnaso Cia Naviera S.A. "The Dominator"* [1959] 1 QB 499, 513; *Inglis v Buttery* [1878] 3 App Cas 552; *Sassoon (MA) & Sons Ltd v International Banking Corp* [1927] AC 711; *Baumvoll Manufactur Von Scheibler v Gilchrest & Co* [1892] 1 QB 253 and *Caffin v Aldridge* [1895] 2 QB 648; *City and Westminster Properties (1934) Ltd v Mudd* [1959] Ch 129; *Compania Naviera S.A. v Tradax Export S.A.* [1965] 1 Lloyd's Rep 198, 204; *Mottram Consultants Ltd v Sunley (Bernard) & Sons Ltd* [1975] 2 Lloyd's Rep 197, 209; *Timber Shipping Co S.A. v London & Overseas Freighter Ltd* [1972] AC 15; *The Golden Leader* [1980] 2 Lloyd's Rep 573 Lloyd; *Jefco Mechanical Services v London Borough of Lambeth* 24 BLR 1; *The C Joyce* [1986] 2 Lloyd's Rep 285; *Wates Construction v Frantham Property* [1991] BLR 23; *Punjab National Bank Ltd v de Boinville* [1992] 1 WLR 1138; *Team Service Plc v Kier Management and Design Ltd* (1993) 63 BLR 76; *Rhodia Chirex v Laker Vent Engineering Ltd* 2004 BLR 75, 84.

> negotiations. The deletion is physically contained in the concluded contract. It is submitted that the court should first construe the retained words. If they are unambiguous, reference to the deletion is unnecessary. If they are ambiguous, reference to deletions from printed documents should be permitted to see whether objectively they throw light on the meaning of the retained words.

Deleted words could then be used to a limited extent for construction purposes. However, the judge admonished that courts must be very careful in drawing inferences from deleted words as it could be the case that the parties:

> have deleted the words because they thought they added nothing to, or were inconsistent with, what was already contained in the document; or because the words that were left were the only common denominator of agreement, or for unfathomable reasons or by mistake. They may have had different ideas as to what the words meant and whether or not the words that remained achieved their respective purposes.

Interestingly, the judge also reported the following words of Morgan J in *Berkeley Community Villages Ltd v Pullen*:[44]

> Even in the cases where the fact of deletion is admissible as an aid to interpretation, there is a great difference between a case where a self contained provision is simply deleted and another case where the draft is amended and effectively re-cast. It is one thing to say that the deletion of a term which provides for "X" is suggestive that the parties were agreeing on "not X"; it is altogether a different thing where the structure of the draft is changed so that one provision is replaced by another provision. Further, where the first provision contains a number of ingredients, some assisting one party and some assisting the other, and that provision is removed, it by no means follows that the parties intended to agree the converse of each of the ingredients in the earlier provision.

It is worth noting that the use of printed forms in the case of complex construction contracts would be unusual. The parties may use contract forms (e.g., FIDIC forms) as a starting point of their negotiations. However, nowadays construction contracts are usually negotiated through the exchange of comments via email. The parties use writing programmes with functions allowing them to keep track of the various revisions made to the draft contract so to make aware the other party of the proposed changes. When the parties eventually agree on the final acceptable version of the contract, they will then "accept" all the revisions and have a clean document which may be then executed. However, there may be cases in which deleted words remain visible in the contract after execution. This may be due to last second amendments or merely to distractions. In such cases, the courts will face issues not dissimilar from the ones described for the case of deletions in printing documents and, possibly, apply the same rules and reasoning.

31.2.2.9 Written words prevail

Where the parties have inserted or filled clauses in writing on a printed contract, and such clauses are inconsistent with the printed words, the written words will prevail over the printed. The rationale is that written words reflect the selection of language and terms

44 *Berkeley Community Villages Ltd v Pullen* [2007] EWHC 1330.

made by the parties to express their meaning.[45] This is unless the printed form expressly states that printed words should prevail, in which case, to the extent the printed words are sufficiently clear, they will prevail.[46] Cases like this are not frequent in the case of contracts for large construction projects. However, it may happen that the parties agree to amend in writing what they considered the final version of their contract right before the contract's signature, but do so without re-reading the whole contract to check whether the new terms may generate inconsistencies.

31.2.2.10 Ejusdem generis rule

This "ejusdem generis" rule dictates that where words of a particular class are followed by general words, the general words shall be treated as referring to matters in the same class (for example, where a force majeure clause contains an express list of force majeure events such as war, riots, flood, epidemic, etc. followed by general words such as "*or any other causes beyond the parties' control*" or a specific category of events such as "*flood, drought, earthquake*" followed by general words for the specific category such as "*or other natural disaster*"). The ejusdem generis rule would normally mean that words of the particular class will guide the court's interpretation of the general words.[47] However, the courts may not always take this position. In *Chandris v Isbrandtsen-Moller Co Inc*[48] Devlin J said:

> The ejusdem generis rule means that there is implied into the language which the parties have used words of restriction which are not there. It cannot be right to approach a document with the presumption that there should be such an implication.

In *Tandrin Aviation Holdings Ltd v Aero Toy Store LLC*,[49] in deciding whether a force majeure clause applied to the "*cataclysmic downward spiral of the world's financial markets*" Mr Justice Hamblen stated that:

> The phrase 'any other cause beyond the Seller's reasonable control' should be read in the context of the entire clause. The specific instances of force majeure in the preceding words are as follows: 'act of God or the public enemy; war; insurrection or riots; fires; governmental actions; strikes or labour disputes; inability to obtain the aircraft materials, accessories; equipment or parts from the vendors'. Whilst there is no requirement to construe the phrase 'any other cause beyond the Seller's reasonable control' ejusdem generis with those earlier specific examples, it is telling that there is nothing in any of those specific examples of force majeure in cl.7.17 which is even remotely connected with economic downturn, market circumstances or the financing of the deal.

This means that a court may consider the specific instances of force majeure in the preceding words as laid out before the general words and determine their effect on the entire clause without necessarily construing the general words ejusdem generis with the specific preceding words.

45 *Robertson v French* [1803] 4 East 130.

46 *Gold v Patman & Fotheringham* [1958] 1 WLR 697 at [701].

47 See, for example, *Sonat Offshore SA v Amerada Hess Development and Texaco (Britain)* [1988] 1 Lloyd's Rep 145.

48 *Chandris v Isbrandtsen-Moller Co Inc* [1949] 83 Ll L Rep. 385 at [392]. See also *Navrom v Callitsis Ship Management SA* [1987] 2 Lloyd's Rep 276.

49 *Tandrin Aviation Holdings Ltd v Aero Toy Store LLC* [2010] EWHC 40.

31.2.2.11 Contra proferentem

The contra proferentem rule requires that where words of a contract are ambiguous or uncertain, the courts should choose the meaning that is less favourable to the party putting the clause forward and relying upon it. The case of *John Lee & Son (Grantham) Ltd v Railway Executive*[50] gives an idea of when the rule applies:

> We are presented with two alternative readings of this document and the reading which one should adopt is to be determined, amongst other things, by a consideration of the fact that the defendants put forward the document. They have put forward a clause which is by no means free from obscurity and have contended . . . that it has a remarkably, if not extravagantly, wide scope and I think that the rule contra proferentem should be applied.

It is worth noting that in the case of complex construction contracts the parties are typically large corporations of equal bargaining power. This gives the contra proferentem rule a limited role in such contracts. In *Persimmon Homes Limited & ors v Ove Arup & Partners Ltd & anr*[51] the Court of Appeal held:

> The contra proferentem rule requires any ambiguity in an exemption clause to be resolved against the party who put the clause forward and relies upon it. In relation to commercial contracts, negotiated between parties of equal bargaining power, that rule now has a very limited role.

He then noted how Lord Neuberger MR had summarised the position in *K/S Victoria Street v House of Fraser (Stores Management) Ltd*[52] where he said that:

> Quite apart from raising abstruse issues as to who is the proferens (and, in particular, whether the issue turns on the precise facts of the case or hypothetical analysis), 'rules' of interpretation such as contra proferentem are rarely decisive as to the meaning of any provisions of a commercial contract. The words used, commercial sense, and the documentary and factual context, are, and should be, normally enough to determine the meaning of a contractual provision.

A similar approach was recently taken in *Transocean Drilling UK Ltd v Providence Resources PLC*[53] where the Court of Appeal held that the contra preferentem rule will not apply where there is no ambiguity and where the clause in question:

> favours both parties equally, especially where they are of equal bargaining power.

Moreover, the rule would not apply where the parties use standard contracts (e.g., FIDIC, ICE or JTC forms of contract). In *Tersons Ltd v Stevenage Development Corporation*[54] a dispute arose out of the ICE conditions (2nd edition). Tersons Ltd ("Tersons"), the contractors, argued that since the conditions had been included in the invitation to tender

50 *John Lee & Son (Grantham) Ltd v Railway Executive* [1949] 2 All ER 581 at [584].

51 *Persimmon Homes Ltd and others v Ove Arup & Partners Ltd and another* [2017] EWCA Civ 373 at [52] – [53].

52 *K/S Victoria Street v House of Fraser (Stores Management) Ltd* [2011] EWCA Civ 904; [2012] Ch 497 at [68].

53 *Transocean Drilling UK Ltd v Providence Resources PLC* [2016] EWCA Civ 372.

54 *Tersons Ltd v Stevenage Development Corporation* [1963] 5 BLR 54.

sent by Stevenage Development Corporation ("SDC"), they should be interpreted contra proferentem the employer and in favour of the contractors. The court rejected this argument. Pearson LJ stated that:

> [Counsel] has contended that the maxim verba fortius accipiuntur contra proferentem should be applied in this case in favour of the contractor against the corporation on the ground that the general conditions were included in the invitation to tender sent by the corporation to the contractor. In my view, the maxim has little, if any, application in this case. The general conditions are not a partisan document or an 'imposed standard contract' as that phrase is sometimes used. It was not drawn up by one party in its own interests and imposed on the other party. It is a general form, evidently in common use, and prepared and revised jointly by several representative bodies including the Federation of Civil Engineering Contractors. It would naturally be incorporated in a contract of this kind, and should have the same meaning whether the one party or the other happens to have made the first mention of it in the negotiations.

The contra proferens rule is particularly relevant in the context of exemption and indemnity clauses. In *Canada Steamship Lines Ltd v The King*[55] Canada Steamship Lines ("Canada") had leased a dock (which included a freight shed) in the Port of Montreal from the Crown. The lease contained: (i) an exemption clause stating that the claimant would not be liable for damages to goods which were stored in the shed; and (ii) a clause stating that the defendant had to maintain the shed and bear the relevant costs. While working for maintaining the shed, an employee of the defendant accidently generated a fire in the shed. This caused significant damage to the claimant. When the claimant sued the defendant, the latter asserted that based on the exclusion clause he had no liability. A dispute then arose on whether the clause excluded the defendant's liability for negligent acts of his employees. The Privy Council held that the exclusion clause was not worded clearly or widely enough to apply to liability for negligence. As a result, it did not exclude the appellant's claim. In doing so, Lord Morton set out the following three-step test to determine if exemption clauses and indemnity clauses effectively provide the protection sought by those in whose favour the clauses are included, i.e., the "*proferens*": (i) if the clause contains language which expressly exempts the person in whose favour it is made (i.e., the proferens) from the consequence of the negligence of his own servants, effect must be given to that provision; (ii) if there is no express reference to negligence, the court must consider whether the words used are wide enough, in their ordinary meaning, to cover negligence on the part of the servants of the proferens. If a doubt arises at this point, it must be resolved against the proferens; (iii) if the words used are wide enough for the above purpose, the court must then consider whether the head of damage may be based on some ground other than negligence. Such other ground must not be so fanciful or remote that the proferens cannot be supposed to have desired protection against it. Subject to this qualification, the existence of a possible head of damage other than that of negligence is fatal to the proferens even if the words used are prima facie wide enough to cover negligence on the part of his servants.

However, the test in *Canada Steamships* (in so far as they survive) are now more relevant to indemnity clauses. Moreover, since *Canada Steamship*, the courts have shown

55 *Canada Steamship Lines Ltd v The King* [1952] AC 192.

a preference for a more commercial approach and the rule has become a guideline rather than a strict rule.

31.2.2.12 Errors

Where the contract agreement contains an obvious error, a court will usually put a sensible meaning on it by correcting the error or interpreting it as if the error had been corrected.[56]

56 *Townsends (Builders) Ltd v Cinema News and Property Management Ltd.* [1982] 20 BLR 118.

PART SIX

CONTRACT EXECUTION

As soon as the negotiations are complete and the parties have an "execution version" of the construction contract ready to be signed, they will typically go through all the checks and formalities necessary to execute the contract. In this phase, the parties will typically go through several checks aimed at ensuring that their contract is valid and enforceable.

The first step is to identify if the other party has capacity to contract and if the signatory has the relevant authority to bind the company he is representing.

The second step is usually to agree on the form of the document ("simple contract" or "deed") and ascertain any required formalities. If the parties do not opt for a deed, they are not bound by any formalities. Provided that the essential components of a contract are present, a contract will be enforceable, even if agreed verbally or by conduct, although agreements made orally or by conduct should be avoided.

The third step would be to agree on whether and how the document will be signed. The options will typically be a traditional wet-ink signature applied to the original, hard copy (or copies, where the agreement is executed in "counterparts") of the document, or by electronic signature. This will depend on several aspects, including where the parties are located, the law applicable to e-signatures and the parties' preference in general.

DOI: 10.4324/9781003387718-38

CHAPTER 32

Capacity

32.1 Capacity in general

Before the contract is executed, each party should seek to ensure that the other party's signatory has the necessary capacity to contract, i.e., the power to bind himself by the contract which is being executed. This is a different thing from authority to contract, which is a person's authority to bind another person (legal or natural) by the contract which is being executed.

The general principle in relation to capacity to contract is that individual adults, companies, partnerships and other legal entities have the right to enter into contracts. However, certain categories of individuals are not regarded as having full capacity (e.g., undischarged bankrupts, minors and persons of unsound mind). As a result, any agreements entered into by such persons may be unenforceable.

In the case of complex construction projects, contracts are usually signed by companies' employees based on powers expressly given to them through powers of attorney which will typically expressly state the subject matter of any contract that such person may sign on behalf of the company and any limits thereof. For this reason, issues relating to the contractual capacity are uncommon.

32.2 Companies

Construction contracts for complex projects are typically entered into between legal persons (typically companies) and not natural persons. A famous definition of "company" was given by Lord Justice Lindley, according to whom:

> A company is an association of many persons who contribute money or monies worth to a common stock and employed in some trade or business and who share the profit and loss arising therefrom. The common stock so contributed is denoted in money and is the capital of the company. The persons who contribute to it or to whom it pertains are members. The proportion of capital to which each member is entitled is his share. The shares are always transferable although the right to transfer is often more or less restricted.

A company is a legal entity that is incorporated under the company law of the country in which it is established.[1] Once registered, a certificate of incorporation is issued by the local companies house. From that moment, the company has legal capacity and powers

1 For English companies, that would be the Companies Act 2006.

DOI: 10.4324/9781003387718-39

of an individual, which are generally exercised in line with its articles of association. Obviously, a company cannot function without natural persons acting as agents to the company. This was well explained in the seventeenth-century legal case of *Sutton's Hospital*[2] where Sir Edward Coke stated:

> A corporation aggregate of many is invisible, immortal, and rests only in intendment and consideration of the law; and therefore . . . cannot have predecessor nor successor. . . . They cannot commit treason, nor be outlawed, nor excommunicate, for they have no souls, neither can they appear in person, but by attorney. . . . A corporation aggregate of many cannot do fealty, for an invisible body cannot be in person, nor can swear . . . it is not subject to imbecilities, nor death of the natural body, and divers other cases.

A company enters into contracts through its agents, i.e., physical persons acting under the company's express or implied authority to contract on behalf of the company.[3]

Legal systems have different rules applying to the execution of documents. Under English law, these aspects are regulated in the Companies Act 2006. Historically, if a company incorporated under the Companies Act entered into a contract which was not within the scope of the objects as set out in its memorandum of association or without following the correct procedure for entering into a contract, the risk was that such contract could be held void for having been made "*ultra vires*" (i.e., "*beyond the powers*"). In *Ashbury Railway Carriage and Iron Co. Ltd v Riche*[4] the directors of Ashbury Railway Carriage and Iron Co. Ltd ("Ashbury") purchased a concession for building a railway in Belgium and contracted Riche to build the line. Ashbury's objects as set out in the company's memorandum were

> to make and sell, or lend on hire, railway carriages and wagons, and all kinds of railway plant, fittings, machinery and rolling stock; to carry on the business of mechanical engineers and general contractors; to purchase, lease, work and sell mines, minerals, land and buildings; to purchase and sell as merchants, timber, coal, metals, or other materials, and to buy any such materials on commission or as agents.

Riche brought an action against Ashbury for breach of contract. The action failed as the House of Lords held that the contract was *ultra vires*, and thus void. This was because the construction of a railway was distinct from "*rolling stock*". Thus, it was an act that the company had no power, in law, to do, and it would be so even if all the company's shareholders had expressed their approval in that respect.

This strict approach to *ultra vires* acts has changed, and the general position is now the one expressed in: (i) Section 39(1) of the Companies Act 200, according to which the validity of an act done by a company shall not be called into question on the ground of lack of capacity by reason of anything in the company's constitution;[5] and (ii) Section 40(1) of the Companies Act 2006,[6] according to which in favour of a person dealing with a company in good faith, the power of the directors to bind the company, or authorise others to do so, is deemed to be free of any limitation under the company's constitution.

2 *Sutton's Hospital* [1612] 77 Eng Rep 960.

3 Companies Act 2006 (UK) section 43(1).

4 *Ashbury Railway Carriage and Iron Co. Ltd v Riche* (1875) LR 7 HL 653. See also *Diggle v The London and Blackwall Railway Co* [1850] 3 Ex 442 [155 ER 193].

5 Section 39(1) of the Companies Act 2006.

6 Section 40(1) of the Companies Act 2006.

In addition, Section 40 (2)(b) of the Companies Act 2006 states that a person dealing with a company (i) is not bound to enquire as to any limitation on the powers of the directors to bind the company or authorise others to do so, (ii) is presumed to have acted in good faith unless the contrary is proved, and (iii) is not to be regarded as acting in bad faith by reason only of his knowing that an act is beyond the powers of the directors under the company's constitution.[7] However, this shall not affect: (i) any right of a member of the company to bring proceedings to restrain the doing of an action that is beyond the powers of the directors;[8] and (ii) any liability incurred by the directors, or any other person, by reason of the directors' exceeding their powers.[9]

It is easy to see why disputes on the validity of a company's actions are rare when a party to the contract is an English company or a company is established in a legal system which follows the same principles, which in fact apply to most modern company laws.

32.3 Joint ventures

In the case of particularly large, costly and complex projects employers or contractors may decide to join forces with peers. In particular: (i) employers may consider joining forces with peers where they are unable to secure financing for the project or where they seek to share costs and risks with other peers considering the amount at stake and the risk of failure deriving from the projects' complexity; (ii) contractors may consider joining forces as they may be unable to secure financing or to obtain the required bank guarantees. They may also be driven by the desire to share risks or increase their buying capacity. In some cases, they may lack the technical capacity required for the project. For example, the tender documents may require a particular expertise (e.g., where the tender documents require that the contractor shall do both the engineering and the construction works) or a track record on similar projects which a single the contractor may not possess. Sometimes the local law may require that contractors can only be awarded a contract in the country if they have a certain amount of local representation or use a certain percentage of local workforce (so-called local content) which they do not have available.

In such cases, employees or contractors may opt to carry out such projects together by creating an incorporated company just for the purpose (a so called special purpose vehicle or "SPV") or an unincorporated joint venture ("JV"). Incorporated SPVs are a legal entity separate from the relevant shareholders and may enter into construction contracts. Conversely, an unincorporated JV does not have a legal identity which is distinct from that of the relevant parties. The parties to a JV will typically formalise their legal relationship by entering into a joint venture agreement (sometimes also called a "consortium" agreement) regulating the JV partners' rights and obligations, including any procedure that the JV shall follow to enter into contracts with third parties (e.g., bid/no-bid procedures and authority to bind the JV). In the case of an unincorporated JV, each JV partner will typically enter into the contract separately from the JV and assume separate

7 Section 40(2)(b) of the Companies Act 2006.
8 Section 40(4) of the Companies Act 2006.
9 Section 40(5) of the Companies Act 2006.

rights and liabilities vis-à-vis the other parties. However, such rights and liability will then be internally regulated by the JV agreement.

32.4 Governments and local authorities

Governments and local authorities are generally allowed to enter into construction contracts. The Local Government Act 1972 provides that local authorities are required to make standing orders when they make contracts for the execution of works. Such orders aim at securing competition and regulate the tender process. In particular, Section 135 of the Local Government Act 1972 states:

(1) A local authority may make standing orders with respect to the making of contracts by them or on their behalf.

(2) A local authority shall make standing orders with respect to the making by them or on their behalf of contracts for the supply of goods or materials or for the execution of works.

(3) Standing orders made by a local authority with respect to contracts for the supply of goods or materials or for the execution of works shall include provision for securing competition for such contracts and for regulating the manner in which tenders are invited, but may exempt from any such provision contracts for a price below that specified in standing orders and may authorise the authority to exempt any contract from any such provision when the authority are satisfied that the exemption is justified by special circumstances.

(4) A person entering into a contract with a local authority shall not be bound to inquire whether the standing orders of the authority which apply to the contract have been complied with, and non-compliance with such orders shall not invalidate any contract entered into by or on behalf of the authority.

32.5 Partnerships

The parties to construction contracts relevant to complex projects are usually companies or government/local authorities. However, smaller projects may see as players people organised in a partnership. Section 1(1) of the Partnership Act 1890 describes a partnership as the relation which subsists between persons carrying on a business in common with a view of profit. A partnership may enter into a construction contract.

32.6 Unincorporated associations

Associations or societies are organisations different from companies and partnerships, who act together for a certain purpose.[10] An example is housing associations, which are largely involved as clients in the housing market in England. When the association is unincorporated,[11] they do not have legal personality[12] separated from their members.

10 S. Furst QC, V. Ramsey QC, *Keating on Building Contracts* (7th edition) Sweet & Maxwell, 2001, at [41].

11 If they are incorporated, they are considered to have legal identity separate from that of the members. Any contract entered into by such association will bind the association and not its members.

12 *Michael John Construction Ltd v Golledge* [2006] EWHC 71 (TCC) at [38].

Unincorporated associations cannot enter into construction contracts. As a result, if a member of the association enters into a contract on behalf of the association, he/she will be personally liable for any the relevant obligations.

32.7 Undischarged bankrupts

Under section 360(1) of the Insolvency Act 1986:

> The bankrupt is guilty of an offence if –
>
> (a) either alone or jointly with any other person, he obtains credit to the extent of the prescribed amount or more without giving the person from whom he obtains it the relevant information about his status; or
>
> (b) he engages (whether directly or indirectly) in any business under a name other than that in which he was [made] bankrupt without disclosing to all persons with whom he enters into any business transaction the name in which he was so adjudged.

Thus, if a contractor is bankrupt, such condition does not affect his capacity to enter into a construction contract per se. However, he will commit an offence if he commits one of two of the criminal offences described.

Construction contracts for complex projects will typically be between companies or government/local authority. As a result, issues relevant to the authority of undischarged bankrupts will be rare.

32.8 Mentally impaired persons

Under Section 2(1) of the Mental Capacity Act 2005:

> a person lacks capacity in relation to a matter if at the material time he is unable to make a decision for himself in relation to the matter because of an impairment of, or a disturbance in the functioning of, the mind or brain.

Traditionally, the common law was that a contract entered into by a person lacking mental capacity was void *ab initio*. It followed that a lunatic could claim his own insanity to avoid an obligation which he had undertaken. This rule has now changed. The present position is that a person may plea his own mental incapacity, in which case the impugned contract will become voidable, but only to the extent that the defendant has actual or constructive knowledge of the incapacity of his contractual counterparty.[13] In *Moulton v Camroux*[14] Pollock CB, in delivering the judgment of the Court of Exchequer Chamber, said that:

> the rule had in modern times been relaxed, and unsoundness of mind would now be a good defence to an action upon a contract, if it could be shown that the defendant was not of the capacity to contract and the plaintiff knew it.

---

13 However, under s. 7 of the Mental Capacity Act 2005: "*(1) If necessary goods or services are supplied to a person who lacks capacity to contract for the supply, he must pay a reasonable price for them. (2) 'Necessary' means suitable to a person's condition in life and to his actual requirements at the time when the goods or services are supplied*".

14 *Moulton v Camroux* [1849] 4 Exch 17.

In the recent case of *Fehily v Atkinson*[15] the High Court set out some important points of principle regarding a person's capacity to enter into a contract. In particular, Stephen Jourdan QC sitting as a Deputy High Court judge said as follows:

> First, in order to understand a proposed transaction, a person needs the mental capacity to recognise the issues that need to be considered, to obtain, receive, understand and retain relevant information, including advice, and to weigh the information (including that derived from advice) in the balance in reaching a decision: Masterman-Lister at [26], see also Cooper at [24], where Lady Hale said that, to be able to make a decision, a person must not only be able to understand the information relevant to making it but also be able to weigh that information in the balance to arrive at a choice.
>
> Second, the question of whether a person lacks capacity is issue specific, to be judged in relation to the particular decision or activity in question and not globally. A person may have sufficient capacity for one type of decision but not another. Some transactions are more complicated and important than others. E.g. a person may have sufficient capacity to instruct solicitors on the conduct of a personal injury action, but not to administer, even with advice, the large sum of money likely to be awarded as damages. A person may have sufficient capacity to decide to authorise someone else to deal with their property on their behalf, but not sufficient capacity to themselves make decisions about what should be done with that property. A person may have capacity to consent to a simple medical procedure but lack capacity to consent to a more complex one. A person may have capacity to conduct a modest personal injury claim but not a very substantial one: Re K, Masterman-Lister at [27 and 62], Sheffield City Council at [38–49], Burgin at [13].
>
> Third, the question may also be time specific, if a person's capacity varies over time. In that case, the court will need to consider the question of capacity in relation to specific times when decisions were required from the person asserting incapacity, taking into account the nature and complexity of those decisions: Haworth [43] and [55].
>
> Fourth, the question is whether the person had the ability to understand the transaction, not whether they actually understood it: Re Beaney at 773A-B, Haworth at [74]. In Manches v Trimborn (1946) 174 LT 344, Hallett J said: 'the question in a case of this kind is not whether the consent was accompanied by reason or deliberation, but whether the person was capable of exercising the reason and deliberation necessary for a true consent'. In Re Smith (Deceased); Kicks v Leigh [2014] EWHC 3926 (Ch), [2015] 4 All ER 329 at [27], Stephen Morris QC, sitting as a deputy High Court judge said: 'Thus the overall test is one of ability to understand, rather than actual understanding. If the maker of the gift does not in fact understand the transaction, in circumstances, where its general purport has not been fully explained, that does not establish lack of capacity. The test is whether he or she would have understood it, if the consequences had been fully explained'. Having said that, if the person did understand the transaction, then obviously they had capacity to understand it, so that evidence of their actual understanding may be highly relevant.
>
> Fifth, the fact that a person needs help in understanding the transaction does not prevent them from having the capacity to understand it. Few people have the capacity to manage all their affairs unaided, and whether they are capable of managing their property and affairs depends on whether they are capable of taking, considering, and acting upon appropriate advice. In a case where a person needs advice to enable them to understand the transaction, the question is whether they have: (1) the insight and understanding to realise that they need advice; (2) the ability to find an appropriate adviser and instruct them with sufficient clarity to get the advice; and (3) to understand and make decisions based on that advice: Masterman-Lister at [18] and [75].

15 *Fehily v Atkinson* [2016] EWHC 3069 (Ch). In this case, the High Court was asked to determine whether a person who had entered into an Individual Voluntary Arrangement (IVA), which subsequently failed, had the relevant mental capacity.

It is worth noting that there is no difference between incapacity caused by a mental condition and incapacity caused by intoxication. Section 3 of the Sale of Goods Act 1979 equally applies to minors and the persons who are mentally incompetent, also by reason of "drunkenness". The same rule would certainly apply also to persons intoxicated by drugs. A contract entered into by the intoxicated person would be considered not binding on that person (unless if he ratified upon such person coming to his senses[16]) where his lack of mental capacity was known to the other party.[17] Such contract would not be void but merely voidable.

32.9 Minors

Intuitively, issues relevant to the capacity of minors to enter into contracts for complex construction projects are rare. In England a minor is a person who is under the age of 18.[18] Minors do not have the necessary capacity to enter into contracts. A contract made by a minor with an adult will be binding on the adult, but not on the minor. The minor may however ratify such contract after attaining his majority by an act confirming the promise that he made when a minor.

There are three exceptions to the principle that minors are not bound by the contracts they enter into, which however do not seem relevant to construction contracts:

(i) The first exception relates to contracts for necessaries. A minor is bound to pay for necessaries supplied to him under a contract. The Sale of Goods Act 1979 s.3, re-enacting the Act of 1893, states that:

> where necessaries are sold and delivered to an infant (or minor) . . . he must pay a reasonable price therefor. 'Necessaries' in this section means goods suitable to the condition of life of such infant (or minor) . . . and to his actual requirements at the time of sale and delivery.

"Necessaries" are generally described as goods without which a person cannot reasonably exist. These include food, clothing, lodging, education or training in a trade and essential services. The "condition of life" of the minor is his social status and wealth. Where a contract for necessaries is entered into by a minor, he will be liable to pay only "a reasonable price" (i.e., not any agreed price) and only for goods "sold and delivered". However, the contract will not be binding if it contains harsh and onerous terms.[19]

(ii) The second exception relates to contracts of service. Minors are allowed to enter into a contract where they provide services, provided that the contract, taken as a whole, is manifestly for their benefit. In *Clements v London & North Western Railway*[20] a minor who was a railway servant, as a condition of his employment joined an insurance society to whose funds the railway company contributed,

---

16 *Matthews v Baxter* [1873] LR 8 Ex 132.

17 *Gore v Gibson* [1845] 13 M & W 621; 153 ER 260.

18 At common law, "infants", i.e., persons under the age of 21, had only a limited capacity to contract. The Family Law Reform Act 1969 reduced the age of majority to 18 and authorised the term "minor" as an alternative to "infant".

19 *Fawcett v Smethurst* (1914) 84 LJKB 473.

20 *Clements v London & North Western Railway* [1894] 2 QB 482.

and agreed to forgo any claims he might have under the Employers' Liability Act Employers' 1880. The court held that the contract was binding as it was for the infant's benefit.

(iii) The third exception applies where a minor acquires property with obligations attached to it, e.g., a leasehold, or shares in a company. In such case, the minor is bound to pay the rent or calls on the shares as long as he retains the subject.[21] In this case, the contract is voidable by the minor who may repudiate it any time during his minority or within a reasonable time thereafter. As to the actions that an adult may take in case he has contracted with a minor who has obtained property under a contract which is not enforceable against him, the Minors' Contracts Act 1987, s3, provides that:

> the court may, if it is just and equitable to do so, require the defendant to transfer to the plaintiff any property acquired by the defendant under the contract or any property representing it.

Section 2 of the Minors' Contracts Act 1987 also provides that a guarantee of a minor's contract is not unenforceable against the guarantor merely because the contract made by the minor is unenforceable against him on the ground that he is a minor. The section does not apply if the contract made by the minor is unenforceable against him for some other reason (e.g., misrepresentation or duress by the adult), in which case the guarantor will not be bound.

21 *London & North Western Railway v M'Michael* (1850) 5 Ex 114.

CHAPTER 33

Authority

The second aspect that the parties should check during the contract execution phase is whether the counterparty's proposed signatory has the necessary authority to bind the party he is signing the contract for.

33.1 Contracts signed "by" or "on behalf" of a company

According to Section 43 (1) of the Companies Act 2006 (the "Companies Act"), a contract may be made "by" a company or "on behalf of" a company. In particular:

(1) Under the law of England and Wales or Northern Ireland a contract may be made –

(a) by a company, by writing under its common seal,[1] or
(b) on behalf of a company, by a person acting under its authority, express or implied.

(2) Any formalities required by law in the case of a contract made by an individual also apply, unless a contrary intention appears, to a contract made by or on behalf of a company.

Section 44 (1) of the Companies Act states that:

(1) Under the law of England and Wales or Northern Ireland a document is executed by a company –

(a) by the affixing of its common seal, or
(b) by signature in accordance with the following provisions.

(2) A document is validly executed by a company if it is signed on behalf of the company –

(a) by two authorised signatories, or
(b) by a director of the company in the presence of a witness who attests the signature.

---

1 Under 45 section (1) and (2) of the Companies Act 2006, "[a] *company may have a common seal, but need not have one*" and "*[a] company which has a common seal shall have its name engraved in legible characters on the seal*".

DOI: 10.4324/9781003387718-40

(3) The following are "authorised signatories" for the purposes of subsection (2) –

(a) every director of the company, and
(b) in the case of a private company with a secretary or a public company, the secretary (or any joint secretary) of the company.

(4) A document signed in accordance with subsection (2) and expressed, in whatever words, to be executed by the company has the same effect as if executed under the common seal of the company.

Therefore, contracts may either be signed: (i) by the company by using its common seal or having them signed by "authorised signatories" as per Section 44 (2) and (3) of the Companies Act referred earlier; or (ii) on behalf of the company, by a person (or persons) having the relevant "authority".

Which of the two is more appropriate will depend on the factual circumstances and the type of agreement. Where a deed is not necessary or desirable the parties will typically have more leeway to decide whether to have the contract signed "by" or "on behalf" of their company. Clearly, having the document executed "by" the company is the safest method as it does not carry all the doubts on the correctness of, and the limits to the authority given by the company to the signatory person(s). On the other hand, the list of authorised signatories under section 44 of the Companies Act is somewhat restricted compared to the more flexible approach that section 43 of the Act provides for execution "on behalf of" the company. This may lead to "logistic" issues in case a company was to adopt the "by" method for all its contracts. If the contract is signed "on behalf" of a company by a person (or persons) with express or implied authority to sign, the best practice is to ensure that the signatories have authority by checking the company's articles of association to see if the transaction is compliant with the relevant provisions. However, a failure to follow internal rules and limitations about signing and delegated levels of authority is usually an internal matter which rarely results in an unenforceable contract.

It is also worth noting that, in case a contract is executed by a foreign company on the basis of the provisions of the Overseas Companies (Execution of Documents and Registration of Charges) Regulations 2009, the parties should consider that the relevant formalities may not be compliant with the laws of the country where the foreign company is incorporated. It is therefore advisable that a legal opinion from a lawyer qualified in the jurisdiction of the foreign company is obtained in order to confirm the validity of the proposed method of execution under the company's local law.

33.2 Authority in general

Authority to contract is the power of one person (the "agent") to bind another (the "principal") by a contract. Thus, an agent may be defined as someone who is given the authority to make one or more contracts with third parties in place and on behalf of the principal. This creates a twofold relation, one between principal and agent and the other between the principal and the third party.

Company employees engaged in the negotiation of construction contracts (e.g., contract managers) will not typically be authorised to execute the construction they have negotiated.[2]

2 *GPN Ltd v O2 (UK) Ltd* [2004] EWHC 2494 (TCC) at [27] and [31].

The power to execute construction contracts will normally rest with the board of directors. Boards will keep the power to authorise execution of construction contracts beyond a certain contract value or those presenting unusual risks (e.g., those providing for guarantees in favour of third parties). Where a contract is such that only the board may authorise execution, the board will usually grant express authority to contract on the company's behalf by way of a board resolution. Boards will also normally give a general power of attorney (or "POA") to chief executive officers ("CEO") authorising them to execute construction contracts with certain limitations (e.g., those up to a certain contract value). Where the POA given to the CEO allows it, the CEO may then subdelegate such general power to company's senior officers, again with limitations (for example, based on contract value). POAs may also be given for specific contracts, in which case the POA will identify: (i) the authorised signatory (or signatories) to whom the power is delegated. In this regard, it is advisable that authority is granted to more than one officer as this will avoid having to repeat the process in case the single signatory becomes unavailable for any reason; (ii) any limitations to authority. In case the content of the construction contract which is the subject matter of the POA is already agreed on, the POA may authorise execution of that specific document (e.g., attaching it to the POA). However, this may not be advisable in case the parties anticipate any last second amendments, although minor, as in this case a new POA may become necessary. For this reason, it is more common for such POAs to identify the construction contract by listing its main terms; (iii) any right to subdelegate the relevant power. When the POA is to the CEO, it is common to give a power to subdelegate. However, POAs relevant to specific contracts will not usually include a power to subdelegate.

The subject of authority is particularly important in the case of construction contracts for complex projects.

Where the construction contract is signed by a person on behalf of the company, the other party will normally check before signing that that counterparty's proposed signatory has the necessary authority to contract. This is not a strict requirement in case the signatory has apparent or ostensible authority. However, in the case of large and complex projects, it is always advisable to put in place a check that such apparent authority is in fact backed by actual authority given in writing. Such checks may be done by requesting evidence such as extracts of board minutes or POAs whereby the person was empowered to sign that specific contract or contracts falling within that specific category. Sometimes a party may also need to request evidence of external consents by third parties such as investors or lenders.

33.3 Actual authority and apparent authority

An agent may possess two types of authority, i.e., actual authority and apparent authority.

33.3.1 Actual authority

Actual authority is a legal relationship between the principal and agent created by an agreement to which the third party with whom the agent deals is not a party. Where such agreement between the agent and the principal is express (e.g., a resolution by the board of directors giving specific powers, expressly conferred by the principal to the agent to act on the principal's behalf on a certain matter, e.g., to appoint architects), a contract entered into between the agent, operating under actual authority, and a third party will be binding on, and create contractual rights and liabilities between the principal and the third party. In the case of *Freeman and Lockyer v Buckhurst Park Properties*[3] the court said that:

> An 'actual' authority is a legal relationship between principal and agent created by a consensual agreement to which they alone are parties. Its scope is to be ascertained by applying ordinary principles of construction of contracts, including any proper implications from the express words used, the usages of the trade, or the course of business between the parties. To this agreement the contractor is a stranger; he may be totally ignorant of the existence of any authority on the part of the agent. Nevertheless, if the agent does enter into a contract pursuant to the 'actual' authority, it does create contractual rights and liabilities between the principal and the contractor.

In that case, Mr Shiv Kumar Kapoor was appointed by the board of directors of Buckhurst Park Properties ("Buckhurst"), the defendant, to manage a land sale. Mr Kapoor was never appointed as managing director. However, he had throughout been acting as such in employing agents and taking other steps to find a purchaser for the estate. This was well known to the board. Mr Kapoor hired Freeman and Lockyer, the plaintiffs, as architects to obtain planning permission on the land. Such appointment was beyond the (actual) authority he was given by the board. The plaintiffs, Mr Freeman and Mr Lockyer, were not paid for the work on developing the real estate, so they brought an action against Buckhurst and Mr Kapoor. The Court of Appeal held that Buckhurst was bound to pay. Although Kapoor had no actual authority to employ the plaintiffs as architects, in doing so he was acting within the scope of his ostensible authority.

Obviously, where an agent enters into a contract in his own name, he will be bound by that contract of which he will be considered a party. In the case of *Sika Contracts Ltd v Gill*[4] an engineer acting as an agent had invited a contractor to quote for repair works at a property owned by its principal. The contractor provided the quote, which the engineer accepted, but without disclosing that he was acting as an agent. The court held that the engineer had contracted personally with the contractor and was responsible for payment to the contractor. An actual authority to enter into a contract may lead to an implied authority to do acts that are incidental to that contract, even if such authority was not expressly indicated in the actual authority.[5]

33.3.2 Apparent or ostensible authority

In the case of apparent or ostensible authority the power of an agent to legally bind the principal with a third party does not arise from an express authority conferred to the agent,[6] but from a representation made by the principal to the third party with whom the agent will deal.[7] The basic principle is that when the principal represents that the agent

3 *Freeman & Lockyer v Buckhurst Park Properties* [1964] 2 QB at [480].

4 *Sika Contracts Ltd v Gill* [1978] 9 BLR 11 at [17].

5 *CRJ Services Ltd v Lanstar Ltd* [2011] EWHC 972 (TCC) at [22].

6 It can both enlarge actual authority or create authority where no actual authority exists. See *First Energy (UK) Limited v Hungarian International Bank* [1993] BCLC 1409.

7 Apparent authority in fact refers to the authority of an agent as it appears to others. See *Hely-Hutchinson v Brayhead Ltd* [1968] 1 QB 549 at 583 [4].

has authority to represent him, the agent can commit the principal to contracts which are within the scope of the agent's authority. If that representation is acted upon by a third party who has relied upon it, it operates as an estoppel, meaning that the principal will be prevented from denying the existence of the agency and will be bound by the contract entered into on his behalf by the agent.

In *Freeman*[8] Lord Diplock said:

> An 'apparent' or 'ostensible' authority . . . is a legal relationship between the principal and the contractor created by a representation, made by the principal to the contractor, intended to be and in fact acted upon by the contractor, that the agent has authority to enter on behalf of the principal into a contract of a kind within the scope of the 'apparent' authority, so as to render the principal liable to perform any obligations imposed upon him by such contract. To the relationship so created the agent is a stranger. He need not be (although he generally is) aware of the existence of the representation but he must not purport to make the agreement as principal himself. The representation, when acted upon by the contractor by entering into a contract with the agent, operates as an estoppel, preventing the principal from asserting that he is not bound by the contract. It is irrelevant whether the agent had actual authority to enter into the contract. The representation which creates 'apparent' authority may take a variety of forms of which the commonest is representation by conduct, that is, by permitting the agent to act in some way in the conduct of the principal's business with other persons. By so doing the principal represents to anyone who becomes aware that the agent is so acting that the agent has authority to enter on behalf of the principal into contracts with other persons of the kind which an agent so acting in the conduct of his principal's business has usually 'actual' authority to enter into.

In *Freeman*[9] Lord Diplock also held that for the third party being able to enforce against a principal a contract entered into on behalf of the principal by an agent who had no actual authority, the third party shall establish:

(i) That a representation that the agent had authority to enter on behalf of the company into a contract of the kind sought to be enforced was made to him.
(ii) That such representation was made by a person or persons who had "actual" authority to manage the business of the company either generally or in respect of those matters to which the contract relates.
(iii) That he was induced by such representation to enter into the contract, that is, that he in fact relied upon it.

According to principles (i) and (ii), for apparent authority to exist the representation must come from the principal, not from the agent. In *Armagas Ltd v Mundogas SA*[10] the plaintiffs, Armagas Ltd. ("Armagas"), wanted to purchase a ship, the "Ocean Frost", from the defendants, Mundogas SA ("Mundogas"). They hired a broker to carry out the negotiations. The plaintiffs made the defendants aware that they wanted to let the ship back to the defendants on a three-year charterparty. However, the defendants were to be only available to enter into a one-year charterparty. The broker bribed the vice president of the defendants, who was carrying out the negotiations with the broker. As a result, the vice president signed a three-year charterparty as sought by the plaintiffs. The vice presi-

8 *Freeman & Lockyer v Buckhurst Park Properties* [1964] 2 QB at [480].
9 *Freeman & Lockyer v Buckhurst Park Properties* [1964] 2 QB.
10 *Armagas Ltd v Mudogas SA* [1986] AC 717.

dent also signed a one-year charterparty, leading the defendants to believe that their conditions had been accepted. When, after a year, the defendants returned the ship to the plaintiffs, the latter sought damages for breach of contract claiming that the defendant's vice president had implied or apparent authority to sign the three-year charterparty. The House of Lords, dismissing the appeal, held that the vice president had no authority to complete the charterparty agreement. The House of Lords stressed that for apparent authority to exist, the representation must come from the principal, not from the agent. In that case, the representation came from the vice president, while there was no representation of authority from the defendants that the vice president had the authority to enter into a three-year charterparty.

According to principle (3), the third party shall be induced by the principal's representation to enter into the contract and have relied upon it. It has been said that such a reliance should be reasonable.[11] However, such approach was challenged in *Thanakarn Kasikorn Thai Chamkat (Mahachno) v Akai Holdings Ltd (No 2)*[12] where the Hong Kong Court of Final Appeal (where Lord Neuberger sat as a non-permanent judge) accepted the position of one of the parties that reliance in the context of apparent authority does not need to be reasonable, but rather lack dishonesty or irrationality. This approach was followed in a number of subsequent English cases[13] until *the* Privy Council restated the traditional position in *East Asia Company Ltd v PT Satria Tirtatama Energindo.*[14] Although a decision of the Privy Council, such position was then cited in several subsequent English judgments.[15]

33.4 Authority of directors to bind the company

Section 40 (1) and (2) of the Companies Act provides that:

(1) In favour of a person dealing with a company in good faith, the power of the directors to bind the company, or authorise others to do so, is deemed to be free of any limitation under the company's constitution.

(2) For this purpose –

  (a) a person "deals with" a company if he is a party to any transaction or other act to which the company is a party,

  (b) a person dealing with a company –

    (i) is not bound to enquire as to any limitation on the powers of the directors to bind the company or authorise others to do so,

    (ii) is presumed to have acted in good faith unless the contrary is proved, and

11 *Marme v Natwest Markets Plc & Ors.* [2019] EWHC 366 (Comm); *Egyptian International Foreign Trade v Soplex Whole Supplies Ltd* [1985] 2 Lloyd's Rep 36.

12 *Thanakarn Kasikorn Thai Chamkat (Mahachno) v Akai Holdings Ltd (No 2)* [2010] HKCFA 63.

13 *Quinn v CC Automotive Group Ltd (t/a Carcraft)* [2010] EWCA Civ 1412.

14 *East Asia Company Ltd v PT Satria Tirtatama Energindo* [2019] UKPC 30.

15 *Ciban Management Corp v Citco (BVI) Ltd* [2020] UKPC 21 at [29]. But see also *Harbour Fund lll LP v Kazakhstan Kagazy Plc* [2021] EWHC 1128 (Comm) at [109–17] where the High Court applied the position in *Akai Holdings.*

(iii) is not to be regarded as acting in bad faith by reason only of his knowing that an act is beyond the powers of the directors under the company's constitution.

Therefore, third parties dealing in good faith with directors of a company are entitled to assume that the internal rules of the company on which behalf the directors act were complied with and are not required to enquire as to any limitation on such powers. However, this does not affect the general principle that ostensible authority cannot be relied on in case the third party dealing with an agent has actual knowledge of some limitation which prevents the authority from arising. Moreover, apparent authority may not be invoked if the third party is "put on enquiry" (i.e., when suspicious circumstances arise that would cause the third party to query the authority of the agent[16]). This will be the case where the third party is aware of the fact that the agent does not have actual authority. As said by *Lord Scott* in *Criterion Properties plc v Stratford UK Properties LLC*:

> If a person dealing with an agent knows that the agent does not have actual authority to conclude the contract or transaction in question, the person cannot rely on apparent authority. Apparent authority can only be relied on by someone who does not know that the agent has no actual authority. And if a person dealing with an agent knows or has reason to believe that the contract or transaction is contrary to the commercial interests of the agent's principal, it is likely to be very difficult for the person to assert with any credibility that he believed the agent did have actual authority. Lack of such a belief would be fatal to a claim that the agent had apparent authority.

It is worth noting that where a contract has been entered into by a purported agent who had no actual or apparent authority, the principal may choose to ratify the unauthorised agreement, in which case the principal and the third party will be bound by the contract.[17] Ratification may also be implicit by conscious and unequivocal conduct.

16 *Criterion Properties plc v Stratford UK Properties LLC* [2004] UKHL 28.

17 *Yona International Ltd v La Reunion Francaise SA* [1996] 2 Lloyd's Rep 84 at 103 and 106; *Sea Emerald SA v Prominvestbank* [2008] EWHC 1979 (Comm) at [102] – [103].

CHAPTER 34

Form and formalities

34.1 Form

34.1.1 Form in general

The general rule under English law is that no particular form or formalities are necessary to enter into a binding contract. A contract may be made in writing, orally, by conduct or any combination of the three.[1]

However, there are statutory exceptions providing that some contracts may only be validly executed by deed (or "under seal" or "speciality")[2] or in writing[3] or may only be evidenced by a written note or memorandum.[4]

There is no statutory requirement under English law that construction contracts for complex projects be executed in writing or as deeds. However, considering the complexity of such agreements it would be uncommon and risky not to reduce the parties' agreement in a written and comprehensive document. Moreover, although not a requirement under English law, employers may require that some agreements relevant to construction projects (such as guarantees, variations, assignments and, although more rarely, the whole construction contract) be executed as deeds.

34.1.2 Written and oral contracts

English law is based on the principle of freedom to contract. The general rule is that contracts can be made in writing or orally or by conduct (or a mix of the three). In the case of complex construction projects, agreements are normally made in writing.

1 E. McKendrick, *Goode on Commercial Law* (5th edition) LexisNexis, 2016, at para 3.29; *Halsbury's Laws of England* (2012) vol 22 (Contract) para 220.

2 E.g., a lease for more than three years as per sections 52, 54(2) of the Law of Property Act 1925.

3 E.g., bills of exchange and promissory notes as per sections 3(1) and 17(2) of the Bills of Exchange Act 1882; bills of sale as per the Bills of Sale Act 1878 (Amendment) Act 1883; consumer credit agreements as per the Consumer Credit Act 1974; contracts for the sale or disposition of an interest in land as per the Law of Property (Miscellaneous Provisions) Act 1989. The Interpretation Act 1978 defines "writing" to include "*typing, printing, lithography, photography and other modes of representing or reproducing words in a visible form*". Where the contract is represented on a screen (e.g., a desktop, laptop, tablet or smartphone) in a manner which enables a person to read its terms properly, it will be "in writing".

4 E.g., contracts of guarantee as per section 4 of the Statute of Fraud 1677 must be in writing, or evidenced by writing, and signed.

DOI: 10.4324/9781003387718-41

The parties shall be aware that written contracts may be validly created via email.[5] For example, in *Golden Ocean Group Limited v Salgaocar Mining Industries PVT Ltd and another*,[6] the Court of Appeal held that the exchange of various e-mails could lead to the conclusion of a binding agreement in writing for the purposes of the Statute of Frauds 1677.

Therefore, where a negotiation is carried out through rounds of e-mail exchanges whereby each party sends its comments to the other, the parties should consider that each of such exchange may constitute an offer or counteroffer to enter into a contract subject of being accepted. Where the contract is still subject to internal approvals, the party sending the proposed version of the contract should qualify the document as "subject to contract" and use clear wording to state that the communication and any relevant attachments are not intended to form an offer or a counteroffer capable of being accepted.

34.1.3 Deeds and "simple" agreements

As mentioned, there is no general requirement under English law that a construction contract be in the form of a deed. Despite that, it is common for the parties to agree that contracts or other ancillary documents be executed as deeds. The benefits of entering into deeds of agreement are that such documents are valid even when no consideration was given for the other party's promise (certain types of guarantees or variations may sometimes lack consideration) and may be enforced for 12 years from the date of the breach of the obligation contained in the deed[7] (contrary to simple contracts which may be enforced for six years from the date of the breach[8]). Such a longer limitation period means that employers have more time to make a claim for defects. As it may take several years for defects to become apparent, this feature may be particularly appealing for employers. For contractors, however, this means a longer period of uncertainty as to their exposure to warranty claims.

A validly executed deed must fulfil the requirements prescribed by Section 1 of the Law of Property (Miscellaneous Provisions) Act 1989:

(2) An instrument shall not be a deed unless –

(a) it makes it clear on its face that it is intended to be a deed by the person making it or, as the case may be, by the parties to it (whether by describing itself as a deed or expressing itself to be executed or signed as a deed or otherwise); and

(b) it is validly executed as a deed by that person or, as the case may be, one or more of those parties.

(2A) For the purposes of subsection (2)(a) above, an instrument shall not be taken to make it clear on its face that it is intended to be a deed merely because it is executed under seal.

(3) An instrument is validly executed as a deed by an individual if, and only if –

5 See *J Pereira Fernandes SA v Mehta* [2006] EWHC 813 (Ch), [2006] 1 WLR 1543 and *Golden Ocean Group Limited v Salgaocar Mining Industries PVT Ltd and another* [2012] EWCA Civ 265.

6 *Golden Ocean Group Limited v Salgaocar Mining Industries PVT Ltd and another* [2012] EWCA Civ 265.

7 Section 8 (1) of the Limitation Act 1980: "*An action upon a specialty shall not be brought after the expiration of twelve years from the date on which the cause of action accrued*".

8 Section 8 (1) of the Limitation Act 1980: "*An action founded on simple contract shall not be brought after the expiration of six years from the date on which the cause of action accrued*".

(a) it is signed –

(i) by him in the presence of a witness who attests the signature; or

(ii) at his direction and in his presence and the presence of two witnesses who each attest the signature; and

(b) it is delivered as a deed

(4) In subsections (2) and (3) above 'sign', in relation to an instrument, includes making one's mark on the instrument and 'signature' is to be construed accordingly.

(4A) Subsection (3) above applies in the case of an instrument executed by an individual in the name or on behalf of another person whether or not that person is also an individual.

Under Section 46 of the Companies Act 2006, a deed is validly executed for the purposes of Section 1 of the Law of Property (Miscellaneous Provisions) Act 1989 if it is duly executed and delivered as a deed. In addition to these statutory requirements, when a deed is by a company, it will be necessary to comply with any formality requirements in the company's constitution.

As mentioned, the deed must be signed in the presence of a witness. A party to a deed cannot be an attesting witness. This includes a person who is named in a document as being someone in whose favour an obligation is to be performed. Moreover, although not a statutory requirement, the standard and best practice is that the witness should be of adult age and independent. A spouse, a child or other family member can witness a person's signature (unless that person is a party to the document itself). It also is generally acceptable for an employee or director of a company who is a party to a deed to witness that party's signature. The witness must be in the physical presence of the signatory when they sign the document. The Law Commission identified that the statutory requirement that deeds be signed "*in the presence of a witness*" means physical presence of the witness when they actually sign the document. This was confirmed in the case of *Man Ching Yuen v Landy Chet Kin Wong*.[9] In this case, a deed was signed by the parties personally at a meeting that took place in Hong Kong. The respondent's solicitor, who acted as a witness for both parties' signatures, attended the meeting via Skype from London. She received a hard copy of the deed a few days later, which she signed as a witness. The two issues were brought to the attention of the court where: (i) whether the deed was valid although the witness was not physically present at the time the parties signed it; and (ii) whether the fact that the witness attested the deed only some days later somehow affected the validity of the deed. On the first issue, the court found that, considering the Law Commission's conclusions regarding the necessary formalities for execution of a deed, a witness' remote presence via video-link or similar would not suffice. On the second issue, the court held that, based on *Wood v Commercial First Business Ltd*,[10] a witness is not required to sign the deed in the presence of the party or the parties whose signature is being attested, so that signing some days later is acceptable.

It is worth noting that, according to Section 47 of the Companies Act 2006 where a deed is executed by attorney on behalf of a company, the power of attorney shall be executed as a deed.

9 *Man Ching Yuen v Landy Chet Kin Wong* [2020] First Tier Tribunal (Property Chamber) 2016/1089.

10 *Wood v Commercial First Business Ltd (In Liquidation)* [2019] EWHC 2205 (Ch).

Where the parties opt for a deed, they must be sure that the formalities referred earlier are complied with. If such requirements are not met the contract will not be a deed, although it may still be binding as a simple contract. However, where the deed was used to have a valid contract despite a lack of consideration, a deed which has not been executed correctly will not be binding as a simple contract. In this case, the parties may be left with no written agreement at all. This may lead to arguments on whether an agreement was in fact reached and on what terms, and may have serious consequences, for example in case of funded projects, where lenders may be unwilling to provide any funding for the project as their ability to recover under the construction documents in the event the project does not go as expected is compromised.

34.2 Formalities

34.2.1 Signature

Under English law signature is not a requirement for contracts to be binding on the parties. In *Balfour Beatty Regional Construction Limited v Van Elle Ltd*[11] Balfour Beatty Regional Construction Limited ("Balfour Beatty") was the main contractor for the design and construction of a sub-sea cable manufacturing facility in Newcastle upon Tyne. Balfour Beatty engaged Van Elle Ltd ("Van Elle") as a subcontractor to carry out the foundational piling. Van Elle carried out part of its scope ("the Northern Carousel") prior to the parties signing a formal subcontract. Balfour Beatty claimed remedial costs against Van Elle arguing that part of their works was defective and asked to be indemnified for any resulting liability that Balfour Beatty may have vis-à-vis the employer. Van Elle argued that the works relevant to the North Carousel were carried out before the parties signed the subcontract. As a result, the agreement between the parties was contained in the written quotation that Van Elle had sent to Balfour Beatty before carrying out that part of the scope, which incorporated Van Elle's standard terms of business. Among such terms, there were several limitations of Van Elle's liability, Balfour Beatty had implicitly accepted such terms by allowing Van Elle to commence the relevant works. The Technology and Construction Court rejected Van Elle's argument that the North Carousel works were governed by the written quotation that Van Elle had sent to Balfour Beatty. According to the court, the works on the North Carousel were regulated by the subcontract, although the parties had not signed it at the time Van Elle had commenced such works.

Despite it not being a legal requirement, having contracts signed is a widespread practice in the construction industry. This is even more so in the case of complex or mega construction projects where the amounts at stake and the general complexity of the contractual terms make signature a valuable means to reduce disputes. This result is attained as signature serves a number of significant scopes. The first advantage of having a construction contract signed is its personal authentication.[12] In the case of *Goodman v J Eban Ltd*[13] the Master of the Rolls clarified that:

---

11 *Balfour Beatty Regional Construction Limited v Van Elle Ltd* [2021] EWHC 794 (TCC).

12 *Pereira Fernandes SA v Mehta* [2006] EWHC 813 (Ch), [2006] 1 WLR 1543 at [29]; *Golden Ocean Group Ltd v Salgaocar Mining Industries PVT Ltd* [2012] EWCA Civ 265, [2012] 1 WLR 3674 at [32].

13 *Goodman v J Eban Ltd* [1954] 1 QB 550, 557.

> The essential requirement of signing is the affixing in some way, whether by writing with a pen or pencil or by otherwise impressing upon the document, one's name or 'signature' so as personally to authenticate the document.

Other substantial benefits of having construction contracts signed include: (i) identifying the author or sender of the document; (ii) showing the parties' intention to be legally bound by the terms of the contract; or (iii) confirming that the signatory has notice of the contents of the contract[14] and accepts it.

34.2.2 Wet-ink signature and e-signature

Under English law, there is no prescribed form of signature. According to the "*2016 practice note on the execution of a document using an electronic signature*" (the "2016 Electronic Signatures Practice Note"):

> The test for determining whether or not something is a signature is whether the mark which appears in a document was inserted in order to give, and with the intention of giving, authenticity to it.

Therefore, the parties are free to agree on the way they intend to execute their contracts. In general, they may either opt for a traditional "wet-ink" signature or an electronic signature (or "e-signature").

34.2.2.1 Wet-ink signature

A "wet ink" signature is the conventional execution practice of having the two parties in the same room "wet ink" signing the same original contract (or more original copies, when signature is in counterparts).

A wet-ink signature would normally indicate the full name of the person signing the document. However, this is not a strict requirement and the English courts have considered as valid signatures expressed with an "X"[15] or initials,[16] stamps of handwritten signatures,[17] printed names,[18] marks[19] and even mere descriptions of the signatory, provided they were sufficiently unambiguous.[20]

The practice of wet-ink signing documents has the intuitive advantage of simplifying contracts' execution as it is considered the traditional, widespread and harmonised way to execute contracts. This is even more so when the wet-ink signatories are in the same room, as this will further reduce the scope of disputes.

This, however, may not always be achievable. For example, the signatories may be located in different countries, or be unwilling or unable to travel or to appoint a power of attorney, or face travel bans or other restrictions. In such situations, where the parties intend to opt for a wet-ink signature, the practice is to exchange the wet-ink signed

14 This function "*distinguishes a 'signature' from the mere writing of a name*". See *J. Pereira Fernandes SA v Mehta* [2006] EWHC 813 (Ch), [2006] 1 WLR 1543 at [26].

15 *Jenkins v Gaisford & Thring* [1863] 3 Sw & Tr 93.

16 *J Pereira Fernandes SA v Mehta* [2006] EWHC 813 (Ch), [2006] 1 WLR 1543 at [26].

17 *Goodman v J Eban LD* [1954] 1 QB 550 at [557].

18 *Brydges (Town Clerk of Cheltenham) v Dix* [1891] 7 TLR 215.

19 *Baker v Dening* [1838] 8 Ad & E 93.

20 *In re Cook* [1960] 1 All ER 689.

original via courier (usually in counterparts). However, this method may carry risks. At a minimum, the document may take a long time to reach the other party while, in the worst case, it may be lost by the courier, so forcing the parties to go through the process again.

34.2.2.2 E-signature

34.2.2.2.1 VALIDITY OF E-SIGNATURE

The term electronic signature includes a broad range of technologies that link an identifiable person to information held in electronic form.

The use of electronic signatures has accelerated as a result of the restrictions to movement and to gatherings imposed by the Covid-19 pandemic and is now routinely adopted in a wide range of commercial transactions, including contracts for complex construction projects. There are however some exceptions, such as where the parties intend to hold a physical meeting and execute a contract in person for publicity reasons.

There is no doubt that documents signed electronically are valid under English law. On 3 March 2020 the Lord Chancellor and Secretary of State for Justice issued a ministerial statement where he held that electronic signatures "*are permissible and can be used in confidence in commercial and consumer documents*".

The courts have confirmed that electronic signatures can be safely used to legally execute documents. In *J Pereira Fernandes SA v Mehta*[21] the court held:

> I have no doubt that if a party creates and sends an electronically created document then he will be treated as having signed it to the same extent that he would in law be treated as having signed a hard copy of the same document. The fact that the document is created electronically as opposed to as a hard copy can make no difference.

Construction contracts are no exception. They may be signed electronically provided that the person signing the document intends to authenticate the document and any execution formalities which may be required under a statute (or statutory instrument) or by agreement of the parties are satisfied.

However, while the use of e-signatures is safe in the case of internal transactions, for cross-border transactions with overseas parties e-signatures may carry the risk that a document wrongly signed may not be enforceable in the relevant jurisdiction. The issue shall be evaluated on a case-by-case basis, possibly by seeking legal advice from a local counsel.

34.2.2.2.2 LEGISLATIVE FRAMEWORK

The Regulation (EU) No 910/2014 of the European Parliament and of the Council of 23 July 2014 on electronic identification and trust services for electronic transactions in the internal market (eIDAS Regulation)[22] established an EU-wide legal framework for e-signatures and other trust services.

The eIDAS Regulation identifies three types of e-signatures: (i) simple electronic signatures (which is currently the most widely used in the UK), defined as "*data in*

21 *J Pereira Fernandes SA v Mehta* [2006] EWHC 813 (Ch), [2006] 1 WLR 1543 at 28. See also *Green (Liquidator of Stealth Construction Ltd) v Ireland* [2011] EWHC 1205 (Ch) at [44].

22 Repealing Directive 1999/93/EC.

electronic form which is attached to or logically associated with other data in electronic form and which is used by the signatory to sign"; (ii) advanced electronic signature (or "AES"), which are e-signatures that: (a) are uniquely linked to the signatory; (b) are capable of identifying the signatory; (c) are created using electronic signature creation data that the signatory can, with a high level of confidence, use under their sole control; and (d) are linked to the data signed therewith in such a way that any subsequent change in the data is detectable. To meet these requirements, most AES currently rely on public key infrastructure and involve a certificate authority as a trusted party to create, manage and store the relevant keys; and (iii) qualified electronic signatures (or "QES"), which are defined as "*an advanced electronic signature that is created by a qualified electronic signature creation device, and which is based on a qualified certificate for electronic signatures*".

Article 25(1) of the eIDAS Regulation provides that an electronic signature shall not be denied legal effect and admissibility as evidence in legal proceedings solely on the grounds that it is in an electronic form or that it does not meet the requirements for qualified electronic signatures.

Article 25(2) of the eIDAS Regulation states that a qualified electronic signature shall have the equivalent legal effect of a handwritten signature.

The Electronic Communications Act 2000 (the "ECA 2000") provides a statutory framework for the admissibility of electronic signatures in England and Wales. Section 7(1) of the ECA 2000 states that in any legal proceedings: (i) an electronic signature incorporated into or logically associated with a particular electronic communication or particular electronic data; and (ii) the certification by any person of such a signature, shall each be admissible in evidence in relation to any question as to the authenticity or integrity of the communication or data.

The United Kingdom left the European Union on 31 January 2020 as a result of Brexit. The eIDAS was then incorporated (with minor amendments) into UK domestic law on 31 December 2020 and became the UK eIDAS. The UK eIDAS: (i) removed references to "Member States"; (ii) repealed the electronic identification (e-ID) provisions of eIDAS Regulation so that the UK lost access to the interoperability framework for e-ID; and (iii) affected the legal framework allowing for mutual recognition of identification systems between Member States. Beyond these, the UK eIDAS substantially mirrors the eIDAS Regulation. In particular, Article 25 of UK eIDAS confirms that an e-signature cannot be denied legal effectiveness solely because of its electronic nature and that e-signatures are admissible as evidence in legal proceedings. Thus, QES remain the most secure type of electronic signature also under the UK eIDAS as, in addition to fulfilling the requirements of an AES, they require Qualified Trust Service Providers ("QTSP") accredited by the United Kingdom Accreditation Service ("UKAS") to issue a Qualified Certificate ("QC") aimed at verifying the identity of the holder, and to prove that he is both a real person and the same individual who has created the account. For this reason, QES are the only electronic signatures having the same legal effect as a handwritten "wet ink" signature, i.e., that carry a presumption of authenticity. However, neither AES nor QES are currently widely used to execute documents governed by English law as the parties to such contracts have shown a preference for simple electronic signatures.

34.2.2.2.3 SIGNATURE REQUIREMENT

For a document to be considered as validly e-signed and binding on the parties a signature should be present. In the case of *J Pereira Fernandes SA v Mehta*[23] the Court of Appeal was called to decide whether an unsigned email might be considered a written and signed memorandum or note as per section 4 of the Statute of Fraud 1677. The Portuguese company J Pereira Fernandes SA ("JPF") supplied some bedding products to Bedcare (UK) Limited ("Bedcare") in July 2002. Bedcare failed to pay for the products. As a result, JPF presented a winding up petition on 12 January 2005. On 20 February 2005, Mr Mehta, a director of Bedcare, asked a member of his staff to send an e mail to JPF's solicitors in the following terms:

> I would be grateful if you could kindly consider the following. If the hearing of the Petition can be adjourned for a period of 7 days subject to the following: (a) A Personal Guarantee to be given in the amount of £25,000 in favour of your client – together with a list of my personal assets provided to you by my solicitor (b) A repayment schedule to be redrawn over a period of six months with a payment of £5000.00 drawn from my personal funds to be made before the adjourned hearing. I am also prepared to give a company undertaking not to sell market or dispose of any company assets without prior consent from your client pending the signing of the Personal Guarantee.

The e-mail was not signed by Mr Mehta, but was described in the header as coming from Nelmehta@aol.com. This e-mail address appeared on other e-mails that Mr Metha had previously sent to JPF's solicitors, which he had signed. Mr Mehta did not honour the guarantee, saying that it was not enforceable as the email was not signed. He had not typed his name at the end of the email and his email address had been automatically inserted into the email header. JPF applied for summary judgment. The district judge concluded that the presence of Mr Mehta's e-mail address constituted a sufficient signature for the purposes of Section 4 of the Statute of Frauds 1677. As a result, he gave summary judgment to JPF in the sum of £24,985.53 and ordered Mr Mehta to pay the costs of the claim. Mr Metha appealed. The Court of Appeal had to decide: (i) whether the e-mail sent by Mr Metha constituted a sufficient note or memorandum of the alleged agreement for the purposes of Section 4 of the Statute of Frauds 1677; and (ii) assuming the e mail was a sufficient note or memorandum, whether it was sufficiently signed by or on behalf of Mr Mehta (i.e., whether the e-mail address included in the e-email could be considered a sufficient signature). As to the first point, the court held that:

> where (as in this case) there is an offer in writing made by the party to be bound which contains the essential terms of what is offered and the party to be bound accepts that his offer has been accepted unconditionally, albeit orally, there is a sufficient note or memorandum to satisfy Section 4 . . . the e mail referred to in Paragraph 3 above is capable of being a sufficient note or memorandum for the purpose of Section 4 because it is in writing, and it is not disputed by Mr Metha that the offer was accepted orally on behalf of JPF.

The judge observed that the e-mail was not signed by anyone in a conventional sense as Mr Mehta's name or initials did not appear at the end of the e-mail or anywhere else in the body of the e-mail. Moreover, the e-mail address at the top of the e-mail was inserted

23 *J Pereira Fernandes SA v Mehta* [2006] EWHC 813 (Ch), [2006] 1 WLR 1543.

automatically and not by the sender of the e-mail in any active sense. Therefore, it was not sufficient to act as authentication of the message. The court also cited *Caton v Caton*[24] where Lord Westbury said that:

> if a signature be found in an instrument incidentally only . . . the signature cannot have legal effect and force which it must have in order to comply with the statute, and to give authenticity to the whole of the memorandum.

As a result, the court concluded that the e-mail sent by Mr Metha did not bear a signature sufficient to satisfy the requirements of Section 4 of the Statute of Fraud 1677. As there was no signature, the guarantee was unenforceable.

In the similar case of *Golden Ocean Group Limited v Salgaocar Mining Industries PVT Ltd and another*[25] the Court of Appeal came to the opposite conclusion. The court had to consider a chain of e-mails between Golden Ocean Group ("GOG") and Trustworth Shipping ("TS") by which they agreed the charter of a vessel. At some point, the correspondence referred to the deal being "*fully guaranteed by*" an affiliate of Trustworth, Salgaocar Mining Industries Ltd ("SMI"). The e-mail in which the guarantee was included contained the name "Guy" (which was the name of Guy Hindley, SMI's broker). When TS repudiated the charterparty, GOG sought to recover from SMI under the purported guarantee. SMI contended that the guarantee was unenforceable under Section 4 of the Statute of Frauds 1677 as it was not an agreement in writing and it was not signed. The name Guy in the e-mail was only a salutation, and moreover one delivered in a "*matey*" or "*familiar fashion*". The Court of Appeal held that although brokers may communicate with one another in a familiar manner, that does not detract from the seriousness of the business they are conducting. The fact that Mr Hindley had included his name in the e-mail indicated that the communication was made under his authority, and that he intended to take responsibility for its contents. This was sufficient to meet the underlying requirement of Section 4 of the Statute of Frauds.

The conclusions in the judgments of *J Pereira* and *Golden Ocean* are not conflicting. The two cases differ in that, while in *J Pereira* the email was unsigned, in *Golden Ocean* the name of the sender was typed in the email. This confirms that it is only in case the email includes the name the document can be considered as showing the signatory's intention to enter into a legally binding relationship. This was confirmed in a number of subsequent judgments such as: (i) *Lindsay v O'Loughnane*,[26] where the judge suggested that an email needs to include a written indication of who is sending the email. This might include signing off with a name, title or even informally with just a forename; (ii) *Green (Liquidator of Stealth Construction Ltd) v Ireland*[27] where the High Court confirmed the distinction between merely having the sender's name in the header or "*from*" line of an e-mail and purposefully affixing one's name to the foot of the message; (iii) *Neocleous & Anor v Rees*,[28] where the High Court held that an automatic email sign-off was proof of signature, provided the automatic signature had the sender's name in the e-mail.

24 *Caton v Caton* [1867] LR 2 HL 127.
25 *Golden Ocean Group Limited v Salgaocar Mining Industries PVT Ltd and another* [2012] EWCA Civ 265.
26 *Lindsay v O'Loughnane* [2010] EWHC 529 (QB).
27 *Green (Liquidator of Stealth Construction Limited) v Ireland* [2011] EWHC 1305 (Ch).
28 *Neocleous and another v Rees* [2019] EWHC 2462 (Ch).

34.2.2.2.4 CATEGORIES OF E-SIGNATURE AND GENERAL GUIDELINES ON ELECTRONIC EXECUTION

There is not a single way to e-sign documents. Some types of e-signatures include, for example: (i) digital signatures based on a public key encryption system managed by a certification authority; (ii) scanned manuscript signatures, where a printed document is wet-ink signed, scanned and sent to the other party (e.g., via email or by uploading it in a shared file); (iii) typing of a name in an electronic communication (e.g., an e-mail); (iv) a digital representation of characteristics, for example, fingerprint or retina scan; (v) a signature created by cryptographic means; (vi) clicking an "*I accept*" tick box on a website;[29] or (vii) the header of a SWIFT message.[30]

The strength of each of them varies based on the type of technology. Aspects that the parties may consider when making a decision as to which form of electronic signature they should opt for are: (i) the level of security and reliability of the chosen technology (for example, the use of an electronic signature platform typically secure, resilient to fraud, and usually generating a tamper-proof completion certificate containing the signing information at the end of the process); (ii) how such technology may help them providing evidence of the signatory's identity and intention to authenticate the document (for example, a QES carries more evidentiary weight than a simple e-signature); (iii) the value of the transaction; (iv) whether the party has an internal policy of using a specific electronic signing platform; (v) whether amendments to the final version of the document may be required (e.g., an "accept and sign" option may create difficulties in case of last minute amendments); (vi) the size of the documents to be signed. In this regard, an electronic signing platform may create some issues. The documents to be signed are uploaded in a container called "envelop". Once all parties have signed the documents, the platform will generate a certificate of completion. The parties may then access such certificate to have information on the audit history of the transaction (documents, signers and other recipients, dates of signature, etc.). However, envelops usually have limits in terms of number of documents and megabyte size.

As there is no single source of law setting out the current English law position on electronic execution of documents, where contracts are executed in England, the parties may follow the various practice notes issued on the subject. In particular:

(i) In 2009, the Law Society Company Law Committee and The City of London Law Society Company Law and Financial Law Committees published a "*Note on execution of documents at a virtual signing or closing*"[31] (the "**2009 Note**") following *R (on the Application of Mercury Tax Group Limited and another v HMRC*,[32] a landmark case that highlighted the need for such guidance. The 2009 Note sets out the so-called Mercury Procedures addressed to "*solicitors who deal with execution of documents at virtual signings or closings where some or all of the signatories involved are not physically present at the same meeting . . .*

29 *Kathryn Bassano v Alfred Toft, Peter Biddulph, Peter Biddulph Ltd, Borro Loan Ltd, Borro Loan 2 Ltd* [2014] EWHC 37 (QB) at [43] and [44].

30 *WS Tankship II BV v Kwangju Bank Ltd and another; WS Tankship III BV v Seoul Guarantee Insurance Co; WS Tankship IV BV v Seoul Guarantee Insurance Co* [2011] EWHC 3103 (Comm) at [155].

31 Which was then amended in 2010 with minor updates.

32 *R (on the Application of Mercury Tax Group Limited and another v HMRC* [2008] EWHC 2721 (Admin).

where it is more convenient to have a virtual signing or closing and wet ink documents are not required for registration".

Paragraphs 6, 7 and 8 of the note identify three ways to execute documents through e-signatures when the parties are not present in the same room: (a) the first method is by e-mailing the final execution copies of the documents as a PDF or Word attachment) and, if convenient, a separate PDF or Word document containing the relevant signature page, to all absent parties and/or their lawyers (as agreed). Each absent signatory should then print and sign the signature page only (there is no need to print off the full document) and return a single e-mail to their lawyer or to the lawyers coordinating the signing/closing (as agreed) attaching both the final version of the PDF or Word document and a PDF copy of the signed signature page.[33] At or shortly after signing/closing, one of the law firms should circulate a final version of the document (together with copies of the executed signature pages) which will constitute an original signed document; (b) the second method is consistent with the first method, with the only difference that each absent party e-mails only its signed signature page as a PDF attachment to their lawyers or to the lawyers coordinating the signing/closing, giving authority to attach it to the final approved version of the document. This method is available for simple contracts and for guarantees (to the extent they are not deeds), but not also for deeds and real estate contracts; (c) the third method is by creating a pre-signed signature page in advance of finalising the document. The law firm coordinating the signing/closing should e-mail or circulate hard copies of the signature pages relating to the documents still being negotiated to each person who will not be present at the signing/closing or their lawyers. Each signature page should clearly identify the document to which it relates. Each of the signatories executes the signature page and returns it to their lawyers or to the law firm coordinating the signing/closing (as agreed), by e-mail (as a PDF attachment) or by courier. The document is then held to the order of the signatory or their lawyers, until authority is given for it to be attached to the document to be signed. When each document has been finalised, the law firm coordinating the signing/closing should e-mail the final version of the document to each absent party and/or their lawyers and obtain confirmation from them or their lawyers, that they have agreed the final version of the document and authorising the relevant law firm to attach the pre-signed signature page to the final version and to date and release the document. The final approved version of the document with the pre-signed signature pages, which have been attached with the prior approval of the parties or their lawyers,[34] will then constitute an original signed document. This method is available for simple contracts and for guarantees (to the extent they are not deeds), but not also for deeds and real estate contracts. As

33 In the case of a deed, the communication should either make clear when delivery is to take place or that it has not been delivered merely because it has been signed and the steps set out earlier followed.

34 According to Paragraph 3.4 of the 2009 Note, it is crucial that there is clear evidence, such as an exchange of e-mails, that the signatories, their lawyers or someone else authorised by the signatory have authorised the attachment of their signatures to the final version of the relevant contract. This will avoid any evidential concerns and show an intention to be legally bound, as well as ensuring the certainty of contractual terms.

to which option a solicitor should prefer, Paragraph 5 of the 2009 Note clarifies that the parties' solicitors should choose which option to follow at their own discretion and according to the facts of each transaction, but that, before choosing one of the options, they should have prior approval and cooperation of all the parties, consider relevant regulatory and tax implications, such as stamp duty, before deciding and avoid conflict with procedures or restrictions particular to certain documents, such as notarisation or escrow conditions. Factors to consider include countries of incorporation of the parties, each party's domestic rules and internal procedures for execution of contracts, the content of board resolutions, whether individual contracts must take effect in a particular sequence, and whether a legal opinion is being issued on a party's due execution of the documents.

(ii) In 2016, the Law Society published a "*Note on the execution of a document using an electronic signature*" (the "**2016 Note**"). Among other things, the 2016 Note clarifies that, for the case of simple contracts (i.e., those that are not required to be executed as deeds) there are no restrictions on the use of electronic signatures as such signatures satisfy the various tests that documents be executed "in writing" (the Interpretation Act 1978 defines "writing" to include "typing, printing, lithography, photography and other modes of representing or reproducing words in a visible form"; where the contract is represented on a screen, including a desktop, laptop, tablet or smartphone, in a manner which enables a person to read its terms properly, it will be "in writing" at that point) or "under hand" (a document is generally understood to have been executed under hand if it has been executed otherwise than by deed) or be "signed" (the test for determining whether or not something is a signature is whether the mark which appears in a document was inserted in order to give, and with the intention of giving, authenticity to it).

The 2016 Note also identifies the following ways to e-sign simple contracts, i.e., typing the person's name into a contract or into an email containing the terms of a contract, electronically pasting the person's signature (e.g., in the form of an image) into a soft copy version of the contract in the appropriate place (e.g., next to the relevant party's signature block), accessing a contract through a web-based electronic signature platform and clicking to have his or her name in a typed or handwriting font automatically inserted into the contract in the appropriate place (e.g., next to the relevant party's signature block), and using a finger, light pen or stylus and a touchscreen to write the person's name electronically in the appropriate place (e.g., next to the relevant party's signature block) in the contract. According to the 2016 Note English law governed documents may be signed using a combination of different methods provided that each party uses a valid signature method. Signing in counterpart may facilitate this. For example, a party could sign a counterpart with an image signature, while another party could sign a counterpart in wet ink. It is possible, depending on the facts, to have multiple originals of a document in both electronic and hard copy form where this does not conflict with other legal requirements. Where parties have signed in counterpart using a combination of signing methods, each counterpart would be an original.

Interestingly, the 2016 Note also clarifies some aspects of what constitutes the "original" when a document is executed electronically. In particular, according to the 2016 Note: (a) originals may be held in hard copy or electronic form, and the parties may create multiple originals; (b) where signature occurs through an electronic signature platform, the signatories who have signed the same document will each be deemed to have signed the same counterpart; (c) where a document has been signed by a combination of methods, a single "composite" original may be created; (d) where a document is undated, a date may be added electronically or through printing out and inserting the date by hand; (e) where an electronic or hard copy original has to be amended, the parties shall follow the same rules for amendments to wet-ink documents.

(iii) In 2019, the Law Commission published a report on the *Electronic Execution of Documents* (the "2019 Report"). The Law Commission confirmed that electronic signatures were valid for most business transactions and legal processes. Nevertheless the 2019 Report also acknowledged the various uncertainties around e-signatures which limited the confidence in their use and could hold back some parties from adopting them. The Report tries to summarise in a concise document the law relating to the validity of e-signatures, including confirmation that: (a) e-signature is capable of being used to validly execute documents and deeds; (b) a document will only be validly executed if the person signing it intends to authenticate the document and any formalities relating to execution are satisfied; (c) deeds must be signed in the physical presence of a witness attesting the signature (i.e., they may not attest signatures by viewing the signing on a screen or through an e-signature platform) even where both the person executing the deed and the witness use e-signatures to execute/attest the document.

(iv) In February 2022, the Industry Working Group on electronic execution, a multidisciplinary group of business, legal and technical experts established by the Government published a report (the "IWG Report") containing recommendations to promote and facilitate the electronic execution of documents. Among others, the IWG Report lists a number of best practice principles intended to "*enable parties to use electronic signatures in a way which best suits their specific requirements*". Those principles can be distilled into five high-level points: (a) agree as early as possible that a document is to be executed electronically and the procedure for doing so. Determine the optimal form of electronic signature for the transaction, and, in particular, which eIDAS category (Qualified, Advanced or Simple) is required. This should be a matter of user choice (depending on nature of parties/risk level/value/personal circumstances) and larger users should establish policies in relation to this; (b) where a signing platform is to be used, choose one that provides at least a minimum set of security/safety/functionality with a strong audit trail that demonstrates an intention to sign by the signatories. Such platforms should at the very least include the ability for signing parties to download/retain executed documents. In particular, storage (so-called shelf life of documents and their audit trail details) should be clearly identified by the signing platform to enable informed choice by signatories; (c) consider whether additional evidence to record the identity of the signatory and the fact that the signatory is approving the document and has the intention to be bound is necessary and/or appropriate, for example simultaneous video recording; (d) where possible, provide multiple options to vulnerable customers or counterparties so that these groups can adopt a method of signing that suits their needs; (e) intention to authenticate should be easier to demonstrate for those with secure digital identities, but the latter should not be essential.

(v) In October 2022, the Company and Financial Law Committees, with input from The Law Society Company Law Committee, issued a note (the "2022 Note") updating the 2016 Note to reflect the increasing use of e-signing platforms and the publication of the 2019 Report. Among other things, the 2022 Note (a) confirms the "Mercury Procedures" as set out in the 2009 Note; (b) confirms the requirement that witnesses be physically present when a signatory signs a deed; (c) suggests that companies formed under the Companies Acts should not to use an e-seal on electronic documents and should not substitute an e-seal for their corporate seal (although, in practice, very few companies now use a seal).

PART SEVEN

DEFENCES FOR NON-PERFORMANCE

Considering the complexity of the projects in question and the fact that the works usually are carried out through several years, this phase is typically characterised by a number of events which may affect the contract's performance or the project in its entirety.

As mentioned, under English law the parties are obliged to honour their contractual obligations. However, there are exceptions to the principle that "*pacta sunt servanda*". Where one of such exceptions occurs, the affected party's non-performance is excused and, depending on the circumstances, may be entitled to claim damages, extensions of time or, in the most extreme cases, bring the contract to an end.

DOI: 10.4324/9781003387718-42

CHAPTER 35

Misrepresentation, illegality, mistake and duress

35.1 Misrepresentation

35.1.1 Misrepresentation in general

A misrepresentation may be defined as an unambiguous false statement made before the contract is entered into whereby one party (the "representor") represents an existing or past fact, or law or both, to another party (the "representee") with an aim of inducing that party to enter into a contract, and which has the effect of inducing the representee to contract.

In the process of offer and acceptance, it is normal for the parties negotiating a construction contract to make statements relating to the contract which may affect the other party's decisions and choices. For example: (i) a contractor may represent that it has the necessary skills, expertise and structure to execute the scope of work of the contract; while (ii) an employer may represent that a project is buildable or that it has secured the funds that are necessary to develop the project.

A pre-contractual statement may be either a term or a representation. While a term is an integral part of an agreement, a representation is a pre-contractual statement made to encourage another party to enter into a contract, which, however, does not form part of that contract. Traditionally, the difference between a term and a representation related primarily to the type of relief available in case of breach. Where a statement had become a term of the contract, in the event of breach the aggrieved party had a remedy under a breach of contract. Conversely, an incorrect or untrue pre-contractual statement which had not become a term of the contract would entitle the aggrieved party to an action for misrepresentation. However, the Misrepresentation Act 1967 has now extended the right to claim misrepresentation and the remedy of rescission also to cases of misrepresentation relating to contractual terms. Section 1 (a) of the Misrepresentation Act 1967 states as follows:

> Where a person has entered into a contract after a misrepresentation has been made to him, and –
>
> (a) the misrepresentation has become a term of the contract; or
> (b) the contract has been performed;

DOI: 10.4324/9781003387718-43

> or both, then, if otherwise he would be entitled to rescind the contract without alleging fraud, he shall be so entitled, subject to the provisions of this Act, notwithstanding the matters mentioned in paragraphs (a) and (b) of this section.

35.1.2 Categories of misrepresentation

The consequences of a misrepresentation will be different depending on the state of mind of the representor. Based on this, a misrepresentation may be innocent, negligent or fraudulent.

35.1.2.1 Fraudulent misrepresentation

A fraudulent misrepresentation occurs when the false statement is made knowingly, or without belief in its truth, or recklessly, careless whether it be true or false.[1] A statement is made recklessly where the statement maker ignores whether the statement is true, but he nonetheless makes it as if it were certainly true.[2]

In this case, the representee does not need to prove dishonesty or fraud, but only that the representor made the statement without caring whether it was true. In the case of *Bradford Third Equitable Benefit Building Society v Borders*[3] a builder represented prospective home purchasers that they were the only builders in Great Britain who, by special arrangement with a leading building society, could offer certain financial conditions. However, the statement was knowingly false. Lord Maugham found the builders guilty of deceit. In his judgment he also set out four main facts which a plaintiff must show to establish a tort of deceit:

> First, there must be a representation of fact made by words, or, it may be, by conduct. The phrase will include a case where the defendant has manifestly approved and adopted a representation made by some third person. On the other hand, mere silence, however morally wrong, will not support an action of deceit. . . . Secondly, the representation must be made with a knowledge that it is false. It must be wilfully false, or at least made in the absence of any genuine belief that it is true. . . . Thirdly, it must be made with the intention that it should be acted upon by the plaintiff, or by a class of persons which will include the plaintiff, in the manner which resulted in damage to him. . . . If, however, fraud be established, it is immaterial that there was no intention to cheat or injure the person to whom the false statement was made. . . . Fourthly, it must be proved that the plaintiff has acted upon the false statement and has sustained damage by so doing.

Moreover, where a statement was true at the time it was made but it then becomes false after it is made, and the statement maker fails to inform the representee of this change in circumstances, such failure may result in a fraudulent misrepresentation (in case he is aware of his duty to notify the representee of the change[4]) or in a negligent misrepresentation (where he is not aware of his duty to notify the representee of the change[5]).

The usual remedies for a fraudulent misrepresentation are rescission of the contract and damages for deceit (common law) and under the Misrepresentation Act 1967, s.2 (1).

---

1 *Derry v Peek* [1889] 14 App Cas 337.
2 *Thomas Witter Ltd v TBP Industries Ltd* [1996] 2 All ER 573.
3 *Bradford Third Equitable Benefit Building Society v Borders* [1941] 2 All ER 205 (HL(E)).
4 *Banks v Cox* (No 2) unreported.
5 *With v O'Flanagan* [1936] Ch 575.

35.1.2.2 Negligent misrepresentation

A negligent misrepresentation occurs when the statement maker makes a false statement in the belief that it was true, but with no reasonable grounds for that belief (i.e., he was careless in reaching such conclusion).

Traditionally, only fraudulent misrepresentation was actionable at common law.[6] However, further to *Hedley Byrne & Co Ltd v Heller & Partners Ltd*[7] negligent statements which cause a pure economic loss became actionable in tort under the common law to the extent a duty of care could be established between the representor and the representee who relied on the farse representation. A duty of reasonable care and skill will typically arise from a "special relationship"[8] between the representor and the representee. In particular, this will be the case when there is an "assumption of responsibility"[9] on the part of the statement maker because he has special knowledge of the subject matter of the representation so that he can reasonably assume that the representee will rely on the representation. It will be irrelevant whether the statement maker is in fact an expert in the subject matter, provided that he holds himself as being an expert. The burden of proof is on the representee. The aggrieved party should prove that a duty of care existed, and that the representor breached it. The remedy available for negligent misrepresentation at common law is rescission.

As an alternative to a claim in tort, an aggrieved party may pursue its negligent misrepresentation claim under Section 2 (1) of the Misrepresentation Act 1967, which states as follows:

> Where a person has entered into a contract after a misrepresentation has been made to him by another party thereto and as a result thereof he has suffered loss, then, if the person making the misrepresentation would be liable to damages in respect thereof had the misrepresentation been made fraudulently, that person shall be so liable notwithstanding that the misrepresentation was not made fraudulently, unless he proves that he had reasonable ground to believe and did believe up to the time the contract was made the facts represented were true.

Moreover, under Section 2 (2) of the Misrepresentation Act 1967 a court has a discretion to refuse rescission and award damages in lieu. The burden of proof is reversed. Contrarily to a common law claim for negligent misrepresentation, it will be for the statement maker to establish that he was not negligent in making the statement, i.e., that he had reasonable grounds to believe the statement was true at the time it was made.[10]

35.1.2.3 Innocent misrepresentation

An innocent misrepresentation occurs when the representor makes a false statement, but he was not negligent in doing so as he honestly and reasonably believed the statement to be true. The usual remedies for an innocent representation are rescission of the contract, or damages in lieu of rescission under the Misrepresentation Act 1967, s.2 (2), while compensatory damages are not available at common law.

---

6 *Walker v Milner* [1866] 4 F&F 745 at [761].
7 *Hedley Byrne & Co Ltd v Heller & Partners Ltd* [1964] AC 465.
8 *Caparo Industries plc v Dickman* [1990] 2 AC 605.
9 *Henderson v Merrett Syndicates Ltd* [1995] 2 AC 145.
10 *Howard Marine & Dredging Co Ltd v A Ogden & Sons (Excavations) Ltd* [1978] QB 574.

35.1.3 Arguing misrepresentation

For there to be an actionable misrepresentation the following elements should be present.

35.1.3.1 Statement

A statement is something communicated to another party to express an opinion. Some of the principles applying to the subject are as follows:

- (i) A statement may be of fact, of law[11] or both.
- (ii) A statement may be made in writing, verbally or by conduct.[12] In *Walters v Morgan*[13] it was held that even a nod or a wink or a shake of the head or a smile may amount to a representation if they are aimed at inducing the other party to believe a certain set of facts.
- (iii) Where there is more than one statement, a court will usually give each episode separate consideration, but it will also have regard to their cumulative effect.[14]
- (iv) For there to be a statement it will be necessary that some kind of positive conduct be present. Silence or non-disclosure will not amount to a statement.[15] There are however exceptions, e.g.: (a) a half-truth (i.e., a deceptive statement which includes some element of truth) may be held to be a misrepresentation;[16] (b) where a statement is true at the time of making, but is rendered false by a change in circumstances, the statement maker has a positive duty to disclose the change by informing the receiving party.[17] However, this does not extend to a party's obligation to inform the other party that the latter is under a mistake which has not been induced by the act of the party that has remained silent;[18] and (c) in the case of the contracts so-called *uberrimae fidei* (i.e., "of the utmost good faith") such as insurance contracts, there is an implied duty on the parties to reveal any information which could reasonably be regarded as relevant for the other party.
- (v) A statement may only relate to the past or the present while a statement of future intention is not usually considered a statement of fact.[19] There is generally no duty to inform the other party of a change of intention[20] unless the

---

11 *Kleinwort Benson v Lincoln CC* [1999] 2 AC 349; *Pankhania v Hackney LBC* [2002] EWHC 2441 (Ch).

12 *Curtis v Chemical Cleaning & Dyeing co Ltd* [1951] 1 KB 805.

13 *Walters v Morgan* [1861] 3 De G.F. and J 718, 723.

14 *Spice Girls Ltd v Aprilia World Service BV* [2002] EWCA Civ 15.

15 *Fletcher v Krell* [1872] 42 LJQB 55.

16 See, e.g., *Nottingham Patent Brick and Tile Co. v Butcher* [1866] 16 QBD 778; *Dimmock v Hallett* [1866] LR 2 Ch App 21 (CA); *Banks v Cox (No.2)* [2000] Unreported; *Inntrepreneur Estates Ltd. v Hollard* [2000] Unreported (CA); *National Guild of Removers and Storers Ltd. v Bee Moved Ltd.* [2016] EWHC 3192 (IPEC); *Leni Gas and Oil Investments Ltd. v Malta Oil Pty Ltd.* [2014] EWHC 893 (Comm); *Burntcopper Ltd. (t/a Contemporary Design Unit) v International Travel Catering Association Ltd.* [2014] EWHC 148 (Comm).

17 *With v O'Flanagan* [1936] Ch 575. On this subject see also *Traill v Baring* [1864] 4 DJ & S 318; *Spice Girls Ltd. v Aprilia World Service BV* [2002] EWCA Civ 15 (CA).

18 *Bell v Lever Bros. Ltd.* [1932] AC 161 (HL) at p. 227. On this subject see also *Keates v The Earl of Cadogan* [1851] 10 CB 591 (Common Pleas); *Smith v Hughes* [1871] LR 6 QB, 597 (DC); *Sykes v Taylor-Rose* [2004] (Unreported) (CA).

19 In *Beattie v Lord Ebury* [1872] 7 Ch. App. 777, 804 Mellish LJ said that "*something will be done in the future, cannot either be true or false at the time it is made*".

20 *Wales v Wadham* [1977] 1 WLR 199.

statement only makes sense as a continuing representation as to the future.[21] However, where statement is made with absolutely no intention at the time of the statement, it may amount to a statement of fact as to the present state of mind of the person making the statement.[22]

(vi) A "mere puff", i.e., a statement favourably describing or extolling goods which by virtue of its vagueness or extravagance would not normally be regarded as something to be taken seriously or as grounding any form of liability,[23] will not normally amount to a misrepresentation.[24]

(vii) An uninformed statement of opinion or belief will not normally amount to a statement of fact[25] and, if false, will usually not be actionable as a misrepresentation. The statement maker is under no duty to carry out enquiries to assess whether the opinion is valid and inform the other party. What is relevant is whether the statement maker had skill and/or knowledge which put him in a better position to know the truth about the subject matter of the statement and whether the other party was aware of this. If the statement maker was in no better position, the statement will likely be considered an opinion rather than a statement of fact even if the statement was unreasonable.[26] There are exceptions in which an opinion may be regarded as a statement of fact, e.g.: (a) where the opinion is either not held or could not be held by a reasonable person with the speaker's knowledge. For example, in the case of *Smith v Land & House Property Corp*[27] the plaintiff trying to sell his hotel stating that it was let to a "most desirable tenant". The defendants agreed to buy the hotel, but then refused to complete the contract when they found out that the tenant was in fact bankrupt. When the plaintiff sued the defendants for specific performance, the Court of Appeal held that the plaintiff's statement was not a mere opinion, but a statement of fact; (b) where the person expressed an opinion which he does not in fact hold, the opinion is regarded as a statement of fact;[28] and (c) where the person giving the opinion has a special skill or experience in the subject matter on which he is giving his informed opinion.[29]

(viii) A court will assess objectively whether a representation has been made, i.e., looking at the impact that the statement may be expected to have on a

21 *Inntrepreneur Pub Co. v Sweeney* [2002] EWHC 1060 (Ch).

22 *Edgington v Fitzmaurice* [1885] 29 Ch D 459. See also *FoodCo UK LLP and others v Henry Boot Developments Ltd* [2010] EWHC 358 (Ch).

23 M.G. Bridge, *Benjamin's Sale of Goods* (10th edition) Sweet and Maxwell, 2017, at 10, s4. On this subject, see also *Magennis v Fallon* [1828] 2 Moll Rep 588; *Dimmock v Hallett* [1866] LR 2 Ch App 21 (CA); *Lichtenstein v Clube Atletico Mineiro* [2005] EWHC 130; *Fordy v Harwood* [1999] Unreported (CA); *Brewer v Mann* [2012] EWCA Civ 246.

24 *Magennis v Fallon* [1828] 2 Moll Rep 588; *Dimmock v Hallett* [1866] LR 2 Ch App 21 (CA); *Lichtenstein v Clube Atletico Mineiro* [2005] EWHC 1300; *Fordy v Harwood* [1999] Unreported (CA); *Brewer v Mann [*2012] EWCA Civ 246.

25 *Bisset v Wilkinson* [1927] AC 177; *Hummingbird Motors v Hobbs* [1986] RTR 726; *Springwell Navigation Corp v JPMorgan Chase Bank (formerly Chase Manhattan Bank)* [2010] EWCA Civ 1221.

26 *Hummingbird Motors Ltd v Hobbs* [1986] RTR 276.

27 *Smith v Land and House Property Corporation* [1884] 28 Ch D 7.

28 *Connolly Ltd v Bellway Homes Ltd* [2007] EWHC 895, [2007] ALL ER (D) 182.

29 *Esso Petroleum v Mardon* [1976] QB 801. See also *Smith v Land & House Property Corporation* [1884] 28 ChD 7 (CA).

reasonable person in the position and with the known characteristics of the actual representee.[30]

35.1.3.2 Unambiguously false

Statements triggering misrepresentation cases are rarely absolutely and completely false. The most common scenario is that a statement includes both false and true information. In such situations, a court may consider the representation true in as much as it is substantially correct.[31] This suggests that the court will look at the substance of the statement to assess how likely it would be that such statement could influence a reasonable person in the receiving party's position. Moreover, the element of falsity may also be found in case a party does not make what is normally considered a statement but takes active steps to deliberately[32] conceal a fact. For example, in the case of *Gordon v Sellico*[33] the Court of Appeal confirmed that the concealment of patches of dry rot in a flat by the estate agents would amount to a misrepresentation if such action was intended to, and had the effect of deceiving the other party, which would not have entered into the contract had he known the truth. This concept was summarised by Goulding J as follows:

> The law must be careful not to run ahead of popular morality by stigmatising as fraudulent every trivial act designed to make buildings or goods more readily saleable, even if a highly scrupulous person might consider it dishonest. But it is to my mind quite a different matter for an intending vendor to hide so sinister and menacing a defect as dry rot.

Moreover, for there to be an actionable misrepresentation, the false statement shall be unambiguous.[34] Thus, if the meaning of a statement is objectively ambiguous and the representee merely misinterprets it, this will not normally trigger an actionable misrepresentation. As stated by Lord Denning in *McInerny v Lloyds Bank Ltd.*:[35]

> No man is to be made liable for not making his meaning clear. If it were so, few of us would escape condemnation.

35.1.3.3 Made to another party intending to enter into a contract

Normally, for a misrepresentation to be actionable the statement should be made to the party that relies upon it and is eventually induced to enter into the contract. However, where a misrepresentation is made to a third party that "passes" it to the other contracting

30 *MCI WorldCom International Inc v Primus Telecommunications Inc* [2004] EWCA Civ 957) 3.

31 *Avon Insurance plc v Swire Fraser Ltd* [2000] 1 All ER (Comm) 573, [2000] CLC 665.

32 Although misrepresentation may be claimed also in case of negligent concealment of a material fact. See, e.g., *Pilbrow v Pearless De Rougemont & Co* [1999] 3 All ER 355 (CA).

33 *Gordon v Sellico* [1986] EGLR 71 (CA).

34 *Chocosuisse Union des Fabricants Suisse de Chocolat & Lindt & Suchard v Cadbury Ltd.* [1999] RPC 826 (CA). On this subject see also *British Broadcasting Corporation v Talk Sport Ltd.* [2001] FSR 6; *GMG Radio Holdings Ltd v Tokyo Project Ltd.* [2005] EWHC 2188; *Phones 4U Ltd. v Phone4U.co.uk Internet Ltd.* [2006] EWCA Civ 244; *L'Oreal SA et al v Bellure NV et al.* [2006] EWHC 2355; *Numatic International Ltd. v Qualtex Ltd.* [2010] EWHC 1237 (Ch); *Woolley v Ultimate Products Ltd.* [2012] EWCA Civ 103; *Fage UK Ltd. and Fage Dairy Industry SA v Chobani UK Ltd.* [2013] EWHC 630 (Ch); *Moroccanoil Israel Ltd. v Aldi Stores Ltd.* [2014] EWHC 1686 (IP Enterprise Court); *Walt Disney v Brightspark Productions Ltd.* [2012] Evening Standard, 6.11.2012; *Simon Cowell v Sharon Gallacher* (2013) Unreported; *Cranford Community College v Cranford College Ltd.* [2014] EWHC 2999 (IP Enterprise Court); *Fenty v. Arcadia Group Brands Ltd.* (t/a Topshop) [2015] 1 WLR 3291 (CA); *Comic Enterprises Ltd v Twentieth Century Fox Film Corp* [2016] EWCA Civ 41.

35 *McInerny v Lloyds Bank Ltd.* [1974] 1 Lloyd's Rep 246 (CA) at [254].

party that, relying on the misrepresentation, enters into the contract, then the representation will be actionable, to the extent the representor intended the false information to be used to induce the contracting party to enter into the contract.[36]

35.1.3.4 Reliance and inducement

A claim for misrepresentation will not succeed in case the representee did not rely upon the false statement (for example, because he relied upon his own information) and was not induced[37] to enter into the contract as a result of that statement[38] (i.e., where he would have entered into the contract regardless of the misrepresentation[39] or knew that the statement was false[40]). In *Francis v Knapper*[41] Andrew Baker J held:

> The essence of the wrongful conduct is making (or procuring the making of) a statement intended to be acted upon, knowing it to be untrue or having no belief in its truth. The tort of deceit protects claimants from the harmful consequences of statements made to them that ought never to have been made. For the claimant, therefore, the essence of the claim is that the making of a statement that ought not to have been made has caused him loss. Hence, it is the claimant's burden to show "that he acted in reliance on the defendant's misrepresentation. If he would have done the same thing in the absence of it, he will fail. What is relevant . . . is what the claimant would have done had no representation at all been made.

However, the representation does not have to be the sole reason why the representee resolved to enter into the contract. In general, it would be enough that it played a "*real and substantial part, though not by itself a decisive part*".[42]

Moreover, the statement should be such that the representee was intended, and was entitled, to rely on. In *Raiffeisen Zentralbank Osterreich AG v Royal Bank of Scotland Plc*[43] the court held that:

> It is also necessary for the statement relied on to have the character of a statement upon which the representee was intended, and was entitled, to rely. In some cases the statement in question may have been accompanied by other statements by way of qualification or explanation which would indicate to a reasonable person that the putative representor was not assuming a responsibility for accuracy or completeness of the statement or was saying that no reliance can be placed upon it. Thus the representor may qualify what might otherwise have been an outright statement of fact by saying that it is only a statement of belief, that it may not be accurate, that he has not verified its accuracy or completeness, or that it is not to be relied on.

It is for the representee to prove that he was induced by the misrepresentation. However, where the representee is able to establish that the misrepresentation was calculated so to induce him to enter into the contract, a presumption will be raised in the representee's

36 *Smith v Chadwick* [1884] 9 App Cas 187; *Cramaso LLP v Ogilvie-Grant* [2014] AC 1093.

37 Or, in the case of fraudulent misrepresentation, "was likely" to induce that person to enter into the contract. See *Fitzroy Robinson Ltd v Mentmore Towers Ltd* [2009] EWHC 1552 (TCC) at [111].

38 *Floods of Queensferry Ltd v Shand Construction Ltd* [2000] BLR 81 at [90].

39 *J.E.B. Fasteners Ltd. v Marks Bloom & Co* [1983] 1 All ER 583; *Welven Ltd. v Soar Group Ltd.* [2011] EWHC 3240 (Comm); *Leni Gas and Oil Investments Ltd. v Malta Oil Pty Ltd.* [2014] EWHC 893 (Comm).

40 *Redgrave v Hurd* (1881) 20 ChD 1 (CA); *Walsh v Staines* [2009] CP Rep 16 (CA); *Smith v Headline Publishing Group Ltd.* [2011] EWHC 2106 (Ch).

41 *Francis v Knapper* [2016] EWHC 3093 (QB)10.

42 *JEB Fasteners Ltd v Marks Bloom* [1983] 1 All ER 583 (CA), at [588–9]. See also *Francis v Knapper* [2016] EWHC 3093 (QB)10.

43 *Raiffeisen Zentralbank Osterreich AG v Royal Bank of Scotland Plc* [2010] EWHC 1392 (Comm), [2011] 1 Lloyd's Rep 123 at [86].

favour, and the burden of proof will shift on the representor. In *Redgrave v Hurd*[44] Sir George Jessel MR held that:

> If it is a material representation calculated to induce him to enter into the contract, it is an inference of law that he was induced by the representation to enter into it, and in order to take away his title to be relieved from the contract on the grounds that the representation was untrue, it must be shown either that he had knowledge of the facts contrary to the representation, or that he stated in terms, or showed clearly by his conduct, that he did not rely on the representation.

The test to prove inducement is a subjective one. The representee will need to establish that he relied on the statement, and not that a reasonable person would have been induced to enter the contract. In *Akerhielm v de Mare*,[45] Lord Jenkins said that:

> The question is not whether the defendant in any given case honestly believed the representation to be true in the sense assigned to it by the court on an objective consideration of its truth or falsity, but whether he honestly believed the representation to be true in the sense in which he understood it albeit erroneously when it was made.

However, in the same judgment Lord Jenkins added that this general proposition is subject to limitations:

> For instance, the meaning placed by the defendant on the representation made may be so far removed from the sense in which it would be understood by any reasonable person as to make it impossible to hold that the defendant honestly understood the representation to bear the meaning claimed by him and honestly believed it in that sense to be true.[46]

Obviously, there will not be reliance in case the representee was not aware of the misrepresentation at the time of the contract but became aware of it after the contract was entered into.[47]

35.2 Illegality

35.2.1 Illegality in general

Illegality may constitute a defence to contractual claims and excuse non-performance of contractual obligations.

A contract may be or become illegal for several reasons. These were summarised as follows by Lord Toulson in *Patel v Mirza*:[48]

> A contract may be prohibited by a statute; or it may be entered into for an illegal or immoral purpose, which may be that of one or both parties; or performance according to its terms may involve the commission of an offence; or it may be intended by one or both parties to be

44 *Redgrave v Hurd* [1881] 20 Ch D 1 (CA). See also *Leni Gas and Oil Investments Ltd. v Malta Oil Pty Ltd.* [2014] EWHC 893 (Comm).

45 *Akerhielm v de Mare* [1959] AC 789 (Privy Council, Eastern Africa) at [805]. See also *Smith v Chadwick* [1884] 9 App Cas 187.

46 *Akerhielm v de Mare* [1959] AC 789 (Privy Council, Eastern Africa) at p. 805. See also *Smith v Chadwick* [1884] 9 App Cas 187.

47 *Horsfall v Thomas* [1862] 1 H&C 9; *Francis v Knapper* [2016] EWHC 3093 (QB).

48 *Patel v Mirza* [2016] UKSC 42.

performed in a way which will involve the commission of an offence; or an unlawful act may be committed in the course of its performance.

35.2.2 Arguing illegality

The law of illegality has changed across the centuries. Traditionally, the courts would strictly apply the common law principle based on the maxim "*ex turpi causa non oritur actio*" (i.e., "*no action can arise from an illegal act*"). The result would be that no court could lend its aid to a man who founds his cause of action upon an immoral or an illegal act.[49] In *Holman v Johnson*[50] Lord Mansfield held:

> If, from the plaintiff's own stating or otherwise, the cause of action appears to arise ex turpi causa, or the transgression of a positive law of this country, there the court says he has no right to be assisted. It is upon that ground the court goes; not for the sake of the defendant, but because they will not lend their aid to such a plaintiff.

The practical result of such an inflexible approach based only on morality was that the courts would "*let the estate lie where it falls*"[51] (i.e., leave *the* claimed property where it stood) without even considering the claim.

This approach changed with the case of *Tinsley v Milligan*[52] which adopted the so-called reliance test based on which, where the claimant had relied on an illegal act to advance his case, this would be sufficient to defeat his claim. Where, instead, the cause of action on which the claimant based his claim was not tainted with the illegality, the claim would not automatically fail, and the claimed property may return to the claimant despite overall transaction being illegal. The reliance test, however, was seen as arbitrary as it did not consider other factors and considerations of the case, which could lead to unjust and unfair results. For example, where the illegality had been committed by both parties the property would be vested in the claimant despite him being one of the wrongdoers. *Tinsley* was then overruled in *Patel v Mirza,*[53] where the Supreme Court indicated a "*trio of considerations*" which courts should have regard to when assessing whether the public interest would be harmed, i.e.: (i) the policies involved; (ii) the public interest; and (iii) the need for proportionality. Lord Toulson held that a court had:

> (a) to consider the underlying purpose of the prohibition which has been transgressed and whether that purpose will be enhanced by the denial of the claim, (b) to consider any other relevant public policy on which the denial of the claim may have an impact and (c) to consider whether denial of the claim would be a proportionate response to the illegality, bearing in mind that punishment is a matter for the criminal courts. Within that framework, various factors may be relevant, but it would be a mistake to suggest that the court is free to decide a case in an undisciplined way. The public interest is best served by a principled and transparent assessment of the considerations identified, rather by than the application of a formal approach capable of producing results which may appear arbitrary, unjust or disproportionate.

---

49 *Holman v Johnson* [1775] 1 Cowp 341, 343.
50 *Holman v Johnson* [1775] 1 Cowp 341, 343.
51 *Muckleston v Brown* [1801] 6 Ves 52, 68–69.
52 *Tinsley v Milligan* [1993] UKHL 3.
53 *Patel v Mirza* [2017] AC 474.

The courts will consider the test established in *Patel* to establish whether to grant the claimed relief. However, this does not displace the "*ex turpi causa non oritur action*" principle, and the courts will continue to refuse assisting a claimant seeking to benefit from his own wrong.

Further guidance was given in *Henderson v Dorset Healthcare University NHS Trust*,[54] where Lord Hamblen, considering each of the considerations in *Patel* as a separate "stage", observed that:

> questions arise as to how under the trio of considerations approach relevant policy considerations are to be weighed. It appears that this must involve a balancing between considerations arising at the first and second stages; the third stage relates to proportionality and factors specific to the case rather than general policy considerations. Stage (a) is directed at policy reasons which support denial of the claim and stage (b) is directed at policy reasons which support denial of the illegality defence . . . stage (b) is meant to operate 'conversely' to stage (a).

He then added that where, after balancing the considerations at stage (a) and stage (b), a court is satisfied that the claim should be denied, it will not be necessary to proceed to stage (c) relevant to the issue of proportionality. In all other cases, the requirement for proportionality could be assessed against the seriousness of the conduct, its centrality to the transaction, whether it was intentional and whether there was a marked disparity in the parties' respective culpability.[55]

In the case of *Grondona v Stoffel & Co*[56] the Supreme Court provided further guidance on the application of the trio of considerations in *Patel*. Lord Lloyd-Jones held that:

> In the application of stages (a) and (b) of this trio a court will be concerned to identify the relevant policy considerations at a relatively high level of generality before considering their application to the situation before the court. . . . The essential question is whether to allow the claim would damage the integrity of the legal system. The answer will depend on whether it would be inconsistent with the policies to which the legal system gives effect. The court is not concerned here to evaluate the policies in play or to carry out a policy-based evaluation of the relevant laws. It is simply seeking to identify the policies to which the law gives effect which are engaged by the question whether to allow the claim, to ascertain whether to allow it would be inconsistent with those policies or, where the policies compete, where the overall balance lies. In considering proportionality at stage (c), by contrast, it is likely that the court will have to give close scrutiny to the detail of the case in hand.

35.3 Mistake

35.3.1 Mistake in general

Mistakes, either common or unilateral, do not automatically affect the validity of a contract unless they are so fundamental to the very existence of a contract to make it void from its inception (so-called operative mistakes).

54 *Henderson v Dorset Healthcare University NHS Trust* [2021] AC 564 at [116].
55 *Henderson v Dorset Healthcare University NHS Trust* [2021] AC 564 at [124].
56 *Grondona v Stoffel & Co* [2021] AC 540 at [26].

35.3.2 Categories of mistake

The three categories of mistake are common mistake, mutual mistake and unilateral mistake.

35.3.2.1 Common mistake

A common mistake occurs where both parties agree on a matter of fact, law or both, but they are mistaken as to the possibility of performing the contract[57] as per their agreement (e.g., where a construction contract is entered into with a company which is not incorporated or where the subject matter of the contract was mistakenly believed to exist). The modern doctrine of common mistake was set out in the case of *Great Peace Shipping Ltd. v Tsavliris (International) Ltd.*[58] where Lord Phillips MR indicated the following key elements:

> The following elements must be present if common mistake is to avoid a contract. (i) there must be a common assumption as to the existence of a state of affairs; (ii) there must be no warranty by either party that that state of affairs exists; (iii) the non-existence of the state of affairs must not be attributable to the fault of either party; (iv) the non-existence of the state of affairs must render performance of the contract impossible; (v) the state of affairs may be the existence, or a vital attribute, of the consideration to be provided or circumstances which must subsist if performance of the contractual adventure is to be possible.

This list was further refined in *Triple Seven Msn 27251 Ltd and another v Azman Air Services Ltd*[59] where the court, having reviewed the case law on the subject, concluded that the elements of a common mistake which has the effect of rendering the contract based on that common mistake void are as follows:

(1) There must have been, at the time of the conclusion of the contract, an assumption as to the existence of a state of affairs substantially shared between the parties.
(2) The assumption itself must have been fundamental to the contract.
(3) That assumption must have been wrong at the time of the conclusion of the contract.
(4) By reason of the assumption being wrong, the contract or its performance would be essentially and radically different from what the parties believed to be the case at the time of the conclusion of the contract; alternatively, the contract must be impossible to perform having regard to or in accordance with the common assumption. In other words, there must be a fundamental difference between the assumed and actual states of affairs.
(5) The parties, or at least the party relying on the common mistake, would not have entered into the contract had the parties been aware that the common assumption was wrong.
(6) The contract must not have made provision in the event that the common assumption was mistaken.

57 *Great Peace Shipping Ltd v Tsavliris Salvage (International) Ltd* [2003] QB 679 at 703 [73] – [76].
58 *Great Peace Shipping Ltd v Tsavliris Salvage (International) Ltd* [2003] QB 679 at 703 [75] – [76].
59 *Triple Seven Msn 27251 Ltd and another v Azman Air Services Ltd* [2018] EWHC 1348 Comm) at [76].

Where such elements are present, a common mistake will render the contract void "*ab initio*" and either party will be entitled to recover any payment made pursuant to it.[60]

It is worth nothing that such a consequence will only apply if the contract contains no provision that covers the situation. Where, instead, on true construction of the contract, a party warrants that the subject matter of the contract exists, or that it will be possible to perform the contract, there will be no scope to hold the contract void on the ground of common mistake.[61]

35.3.2.2 Mutual mistake

A mutual mistake occurs where the parties negotiate under a misunderstanding as to each other's intentions. In such cases, they are said to have talked at cross-purposes with one another. As this negates "*consensus ad idem*" (or "*meeting of the minds*"), the agreement will be void ab initio as no agreement was ever reached in the first place[62] (although the courts will strive to find a reasonable interpretation of the contract to preserve it, if possible[63]).

35.3.2.3 Unilateral mistake

A unilateral mistake occurs where only one contractual party is mistaken as to the terms or subject-matter of that contract. In such cases, the courts will not uphold that contract only in case the non-mistaken party knows that the other has made a fundamental mistake and tried to take advantage from that mistake.[64] However, this will not apply to mistakes as to facts known or assumed by the parties. In the case of a construction contract, for example, a contractor may not normally avoid a contract which it has been awarded as a result of an erroneously understated price[65] or a mistake as to the volume of work to be performed.[66]

35.4 Duress[67]

35.4.1 Duress in general

A contract is said to have been made under duress when one party exerts some form of pressure or threat to persuade or coerce another party to enter into that contract and this has the effect of depriving such party of a practical choice and, ultimately, of inducing him to enter into the contract.

In *DSND Subsea Ltd v Petroleum Geo-Services ASA*[68] Dyson J held that the ingredients of actionable duress are that there must be pressure: (i) whose practical effect is that there

60 *McGlinn v Waltham Contractors Ltd (No 3)* [2007] EWHC 149 (TCC) at [961] – [962].

61 *Great Peace Shipping Ltd v Tsavliris Salvage (International) Ltd* [2003] QB 679 at 703 at [73] – [76].

62 *Raffles v Wichelhaus* [1864] 2 H&C 906.

63 *Raffles v Wichelhaus* [1864] 2 H&C 906.

64 *Smith v Hughes* [1871] LR 6 QB 597.

65 *Seaton Brick and Tile Co Ltd v Mitchell* [1900] 2 F 550.

66 *Inglis v Buttery* (1878) 3 App Cas 552.

67 The doctrine of duress is a common law doctrine which finds its equity alter ego in the doctrine of undue influence. The key differing factor is that, while duress is triggered by a threat, undue influence is triggered by the exploitation of a relationship (e.g., father and child). For this reason, it is unlikely that undue influence will play a role in construction projects, which are commonly between parties to be capable of looking after their own interests.

68 *DSND Subsea Ltd v Petroleum Geo-Services ASA* [2000] BLR 530 at [545].

is compulsion on, or a lack of practical choice for, the victim; (ii) which is illegitimate; and (iii) which is a significant cause, inducing the claimant to enter into the contract.

In determining whether there has been illegitimate pressure, the court takes into account a range of factors including: (i) whether there has been an actual or threatened breach of contract; (ii) whether the person allegedly exerting the pressure has acted in good or bad faith; (iii) whether the victim had any realistic practical alternative but to submit to the pressure; (iv) whether the victim protested at the time; and (v) whether he affirmed and sought to rely on the contract. Interestingly, the judge also highlighted that illegitimate pressure must be distinguished from the rough and tumble of the pressures of normal commercial bargaining.

If duress is established, the contract will be voidable.[69] The remedy for the threatened party is rescission.

35.4.2 Arguing duress

35.4.2.1 Pressure or threat

Depending on the type of pressure exerted, a distinction may be drawn between duress to the person, duress to property and economic duress. In particular: (i) duress to the person involves threats to the life, health or liberty aimed at persuading someone to enter into a contract. The leading case on duress to the person is *Barton v Armstrong*[70] where the Privy Council held that if the victim can establish that physical threats "*contributed*" to his decision to enter into the contract, the courts will find that that contract was entered under duress without the victim having to show that he would not have entered into the contract but for the threat (i.e., the threats will merely need to be one of the factors, and not a decisive factor, influencing the victim). The burden of proof will be on the party who exerted the pressure to show the threats did not contribute to the victim's decision to enter into the contract; (ii) duress to property (or to goods) occurs where the threat concerns seizure of or damage to the victim's property;[71] and (iii) economic duress occurs where the threat concerns the victim's economic or commercial interests such as rights someone has under a contract.

Economic duress is the most common type of duress in the construction sector, and also the latest to be recognised by the courts. Historically, duress would lead to the avoidance of a contract only in cases of duress to the person or to property. The relevance of economic duress was first recognised in the cases of *Occidental Worldwide Investment Corp v Skibbs A/S Avanti*[72] and *North Ocean Shipping Co Ltd v Hyundai Construction Co Ltd*[73] and was then authoritatively accepted by the House of Lords in *Universe Tankships Inc of Monrovia v International Transport Workers Federation (The Universe Sentinel)*.[74]

A typical example of economic duress in the context of a construction contract is where the contractor threatens to discontinue works which are critical to completion of the project

69 *North Ocean Shipping Co. Ltd. v Hyundai Construction Ltd* [1978] 3 All ER 1170 (QB) 1183.

70 *Barton v Armstrong* [1976] AC 104.

71 *Occidental Worldwide Investment Corp v Skibs A/S Avanti* [1976] 1 Lloyd's Rep 293 (QB) 335.

72 *Occidental Worldwide Investment Corp v Skibbs A/S Avanti* [1976] 1 Lloyd's Rep 293.

73 *North Ocean Shipping Co Ltd v Hyundai Construction Co Ltd* [1979] QB 705.

74 *Universe Tankships Inc of Monrovia v International Transport Workers Federation (The Universe Sentinel)* [1983] 1 AC 366.

unless the employer agrees to pay extra money. In *Carillion Construction Ltd v Felix (UK) Ltd*,[75] Carillion Construction Ltd ("Carillion") had subcontracted some cladding works to Felix (UK) Ltd ("Felix"). During the works, Felix threatened to stop supplies unless Carillion agreed to pay the final account. A note disclosed by Felix during the proceedings indicated as one of the "*Carillion weaknesses*" that "*They need to finish the work*" and "*No deliveries until we get agreement*". The judge found that there had been duress as Felix knew that Carillion would be unable to complete the main contract works without the cladding and could not find an alternative supplier to finish the works in time.

It is worth noting that such arguments of economic duress may not succeed where the defendant shows that the claimant spontaneously offered to make the extra payment. In *Williams v Roffey Bros and another*,[76] the contractor, Roffey Bros, was contracted by Shepherds Bush Housing Association to refurbish a block of 27 flats. The main contract provided for liquidated damages in case of delay. Roffey Bros subcontracted part of the works to Williams at a certain price. Once the works were commenced, Williams realised that they would be unable to complete at the agreed price. Recognising that the price was particularly low and considering its exposure to delay damages, Roffey Bros agreed to a price increase. When Roffey Bros eventually refused to pay part of the additional amount, Williams then refused to continue the works unless payment was made. The Court of Appeal held that there was no finding of duress on the facts as Roffey Bros had offered to pay the additional sum.

35.4.2.2 Illegitimacy of the pressure or threat

For there to be an actionable duress, the pressure or threat should be illegitimate.[77] In the case of *Universe Tankships Inc of Monrovia v International Transport Workers' Federation*[78] Lord Scarman observed that in determining what is legitimate the matters to be considered are the nature of the pressure and the nature of the demand which the pressure is applied to support. This suggests that a pressure may be illegitimate either when the conduct that is threatened is unlawful (e.g., a threat to commit a crime) or when the conduct that is threatened is lawful, but the pressure is exerted in an illegitimate way. Cases in which the threatened conduct is unlawful (e.g., a threatened breach of contract or tort) may be easily identified as economic duress. However, where what is threatened is lawful (so-called lawful act duress), courts will typically be reluctant to consider the contract voidable. The issue of "lawful act duress" was recently dealt with by the Supreme Court in the case of *Pakistan International Airline Corporation v Times Travel (UK) Ltd*.[79] Times Travel (UK) Ltd ("Times") was a travel agency whose main activity was selling plane tickets for flights between the UK and Pakistan. At the relevant time, Pakistan International Airline Corporation ("PIAC") was the only airline operating flights between the two countries. When Times raised claims against PIAC for unpaid commissions, PIAC terminated the agreement with Times and offered to enter into a new contract providing for a release of all claims that Times had against PIAC and a reduction of

75 *Carillion Construction Ltd v Felix (UK) Ltd* [2001] BLR 1.

76 *Williams v Roffey Bros & Nicholls (Contractors) Ltd* [1991] 1 QB 1.

77 *Universe Tankships Inc. of Monrovia v International Transport Workers' Federation and Laughton* [1983] AC 366 (HL) [384] and [400].

78 *Universe Tankships Inc of Monrovia v International Transport Workers' Federation* [1983) AC 366 (HL).

79 *Pakistan International Airline Corporation v Times Travel (UK) Ltd.* [2021] UKSC 4.

ticket allocation from 300 to 60. Times agreed to the new terms and brought proceedings against PIAC for the unpaid commissions on grounds of economic duress. Lord Hodge (with whom Lord Reed, Lord Lloyd-Jones and Lord Kitchin agreed) made the following point about the impact that the lack of a general principle of good faith under English law has on lawful act duress:

> English law has never recognised a general principle of good faith in contracting. Instead, English law has relied on piecemeal solutions in response to demonstrated problems of unfairness. . . . The absence of these doctrines restricts the scope for lawful act economic duress in commercial life. . . . Against this commercial background the pressure applied by a negotiating party will very rarely come up to the standard of illegitimate pressure or unconscionable conduct. It will therefore be a rare circumstance that a court will find lawful act duress in the context of commercial negotiation.

The Supreme Court concluded its judgment with the following guidance:

> One can summarise the analysis of the law set out in this judgment as follows:
>
> (i) Lawful act duress, including lawful act economic duress, exists in English law.
> (ii) Three elements need to be established for lawful act economic duress: an illegitimate threat; sufficient causation; and that the threatened party had no reasonable alternative to giving in to the threat.
> (iii) As the threat is lawful, the illegitimacy of the threat is determined by focusing on the justification of the demand.
> (iv) A demand motivated by commercial self-interest is, in general, justified. Lawful act economic duress is essentially concerned with identifying rare exceptional cases where a demand, motivated by commercial self-interest, is nevertheless unjustified.
> (v) In relation to a demand for a waiver by the threatened party of a claim against the threatening party, a demand is unjustified, so that the lawful act economic threat is illegitimate, where, first, the threatening party has deliberately created, or increased, the threatened party's vulnerability to the demand and, secondly, the 'bad faith demand' requirement is satisfied. The demand is made in bad faith where the threatening party does not genuinely believe that it has any defence (and there is no defence) to the claim being waived.[80]

35.4.2.3 Lack of practical choice but to submit

An actionable duress will require the pressure to be so great that it caused the victim to realise that he has no other practical choice but to enter into the contract.[81] What is relevant is whether the victim had a reasonable alternative to giving in to the threat and ultimately entering into the contract (also considering the physical and mental condition of the victim[82]). In the case of *Pao On v Lau Liu Long*[83] Lord Scarman suggested that, in addition to the alternatives test:

> it is material to inquire whether the person alleged to have been coerced did or did not protest; whether he was independently advised; and whether he later took steps to avoid the contract.

80 *Pakistan International Airline Corporation v Times Travel (UK) Ltd.* [2021] UKSC 4 at [136].
81 *Universe Tankships Inc of Monrovia v International Transport Workers' Federation* [1983] 1 AC 366 (HL) 400.
82 *Scott v Sebright* [1886] 57 LT 421 (Probate Divorce and Admiralty Division) 424.
83 *Pao On v Lau Liu Long* [1980] AC 614 (PC) 635.

However, in cases where the threat concerns a criminal offence (e.g., physical violence) the courts will typically consider that even a lower impact of the threat on the victim's choice to enter into the contract may be relevant and entitle the victim to rescind the contract.

35.4.2.4 Causation

Duress may be established only where the pressure or threat was significant cause inducing the claimant to enter into the contract. The causation element will vary depending on the type of duress involved. In the case of duress to the person it will be sufficient that the pressure was one of the contributing factors inducing the victim to enter into the contract.[84] In the case of duress to property[85] and economic duress[86] the pressure must have been a significant cause of the victim's decision to contract. Moreover, unlike duress to person and duress to property, in the case of economic duress it seems unlikely that the victim will have the benefit of the reversed burden of proof.[87]

84 *Barton v Armstrong* [1976] AC 104 (PC) 120.
85 *Dimskal Shipping Co SA v ITWI* [1992] 2 AC 152 (HL) 165.
86 In *Dimskal Shipping Co. SA v I.T.W.I.* [1992] 2 AC 152 (HL) 165.
87 H.G. Beale, *Chitty on Contracts* (28th edition) Sweet & Maxwell, 1999, at 7–018.

CHAPTER 36

Prevention and force majeure

36.1 Prevention

36.1.1 Prevention in general

An employer's act of prevention may excuse the contractor's failure to complete the works within the agreed completion date.

The doctrine of prevention is based on the principle that an employer may not hold a contractor to a specific completion date if the employer has, by its own act or omission, prevented the contractor from completing by that date[1] regardless of any bad faith from the employer.[2]

This principle is based on the well-established and more general rule that, in the absence of clear terms to the contrary, a party is prevented from taking advantage of its own wrong. This principle was clearly formulated in *Cheall v A.P.E.X.*[3] where Lord Diplock held that:

> except in the unlikely case that the contract contains clear express provisions to the contrary, it is to be presumed that it was not the intention of the parties that either party should be entitled to rely upon his own breaches of his primary obligations as bringing the contract to an end, i.e. as terminating any further primary obligations on his part then remaining unperformed.

In *Keating on Construction Contracts*[4] the basis of the prevention principle is identified as

> the notion that a promise cannot insist upon the performance of an obligation which it has prevented the promisor from performing.

The doctrine has undergone a development process through the decades. In the early case law, the doctrine of prevention was intended as precluding the employer from relying on any liquidated damages provision in the contract in circumstances where the employer had acted in a manner which required the contractor to do more than what was contractually agreed and, as a result of that, the contractor failed to meet the scheduled completion date. In *Dodd v Churton*,[5] Lord Esher held that:

1 *Jerram Falkus Construction Ltd v Fenice Investments, Inc* [2011] EWHC 1935 (TCC) at [47] – [50].

2 *SMK Cabinets v Hili Modern Electrics Pty Ltd* [1984] VR 391.

3 *Cheall v A.P.E.X.* [1983] 2 AC 180 at p. 188. See also *Alghussein Establishment v Eton College* [1988] 1 WLR 587.

4 S. Furst, V. Ramsey, *Keating on Construction Contracts* (10th edition) Sweet & Maxwell, at 8–014.

5 *Dodd v Churton* [1867] 1 QB 566.

DOI: 10.4324/9781003387718-44

> if the building owner has ordered extra work beyond that specified by the original contract which has necessarily the time requisite for finishing the work, he is thereby disentitled to claim the penalties for non-completion provided by the contract. The reason for that rule is that otherwise a most unreasonable burden would be imposed upon the Contractor.

A more modern view of the doctrine is the one that has introduced the concept of "time at large". In *Trollope & Colls Ltd v North West Metropolitan Regional Hospital Board*[6] Lord Denning held that:

> It is well settled that in building contracts – and in other contracts too – when there is a stipulation for work to be done in a limited time, if one party by his conduct – it may be quite legitimate conduct, such as ordering extra work – renders it impossible or impracticable for the other party to do his work within the stipulated time, then the one whose conduct caused the trouble can no longer insist upon strict adherence to the time stated. He cannot claim any penalties or liquidated damages for non-completion in that time.

The current view on the prevention principle is the one established in *Multiplex Constructions (UK) Ltd v Honeywell Control Systems Ltd (No 2)*[7] where Jackson J held that:

> In the field of construction law, one consequence of the prevention principle is that the employer cannot hold the contractor to a specified completion date, if the employer has by act or omission prevented the contractor from completing by that date. Instead, time becomes at large and the obligation to complete by the specified date is replaced by an implied obligation to complete within a reasonable time. The same principle applies as between main contractor and sub-contractor.
>
> 49. It is in order to avoid the operation of the prevention principle that many construction contracts and sub-contracts include provisions for extension of time. Thus, it can be seen that extension of time clauses exist for the protection of both parties to a construction contract or sub-contract.

The most common case of prevention is when the employer instructs variations to the work.[8] If the employer variates the works and this has an impact on the time necessary to perform the work as resulting from the variation, it is said that the employer has prevented the contractor from completing in time. Other common examples where the prevention principle may apply are the employer's failure to provide timely access to the site[9] or to issue progress payments[10] or to award an extension of time which was to be awarded.[11]

It is worth noting that the very existence of the principle of prevention has been subject to various criticism. For example, in *Bluewater Energy Services v Mercon*[12] Ramsey J stated that:

> The principle is of some antiquity and has a surprising effect on the contractual obligations as to the time of completion.

Another example of criticism can be found in the case of *Balfour Beatty v Chestermount*[13] where Coleman J stated that:

6 *Trollope & Colls Ltd v North West Metropolitan Regional Hospital Board* [1973] 1 WLR 601.
7 *Multiplex Constructions (UK) Ltd v Honeywell Control Systems Ltd (No 2)* [2007] EWHC 447 (TCC) at [48].
8 *Dodd v Churton* [1867] 1 QB 566.
9 *Holme v Guppy* [1838] 150 ER 1195.
10 *Fernbrook Trading Co Ltd v Taggart* [1979] 1 NZLR 556 at [568].
11 *Hawl-Mac Construction v Campbell River* (1985) 60 BCLR 57 at [16].
12 *Bluewater Energy Services v Mercon* [2014] EWHC 2132 (TCC) at [518].
13 *Balfour Beatty v Chestermount* 62 BLR 1 [1993] at 3.

> The remarkable consequences of the application of this principle could therefore be as if . . . the contractor fell well behind the clock and overshot the completion date . . . if the architect then gave an instruction for the most trivial variation, representing perhaps only a day's extra work, the employer would thereby lose all right to liquidated damages for the culpable delay . . . what might be a trivial variation instruction would destroy the whole liquidated damages regime.

36.1.2 Consequences of prevention

Where the contractor is successful in showing that the employer's act prevented completion within the agreed completion date, so critically delaying the project,[14] time becomes "at large" (unless the parties have expressly agreed that the contractor shall be liable notwithstanding the prevention principle[15]). The consequences of time becoming at large are that: (i) contractor is entitled (and obliged) to complete the works within reasonable time after the agreed completion date,[16] but may not claim any prolongation costs or any early completion bonuses or other incentives that it would have received had the act of prevention not occurred;[17] (ii) the employer loses its entitlement to apply liquidated damages. However, in case the act of prevention occurs after the completion date has passed, the employer will keep its right to apply liquidated damages for any amounts already accrued as a result of the contractor's failure to complete within the agreed date.[18] Moreover, in case the contractor fails to complete the work within reasonable time, the employer may still claim unliquidated damages for any actual losses suffered as a result of such delay.[19]

36.1.3 Prevention and extension of time clauses

The application of the prevention principle should be considered in the light of any extension of time clause contained in the contract. Where the contract contains an extension of time clause, in case of employer's acts of prevention, time will not become "at large" (i.e., the contractor will not be entitled to complete within reasonable time). Rather, the clause will apply, so entitling the contractor to complete within the new completion date, as extended as a result of the extension of time granted by the employer. Where the contract does not contain a clear or effective mechanism to extend time for completion in case of delays caused by the employer, or where the extension of time clause is drafted too narrowly, the contractor may also claim an extension of time based on the general principle of contract law that an aggrieved party can claim damages for breach of contract, which may relate either to an express term or an implied term. In such cases the prevention principle may still operate. In *Multiplex Constructions (UK) Ltd v Honeywell Control Systems Ltd (No 2)*[20] the main contractor issued directions to the subcontractor which prevented the subcontractor from completing within the agreed completion date. It was

14 *Adyard Abu Dhabi v SD Marine Services* [2011] EWHC 848 (Comm) at [243].
15 *SMK Cabinets v Hili Modern Electrics Pty Ltd* [1984] VR 391.
16 *Trollope & Colls Ltd v Northwest Metropolitan Regional Hospital Board* [1973] 1 WLUK 456.
17 *Castle Trustees Ltd v Bombay Palace Restaurant* [2018] EWHC 1602 (TCC) at [313].
18 *SMK Cabinets v Hili Modern Electrics Pty Ltd* [1984] VR 391.
19 *Peak Construction (Liverpool) Ltd v McKinney Foundations Ltd* [1971] 1 WLUK 456.
20 *Multiplex Constructions (UK) Ltd v Honeywell Control Systems Ltd (No 2)* [2007] EWHC 447 (TCC).

argued that, as the extension of time clause in the contract omitted to identify such instructions as an event justifying an extension of time, they constituted an act of prevention which rendered time at large. Jackson J disagreed. In doing so, he summarised the application of the prevention principle to extension of time clauses in the following terms:

(i) Actions by the employer which are perfectly legitimate under a construction contract may still be characterised as prevention, if those actions cause the delay beyond the contractual completion date.
(ii) Acts of prevention by an employer do not set time at large, if the contract provides for an extension of time in respect of those events.
(iii) Insofar as the extension of time clause is ambiguous, it should be construed in favour of the contractor.

The third principle is of particular interest as it confirms that an ambiguous extension of time clause will be construed against the employer,[21] which would lead to time becoming "at large" in the event an employer's conduct is considered an act of prevention.[22]

In *North Midland Building Ltd v Cyden Homes Ltd*,[23] Coulson LJ clarified that the principle of prevention operates as an implied term:

> If the parties do not stipulate that a particular act of prevention triggers an entitlement to an extension of time, then there will be no implied term to assist the employer and the application of the prevention principle would mean that, on the happening of that event, time was set at large.

36.1.4 Cases in which the prevention principle does not apply

The doctrine of prevention will not apply in a number of cases, including:

(i) Where the parties have contracted out of the principle. The parties' right to exclude or modify the application of the principle was confirmed, for example, in *BDW Trading Limited v JM Rowe (Investments) Limited*[24] where Patten LJ held:

> Although there has been a certain amount of academic discussion as to whether the principle has the status of a rule of law which is imposed upon the parties to a contract almost regardless of what they have agreed, it is now clear as a matter of authority that the application of the principle can be excluded or modified by the terms of the contract and that its scope in any particular case will depend upon the construction of the relevant agreement.

This position was confirmed in *North Midland Building Ltd v Cyden Homes Ltd*[25] where Coulson LJ stated that:

> Clause 2.25.1.3(b) was an agreed term. There is no suggestion in the authorities noted above that the parties cannot contract out of some or all of the effects of the

21 Based on the "*contra proferentem*" construction rule.
22 See also *Peak Construction (Liverpool) v McKinney Foundations Ltd* [1970] 1 BLR 114 at [121].
23 *North Midland Building Ltd v Cyden Homes Ltd* [2018] EWCA Civ 1744.
24 *BDW Trading Limited v JM Rowe (Investments) Limited* [2011] EWCA Civ 548.
25 *North Midland Building Ltd v Cyden Homes Ltd* [2018] EWCA Civ 1744 at [36].

> prevention principle: indeed, the contrary is plain. Salmon LJ's judgment in Peak v McKinney . . . expressly envisaged that, although it had not happened in that case, the parties could have drafted an extension of time provision which would operate in the employer's favour, notwithstanding that the employer was to blame for the delay.

However, as stated in *Richco International v Alfred C. Toepfer International*[26] for the prevention principle to be disapplied, there must be:

> clear contractual intention to be gathered from the express provisions of the contract.

Thus, the intention to give up such right should clearly result from an express provision of the contract. The courts may not presume the parties' intention to abandon their rights under the general law without clear words to the contrary.[27]

(ii) Where a contractor fails to notify its claim in compliance with the contract's requirements, the contractor may lose its entitlement to an extension of time even where the delay was caused by an employer's act of prevention. In *Multiplex Constructions (UK) Ltd v Honeywell Control Systems Ltd (No 2)*[28] Jackson J held that:

> Contractual terms requiring a contractor to give prompt notice of delay serve a valuable purpose; such notice enables matters to be investigated while they are still current. Furthermore, such notice sometimes gives the employer the opportunity to withdraw instructions when the financial consequences become apparent.

(iii) There is considerable debate as to whether the prevention principle applies in the context of offshore construction contracts, with specific reference to shipbuilding contracts. This different approach is explained by the fact that, traditionally, shipbuilding contracts followed a sale-of-goods approach based on which a shipbuilder may not be prevented from delivering the vessel on time as a result of a purchaser's act of prevention (i.e., an instruction to variate the contract) as the shipbuilder has always a right to refuse to make changes to the design which may be requested by the purchaser, and is not expected to take into account any defects or punch list items issued by the purchaser to the extent the shipbuilder obtains the approval of class. Where the shipbuilder does not deliver the vessel within the agreed delivery date, the purchaser may simply cancel the order and be repaid of any amount already paid. However, recent case law has shown a new trend. In *Adyard Abu Dhabi v SD Marine Services*[29] Hamblen J held that:

> (1) In a basic shipbuilding contract, which simply provides for a Builder to complete the construction of a vessel and to reach certain milestones within specific periods

---

26 *Richco International v Alfred C. Toepfer International* [1991] 1 Lloyd's Rep 136 at [144].

27 *Gilbert-Ash (Northern) Ltd v Modern Engineering (Bristol) Ltd* [1974] AC 689 and *Stocznia Gdynia v Gearbulk* [2010] QB 27.

28 *Multiplex Constructions (UK) Ltd v Honeywell Control Systems Ltd* (No 2) [2007] EWHC 447 (TCC) at [103].

29 *Adyard Abu Dhabi v SD Marine Services* [2011] EWHC] 848 (Comm) at 242. See also *Zhoushan Jinhaiwan Shipyard Co Ltd v Golden Exquisite Inc.* [2011] EWHC] 848 (Comm) at [242] and *Jiangsu Guoxin Corporation Ltd (formerly known as Sainty Marine Corporation Ltd) v Precious Shipping Public Co. Ltd* [2020] EWHC 1030 (Comm) at [32].

of time, the Builder is entitled to the whole of that period of time to complete the contract work.

(2) In the event that the Buyer interferes with the work so as to delay its completion in accordance with the agreed timetable, this amounts to an act of prevention and the Builder is no longer bound by the strict requirements of the contract as to time.

(3) The instruction of variations to the work can amount to an act of prevention.

36.2 Force majeure

36.2.1 Force majeure in general

Force majeure events may excuse non-performance of a party's contractual obligation. However, force majeure arguments are not always easy to prove, and the relevant onus is on the party seeking to rely upon the force majeure clause to demonstrate that the facts of the case fall within the terms of the clause.[30]

36.2.2 Arguing force majeure

The elements that the party seeking to rely on the force majeure clause needs to prove will vary based on the exact wording of the clause. Typically, in the case of construction contracts, such elements include the following:

36.2.3 Existence of a force majeure provision

Under English law force majeure may only be relied on if the parties have expressly provided for it in their contract. In the absence of a force majeure provision, the courts will be reluctant to imply one.

36.2.4 Occurrence of a force majeure event

The affected party seeking to rely on a force majeure clause shall establish whether an event has occurred which falls within the meaning of the relevant clause.

A force majeure clause will usually expressly state what events shall, and shall not be considered force majeure events under the contract. Therefore, a party seeking to rely on the force majeure clause should first ascertain if the force majeure clause expressly includes or excludes the specific event on which that party intends to rely: (i) where the clause expressly excludes that the occurred event may constitute a force majeure event, any force majeure argument will unlikely be successful; (ii) where the event is expressly mentioned as a possible force majeure event, then the next step is to ascertain whether any other requirements stated in the clause are satisfied; (iii) where the event is neither expressly included nor excluded, the claimant shall verify whether the list is exclusive or non-exclusive. Where the list is non-exhaustive, and all other requirements are met, it may still be possible for a party to rely on the force majeure clause in case the event

30 *Channel Island Ferries Ltd v Sealink UK Ltd* [1988] 1 Lloyd's Rep; *Tandrin v Aero* [2010] 2 Lloyd's Rep 668 at [48].

had consequences which fall within the scope of the clause. For example, in case a clause does not expressly refer to "pandemic" or "epidemic" as force majeure events, but a government issues orders or laws as a consequence of such events which have the effect of preventing the performance of one party's obligations under the contract, the affected party may rely on the government's order to argue that these constitute a force majeure event under the contract.

36.2.5 Causation

The second requirement for a party to rely on a force majeure clause is that the event must be the cause of the affected party's non-performance of its contractual obligation. Typically, a force majeure clause will state that the affected party may only invoke force majeure if it was "prevented" from performing its contractual obligations as a result of the force majeure event. However, the word "prevented" is sometimes replaced or accompanied by words such as "hindered", "delayed" or other similar language aimed at lowering the level of impediment caused by the force majeure event. The parties may also agree that for a force majeure clause to be relied on, the force majeure event shall be the sole cause of the non-performance.

36.2.6 Prevented, hindered, delayed and unprofitable

Typically, a force majeure clause will state that the force majeure may be invoked only if the force majeure event has "prevented" the affected party from performing its obligations under the contract. In *Tennants (Lancashire) Ltd v G.S. Wilson & Co. Ltd*[31] the court concluded where a force majeure clause provides that the force majeure event must "prevent" performance the affected party must prove that the performance of its obligations has not become just difficult or unprofitable, but legally or physically impossible.

Conversely, where a force majeure clause states that a party may invoke force majeure simply because the relevant triggering event has "hindered" the performance of its contractual obligations, the affected party is typically required to merely demonstrate that its obligations became substantially more onerous as a result of the force majeure event having occurred. Therefore, force majeure clauses using the words "hindered", "impeded", "impaired", "interfered with"[32] or other similar language impose a lower standard than those using the word "prevented". This may include situations where the party claiming force majeure may perform only by dislocating its business or breaking other contracts.[33] In *Tennants (Lancashire) Ltd v CS Wilson & Co Ltd*[34] the seller of magnesium chloride could rely on a force majeure clause giving them the right to suspend performance due to circumstances beyond their control "*preventing or hindering the manufacture or delivery*" when their principal source of supply in Germany became unavailable due to the outbreak of the First World War and despite an English source remained still available.

31 *Tennants (Lancashire) Ltd v G.S. Wilson & Co. Ltd* [1917] AC 495; see also *Mamidoil-Jetoil Greek Petroleum Co SA v Okta Crude Oil Refinery AD* [2003] 1 Lloyd's Rep 1.

32 H.G. Beale, *Chitty on Contracts* (33rd edition) Sweet & Maxwell, 2018, at para 15–158.

33 *Reardon Smith Line v Ministry of Agriculture* [1962] 1 QB 42.

34 *Tennants (Lancashire) Ltd v CS Wilson & Co Ltd* [1917] AC 495.

Where the event has made the performance simply unprofitable, including due to a rise in prices,[35] this will not typically constitute hindrances sufficient to claim force majeure,[36] unless the parties have expressly agreed otherwise. For example, in *Thames Valley Power Ltd v Total Gas & Power Ltd*,[37] where the gas supply contract included a force majeure clause providing for release of contractual obligations in the event of inability to perform, the court held the clause would excuse non-performance where performance had merely become economically more burdensome.

Where a force majeure clause refers to the force majeure event as an event that has "delayed" performance,[38] the meaning of the word "delayed" will depend on context and any other words used in the contract, and will not be necessarily interpreted the same as "prevented".[39]

36.2.7 Force majeure as sole cause of non-performance

Where a force majeure clause states that a party may successfully invoke force majeure only if it can show that it would have performed its obligations under the contract but for the force majeure event[40] ("but for" test), this means that the force majeure event shall be the sole effective cause of the affected party's inability to perform. Whether the "but for" test applies will depend on the language of the clause.[41]

In *Seadrill Ghana Operations Ltd v Tullow Ghana Ltd*[42] the Hight Court held that an event may only constitute a force majeure event if the force majeure is the sole operative cause of the failure of the affected party to perform its obligations, unless the force majeure clause includes express wording to the contrary. The case concerns a contract for the hire of an oil rig. Tullow Ghana Limited ("Tullow") had interests in two offshore petroleum licenses or concessions about 60 km off the coast of Ghana. One of the platforms included the Jubilee oilfield, while the other included three oilfields collectively known as "TEN". Tullow was the operator of both Jubilee and TEN. Both concessions were granted by the Government of Ghana. On 3 November 2011, Tullow hired the West Leo rig from Seadrill Ghana Operations Limited ("Seadrill"). Tullow intended to use the West Leo initially in TEN and then in the Jubilee field. Pursuant to the contract between Tullow and Seadrill, Tullow was obliged to pay a daily operating rate of hire of the order of US$600,000. The contract included a force majeure provision (Section A Clause 27) requiring a force majeure event to be the sole effective cause of the invoking party's inability to perform. The contract (as extended) was to run until June 2018. In May 2013 the Government of Ghana approved the TEN Plan of Development. In September 2014 Ghana and Cote d'Ivoire entered into an arbitration to determine the precise offshore boundaries of the

35 *Tennants (Lancashire) Ltd v G.S. Wilson & Co. Ltd* [1917] AC 495.

36 *Blythe & Co v Richards* [1916] 114 LT 753; *Tennants (Lancashire) Ltd v G.S. Wilson & Co. Ltd* [1917] AC 495; *Navrom v Callitsis Ship Management SA* [1987] 2 Lloyd's Rep 267, 281, 282; *Thames Valley Power Ltd v Total Gas & Power Ltd* [2005] EWHC 2208 (Comm); *Tandrin Aviation Holdings Ltd v Aero Toy Store LLC and others* [2010] EWHC 40 (Comm); *Triple Point v PTT* [2017] EWHC 2178 (TCC) at [221].

37 *Thames Valley Power Ltd v Total Gas & Power Ltd* [2005] EWHC 2208.

38 *Fairclough Dodd & Jones v Vantol (JH)* [1957] 1 WLR 136.

39 H.G. Beale, *Chitty on Contracts* (33rd edition) Sweet & Maxwell, 2018, at para [15–159].

40 *Intertradex v Lesieur* [1978] 2 Lloyd's Rep 509.

41 *Seadrill Ghana Operations Ltd v Tullow Ghana Ltd* [2019] 1 All ER (Comm) 34 at [79].

42 *Seadrill Ghana Operations Ltd v Tullow Ghana Ltd* [2019] 1 All ER (Comm) 34 at [52] – [53].

two states. The TEN oilfield, but not also the Jubilee, fell within the contended waters. Cote d'Ivoire obtained a provisional measure order (the "PMO") whereby Ghana was ordered to "*take all necessary steps to ensure that no new drilling either by Ghana or under its control takes place in the disputed area*". Following the publication of the PMO, the Government of Ghana wrote to Tullow instructing it not to carry on with any further drilling in TEN. Before the PMO, Tullow had planned to use West Leo in the disputed area (TEN) until October 2016 and then to move the rig to the Jubilee oilfield and use it until conclusion of the hire contract in June 2018. However, in February 2016, a technical problem occurred on the FPSO (Floating Production Storage and Offloading) which was being used in the Jubilee field and the Government of Ghana refused the necessary permissions for West Leo to drill in the Jubilee oilfield (which also included other oil fields and was therefore referred to as the "Greater Jubilee Plan"). Tullow failed to issue a drilling programme for West Leo from October onwards and, in December 2016, invoked force majeure and terminated the hire contract. Tullow argued that the combination of the PMO and the instruction from the Ghanaian Government amounted to a drilling moratorium, which was considered a force majeure event under the force majeure provision (Section A Clause 27). Seadrill rejected that position arguing that: (i) the PMO did not amount to a moratorium: (ii) the only effective cause preventing the performance of the contract was the Ghanian Government's failure to approve the development Greater Jubilee Plan; (iii) even if the moratorium was one of the two causes, it was insufficient as it had to be the sole cause of the force majeure; (iv) the truth was that Tullow had terminated due to falling hire rates for rigs like West Leo. Tullow's termination was in fact a termination for convenience. As a result, Tullow was obliged to pay the contractual termination fee in excess of US$270 million. Teare J held that the question of whether a force majeure event must be the sole cause of the failure to perform is one of construction of the force majeure clause. According to the judge, Section A Clause 27 required the force majeure event to be the sole effective cause of Tullow's inability to perform. However, the judge disagreed with the argument that the only effective cause of Tullow's inability to provide drilling instructions to Seadrill was the failure of the Ghanian Government to approve the Greater Jubilee Plan. It was true that that failure was a much greater impediment to Tullow's plans than the moratorium, but both the moratorium and the failure of the Government to approve the Greater Jubilee Plan were, on a broad common sense view of the position, causative of Tullow's inability. There were, therefore, two effective causes of Tullow's inability to issue a drilling programme for West Leo, i.e., the PMO and Tullow's failure to secure permission from the Ghanian Government to drill the other oilfield. As only the first cause was a force majeure event, it could not be said that such force majeure event was the sole effective cause of Tullow's inability to perform. Therefore, the force majeure clause was not engaged.

However, the application of the "but for" test to construction projects presents a few hurdles due to the nature of force majeure clauses in construction contracts and the consequence flowing from force majeure events. In previous English cases like *Bremer Handelsgesellschaft v Westzucker*[43] it was held that force majeure clauses which were based on the common law doctrine of frustration (so-called contractual frustration clauses)

43 See for example *Bremer Handelsgesellschaft v Westzucker* [1981] 2 Lloyd's Rep 130.

and gave a right to terminate the contract (which is the case for the vast majority of force majeure clauses in construction contracts) did not require a "but for" test for causation to be satisfied even where they included causative language (e.g., words like "prevented"). This was in line with the common law doctrine of frustration. However, in the case of *Classic Maritime Inc v Limbungan Makmur Sdn Bhd*[44] the Court of Appeal clarified that in case the force majeure clause contains causative language, the "but for" test shall apply. Classic Maritime (the "Owners") and Limbungan (the "Charterers") entered into a long-term contract of affreightment (the "Contract") for the shipment of iron ore pellets from Brazil to Malaysia. The Contract included a force majeure clause (Clause 32) stating that:

> Neither the Vessel, her Master or Owners, nor the Charterers, Shippers or Receivers shall be responsible for loss or damage to, or failure to supply, load, discharge or deliver the cargo resulting from: act of God . . . floods . . . landslips . . . accidents at mine or production facility . . . or any other causes beyond the Owners', Charterers', Shippers' or Receivers' control; always provided that such events directly affect the performance of either party under This Charter Party. If any time is lost due to such events or causes such time shall not count as Laytime or demurrage (unless the Vessel is already on demurrage in which case only half time to count).

When the Charterers failed to provide some shipments, the Owners brought legal proceedings against the Charterers for breach of contract. The Charterers contended that in the light of Clause 32 they had no liability for failing to provide a number of those shipments as such failure was due to a dam burst at the shipper's (Samarco) mine which had halted the iron ore pellets' production. The dam burst was an "*accident at mine*" which was "*beyond the . . . Shippers' control*". However, as it was undisputed that the Charterer would have defaulted regardless of the dam burst (i.e., that the dam burst was not the sole effective cause of its inability to perform), the court was asked to determine whether the "but for" test applied to Clause 32. If it applied, the Charterer could not rely on the force majeure clause. The case focused on whether the force majeure clause was a frustration clause, as in that case the "but for" test would not apply.[45] Both the judge of first instance and the Court of Appeal held that the "but for" test would apply. Clause 32 was not a contractual frustration clause as, among other things, it did not contemplate the affected party's right to terminate the Contract following the occurrence of a force majeure event. Rather, it was an "exceptions clause", which only provided a defence to a claim for damages following a failure to perform, while leaving the contract subsisting. Both courts found in favour of the Owners as the Charterers were unable to demonstrate that their breach of the Contract was "*resulting from*" or "*directly affected by*" the dam burst. The Court of Appeal also held that there is no general principle that "but for" causation is not required in cases of "contractual impossibility" and that regardless of the their label ("*what matters is not the label but the content of the tin*"), force majeure clause shall be interpreted like any other contractual clause, i.e. as a whole and in accordance with the "*modern iterative approach*" to construction as set out in *Wood v Capita Insurance Services Ltd.*[46] Applying aforementioned principle, the Court of

44 *Classic Maritime Inc v Limbungan Makmur Sdn Bhd* [2019] EWCA Civ 1102.
45 Based on *Bremer Handelsgesellschaft v Westzucker* [1981] 2 Lloyd's Rep 130.
46 *Wood v Capita Insurance Services Ltd* [2017] UKSC 24.

Appeal distinguished this case from those following *Bremer Handelsgesellschaft v Westzucker*. Upon construction, Clause 32 included causative language which indicated that the "but for" causation was required.

36.2.8 "Beyond reasonable control"[47]

The party seeking to rely on a force majeure clause shall demonstrate that the circumstances which led to the force majeure event were beyond the invoking party's reasonable control.[48] "Reasonable control" is not to be confused with "foresight". Although a force majeure clause may expressly require that the force majeure event be "unforeseeable" for the affected party to invoke the relevant remedy, this is not a requirement under English law. In *Great Elephant Corporation v Trafigura Beheer BV*[49] (The "Crudesky") it has been held that the word "*unforeseeable*" does not add much to the concept of "reasonable control" as once it has been determined that a certain event is within a party's reasonable control, it is very likely that the same event will be foreseeable.

The *Crudesky* gives good insights on the meaning of reasonable control means in force majeure clauses. Trafigura Beheer BV ("Trafigura") were free on board ("FOB") buyers in a chain of contracts for the sale of crude oil from Nigeria. They had bought the cargo from Vitol SA. Vitol SA had bought from Vitol Asia Pte Ltd, which, in turn, had bought from China Offshore Oil (Singapore) International Pte Ltd ("COOSI"). Trafigura had chartered a vessel called "Mv Crudesky", from the owners Great Elephant Corporation ("Great Elephant"), which Trafigura intended to use to load the cargo at the Akpo oil terminal, operated by Total. The charterparty agreement was based on BPVoy3 form. Clause 21 (Laytime/Demurrage/Force Majeure) of the contract stated that:

> Any delay(s) arising from . . . arrest or restraint of princes, rulers or peoples shall, provided always that the cause of the delay(s) was not within the reasonable control of Charterers or Owners or their respective servants or agents, count as one half laytime or, if the Vessel is on demurrage, at one half of the demurrage rate.

Local regulations required that a representative of the Nigerian Department of Petroleum Resources ("DPR") had to be present at the terminal during loading and a documentary authorisation had to be obtained from the DPR office in Lagos. However, the loading was carried out in breach of such regulations as Total believed that the DPA's local office in Port Harcourt had verbally authorised it. As a result, the Nigerian authorities detained the Crudesky in the terminal for a month and a half and released it only after Total had paid a "fine" of US$12 million to the Nigerian Ministry of Oil. Great Elephant sued Trafigura for demurrage and additional losses due to the Crudesky's detention. Trafigura sought to pass on its liability, if any, to its sellers Vitol S.A. based on a force majeure clause (Article 21) in their FOB sale contract, which was on the NNPC (Nigerian National Petroleum Corporation), which stated that:

> Neither the Seller nor the Buyer shall be held liable for failure or delay in the performance of its obligations under this Contract, if such performance is delayed or hindered by the occurrence of

47 *Sonat Offshore SA v Amerada Hess Developments Ltd* [1988] 1 Lloyd's Rep 323, 327.
48 H.G. Beale, *Chitty on Contracts* (33rd edition) Sweet & Maxwell, 2018, at para 15–164.
49 *Great Elephant Corporation v Trafigura Beheer BV* [2013] EWHCA Civ 905.

> an unforeseeable act or event which is beyond the reasonable control of either party ("Force Majeure"). . . . The act or event constituting Force Majeure shall include, but not [be] limited to:
>
> i. Act of God
> ii. Act of Government intervention, directive, or policy (whether war, Federal or State Government).

Vitol Asia in turn sought to pass its liability to its supplier COOSI, while there was no dispute between the Vitol companies due to the back-to-back nature of their agreements. Among other things, the court had to consider whether the event that had caused the delay at the terminal was "*beyond reasonable control*" of Total or the other parties in the chain of sales. If the answer was positive, then the force majeure clause would operate excusing such parties from liability. In its judgment of first instance, Teare J found that the delay was the consequence of the unlawful imposition of a "fine" by the Nigerian Ministry of Oil. This was to be considered a "restraint of princes" as per Clause 21 of the charterparty contract between Trafigura and Great Elephant. The Court of Appeal (Longmore, Tomlinson, Underhill LJJJ) disagreed. According to the court, the delay was not beyond Total's reasonable control as Total had chosen to rely on an oral communication by the local DPR authority in Port Harcourt rather than follow the official channel of communication and obtain clearance by way of documentary authorisation from the DPR authority in Lagos before the Crudesky began to load. The court held that:

> Exercising a choice which carries a risk is doing something which is within one's control. Using the usual channels which would carry no risk is also within one's control. It was not beyond Total's reasonable control to exercise one choice rather than another.

36.2.9 Mitigation

The party invoking force majeure shall show that it has taken reasonable steps to mitigate the event and its results. In *Channel Island Ferries Ltd v Sealink*[50] the Court of Appeal held that a force majeure clause which includes language referring to events "*beyond the control of the relevant party*" for the affected party being able to rely on the clause, such party:

> must not only bring himself within the clause but must show that he has taken all reasonable steps to avoid its operation or mitigate its results.

In that specific case, the purported force majeure event was a series of strikes which could have been avoided or settled by taking reasonable steps, for example increasing wages.

Force majeure clauses typically include language requiring a party to mitigate the force majeure event and/or its effects. In the lack of such express wording, the courts would usually imply an obligation on the party seeking to rely on the force majeure clause to show that it took reasonable steps to avoid the operation of the force majeure or mitigate the consequences.[51]

The rationale behind this is that where an event which would be capable in principle to be considered a force majeure event may be avoided or mitigated by the affected party

50 *Channel Island Ferries Ltd v Sealink UK Ltd* [1988] 1 Lloyd's Rep 323. See also *B&S Contracts and Design v Victor Green Publications* [1984] ICR 419.

51 H.G. Beale, *Chitty on Contracts* (33rd edition) Sweet & Maxwell, 2018, at para 15–155.

by taking steps which are reasonable in the circumstances, a court will consider that that party has brought itself within the force majeure clause, which would make it impossible for that party to rely on the avoidable event to invoke force majeure, so precluding reliance on the clause.[52]

Moreover, where the contract itself provides that a party may perform an obligation in different ways, that party has a duty to perform such obligation in one of the alternative ways permitted under the contract[53] and may not claim under a force majeure clause where this would bar one of such available methods of performance, even where such method would be unprofitable. In the *Seadrill Ghana Operations Ltd v Tullow Ghana Ltd*[54] case discussed earlier, the force majeure clause (Clause 27) expressly mandated Tullow to use "*reasonable endeavours*" to circumvent the force majeure event. Teare J held that four other oilfields were undisputed and hence available for Tullow to drill. As Tullow decided to claim force majeure rather than opting for such available alternative method whereby it would have circumvented the force majeure event, Tullow had failed to discharge its obligation to use "*reasonable endeavours*". In doing so, Tullow had disregarded Seadrill's interests. The fact that the available oilfields were less profitable had no bearing on Tullow's obligation to mitigate.

The burden of proof on the party seeking to claim force majeure that it has complied with its obligation to mitigate is clearly a heavy one as the courts will typically consider all possible alternatives and mitigating measures that a party may have taken to avoid the event or reduce its consequences. For example, in the case of *Classic v Limbungan*[55] discussed earlier, before reaching its conclusion that the party seeking to rely on the force majeure clause had no means of avoiding or mitigating the dam-burst and its effect on supplies of Brazilian iron ore, the court went through an exhaustive analysis of all possible sources of supply (e.g., going into the market, alternative routes, etc.).

The issue of mitigation was also recently considered in the case of *MUR Shipping BV v RTI LTD*[56] in the context of sanctions. The case relates to a shipping contract where the charterers' parent company became subject to sanctions imposed by the United States to Russia in 2018. MUR Shipping BV (the "Owners") and RTI Ltd (the "Charterers") entered into a Contract of Affreightment ("COA") in June 2016 to carry a certain cargo from Guinea to Ukraine. The force majeure clause in the COA provided that neither the Owners nor the Charterers would be liable to one another for loss, damage, delay or failure in performance caused by a force majeure event. A "*force majeure event*" was defined as an event or state of affairs satisfying each of the following criteria:

a) It is outside the immediate control of the Party giving the Force Majeure Notice;
b) It prevents or delays the loading of the cargo at the loading port and/or the discharge of the cargo at the discharging port;
c) It is caused by one or more of acts of God, extreme weather conditions . . . any rules or regulations of governments or any interference or acts or directions of

52 See also *Channel Island Ferries Ltd v Sealink UK Ltd* [1988] 1 Lloyd's Rep 323.
53 *Reardon Smith Line v Ministry of Agriculture, Fisheries and Food* [1963] AC 691.
54 *Seadrill Ghana Operations Ltd v Tullow Ghana Ltd* [2018] EWHC 1640 (Comm).
55 *Classic Maritime Inc v Limbungan Makmur Sdn Bhd* [2019] EWCA Civ 1102.
56 *MUR Shipping BV v RTI LTD* [2022] EWHC 467 (Comm).

governments, the restraint of princes, restrictions on monetary transfers and exchanges;

d) It cannot be overcome by reasonable endeavours from the Party affected.

When the Charterers' Russian parent company, United Company Rusal plc, was sanctioned by the US on 6 April 2018, the Owners sent a force majeure notice stating that due to the sanctions they would be prevented from paying in USD, which was the currency stipulated under the COA. This prevented them from performing under the COA as they could not be expected to load and discharge cargo without payment. In response, the Charterers contended that: (i) the sanctions did not affect the cargo operations; (ii) the sanctions applied to any "US person" while the Owners were a Dutch company; and (iii) the Owners could make the payment in Euros. When the Owners confirmed their position, the Charterers obtained alternative tonnage and commenced arbitration proceedings against the Charterers for the additional costs incurred. The arbitral tribunal found in favour of the Charterers as the Owners were in the position to overcome the event by using reasonable endeavours. Such reasonable endeavours took the form of a payment in Euros, which, according to the tribunal, was a "*completely realistic alternative that [the Owners] could have adopted with no detriment to them*". The Owners appealed under Section 69 of the Arbitration Act 1996. The question of law was whether "*reasonable endeavours*" extended to the Owners having to accept a payment in Euros in contrast with the contractual obligations. The Charterers contended that in deciding the question of reasonable endeavour in a force majeure context several factors had to be weighted and that contractual obligations were simply one of those factors. The Commercial Court rejected this argument and stated that there is no authority which supports this broad proposition, and that the charterers' contention went against the principles laid down in *Bulman v Fenwick*[57] and *Vancouver Strikes*[58] (in which the parties' contractual obligations were regarded as paramount and determinative and not just one of the factors to consider in assessing reasonableness). Although not a construction case, this decision shows that a force majeure claim may not be defeated by an argument that the affected party could have taken reasonable steps by accepting a non-contractual performance.

36.2.10 Form, notices and conditions precedent

The force majeure clause will usually prescribe that, to rely on the provision, the claimant shall have complied with any contractual claim procedure. For example, the clause may state that the notice shall: (i) be in a particular form; (ii) be sent within a certain time limit; (iii) be addressed to a certain addressee; (iv) be sent in a certain manner (e.g., via courier, email, etc.); (v) indicate the contractual clause under which the claim is being made; (vi) clearly describe the event, the date on which it has occurred, the relevant causes and the impact on performance; (vii) state the estimated duration of the inability to perform and the relief sought.

Force majeure clauses in contracts for complex construction projects will typically include the requirement to give notice and may include language aimed at making

57 *Bulman & Dickson v Fenwick & Co* [1894] 1 QB 179.

58 *Reardon Smith Line Ltd v Ministry of Agriculture, et al.* [1963] AC 691.

compliance with such requirement a condition precedent to reliance on the relevant clause. In such case, failure to provide notice in compliance with the contract may prevent the party seeking to rely on the clause from benefiting from the force majeure relief. Where the parties intend to exclude the right to relief in case of non-compliance with any notice requirements, they should clearly express their intent for such requirement to be upheld as a condition precedent.[59] It should be clear from the language of the clause that the force majeure relief is contingent on the compliance with the notice requirements, so creating a "*conditional link*".[60] However, where the clause uses express and clear language aimed at making the satisfaction of a certain obligation a condition precedent with respect to a certain relief, the courts will typically hold the clause a condition precedent and give effect to it, even if the language "*condition precedent*" is not present. This approach was confirmed in *Mamidoil-Jetoil Greek Petroleum Company SA v Okta Crude Oil Refinery*[61] where a force majeure clause stating that the party seeking to rely on the clause had to "*give prompt notice to the other party*" with no mention of a fixed time limit within which notice had to be given was held to be a condition precedent as the notice had the scope to allow the party receiving it to investigate the matter and challenge the claim, if necessary.

However, a court may find that a conditional link is not present where a clause does not include the words "*condition*" or "*precedent*", which are however present elsewhere in the contract for the purposes of creating a condition precedent.[62]

59 *Scottish Power UK Plc v BP Exploration Operating Co Ltd* [2016] 1 All ER (Comm) 536.

60 *Aspen Insurance UK Ltd v Pectel Ltd* [2009] 2 All ER (Comm) 873.

61 *Mamidoil-Jetoil Greek Petroleum Co SA v Okta Crude Oil Refinery* [2001] EWCA Civ 406, [2001] 2 Lloyd's Rep 76. See also *O'Brien v TTT Moneycorp Ltd* [2019] EWHC 1491.

62 *Davy Offshore Ltd v Emerald Field Contracting Ltd* [1991] 55 BLR at 79; *Bremer Handelgesellschaft v Vanden Avennelzegem* [1978] 2 Lloyd's Rep 109.

CHAPTER 37

Suspension, termination and set-off

37.1 Suspension

Timely and correct payments are crucial for contractors in the context of complex and high-value contracts as they assure that contractors have the necessary cash flow to bear all the project costs necessary to carry on with the works in a timely fashion and avoid the burden on contractors of having to ultimately "finance" the project for the employer. For this reason, where an employer fails to make payments that a contractor considers due, the contractor is left with the dilemma of continuing with the works in the hope that a payment will be made at some point or suspending the works (or threat to do so) unless and until payment is made. In some cases, suspension is considered by contractors as the only way to put pressure on the employer and attain an early payment, even more so where the contractor has doubts as to whether the employer will ever be able to make the payment considering its deteriorated financial condition.

Where a construction contract falls within the description in Part II of the Housing Grants, Construction and Regeneration Act 1996 (the "HGCR Act") and relates to the carrying out of construction operations in England, Wales or Scotland (whether or not the law of England and Wales or Scotland is otherwise the applicable law in relation to the contract), Section 112 of the HGCR Act entitles the party to which the sum is due (without prejudice to any other right or remedy) to suspend performance of any or all of its obligations under the contract to the party in default by first giving to such party at least seven days' notice of intention to suspend performance, stating the ground or grounds on which it is intended to suspend performance. The suspension will entitle the innocent party to an extension of time. While Section 112 of the HGCR Act seems to indicate that party of the contract may suspend its performance in case of non-payment, the courts[1] have taken the view that the provision is limited to the case of non-payment by the employer.

In cases where the HGCR Act does not apply (or where it applies but the employer disputes that the payment be due), suspending the works may be unattractive for a contractor considering the severe risks and consequences deriving from a wrongful suspension amounting to a repudiatory breach of contract.

1 *Melville Dundas Ltd (In Receivership) v George Wimpey UK Ltd* [2007] UKHL 18 (HL); [2007] Bus LR 1182; [2007] 1 WLR 1136 at [21]. *Balfour Beatty Construction Northern Ltd v Modus Corovest (Blackpool) Ltd* [2008] EWHC 3029 (TCC) at [107]; [2009] CILL 2660.

 DOI: 10.4324/9781003387718-45

It is worth noting that the mere fact that the employer has not made an interim payment will not normally be regarded as a repudiatory breach of contract from the employer.[2] As a result, should a contractor seek to suspend the works and terminate the contract as a consequence thereof, this may be regarded as a breach of contract[3] which may amount to a repudiation. This, however, will not be an automatic consequence, but rather depend on the circumstances of the case. In case of *Mayhaven Healthcare Limited v Bothma & Anor (t/a DAB Builders)*[4] a dispute arose between the employer, Mayhaven Healthcare Limited ("Mayhaven"), and the contractor, Bothma & Anor (t/a DAB Builders) ("DAB"), over a payment under a JCT Intermediate Form of Building Contract (1998) Edition contract. The dispute was referred to adjudication. The adjudicator ordered the employer to pay the contractor a certain sum. The contractor then suspended the works on the mistaken belief that the employer had not paid the amount due. The employer notified the contractor that the suspension was wrongful and that it constituted a repudiatory breach of contract, which was accepted by the employer. The matter was then referred to arbitration. In the arbitration the contractor conceded that its suspension was wrongful as it was based on a mistake, but disagreed on the contention that it amounted to a repudiatory breach. The arbitrator held that whether the wrongful suspension was in fact a repudiatory breach depended on the nature of the breach and the facts and circumstances of the case. He then concluded the breach did not amount to a repudiation as the contractor was willing to complete the works, as shown by the fact that it did not absolutely refuse to do it. The matter reached the Technology and Construction Court. Ramsey J, having examined the relevant law, stated that:

> If a contractor under a construction contract breaches that contract by wrongfully suspending the works, does such conduct amount to a repudiatory breach of contract? As I observed in argument, the answer to that question whether a contractor's wrongful suspension of the works amounts to a repudiatory breach will depend on the terms of the contract, the breach or breaches of the contract and all the facts and circumstances of the case. The question is not capable of a simple answer, as a matter of general principle.

However, a wrongful suspension may still have severe consequences for a contractor. Where there is a dispute between the parties as to whether a payment is due, the contractor may prefer opting for different remedies such as bringing a claim for breach of contract. Where the contractor intends to suspend the works, it shall ensure that it is entitled to do so (e.g., under an express provision of the contract) and expressly inform the employer that the suspension is only temporary and shall not be considered as an absolute refusal to complete the work. This may ultimately assist the contractor in defending any employer's allegation of repudiatory breach resulting from a wrongful suspension.

2 *Mersey Steel and Iron v Naylor* [1884] 9 App Cases 434. See also *Decro Wall v Practitioner in Marketing* [1971] 2 All ER 216.

3 *Supamarl v Federated Homes* [1981] 9 ComLR 25 at 28; *Channel Tunnel Group Ltd v Balfour Beatty* [1992] 1 QB 656 at 666H. *Canterbury Pipe Lines v Christchurch Drainage Board* [1981] 16 BLR 76 at [88] – [94].

4 *Mayhaven Healthcare Limited v Bothma & Anor (t/a DAB Builders)* [2009] EWHC 2634 (TCC).

37.2 Termination

Termination is a drastic measure which is typically seen by the parties as a remedy of last resort. It will usually lead to complex disputes relevant to the terminating party's right to terminate as well as to significant delays to the project and substantial increase in cost, in particular where the contract is terminated by an employer which intends to replace the terminated contractor with a third-party contractor. For this reason, parties contemplating terminating a construction contract will usually carefully consider a number of aspects, including how termination will affect the commercial relationship with the other party, whether it may be more profitable to continue with the contract and whether viable alternatives are available (e.g., a partial de-scoping or the recovery of losses through the retention of due amount or the call of a performance bond or a formal dispute resolution process) as once given, a termination notice may not be revoked.

Moreover, it is crucial that the party purporting to terminate the contract does it in the correct way as an invalid termination may amount to a repudiatory breach of contract. This may clearly have unexpected and unwanted consequences on the terminating party.

It is also important that, while pondering its options, the party considering termination does not act in a way which is inconsistent with its intention to terminate the contract as such actions may have the effect of affirming the contract. Therefore, any actions indicating that the party is enforcing the contract (e.g., issuing pay less notices) should be taken without prejudice to that party's right to terminate and reserving all rights under the contract and at law.

There is no mandatory procedure to follow to terminate a construction contract. However, a party considering termination should endeavour to ensure that the choice is pondered and implemented in an ordinate fashion to avoid the risk of unexpected results. The steps that are usually taken before construction contracts are terminated include the following:

(i) The first step that a party intending to terminate a contract should take is seeking legal advice to assess whether the contract or the law entitles it to terminate in the specific circumstances. The right to terminate is a complex area of the law which shall be considered carefully as a wrongful termination may have severe consequences on the party purporting to terminate the contract.

(ii) Where the party considers itself entitled to terminate, it should assess the contract to identify any contractual requirements for a valid termination. The party purporting to terminate a construction contract is usually required to give notice to the breaching party. Where a notice is required, the terminating party should consider the following aspects:

   (a) Where the contract affords to the breaching party a right to cure the breach before the contract may be validly terminated, the terminating party should inform the breaching party of its intention to terminate the contract unless the breach is cured in accordance with, and within the terms of the contract. The notice shall be sufficiently clear and unambiguous. In *QOGT Inc v International Oil & Gas Technology Limited*[5] Popplewell J stated:

5 *QOGT Inc v International Oil & Gas Technology Limited* [2014] EWHC 1628 (Comm) at [113].

> Accordingly in the current context I would formulate the general principle as being that the notice must be sufficiently clear and unambiguous to enable a reasonable recipient (that is to say one having all the background knowledge reasonably available to the recipient at the time of the notice) to understand the contractual basis for the notice and the nature of the breach which is alleged to have occurred, so as to be able to assess the validity of the notice and take such steps as are open to him to remedy the alleged breach.

(b) A party may terminate the contract at common law (i.e., by acceptance of a repudiatory breach) or under the contract (i.e., pursuant to specific contractual provisions). Normally, it will not be necessary for the terminating party to specify whether it is terminating at common law or under the contract as these two forms of termination have usually the same consequences. However, where the contract expressly departs from the normal consequences under the general law of termination (for example, sets out specific remedies arising out of the termination or establishes that some obligations will survive the termination), the terminating party should use precise terms[6] in the termination notice to elect the type of termination right it is seeking to exercise with that notice.[7] Where the notice merely refers to a contractual clause entitling the party to terminate the contract, this will usually suggest that the termination is intended to be contractual.[8]

(c) If termination is contractual, the terminating party should carefully verify the notice provisions for any formalities on how (e.g., by courier and/or hand and/or email, etc.) and to whom (for example, some contracts may provide that any termination notice shall be sent also to the project's lenders) the termination should be delivered.

(d) The notice shall strictly comply with the contractual requirements. As stated in *Mannai Investments Co Ltd v Eagle Star Assurance*:[9]

> if the clause had said that the notice had to be on blue paper, it would have been no good serving a notice on pink paper, however clear it might have been that the tenant wanted to terminate the lease.

(e) The notice should be sufficiently clear and unambiguous for a reasonable recipient. In *Mannai*[10] Lord Steyn held that:

> all notices exercising rights reserved under a contract should be construed in the same way: they must be sufficiently clear and unambiguous to leave a reasonable recipient in no reasonable doubt as to the contractual right being invoked; and as to how and when the notice is intended to operate.

(iii) The termination of a contract for breach will typically be accompanied by a claim for damages. The terminating party will typically assess any entitlement to damages for breach of contract before terminating the contract. Where the

6 *Stocznia Gdynia SA v Gearbulk Holdings Ltd* [2014] EWHC 661 (Comm) at [44].
7 *Newland Shipping and Forwarding limited v Toba Trading FZC* (1997) 55 Con LR 1; 86 BLR 70 at [53] – [54].
8 *Shell Egypt West Manzala GMBH & Ors v Dana Gas Egypt Limited* [2010] EWHC 465 (Comm).
9 *Mannai Investments Co Ltd v Eagle Star Assurance* [1997] AC 749 at [776].
10 *Mannai v Eagle Star Assurance Ltd* [1997] AC 749 at [768F-H].

terminating party is the contractor, damages may include its loss of profit. Where the contract is terminated by the employer, the damages may include the costs to complete the works.

(iv) An employer terminating a construction contract may also consider: (a) making an immediate assessment of the work done and the equipment and the materials at the site. This is aimed at crystallising the actual progress achieved and fulfilment of the contractor's obligations at the date of termination; (b) assessing whether any retention money are available and any bonds and/or other forms of securities provided by the contractor are still valid and whether there are valid grounds to call such guarantees and for what amount; (c) ensuring that the contractor's insurance policies are replaced seamlessly; (d) taking immediate control of the site and securing it as quickly as possible to avoid damages and prevent unpaid subcontractors and creditors from removing plant, equipment and materials until title in the goods has been established; (d) novating in the employer's favour any agreements that the contractor has with subcontractors and suppliers; (e) assessing any rights over, and requesting the contractor to deliver any manuals, drawings, books and records; (f) assessing any entitlement to deduct liquidated damages (or other costs arising from termination) from any final account due to the contractor (if any). In this regard, employers should consider that in the case of *Triple Point Technology, Inc v PTT Public Company Ltd*[11] the Supreme Court clarified that accrual of liquidated damages will come to an end upon termination of the contract (although the rights already accrued as at the date of termination will survive) regardless of whether the liquidated damages clause expressly provides for such an outcome.[12] Therefore, once the contract is terminated, the party will be entitled to seek "only" general (unliquidated) damages for breach of contract.

37.3 Set-off

Set-off may constitute a defence for non-payment of amounts due. This means that a party validly refusing to make a payment on grounds of set-off will not commit a breach of contract.

Where a party to a construction contract intends to set-off between amounts due and owed under the contract it will first need to ascertain whether it is entitled to do so.

As seen, under English law there are different categories of set-off, although the most relevant to construction contracts are contractual set-off and equitable set-off. Based on this, the two scenarios that a party may face when applying set-off are as follows:

(i) Where the parties included a set-off clause in their construction contract, then the party intending to rely on such clause (typically the employer) should consider if the clause applies to the actual circumstances and whether the clause expressly excludes set-off in cases such as the one in question. Where set-off is allowed, the next step will be to look at the contract to ensure that any contractual

11 *Triple Point Technology, Inc v PTT Public Company Ltd* [2021] UKSC 29.
12 *Triple Point Technology, Inc v PTT Public Company Ltd* [2021] UKSC 29 at [35].

formalities are complied with (e.g., notices whereby the party informs the other party that the amount due will be set-off against the amount owed).

(ii) Where the contract does not contain any express set-off provisions (either allowing or prohibiting set-off), the party intending to apply set-off may consider any entitlement to set-off in equity.

The courts will assess the availability of equitable set-off on the facts of the case and have a high degree of discretion in making their assessment. However, it may be said that equitable set-off is usually available where there is a close connection between the claim and the counterclaim so that it would be unjust to enforce the claim without taking into account the counterclaim.

It is also worth noting that, where the parties are engaged in multiple contracts, a cross contract set-off is potentially possible. In *Geldof Metaalconstructie NV v Simon Carves Ltd* it was said that cross-contracts set-off is possible provided that the party seeking to set-off a sum due under a contract with a sum owed under a different contract can show that the claim is:

> so closely connected with [other party's] demands that it would be manifestly unjust to allow him to enforce payment without taking into account the cross-claim.[13]

13 *Geldof Metaalconstructie NV v Simon Carves Ltd* [2010] EWCA Civ 667.

PART EIGHT

REMEDIES

When a wrongful act is inflicted on another party, the injured party will be entitled to choose among various remedies, i.e., means which the legal system makes available to such party to be redressed of the harm or loss suffered as a result of the wrongful act. Such remedies are traditionally divided into the two categories of legal remedies (i.e., monetary damages) and equitable remedies.

DOI: 10.4324/9781003387718-46

CHAPTER 38

Remedies

38.1 Damages

38.1.1 Damages in general

Damages are the default and most common remedy under English law in case of breach of contract. The obligation to pay damages (which is the secondary obligation) arises directly from the non-performance of a contractual obligation (which is the primary obligation). As stated by Lord Diplock in *Photo Production Ltd v Securicor Transport Ltd*:[1]

> Every failure to perform a primary obligation is a breach of contract. The secondary obligation on the part of the contract breaker to which it gives rise by implication of the common law is to pay monetary compensation to the other party for the loss sustained by him in consequence of the breach.

Under English law, damages have a compensatory purpose in that they are aimed at compensating the claimant for a loss under a contract. It would be very exceptional for an English court to award non-compensatory damages (such as punitive damages), which are not a direct consequence of the breach, but that are rather awarded to penalise the party in breach and compensate the claimant in consideration of the particular conduct of the breaching party.

The purpose of an award of damages for breach of contract is different from the purpose of damages in tort (e.g., negligence) as: (i) damages for breach of contract are aimed at putting the aggrieved party in the position he would have been in had the contract been duly performed;[2] while (ii) damages in tort are aimed at putting the aggrieved party in the position he would have been in had the tort not been committed.[3]

38.1.2 Claiming damages for breach of contract

When the parties have not agreed that a certain breach event will be compensated by way of liquidated damages, the elements that should be considered when general damages for breach of contract are claimed are the following:

---

1 *Photo Production Ltd v Securicor Transport Ltd* [1980] AC 827.
2 *Robinson v Harman* [1848] 1 Exch 850 at [855].
3 *Livingstone v Rawyards Coal Co* [1880] 5 App Cas 25 at [39].

DOI: 10.4324/9781003387718-47

38.1.2.1 The loss

A party may claim damages for breach of contract only in case that party has suffered a loss. The loss suffered by the claimant may either be an expectation loss (i.e., a loss of profits) or a reliance loss. A third type of loss is the loss of opportunity.

38.1.2.1.1 EXPECTATION LOSS

An expectation loss is based on the so-called expectation rule stated by Baron Parke in *Robinson v Harman*:[4]

> The rule of the common law is, that where a party sustains a loss by reason of a breach of contract, he is, so far as money can do it, to be placed in the same situation, with respect to damages, as if the contract had been performed.

This means that, where under the contract the claimant was supposed to earn a certain amount of profit which was reduced due to a breach of contract by the defendant, the claimant will be entitled to damages equal to the difference in value between the expected profit and the actual profit, i.e., the loss of profit.

However, in the case of construction projects the innocent party may have an interest to recover damages as a "cost of cure", which are quantified to remedy a defect rather than recover the economic loss calculated as a difference in value. In such cases, where the "cost of cure" is higher than the "difference in value" the courts will usually award the latter as the claimant could otherwise be in a better position than he would have been had the other party not breached the contract (e.g., in case the claimant cashes the extra money without fixing the defect). In *Phillips v Ward*[5] a surveyor failed to draw his client's attention to a defect in the house his client was about to buy. As a result, the client paid for the house more than its actual value. Considering that the repairs would cost more than the difference in value, the court held that the client was not entitled to the full amount for the repairs as:

> The general rule is that the injured person is to be fairly compensated for the damage he has sustained, neither more nor less.

However, the courts will look at the circumstances of the case to decide whether the rule should be applied. For example, in *Radford v De Froberville*[6] De Froberville failed to fulfil a covenant to build a brick wall aimed at marking the boundary between her land and that of Radford. When Radford sued for the cost of doing the work, De Froberville contended that the absence of the wall had not diminished the value of Radford's land, and that a boundary could be marked by using a cheap prefabricated fence. Considering that De Froberville had expressly covenanted to build a brick wall, the court held that it would have been unjust awarding Radford the mere cost of a prefabricated fence plus the nominal diminution in property value. As a result, De Froberville was condemned to pay the price of a brick wall. Oliver J held:

4 *Robinson v Harman* [1848] 1 Ex 850 at [855].

5 *Phillips v Ward* [1956] 1 WLR 471 (CA) at [473].

6 *Radford v De Froberville* [1977] 1 WLR 1262. See also *East Ham Corporation v Bernard Sunley & Sons Ltd.* [1966] AC 406 (HL) at [126].

> if the contract had been performed according to its terms, the plaintiff would have had his property bounded and enclosed by a wall of a particular height which did not obtrude into his land; which was maintainable wholly by his neighbour and which was constructed to a specification and design approved by the plaintiff as suitable for his adjoining property. What he is left with in fact, after eight years of patient endeavour and four years of exasperated litigation, is no wall at all, no right to demand one, no control over what is erected along his boundary, the expense of putting up a wall or fence of his own if he wants one and, for his trouble, the sum of 40 shillings or its decimal equivalent and the consolation of knowing that he has parted irrevocably with his adjoining land and his right of pre-emption for a consideration part of which has, in the event, turned out to be totally illusory. . . . The purpose of the law is to remedy wrongs, not to perpetuate injustices.

One of the factors that a court may consider in assessing the sum of damages due as a result of a breach of contract is whether the costs of reinstatement are reasonable. The question of the reasonableness of reinstatement costs was considered in *Ruxley Electronics and Construction Ltd. v Forsyth.*[7] Stephen Forsyth ("Forsyth") contracted Ruxley Electronics ("Ruxley") to build a swimming pool in his garden. According to the contract, the pool's diving area had to be 7 feet 6 inches deep. When the works were complete, the diving area was only 6 feet deep. This, however, did not diminish the value of the pool. Forsyth sued Ruxley for the full cost of remedying the defect arguing that the pool was too shallow and thus unsafe for him considering his size. The Court of Appeal awarded Forsyth the full cost of reinstatement, which meant demolishing the pool and building another one 7 feet 6 inches deep. The House of Lords overturned the Court of Appeal's decision. The cost of reinstatement was not the appropriate measure of damages in that case as the expenditure would be "*out of all proportion to the good to be obtained*". As a result, they awarded Forsyth the difference in value, even though it would result in a nominal award. Lord Jauncey distinguished between: (i) cases in which the contract breaker has entirely failed to achieve the contractual objective, in which case a court may easily conclude that the loss is the necessary cost of achieving that objective (for example, where a building is constructed so defectively that it is of no use for its designed purpose, the loss will be the cost of reconstructing); and (ii) cases in which the contractual objective has been achieved to a substantial extent, in which case the court's position may be very different.[8] He then held that damages are designed to compensate for an established loss and not to provide a gratuitous benefit to the aggrieved party. As a consequence, the reasonableness of an award of damages is to be linked directly to the loss sustained. Where the loss sustained does not extend to the need to reinstate, it will be unreasonable to award the cost of reinstatement. Where the breaching party has failed to achieve the precise contractual objective, this will not necessarily mean that the resulting loss will be the same occasioned by a total failure.[9] The following example given in the judgment clarifies the court's reasoning:

> A man contracts for the building of a house and specifies that one of the lower courses of brick should be blue. The builder uses yellow brick instead. In all other respects the house conforms to the contractual specification. To replace the yellow bricks with blue would involve

---

7 *Ruxley Electronics and Construction Ltd. v Forsyth* [1996] AC 344 (HL). See also *McGlinn v Waltham Contractors* [2007] 111 Con LR 1.

8 *Ruxley Electronics and Construction Ltd. v Forsyth* [1996] AC 344 (HL) at [258].

9 *Ruxley Electronics and Construction Ltd. v Forsyth* [1996] AC 344 (HL) at [357].

> extensive demolition and reconstruction at a very large cost. It would clearly be unreasonable to award to the owner the cost of reconstructing because his loss was not the necessary cost of reconstruction of his house, which was entirely adequate for its design purpose, but merely the lack of aesthetic pleasure which he might have derived from the sight of blue bricks.

Applying this reasoning to the case in question, Lord Jauncey held that, considering that the swimming pool was perfectly serviceable (albeit lacking the specified depth) Forsyth's loss was not the cost to construct a new pool as, were he to receive the cost of building a new one and retain the existing one he would have recovered not compensation for loss but a very substantial gratuitous benefit, something which damages are not intended to provide.[10] However, he clarified that a court will not normally be concerned with the issue of whether the claimant will actually spend the sum of damages awarded on rectifying the breach and that:

> Intention, or lack of it, to reinstate can have relevance only to reasonableness and hence to the extent of the loss which has been sustained. Once that loss has been established intention as to the subsequent use of the damages ceases to be relevant.[11]

38.1.2.1.2 RELIANCE LOSS

When claiming damages, the claimant may elect to recover the wasted expenses incurred in reliance on the contract rather than the expectation loss. The two remedies are alternative and cannot be cumulated.[12]

A claim for wasted expenditure may include both the expenditure incurred after the contract was concluded and the expenditure incurred before the contract, provided that it was such as would reasonably be in the contemplation of the parties as likely to be wasted if the contract were broken.[13] The rationale of this was explained by Lord Denning MR in *Anglia Television Ltd. v Reed*[14] where he held:

> It is true that, if the defendant had never entered into the contract, he would not be liable, and the expenditure would have been incurred by the plaintiff without redress; but, the defendant having made his contract and broken it, it does not lie in his mouth to say he is not liable, when it was because of his breach that the expenditure has been wasted.

However, the reliance measure of damages may not be claimed where the defendant can prove that it would exceed the claimant's expectation loss.[15] Moreover, the defendant will not have to pay damages for reliance loss if he can prove that his breach has given the claimant a financial advantage.[16]

38.1.2.1.3 LOSS OF OPPORTUNITY

Damages for loss of opportunity are aimed at compensating the claimant for the benefit he would have gained had the contract been performed. These damages are not easy to prove and/or quantify due to their speculative nature. However, this does not mean that

10 *Ruxley Electronics and Construction Ltd. v Forsyth* [1996] AC 344 (HL) at [358].
11 *Ruxley Electronics and Construction Ltd. v Forsyth* [1996] AC 344 (HL) at [359].
12 *Anglia Television Ltd. v Reed* [1972] 1 QB 60 (CA) at [64].
13 *Anglia Television Ltd. v Reed* [1972] 1 QB 60 (CA) at [64].
14 *Anglia Television Ltd. v Reed* [1972] 1 QB 60 (CA) at [64].
15 *C & P Haulage v Middleton* [1983] EWCA Civ 5.
16 *C & P Haulage v Middleton* [1983] 3 All ER 94 (CA) at [98] – [99]; *Omak Maritime Ltd. v Mamola Challenger Shipping Co.* [2011] 1 Lloyd's Rep 47.

they are impossible to ascertain. In *Simpson v The London and North Western Railway Co.*[17] Cockburn CJ held:

> As to the supposed impossibility of ascertaining the damages, I think there is no such impossibility; to some extent, no doubt, they must be a matter of speculation, but that is no reason for not awarding any damages at all.

38.1.3 Causation

38.1.3.1 Causation in general

For a loss to be actionable, the mere suffering of that loss will not be enough. The claimant will also need to show causation. The nature of causation is somehow uncertain and has been the subject of debate. In *Alphacell v Woodward*[18] Lord Salmon said:

> The nature of causation has been discussed by many eminent philosophers and also by a number of learned judges in the past. I consider, however, that what or who has caused a certain event to occur is essentially a practical question of fact which can best be answered by ordinary common sense rather than by abstract metaphysical theory.

A claim will fail for lack of causation where the claimant is unable to establish that the event relied upon caused the lamented loss (or falls within the contractual mechanism for the award of an entitlement). This applies to damages for both breach of contract and in tort.

38.1.3.2 The "but for" test

In the case of claims for breach of contract, the test for causation will typically be the "but for" test, i.e., the claimant will need to demonstrate that "but for" the defendant's breach of contract it would not have suffered the loss. This could however cause injustice in cases where there are multiple independent causes, and each of them could separately be sufficient to cause the loss.[19]

In *Quinn v Burch Bros*[20] the defendant was contracted by the claimant to do some construction works. Based on the agreement between the parties, the defendant had to supply the equipment necessary for the works. As the defendant failed to supply a stepladder, the claimant had to improvise an alternative solution, which collapsed causing him injury. Although the defendant was in breach of contract, the claimant's case failed for lack of causation. Sellers LJ held:

> this cannot be said to be an accident which was caused by the defendants' breach of contract. No doubt that circumstance was the occasion which brought about this conduct of the plaintiff but it in no way caused it. It was in no way something flowing probably and naturally from the breach of contract.

This was clarified as follows by Salmon LJ:

> But it seems to me quite impossible to say that in reality the plaintiff's injury was caused by the breach of contract. The breach of contract merely gave the plaintiff the opportunity to

17 *Simpson v The London and North Western Railway Co.* [1876] I QBD 274 at [277].
18 *Alphacell v Woodward* [1972] AC 824 at [847].
19 *Greenwich Millennium Village Ltd v Essex Services Group Ltd* [2013] EWHC 3059 (TCC).
20 *Quinn v Burch Brothers (Builders) Ltd.* [1966] 2 QB 370.

> injure himself and was the occasion of the injury. There is always a temptation to fall into the fallacy of post hoc ergo propter hoc; and that is no less a fallacy even if what happens afterwards could have been foreseen before it occurred.[21]

38.1.3.3 Effective cause

The event causing the loss must be an effective cause and not just the occasion of the loss. However, it need not be the "dominant" or "proximate" cause.[22]

A recent construction case showing how a court may assess whether an event is the effective cause of a loss is *Beattie Passive Norse Limited (2) NPS Property Consultants Ltd v Canham Consulting Ltd.*[23] Canham Consulting Limited ("Canham") was contracted as a consulting engineer to Beattie Passive Norse Limited ("BPN") and NPS Property Consultants Limited ("NPS"), a shareholder of BPN, for the design of foundations of two PassivHaus blocks (Blocks A and B) of terraced housing in Burwash, Sussex. The main contractor for the construction works was Beattie Passive Construction Ltd ("Beattie Construction"), which had subcontracted the foundation works to Foxdown Engineering Ltd ("Foxdown"). Canham had provided BPN with two sets of design drawings for the foundations, Revisions A and B. However, Beattie Construction had only provided Foxdown with Revision A (which provided for shallower and smaller foundation pads, and were superseded by Revision B). As the Revision A design was issued to Foxdown "*for construction*", they were used by them to build the blocks. During the construction it was discovered that both blocks had defective sub-structures and superstructures. The defects also included the absence, in both Revision A and B, of dowel connections between pads and beams. As a result, both blocks were demolished. BNP and NPS then brought a £3.7 million professional negligence claim against Canham alleging defects in the designed had led to the need to demolish and rebuild both blocks. Canham argued that: (i) the foundations had not been constructed in accordance with the Revision B design, and (ii) the two blocks would have had to be demolished notwithstanding Canham's negligence as they presented other defects; (iii) the absence of dowels could have been remedied without the need to demolish the blocks. The court found that, although Canham's designs were negligent, they had not caused Block A's demolition. The real cause of demolition was the combination of the use of the wrong revision drawings and the other widespread construction defects (which had not been caused by Canham's design). For Block B, the court found that the only defect attributable to Canham was the absence of dowels, which could have been remedied at a cost of approximately £4,000, while the demolition of Block B was caused by the widespread failures caused by Beattie Construction during the construction phase. Therefore, Canham's breaches were not an effective cause of the decision to demolish the two blocks. As a result, BPN was awarded the sum for the remedial works to Block B that were performed prior to the decision to demolish that block. In achieving this conclusion, the court also cited

21 *Quinn v Burch Bros (Builders) Ltd* [1966] 2 QB 370 at [394–5].

22 *Wayne Tank and Pump Co Ltd v Employers Liability Assurance Corpn Ltd* [1994] 1 WLR 1360; *Galoo v Bright Grahame Murray* [1994] 1 WLR 1360; *County Ltd v Girozentrale Securities* [1996] 3 All ER 834; *Supershield Ltd v Siemens Building Technologies FE Ltd* [2010] EWCA Civ 7; *Petroleo Brasileiro SA v ENE Kos 1 Ltd* [2012] UKSC 17, [2012] 2 AC 164.

23 *Beattie Passive Norse Limited (2) NPS Property Consultants Ltd v Canham Consulting Ltd* [2021] EWHC 1116 (TCC).

Board of Governors of the Hospital for Sick Children v McLaughlin & Harvey plc[24] where HHJ Newey QC said:

> However reasonably the plaintiff acts, he can only recover in respect of loss actually caused by the defendant. If, therefore, part of a plaintiff's claim does not arise out of the defendant's wrongdoing, but is due to some independent cause, the plaintiff cannot recover in respect of that part.

There might be cases in which one party's conduct has not directly caused the loss, but has somehow indirectly contributed to the relevant circumstances. In *Stansbie v Troman*[25] a painter failed to lock his client's house and went out to buy some wallpaper. Thieves then broke in and stole some goods. Tucker LJ held:

> It seems clear that the negligence of the decorator was not the direct cause of the householder's loss. The direct cause was the crime of the thief. The decorator was no party to the crime, which was a thing that he never intended. On the other hand, the main purpose of the latch is to keep out thieves, so far as the latch will serve. If the latch be fastened back, the house really needs watching; and therefore the negligence of the decorator really consisted in failure to take reasonable care to guard against the very thing that happened. Forcing a door or breaking a window takes time and may attract attention. The decorator's negligence increased the problematic risk of the theft; and the risk matured into a certainty.

38.1.3.4 Breach of causation chain

In case the chain of factual causation is broken due to the occurrence of an intervening event, the claimant's claim will fail for lack of causation. The chain of causation is broken when the intervening event has such an impact that the wrongdoing of the defendant can no longer be said to be an effective cause of the claimant's loss. In the negligence case of *Corr v IBC Vehicles Ltd*[26] Lord Bingham explained this as follows:

> The rationale of the principle that a novus actus interveniens [Latin for new intervening act] breaks the chain of causation is fairness. It is not fair to hold a tortfeasor liable, however gross his breach of duty may be, for damage caused to the claimant not by the tortfeasor's breach of duty but by some independent, supervening cause (which may or may not be tortious) for which the tortfeasor is not responsible.

In *Borealis AB v Geogas Trading SA* Gross LJ held that:[27]

> the question of whether there has been a break in the chain of causation is fact sensitive . . . 'it is almost impossible to generalise'.

The judge then went on giving a thorough explanation on how to establish whether a chain of causation was broken:

---

24 *Board of Governors of the Hospital for Sick Children v McLaughlin & Harvey plc* [1987] 19 Con LR 25 at [96].

25 *Stansbie v Troman* [1948] 2 KB 48 (CA) at [51].

26 *Corr v IBC Vehicles Ltd* [2008] 1 AC 884.

27 *Borealis AB v Geogas Trading SA* [2010] EWHC 2789 (Comm), [2011] 1 Lloyd's Rep 482 at [47].

First, although an evidential burden rests on the Defendant insofar as it contends that there was a break in the chain of causation, the legal burden of proof rests throughout on the Claimant to prove that the Defendant's breach of contract caused its loss.

[44] Secondly, in order to comprise a novus actus interveniens, so breaking the chain of causation, the conduct of the Claimant 'must constitute an event of such impact that it 'obliterates' the wrongdoing' of the Defendant: Clerk & Lindsell on Torts (19th ed), at para 2–78. The same test applies in contract. For there to be a break in the chain of causation, the true cause of the loss must be the conduct of the Claimant rather than the breach of contract on the part of the Defendant; if the breach of contract by the Defendant and the Claimant's subsequent conduct are concurrent causes, it must be unlikely that the chain of causation will be broken. In circumstances where the Defendant's breach of contract remains an effective cause of the loss, at least ordinarily, the chain of causation will not be broken: County Ltd v Girozentrale [1996] 3 All ER 834, at p. 849b-c, [1996] 1 BCLC 653, per Beldam LJ and at pp. 857f-g and 858b-c, per Hobhouse LJ (as he then was). . . .

[45]Thirdly, it is difficult to conceive that anything less than unreasonable conduct on the part of the Claimant would be capable of breaking the chain of causation. It is, however, also plain that mere unreasonable conduct on a Claimant's part will not necessarily do so – for example where the Defendant's breach remains an effective cause of the loss, albeit in combination with the Claimant's failure to take reasonable precautions in its own interest. . . .

[46] Fourthly, the Claimant's state of knowledge at the time of and following the Defendant's breach of contract is likely to be a factor of very great significance. For the chain of causation to be broken, the Claimant need not have knowledge of the legal niceties of the breach of contract; nor, as it seems to me, will the chain of causation only be broken if the Claimant has actual knowledge that a breach of contract has occurred – otherwise there would be a premium on ignorance. However, the more the Claimant has actual knowledge of the breach, of the dangerousness of the situation which has thus arisen and of the need to take appropriate remedial measures, the greater the likelihood that the chain of causation will be broken. Conversely, the less the Claimant knows the more likely it is that only recklessness will suffice to break the chain of causation. . . .

[47] Fifthly and ultimately, the question of whether there has been a break in the chain of causation is fact sensitive, involving as it does a practical inquiry into the circumstances of the Defendant's breach of contract and the Claimant's subsequent conduct.

38.1.3.5 Mitigation

The issue of causation is strictly linked to the one of mitigation as a breaching party may argue that, although the breach caused the original loss, his responsibility is removed or reduced as a result of the claimant's failure to mitigate the loss.

For this reason, under English law a claimant has a duty of taking all reasonable steps to mitigate the loss resulting from a breach and may not claim damages resulting from his failure to do so. The burden of proving that the claimant failed to mitigate his losses is on the defendant.

This rule was summarised in *British Westinghouse Electric and Manufacturing Co. Ltd. v Underground Electric Railways Co. of London Ltd.*[28] where Viscount Haldane LC held:

> The fundamental basis is thus compensation for pecuniary loss naturally flowing from the breach; but this first principle is qualified by a second, which imposes on a plaintiff the duty of taking all reasonable steps to mitigate the loss consequent on the breach, and debars him from claiming any part of the damage which is due to his neglect to take such steps.

28 *British Westinghouse Electric and Manufacturing Co. Ltd. v Underground Electric Railways Co. of London Ltd.* [1912] AC 673 (HL) at [689].

However, the mitigation steps should be reasonable in the circumstances. In *British Westinghouse Electric and Manufacturing Co. Ltd. v Underground Electric Railways Co. of London Ltd.*[29] Viscount Haldane LC clarified that:

> The principle does not impose on the plaintiff an obligation to take any step which a reasonable and prudent man would not ordinarily take in the course of his business.

38.1.4 Loss not too "remote"

Under English law, not every loss, however remote, is recoverable, but only those that are not "too remote". The modern test for remoteness of damages in contract law is founded on the case of *Hadley v Baxendale*.[30] Hadley, the owner of a mill in Gloucester, contracted Baxendale to deliver Hadley's only crankshaft, which had broken, to a firm in Greenwich for replacement. The deliver took a week, albeit the parties had agreed it to be done the following day. As a result, Hadley lost a week's profits, which they claimed from Baxendale. The claim failed. Alderson B stated as follows:

> Where two parties have made a contract which one of them has broken, the damages which the other party ought to receive in respect of such breach of contract should be such as may fairly and reasonably be considered either arising naturally, i.e. according to the usual course of things, from such breach of contract itself, or such as may reasonably be supposed to have been in the contemplation of both parties, at the time they made the contract, as the probable result of the breach of it.
>
> . . . If the special circumstances under which the contract was actually made were communicated by the plaintiffs to the defendants, and thus known to both parties, the damage resulting from the breach of such a contract, which they would reasonably contemplate, would be the amount of injury which would ordinarily follow from a breach of contract under those special circumstances so known and communicated.
>
> . . . But, on the other hand, if these special circumstances were wholly unknown to the party breaking the contract, he, at most, could only be supposed to have had in his contemplation the amount of injury which would arise generally, and in the great multitude of cases not affected by any special circumstances, from such a breach of contract. For, had the special circumstances been known, the parties might have specially provided for the breach of contract by special terms as to the damages in that case; and of this advantage it would be very unjust to deprive them.

Summarising the rule in *Hadley*, damages for breach of contract are recoverable where the loss: (i) flows naturally from the breach, so that it was fairly and reasonably in the contemplation of the parties when the contract was entered into (the so-called first limb, which defines what are commonly known as "direct losses"); or (ii) does not flow naturally from the breach, but was in the contemplation of the parties at the time of the contract, so requiring actual knowledge of specific circumstances outside the ordinary course of things (the so-called second limb, which defines what are commonly known as "indirect losses" or "consequential losses").[31]

29 *British Westinghouse Electric and Manufacturing Co. Ltd. v Underground Electric Railways Co. of London Ltd.* [1912] AC 673 (HL) at [689].

30 *Hadley v Baxendale* [1854] EWHC Exch J70.

31 However, since *Hadley*, the test for remoteness of damages has been refined by a number of cases.

The rule in *Hadley* was then applied and further developed in several subsequent decisions.

In the case of *Victoria Laundry (Windsor) Ltd v Newman Industries*[32] the meaning of the "second limb" was further clarified. The claimant bought a boiler from the defendants. Although the defendants knew that the boiler was required for immediate use, they delivered it five months late, which caused the claimants losing some profits. As a result, the claimants sought to recover the usual profits that they could have made from normal customers and the profits that would result from a special contract with the Ministry of Supply. The Court of Appeal applied the rule in *Hadley*.[33] Asquith LJ said:

> (1) It is well settled that the governing purpose of damages is to put the party whose rights have been violated in the same position, so far as money can do so, as if his rights had been observed. . . . This purpose, if relentlessly pursued, would provide him with a complete indemnity for all loss de facto resulting from a particular breach, however improbable, however unpredictable. This, in contract at least, is recognized as too harsh a rule. Hence,
>
> (2) In cases of breach of contract the aggrieved party is only entitled to receive such part of the loss actually resulting as was at the time of the contract reasonably foreseeable as liable to result from the breach.
>
> (3) What was at that time reasonably foreseeable depends on the knowledge then possessed by the parties or, at all events, by the party who later commits the breach.
>
> (4) For this purpose, knowledge 'possessed' is of two kinds; one imputed, the other actual. Everyone, as a reasonable person, is taken to know the 'ordinary course of things' and consequently what loss is liable to result from a breach of contract in that ordinary course. This is the subject matter of the 'first rule' in Hadley v Baxendale. But to this knowledge, which a contract-breaker is assumed to possess whether he actually possesses it or not, there may have to be added in a particular case knowledge which he actually possesses, of special circumstances outside the 'ordinary course of things' of such a kind that a breach in those special circumstances would be liable to cause more loss. Such a case attracts the operation of the 'second rule' so as to make additional loss also recoverable.
>
> (5) In order to make the contract-breaker liable under either rule it is not necessary that he should actually have asked himself what loss is liable to result from a breach. As has often been pointed out, parties at the time of contracting contemplate not the breach of the contract, but its performance. It suffices that, if he had considered the question, he would as a reasonable man have concluded that the loss in question was liable to result.
>
> (6) Nor, finally, to make a particular loss recoverable, need it be proved that upon a given state of knowledge the defendant could, as a reasonable man, foresee that a breach must necessarily result in that loss. It is enough if he could foresee it was likely so to result. It is indeed enough . . . if the loss is a 'serious possibility' or a 'real danger'. For short, we have used the word 'liable' to result. Possibly the colloquialism 'on the cards' indicates the shade of meaning with some approach to accuracy.

32 *Victoria Laundry (Windsor) Ltd v Newman Industries* [1949] 2 KB 528 at [539].

33 The court distinguished the approach relevant to foreseeability of the loss taken in claims for damages under contract (where foreseeability is to be assessed with reference to the time when the contract was entered into) and tort (where the question of foreseeability is addressed to the time when the tort was committed).

The two-part test in *Hadley* was also discussed in *Koufos v C. Czarnikow Ltd. (The Heron II)*[34] in which the House of Lords seemed to slightly depart from the previous decisions on the subject. Koufos was contracted by C. Czarnikow Ltd. ("Czarnikow") for a delivery of sugar which Czarnikow intended to sell immediately upon delivery. The delivery was made nine days late. During the delay, the price of sugar plummeted and Czarnikow sued Koufos for the resulting loss of profit. The court found in favour of the Czarnikow. Lord Reid considered the judgment of Asquith LJ in *Victoria Laundry (Windsor) Ltd. v Newman Industries Ltd.* and held:

> What is said to create a 'landmark' is the statement of principles by Asquith L.J. This does to some extent go beyond the older authorities and in so far as it does, I do not agree with it. In paragraph (2) it is said that the plaintiff is entitled to recover 'such part of the loss actually resulting as was at the time of the contract reasonably foreseeable as liable to result from the breach'. To bring in reasonable foreseeability appears to me to be confusing measure of damages in contract with measure of damages in tort. A great many extremely unlikely results are reasonably foreseeable: it is true that Lord Asquith may have meant foreseeable as a likely result, and if that is all he meant I would not object further than to say that I think that the phrase is liable to be misunderstood. For the same reason I would take exception to the phrase 'liable to result' in paragraph (5). Liable is a very vague word but I think that one would usually say that when a person foresees a very improbable result he foresees that it is liable to happen. I agree with the first half of paragraph (6). For the best part of a century it has not been required that the defendant could have foreseen that a breach of contract must necessarily result in the loss which has occurred. But I cannot agree with the second half of that paragraph. It has never been held to be sufficient in contract that the loss was foreseeable as 'a serious possibility' or 'a real danger' or as being 'on the cards'. It is on the cards that one can win £100,000 or more for a stake of a few pence – several people have done that. And anyone who backs a hundred to one chance regards a win as a serious possibility – many people have won on such a chance. . . . It appears to me that in the ordinary use of language there is a wide gulf between saying that some event is not unlikely or quite likely to happen and saying merely that it is a serious possibility, a real danger, or on the cards.

Thus, according to Lord Reid, although the respondent did not know of the intention to sell the sugar immediately, if he had thought about the matter, he must have realised at least that it was not unlikely that the sugar would be sold in the market at market price on arrival.[35]

In *Jackson v Royal bank of Scotland,*[36] the House of Lords held that the extent of the loss need not be foreseeable provided the "kind" or "type" of the loss was foreseeable.

In the shipping case of *Transfield Shipping Inc v Mercator Shipping Inc (The "Achilleas"),*[37] Lord Hoffman and Lord Hope suggested that the appropriate test in that case was whether the breach could be referred to obligations for which the contractor could reasonably be expected to have assumed responsibility rather than foreseeability of the loss.

34 *Koufos v C. Czarnikow Ltd. (The Heron II)* [1969] 1 AC 350 (HL) at [389].

35 However, the other Lords used different language. In particular: (i) Lord Morris used the words "*the result was liable to be or at least the result was not unlikely to be* "; (ii) Lord Hodson used the words "*the result was liable to be*"; and (iii) Lord Pearce and Lord Upjohn used the words "*there was a serious possibility or a real danger*".

36 *Jackson v Royal bank of Scotland* [2005] 1 WLR 377.

3737 *Transfield Shipping Inc v Mercator Shipping Inc (The "Achilleas")* [2009] 1 AC 61 at [68–14] – [69–15].

One year later, in the *Sylvia Shipping Co Limited v Progress Bulk Carriers Limited* (The "Sylvia")[38] Hamblen J, considering the previous decisions on the subject, including The Achilleas, held that:

> In my judgment, the decision in The "Achilleas" results in an amalgam of the orthodox and broader approach. The orthodox approach remains the general test of remoteness applicable in the great majority of cases. However, there may be "unusual" cases, such as The "Achilleas" itself, in which the context, surrounding circumstances or general understanding in the relevant market make it necessary specifically to consider whether there has been an assumption of responsibility. This is most likely to be in those relatively rare cases where the application of the general test leads or may lead to an unquantifiable, unpredictable, uncontrollable or disproportionate liability or where there is clear evidence that such a liability would be contrary to market understanding and expectations.

He also added that in the great majority of cases, it will not be necessary specifically to address the issues of assumption of responsibility. This approach is consistent with other post-Achilleas decisions in non-shipping cases.[39]

38.2 Equitable remedies

38.2.1 Equitable remedies in general

Equity is a body of law allowing the courts to provide a discretionary remedy in situations where the strict application of the common law would lead to injustice. Historically, the common law was administered in the King's courts, while equity remedies were administered by the Lord Chancellor and then by the Chancery Division of the High Court. However, with the Judicature Acts of 1873 and 1875, the two systems were fused so that both legal and equitable remedies can now be provided by all English courts.

As said, equitable remedies are discretionary remedies (i.e., they are not available as a remedy as of right) available to the aggrieved party in cases where damages, assessed by reference to financial loss, are not considered "adequate". The purpose of such relieves was summarised by Lord Nicholls in *Attorney General v Blake*:[40]

> It is . . . well established that an award of damages, assessed by reference to financial loss, is not always 'adequate' as a remedy for a breach of contract. The law recognises that a party to a contract may have an interest in performance which is not readily measurable in terms of money. On breach the innocent party suffers a loss. He fails to obtain the benefit promised by the other party to the contract. To him the loss may be as important as financially measurable loss, or more so. An award of damages, assessed by reference to financial loss, will not recompense him properly. For him a financially assessed measure of damages is inadequate. . . . The court may make orders compelling the party who has committed a breach of contract, or is threatening to do so, to carry out his contractual obligations. To this end the court has wide powers to grant injunctive relief. The court will, for instance, readily make orders for the specific performance of contracts for the sale of land, and sometimes it

38 *Sylvia Shipping Co Limited v Progress Bulk Carriers Limited* (The "Sylvia") [2010] EWHC 542 Comm.
39 See, e.g., *Supershield Ltd v Siemens Building Technologies* [2010] EWCA Civ 7.
40 *Attorney General v Blake* [2001] 1 AC 268 (HL) at [282].

> will do so in respect of contracts for the sale of goods. In Beswick v Beswick [1968] AC 58 the court made an order for the specific performance of a contract to make payments of money to a third party. . . . Likewise, the court will compel the observance of negative obligations by granting injunctions. This may include a mandatory order to undo an existing breach, as where the court orders the defendant to pull down building works carried out in breach of covenant.

Equitable remedies include recission, rectification, specific performance, injunction and estoppel.

38.2.2 Rescission

Rescission is an equitable relief allowing the parties to treat the contract as if it had never been entered into. The contract is not void, but rather voidable. This means that it will remain a valid contract unless and until the aggrieved party elects to void it. Rescission is the typical remedy for cases of misrepresentation.[41]

The remedy has a number of limits, including that: (i) courts have discretion to grant damages in lieu of rescission; and (ii) rescission is not available where it is no longer possible to put the parties in the position they were before the contract was entered into (e.g., because the so-called counter restitution or restitutio in integrum is not possible[42] because the property has lost its original value or an innocent third party has gained rights over it); (iii) rescission is not available where the innocent party, having knowledge of its rights, has affirmed the contract;[43] (iv) in case rescission is sought as a result of an innocent or negligent misrepresentation, the relevant claim should be made within a reasonable time.[44]

Rescission should not be confused with variation, although sometimes the parties to a rescinded contract may enter into a new agreement regulating the same subject. This issue was touched on in *Morris v Baron & Co*[45] where the court held:

> The difference between variation and rescission is a real one and it is tested to my thinking by this: in the first case there are not such executory clauses in the second arrangement as will enable you to sue upon that alone if the first did not exist; in the second you could sue on the second arrangement alone, and the first contract is got rid of either by express words to that effect or, because of the second dealing with the same subject matter as the first but in a different way, it is impossible that the two should both be performed.

38.2.3 Rectification

Rectification is the normal remedy in case of mistake. Where a contract does not record the true agreement between the parties, they may apply for the equitable remedy of rectification to have the document rectified or altered by the court.

41 *Salt v Stratstone Specialist Ltd. t/a Stratstone Cadillac Newcastle* [2015] EWCA Civ 745.
42 *Clarke v Dickson* [1858] EB&E 148.
43 *Long v Lloyd* [1958] 1 WLR 753 (CA).
44 *Leaf v International Galleries* [1950] 2 KB 86 (CA).
45 *Morris v Baron & Co* [1918] AC 1, HL.

Rectification has some limits, including that: (i) the courts have discretion as to whether to allow rectification; (ii) rectification is only available in case of common mistake or unilateral mistake, but not also in case of mutual mistake;[46] (iii) only mistakes of drafting (those as to the way in which the parties' agreement was put into writing) can be rectified and not also mistakes in the transaction. In *F.E. Rose (London) Ltd. v W.H. Pim Jnr. & Co. Ltd.*[47] it was held that:

> Rectification is concerned with contracts and documents, not with intentions. In order to get rectification, it is necessary to show that the parties were in complete agreement on the terms of their contract, but by an error wrote them down wrongly.; and in this regard, in order to ascertain the terms of their contract, you do not look into the inner minds of the parties-into their intentions-any more than you do in the formation of any other contract.

38.2.4 Specific performance

Specific performance is an equitable remedy whereby a court orders a party to perform a specific act.

In the context of construction contracts, specific performance may be ordered, for example, in cases where:[48] (a) damages would not adequately compensate the claimant; (b) the claimant cannot work because the defendant is in possession of the land; (c) the work is adequately particularised.

Specific performance has a number of limits:[49] (i) the court has discretion to award damages in lieu of it;[50] (ii) specific performance will not be awarded in a number of cases, including where: (a) it would cause a severe hardship to the defendant; (b) the contract was unconscionable; (c) performance would require constant supervision by the court;[51] (d) the service to be performed has a personal nature (as this would restrict an individual's freedom); (e) the contract is not mutual or lacks consideration.

38.2.5 Injunction

Injunction is an alternative remedy to damages aimed at restraining the defendant from doing something ("prohibitory" injunction) or compelling him to perform an act ("mandatory" injunction). As an equity relief, the courts have discretion on whether to grant it and will do it in all cases in which it appears just and convenient to do so.[52]

Injunctions may be "final" (or "perpetual") or "interlocutory" (or "interim"): (i) final injunctions are granted at the conclusion of proceedings and may last up to a specified date, or indefinitely; while (ii) interim injunctions are usually obtained "ex parte" (i.e., without the defendant being present) before the hearings and are only temporary. They remain in force for a particular period of time, which will usually be until the defendant

46 Although the contract may be rescinded in case the mistake is fundamental.
47 *F.E. Rose (London) Ltd. v W.H. Pim Jnr. & Co. Ltd.* [1953] 2 QB 450 (CA) at [461].
48 J. Uff, *Construction Law* (12th edition) Sweet & Maxwell, 2017, at p. 225.
49 C. Chern, *The Law of Construction Disputes* (3rd edition) Routledge, 2020, at p. 255.
50 Section 50 of the Senior Courts Act 1981.
51 *Co-Operative Insurance Society Ltd v Argyll Stores (Holdings) Ltd* [1997] UKHL 17, [1998] AC 1.
52 *Beddow v Beddow* [1878] LR 9 Ch Div 89.

can be heard. At that point, the court will decide whether the injunction should be revoked or should continue (e.g., until the matter comes to trial).

The purpose of interim injunctions is to preserve the status quo between the parties and avoid injustice until the outcome of the trial. In *American Cyanamid v Ethicon*[53] the Lord Diplock gave the following guidance as to what a court should consider when deciding whether to grant an interim injunction:

(i) First a court should consider if there is a serious issue to be tried, while it will not be necessary for the claimant that he has a "prima facie" case:

> Your Lordships should in my view take this opportunity of declaring that there is no such rule. The use of such expressions as 'a probability', 'a prima facie case', or 'a strong prima facie case' in the context of the exercise of a discretionary power to grant an interlocutory injunction leads to confusion as to the object sought to be achieved by this form of temporary relief. The court no doubt must be satisfied that the claim is not frivolous or vexatious, in other words, that there is a serious question to be tried.
>
> It is no part of the court's function at this stage of the litigation to try to resolve conflicts of evidence on affidavit as to facts on which the claims of either party may ultimately depend nor to decide difficult questions of law which call for detailed argument and mature considerations. These are matters to be dealt with at the trial. One of the reasons for the introduction of the practice of requiring an undertaking as to damages upon the grant of an interlocutory injunction was that 'it aided the court in doing that which was its great object, viz. abstaining from expressing any opinion upon the merits of the case until the hearing': Wakefield v Duke of Buccleugh (1865) 12 LT 628, 629.

(ii) Second, a court should consider whether damages are an adequate remedy:

> the governing principle is that the court should first consider whether, if the plaintiff were to succeed at the trial in establishing his right to a permanent injunction, he would be adequately compensated by an award of damages for the loss he would have sustained as a result of the defendant's continuing to do what was sought to be enjoined between the time of the application and the time of the trial. If damages in the measure recoverable at common law would be adequate remedy and the defendant would be in a financial position to pay them, no interlocutory injunction should normally be granted, however strong the plaintiff's claim appeared to be at that stage. If, on the other hand, damages would not provide an adequate remedy for the plaintiff in the event of his succeeding at the trial, the court should then consider whether, on the contrary hypothesis that the defendant were to succeed at the trial in establishing his right to do that which was sought to be enjoined, he would be adequately compensated under the plaintiff's undertaking as to damages for the loss he would have sustained by being prevented from doing so between the time of the application and the time of the trial. If damages in the measure recoverable under such an undertaking would be an adequate remedy and the plaintiff would be in a financial position to pay them, there would be no reason upon this ground to refuse an interlocutory injunction.

(iii) Third, a court should consider where the "balance of convenience" lays:

> It is where there is doubt as to the adequacy of the respective remedies in damages available to either party or to both, that the question of balance of convenience arises.

53 *American Cyanamid v Ethicon* [1975] AC 396 at [400].

> It would be unwise to attempt even to list all the various matters which may need to be taken into consideration in deciding where the balance lies, let alone to suggest the relative weight to be attached to them. These will vary from case to case.
>
> Where other factors appear to be evenly balanced it is a counsel of prudence to take such measures as are calculated to preserve the status quo. If the defendant is enjoined temporarily from doing something that he has not done before, the only effect of the interlocutory injunction in the event of his succeeding at the trial is to postpone the date at which he is able to embark upon a course of action which he has not previously found it necessary to undertake; whereas to interrupt him in the conduct of an established enterprise would cause much greater inconvenience to him since he would have to start again to establish it in the event of his succeeding at the trial.

(iv) Fourth, the court should consider whether there are any other special factors:

> I would reiterate that, in addition to those to which I have referred, there may be many other special factors to be taken into consideration in the particular circumstances of individual cases.

In the case of *Series 5 Software Ltd v Clark*[54] Laddie J held that the merit of the case should not be considered only in case the facts or the law involved rendered the issues particularly intractable. Conversely, the court should consider the merits in cases where credible written evidence could allow them to form a view as to the strength of the case. In his judgment, Laddie J stated the following principles, which may be seen as supplementing the Lord Diplock's guidelines in *American Cyanamid*: (i) the grant of an interlocutory injunction is a matter of discretion and depends on all the facts of the case; (ii) there are no fixed rules as to the exercise of discretion; (iii) the court should rarely attempt to resolve complex issues of fact or law at the interim stage; (iv) the court should bear in mind: (a) to what extent damages is an adequate remedy and the other party's ability to afford to pay them; (b) the balance of convenience; (c) the maintenance of the status quo pending the full trial; and (d) any clear view that the court may reach as to the relative strength of the parties' cases.

38.2.6 Estoppel

38.2.6.1 Categories of estoppel

38.2.6.1.1 PROMISSORY ESTOPPEL

Promissory estoppel is an equitable doctrine based on which one party is prevented from withdrawing a promise made to another party which has reasonably relied on that promise.

In the case of *Central London Property v High Trees*[55] Denning J defined estoppel as:

> a promise was made which was intended to create legal relations and which, to the knowledge of the person making the promise, was going to be acted on by the person to whom it was made and which was in fact so acted on.

54 *Series 5 Software Ltd v Clark* [1996] 1 All ER 853.

55 *Central London Property v High Trees* [1947] KB 130.

For there to be a promissory estoppel it will be necessary that: (i) the representor made a clear and unequivocal[56] representation, either by words or conduct, which induced the representee to assume something;[57] (ii) the representee relied on that promise made by the representor; (iii) it would be unconscionable for the promisor to go back on that promise.[58] This will usually be the case where the representee, who relied on the representor's promise, would suffer a detriment as a result of the promisor departing from that promise.[59]

Promissory estoppel may only be used as a defence, while it cannot give rise to a cause of action. The burden of proof is on the representee to show that the representor induced him to adopt a particular assumption to the representee's detriment.

38.2.6.1.2 ESTOPPEL BY CONVENTION

Estoppel by convention is a type of common law estoppel.

The nature of estoppel by convention was explained in *Amalgamated Investment and Property Co Ltd (in Liq) v Texas Commerce International Bank Ltd*[60] where Lord Denning MR said:

> When the parties to a transaction proceed on the basis of an underlying assumption – either of fact or of law – whether due to misrepresentation or mistake makes no difference – on which they have conducted the dealings between them – neither of them will be allowed to go back on that assumption when it would be unfair or unjust to allow him to do so. If one of them does seek to go back on it, the courts will give the other such remedy as the equity of the case demands.

and

> If parties to a contract, by their course of dealing, put a particular interpretation on the terms of it – on the faith of which each of them – to the knowledge of the other – acts and conducts their mutual affairs – they are bound by that interpretation just as much as if they had written it down as being a variation of the contract. There is no need to inquire whether their particular interpretation is correct or not – or whether they were mistaken or not – or whether they had in mind the original terms or not. Suffice it that they have, by their course of dealing, put their own interpretation on their contract, and cannot be allowed to go back on it.

Thus, for there to be an estoppel by convention it will be necessary that: (i) the parties conduct their dealings on the basis of an underlying assumption, either of fact or of law; (ii) it would be unfair or unjust to allow one of the parties to depart from that assumption.

The consequence of estoppel by convention is that the parties will be bound to continue their dealings on the basis of that assumption, even if that assumption was due to misrepresentation or mistake.

---

56 *Woodhouse AC Israel Cocoa Ltd CSA v Nigerian Produce Marketing Co Ltd* [1972] AC 741, [1972] 2 All ER 271.

57 *Spliethoff's Bevracthingskantoor BV v Bank of China Ltd* [2015] EWHC 999 (Comm) at [156].

58 *Thompson v Palmer* [1933] 49 CLR 507 at 547.

59 *Borough of Blaenau Gwent v Robinson Jones Design Partnership Ltd* [1997] 53 Con LR 31.

60 *Amalgamated Investment and Property Co Ltd (in Liq) v Texas Commerce International Bank Ltd* [1982] QB 84, [1981] 1 All ER 923, [1981] 2 WLR 554, [1982] 1 Lloyd's Rep 27.

CHAPTER 39

Breach of contract and negligence

A claim may be contractual, where the relevant entitlement results from express or implied terms of the construction contract, or "extra-contractual", where the relevant entitlement results from a provision of law.

Typically, contractual claims are claims for breach of contract while extra-contractual claims are said to be in tort. In the case of construction contracts, the most relevant category of claim in tort is negligence.

39.1 Breach of contract

39.1.1 Breach of contract in general

A breach of contract occurs when one of the parties fails to fulfil one or more of its primary obligations under the contract.[1] In the case of construction contracts, for example: (i) a contractor is in breach of contract if it fails to execute the work specified in the contract or fails to complete within the agreed completion date[2]; and (ii) an employer is in breach of contract if it fails to pay the contractor for work performed in compliance with the contract, in both cases. In such cases the innocent party has a claim for breach of contract against the breaching party.

A claim "for breach of contract" shall not be confused with a claim "under the contract". A claim for breach of contract is a claim which arises as a result of a contractual breach which entitles the innocent party to claim any relief it is entitled to under the contract or at law. A claim under the contract arises when a party claims a contractual remedy following the occurrence of a certain event, which may or may not constitute a breach of contract. The two categories often overlap but are not the same thing. For example, an EOT claim arising from a force majeure event would be a claim under the contract, but not a claim for breach of contract. This is because the force majeure event entitles the contractor to claim extra time under the contract but is not the result of an employer's failure to fulfil its obligations under the contract.

39.1.2 Claiming breach of contract

In very broad and basic terms, for a successful breach of contract argument, the claimant shall be able to establish: (i) that a legally binding agreement existed between the parties.

1 A primary obligation is the obligation arising from a contract and not from a breach of contract. A secondary obligation, instead, arises when the primary obligation has not been fulfilled.

2 *Kaye v Hosier & Dickinson* [1972] 1 WLR 146.

DOI: 10.4324/9781003387718-48

This may become a problem in case the contractor has commenced the works on the basis of some verbal instruction without the formal contract having been yet entered into. In such cases, a contractor may still be entitled to a claim in quantum meruit; (ii) that the contract was subsequently broken and the party in breach failed to fulfil its obligations in compliance with the contract; (iii) that the claimant suffered a loss which: (a) was a foreseeable consequence of the subsequent breach at the time of the contract; and (b) is a direct consequence of the breach of contract; (iv) that the claimant has taken reasonable steps to mitigate its loss; (v) the quantum of the loss resulting from the breach.

39.1.3 Consequences of a breach of contract

A breach of contract will typically entitle the innocent party to recover damages. In the case of *Photo Production Ltd v Securicor Transport Ltd*[3] Lord Diplock held:

> Every failure to perform a primary obligation is a breach of contract. The secondary obligation on the part of the contract breaker to which it gives rise by implication of the common law is to pay monetary compensation to the other party for the loss sustained by him in consequence of the breach.

However, where the breach is sufficiently serious, the innocent party may have an option to consider the contract as repudiated by the party in breach. Where the repudiation is accepted, the contract is terminated, and the innocent party is typically also entitled to recover damages.

39.2 Negligence

39.2.1 Negligence in general

In the case of construction contracts, negligence is the most relevant area of law within tort.[4] A typical example of tort claims relevant to the construction industry is represented by claims for personal injury that occurred during the performance of the works. In such cases, the injured person may sue in negligence.

39.2.2 Claiming negligence

39.2.2.1 Existence of a duty of care

The first element that a claimant shall prove to succeed in a tort claim, including negligence, is that the defendant owed the claimant a duty of care.

In *Donoghue v Stevenson*[5] the House of Lords generalised the concept of duty of care. Lord Atkin said:

> The rule that you are to love your neighbour becomes in law, you must not injure your neighbour; and the lawyers' question, 'Who is my neighbour?' receives a restricted reply. You must take reasonable care to avoid acts or omissions which you can reasonably foresee would

3 *Photo Production Ltd v Securicor Transport Ltd* [1980] AC 827 at [849].
4 The other two areas are nuisance and trespass.
5 *Donoghue v Stevenson* [1932] AC 562.

> be likely to injure your neighbour. Who, then, in law is my neighbour? The answer seems to be – persons who are so closely and directly affected by my act that I ought reasonably to have them in contemplation as being so affected when I am directing my mind to the acts or omissions which are called in question.

In *Caparo v Dickman*[6] Lord Bridge set out a test to be applied in cases of pure economic loss known as the "threefold test" or the "Caparo test", based on which a court will find a duty of care if the claimant can show: (i) that the damage suffered by the claimant was foreseeable; (ii) that there was sufficient proximity between the claimant and the defendant; and (iii) that in all the circumstances it is fair, just and reasonable to impose a duty of care on the defendant.

A duty of care may also arise when a party relies on a special skill that the other party has undertaken to apply in the relation with the party that has relied on it. In the case of *Hedley Byrne & Co Ltd v Heller & Partners Ltd*[7] Lord Morris held that:

> if someone possessed of a special skill undertakes, quite irrespective of contract, to apply that skill for the assistance of another person who relies upon such skill, a duty of care will arise.

39.2.2.2 Breach of a duty of care

If the claimant can show that a duty of care exists, the second element to show to succeed in claiming negligence is fault, i.e., that the defendant breached such duty of care. To do so, the first step will be determining the standard of care that the defendant owed the claimant (which is a question of law). In general, the standard of care will be the one expected from a "reasonable person" carrying out the profession, occupation or activity in question. In the context of the construction industry, the standard of care will vary based on what the party purports to be, and the actual level of skill, knowledge and experience possessed. For example, where a contractor is particularly skilful, experienced and qualified for a specific project or purports to be such, the level of care expected of that contractor will be higher.

Having determined the standard of care, the next step will be determining if the defendant reached such standard with its actions (which is a question of fact).

39.2.2.3 Causation

The third element that the claimant should show in claiming negligence is causation, i.e., that the defendant's breach of the duty of care caused a loss. This will be achieved though the "but for" test based on which, but for the defendant's tort the claimant would not have suffered the loss. However, the defendant will not be liable where the damages: (i) are too remote a consequence of the defendant's negligence; (ii) could not be reasonably foreseen;[8] or (iii) were caused by the wilful wrongdoing of a third party.[9] Moreover, the defendant will not be liable where the claimant did not rely on the defendant to exercise reasonable skill and care in performing the works.[10]

---

6 *Caparo v Dickman* [1990] 2 AC 605.
7 *Hedley Byrne & Co Ltd v Heller & Partners Ltd* [1964] AC 465.
8 *The Wagon Mound (No.1)* [1961] AC 388.
9 See, e.g., *Gray v TP Bennett & Son* [1987] 43 BLR 63.
10 *Williams v Natural Life Health Foods Ltd* [1998] 1 WLR 830.

PART NINE

CLAIMS

Complex construction projects will typically involve several parties performing a multitude of activities. Such activities will normally give rise to numerous claims of various nature and magnitude which, if not settled, may eventually result in disputes.

A claim may be contractual, where the relevant entitlement results from the express or implied terms of the construction contract, or "extra-contractual", where the relevant entitlement results from a provision of law. Good claim management procedures are pivotal for the success of a construction project. The claiming party should present its demands to the other party in a professional manner, detailing all the relevant aspects including the grounds of the claim, the amount sought and the relevant calculations, and providing the necessary supporting evidence so to enable the party to which the claim is addressed to assess the claim in a timely fashion and decide whether and to what extent the request shall be agreed with.

The preparation of construction claims may be time consuming and costly. Moreover, considering the general complexity of the typical issues arising under such contracts and projects, the parties may come to different conclusions based on their experts' and counsels' respective advice. The high amounts at stake do not allow the parties to lightly accept or dismiss their counterparty's claims. As a result, negotiations will typically be tough and protracted. In some cases, the parties' positions may be driven by elements other than the technical or legal aspects of the claim. There may be cash flow issues, external pressures and inferences (e.g., by lenders), general market and industry conditions affecting the parties' financial strength, losses on other projects, etc. Such complexity may lead to the proliferation of disputes, which may be either dealt with during the construction phase or at the end of the project. The parties are usually mandated to go through a number of steps before the dispute may land to arbitration or litigation. These steps, which may be agreed between the parties or mandated by the applicable law, include mandatory negotiation, mediation and adjudication (and many others).

DOI: 10.4324/9781003387718-49

CHAPTER 40

General aspects of claims in construction contracts

40.1 Typical content and submission

Although employers are entitled to claim under a construction contract, in the context of complex projects most of the claims will be made by the contractors.

Claims submitted by a contractor to the employer (or the engineer) are usually divided into sections. Such sections may include:

(i) An introduction of the claim stating the parties' names, the details of the contract, information relevant to the tender, any relevant contractual dates (e.g., commencement date, completion date and relevant milestones) and a summary of the claim (e.g., time and/or money claimed).

(ii) The basis on which the claim is being submitted. In this section the contractor will typically state the event or events that gave rise to the claim and the delay and/or loss and/or extra costs and/or damages flowing from such events.

(iii) The most important section is the one where the contractor gives the details of its claim. For example, in the case of an extension of time the contractor may include details of the event or events that generated the delays (force majeure, variations, etc.), the relevant responsibility (e.g., if the delays are solely attributable to the employer or there has been concurrency and to what extent), the impact of such events on the progress, the specific extension of time sought and any supporting documents/analysis (e.g., a critical path analysis).

(iv) If the contractor is claiming money (e.g., prolongation costs or costs deriving from disruption events), it will present a monetary valuation of the claim (the "quantum"). To prove the "quantum" of the claim, the claimant must show: (a) that there is causal link between the event that has caused the "loss" (e.g., a breach or a variation) and the loss incurred as a result of such causing event (e.g., damages or additional costs following a variation); (b) that the loss was actually and properly incurred as a result of the causing event; (c) that the contractor has taken reasonable steps to mitigate the event or its effects.

(v) Any backup documentation aimed at substantiating the claim (e.g., contemporary records).

40.2 The importance of contemporary records

A claim is likely to fail if not properly documented. Evidence of a claim should be given by submitting contemporary records which give a picture of the events occurring on site

DOI: 10.4324/9781003387718-50

at the relevant time and how the parties reacted to such events. These may include documents such as internal and external correspondence (emails, letters and even instant messages), minutes of meetings, progress reports, site documents, programmes, personal notebooks, etc. The importance of contemporary documents should not be underestimated. In *Van Oord and another v Allseas UK Ltd*[1] contemporary documents were defined as:

> a useful starting point when trying to work out what was happening on site at any given time, and what the relevant individuals thought were the important events on site during the works.

This is even more so in the case of complex construction projects, which typically take many years to be completed. The parties should endeavour to properly record events as soon as they occur and keep such records in an organised manner. Proving a claim based on events which occurred in retrospect may prove difficult, if not impossible. A contractor failing to keep good records may encounter several hurdles when trying to retrospectively gather documents to prove its claim. For example, a contractor may find it difficult to: (i) collect the necessary information, in particular in cases where no records are available as the claim was not notified contemporaneously; (ii) obtain or extract the necessary documents, in particular where contractual documents are only available in hard copy or project communications are not properly stored in a systematic manner; (iii) obtain first-hand information from project people, in particular where those people have been assigned to different projects or, worse, have left the company; (iv) obtain the cooperation of subcontractors and/or vendors, in particular where the contractor is in dispute with them or where the information/documents they are requested to provide may undermine their position and expose them to indemnity claims.

However, despite the importance of contemporary documents, there is often a lack of good record keeping in construction projects. For this reason, the parties should endeavour to reach a clear and documented agreement on this point[2] and possibly record such agreement in their contract.

40.3 Notice of claim

Construction contracts for complex projects will normally include provisions stating that contractual claims shall be notified in certain ways, in compliance with certain formalities, and within specific timelines.

Such provisions serve several scopes, including: (i) encouraging effective communication between parties; (ii) allowing the issues on which claims are based to be identified and investigated promptly; (iii) allowing employers to be informed about project issues at an early stage and take any steps to mitigate the relevant effects; and (iv) bringing certainty to the parties by avoiding that contractors' claims build up during the project and are only raised at the end as an expensive final account, which an employer may be less inclined to pay when the project is complete.

1 *Van Oord and another v Allseas UK Ltd* [2015] EWHC 2074 (TCC).

2 *Society of Construction Law Delay and Disruption Protocol* (2nd edition) February 2017, www.scl.org.uk, at p. 12.

40.3.1 Condition precedents and time bars

Notices of claims are almost invariably the subject of disputes as contractors may find it difficult to comply with the strict requirements that such clauses impose.

Depending on how the relevant clause is worded, the notice may constitute a condition precedent. In this case, non-compliance with the requirement of the notice, particularly as to the relevant timing, may be fatal for the claim regardless of the relevant merits.

However, when considering the question of time bars, the English courts have typically taken the view that, unless the contract expressly states that a non-compliance notice will affect the contractor's right to claim, notice requirements in construction contracts are not mandatory. As stated in *Keating on Construction Contracts*:[3]

> Many contracts provide that the contractor's entitlement to an extension of time is dependent upon, amongst other things, the service of a notice within a stipulated time of an event causing delay. Courts are normally reluctant to construe the requirements as to the form and content of the notice required under such clauses too strictly and are unlikely to treat them as condition precedent to the making of any claim (as opposed to procedural requirements) absent clear language to this effect.

Therefore, where the parties' intent is to extinguish the contractor's right to relief in cases of non-compliance, the clause shall expressly provide that, should the contractor fail to serve the claim notice within the period specified in the clause, then the claim will become time barred and the contractor will irremediably lose its right to the relevant relief. To the extent the clause expressly reflects the parties' intent, it will be enforced as a condition precedent[4] as opposed to an option (although the courts will usually interpret the clause in the context of the contract as a whole).

The courts will generally uphold a condition precedent if it clearly states the "conditional link" between the relief or obligation and the performance of certain obligations. In A*spen Insurance UK Limited, Brit Insurance Holding Limited, DA Constable v Pectel Limited*[5] Pectel Limited ("Pectel"), a specialist contractor experienced in the removal of asbestos from commercial and government property, was engaged by AMEC as subcontractor to work on a tunnel facility in Manchester, which had been commissioned by BT. Pectel contracted an insurance coverage with Aspen Insurance UK Limited ("Aspen"). Condition 4(a) of the policy required the insured to give insurers "*immediate written notice with full particulars of . . . any occurrence which may give rise to indemnity under this insurance*", while condition 13 stated that "*the liability of Underwriters shall be conditional on . . . the Assured paying in full the premium demanded and observing the terms and conditions of this insurance*". During preparatory work a fire broke out on the project. In the following months, an investigation and some tests were carried out by AMEC, also with the support of Pectel. AMEC informed the insurer that BT was claiming damages from them in the amount of about £15 million as Pectel was responsible for the fire. At that point, Pectel notified its insurers who denied any liability on the grounds that the

3 S. Furst, V. Ramsey, *Keating on Construction Contracts* (10th edition) Sweet & Maxwell, 2016, at para 8–031.

4 *Scottish Power UK Plc v BP Exploration Operating Co Ltd* [2016] 1 All ER (Comm) 536. See also *Adyard Abu Dhabi v SD Marine Services* [2011] EWHC 848 Comm.

5 *Aspen Insurance UK Limited, Brit Insurance Holding Limited, DA Constable v Pectel Limited* [2008] EWH 2804 (Comm).

claim was three years late and that Pectel had breached a notification clause which, as per condition 13, was a condition precedent to their liability. The cases ended in court. The court found that it was a condition precedent that the insured notify the occurrence immediately. Condition 13, when read in conjunction with condition 4(a), made it clear that the parties intended there to be a conditional link between the insured's obligation to give notice and insurers' obligation to pay the claim. In addition, there was an objective commercial purpose in the notification provisions as they aimed at enabling the insurers to investigate the potential claim at the earliest opportunity. As the insured was in breach of a condition precedent, the insurers were entitled to decline liability.

For time bars language to be considered a condition precedent and have the effect of preventing late claims it is crucial that the parties use clear words to express such intention. The courts will look at the clause and the contract as a whole to determine the real nature of the provision. In *Bremer Handels GmbH v Vanden-Avenne Izegem PVBA*[6] Lord Wilberforce held that an automatic and invariable treatment of a clause such as the one in question would be contrary to the approach, which modern authorities recognise, of treating such a provision as having the force of a condition (giving rise to rescission or invalidity), or of a contractual term (giving rise to damages only) according to the nature and gravity of the breach. He gave three factors that determined whether a notice provision was a condition precedent. These are the form of the clause itself, which shall be clearly framed as a condition precedent, the relation of the clause to the contract as a whole (e.g., in case provisions elsewhere in the contract suggest that clause is not intended as a condition) and general considerations of law. In that specific case, the court did not find that the clause was a condition precedent as, among other things, contrarily to another clause in the contract, the provision in question did not give a fixed or definite time limit for giving of notice.

The parties should expressly state in the clause the time in which the notice should be served to be considered compliant with the clause and the consequences in case of non-compliance.

As to the first aspect, in *Bremer Handels GmbH v Vanden-Avenne Izegem PVBA*[7] Lord Salmon said:

> Had it been a condition precedent, I should have expected the clause to state the precise time within which the notice was to be served and to have made plain by express language that unless the notice was served within the time, the sellers would lose their rights under the clause.

However, a precise time limit to give notice is not always necessary for a provision to be considered a condition precedent. In the case of *Mamidoil-Jetoil Greek Petroleum Company SA v Okta Crude Oil Refinery*[8] a force majeure clause in the contract stated that the party invoking the force majeure "*shall give prompt notice to the other party*" without mentioning a fixed time limit to do so. The court held that the clause was in fact a condition precedent.

6 *Bremer Handels GmbH v Vanden-Avenne Izegem PVBA* [1978] 2 Lloyd's Rep 109.
7 *Bremer Handels GmbH v Vanden-Avenne Izegem PVBA* [1978] 2 Lloyd's Rep 109.
8 *Mamidoil-Jetoil Greek Petroleum Company SA v Okta Crude Oil Refinery* [2002] EWHC 2210 (Comm).

As to the second aspect, although advisable, express language as to the consequences of non-compliance with the time limit set out in the clause is not usually considered a perquisite for a clause to be a condition precedent. In the case of *Steria v Sigma Wireless Communications*[9] the extension of time clause provided that the contractor had to give notice for extension of time within a reasonable time, but failed to expressly state that failure to give notice would exclude an extension of time. HHJ Davies held that a notification requirement may operate as a condition precedent even though it does not contain an express warning as to the consequence of non-compliance.

Whether a notice may be considered a condition precedent is a delicate issue, particularly in the case of extension of time clauses. Employers should not lightly disregard late notices on the assumption that the obligation to notify is a condition precedent as, should such assumption prove wrong, this may cause time to become "at large" and result in the employer losing its right to liquidated damages. As stated in *Keating on Building Contracts*:[10]

> If the Architect wrongly assumes that a notice by the contractor is a condition precedent to the performance of the duty of the Architect to form an opinion and take appropriate steps and in consequence refuses toper form such duties the employer loses his right to liquidated damages. It may therefore be against the employer's interests for an Architect not to consider a cause of delay of which late notice is given or of which he has knowledge despite lack of notice.

The timing by which a contractor shall send a valid notice is a matter of contract. Claim clauses will usually state that the contractor shall give the notice as soon as possible/practicable and in any case within a certain timeframe (28 days being a common one). The clause will also commonly state when "the clock will start ticking". This will typically be after the contractor becomes aware, or should have become aware, of the event or circumstance giving rise to the claim. This starting point may be considered from a prospective or retrospective point of view. In the case of *Obrascon Huarte Lain SA v Her Majesty's Attorney General for Gibraltar*[11] the court was called to decide on a clause (Clause 20.1) stating that, in the event the contractor intended to claim an extension of time and/or an additional payment, it had to: "*give notice to the Engineer, describing the event or circumstance giving rise to the claim. The notice shall be given as soon as practicable, and not later than 28 days after [the contractor] became aware, or should have become aware, of the event or circumstance*", failing which the contractor would not be entitled to any extension of time or additional payment. Clause 8.4 of the same contract stated that: "*The Contractor shall be entitled subject to Sub-Clause 20.1 . . . to an extension of the Time for Completion if and to the extent that the completion . . . is or will be delayed*". Akenhead J held that Clause 20.1 had to be construed broadly and taking into account Clause 8.4. Therefore, although Clause 20.1 stated that the 28-day timeframe commenced when the contractor "*became aware, or should have become aware*" of the event or circumstance, the language "*is or will be delayed*" meant that an

9 *Steria v Sigma Wireless Communications* [2007] EWHC 3454 (TCC); [2008] BLR 79.

10 Keating, J. Uff, *Keating on Building Contracts* (4th edition) Sweet & Maxwell, 1984 at p. 346.

11 *Obrascon Huarte Lain SA v Her Majesty's Attorney General for Gibraltar* [2014] EWHC 1028 (TCC).

extension of time claim could be made either retrospectively (i.e., when the delay had already occurred) or prospectively (i.e., when it was clear that a delay would occur).

40.3.2 Content of a claim notice

The parties are free to agree in the contract on the content that a notice of claim shall have, including the specific time by which the notice shall be sent. Where the clause does not expressly give any specific indication, the courts will typically consider that the contractor is merely required to do his best as soon as he reasonably can to provide supporting details of which he has knowledge and information available to the contractor at the time. This approach was confirmed in the case of *Multiplex Constructions (UK) Ltd v Honeywell Control Systems Ltd (No2)*[12] where the Technology and Construction Court considered a clause stating as follows:

> 11.2.1 If and whenever it becomes apparent or should have become apparent to an experienced and competent Sub-Contractor that the commencement, progress or completion of the Sub-Contract Works or any part thereof is being or is likely to be delayed, the Sub-Contractor shall forthwith give written notice to the Contractor of the material circumstances including, in so far as the Sub-Contractor is able, the cause or causes of the delay and identify in such notice any event which in his opinion is a Relevant Event.
>
> 2 In respect of each and every Relevant Event, and identified in the notice given in accordance with clause 11.2.1, the Sub-Contractor shall, if practicable in such notice, or otherwise in writing as soon as possible after such notice:
>
> .1 give particulars of the expected effects thereof; and
>
> .2 estimate the extent, if any, of the expected delay in the completion of the Sub-Contract Works beyond the expiry of the period or periods stated in the Appendix Part 4 or beyond the expiry of any extended period or periods previously fixed under clauses 11 or 4.6 which results therefrom not double counting delay caused by another Relevant Event or taking into account delay to the completion of the Sub-Contract Works for which the Sub-Contractor is responsible or bears the risk which in either case is concurrent with delay caused by such Relevant Event; and
>
> .3 the Sub-Contractor shall give further written notices to the Contractor as may be necessary or as the Contractor may reasonably require for keeping up-to-date the particulars and estimate referred to in clause 11.2.2.1 and .2 including any material change in such particulars or estimate.

Mr. Justice Jackson held that:

> This clause does not require the sub-contractor to provide information which is not available to him at the time of the notice, or indeed at any later time. Clause 11.2.2 requires the sub-contractor to provide the specified information 'if practicable' in his notice or otherwise 'as soon as possible'.
>
> 80. Standing back for a moment from the various sub-sub-clauses, I construe clause 11.2 as requiring the sub-contractor to do his best as soon as he reasonably can. I do not read

12 *Multiplex Constructions (UK) Ltd v Honeywell Control Systems Ltd (No2)* [2007] EWHC 447 (TCC) at [79] and [80].

clause 11.2 as requiring the sub-contractor to serve notices or to provide supporting details which go beyond the knowledge and information available to him.

40.3.3 Practical aspects of claim notices

A claim notice should reflect the contractual requirements as being as precise and unambiguous as possible. Before serving it, the claimant shall consider the relevant clause and the whole contract to ascertain and ensure that the notice: (i) contains all the required information at the level of detail required by the contract; (ii) is sent within the time limit set out in the contract; (iii) is delivered through one of the means allowed by the contract (e.g., courier, email, etc.). Where the contract refers to "any effective means", this will likely be interpreted by the courts as including post or couriers, emails, fax or even hand delivery, to the extent delivery can be proved; (iv) is delivered to the right recipient. Particular attention should be paid in case the clause provides that different types of communications should be sent to different recipients.

Moreover, once the notice is sent, the sender should obtain and keep evidence that it was validly served (e.g., through the relevant courier delivery slip, email delivery receipt, fax transmission report, etc.).

CHAPTER 41

Claims against the employer

41.1 Extension of time claims

41.1.1 Extensions of time claims in general

Time for completion and consequences of delay are pivotal aspects for contractors. A delayed project may lead to increased costs resulting from the prolonged permanence at the site and to the distraction of resources which the contractor may use on other projects (new projects or projects already awarded which may overlap with the delayed project).

A contractor will normally be required to complete the originally contracted scope of works within the agreed completion date (or within a specified time) as defined in the construction contract. Failure to comply with this obligation will result in a critical delay (i.e., a delay affecting the project's completion date) and will typically expose the contractor to delay damages, which may either be liquidated or general (i.e., unliquidated). However, a contractor may avoid or reduce its exposure to damages by claiming an extension of time for completion ("EOT") where contractually or legally entitled to do so.

An EOT claim is aimed at obtaining a new extended completion date. It has the effect to relieve the contractor of any liability to pay damages for delays accrued prior to the extended completion date and avoids time becoming "at large".[1]

41.1.2 Extensions of time and prolongation costs

It is worth noting that the entitlement to an EOT will not automatically carry an entitlement to any resulting prolongation costs. As stated in the Society of Construction Law Delay and Disruption Protocol ("SCL Protocol"):[2]

> It is often incorrectly thought that an entitlement to an EOT automatically carries with it an entitlement to compensation for prolongation costs during the period of the EOT. The main effect of an EOT is that the Contractor is relieved of its liability for liquidated damages during the period of the extension and is able to reprogramme its works to completion. Its entitlement to compensation is usually to be found in other provisions of the contract or at law. The benefit of an EOT for the Employer is that it establishes a new contract completion date, prevents time for completion of the works becoming 'at large' and allows for coordination/planning of its own activities, such as training operational staff.

1 In which case, the contractor shall complete the works within a reasonable timeframe.

2 *Society of Construction Law Delay and Disruption Protocol* (2nd edition) February 2017, www.scl.org.uk, at p. 22.

DOI: 10.4324/9781003387718-51

The correlation between EOTs and prolongation costs claims was also clearly stated in the case of *Costain Limited v Charles Haswell & Partners Limited*,[3] where it was held:

> When an extension of time of the project completion date is claimed, the contractor needs to establish that a delay to an activity on the critical path has occurred of a certain number of days or weeks and that that delay has in fact pushed out the completion date at the end of the project by a given number of days or weeks, after taking account of any mitigation or acceleration measures. If the contractor establishes those facts, he is entitled to an extension of time for completion of the whole project including, of course, all those activities which were not in fact delayed by the delaying events at all, i.e. they were not on the critical path.
>
> But a claim for damages on account of delays to construction work is rather different. There, in order to recover substantial damages, the contractor needs to show what losses he has incurred as a result of the prolongation of the activity in question. . . . Simply because the delaying event itself is on the critical path does not mean that in point of fact it impacted on any other site activity save for those immediately following and dependent upon the activities in question.

41.1.3 Claiming extensions of time

Whether a contractor is entitled to an extension of time will depend on the type of delay and how the contract regulates the subject.

Critical delays may fall within one of the following three categories: (i) excusable delays, for which the contractor is contractually and/or legally entitled to an EOT and excused from having to pay delay damages. Such delays are those at the employer's risk (for this reason they are also known as "employer delays") and are typically caused by one or more employer's acts (e.g., acts of prevention, variations, etc.) or due to the occurrence of neutral events for which the employer is contractually or legally responsible (i.e., events outside the parties' control such as force majeure events); (ii) compensable delays, for which the contractor is contractually and/or legally entitled to recover costs or losses incurred as a result of such delays (possibly, in addition to any EOT). Such delays are usually caused by one or more employer's acts and will not normally extend to neutral events (although the parties may agree otherwise and make delays due to neutral events compensable); and (iii) unexcused delays, for which the contractor is not entitled to any EOT and/or compensation, e.g., because it had assumed the relevant risk.

A contractor claiming an EOT shall show a number of elements, including the following:

41.1.3.1 Entitlement

Almost invariably, construction contracts relevant to large projects contain EOT clauses which set a mechanism for extending the time for completion in case of contractor excusable delays. Where the contract does not provide for such a mechanism[4] or the EOT clause contained in the contract does not apply to the specific delay event, a contractor may base its claim on the doctrine of prevention or run a more general claim for breach of an express or implied term of the contract.

---

3 *Costain Limited v Charles Haswell & Partners Limited* [2009] EWHC 3140 (TCC).

4 If the contract provides for an extension of time mechanism for the specific events, the prevention principle does not apply. See *Adyard Abu Dhabi v SD Marine Services* [2011] EWHC 848 (Comm) at [243].

41.1.3.2 Employer risk event

The second element that a contractor must show to get an EOT is that the delay was caused by an event which under the contract is at the risk and responsibility of the employer. These will typically be delays caused by the employer or by neutral events.[5]

41.1.3.2.1 DELAYS CAUSED BY THE EMPLOYER

Delays caused by the employer may be due, for example, to variations or employer's breaches of contract (for example, the employer may delay the project as a result of a breach of its contractual obligation to grant the contractor access to the site within a certain date).

Such delays are usually both excusable (i.e., entitling the contractor to an EOT and reducing liquidated damages) and compensable (i.e., entitling the contractor to also recover prolongation costs in addition to an EOT).

41.1.3.2.2 DELAYS CAUSED BY NEUTRAL EVENTS

Neutral events are events which are not in the parties' control (e.g., force majeure events such as wars, floods, pandemics, etc.). They typically lead to delays that are excusable, but not also compensable, the rationale being that, whilst it would be unfair for a contractor to pay liquidated damages for delays due to events which were not in its control, it would also be unfair for an employer to bear the economic consequences deriving from delays for which it is not responsible. As said by Judge Edgar Fay QC in the case of *Henry Boot Construction Ltd v Central Lancashire New Town Development Corp*:[6]

> There are cases where the loss should be shared, and there are cases where it should be wholly borne by the employer. There are also cases which do not fall within either of these conditions and which are the fault of the contractor. But in cases where the fault is not that of the contractor the scheme clearly is that in certain cases the loss is to be shared: the loss lies where it falls. But in other cases the employer has to compensate the contractor in respect of the delay, and that category, where the employer has to compensate the contractor, should, one would think, clearly be composed of cases where there is fault upon the employer or fault for which the employer can be said to bear some responsibility.

However, there may be instances in which a contractor may be unable to claim an EOT even for delays caused by neutral events, for example in case of unforeseen site conditions, where the contract does not contemplate the granting of an EOT[7] or where the neutral event occurs when the works are already in delay due to the contractor's fault. In such case, the contractor may not be entitled to claim an EOT where, had it completed the works within the stipulated completion date, the effects caused by the neutral event would have been avoided.[8]

5 "*sometimes misleadingly called 'neutral events'; in fact, they are only neutral in the sense that one party [the employer] bears the time risk and the other party [the contractor] bears the cost risk*". See *Society of Construction Law Delay and Disruption Protocol* (2nd edition) February 2017, www.scl.org.uk, at p. 37. A classic example is delay resulting from adverse weather conditions.

6 *Henry Boot Construction Ltd v Central Lancashire New Town Development Corp* [1980] 15 BLR 1 (QBD) at [12].

7 *Bacal Construction (Midlands) Ltd v Northampton Development Corporation* [1975] 8 BLR 88 at [100].

8 *Balfour Beatty Building Ltd v Chestermount Properties Ltd* [1993] 62 BLR 1 at [34] – [35].

41.1.3.3 Causation

41.1.3.3.1 CAUSATION IN GENERAL

The contractor must prove that the delay event caused a critical delay (i.e., causation). A delay is critical when it is a delay to progress of any work activity falling on the "critical path" which results in the overall project duration being extended.

Causation is not easy to prove in case of complex construction projects, which are the result of a myriad of work activities. While some of such work activities may be performed in parallel, the majority of them may only be commenced after completion of other work activities in the same chain. In the first case, a delay affecting one of the work activities will not usually affect the contractor's ability to perform the others. In the second case, a delay event affecting one work activity will generate several constrains impacting the timing of the next work activities in the chain, up to completion. Where such work activities are on the critical path, this will create a critical delay. An explanation of this may be found in *Cleveland Bridge UK Ltd v Severfield-Rowen Structures Ltd*:[9]

> on a simple house construction, a delay in the provision of the foundations will, generally and obviously, cause delay to all the following trades so that for instance the brickwork and blockwork which may rest on the foundations in question cannot commence and the windows and the roof cannot go until the brickwork and blockwork are done; that is logical and to be expected. However, the position becomes much more complex when one is looking at a building like the Shard. Certain it is that at least some steelwork has to be in place before follow on trades, such as concrete flowing and glazing or curtain walling, can be commenced; it is not the case that all the steelwork needs to be in place before such follow on trades can commence. Thus, the fact that the steel work is finished late does not, necessarily, mean that the overall project would be late.

The level of complexity is even higher in cases where delay is the result of a multitude of simultaneous and/or consecutive causes overlapping each other, and delays are "concurrent" (meaning that the contractor and the employer are each responsible for some of the delay events).

41.1.3.3.2 CONCURRENT DELAY

(A) MEANING OF CONCURRENT DELAY In the case of complex construction projects, it is not unusual for more delay events to concur in determining a delay. Under English law there is no agreed meaning of concurrent delay. One famous definition is the one coined by John Marrin QC according to which concurrent delay is:

> a period of project overrun which is caused by two or more effective causes of delay which are of approximately equal causative potency.[10]

This definition was accepted in *North Midland Building Ltd v Cyden Homes Ltd*[11] which, being a Court of Appeal decision, binds lower courts, as well as arbitrators and adjudicators.

9 *Cleveland Bridge UK Ltd v Severfield-Rowen Structures Ltd* [2012] EWHC 3652 (TCC) at [121].

10 J. Marrin QC, *"Concurrent Delay"* (2002) 18(6) Construction Law Journal 436. This definition was then adopted by Hamblen J in *Adyard Abu Dhabi v SD Marine Services* [2011] EWHC 848 (Comm) and subsequently by Coulson LJ in *North Midland Building Ltd v Cyden Homes Ltd* [2018] EWCA Civ 1744.

11 *North Midland Building Ltd v Cyden Homes Ltd* [2018] EWCA Civ 1744.

A consequence of this approach would be that the existence of a concurrent delay may be assessed by performing a critical path analysis whereby the delay expert will consider whether a critical delay would still occur after having eliminated all the competing causes of delay: (i) which have not impacted the critical path; and (ii) which have impacted the critical path, but are of markedly different causative potency (i.e. are minor causes of delay), which will be treated as they were not causative at all.[12]

(B) TIMING OF THE DELAY EVENTS In the case of *Royal Brompton Hospital National Health Service Trust v Frederick Hammond and Others and Taylor Woodrow Construction (Holdings) Limited*[13] Seymour J took the position that two or more competing events would determine a situation of concurrent delay only where all events start and release their effects at the same time. In the SCL Protocol[14] this narrow definition of concurrent delay, which is described as "*true concurrent delay*",[15] is said to rarely occur, while situations of mere concurrent delay, where the delay events arise at different times, but their effects are felt at the same time, are more common.

It is now generally accepted that for a concurrent delay to occur it is not necessary that the two or more delay events have occurred at the same time, but the relevant delaying effects must be contemporaneous.

(C) CONSEQUENCES OF CONCURRENT DELAY Under English law, the parties are free to allocate risk in their contract as they deem appropriate. This includes the risks and consequences deriving from situations of concurrent delay. Although it would not be usual for a construction contract to expressly address the issue of concurrent delay, the courts will be inclined to uphold the parties' choice and hold them to their bargain.[16] Thus, how concurrent delay is treated will ultimately depend on relevant contract terms and their application to the circumstances of the case.

Where the contract does expressly cover the subject of concurrent delay, the court will be called to determine the consequences of concurrency on the contractor's EOT claim.

The issue of concurrency is far from being resolved. In *Walter Lilly* Mr Justice Akenhead mentioned two schools of thought:[17] (i) the English school, based on which the contractor is entitled to a full EOT for the delay caused by the two or more events (i.e., the so-called Malmaison approach); and (ii) the Scottish school based on which the contractor is only entitled to an EOT on the basis of a reasonable apportionment of the concurrently caused delay.

The Scottish approach derives from the case of *City Inn Ltd v Shepherd Construction Ltd*[18] where the Scottish appeal court held that in cases where there are two concurrent

12 J. Marrin QC, "*Concurrent Delay*" (2002) 18(6) Construction Law Journal 436; J. Marrin QC "*Concurrent Delay Revisited*" (2013) The Society of Construction Law, February, Paper 179.

13 *Royal Brompton Hospital National Health Service Trust v Hammond and Others and Taylor Woodrow Construction (Holdings) Limited* [2002] UKHL 14.

14 *Society of Construction Law Delay and Disruption Protocol* (2nd edition) February 2017, www.scl.org.uk, at p. 30.

15 *Society of Construction Law Delay and Disruption Protocol* (2nd edition) February 2017, www.scl.org.uk, at p. 30.

16 *North Midland Building Ltd v Cyden Homes Ltd* [2017] EWHC 2414 (TCC).

17 *Walter Lilly & Co Ltd v Mackay* [2012] EWHC 1773 (TCC); [2012] BLR 503.

18 *City Inn Ltd v Shepherd Construction Ltd* [2010] ScotCS CSIH 68.

delay events, one of which is a "relevant event" (i.e., an event that would entitle the contractor to an EOT) and the other an event for which the contractor is liable, but no dominant cause of delay may be identified, it would be appropriate to apportion the delay between the parties in a fair and reasonable manner. The court said:

> Where a situation exists in which two causes are operative, one being a relevant event and the other some other event for which the contractor is to be taken to be responsible, and neither of which could be described as the dominant cause, the claim for extension of time will not necessarily fail. In such a situation, which could, as a matter of language, be described as one of concurrent causes, in a broad sense, it will be open to the decision-maker, whether the architect, or other tribunal, approaching the issue in a fair and reasonable way, to apportion the delay in the completion of the works occasioned thereby as between the relevant event and the other event.

The "Malmaison principle" was formulated by Mr Justice Dyson in *Henry Boot Construction (UK) Ltd v Malmaison Hotel (Manchester) Ltd*:[19]

> It is agreed that if there are two concurrent causes of delay, one of which is a relevant event and the other is not, then the contractor is entitled to an extension of time for the period of delay caused by the relevant event notwithstanding the concurrent effect of the other event. Thus, to take a simple example, if no work is possible on a site for a week not only because of exceptionally inclement weather (a relevant event), but also because the contractor has a shortage of labour (not a relevant event), and if the failure to work during that week is likely to delay the works beyond the completion date by one week, then if he considers it fair and reasonable to do so, the architect is required to grant an extension of time of one week. He cannot refuse to do so on the grounds that the delay would have occurred in any event by reason of the shortage of labour.

The effect of the Malmaison principle is that it would be sufficient that one of the concurrent causes of the delay be an employer delay for the contractor to be entitled to an EOT for the whole period of delay irrespective of the fact that the contractor was responsible for part of the delay (i.e., the existence of a delay event for which the contractor is responsible is irrelevant to the assessment of an EOT).

The Malmaison approach was supported in various subsequent cases. In *De Beers v Atos Origin IT Services UK Ltd*[20] Mr Justice Edwards Stuart said:

> The general rule in construction and engineering cases is that where there is concurrent delay to completion caused by matters for which both employer and contractor are responsible, the contractor is entitled to an extension of time but he cannot recover in respect of the loss caused by the delay. In the case of the former, this is because the rule where delay is caused by the employer is that not only must the contractor complete within a reasonable time but also the contractor must have a reasonable time within which to complete. It therefore does not matter if the contractor would have been unable to complete by the contractual completion date if there had been no breaches of contract by the employer (or other events which entitled

19 *Henry Boot Construction (UK) Ltd v Malmaison Hotel (Manchester) Ltd (1999)* 70 Con LR 32 at paragraph 13. Although in that case the judge "*was simply repeating the common ground between the parties rather than reach a considered decision on the issue*" *(Walter Lilly & Company Limited v Giles Patrick Cyril Mackay* [2012] EWHC 1773 (TCC); [2012] BLR 503 at paragraph 370), "*Nonetheless the fact that he, as a judge with such wide experience in the field, noted the agreement without adverse comment is a strong indication that he considered that it correctly stated the position*" (*Steria Ltd v Sigma Wireless Communications Ltd* [2008] BLR 79 (TCC), 118 Con LR 177, [2008] CILL 2544 at [131].

20 *De Beers v Atos Origin IT Services UK Ltd* [2011] BLR 274 at [177].

> the contractor to an extension of time), because he is entitled to have the time within which to complete which the contract allows or which the employer's conduct has made reasonably necessary.

In *Adyard Abu Dhabi v SD Marine Services*[21] Mr Justice Hamblen quoted as good law the words of Mr Justice Dyson in the *Henry Boot* case:

> It is to be noted that this example involves a relevant event which caused a period of actual delay to the progress of the works – no work could be done for a week due to the weather. If that is established then the contractor is entitled to his extension of time even if there is another concurrent cause of that same delay. A useful working definition of concurrent delay in this context is "a period of project overrun which is caused by two or more effective causes of delay which are of approximately equal causative potency".

In *Walter Lilly & Company Limited v Giles Patrick Cyril Mackay*[22] Mr Justice Akenhead said:

> In any event, I am clearly of the view that, where there is an extension of time clause such as that agreed upon in this case and where delay is caused by two or more effective causes, one of which entitles the Contractor to an extension of time as being a Relevant Event, the Contractor is entitled to a full extension of time.

Thus, based on the Scottish and the Malmaison approaches, delays caused by two or more concurrent causes, only one of which entitles the contractor to an EOT, the contractor will always be entitled to an extension EOT, which may either be "apportioned" or "full", depending on the chosen approach.

(D) CONCURRENT DELAY AND PREVENTION PRINCIPLE Based on the prevention principle a party A may not require the other B to comply with a contractual obligation in circumstances where that party A has prevented party B from complying with that obligation.

In the context of delays, in *Holme v Guppy*[23] Parke B noted that there were clear authorities to the effect that:

> if the party be prevented by the refusal of the other contracting party from completing the contract within the time limited he is not liable in law for the default.

In general terms, an employer that has prevented the contractor from achieving completion within the agreed completion date may not hold the contractor to that date. In such cases, where the contract does not include any mechanism to extend time for completion, time may become "at large" (i.e., the contractor shall complete the works within a reasonable time and the employer may not apply liquidated damages (unless the employer subsequently makes time of the essence).

In *Multiplex Constructions (UK) Ltd v Honeywell Control Systems Ltd*[24] the court said:

---

21 *Adyard Abu Dhabi v SD Marine Services* [2011] EWHC 848 Comm at [277].

22 *Walter Lilly & Company Limited v Giles Patrick Cyril Mackay* [2012] EWHC 1773 (TCC); [2012] BLR 503 at [370].

23 *Holme v Guppy* [1838] 3 M&W 387.

24 *Multiplex Constructions (UK) Ltd v Honeywell Control Systems Ltd* [2007] EWHC 447 (TCC), [2007] BLR 195, 111 Con LR 78, [2007] CILL 2458 at [47]; note 19 at [56].

From this review of authority I derive three propositions:

1. Actions by the employer which are perfectly legitimate under a construction contract may still be characterised as prevention, if those actions cause delay beyond the contractual completion date.
2. Acts of prevention by an employer do not set time at large, if the contract provides for an extension of time in respect of those events.
3. Insofar as the extension of time clause is ambiguous, it should be construed in favour of the contractor.

Thus, applying the prevention principle to cases of concurrent delays would mean that time becomes "at large".

However, whether the prevention principle applies in cases of concurrent delay is not an agreed topic.

In *Peak Construction (Liverpool) Ltd v McKinney Foundations Ltd*[25] Salmon LJ observed that the prevention principle applies to concurrent delay:

> If the failure to complete on time is due to the fault of both the employer and the contractor, in my view the clause (giving the employer liquidated damages) does not bite. I cannot see how, in the ordinary course, the employer can insist on compliance with a condition if it is partly his own fault that it cannot be fulfilled. . . . I consider that unless the contract expresses a contrary intention, the employer, in the circumstances postulated, is left to his ordinary remedy; that is to say, to recover such damages as he can prove flow from the contractor's breach.

In *Hudson's Building and Engineering Contracts*[26] the authors say:

> Thus, it is well established that an Employer is not entitled to liquidated damages if by their acts or omissions they have prevented the Contractor from completing their work by the completion date. Whether concurrent with another Contractor delay or not, there is no reason why the principle should not be the same.

Another position is that in cases of concurrent delay where the employer's prevention is concurrent with the contractor delay the prevention principle does not apply as the delay would have occurred regardless of the employer's acts of prevention. Thus, in such cases, the contractor should take responsibility for the delays regardless of the employer delay.

In *Adyard Abu Dhabi v SD Marine Services*[27] the court held that for the principle of prevention to apply the act of prevention must render it impossible or impractical for the other party to do his work within the stipulated time, which is not the case in situations of concurrent delay where the contractor is already in culpable delay.

In *Jerram Falkus Construction Ltd v Fenice Investments Inc*[28] the court held that the prevention principle could apply only where the contractor is able to demonstrate that the employer's acts or omissions prevented the contractor from completing earlier than the agreed completion date, which may not occur in situations of concurrent delay where the contractor is not able to complete earlier due to its own concurrent delays. The court said:

25 *Peak Construction (Liverpool) Ltd v McKinney Foundations Ltd* [1970] 1 BLR 111.

26 N. Dennys, M. Reaside, R. Clay (general editors), *Hudson's Building and Engineering Contracts* (12th edition) Sweet & Maxwell, 2010, at para 6–060.

27 *Adyard Abu Dhabi v SD Marine Services* [2011] EWHC 848 (Comm).

28 *Jerram Falkus Construction Ltd v Fenice Investments Inc* [2011] EWHC 1935 (TCC).

> Accordingly, I conclude that, for the prevention principle to apply, the contractor must be able to demonstrate that the employer's acts or omissions have prevented the contractor from achieving an earlier completion date and that, if that earlier completion date would not have been achieved anyway, because of concurrent delays caused by the contractor's own default, the prevention principle will not apply.

On the point, *Keating on Construction Contracts*[29] takes the following view:

> However, where there are concurrent causes of delay (one the contractor's responsibility and the other the employer's) the prevention principle would not be triggered because the delay would have occurred anyway absent the employer delay event.

The subject was recently considered by the Court of Appeal in the case of *North Midland Building Ltd v Cyden Homes Ltd.*[30] The contractor argued that an EOT clause excluding the right to claim EOTs in cases of concurrent delay was void by operation of the prevention principle. According to the contractor, by operation of the prevention principle, which is a rule of law, the contractor could not be held to a completion date which the employer had prevented it from achieving. The Court of Appeal disagreed and held that where a contract is silent on whether an employer's act of prevention entitles a contractor to an extension of time, the prevention principle will apply to cases of concurrent delay. According to Coulson LJ the prevention principle should be considered as an implied term rather than an overriding rule of public or legal policy. As express terms in the contract (the extension of time clause) can override implied terms, the functioning of the extension of time in concurrent cases did not offend the prevention principle.

(E) CONCURRENT DELAYS AND PROLONGATION COSTS In cases of concurrent delay, a contractor will not be entitled to recover delay damages (i.e., prolongation costs) if it would have suffered the same loss as a result of delays caused by events it is contractually responsible for.[31] The rationale is that in such cases the contractor has not satisfied the "but for" test, i.e., it has not shown that it would not have suffered the damages but for the employer's delay.

In cases where the contractor is able to satisfy the "but for" test, it will be entitled to recover compensation only to the extent it can separate the additional costs caused by the employer delay from those caused by the contractor delay.[32]

41.1.3.3.3 MITIGATION

Under English law, an injured party is required to mitigate its loss, i.e., to take all reasonable measure to minimise such loss. A failure to take reasonable mitigating measures will prevent the injured party from recovering damages that could have been avoided had such measures been taken.

In the context of EOT claims, contractors have a duty to mitigate delays and the resulting losses, for example by resequencing and/or accelerating the works (e.g., by increasing workforce or working hours). This obligation is twofold as contractors are required to

29 S. Furst, V. Ramsey, *Keating on Construction Contracts* (10th edition) Sweet & Maxwell, at para 8–014.

30 *North Midland Building Ltd v Cyden Homes Ltd* [2018] EWCA Civ 1744.

31 *De Beers v Atos Origin IT Services UK Ltd* [2011] BLR 274.

32 *Society of Construction Law Delay and Disruption Protocol* (2nd edition) February 2017, www.scl.org.uk, at p. 7.

take reasonable steps aimed at minimising their losses and not take unreasonable steps that may increase such losses.[33] The costs sustained for the mitigation measures will be recoverable even where the contractor was not successful.[34] However, the SCL Protocol[35] suggests that:

> The Contractor does not have a duty to carry out any change in scope any more efficiently than the original scope. Neither is the Contractor obliged to expend money in order to attempt to mitigate the effect of an Employer Risk Event. If the Employer wishes the Contractor to take measures to mitigate the Employer Delay (whether by adding extra resources, by working outside its planned working hours or otherwise), the Employer should agree to pay the Contractor for the costs of those efforts.

41.1.3.3.4 COMPLIANCE WITH CONTRACTUAL REQUIREMENTS

A contractor claiming an EOT should make sure that it has complied with all the requirements mandated by the contract. These include but are not limited to the provisions on the content of the claim, any notification time limits, and any formalities relevant to the notification (e.g., the relevant means and addressee).

41.1.4 Delay analysis

A delay analysis is a type of technical analysis aimed at ascertaining the delay events and assessing their impact on the project to evaluate whether and how such events delayed completion (i.e., were critical).

In *Cleveland Bridge UK Limited v Severfield – Rowen Structures Limited*[36] Mr Justice Akenhead observed that:

> The science or art of delay analysis is one which is based in logic, albeit in a construction context. Thus, on a simple house construction, a delay in the provision of the foundations will, generally and obviously, cause delay to all the following trades so that for instance the brickwork and blockwork which may rest on the foundations in question cannot commence and the windows and the roof can not go on until the brickwork and blockwork are done; that is logical and to be expected. However, the position becomes much more complex when one is looking at a building like the Shard. Certain it is that at least some steelwork has to be in place before follow on trades, such as concrete flooring and glazing or curtain walling, can be commenced; it is not the case that all the steelwork needs to be in place before such follow on trades can commence. Thus, the fact that the steel work is finished late does not, necessarily, mean that the overall project would be late.[37]

Almost invariably, in disputes concerning time and delay in complex construction projects a delay analysis will be carried out (although a claim will not necessarily fail in the absence of such evidence[38]).

33 *Society of Construction Law Delay and Disruption Protocol* (2nd edition) February 2017, www.scl.org.uk, at p. 40.

34 *Cleveland Bridge UK Ltd v Severfield-Rowen Structures Ltd* [2012] EWHC 3652 (TCC).

35 *Society of Construction Law Delay and Disruption Protocol* (2nd edition) February 2017, www.scl.org.uk, at p. 40.

36 *Cleveland Bridge UK Ltd v Severfield-Rowen Structures Ltd* [2012] EWHC 3652 (TCC) at [121].

37 *Cleveland Bridge UK Ltd v Severfield-Rowen Structures Ltd* [2012] EWHC 3652 (TCC) at [121].

38 *City Inn Ltd v Shepherd Construction Ltd* [2007] ScotCS CSOH 190, [2008] BLR 269, (2008) 24 Const LJ 590.

Delay analysis may be carried out in using different methods. The main difference is between: (i) "cause and effect" methods, which start by identifying and describing the event that has caused the delay to establish the delaying effect that such events have had on the project's completion. As the analysis is made retrospectively, these methods consider all the potential causes of the delay. For this reason, they are more reliable in cases where the assessment is made after the works have been completed or significantly after the effects of the delaying event; and (ii) "effect and cause" methods, which start from the critical delay to establish the relevant cause. As the analysis is made prospectively, these methods do not consider all the actual delaying events. For this reason, they are usually used in cases where the assessment is made at the same time of the occurrence of the delaying events.[39]

A delay analysis will normally require the delay expert to identify the critical path (although there may be more than one critical path[40]) to the completion date. In *Mirant Asia-Pacific Construction (Hong Kong) Limited v Ove Arup and Partners International Limited v Ove Arup International Limited and Ove Arup Partners Hong Kong Limited*[41] Judge Toulmin CMG, QC defined the "critical path" as:

> the sequence of activities through a project network from start to finish, the sum of whose durations determines the overall project duration.

The assessment may be made: (i) prospectively, in which case the delay expert does not take into consideration the actual progress achieved by the contractor; (ii) contemporaneously, in which case the delay expert considers progress and the perspective impact that changes in the strategy may have on predicted criticality (e.g., any attempted acceleration or re-sequencing of the works or redeployment of resources); or (iii) retrospectively, in which case the delay expert adopts the perspective at the project's completion.[42]

Once the critical path is determined, the delay expert will determine the delay impact. This may be done: (i) prospectively, in which case the delay expert will endeavour to establish the likely impact that actual progress and/or delay events already occurred may have on the achievement of completion by the completion date; or (ii) retrospectively, in which case the delay expert will consider the actual impact that the delay events had on the critical path.[43]

The SCL Protocol[44] identifies the following six commonly used methods of delay analysis:

(i) The "impacted as-planned analysis" which:

> involves introducing delay event sub-networks into a logic-linked baseline programme and its recalculation using CPM [Critical Path Method] programming

39 *Society of Construction Law Delay and Disruption Protocol* (2nd edition) February 2017, www.scl.org.uk, at p. 32.

40 *Mirant Asia-Pacific Construction (Hong Kong) Limited v Ove Arup and Partners International Limited v Ove Arup International Limited and Ove Arup Partners Hong Kong Limited* [2007] EWHC 918.

41 *Mirant Asia-Pacific Construction (Hong Kong) Limited v Ove Arup and Partners International Limited v Ove Arup International Limited and Ove Arup Partners Hong Kong Limited* [2007] EWHC 918.

42 *Society of Construction Law Delay and Disruption Protocol* (2nd edition) February 2017, www.scl.org.uk, at p. 33.

43 *Society of Construction Law Delay and Disruption Protocol* (2nd edition) February 2017, www.scl.org.uk, at p. 33.

44 *Society of Construction Law Delay and Disruption Protocol* (2nd edition) February 2017, www.scl.org.uk, at p. 34–37.

> software in order to determine the prospective impact these events have on the predicted contract completion dates shown within the baseline programme.[45]

This is a simple method, which can be used either for retrospective or for prospective analysis, whereby the analyst examines the impact of single events (or groups of events) on the planned programme. The software[46] simply calculates the likely effect that the selected delay events may have on the baseline programme without considering actual progress and changes that occurred throughout the project. This type of analysis assumes that, but for the events of delay caused by the employer, the contractor would have completed the works within the planned period.[47] There are obvious limitations which render this analysis just hypothetical and thus sufficient only in limited circumstance.[48] In *Great Eastern Hotel Co Ltd v John Laing Construction Ltd*[49] the court held that impacted as-planned analysis takes:

> no account of the actual events which occurred on the Project and gives rise to hypothetical answer when timing of design release is compared against the original construction programme.

(ii) The "time impact analysis" which:

> involves introducing delay event subnetworks into a logic-linked baseline programme and recalculation of this updated programme using CPM programming software in order to determine the prospective impact the delay event would have on the then predicted completion dates. The baseline programme for each analysis can be either a contemporaneous programme or a contemporaneously updated baseline programme (i.e. an Updated Programme), the difference being the revised contemporaneous programme may have logic changes/activity/resource changes from the original baseline programme.[50]

This is a prospective analysis whereby the delay expert updates the contractor's programme to reflect the progress achieved at the time of the delaying event and then calculates the anticipated completion dates with and without the delaying events.[51]

Compared to the impacted as-planned analysis, the time impact analysis is more accurate as the delay event is inserted in the baseline schedule which existed at the time of the event (which includes any contractor delay that occurred prior to the event). Time impact analysis has the limit of being a prospective

45 *Society of Construction Law Delay and Disruption Protocol* (2nd edition) February 2017, www.scl.org.uk, at p. 34–35.

46 Although this analysis may be performed without computer software.

47 K. Rosemberg, E. Miller Rankin, B. Dayton, *Dealing With Delay and Disruption on Construction Projects* (1st edition) Sweet & Maxwell, 2020, at p. 87.

48 "*Such circumstances include where the impacted as-planned method is dictated by the terms of the contract and/or where the delay events being considered occurs right at the outset of the works*". (*Society of Construction Law Delay and Disruption Protocol* (2nd edition) February 2017, www.scl.org.uk, at p. 35)

49 *Great Eastern Hotel Co Ltd v John Laing Construction Ltd* [2005] EWHC 181 (TCC) at [184].

50 *Society of Construction Law Delay and Disruption Protocol* (2nd edition) February 2017, www.scl.org.uk, at p. 35.

51 B. Eggleston, *Liquidated Damages and Extensions of Time in Construction Contracts* (3rd edition) Wiley-Blackwell, 2009, at p. 321.

analysis, which makes the relevant outcome a forecast that does not consider the subsequent progress of the works and the eventual actual delay caused by the relevant delay events.

(iii) The "time slice analysis", which:

> requires the analyst to verify (or develop) a reliable series of contemporaneously updated baseline programmes or revised contemporaneous programmes reflecting an accurate status of the works at various snapshots (being the time slices) throughout the course of the works.[52]

A delay expert performing a time slice analysis will divide the progress of the works (as updated from time to time) into "time slices" (typically monthly windows) so to show the contemporaneous critical path and the critical delay incurred in each window and then look at the project records to determine what events might have caused the identified critical delay in each time slice period, and who bears the relevant responsibility.

The limit of this method is that it is heavily dependent on how precise the cotemporaneous schedule updates are as they shall reflect the progress of all key activities and the occurrence of all significant events. Moreover, when performed forensically this method is the most costly and time-consuming.

(iv) The "as-planned versus as-built windows" in which:

> the duration of the works is broken down into windows.[53] Those windows are framed by revised contemporaneous programmes, contemporaneously updated programmes, milestones or significant events. The analyst determines the contemporaneous or actual critical path in each window by a common-sense and practical analysis of the available facts.

In this case, the delay expert: (a) divides the updated progress of the works into windows; (b) determines the incidence and extent of critical delay in each window by comparing key dates along the contemporaneous or actual critical path against corresponding planned dates in the baseline programme; and (c) looks at the project records to determine what events might have caused the identified critical delay in each time slice period, and who bears the relevant responsibility.

It is a retrospective method of delay analysis which examines the progress actually achieved against the progress as planned. Compared to the time slice analysis, the as-planned versus as-built windows is less reliant on programming software and more focused on a common-sense and practical analysis of the facts. As such, it is more suitable where there are concerns over the reliability of the baseline programme or where there are no reliable or there are too few contemporaneously updated programmes.

(v) The "retrospective longest path analysis" which:

---

52 *Society of Construction Law Delay and Disruption Protocol* (2nd edition) February 2017, www.scl.org.uk, at p. 35.

53 Time slice analysis and as-planned versus as-built windows are indeed called windows analysis methods.

> involves the determination of the retrospective as-built critical path (which should not be confused with the contemporaneous or actual critical path identified in the windows methods above). In this method, the analyst must first verify or develop a detailed as-built programme. Once completed, the analyst then traces the longest continuous path backwards from the actual completion date to determine the as-built critical path.[54]

In this case, once the delay expert has determined the as-built critical path, he will compare key dates along the as-built critical path against corresponding planned dates in the baseline programme in order to determine incidence and extent of critical delay, and then investigate the project records to establish what events might have caused the identified critical delay and who is responsible for them. Limitations to this method are that it is overly subjective as it relies on the analyst's interpretation of the project records and facts[55] and has a limited capacity to recognise and allow for switches in the critical path across the works.[56]

(vi) The "collapsed as-built (or "but for") analysis" which:

> involves the extraction of delay events from the as-built programme to provide a hypothesis of what might have happened had the delay events not occurred.

This is a retrospective method where the delay expert extracts (or collapses out) delays from the as-built programme to assess when the contractor would have achieved completion but for the delaying effects attributable to the employer or to the contractor. The expert does not use as as-built schedule the last baseline schedule update, but rather re-creates the schedule with software by logically creating and linking all the as-built activities. Once the as-built schedule is complete, the analyst identifies the delay events and extracts them to determine the relevant impact of each event.

Which method should be preferred will depend on the type of project and EOT claim. As a general guidance, in *Mirant Asia-Pacific Construction (Hong Kong) Limited v Ove Arup and Partners International Limited v Ove Arup International Limited and Ove Arup Partners Hong Kong Limited*[57] Judge Toulmin CMG, QC indicated that: (i) a windows analysis, which involves regular reviews and updates on the progress of a project for set intervals of time (usually a month), is an excellent and the most accepted method of critical path analysis as it enables the employer and contractor quickly to identify and deal with delays; while (ii) a watersheds analysis, where the critical path analysis is only undertaken at critical benchmarks in a project (usually months apart) is less reliable as

54 *Society of Construction Law Delay and Disruption Protocol* (2nd edition) February 2017, www.scl.org.uk, at p. 36.

55 K. Rosemberg, E. Miller Rankin, B. Dayton, *Dealing With Delay and Disruption on Construction Projects* (1st edition) Sweet & Maxwell, 2020, at p. 112.

56 *Society of Construction Law Delay and Disruption Protocol* (2nd edition) February 2017, www.scl.org.uk, at p. 36.

57 *Mirant Asia-Pacific Construction (Hong Kong) Limited v Ove Arup and Partners International Limited v Ove Arup International Limited and Ove Arup Partners Hong Kong Limited* [2007] EWHC 918.

it provides only a "snapshot" of the time at which it is undertaken and does not take account of the events between the watersheds.

It should be borne in mind that construction disputes will typically also focus on the delay analysis methodology chosen by the counterparty. To avoid such type of arguments, the parties should endeavour to agree an appropriate method of delay analysis before each embarks upon significant work on an after the event delay analysis.[58]

41.2 Prolongation claims

41.2.1 Prolongation claims in general

A claim for prolongation costs is a claim for time-related loss and expense incurred by a contractor as a result of one or more compensable delay events generating a critical delay for which an EOT was granted.

The aim of prolongation costs claims is to put the contractor in the same financial position it would have been had the employer delay event not occurred.[59]

In *Costain Limited v Charles Haswell & Partners Limited*[60] it was held that a contractor entitled to prolongation costs will be able to recover:

> the increased and additional costs of carrying out the delayed activity itself as well as the additional costs caused to other site activities as a result of the delaying event. But the contractor will not recover the general site overheads of carrying out all the activities on site as a matter of course unless he can establish that the delaying event to one activity in fact impacted on all the other site activities.

It should be noted that prolongation costs claims are not an automatic consequence of EOT claims as there may be cases in which a contractor may be entitled to an EOT, but not also to the prolongation costs deriving from the delay event that has generated the right to the EOT. Moreover, it often occurs that contractors which are entitled "in principle" to recover their prolongation costs, are awarded an EOT, but are unsuccessful, in part or in full, in their efforts to recover the relevant prolongation costs due to poor quality of their claims and/or records.

41.2.2 Claiming prolongation costs

The elements that a contractor should prove to succeed in claiming its prolongation costs were clearly summarised by Akenhead J in *Walter Lilly & Company Limited v Giles Patrick Cyril Mackay*:[61]

> Ultimately, claims by contractors for delay or disruption related loss and expense must be proved as a matter of fact. Thus, the Contractor has to demonstrate on a balance of probabilities that, first, events occurred which entitle it to loss and expense, secondly, that those events

58 *Society of Construction Law Delay and Disruption Protocol* (2nd edition) February 2017, www.scl.org.uk, at p. 37.

59 *Society of Construction Law Delay and Disruption Protocol* (2nd edition) February 2017, www.scl.org.uk, at p. 20.

60 *Costain Limited v Charles Haswell & Partners Limited* [2009] EWHC 3140 (TCC).

61 *Walter Lilly & Company Limited v Giles Patrick Cyril Mackay* [2012] EWHC 1773 (TCC) at [486].

caused delay and/or disruption and thirdly that such delay or disruption caused it to incur loss and/or expense (or loss and damage as the case may be).

In addition to that, contractors should ensure that they have complied with any contractual requirements, including any notice provisions.

41.2.2.1 Entitlement

A contractor should show that it is entitled to claim prolongation costs under the contract or at law.

41.2.2.2 Compensable delay event

A contractor seeking to recover prolongation costs should show that the delay event triggering the right to the EOT was a compensable delay event.

As mentioned, not all delay events which justify an EOT also trigger an obligation on the employer to compensate the contractor for the losses and costs sustained throughout the delay period.

Compensable delay events will typically include those caused by the employer (e.g., breach of contract) and exclude neutral events (e.g., force majeure events). The first source of information to assess whether a delay event is compensable is the contract.

41.2.2.3 Causation

The contractor shall establish causation, in that it should prove "on a balance of probabilities": (i) that the compensable delay event prolonged the works, which resulted in additional loss and/or costs for the contractor; and (ii) that the contractor would not have incurred such losses and/or costs but for the occurrence of that compensable delay event. Thus, a contractor may not recover as prolongation costs those costs which do not have a direct causal link with the delay and/or which the contractor would have incurred regardless of the prolongation in the duration of the works caused by compensable delay event[62] (so-called task-related costs).

Claims for prolongation costs which do not establish causation, but rather which assume a link between the claimed prolongation costs and the delay event (so-called global claims) will be likely to fail.

41.2.2.4 Recoverability of costs

The contractor shall show that the prolongation costs it is claiming were actually incurred and recoverable. In particular: (i) as to the first requirement, the contractor may only recover costs for work actually done, time actually taken up or loss and/or expense actually suffered,[63] and must give sufficient evidence that such costs were actually incurred as a result of the delay. This is typically done using the project cost records. Such evidence will typically be prepared by the contractor, although contractors may opt to involve a "quantum expert". The claim should be as detailed as possible, although not

62 *Society of Construction Law Delay and Disruption Protocol* (2nd edition) February 2017, www.scl.org.uk, at p. 7.

63 *Society of Construction Law Delay and Disruption Protocol* (2nd edition) February 2017, www.scl.org.uk, at p. 8.

up to any conceivable detail.[64] Moreover, contractors should be careful not to breach any confidentiality obligations (e.g., where they are seeking to recover costs paid to third parties) and competition laws (e.g., where work rates are disclosed, and the dispute is between competitors); while (ii) as to the requirement that the claimed prolongation costs be recoverable heads of costs, for example a contractor may not recover so-called task-related costs, i.e., costs that the contractor would have incurred in any event in order to complete the work.

Typical costs that contractors seek to recover with prolongation claims are as follows:

41.2.2.4.1 ON-SITE OVERHEADS

On-site overheads are site-related costs incurred by the contractor as a result of a compensable delay event. These may include: (i) labour costs for personnel that the contractor had to maintain at the site or hire and send to the site during the period of delay; (ii) costs for hired or owned plant and equipment that the contractor had to maintain at the site during the period of delay. For hired plant and equipment, it will usually be the relevant hire charges. For owned plant and equipment, the contractor may claim the loss of opportunity to hire such plant and equipment to third parties,[65] depreciation in value or maintenance costs incurred during the period of delay; (iii) costs for preliminaries, i.e., those items which are not part of the works, but are indicated by the contractor, usually in the bill of quantities, as necessary to complete the works. These may include, for example, any costs for scaffolding, water, utilities for power and water to the site, site fencing, etc.

41.2.2.4.2 OFF-SITE OVERHEADS

A contractor may also be entitled to recover off-site costs or head office overheads (e.g., head office utilities, head office rent, etc.) in cases where: (i) such costs have increased as a result of the compensable delay event (although a project delay rarely affects head office costs); or (ii) there was a lost recovery of office overheads, subject to the contractor being able to show that, but for the delay, the contractor would have employed its workforce on a different project, which would have contributed to fund its head office overheads during the delay period. This concept was summarised in *JF Finnegan Ltd v Sheffield City Council*[66] as follows:

> It is generally accepted that, on principle, a contractor who is delayed in completing a contract due to the default of his employer, may properly have a claim for head office or off-site overheads during the period of delay, on the basis that the work-force, but for the delay, might have had the opportunity of being employed on another contract which would have had the effect of funding the overheads during the overrun period.

To succeed in a claim for lost recovery a contractor should be able to show that, but for the delay, it would have secured alternative work. This may be achieved, for example, by proving: (i) that the contractor had not tendered for another project due to a lack or insufficiency of resources which were in fact employed on the delayed project;[67] or (ii)

64 *Walter Lilly & Company Limited v Giles Patrick Cyril Mackay* [2012] EWHC 1773 (TCC).
65 *Alfred McAlpine Homes North Ltd v Property and Land Contractors Ltd* [1995] 76 BLR 59.
66 *JF Finnegan Ltd v Sheffield City Council* [1988] 43 BLR 124.
67 *Walter Lilly & Co Ltd v Mackay* [2012] EWHC 1773 (TCC); [2012] BLR 503.

that the delay has resulted in a diminution of turnover or cash flow which has prevented the contractor from tendering for other available projects.

41.2.2.4.3 LOSS OF PROFIT

The construction contract may allow the contractor to recover the profit it has been deprived of earning due to the delay. Such loss of profit corresponds to the diminution of the contractor's turnover profitability resulting from the fact that the delay has prevented it from carrying out work on one or more different contracts. However, also in this case, the contractor should prove on the balance of probabilities, that: (i) such projects were available;[68] (ii) the compensable delay event prevented the contractor from tendering for and working on such projects; (iii) the contractor would have secured such project but for the compensable delay event;[69] and (iv) at the time of the delay, the contractor could have used the lost turnover profitably.[70]

41.2.2.4.4 INCREASED COSTS

Where a contract includes a so-called escalation clause, a contractor may be entitled to claim the loss resulting from an increase in material and labour costs occurred throughout the delay period. In such cases, the loss will typically be calculated by reference to published inflation indexes included in the clause. Should the clause not include any mechanisms or formulae, a contractor may use its records to demonstrate the actual increases in its costs during the period of delay.

41.2.2.4.5 INTEREST

A contractor may typically claim any interest it paid on bank borrowings or unearned on bank deposits as a result of the loss and expenses suffered due to the compensable delay event.

The construction contract may clearly state the circumstances in which such amounts are payable and the relevant interest rates. Such clauses will typically be upheld by the courts penal. As stated in the SCL Protocol[71] an interest rate is penal in nature where it is:

> out of all proportion to the legitimate interests of the Contractor in receiving the timely payment of compensation that is due for delay and disruption.

Moreover, the parties should consider the various statutes and statutory rights on the subject, such as the Late Payment of Commercial Debts (Interest) Act 1998, the Senior Court Act 1981, the Arbitration Act 1996 and the Judgments Act 1838.

68 As stated in *Walter Lilly & Co Ltd v Mackay* [2012] EWHC 1773 (TCC); [2012] BLR 503 at 543, the contractor should show that during the delay period the contractor "*had to and did decline a number of tendering opportunities: that was not said vaguely, or in a vacuum of support: the opportunities received and declined were precisely detailed on a comprehensive schedule*".

69 S. Furst, V. Ramsey, *Keating on Construction Contracts* (9th edition) Sweet & Maxwell, 2012, at 9–033.

70 S. Furst, V. Ramsey, *Keating on Construction Contracts* (9th edition) Sweet & Maxwell, 2012, at 9–033.

71 *Society of Construction Law Delay and Disruption Protocol* (2nd edition) February 2017, www.scl.org.uk, at p. 54.

In order to successfully claim interest on prolongation costs, the contractor should prove that such loss has "actually" been suffered and was within the reasonable contemplation of the parties at the time the contract was entered into. According to the SCL Protocol:[72]

> it is recognised that, in the construction industry, it will always be in the contemplation of the parties at the time they enter into their contract that if deprived of money the Contractor will pay interest or lose the ability to earn interest. Contractors therefore need only establish that the loss was actually suffered.

41.2.2.5 Compliance with contractual requirements
The contractor shall have complied with all the requirements of the contract, including any notice obligations.[73]

41.2.3 Valuation of prolongation claims

The amount due to the contractor as prolongation costs will be calculated by reference to the period of time when the effect of the delay event was felt rather than by reference to the extended period at the end of the contract, and considering any agreement between the parties as to the amount.[74]

41.3 Disruption claims

41.3.1 Disruption claims in general

Disruption may be defined as a loss of productivity caused by unanticipated disturbance, hindrance or interruption to a contractor's normal working methods affecting the progress of works and resulting in lower work efficiency, so ultimately increasing the costs to carry out the relevant disrupted work.

Where the employer is (wholly or partially) responsible for the disruption, the contractor may be entitled to recover the loss and expense suffered in relation to the disrupted labour and equipment hours. Examples may be fragmentary site access, intermittent working, out-of-sequence work, extended working hours and overtime leading to physical fatigue, etc.

It should be noted that, although disruption may cause delay, the two concepts are different as delay refers to lateness in the performance of the works, while disruption refers to a loss of productivity to specific works undertaken by the contractor.

41.3.2 Claiming disruption

A contractor claiming disruption should establish a loss of productivity, i.e., that it incurred in financial loss and expense in carrying out the disrupted work activities which was over

72 *Society of Construction Law Delay and Disruption Protocol* (2nd edition) February 2017, www.scl.org.uk, at p. 54.

73 *Van Oord and another v Allseas UK Ltd* [2015] EWHC 2074 (TCC).

74 *Society of Construction Law Delay and Disruption Protocol* (2nd edition) February 2017, www.scl.org.uk, at p. 53.

and above the loss and expense it would have been incurred were it not for the disruption events for which the employer is responsible.[75]

The elements of a disruption claims that a contractor should prove on a balance of probabilities are:

41.3.2.1 Entitlement

The contractor shall prove that it is entitled to recover compensation for disruption under the contract or at law for breach of an express or implied term of the contract or a breach of law (although disruption is not *per se* a cause of action at law).

Construction contracts do not usually include a single express term for the recovery of disruption costs, but rather deal with the issue in standalone provisions relevant to specific events (e.g., those providing for compensation in case of unforeseen ground conditions).

Subject to the terms of the contract, a contractor may claim disruption under different grounds of entitlement. For example, in *Van Oord UK Ltd v Allseas UK Ltd*[76] the contractor advanced its disruption claim both as a contractual variation and by contending a breach of an implied term of the contract.

41.3.2.2 Disruption event

A contractor should prove that a disruption event or series of events occurred. In the case of complex construction projects, proving disruption may be difficult as disruption will not typically be the result of a single event, but rather a multitude of events concurring, overlapping and/or mixing with each other.

41.3.2.3 Causation

The contractor should prove that the event or series of events caused disruption, which ultimately led to the claimed loss. In particular, the contractor will need to show: (i) the disruption event or events affecting the works caused a loss of productivity; and (ii) the causal link between the loss of productivity and each category of loss and expenses that the contractor suffered over and above what the contractor would have incurred but for the disruption events for which the employer is responsible.

41.3.2.4 Compliance with the contractual requirements

The contractor shall show that it complied with the relevant contractual requirements, including those stated in any notification provisions.

41.3.3 Disruption analysis

Disruption is usually proved by performing a disruption analysis. As explained in the SCL Protocol,[77] a disruption analysis is composed of three phases: (i) the first phase is

75 *Society of Construction Law Delay and Disruption Protocol* (2nd edition) February 2017, www.scl.org.uk, at p. 43.

76 *Van Oord UK Ltd v Allseas UK Ltd* [2015] EWHC 3074 (TCC).

77 *Society of Construction Law Delay and Disruption Protocol* (2nd edition) February 2017, www.scl.org.uk, at p. 44.

aimed at determining when the contractor achieved lower productivity and what work activities were impacted; (ii) the second phase is aimed at understanding the works that were carried out, the moment when they were carried out and the resources used; (iii) the third phase consists in a review of the financial loss incurred.

Lost productivity resulting from disruption events may be calculated by using several methods. The main distinction[78] is between "productivity-based" methods, which aim at measuring the loss of productivity and then to price such loss, and "cost-based" studies, which look at the difference between actual cost and planned cost.

41.4 Global claims

41.4.1 Global claims in general

Keating on Construction Contracts[79] defines a global claim as:

> one that provides an inadequate explanation of the causal nexus between the breaches of contract or relevant events/matters relied upon and the alleged loss and damage or delay that relief is claimed for.

In *Hudson's Building and Engineering Contracts*[80] global claims are defined as:

> those where a global or composite sum, however computed, is put forward as the measure of damage or of contractual compensation where there are two or more separate matters of claim or complaint, and where it is said to be impractical or impossible to provide a breakdown or sub-division of the sum between those matters.

According to the SCL Protocol[81] a global claim is:

> one in which the Contractor seeks compensation for a group of Employer Risk Events but does not or cannot demonstrate a direct link between the loss incurred and the individual Employer Risk Events.

Thus, a global claim is a claim for extra time and/or extra money where the contractor does not adduce evidence to prove causation, but rather presents the events that purportedly caused loss and expense compiled together along with the total amount of loss incurred, and claims that such set of events, taken together, caused the loss or expense it is claiming. In doing so, the contractor asks the court to infer causation, rather than proving it.

Although a global claim may not be the orthodox way to present a claim, courts may allow such claims where the complexity of the case makes it reasonable to do so. For example, where the loss and expense suffered by the contractor is caused by a combination of complex disruption events (e.g., late access to site, variations, delays in providing

78 *Society of Construction Law Delay and Disruption Protocol* (2nd edition) February 2017, www.scl.org.uk, at p. 45.

79 S. Furst, V. Ramsey, *Keating on Construction Contracts* (11th edition) Sweet & Maxwell, 2021, at para 9–064.

80 I.N. Duncan Wallace, *Hudson's Building and Engineering Contracts* (11th edition) Sweet & Maxwell, 1995.

81 *Society of Construction Law Delay and Disruption Protocol* (2nd edition) February 2017, www.scl.org.uk, at p. 64.

design information, etc.) for which the employer is responsible, the contractor may not have any other way to be compensated other than by making a global claim.

In *Crosby v Portland UDC*[82] Donaldson J held that:

> Since, however, the extent of the extra cost incurred depends upon an extremely complex interaction between the consequences of the various denials, suspensions and variations, it may well be difficult or even impossible to make an accurate apportionment of the total extra cost between the several causative elements. An artificial apportionment could of course have been made: but why (the contractor asks) should the arbitrator make an apportionment which has no basis in reality? I can see no answer to this question . . . provided (the arbitrator) ensures that there is no duplication, I can see no reason why he should not recognise the realities of the situation and make individual awards in respect of those parts of individual items of the claim which can be dealt with in isolation and a supplementary award in respect of the remainder of these claims as a composite whole.

Historically, the use of global claims was restricted by the courts.[83] This approach has changed in recent years, and the courts have started taking a more lenient approach when considering such claims. For example, in the case of *Walter Lilly & Company Limited v Giles Patrick Cyril Mackay*,[84] Mr Justice Akenhead said that:

> in principle, unless the contract dictates that a global cost claim is not permissible if certain hurdles are not overcome, such a claim may be permissible on the facts and subject to proof.

41.4.2 Structuring global claims

In *Walter Lilly & Company Limited v Giles Patrick Cyril Mackay*[85] Akenhead J gave the following seven principles for a global claim to succeed.

(i) The contractor should prove, on a balance of probabilities, the following three elements:

> first, events occurred which entitle it to loss and expense, secondly, that those events caused delay and/or disruption and thirdly that such delay or disruption caused it to incur loss and/or expense.[86]

This approach represented a change in direction from previous authority. For example, in *Bernhard's Rugby Landscapes Ltd v Stockley Park Consortium Ltd*[87] where the court held:

> I do not accept that, as a matter of principle, it has to be shown by a claimant contractor that it is impossible to plead and prove cause and effect in the normal way or that such impossibility is not the fault of the party seeking to advance the global claim.

82 *Crosby v Portland UDC* [1967] 5 BLR 121, as reported in J. Uff, *Construction Law* (12th edition) 2017.

83 In *Wharf Properties v Eric Cumine Associates* (No.2) [1991] 52 BLR 503 a global claim was defined by Lord Oliver as "*hopelessly embarrassing*". See also *London Borough of Merton v Stanley Hugh Leach Ltd* [1985] at [475]; *Wharf Properties Ltd v Eric Cumine Associates* [1991] 52 BLR 1; *John Holland Construction & Engineering Pty Ltd v Kvaerner RJ Brown Pty Ltd and Another* [1997] 82 BLR 81.

84 *Walter Lilly & Company Limited v Giles Patrick Cyril Mackay* [2012] EWHC 1773 (TCC).

85 *Walter Lilly & Company Limited v Giles Patrick Cyril Mackay* [2012] EWHC 1773 (TCC).

86 *Walter Lilly & Company Limited v Giles Patrick Cyril Mackay* [2012] EWHC 1773 (TCC) at [486(a)].

87 *Bernhard's Rugby Landscapes Ltd v Stockley Park Consortium Ltd* [1997] 82 BLR 39.

The contractor is not required to prove that it would be impossible or impractical to plead and prove cause and effect for every event.[88] However, the contractor will still have to show causation by proving that the loss it suffered would not have been incurred in any event. There is not one way for contractors to prove the three elements of their claim. They are free to prove their global claim and meet the requisite standard of proof by using whatever evidence will satisfy the tribunal.

(ii) The contractor shall have complied with any contractual requirements such as notices and conditions precedent.[89]

(iii) Global claims present added evidential difficulties which a contractor should overcome.[90] For example, the contractor should prove that it would not have incurred the loss in any event. In this regard, Akenhead J held that employers may:

> adduce evidence that suggests or even shows that the accepted tender was so low that the loss would have always occurred irrespective of the events relied upon by the claimant contractor or that other events . . . occurred may have caused or did cause all or part of the loss.

(iv) In cases where part of the loss and expense suffered by the claimant are caused by events for which the employer is not responsible (e.g., are due to erroneous programming or unrealistic bid pricing or contractor's own inefficiencies) the contractor will not be able to claim that specific portion, but the global claim will not necessarily fail in its entirety. In this regard, Akenhead J said:

> The fact that one or a series of events or factors (unpleaded or which are the risk or fault of the claimant contractor) caused or contributed (or cannot be proved not to have caused or contributed) to the total or global loss does not necessarily mean that the claimant contractor can recover nothing. An example would be where, say, a contractor's global loss is £1 million and it can prove that but for one overlooked and unpriced £50,000 item in its accepted tender it would probably have made a net return; the global loss claim does not fail simply because the tender was underpriced by £50,000; the consequence would simply be that the global loss is reduced by £50,000 because the claimant contractor has not been able to prove that £50,000 of the global loss would not have been incurred in any event.[91]

(v) The court does not need to go down the global or total cost route if the actual cost attributable to individual events can be readily or practicably determined (although this does not prevent a contractor from making a global or total cost claim). However, Akenhead J clarified that a tribunal might be:

> more sceptical about the global cost claim if the direct linkage approach is readily available but is not deployed.

(vi) A global claim should not be rejected on the basis that the contractor has caused the impossibility of disentanglement. In this regard, the judge said:

88 *Walter Lilly & Company Limited v Giles Patrick Cyril Mackay* [2012] EWHC 1773 (TCC).
89 See also *London Borough of Merton v Stanley Hugh Leach* [1985] 32 BLR 51.
90 This was also confirmed in *John Sisk & Son Ltd v Carmel Building Services* [2016] EWHC 806 (TCC).
91 *Walter Lilly & Company Limited v Giles Patrick Cyril Mackay* [2012] EWHC 1773 (TCC) at [486(e)].

> In principle, unless the contract dictates that a global cost claim is not permissible if certain hurdles are not overcome, such a claim may be permissible on the facts and subject to proof.[92]

In practice, global claims are often used in cases where contractors lack the documents necessary to prove causation as they have failed to keep adequate project records. Moreover, global claims are sometimes preferred as they are quicker and relatively inexpensive. However, although the courts have taken a more lenient approach to global claims, contractors should be cognisant of the need to comply with requirements set out in the *Walter Lilly* case and how this will affect the chances of success of their global claim. On the other hand, employer may seek to contractually restrict the use of such claims. In *Walter Lilly* Akenhead J stated that:

> One needs to see of course what the contractual clause relied upon says to see if there are contractual restrictions on global cost or loss claims.[93]

41.4.3 Total cost claims

"Total cost" claims are an extreme type of global claims where the contractor merely offers evidence of the total cost sustained to execute the contract (or a specific part of it) and claims its over-run of costs quantified as the difference between the total actual costs and the contract price (or the specific part of contract price relevant to the part for which the contractor is claiming the relevant loss).

However, while such type of claim may help the parties and/or the court to set a limit on the amount the contractor may be entitled to claim (as the contractor will not typically be entitled to claim more than its actual total loss), unless they are specifically particularised and supported by clear evidence (e.g., that the loss is to be referred to breaches of contract on the part of the employer or change orders and that the claimed overrun costs are wholly attributable to the employer), the likelihood of success is low as such claims would be too generic and lack the very basic elements of a valid claim.

Where a court is persuaded that the contractor's global claim is admissible, the relevant value will be quantified on the basis of the evidence submitted.

41.5 Finance claims

41.5.1 Finance claims in general

Unless the contract provides otherwise, a contractor will not normally be entitled to suspend the works or terminate the contract in case the employer fails to pay a disputed claim or variation, but would rather be expected to proceed the works diligently, so effectively financing the works for the employer.

The contractor may sustain such cost by: (i) resorting to financing, either external (e.g., borrowing money from a bank) or internal (e.g., borrowing money from another

92 *Walter Lilly & Company Limited v Giles Patrick Cyril Mackay* [2012] EWHC 1773 (TCC) at [486(g)].
93 *Walter Lilly & Company Limited v Giles Patrick Cyril Mackay* [2012] EWHC 1773 (TCC) at [486(a)].

company of its group, usually the parent). In both cases, the contractor will typically pay interest on such borrowings that it would not have made but for the employer's delay in making the due payment; or (ii) by using its internal resources (where the contractor is self-financed), in which case the contractor will be deprived of the interest that it would have earned from its bank had such amount been left on its bank account. In addition, the contractor will be deprived of the possibility to invest such money in a different way (e.g., in another project) and earn interest or other type of profits.

The parties may agree in the construction contract the circumstances in which interest will be payable and the relevant rate. Where the contract includes express provisions covering finance charges, the contractor will usually claim under the contract. Alternatively, a contractor may claim finance charges at common law. In such cases, the finance charges will be recoverable as damages by quantifying the relevant cost of finance.

41.5.2 Claiming finance costs

A contractor seeking to recover finance charges as damages should prove:

(i) That the relevant loss has actually been suffered.
(ii) That the loss falls within the first limb of the test in *Hadley v Baxendale*[94] (i.e., it was within the reasonable contemplation of the parties at the time of contracting). According to the SCL Protocol, in the construction industry it is recognised that this will always be the case.[95]

41.5.3 Quantification of finance claims

When the claim is for interest, the contractor should calculate the relevant amount by identifying both the applicable rate and the period of time when interest is incurred.

The interest rate should reflect the actual cost of borrowing charged by the bank or its group company for that specific project. An alternative may be using reasonable commercial interest rates. The parties should consider the various statutory rights to interest applicable to the case, including the Late Payment of Commercial Debts (Interest) Act 1998, section 35A of the Senior Court Act 1981, the Arbitration Act 1996 and the Judgments Act 1838.

The appropriate starting date will depend on the circumstances of the case. Normally, the period of the finance charges will start from the date on which the payment became due and will run until the payment is made, subject to any notice requirements in the contract.

It is worth noting that a finance claim for loss of opportunity may be more difficult to prove due to the intrinsic speculative nature of such claims.

94 *Hadley v Baxendale* [1854] EWHC Exch J70.
95 *Society of Construction Law Delay and Disruption Protocol* (2nd edition) February 2017, www.scl.org.uk, at p. 54.

41.6 Quantum meruit claims

41.6.1 Quantum meruit claims in general

Under English law the basic position is that a party is not obliged to make payment to a service provider unless and until a binding contract is entered into. Quantum meruit claims are an exception to such position and are aimed at preventing unjust enrichment.

The literal translation of the Latin words "quantum meruit" is "the amount deserved". A quantum meruit claim is a claim for a reasonable sum for works performed when one of the parties was unjustly enriched.

Quantum meruit claims may be distinguished in: (i) contractual, where the parties have entered into a construction contract which does not state the price for the works; or (ii) non-contractual (or "restitutionary"), where works are performed without a contract or under a contract which was void ab initio, or which became unenforceable during the project.

Some examples of situations which may entitle a contractor to a quantum meruit payment are:

(i) Where the contractor commenced the works on the assumption that a contract would be entered into and that such work would be paid for (e.g., were works are performed on the basis of a letter of intent). In such cases, where the employer receives a benefit from the works, the contractor would be able to claim in unjust enrichment. In *British Steel Corp v Cleveland Bridge & Engineering Co Ltd*[96] the contractor performed some of the works at the employer's request despite the contract still being in the negotiation stage. Goff J held that there was no contract between the parties, but that the contractor was entitled to payment in restitution for the work performed. He said:

> Both parties confidently expected a formal contract to eventuate. In these circumstances, to expedite performance under that anticipated contract, one requested the other to commence the contract work, and the other complied with that request. If thereafter, as anticipated, a contract was entered into, the work done as requested will be treated as having been performed under that contract; if, contrary to their expectation, no contract was entered into, then the performance of the work is not referable to any contract the terms of which can be ascertained, and the law simply imposes an obligation on the party who made the request to pay a reasonable sum for such work as has been done pursuant to that request, such an obligation sounding in quasi contract or, as we now say, in restitution.

(ii) Where the contractor carried out works beyond the contract's term,[97] in which case such works will not usually be regarded as having been performed under the expired contract and the relevant right to payment will be based on unjust enrichment.

96 *British Steel Corp v Cleveland Bridge and Engineering Co Ltd* [1984] 1 All ER 504.
97 *ERDC Group Ltd v Brunel University* [2006] EWHC 687 (TCC).

41.6.2 Claiming in quantum meruit

In the case of *Benedetti v Sawiris*[98] the Supreme Court held that, when assessing unjust enrichment claims a court should consider whether: (i) one party was enriched; (ii) the enrichment was at the other party's expense and unjust; and (iii) the enriched party may rely on any defences.

In the more recent case of *Moorgate Capital (Corporate Finance) Limited v H.I.G. European Capital Partners LLP*,[99] the court identified the following three essential elements that a claimant must satisfy to establish a prima facie entitlement to a payment by way of quantum meruit for services carried out in the absence of a binding contract: (i) a party shall have been enriched as a consequence of the work done or the services provided; (ii) the enrichment shall be at the expense of the service provider; and (iii) the retention of the enrichment must be unjust unless the beneficiary of the work pays for it.

41.6.3 Quantification of quantum meruit claims

Where a quantum meruit claim is successful, the claimant will be entitled to a reasonable sum. There are no finite rules as to what constitutes a reasonable sum.

In determining reasonableness, a court:

(i) May not take into account the terms of a contract which is later found void.[100]

(ii) May look at the abortive negotiations between the parties to determine reasonableness. In *Way v Latilla*[101] the court held:

> if no trade usage assists the court as to the amount of the commission, it appears to me clear that the court may take into account the bargainings between the parties, not with a view to completing the bargain for them, but as evidence of the value which each of them puts upon the services.

(iii) May consider prices for similar work in a related contract.[102]

(iv) May consider expert evidence as to the value of work performed. However, this will not be strictly necessary, and evidence need not be produced by an independent expert, although a court may consider this aspect when weighing such evidence. In *Lusty v Finsbury Securities Ltd*[103] the claimant sought to prove the value of the work carried out through one of its own surveyors. The court held that the evidence was admissible. The fact that the surveyor was an interested party merely impacted the weight of his evidence.

(v) May look at the price already agreed during the negotiations as an indicator of what could constitute a reasonable price, even more so if the price was already paid. In *Ipswich Town Football Club v Suffolk Constabulary*[104] the court held:

98 *Benedetti v Sawiris* [2013] UKSC 50 at [178].
99 *Moorgate Capital (Corporate Finance) Limited v H.I.G. European Capital Partners LLP* [2019] EWHC 1421.
100 *Rover International Ltd v Cannon Film Sales Ltd (No 3)* [1989] 1 WLR 912.
101 *Way v Latilla* [1937] 3 All ER 759 at [764].
102 *Banque Paribas v Venaglass Ltd* [1994] CILL 918.
103 *Lusty v Finsbury Securities Ltd* [1991] 58 BLR 66.
104 *Ipswich Town Football Club v Suffolk Constabulary* [1984] 1 All ER 504.

> The price actually paid for services under the contracts in dispute reflects the best and most compelling evidence of market value. . . . The starting point must be that the price set at the time and reflected in the contract was a fair one.

(vi) May not take the tender price as the starting point for valuing the work. In *Serck Controls Ltd v Drake & Scull Engineering Ltd*[105] Judge Hicks QC, although acknowledging that the tender price may be of some evidential value, disagreed with D&S' argument that it should form the starting point for assessment held:

> first because that would be to treat it as contractual, which it is not, and secondly because there is no accessible specification, programme, terms and conditions to which it applied and from which departures can be priced.

(vii) May use the price estimated by the contractor to set the upper limit of the amount which the contractor could reasonably claim even where such price would have resulted in a loss for the contractor (as the contractor should not find itself in a better position as a result of a failure to conclude the contract).[106] However, where the estimate is unclear (e.g., where the contractor does not give a fixed price but only an approximate estimate) the court may consider that the contractor had been purposefully ambiguous and use actual costs to assess a reasonable price, so disregarding the estimate or using it only as an aid.[107]

(viii) May not wholly ignore the contractor's performance. This subject attains to the following "*crucial question of law*" formulated by Slade LJ in *Crown House Engineering Ltd v Amec Projects Ltd.*[108] (but then remained unanswered):

> On the assessment of a claim for services rendered based on a quantum meruit, may it in some circumstances (and, if so, what circumstances) be open to the defendant to assert that the value of such services falls to be reduced because of their tardy performance, or because the unsatisfactory manner of their performance has exposed him to extra expense or claims by third parties?

In the recent case of *Serck Controls Ltd v Drake & Scull Engineering Ltd* the subcontractor, Serck Controls Ltd ("Serck") carried out design and installation works for the mechanical and electrical contractor, Drake & Scull Engineering Ltd ("D&S"), on a project for British Nuclear Fuels Ltd. The works were carried out under a letter of intent entered into June 1994 which provided that if no contract was agreed D&S would "*reimburse [Serck] with all reasonable costs incurred*". A dispute arose on the valuation of the works carried out by Serck. The court was then asked to assess the reasonable remuneration for the execution of the work. D&S' position was that, in valuing the works, the court had to consider Serck's inefficiencies. Judge Hicks held that Serck was not obliged to work in accordance with

105 *Serck Controls Ltd v Drake & Scull Engineering Ltd* [2019] EWHC 1421.
106 *Lachhani v Destination Canada (UK) Ltd* [1997] 13 Const LJ 279.
107 *Sykes v Packham (t/a Bathroom Specialist)* [2011] EWCA 608.
108 *Crown House Engineering Ltd v Amec Projects Ltd.* [1990] 48 BLR 32.

the contract programme. However, the judge was not persuaded that a firm working on a quantum meruit basis on a complex construction site can wholly ignore the desirability of cooperation with others at work there. He held:

> There must at least be a duty not unreasonably to interfere with the carrying out of other works, and I believe that, more positively, there is an obligation to be aware of the progress of other trades and, so far as consistent with the firm's own legitimate commercial interests, to co-operate in efficient working practices. There may also be more specific duties, for example in relation to compliance with health and safety legislation and the directions of persons having powers under it.

41.7 Variation claims

41.7.1 Variation claims in general

The high complexity of some construction projects will usually generate several changes to the original project scope of work agreed between the parties.

Some variations may be necessary (e.g., where the design does not include an item which is necessary to complete the project) or just desirable (e.g., when the change is made merely for aesthetical purposes, or the employer seeks to change some architectural features).

There may be situations in which the parties are not in agreement as to whether certain works constitute a variation. This typically occurs where the scope of work agreed in the contract is ambiguous. In such cases, contractors may take the position that certain activities do not fall in the original scope of work and may be performed only upon a payment of the resulting extra costs, whilst employers may argue that the original scope of work did include such works, albeit impliedly or as a result of a certain construction of the relevant documents.

41.7.2 Claiming variations

Construction contracts will typically contain a variation clause setting out the procedure that contractors should follow to claim the extra costs and time resulting from the performance of variations. It is crucial that contractors strictly comply with the requirements of such provisions as a failure to do so may result in a waiver of their entitlement to the relevant payment.

When a variation is instructed, the employer will normally issue a variation order (or "VO"). The contractor will usually be compelled under the contract to comply with the VO and carry out the instructed work, but it will also be eligible to claim any additional costs it will incur as a result of the VO and any extension of time for completion necessary to execute the VO. The contractor will do so by submitting a claim for variation in accordance with the contract. The parties will then endeavour to agree on the contractor's entitlement to extra time and costs, and on the relevant valuation.

There is not a standard way to present a variation claim and how to do it will depend on the contract. However, there are some steps that are commonly taken which, if complied with, may help contractors in increasing their chances of reaching an agreement with employers on variation claims, and possibly saving time and avoiding costly disputes. Such steps include the following.

41.7.2.1 Complying with the contractual requirements

Contractors should first read and understand the variation clause and the relevant requirements. Moreover, they should consider the whole contract and look for any connected provisions which may affect the right to claim variations in certain circumstances.

Contractors should ensure that they adhere with the contractual requirements as failure to do so may severely affect a variation claim. Among others, the contractor should also try to assess whether certain requirements are a condition precedent so that any recovery will be precluded if such requirements are not complied with (particularly where the variation claim notice is to be sent within a certain notification period).

41.7.2.2 Assessing the original work scope

Normally, a variation will only be considered as such and entitle a contractor to an extra payment and time if the varied works fall outside the original scope. Thus, before submitting a variation claim, the contractor should carefully review the contractual work scope so to ensure that the works are not already part of the scope.

41.7.2.3 Ensuring that a written instruction is issued before commencing the varied works

The construction contract will usually state that the contractor should not carry out any extra works unless the employer has first issued an instruction in writing (a draft variation will not typically satisfy this requirement). In the absence of a proper instruction, any costs borne by the contractor to carry out the extra works may be unrecoverable, and any resulting extension of time claim may fail.

41.7.2.4 Assessing that the instruction is compliant with the contract

The contractor shall review the instruction to assess whether it may be considered a valid variation instruction under the contract, e.g., whether: (i) the works align with the type of work contemplated in the contract; (ii) the instruction is issued within any longstop date provided in the contract; or (iii) in case of a purportedly negative variation, the contract allows such type of variations.

41.7.2.5 Objecting an instruction

Typically, a contractor will only be entitled to object an instruction in limited circumstances, e.g., in case the variation is impossible or illegal. In such cases, the objection shall be submitted in a timely fashion and clearly explain the relevant reasons.

41.7.2.6 Submit an application for variation

A construction contract will typically provide that the contractor shall submit a written application for the variation (or variation notice) within a certain time limit and in a certain format before it carries out any additional work. A variation notice is not the actual variation claim, but rather a proposal that the contractor makes to the employer as to the amount of money necessary to carry out the extra work and the time to complete it and sets out the grounds for the variation claim that will follow once the work is done. The contractor shall submit its variation notice in compliance with the contract, including any time limits and content requirements.

41.7.2.7 Carrying out the works
Once the instruction is formally issued (and, possibly, the relevant terms are agreed), and in any case within the term set out in the instruction, the contractor shall carry out the works in accordance with the instruction.

41.7.2.8 Submitting the detailed variation claim
The contractor shall then submit its detailed variation claim. A variation claim should set out at least the following elements: (a) a summary of the claim including the relevant background; (b) the source of the contractor's entitlement to extra money and/or time. This may either be the contract or the law (in each case, the contractor should clearly identify the contractual clause it is relying upon or the legal principle it contends the employer has breached); (c) the events on which the contractor is basing the claim and how such events affected the performance of the contract and led to the extra costs and/or time; (d) the resulting extension of time and monetary compensation.

41.7.3 Valuation of variations

How variations should be valuated is a matter of the contract. In general, the parties may either use the rates and prices broken down in the bill of quantities on which the contract price has been agreed or use rates and prices which are "unrelated" to the contract and agreed in a separate document.

The monetary valuation method the parties should use may also depend on the type of works to be performed. For example: (i) where the extra works are identical to works already priced in the original scope of work, the parties may agree to use the contract rates and prices included in the bill of quantities; (ii) where the additional works are analogous, but not identical, to works for which the parties have already agreed a price, they may agree to calculate the new rates and prices by using the existing contract rates as a starting point; (iii) where the contract does not provide for rates and prices which are applicable to the additional scope of work, the parties may need to agree on new rates and prices (e.g., market rates or actual costs plus a reasonable profit and any overhead allowance); (iv) where the variation claim constitutes a claim for damages deriving from a breach of contract, the contractor may have to base its variation claim on the actual costs sustained as a consequence of the breach.

The valuation of a variation claim is usually negotiated and agreed between the parties. The parties should take particular care when negotiating variations. In the recent case of *A&A Mechanical Contractors v Petroleum Company of Trinidad and Tobago*[109] the employer, Petroleum Company of Trinidad and Tobago ("Petrotrin"), engaged A&A Mechanical Contractors ("A&A") as contractor to perform some steelworks as part of a project in the "Soldado" oilfield, in the Caribbean Sea. The contract provided that the

109 *A&A Mechanical Contractors v Petroleum Company of Trinidad and Tobago* [2022] UKPC 39.

value of variations had to be agreed between the parties by using the contract rates and prices. In case such rates and prices were not applicable, the employer had to pay a reasonable sum for the variations. After a negotiation the parties achieved an agreement on the valuation of some variations. However, when A&A submitted more variations, Petrotrin sought to revoke the concessions made during the negotiations and contended that the relevant discussions were "without prejudice". As such, they were not admissible as evidence in the legal proceedings between the parties. The Privy Council found that the meetings and discussion between the parties were not aimed at settling an ongoing discussion, but rather at agreeing on the value of A&A's variation claims as per the valuation procedure mandated in the contract. As a result, the discussions were admissible in court.[110] The Privy Council also added that, in any case, the discussion would be admissible to determine whether an agreement had been reached regardless of whether they were without prejudice.[111] Moreover, the Privy Council found that the contractual provision mandating that variations be valuated based on their reasonable value in case of the parties' failure to agree on a value implied an obligation to negotiate the value of variations in good faith.[112]

110 *A&A Mechanical Contractors v Petroleum Company of Trinidad and Tobago* [2022] UKPC 39 at [69].
111 *A&A Mechanical Contractors v Petroleum Company of Trinidad and Tobago* [2022] UKPC 39 at [71].
112 *A&A Mechanical Contractors v Petroleum Company of Trinidad and Tobago* [2022] UKPC 39 at [15] – [19].

CHAPTER 42

Claims against the contractor

42.1 Liquidated damages claims

For employers, a delay in the completion of the work may mean delaying the moment when the project starts generating revenues, and could lead to important financial consequences such as loss of profits, exposure to damages to third parties and loss of financing. The redress for employers in cases where contractors are responsible for the delays is damages, which may either be liquidated or unliquidated, although, in the case of complex construction projects, the contract will typically provide for liquidated damages.

Liquidated damages ("LDs") or liquidated and ascertained damages ("LADs") for delay are a pre-agreed amount that the contractor should pay in case of delay in completing the works (or a key milestone) within the relevant agreed date.

In order to succeed in claiming LDs, an employer should prove that: (i) the contract provides for a completion date; (ii) the contractor did not complete the works within such completion date; (iii) the contract contains a LD clause; (iv) the employer has complied with the formalities and requirements set forth in the contract (such as any obligation to give the contractor a time to remedy or any notice requirements); and (v) the quantum the employer is claiming as LDs is consistent with the formula stated in the contract (e.g., X amount multiplied for X days of delay).

Where the employer is successful in proving the aforementioned, it will not be required to prove causation and quantum, and the relevant burden of proof will shift to the contractor, which may reduce or remove any liability by showing (by way of an EOT claim) that the whole or a part of the delay was due to events for which the employer is responsible. The contractor may also avoid the payment of LDs by proving that the LD clause is in fact a penalty, in which case the employer may still be entitled to general damages. Where the contractor is not successful in proving that delay is excusable (or where the employer does not accept the contractor's claim), the contractor will be obliged to pay the LDs amount within the time specified in the contract. Should the contractor fail to make the payment, the employer may, depending on the terms of the contract, recover the relevant amount by: (i) retaining/setting off money payable to the contractor for works performed or to be performed; (ii) calling on the contractor's performance bonds.

42.2 Defective work claims

Claims for defective work are normal in highly complex and high value construction projects.

 DOI: 10.4324/9781003387718-52

Defects may be discovered before or after completion (i.e., during the so-called warranty period): (i) by the employer (or the engineer), for example during the various inspections and tests made throughout the project or at/before handover; or (ii) by the contractor itself, which will typically have a contractual obligation to inform the employer of any defects to the works that he detects during the performance of the contract.

42.2.1 Patent defects and latent defects

The employer's right to claim against the contractor for defective work depends on the type of defect, the seriousness of the relevant consequences, how discoverable the defect is upon reasonable inspection, and the moment in which it is detected and notified to the contractor.

42.2.1.1 Patent defects

Patent defects are defects that are detectable upon reasonable inspection. A construction contract will usually entitle the employer to have the works inspected in order to timely identify any patent defects and notify the contractor accordingly. In such cases, the contractor will have a duty to rectify at its own cost. The employer will also be entitled to notify defects discovered after practical completion (i.e., after the employer has taken over the works), but within a fixed period defined as the "defects liability period" or "rectification period". Where the employer notifies the existence of one or more defects to the contractor within the defects liability period, failure to return to site and rectify the defects will expose the contractor to liability for the cost of another contractor having to remedy those defects. On the other hand, an employer's failure to notify the contractor of any defects the employer becomes aware of during the defects liability period would deprive the contractor of the opportunity to rectify. This may affect any subsequent employer's claim for damages as its failure to notify could amount to a failure to mitigate its losses.

42.2.1.2 Latent defects

Latent defect are defects which are not apparent or readily detectable upon a reasonable inspection of the works, so that the employer may become aware of their existence only after the defects liability period has expired. Where a latent defect becomes patent before the expiry of the defects liability period, the employer may notify the contractor accordingly and ask that the defect be rectified at the contractor's cost. However, in cases where a latent defect becomes patent only after the defects liability period has expired, unless the contract states otherwise the contractor will neither have a duty nor a right to rectify such defect, although the employer may still have a cause of action against the contractor and be entitled to damages arising from the defective works.[1] Where, instead, the construction contract allows the contractor back on site to rectify the defect at its own cost in cases where latent defect become patent after project handover, the employer's refusal to allow the contractor remedying a defect may amount to a failure to mitigate and limit the employer's recovery right to the cost the original contractor would have incurred had it been allowed to carry out the remedial work itself.

---

1 *Hancock v BW Brazier (Anerley) Ltd* [1966] 1 WLR 1317 at [1334].

The subject of the employer's failure to mitigate its losses was considered in *Woodlands Oak Ltd v Conwell*.[2] Although the construction contract did not provide for any mechanism for dealing with post-completion defects, the contractor had informed the employer of its intention to rectify any such defects at its own expense. When defects materialised after completion, the employer had third-party contractors correcting them, and then sought to recover the relevant cost from the original contractor. In its defence the original contractor argued it had not been given an opportunity rectify the defective works. The Court of Appeal held that despite the absence of an express defects liability mechanism, the employer had failed to take reasonable steps to notify the contractor about defects, so depriving it of the opportunity to rectify. As a result, the court did not award any costs to the employer as, had it asked the original contractor to rectify the defects, they would have done it at no cost. In other words, by engaging third-party contractors the employer had failed to mitigate its losses. However, whether an employer has in fact failed to mitigate will depend upon the facts and the circumstances of the case. For example, in the case of *Mul v Hutton Construction Ltd*[3] Akenhead J suggested (obiter) that an employer engaging a third-party contractor to rectify defects would not be failing to mitigate its losses in the following situations: (i) where the defects are so whole scale that no reasonable employer could be expected to have that contractor back on site; (ii) where there has been fraudulent behaviour on the part of the contractor relating to the works; and (iii) where the contractor has made it clear that it was not prepared to return to rectify the alleged defects.

42.2.2 Contractor's possible defences to defects claims

A contractor accused of having carried out defective works may try arguing that:

(i) The works that the employer is alleging being defective are not in fact such. This defence may succeed or fail based on the how the contract documents define defects and the technical analysis of the defective works.
(ii) The defects were not a "breach of contract", but a mere "temporary disconformity" which the contractor intended to rectify before practical completion. This defence, which only applies to defects discovered before completion, is based on the so-called temporary disconformity theory according to which, in case the contractor's works are defective, this will not constitute a breach of contract until the works are completed and handed over to the employer. The theory originates from the following passage of Lord Diplock's dissenting speech in *P&M Kaye Ltd v Hosier & Dickinson Ltd*:[4]

> The contract places upon the contractor the obligation to comply with any instructions to remedy any temporary disconformity with the requirements of the contract. If it is remedied no loss is sustained by the employer unless the time taken to remedy it results in practical completion being delayed beyond the date of completion designated in the contract. In this event the only loss caused is that the employer

2 *Woodlands Oak Ltd v Conwell* [2011] EWCA Civ 254.
3 *Mul v Hutton Construction Ltd* [2014] EWHC 1797 (TCC).
4 *P&M Kaye Ltd v Hosier & Dickinson Ltd* [1972] 1 WLR 146 at [166].

> is kept out of the use of his building beyond the date on which it was agreed that is should be ready for use. For such delay liquidated damages at an agreed rate are payable under condition 22 of the contract.
>
> Upon a legalistic analysis it might be argued that temporary disconformity of any part of the works with the requirements of the contract even though remedied before the end of the agreed construction period constituted a breach of contract for which nominal damages would be recoverable. I do not think that makes business sense. Provided that the contractor puts it right timeously I do not think that the parties intended that any temporary disconformity should of itself amount to a breach of contract by the contractor.

The theory has divided the courts, which have followed[5] it in some cases, and criticised it in others.[6]

In *Hudson's Building and Engineering Contracts*[7] the author takes the following position:

> on grounds of both principle and practicality, a contractor will be in immediate breach of contract whenever his work fails to comply with the contract descriptions or requirements, although no doubt, as envisaged by Lord Diplock, the damages will be at best nominal in a case where he can show that he intends to rectify it at some more convenient time before completion without affecting the quality of the remaining work. Subject to this, it is submitted that there is effectively an implied entitlement of the owner to call for prompt and timeous contract compliance, and that refusal to comply would be a repudiation by the contractor entitling the owner to rescind.

(iii) The works were simply impossible to build in accordance with the relevant specifications. However, this defence may not be successful in case the contractor has undertaken an obligation of result (e.g., that the resulting works be fit for purpose) as, in such case, unless the parties agreed otherwise, the contractor is considered having warranted its ability to achieve the specific result (i.e., the fact that the result turns out being impossible to achieve will not be a justification). Moreover, this subject shall be considered in conjunction with the principles of "frustration" and "impossibility of performance" in cases where subsequent events made performance impossible.

(iv) The employer accepted works (e.g., by issuing a final acceptance certificate) without raising any issues as to defects. Whether this defence be successful will depend on the language of the contract or the certificate itself. Arguably, the parties shall use clear words if they intend to exclude by express agreement a remedy provided by law for breach of contract as, in construing such a contract, the courts will presume that neither party intended to abandon such remedies.[8] So, for example, in the case of *Colbart v Kumar*,[9] which concerned the execution

5 E.g., in *Davy Offshore Ltd v Emerald Field Contracting Ltd* [1991] 55 BLR 1 at 84–85 and in *McGlinn v Waltham Contractors Ltd (No 3)* [2007] EWHC 149 (TCC) at [262].

6 E.g., in *Lintest Builders Ltd. v Roberts* (1978) 10 BLR 120, at p. 128; (1979) 13 BLR 38, at p. 44, C.A. where Roskill LJ said: "*I respectfully question whether his Lordship [Lord Diplock] on any view intended it to be of universal application*".

7 I.N. Duncan Wallace QC, *Hudson's Building and Engineering Contracts* (11th edition) Sweet & Maxwell, 1994.

8 *Gilbert-Ash (Northern) Ltd v Modern Engineering (Bristol) Ltd* [1974] 1 AC 689, 718.

9 *Colbart v Kumar* [1992] 59 BLR 89.

of refurbishment works carried out under the JCT IFC form of contract (the "Contract"), the court had to decide whether the employer could recover any amount for defects after the final certificate had been issued. The court held that the final certificate was in fact conclusive as, according to the Contract, the allegations of defective work were reserved to the opinion of the architect. In that case, therefore, the Contract expressly covered the issue and the court decided by simply upholding the Contract. The Court of Appeal said:

> Where the final certificate does become conclusive evidence, the effect is that any claim in an arbitration (brought after 28 days) which seeks to support some provision of the final certificate is bound to succeed and any claim which seeks to challenge a provision of the final certificate is bound to fail, without any hearing on the merits.

Another case on the subject is *Matthew Hall Ortech Ltd v Tarmac Roadstone Ltd*[10] where the contract (based on an IChemE Red Book) stated that the Final Certificate was "*conclusive evidence . . . that the Contractor had completed the Works and made good all defects*". Based on this language, the court considered that the Final Certificate was in fact conclusive evidence that the works had been completed in accordance with the contract although precising that the employer was still entitled to claim for latent defects.

42.3 Demands under a guarantee

42.3.1 Bond calls in general

It is common for a contractor to disagree on the employer's entitlement to a certain claim (e.g., relevant to poor performance or delays) and/or the relevant quantum. Where the parties' negotiations on the subject have proven unsuccessful, the employer may seek to recover the amount it believes it is entitled to by calling on a bond, so de facto by-passing the need for any further contractual negotiations. Normally, the guarantor (usually a bank or other financial institution) receiving a demand under an on-demand performance bond will inform the contractor (although it is not usually obliged to do so) and pay the demanded amount within a certain number of days without investigating whether the demand was grounded under the underlying contract. The guarantor will then recovery the amount paid from the contractor. At that point, the contractor may try recovering the amount paid to the guarantor by bringing legal proceedings against the employer.

There is not a precise procedure to call on a guarantee. However, steps that an employer should consider before making a demand include:

(i) Considering all the guarantees in the employer's possession (e.g., performance bonds, retention bonds, etc.) and ascertain which one is aimed at covering the specific breach for which the employer intends making the demand (e.g., in case of liquidated damages, the employer should make a demand under the performance bond rather than the retention bond).

10 *Matthew Hall Ortech Ltd v Tarmac Roadstone Ltd* [1997] 87 BLR 96.

(ii) Assessing the exact amount due by the contractor to ensure that the demand is made for a valid sum.

(iii) Reviewing the relevant instrument to determine any formalities required (e.g., any specific language that shall be used in the communication to the guarantor) to ensure that the demand complies with the requirements set out in the guarantee.

42.3.2 Resisting a bond call

A contractor considering that the employer's demand be illegal may try to apply to the competent courts immediately after it is made aware of such demand to obtain an interim injunction aimed at restraining the employer from proceeding with the demand and/or the guarantor from making the payment.

Historically, the English courts have been reluctant in granting injunctions preventing payment of on-demand bonds and have maintained a very high burden of proof for claimants, mostly in recognition of the fact that such guarantees play a vital role in international trade including, and even more in the construction industry. The reason of such a strict position is that bonds are considered equivalent to cash that can be collected by the beneficiary regardless of a dispute between the parties under the underlying contract and that an injunction, if granted, would force the guarantor to dishonour its promise to pay, and risk damaging its reputation.[11] Consequently, the traditional position on this subject has always been that a court should refuse to look at underlying questions of contractual liability and may only grant an injunction provided that the contractor is able to prove fraud.

Although the English courts had started taking a more lenient approach on the subject,[12] recent judgments[13] seem to show a return to the strict test for establishing whether a demand on a bond should be restrained. However, despite the difficulty of obtaining an injunction restraining a guarantor from paying or a beneficiary from making a call, such applications remain common considering the drastic consequences of a bond call.

Possible arguments that contractors may use to try preventing an unlawful call on a bond include the following.

42.3.2.1 The fraud exception

A contractor may argue that the employer's demand was fraudulent. A demand is fraudulent when: (a) the beneficiary could not honestly believe that it was entitled to make the demand; and (b) the guarantor was aware of the fraudulent nature of its demand.[14]

---

11 *Shapoorji Pallonji & Company Private Ltd v Yumn Ltd & Anor* [2021] EWHC 862 (Comm).

12 See *Simon Carves Ltd v Ensus UK Ltd* [2011] EWHC 657 (TCC) and *Doosan Babcock Ltd v Comercializadora de Equipos y Materiales Mabe Lda (formerly Mabe Chile Lda)* [2013] EWHC 3010 (TCC).

13 See *MW High Tech Projects UK Ltd v Biffa Waste Services Ltd* [2015] EWHC 949 (TCC); *Yuanda (UK) Company Ltd v Multiplex Construction Europe Ltd & Anor* [2020] EWHC 468 (TCC).

14 *Edward Owen Engineering v Barclays Bank International Ltd* [1978]1 QB 159. See also *Alternative Power Solution Ltd v Central Electricity Board & Anr* [2014] UKPC 31.

Fraud is hard to prove as the contractor shall show a strong case that it is entitled to the injunction (i.e., that the call is not permitted). For example, in *MW High Tech Properties v Biffa Waste Services Ltd*[15] Stuart-Smith J held that:

> it must be positively established [by the applicant] that [the beneficiary] was not entitled to draw down under the underlying contract.

This approach was confirmed in the recent case of *Shapoorji Pallonji & Company Private Ltd v Yumn Ltd & Anor*[16] where the court referred to the need to satisfy burden of proof at an "*enhanced merits*"[17] standard.

Moreover, the proof of the fraud must be established and obvious.[18] As summarised by Akenhead J in *Simon Carves v Ensus UK*:[19]

> Unless material fraud is established at a final trial or there is clear evidence of fraud at the without notice or interim injunction stage, the Court will not act to prevent a bank from paying out on an on demand bond provided that the conditions of the bond itself have been complied with (such as formal notice in writing).

42.3.2.2 The conditional guarantee exception

A contractor may try arguing that the guarantee is a conditional rather than an on-demand guarantee, and that the employer has not complied with the relevant requirements.

In assessing the nature of a guarantee, a court will first look at the words used in the instrument. For example, a bond requiring the employer to show loss and causation before making a demand or allowing the guarantor to make independent enquiries into the underlying events which led to the call on the bond may be held a conditional guarantee. The courts will interpret the instrument against the background matrix of both the bond and the underlying contract and, if necessary, resort to customary market practice.

In *Sirius International Insurance Co v FAI General Insurance Ltd*[20] the Court of Appeal held that:

> The terms included express contractual restrictions on the circumstances in which Sirius would be entitled to draw on the letter of credit. To that extent the letter of credit was less than the equivalent of cash and Sirius's security was correspondingly restricted.

Another interesting case where this exception was applied is the case of *Simon Carves Ltd v Ensus UK Ltd*.[21] In that case the Technology and Construction Court was called to decide whether a call on a bond should continue to be restrained even after an acceptance certificate had been issued (which should have resulted in the return of the performance bond to the contractor). Akenhead J ordered that the injunction should continue as there was a strong case on the evidence that the bond was null and void and should

15 *MW High Tech Projects UK Ltd v Biffa Waste Services Ltd* [2015] EWHC 949 (TCC).
16 *Shapoorji Pallonji & Company Private Ltd v Yumn Ltd & Anor* [2021] EWHC 862 (Comm).
17 *Shapoorji Pallonji & Company Private Ltd v Yumn Ltd & Anor* [2021] EWHC 862 (Comm).
18 *Edward Owen Engineering Ltd v Barclays Bank International Ltd* [1978] QB 159 at [169].
19 *Simon Carves Ltd v Ensus UK Ltd* [2011] EWHC 657 (TCC). See also *Edward Owen Engineering Limited v Barclays Bank International* [1978] 1 All ER 976 (CA).
20 *Sirius International Insurance Co v FAI General Insurance Ltd* [2003] 1 WLR 2214.
21 *Simon Carves Ltd v Ensus UK Ltd* [2011] EWHC 657 (TCC).

have been returned to the contractor. The judge then gave the following useful example as to when a court might restrain a call on an on-demand bond:

> on a commercial contract in which there is a bond in favour of the beneficiary party, the parties reach a full and final settlement which expressly requires the bond to be returned to the other party and no further calls to be made on the bond. If the beneficiary party in those circumstances seeks to call on the bond, in breach of the settlement terms, the Court could properly restrain the beneficiary from doing either because it is committing a straight breach of contract or because it is or should be taken to be clear fraud by the beneficiary.

This approach was applied in the case of *Doosan Babcock Ltd v Comercializadora de Equipos y Materiales Mabe Lda (formerly Mabe Chile Lda)*[22] where the court granted an injunction preventing the call on two on-demand bonds due to the employer's wrongful refusal to take over two units of the plant in breach of the underlying contract.

This approach was confirmed in the case of *Shapoorji Pallonji & Co Pvt Ltd v Yumn Ltd and Standard Charter Bank*[23] where the court held that:

> a court will generally grant an injunction to restrain a beneficiary from breaching an express obligation contained in the underlying commercial agreement not to make demand other than in defined circumstances.

However, as noted, there is following case law[24] questioning this approach and marking a return to the traditional strict position.

42.3.2.3 Procedural requirements

Where an on-demand bond provides for a specific pre-agreed procedure to make a demand and such procedure has not been complied with by the employer, the courts may grant an injunction to prevent the call (or reinstate the status quo ante in case the payment has already been made). In *Franz Maas (UK) Limited v Habib Bank AG Zurich*[25] the procedure for calling on the bond provided the need to specify that the contractor had "*failed to pay . . . under [its] contractual obligations*". As the actual demand made by the employer referred only to a failure "*to meet contractual obligations*", the call was successfully resisted by the contractor. However, in cases where the injunction is only based on a formal defect of the call, the employer would be usually entitled to make another demand in compliance with the instrument's formalities.

42.3.2.4 Pre-existing foreign judgments

Where a bond demand was already successfully resisted in a foreign court, the foreign injunction may prevent practical enforcement of an on-demand bond by the English courts. In *AES-3C Maritza East 1 Eood v Crédit Agricole Corporate and Investment Bank &*

22 *Doosan Babcock Ltd v Comercializadora de Equipos y Materiales Mabe Lda (formerly Mabe Chile Lda)* [2013] EWHC 3201 (TCC).

23 *Shapoorji Pallonji & Co Pvt Ltd v Yumn Ltd and Standard Charter Bank* [2021] EWHC 862 (Comm) at [20].

24 See for example *MW High Tech Projects UK Ltd v Biffa Waste Services Ltd* [2015] EWHC 949 and *Yuanda (UK) Company Ltd v Multiplex Construction Europe Ltd & Anor* [2020] EWHC 468 (TCC).

25 *Franz Maas (UK) Limited v Habib Bank AG Zurich* [2001] Lloyd's Rep 14.

Anor[26] a French court had issued an order preventing the guarantor bank from paying out under a bond. The Technology and Construction Court found in favour of the claimant, but stayed enforcement until the pre-existing order was lifted. The rationale of such position was that the payment was to be performed in France, and an English court would not enforce a judgment which requires the performance of an act which would be illegal in the country of performance.[27]

26 *AES-3C Maritza East 1 Eood v Crédit Agricole Corporate and Investment Bank & Anor* [2011] EWHC 123 (TCC).

27 *Ralli Brothers v Compania Naviera Sota y Aznar* [1920] 2 KB 287.

PART TEN

DISPUTES

Disputes in complex and high-value construction projects are common. The amounts at stake and the technical complexity of the subject matter of such disputes often affect the parties' ability to agree on their claims and counterclaims. In some cases, triggering the dispute resolution clause in the contract is the only way to bring the other party to the negotiation table in the hope of an early settlement that will save the parties from the hassles and costs of arbitration or litigation. In fact, many construction disputes are settled only after some form of dispute resolution process has commenced and the parties have more clarity as to their respective positions and available evidence.

DOI: 10.4324/9781003387718-53

CHAPTER 43

Litigation, arbitration and alternative dispute resolution

Traditionally, disputes, including construction disputes, were resolved through court litigation. However, the number and types of dispute resolution mechanisms have increased in recent years. Litigation is no longer the most widely used method to resolve construction disputes, while arbitration is generally perceived more aligned with the parties' needs. Moreover, alternative dispute resolution methods or "ADR" are more and more frequently used to deal with construction disputes.

43.1 Litigation

43.1.1 Litigation in general

In the case of court litigation disputes are decided by the courts of law. Litigation presents several advantages which include the specialisation of the courts (e.g., the Technology and Construction Court), the wide powers that courts have compared to arbitral tribunals to compel the parties to comply with their obligations and the defined rights of appeal for errors of fact or law. However, such advantages may be perceived as outbalanced by various disadvantages such as the formality of the proceedings, the greater costs, the longer time to obtain a judgment, the lack of confidentiality and the appealability of the judgment.

43.1.2 Litigation procedure

43.1.2.1 The Civil Procedural Rules and the "overriding objective"

English courts will be competent to hear disputes arising out of construction contracts where the parties have so agreed in the dispute resolution clause, or the English courts have considered themselves competent to hear the dispute where parties have made no express choice.

The procedural steps of litigation in England and Wales are set out in the Civil Procedural Rules ("CPR") and the relevant practice directions.

An important principle applying to all litigation cases dealt in the English courts is the so-called overriding objective set out at CPR 1.1 based on which the court should endeavour to ensure that all cases are dealt with justly and at proportionate cost. This includes: (i) ensuring that the parties are on an equal footing; (ii) taking all practicable steps to save expenditure; dealing with the dispute in ways which are proportionate to the size of the claim and cross-claim and the importance of the case to the parties; (iii)

DOI: 10.4324/9781003387718-54

managing the case throughout in a way that takes proper account of its complexity and the different financial positions of the parties; (iv) ensuring expedition, and to allot to each case an appropriate share of the court's resources.[1]

43.1.2.2 The Technology and Construction Court[2]

Complex construction disputes will almost invariably be heard in the Technology and Construction Court ("TCC"), which is a specialist court within the High Court of Justice.

Examples of claims which may be appropriate to bring as TCC claims are:[3] (i) building or other construction disputes, including claims for the enforcement of the decisions of adjudicators under the Housing Grants, Construction and Regeneration Act 1996; (ii) engineering disputes; (iii) energy disputes, including claims concerning oil and gas pipelines and facilities, onshore and offshore windfarms, waste to energy plants and other renewables; (iv) public procurement claims; (v) claims by and against engineers, architects, surveyors, accountants and other specialised advisors relating to the services they provide for duties concerning the development of land or the construction of buildings; (vi) claims relating to the environment (for example, pollution cases); (vii) challenges to decisions of arbitrators in construction and engineering disputes including applications for permission to appeal and appeals.

The main phases of a dispute in the TCC are as follows:[4]

43.1.2.3 The Pre-Action Protocol

There is a Pre-Action Protocol for Construction and Engineering Disputes ("the Protocol") that aims at: (i) encouraging the frank and early exchange of information about the prospective claim and any defence to it; (ii) enabling parties to avoid litigation by agreeing a settlement of the claim before the commencement of proceedings; and (iii) supporting the efficient management of proceedings where litigation cannot be avoided. The steps provided in the Protocol are as follows: (i) before commencing proceedings, the claimant should first issue a letter of claim to the respondent. The letter of claim should, amongst other things, summarise the facts and the grounds of the claim and give details of the relief sought; (ii) the defendant should then acknowledge the letter of claim within 14 days of receipt and respond within 28 days (the parties may agree on an extension of up to a maximum of three months), failing which the claimant will be entitled to commence proceedings. The letter of response should, amongst other things, state the claims that are accepted or rejected and the relevant basis, and set out any counterclaim advanced by the defendant; (iii) the parties should then meet to attempt resolving the dispute without recourse to litigation and endeavour to agree which form of alternative dispute resolution to adopt, if more suitable. Any discussion at the meetings and/or any note of the meeting is without prejudice and cannot be referred to the court unless all parties agree. However, the letter of claim, the defendant's response and the information relating to attendance at

1 *The Technology and Construction Court Guide* (October 2022) Sub-section 1.1.4.
2 This section borrows heavily or verbatim from *The Technology and Construction Court Guide* (October 2022).
3 *The Technology and Construction Court Guide* (October 2022) Sub-section 1.3.1.
4 This section relies heavily or verbatim on *The Technology and Construction Court Guide* (October 2022).

the meeting (or refusal to attend and relevant grounds) are not considered confidential or "without prejudice".

43.1.2.4 Commencement

The proceedings are started using a claim form which is then to be served by the claimant. The defendant must then file an acknowledgment of service within 14 days of the service of the claim form.

43.1.2.5 First case management conference

When the case is commenced in or transferred to the TCC the listing office will send all parties a case management information sheet ("CMIS") which they should complete. The CMIS will include questions on possible settlement, location of trial, compliance with the Protocol, witnesses, experts, disclosure, costs, etc. The court will then set up a first case management conference ("CMC"), which may also be held remotely or by hybrid hearing, to discuss any areas of potential debate arising from the case management information sheet and give general procedural directions. Issues that may be considered and discussed at the first CMC are: (i) the need for any further statements of case; (ii) the outcome of the Protocol process and the possible further need for alternative dispute resolution;[5] (iii) the need for a preliminary issue hearing; (iv) the request to the parties to provide a list of issues and update it during the course of the proceedings, e.g., in the form of a Scott Schedule (which *The Technology and Construction Court Guide* defines as "*a table, often in landscape format, in which the Claimant's case on liability and quantum is set out item by item in the first few columns and the Defendant's response is set out in the adjacent columns*"[6]); (v) whether the trial should be in stages (e.g., dealing first with liability and causation and then with quantum); (vi) evidence, including disclosure, exchange of written witness statements and expert evidence; (vii) costs budgets.

43.1.2.6 Preliminary issues

In some cases, a preliminary issues hearing may be necessary or desirable, for example[7] in cases where the dispute is on: (a) whether or not there was a binding contract between the parties; (b) the documents constituting the contract between the parties; (c) the contents or relevance of any conversations relied on as having contractual status or effect; (d) the proper construction of the contract documents or the effect of an exclusion or similar clause; (e) the correct application of a statute or binding authority to a situation where there is little or no factual dispute.

43.1.2.7 The further exchanges

The parties will then exchange further pleadings where they will refine their relevant positions and reply to the other party's claims and counterclaims. These are usually lengthy documents where the parties put forward their legal arguments and their technical

5 E.g., early neutral evaluation, which is carried out by any appropriately qualified person, or court settlement process, which is a form of mediation carried out by TCC judges. See *The Technology and Construction Court Guide* (October 2022) Sub-section 7.5 and 7.6.

6 *The Technology and Construction Court Guide* (October 2022) Sub-section 5.6.1.

7 *The Technology and Construction Court Guide* (October 2022) Sub-section 8.3.

arguments and clarify their position. The parties may also refine their positions from time to time by reducing or increasing their claims and/or admitting their counterparties' claims in whole or in part.

43.1.2.8 Evidence

Evidence in the TCC is usually given through disclosure of documents, factual evidence and expert evidence.

43.1.2.8.1 DISCLOSURE[8]

The parties are obliged to disclose (i.e., identify and make available) documents that are relevant to the issues in the proceedings. Disclosure in the TCC is subject to the rules set out in Practice Direction 57AD (with some exceptions).

The parties will typically take the following steps: (i) give "initial disclosure" of key documents at the same time as serving their statements of case; (ii) indicate whether they seek an "extended disclosure" on any specific issues; (iii) conduct a search for documents; and (iv) produce copies of the documents.

The term "document" includes any record of any description containing information and may take any form including paper or electronic held by computer or on portable devices (such as memory sticks or mobile phones or within databases, electronic communications such as emails, text messages, webmail, social media and voicemail, audio or visual recordings) or stored on servers and back-up systems and electronic information that has been "deleted" (including metadata, and other embedded data which is not typically visible on screen or a printout). The duty of disclosure extends to: (i) "adverse" documents, i.e., those whose content contradicts or materially damages the disclosing party's contention or version of events on an issue in dispute, or supports the contention or version of events of an opposing party on an issue in dispute, whether or not that issue is one of the agreed issues for disclosure; and (ii) documents within a party's control, (where "control" extends to documents of which a party has, or had, physical possession, or to which they have, or had, a right to possession or to inspect or to take copies. This will include documents in the possession of an employee or agent, over which a party has control. It may also include documents held by subsidiary companies, professional agents and ex-employees).

Unless privilege applies, any relevant documents must be disclosed regardless of whether they are confidential. It may be possible for sensitive information which is irrelevant to the dispute, and which is contained in a document that has to be disclosed to be redacted or blacked out, and in some cases, there will be an obligation to do so.

The parties have a number of continuing (i.e., that last until the conclusion of the proceedings, including any appeal, or until it is clear there will be no proceedings) disclosure duties, which include: (i) taking reasonable steps to preserve documents in the party's control that may be relevant to any issue in the proceedings; (ii) disclosing "known adverse documents" (i.e., documents, other than privileged documents, that a party is actually aware, without undertaking any further search for documents than it has already undertaken or caused to be undertaken, both are or were previously within its

8 Practice Direction 57AD and *The Technology and Construction Court Guide* (October 2022) Section 11.

control and are adverse), regardless of whether or not any order for disclosure is made; (iii) undertaking any search for documents in a responsible and conscientious manner to fulfil the stated purpose of the search; (iv) acting honestly in relation to the process of giving disclosure and reviewing documents disclosed by the other party; (v) using reasonable efforts to avoid providing documents to another party that have no relevance to the "issues for disclosure" in the proceedings. The court can impose sanctions on a party that does not comply with its disclosure obligations.

43.1.2.8.2 FACTUAL EVIDENCE[9]

Fact witnesses are persons who have knowledge of the facts in dispute based on their contemporaneous involvement in the project (e.g., project managers, contract managers, site managers, etc.). Witnesses of fact will be asked to prepare a witness statement setting out the matters of fact of which the witness has personal knowledge that are relevant to the case. The witness should include in his witness statement the complete evidence relevant to the issues in the case and not also evidence on the basis that it might be needed depending on what the other party's witnesses might say (as this may be addressed in supplementary witness statements).

43.1.2.8.3 EXPERT EVIDENCE

Expert witnesses are technical experts who give opinion to the tribunal on technical matters in their field of expertise (e.g., in the case of construction disputes, delay analysis, quantum analysis, engineering, etc.). They have a duty to help the court on matters within their expertise. This duty overrides any duty to the experts' clients. Thus, the experts' reports must be independent and unbiased. The court may direct that the parties' expert hold without prejudice meetings at all stages of the pre-trial preparation to produce a document whose contents are agreed, and which defines common positions or each expert's differing position. The result will be a signed statement setting out the issues which have been agreed, and those issues which have not been agreed, together with a short summary of the reasons for their disagreement.

43.1.2.9 The trial

After a pre-trial review aimed at discussing and agreeing on issues of trial management, the trial will take place. The trial will normally start with each party's advocate giving an opening note outlining that party's case. The parties will then give an opening speech. The claimant will usually highlight the main features of the party's case and/or dealing with matters raised in the other parties' opening notes, whilst the respondent will emphasise the main features of his case and/or respond to matters raised in the claimant's opening speech.

Then, the parties will introduce their oral evidence. Evidence of fact will usually precede expert evidence. Experts evidence will normally be given in groups with all experts in a particular discipline giving their evidence in sequence. Each party will have an overall length of time for the trial and overall lengths of time within that period for the evidence and submissions. This will be established by the court or agreed between the parties.

9 *The Technology and Construction Court Guide* (October 2022) Section 12.

The trial will end with the closing submissions, which may take the form of: (a) oral closing speeches; or (b) written submission alone; or (c) written submissions supplemented by oral closing speeches.

Although the judge may give judgment orally immediately or soon after closing speeches (unless closing submissions are required), in the case of complex disputes the judge will usually deliver a reserved judgment in writing at a later date. The judge will then release a confidential draft judgment in advance of the formal hand down to parties and their legal advisers. The judgment will also determine which party can be properly described as "the successful party" for cost purposes, unless the parties agreed otherwise.

43.1.2.10 Appeals

Appeals will be heard by the Civil Division of the Court of Appeal subject to obtaining "permission", which may be granted by the court below or, more usually, by the Court of Appeal itself.

The prospective appellant should be able to show that the proposed appeal stands a realistic prospect of success. If permission is granted, the appeal will be heard, usually by a court composed by three judges. Normally, the parties may not introduce new evidence. The Court of Appeal will then usually issue the judgment in writing.

Appeals to the Supreme Court (i.e., the highest court in England, Wales and Northern Ireland) will need permission, which will usually be given only in relation to cases involving important points of principle.

43.2 Arbitration

43.2.1 Arbitration in general

Arbitration is the most widely used method to solve disputes arising out of construction contracts for complex projects. It may be defined as a consensual method of dispute resolution where the parties agree to have their contractual disputes resolved outside of the traditional court system by a third-party arbitrator or arbitral tribunal, by whose decision (or award) they agree to be bound, in line with a set of rules agreed between the parties or which the parties have referred to in the relevant arbitration agreement.

The third-party arbitrator or arbitral tribunal, acting in a judicial manner, runs the process by examining the parties' evidence and submissions and comes to a decision which, except for the possibility to appeal for very limited issues of law, will be final and binding on the parties.

In most countries the legislation governing arbitrations is based on the UNCITRAL Model Law on International Commercial Arbitration. English law arbitration is governed by the Arbitration Act 1996, which applies where the seat of the arbitration is in England and Wales or Northern Ireland. The general principles of arbitration are well summarised in Section 1 of the Arbitration Act 1996, according to which: (a) the object of arbitration is to obtain the fair resolution of disputes by an impartial tribunal without unnecessary delay or expense; (b) the parties should be free to agree how their disputes are resolved, subject only to such safeguards as are necessary in the public interest; (c) the courts should not intervene except as expressly provided by the Arbitration Act 1996.

43.2.2 Arbitration and litigation

Arbitration is a private alternative to litigation. The two dispute resolution means are usually very similar, and the outcome is in both cases a binding decision, although it could be argued that arbitration is "more final" than litigation as an arbitral award may be only challenged in limited circumstances.

The parties to complex construction contracts often prefer arbitration to litigation for several reasons, including that: (i) arbitration is generally perceived as more neutral than court litigation. For example, litigation may carry a risk of bias or favouritisms where one of the parties is a local government or a publicly owned company or a party that may somehow have an influence on a local court. In such cases, arbitration may be preferred as the parties will be able to agree that the arbitrators composing the tribunal shall have nationality that is different from those of the parties; (ii) arbitration awards can be enforced abroad more easily than court judgments because of the Convention on the Recognition and Enforcement of Foreign Arbitral Awards (the "New York Convention"); (iii) arbitration typically ensures that disputes are heard by persons with expertise in the construction industry; (iv) arbitration offers higher procedural flexibility compared with court litigation; (v) arbitration awards do not set a precedent; and (vi) arbitration proceedings are generally private and confidential (although this is not the default position under the Arbitration Act 1996). This is an important aspect as confidentiality is usually crucial both for employers (which may not want to disclose issues relevant to their project) and contractors (which may want to avoid any bad publicity deriving from them being perceived as litigious vis-à-vis clients and/or the disclosure of confidential trade information such as prices, costs and technologies used for the project).

Arbitration constitutes an alternative to litigation. However, there may be situations in which the two dispute resolution methods conflict. This may occur, for example: (i) when one of the parties has commenced court litigation when arbitration proceedings were still pending in relation to the same claims (or vice-versa). In such cases, the defendant may apply to the court for a stay or dismissal of the arbitration proceedings (and vice-versa);[10] (ii) when a party seeks to pursue proceedings in a foreign court despite and in breach of an arbitration agreement providing for arbitration seated in England, the defendant may apply for an anti-suit injunction aimed at restraining such foreign proceedings; (iii) when the dispute resolution clause refers to both litigation and arbitration without specifying how disputes shall be allocated between the two. In the case of *OOO Abbott & anr v Econowall UK Ltd & ors*,[11] the dispute resolution clause in the contract stated as follows:

> The Agreement shall be governed by and construed and interpreted in accordance with the laws of England and the parties hereby submit to the exclusive jurisdiction of the English courts. The parties agree to be subject to be arbitration should there be a disagreement between them.

The defendants contended that the disputes were to be referred to arbitration in line with *Sulamérica Cia Nacional de Seguros S.A. and others v Enesa Engenharia S.A.*[12] and *Ace*

10 *Lloyd v Wright* [1983] QB 1065.
11 *OOO Abbott & anr v Econowall UK Ltd & ors* [2016] EWHC 660.
12 *Sulamérica Cia Nacional de Seguros S.A. and others v Enesa Engenharia S.A.* [2012] EWCA Civ 638.

Capital Ltd v CMS Energy Corporation,[13] which involved similar issues and were both decided in favour of arbitration. The contract included a "severability" clause reading as follows:

> If any clause or any part of any clause in this Agreement is declared invalid or unenforceable by the judgment or decree, by consent or otherwise of a court of competent jurisdiction from whose decisions no appeal is or can be taken all other clauses or parts of clauses in this Agreement shall remain in full force and effect and shall not be affected thereby for the term of this Agreement.

HHJ Hacon held that this was consistent with the dispute resolution clause in the contract, which gave exclusive jurisdiction to English courts, but not with the arbitration clause. As a result, he concluded that it was likely that the parties intended to give the English courts jurisdiction over disputes relating to the agreement. The arbitration clause was "permissive", meaning that the parties could jointly elect to refer any dispute to arbitration to the extent that no court proceedings were already pending in respect of that same dispute.

43.2.3 Arbitration and adjudication

Arbitration has some features in common with adjudication (e.g., both end with a binding decision), but there are also substantial differences between the two. For example: (i) arbitrations awards are final and readily enforceable, while an adjudicator's decisions are usually binding, but susceptible to a rehearing; (ii) adjudication is usually subject to stringent time limits, while a typical arbitration's length is comparable to the one of court proceedings.

43.2.4 Arbitration and mediation

Like mediation, arbitration is consensual, and the parties are usually entitled to choose the third-party arbitrators and the procedural rules applying to the arbitration. However, arbitration is an adversarial method of dispute resolution which ends with a final and binding award. This differentiates arbitration from mediation, where the mediator has no power to bind the parties and the outcome is a mediated agreement which becomes binding on the parties only upon them formalising it in a formal document.

43.2.5 "Ad hoc" and institutional arbitration

The parties to a construction contract opting for arbitration shall first agree between institutional or "ad hoc" arbitration.

In the case of institutional arbitration, a specialised institutional provider of dispute resolution services oversees the arbitration process, typically based on its own set of arbitration rules. Among the most common institutional providers are the International Chamber of Commerce ("ICC"), the London Court of International Arbitration ("LCIA"), the International Centre for Dispute Resolution ("ICDR") and the Singapore International Arbitration Centre ("SIAC"). Institutional arbitration has a number of advantages such as:

13 *Ace Capital Ltd v CMS Energy Corporation* [2008] EWHC 1843 (Comm).

(i) the possibility to adopt and incorporate into the contract the pre-established and tested set of rules which will save or reduce (where the parties intend to make amendments) the parties' efforts and costs in establishing the applicable arbitration procedure; (ii) in case of doubts and/or disagreements, the parties may request the institution to intervene and provide administrative assistance; (iii) such institutions usually have a roster of qualified, impartial and "tested" arbitrators to choose from based on the type of dispute, the necessary skillset, experience and expertise, the law regulating the contract and the language of the dispute; (iv) the institution will typically be allowed to scrutinise the draft award before the final award is issued which has the effect of reducing the risk of mistakes. However, institutional arbitration also presents some disadvantages. Among these, the most significant is certainly that it is usually more costly as the parties: (i) will need to pay the administrative fees for the services provided by the institution and for the use of the institution's facilities (although they may opt for different solutions, like having the hearings taking place at the office of one of the law firms assisting them); and (ii) will not be allowed to negotiate the arbitrators' fees (as these are usually fixed by the institution).

Where the parties agree to institutional arbitration, one of the main points of discussion is what institution should administer the proceedings. When making this choice the parties may want to consider the following aspects: (i) whether the institution has a good reputation and experience in the subject matter of the dispute (e.g., by looking at the arbitrators' roster); (ii) whether the rules of that institution align with the parties' needs; (iii) whether the institution has international standing; (iv) the fees and costs applied and the how are they are quantified.

Where the parties do not intend to opt for administered arbitration, they may choose "ad hoc" arbitration and agree between them all aspects of the arbitration, including the relevant procedure, the number of arbitrators and how to appoint them, the language of the arbitration, the law of the arbitration agreement, etc. Arguably, ad hoc arbitration has some advantages. For example it is relatively more flexible (as the parties are completely free to set out the arbitration procedure) and less expensive (as the parties will be able to negotiate the arbitrators fees directly with the arbitrators and will not have to pay any fee to the institution, although that may be counterbalanced, at least in part, by the fact that the parties will have to negotiate the whole set of rules, which may result in more legal fees). However, such advantages may be counterbalanced by important disadvantages, including that: (i) the negotiation of the arbitration procedure may require a greater degree of effort and be particularly time-consuming where the parties are not willing to cooperate and/or lack the necessary expertise; (ii) the parties may bear additional legal costs to ensure that the clause is properly drafted as a poorly drafted clause may create uncertainties or fail to address all eventualities; (iii) the parties will need to engage directly with the arbitrators in relation to their fees, but may not want to enter into tough negotiations with those who will eventually decide on their dispute; (iv) in case of any issues regarding the arbitral tribunal (e.g., conflict of interest, delays in writing the award, lack of availability, etc.) a party will not be able to refer to an administering institution, but may need to seek court intervention, which will lead to more costs and further delays; and (v) in the case of complex construction arbitrations the tribunal may seek to appoint a secretary to assist in relation to the administrative work involved, which will make the procedure more costly. All such reasons make ad hoc arbitration less popular in the construction industry. However, in case the parties wish to opt for it, they should borrow from an existing set of rules (like the Arbitration Act 1996 or the UNICITRAL Arbitration Rules) to establish the arbitration procedure, but should refrain from referring to institutions' rules (like the "ICC" or the "LCIA" rules) considering that such rules are usually tailored to the provider's specific arbitration procedure, so that incorporating them into ad hoc proceedings may create ambiguities, or even unintentionally agree to an institutional arbitration process.

43.2.6 Arbitration procedure

The procedure applying to each specific arbitration will depend on a number of factors, including whether it is an institutional or ad hoc arbitration, the arbitration agreement, the arbitration rules or the arbitral tribunal's style. The whole process is usually tailored to meet the peculiarities of such complex disputes, including the technical nature of the issues involved and the large amount of evidence necessary to prove the parties' claims and counterclaims.

However, there are some steps that are common to almost all institutional construction arbitrations (while in ad hoc arbitration the procedure may vary as there is not a pre-agreed set of rules and administering entity assisting the parties during the process). These include the following:

43.2.6.1 Commencement and initial exchanges

First the claimant will submit a request for arbitration to the administering institution's secretariat, which will then transmit a copy to the respondent. The respondent will then have a certain number of days from receipt of the request for arbitration (30 being the most common timeframe) to submit an answer to the request for arbitration and counterclaim (although such term may be extended, typically by an additional 30 days).

43.2.6.2 Constitution of the arbitral tribunal

The arbitral tribunal will then be constituted in accordance with the arbitration agreement and the rules chosen by the parties. Any perspective arbitrator will be required to disclose facts or circumstances which might affect his independence and/or impartiality, and each party will be entitled to challenge the appointment of an arbitrator on such grounds. Should the challenge be accepted, the arbitrator will be replaced.

43.2.6.3 Preliminary issues

As soon as the tribunal is constituted, it will review the file with an aim of identifying any preliminary issues that may need to be addressed (e.g., relevant to jurisdiction, interim measures, etc.).

43.2.6.4 Case management conference

The arbitral tribunal will then organise a case management conference ("CMC") aimed at agreeing the conduct of the proceedings including the terms of reference, the procedural timetable and the procedural rules applying to the proceedings. In particular:

(i) The terms of reference may be defined as a summary of the main aspects of the dispute, including the parties, their representatives, the arbitration agreement, the applicable law and the parties' claims and defences. The document is prepared by the arbitral tribunal based on information and comments provided by the parties. The document should be eventually agreed between the parties. The purpose of the document is to clarify the case and the parties' positions.

(ii) The procedural timetable sets out the proceedings' timeline. A specific date will be agreed for each step of the proceedings, including claimant's statement of claim, the defendant's statement of defence and counterclaim, the document production and disclosure phase, the various further exchanges between the parties (also called rejoinders), the hearing dates, the post-hearing briefs and/or closing arguments, the parties' submissions on costs. In some cases, the proceedings may be bifurcated in two phases (e.g., the first phase on entitlement and the second on quantum). The main objective of bifurcation is to spare the parties from having to spend time and money on fully defending dubious claims where lack of entitlement would defeat the claim, so rendering the quantum unnecessary. For example, in the context of a construction project a prolongation claim that may be time barred may benefit from a bifurcation so that, should the claimant fail to prove entitlement (i.e., should the claimant fail to prove that the notices of claim were timely issued), the tribunal will issue a partial award rejecting the claim, so saving the parties the time and money of having to pursue and/or defend the quantum part of the claim. The proceedings will then continue on all other claims and counterclaims (if any).

(iii) The procedural aspects that are not covered by applicable arbitration rules (institutional rules and law applicable to the proceedings), e.g., on how filings should be prepared (including any limits, e.g., on length and time) and exchanged, the need of any translations, the need of a "Scott Schedule", the rules on disclosure to be adopted (e.g., the use of a so-called Redfern Schedule, which is a schematic document summarising the parties' positions on requests for disclosure which is made of various columns that the parties fill with information on the documents that the party is requesting to be disclosed and reasons why it should be disclosed, the responding party's position on each request and the arbitrators' decision on the requirement for disclosure), etc.

43.2.6.5 Further exchanges

The parties will then exchange further pleadings or memorials setting out their case and responding to the other party's contentions.

43.2.6.6 Evidence

Evidence in the arbitration is usually given through disclosure of documents, factual evidence and expert evidence. In addition, the tribunal may ask or the parties may agree to have members of the tribunal visiting the site.

43.2.6.6.1 DISCLOSURE

The parties' submissions will usually be accompanied by large amounts of supporting documentation mainly consisting in contemporaneous records and documents such as communications (e-mails, letters, text messages, etc.), meetings notes, project reports, photographs, drawings, etc. In parallel, the parties will engage in the process of disclosure the extensiveness of which will depend on the type of arbitration and the agreement of the parties and the applicable rules (e.g., whether the parties have agreed on the use of the IBA Rules on the Taking of Evidence in International Arbitration). However, documents are not the only evidence the parties will use to prove their case and disprove their counterparties' cases.

43.2.6.6.2 FACTUAL EVIDENCE

Fact witnesses will usually produce a written witness statement (with the assistance of the relevant party's lawyers) setting out their recollection of the events.

43.2.6.6.3 EXPERT EVIDENCE

Technical experts will prepare their respective expert reports that will then be presented to the tribunal and may be revised during the proceedings based on further documents and information available. Often, the parties' experts will cooperate to try narrowing the points in dispute work together at a joint report setting out the main point of agreement and disagreement.

43.2.6.6.4 SITE VISITS

Site visits are advisable where the members of the arbitral tribunal could benefit from a direct knowledge of the facts in dispute by visiting the site and the project (e.g., in case of defects claims where the tribunal may observe the defect and any possible consequences).

43.2.6.7 Hearings

The hearings will be held on the dates and in the location (although they may be held virtually) set out in the procedural timetable and will be based on a pre-agreed hearing agenda. The hearings will start with the parties' opening statements where they will set out their cases. The various claims and issues will be heard on the basis of the hearing agenda. The factual and expert witnesses will be heard (examined, cross-examined and re-examined) based on a pre-agreed order of appearance. Typically, each party will be allowed an equal amount of time in presenting its arguments and examining witnesses. Everything said at the hearings will be recorded and the transcripts will be sent to the parties at the end of each hearing day for them to check any inaccuracies.

43.2.6.8 Closing submissions

Closing submissions may be presented orally (closing oral arguments), in writing (post-hearing briefs and rebuttal, if so agreed) or both. In the closing submissions each party will summarise its position and highlight the strengths of its case and weaknesses of the counterparty's case as emerged during the proceedings (e.g., any documents disclosed by the other party undermining their case, any concession made by witnesses at the hearings, etc.).

43.2.6.9 The award

The arbitral tribunal will then reach a decision on the various claims and counterclaim and draft the award. Where the decision is not unanimous, the award will reflect the position of the majority of the arbitral tribunal's members, although the dissenting arbitrator may ask to have his dissenting opinion included in the award. Depending on the rules applicable to the proceedings, the draft award may be sent to the administering institution for a scrutiny, which, however, shall not affect the arbitral tribunal's liberty of decision. According to Section 52 of the Arbitration Act 1996 (the "Arbitration Act") the parties are free to agree on the form of an award.

In the absence of such agreement, the award: (a) shall be in writing signed by all the arbitrators or all those assenting to the award; (b) shall contain the reasons for the award unless it is an agreed award or the parties have agreed to dispense with reasons; (c) shall state the seat of the arbitration and the date when the award is made. Section 54 of the Arbitration Act states that, unless otherwise agreed by the parties, the tribunal may decide what is to be taken to be the date on which the award was made. In the absence of any such decision, the date of the award shall be taken to be the date on which it is signed by the arbitrator or, where more than one arbitrator signs the award, by the last of them. The award is then notified to the parties. In this regard, Section 55 (1) and (2) of the Arbitration Act states that the parties are free to agree on the requirements as to notification of the award to the parties. Absent such agreement, the award shall be notified to the parties by service on them of copies of the award, which shall be done without delay after the award is made.

Section 61 of the Arbitration Act states that the tribunal may make an award allocating the costs of the arbitration as between the parties, subject to any agreement of the parties. Unless the parties otherwise agree, the tribunal shall award costs on the general principle that costs should follow the event except where it appears to the tribunal that in the circumstances this is not appropriate in relation to the whole or part of the costs.

43.2.6.10 Award corrections and challenges

According to Section 57 (1), (2) and (3) of the Arbitration Act, the parties are free to agree on the powers of the tribunal to correct an award or make an additional award. Absent such agreement, the tribunal may on its own initiative or on the application of a party: (i) correct an award so as to remove any clerical mistake or error arising from an accidental slip or omission or clarify or remove any ambiguity in the award; or (ii) make an additional award in respect of any claim (including a claim for interest or costs) which was presented to the tribunal but was not dealt with in the award.

An award may be challenged in the following three circumstances:

(i) Because the arbitral tribunal did not have substantive jurisdiction.[14] Sections 82(1) and 30(1) of the Arbitration Act define "*substantive jurisdiction*" by reference to whether there is a valid arbitration agreement, the tribunal is properly constituted and the matters submitted to arbitration are in accordance with the arbitration agreement. On such an appeal the court has the power to confirm, vary or set aside (in whole or in part) the award.

(ii) On the ground of serious irregularity affecting the tribunal, the proceedings or the award which the court considers has caused or will cause substantial injustice to the applicant.[15] This applies in particular to circumstances of failure by the

14 Sections 67 of the Arbitration Act 1996.
15 Sections 68 of the Arbitration Act 1996.

tribunal to comply with the general duty of a tribunal under Section 33 of the Arbitration Act (i.e., the duty to act fairly and impartially as between the parties, giving each party a reasonable opportunity of putting his case and dealing with that of his opponent,[16] and adopt procedures suitable to the circumstances of the particular case, avoiding unnecessary delay or expense, so as to provide a fair means for the resolution of the matters falling to be determined), the tribunal exceeding its powers, failure by the tribunal to conduct the proceedings in accordance with the procedure agreed by the parties, failure by the tribunal to deal with all the issues that were put to it, any arbitral or other institution or person vested by the parties with powers in relation to the proceedings or the award exceeding its powers, uncertainty or ambiguity as to the effect of the award, the award being obtained by fraud or the award or the way in which it was procured being contrary to public policy, failure to comply with the requirements as to the form of the award; or any irregularity in the conduct of the proceedings or in the award which is admitted by the tribunal or by any arbitral or other institution or person vested by the parties with powers in relation to the proceedings or the award. On such an appeal the court has the power to remit the award to the tribunal (in whole or in part) for reconsideration, set the award aside (in whole or in part) or declare the award to be of no effect (in whole or in part).

(iii) On point of law arising out of the award (unless otherwise agreed by the parties).[17] Such appeals may only be brought with the agreement of all the other parties to the proceedings or with the leave of the court. Leave to appeal shall be given only if the court is satisfied that: (a) the determination of the question will substantially affect the rights of one or more of the parties; (b) the question is one which the tribunal was asked to determine; (c) on the basis of the findings of fact in the award, the decision of the tribunal on the question is obviously wrong or the question is one of general public importance and the decision of the tribunal is at least open to serious doubt; (d) despite the agreement of the parties to resolve the matter by arbitration, it is just and proper in all the circumstances for the court to determine the question. On such an appeal the court has the power to confirm, vary or set aside the award (in whole or in part), or remit it to the tribunal (in whole or in part) for reconsideration in the light of the court's determination.

The recent case of *WSB v FOL*[18] has confirmed that applications under Sections 67–69 of the Arbitration Act are narrow in scope, and subject to strict procedural requirements. Moreover, Calver J confirmed the guidance in *Midnight Marine Ltd & Another v Thomas Miller Speciality Underwriting Agency Ltd (The "Labhauler")*[19] where Mr Justice Butcher recommended procedures to dispose of unmeritorious challenges quickly and cheaply:

---

16 See, for example *P (a company incorporated in Country A) v D (a company incorporated in Country B) and others* [2019] EWHC 1277 (Comm).

17 Section 69 of the Arbitration Act 1996.

18 *WSB v FOL* [2022] EWHC 586 (Comm).

19 *Midnight Marine Ltd & Another v Thomas Miller Speciality Underwriting Agency Ltd (The "Labhauler")* [2018] EWHC 3431 [2019] 1 Lloyd's Rep 399 [2018] 12 WLUK 157 at [36].

The importance of arbitral finality is well known and the court is required by section 1(a) of the 1996 Act to have regard to the need to avoid unnecessary delay and expense.

43.3 Alternative dispute resolution

Alternative dispute resolution or "ADR" refers to the various methods to resolve disputes which are "alternative" to litigation and arbitration. These include methods such as mediation and adjudication.

The fact that all such procedures are typically included in the ADR category despite the substantial differences among them makes it harder to precisely define ADR. However, as the name suggests, an attempt to define ADR may be done by referring to the key aspects which make ADR procedures "alternative" to litigation and arbitration. In general, the key differences are as follows:

(i) While in the case of litigation and arbitration the deciding body (i.e., the court and the arbitral tribunal respectively) has coercive or directive powers, ADR methods are said to be "consensual" in that the relevant outcome may only be enforced provided that the parties so agree (although in the case of adjudication the adjudicator's decision will usually be provisionally binding).

(ii) While litigation and arbitration are more formal (this is particularly true for litigation), ADR procedures are relatively more informal and "tailorable" based on the parties' needs.

The parties shall use particular care when opting for ADR in their contract. Simply referring to ADR may not suffice and make the clause unenforceable for uncertainty. In *Cable & Wireless v IBM*[20] the dispute resolution clause in the contract stated that the parties "*shall attempt in good faith to resolve the dispute or claim through an . . . (ADR) procedure as recommended to the Parties by the Centre for Dispute Resolution*". Colman J held that the clause was enforceable considering that the ADR procedure to be used was sufficiently certain. He also clarified that had the clause not referred to the recommendation of the Centre for Dispute Resolution, a simple obligation to attempt in good faith to settle a dispute would have been unenforceable due to uncertainty. This is because the court would not have had any "*objective criteria*" to decide if the parties had complied with such provision.

43.3.1 Mediation

43.3.1.1 Mediation in general

Mediation is a private, consensual, informal and non-adjudicative ADR process where the parties engage a neutral third party (the "mediator") to assist them achieving a negotiated solution which, if acceptable to all parties, will form the terms of a legally enforceable contract between the parties.

The difference with negotiation is the addition of the mediator who, acting as a contract facilitator, aids the parties in dispute to achieve an agreed solution without deciding the outcome of the dispute. The common feature with negotiation is that whether or not a

20 *Cable & Wireless v IBM* [2002] EWHC 2059 (Comm).

settlement is achieved lies ultimately with the parties. This differentiates mediation from other adversarial methods of dispute resolution such as litigation, arbitration and adjudication where the control of the dispute is relinquished to a court, a tribunal or an adjudicator that has no interest in preserving the parties' relationships or the smooth continuation and completion of the project. As mentioned, the parties will be the sole decision makers as the mediator does not have the power to bind the parties to any outcome. This is a particularly useful feature in the construction industry where the parties may have an interest in preserving their relationship during an ongoing construction phase and not to spoil their relationship for future construction projects.

Mediation is also particularly useful to re-open or facilitate the communications between the parties in case negotiations have been dragging for a long time with no positive results and the parties have lost mutual trust. Another benefit of mediation is that chances of resolving the dispute are increased by the fact that the mediator may "bring on the table" arguments which are unrelated to the facts but may nonetheless encourage the parties achieving a mutual satisfactory agreement (e.g., future projects or discounts).

The importance of mediation in the English legal system was confirmed in various cases where the courts showed to take into serious account the parties' refusal to mediate their disputes without good reason.

For example, *Dunnett (Susan) v Railtrack PLC*,[21] in granting permission to appeal the judge suggested that the parties tried mediation or a similar process. Railtrack refused to engage in mediation without good reason. When Railtrack won the appeal, the court held that no costs order should be made against the claimant. In particular, the court held that:

> When asked by the Court why his clients were not willing to contemplate alternative dispute resolution, said that this would necessarily involve the payment of money, which his clients were not willing to contemplate, over and above what they had already offered. This appeared to be a misunderstanding of the purpose of alternative dispute resolution. Skilled mediators are now able to achieve results satisfactory to both parties in many cases which are quite beyond the powers of lawyers and the courts alike.

Thus, refusing to mediate without good reason may have consequences in terms of costs. Typically, arguments relevant to costs already incurred and seriousness/ground of the other party's allegations will not suffice,[22] while the courts may consider, for example: (i) the absence of real prospects of a successful mediation considering the other party's litigious attitude;[23] and (ii) the previous negotiations between the parties, where one of them has made real efforts to settle the dispute through reasonable offers which have been always rejected by the other party, which has unreasonably asked for substantial payments.[24]

Mediation shall not be confused with conciliation, where the parties appoint a third-party conciliator to express his provisional view on the merits of the dispute (typically in the form of a recommendation) and typically agree that the conciliator's decision will become binding unless any of the parties escalates the dispute to the next dispute resolution stage envisaged in the contract. Another difference is that mediation is typically a

21 *Dunnett (Susan) v Railtrack PLC* [2002] EWCA Civ 302.

22 *Hurst v Leeming* [2002] EWCH 1051.

23 *Hurst v Leeming* [2002] EWCH 1051.

24 *Alan Valentine v (1) Kevin Allen (2) Simon John Nash (3) Alison Nash* [2003] ADR LR 07/04.

facilitative process (i.e., the mediator facilitates the settlement process without necessarily evaluating the parties' positions), while conciliation is usually an evaluative process (i.e., the conciliator enters into the details of the subject matter).

Mediation is also different from the so-called Med-Arb where, following an unsuccessful mediation, the dispute is decided through an arbitration procedure in which the mediator assumes the role of arbitrator.

43.3.1.2 The mediated agreement

As the outcome of a successful mediation is a contract, the parties will be obliged to comply with the relevant terms based on the principle that "*pacta sunt servanda*". However, this will also mean that the mediated agreement will be subject to the usual rules relevant to the validity of contracts, including those allowing the parties to have a vitiated agreement set aside (e.g., in cases of mistake[25] or duress[26]).

A mediated settlement agreement is not an arbitral award and may not be enforced internationally like an arbitral award under the 1958 New York Convention on the Recognition and Enforcement of Foreign Arbitral Awards (the "New York Convention"). However, the parties may seek a so-called consent award, i.e., an arbitral award recording the content of a mediated settlement agreement. In this case, under certain circumstances, the mediated agreement recorded in the consent award may be enforceable under the New York Convention. Moreover, the "*Directive 2008/52/EC of the European Parliament and of the Council of 21 May 2008 on certain aspects of mediation in civil and commercial matters*" (the "Mediation Directive") has resulted in many EU countries having enacted legislation aimed at ensuring that mediated settlement agreements are recognisable and enforceable from one Member State to another as if they were court judgments or orders and provide for a "*mediated settlement enforcement orders*". In addition to this, the Singapore Convention on Mediation[27] (the "Singapore Convention") has given a framework for international settlement agreements resulting from mediation. The Singapore Convention applies to international settlement agreements resulting from mediation, concluded by parties to resolve a commercial dispute. The Convention has the scope to "*facilitate international trade and commerce by enabling disputing parties to easily enforce and invoke settlement agreements across borders. Businesses will benefit from mediation as an additional dispute resolution option to litigation and arbitration in settling cross-border disputes*".[28] It applies to the enforcement of settlement agreements resulting from mediation which are commercial[29] (i.e., disputes arising from transactions by consumers for personal, family or household purposes, or relating to family, inheritance or employment law will be excluded) and international in character[30] while settlement agreements that are enforceable as a judgment or arbitral award will be excluded.[31] Based on the Singapore Convention, settlement agreements are directly enforceable in the competent authority of

25 See for example *Brennan v Bolt Burden* [2004] EWCA Civ 1017; [2004] 3 WLR 1321.
26 See for example *Farm Assist v Minister for the Environment* [2009] BLR 399.
27 As of 24 February 2023, the Convention has 55 signatories, of which eight are parties to the Convention.
28 See www.singaporeconvention.org.
29 Art 1(2) of the Singapore Convention.
30 Art 1(1) of the Singapore Convention.
31 Art 1(3)(b) of Singapore the Convention.

a party state[32] and may be invoked as evidence in case of disputes on matters resolved by the agreement.[33] However, the competent authority of a party state is not obliged to grant relief in a number of cases, including where: (i) one of the parties was incapable;[34] (ii) the settlement agreement is not binding, or is null and void, inoperative or incapable of being performed under the law to which it is subjected, or has been subsequently modified;[35] (iii) the mediator is culpable of a serious breach of the mediator standards[36] or has failed to disclose circumstances that raise doubts as to his/her impartiality or independence;[37] or (iv), granting the relief would be contrary to the public policy of the party state.[38]

43.3.1.3 Mediation procedure

There is not one agreed procedure to conduct mediation. The relevant process may vary based on the parties' agreement, any mediation rules chosen by the parties and/or the mediator's style. However, there are certain steps that are common to most mediations. These include the following:

(i) The party seeking to commence the mediation will send the other party the relevant notice in compliance with the requirements set forth in the contract.
(ii) The mediator will then be appointed in accordance with the procedure and the requirements set forth in the mediation clause.
(iii) As soon as the mediator is appointed, he may schedule one or more pre-mediation meetings with the parties' counsels aimed at discussing the conduct of the mediation, such as fees and payments, mediation place and language, duration, number and frequency and conduct of meetings (e.g., whether they will be held physically and/or via conference calls or video conferences so to reduce the costs associated with physical meetings), submissions of written documents, mediation date(s) and relevant attendees, etc. At this meeting the mediator may also describe the mediation process, e.g., by explaining that: (a) the mediator may have joint sessions which all the parties will be allowed to attend (although, such sessions may be postponed or avoided in case the parties are hostile to each other) and private conferences held between the mediator and each of the parties; (b) as the meditation is private and confidential (unless the parties agree otherwise), the parties should be encouraged to act freely as discussions, communications, statements, documents, including any settlement offers, which are disclosed by and/or to a party or the mediator during the process will be kept confidential (the parties may be requested to sign a confidentiality statement) and will be considered without prejudice (i.e., may not be disclosed in court or arbitration in case the mediation fails).
(iv) The mediator may then schedule a meeting for the parties' counsels to present their respective positions, including their view of the facts in dispute, their

32 Art 3(1) of the Singapore Convention.
33 Art 3(2) of the Singapore Convention.
34 Art 5(1)(a) of the Singapore Convention.
35 Art 5(1)(b) of the Singapore Convention.
36 Art 5(1)(e) of the Singapore Convention.
37 Art 5(1)(f) of the Singapore Convention.
38 Art 5(2)(a) of the Singapore Convention.

position on liability and damages and their expectation in terms of outcome, although it is more frequent for mediators to ask the parties to submit written confidential memorandums (the mediator will typically indicate the maximum length of such document and term for the relevant submission).

(v) Once the mediator has understood the parties' respective positions, drivers and expectations, the mediation will proceed with private conferences with each party in separate conference rooms in which the mediator will endeavour to identify any common grounds and understand whether a mediated solution is possible, and on what terms. The mediator may also convey to one party any messages or proposals he has received from the other party, provided that such party has allowed him to do so.

(vi) If the mediator succeeds in finding common grounds and narrowing the parties' differences to the point that a settlement becomes achievable, the mediator may organise a joint session where the parties (the mediator may expressly ask that each party is represented by someone with authority to settle the dispute) and their respective counsels may discuss any points still open and agree on the possible settlement.

(vii) To the extent an agreement is reached "in principle", the parties will then work together in order to record the relevant terms in a formal mediated settlement agreement.

43.3.2 Adjudication

43.3.2.1 Adjudication in general

Adjudication is among the most widely used means for the resolution of construction disputes. It is an ADR process where a neutral third party, the adjudicator, gives a decision which binds on the parties unless or until it is revised in litigation or arbitration. In *Wimbledon Construction Company 2000 Limited v Vago*[39] adjudication was said to be:

> designed to be a quick and inexpensive method of arriving at a temporary result in a construction dispute.

The main advantages of adjudication are that:

(i) The adjudicator's decision will be binding on the parties unless and until any of them refers it to another available dispute resolution process and a final and binding judgment or award or other form of decision is issued as a result thereof. The need of quick, albeit "rough" decisions is mainly driven by the need to continue with the work and avoid any cash flow issues to contractors. An adjudicator's decision that is not complied with voluntarily may be enforced by the party in whose favour the decision was issued. This differentiates adjudication from other means of dispute resolution which do not end with a binding decision (such as mediation) and makes it more akin to an arbitration award, although an adjudicator's decision does not have the same legal status of an arbitration

39 *Wimbledon Construction Company 2000 Limited v Vago* [2005] EWHC 1086.

award, and may not be enforced as such[40] unless the parties expressly agree that the adjudicator's decision shall be conclusive (i.e., that the parties have no recourse to the courts or arbitration to finally determine the dispute). In practice, only a small percentage of adjudications lead to further proceedings as the parties will typically either accept the adjudicator's decision or use it as a basis to settle their dispute amicably.

(ii) Unlike other means of dispute resolution such as arbitration or litigation, adjudication is quicker thanks to the limited time that the parties have to appoint the adjudicator and that the adjudicator has to reach a decision.

(iii) Adjudication is typically cheaper than litigation and arbitration considering the relevant length and level of detail.

Payment disputes (e.g., interim payments or final account) are probably best suited for adjudication. However, adjudication is now used for any type of contentious matters including those of variations, delays, back-charges, negligence, wrongful termination, defects, etc.

43.3.2.2 Statutory, contractual and "ad hoc" adjudication

A distinction must be made between statutory adjudication, contractual adjudication and "ad hoc".

43.3.2.2.1 STATUTORY ADJUDICATION

Statutory adjudication was introduced by the Housing Grants, Construction and Regeneration Act 1996 as subsequently amended by the Local Democracy, Economic Development and Construction Act 2009 (the "HGCR Act"). The HGCR Act sets out a framework for the adjudication process and applies whether or not the law of England and Wales or Scotland is otherwise the applicable law in relation to the contract, provided that all the following criteria are met: (i) the dispute involves a "construction contract" as defined at Section 104 of the HGCR Act, i.e., contracts relating to the carrying out of construction operations, arranging for the carrying out of construction operations by others (under subcontract or otherwise) and/or providing labour, or the labour of others, for the carrying out of construction operations, in England, Wales or Scotland. This includes agreements to do architectural, design or surveying work, or to provide advice on building, engineering, interior or exterior decoration or on the laying-out of landscape, in relation to construction operations, while contracts of employment (within the meaning of the Employment Rights Act 1996) are excluded. The meaning of "construction operations" is then defined at Section 105 of the HGCR Act. Interestingly, the definition of construction operations excludes: (a) drilling for, or extraction of, oil or natural gas; (b) extraction (whether by underground or surface working) of minerals; tunnelling or boring, or construction of underground works, for this purpose; (c) assembly, installation or demolition of plant or machinery, or erection or demolition of steelwork for the purposes of supporting or providing access to plant or machinery, on a site where the primary activity is nuclear processing, power generation, or water or effluent treatment, or the production,

40 See *Cameron v Mowlem* [1990] 52 BLR 24, where the Court of Appeal stated that the decision of the adjudicator had "*an ephemeral and subordinate character*".

transmission, processing or bulk storage (other than warehousing) of chemicals, pharmaceuticals, oil, gas, steel or food and drink; (d) manufacture or delivery to site of building or engineering components or equipment, materials, plant or machinery, or components for systems of heating, lighting, air-conditioning, ventilation, power supply, drainage, sanitation, water supply or fire protection, or for security or communications systems, except under a contract which also provides for their installation; (e) the making, installation and repair of artistic works, being sculptures, murals and other works which are wholly artistic in nature; (ii) the construction contract is not with a residential occupier, i.e., it does not principally relate to operations on a dwelling which one of the parties to the contract occupies, or intends to occupy, as his residence; (iii) if the contract was formed prior to 1 October 2011, then the contract is a "contract in writing".[41]

Where all such requirements are met, disputes will be adjudicated based on the statutory adjudication procedure set out in the Scheme for Construction Contracts (England and Wales) Regulations (the "Scheme"). However, there may be situations in which an agreement is a "hybrid" that relates to construction operations "*and other matters*", in which case, the Scheme will only apply to the part relating to construction operations.[42]

Section 108 of the HGCR Act contains the provisions which a construction subject to the HGCR Act contract shall include (in writing). In particular, the contract shall: (i) enable a party to give notice at any time of his intention to refer a dispute to adjudication; (ii) provide a timetable with the object of securing the appointment of the adjudicator and referral of the dispute to him within seven days of such notice; (iii) require the adjudicator to reach a decision within 28 days of referral or such longer period as is agreed by the parties after the dispute has been referred; (iv) allow the adjudicator to extend the period of 28 days by up to 14 days, with the consent of the party by whom the dispute was referred; (v) impose a duty on the adjudicator to act impartially; (vi) enable the adjudicator to take the initiative in ascertaining the facts and the law; (vii) provide in writing that the decision of the adjudicator is binding until the dispute is finally determined by legal proceedings, by arbitration (if the contract provides for arbitration or the parties otherwise agree to arbitration) or by agreement (although the parties may agree to accept the decision of the adjudicator as finally determining the dispute); (viii) include provision in writing permitting the adjudicator to correct his decision so as to remove a clerical or typographical error arising by accident or omission; (ix) provide in writing that the adjudicator is not liable for anything done or omitted in the discharge or purported discharge of his functions as adjudicator unless the act or omission is in bad faith, and that any employee or agent of the adjudicator is similarly protected from liability. Where a construction contract subject to statutory adjudication does not comply with the said requirements, the right to adjudicate will be implied into the contract as a matter of law by the HGCR Act, and the fallback procedure set out in the Scheme will apply.[43]

43.3.2.2.2 CONTRACTUAL ADJUDICATION

The parties may include in the contract detailed provisions aimed at providing for adjudication as a dispute resolution method in their contract. They could achieve such a result

41 Section 107 of the HGCR Act (now repealed).

42 See, e.g., the case of *Severfield v Duro* [2015] EWHC 3352 (TCC), which involved a case of a hybrid contract.

43 Section 108 (5) of the HGCR Act.

by adopting the Scheme in full, negotiating their own set of bespoke rules or adopting a ready set of rules of one of the several institutions that have made them available such as the Institution of Civil Engineers ("ICE") Adjudication Procedure, the Centre for Effective Dispute Resolution ("CEDR") Rules for Adjudication, the Institution of Chemical Engineers ("IchemE") Adjudication Rules, etc. Where the parties have adopted a standard forms contract (e.g., a "FIDIC" form contract) the adjudication rules will typically be set out in the contract.

43.3.2.2.3 AD HOC ADJUDICATION

The parties may agree that a dispute under their construction contract be settled by "ad hoc" adjudication after the dispute has crystallised even where adjudication was not included in the contract as a method of resolution of contractual disputes. The courts will normally uphold such agreements. In the case of *Nordot Engineering Services v Siemens*[44] it was held that:

> if the parties with their eyes open enter into an agreement to the effect that 'The adjudicator will decide this question and we will be bound by his decision' why should the court not give effect to that agreement? There can be no public policy against that and the mere fact that the system of adjudication is enshrined in statute does not, it seems to me, make any difference.

Also in this case, the parties may either adopt the Scheme in full or opt for a bespoke and more tailored approach, possibly using the Scheme as a starting point.

43.3.2.3 Adjudication procedure

There is no standard adjudication procedure, and the relevant phases and process will typically vary based on the type of adjudication (statutory or contractual), the parties' agreement and the adjudicator's style. However, there are some steps that are common to all adjudications. These include the following:

(i) Adjudications will normally commence when one party issues a notice of adjudication ("NOA") to the other party. This is the document giving the adjudicator jurisdiction over the dispute. The purpose of a NOA is to: (a) inform the other party of the referring party's intention to refer the dispute to adjudication; and (b) set out the terms of the dispute to be adjudicated. A NOA is usually a brief document which describes the contract, sets out the dispute and sets forth the relief sought.

(ii) The next step will be the appointment of the adjudicator (or dispute board). The relevant process and timing will depend on the type of adjudication (statutory or contractual), what the parties have agreed in their contract and whether the parties are able to reach an agreement on the adjudicator to be appointed.

(iii) As soon as the adjudicator is appointed, he will inform the parties above the terms of business and give indications on how the adjudication should be conducted (e.g., the initial timetable, information on how submissions should

44 *Nordot Engineering Services v Siemens* [2001] CILL 1788.

be made and exchanged, amount, timing and apportionment of adjudicator's fees and expenses, etc.).

(iv) The referring party will then send the so-called notice of referral (the "Referral") to the adjudicator. A Referral is the equivalent of what a statement of case is in litigation/arbitration, i.e., a document setting out the legal and factual components of the referring party's claim in more detail. The Referral is usually accompanied by the relevant supporting documentary evidence including: (a) the construction contract; (b) any contemporaneous documentation (e.g., minutes of meeting, communications, etc.); and (c) any witness or expert evidence (if allowed).

(v) The defendant will then provide a response (the "Response") to Referral within the term set out by the adjudicator or under the contract. The Response is a document setting out, typically in a "paragraph-by-paragraph" format, the defence (along with any counterclaim, where permitted), and is normally accompanied by the supporting documentary evidence.

(vi) The adjudicator may then permit further exchanges based on the complexity of the case and the parties' agreement. Where permitted, further submissions are: (a) the reply to Response whereby the referring party responds to the arguments set out in the Response; and (b) the rejoinder and the surrejoinder, submitted by the respondent and the referring party, respectively.

(vii) In cases where further submissions are not allowed or the parties' positions are still unclear, the adjudicator may invite the parties to attend an oral hearing where they will clarify any outstanding aspects and exhaust their arguments. In case of complex adjudications, witnesses and independent experts may also need to be heard.

(viii) The adjudicator will then give his decision within the term agreed by the parties or set out in the contract (or within the statutory limit, in case of statutory adjudication). Unless otherwise agreed between the parties, the decision will be temporarily binding on the parties who should comply with it. They may neither "appeal" nor have the same dispute re-adjudicated, although they may have the adjudicator's decision overturned in arbitration or litigation (depending on the dispute resolution clause in the contract).

INDEX